INSTITUTE OF GOVERNMENTAL STUDIES
University of California · Berkeley
TODD LA PORTE, *Acting Director*

THE
SAN FRANCISCO
BAY AREA

Its Problems and Future

Edited by

STANLEY SCOTT
Assistant Director

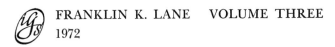 FRANKLIN K. LANE   VOLUME THREE
1972

Library of Congress Cataloging in Publication Data
Main entry under title:

The San Francisco Bay area.

([The] Franklin K. Lane [project])
A collection of monographs also issued separately by the Institute of
Governmental Studies, University of California, Berkeley.

Includes bibliographical references.

1. San Francisco Bay Region—Collections. I. Scott,
Stanley, 1921–   ed. II. California. University.
Institute of Governmental Studies.   III.   Series.
HN80.S4C3   309.17946   66–7975
ISBN O-87772-151-3

$8 (paperbound)
$11 (clothbound)

FOREWORD

The Institute of Governmental Studies is pleased to present this volume bringing together four of the Franklin K. Lane monographs dealing with the problems and future of the San Francisco Bay Area. The series takes its name from Franklin Knight Lane (1864–1921), a distinguished Californian who was successively New York correspondent for the San Francisco *Chronicle*, City and County Attorney of San Francisco, member and later Chairman of the U. S. Interstate Commerce Commission, and Secretary of the Interior in the cabinet of President Woodrow Wilson.

Shortly after Franklin K. Lane's death, a group of friends arranged for the establishment of a fund to be held and invested by Herbert Hoover, Adolph C. Miller and Franklin D. Roosevelt for the benefit of Mr. Lane's widow during her lifetime, and thereafter for some purpose to perpetuate his memory. In 1939, the three trustees acted to establish the Franklin K. Lane Memorial Foundation at the University of California, Berkeley; the income was subsequently allocated to the Institute of Governmental Studies.

The general purposes of the fund are to promote "better understanding of the nature and working of the American system of democratic government, particularly in its political, economic and social aspects," and the "study and development of the most suitable methods for its improvement in the light of experience."

Since its inception, the fund has supported a wide variety of studies in its review of major problems and prospects for the future of the San Francisco Bay Area. To date, the Bay Area series has produced 17 monographs. All are available as individual paperbacks, and in addition, have also been bound into Volumes I, II and III, *The San Francisco Bay Area—Its Problems and Future*. The six monographs in Volume I deal with local government finance, social dependency, economic trends, minority groups and intergroup relations, public education, and support of the arts. The seven studies in Volume II discuss future demographic growth of the area, city and regional planning, resource management, managing man's environment, geography and urban evolution, housing, and urban transportation. Volume III treats open space, the region's press, regional government, and problems of seismic safety.

STANLEY SCOTT
Editor

CONTENTS

I

T. J. KENT, JR.

OPEN SPACE . . .

Open Space for the San Francisco Bay Area:
Organizing to Guide Metropolitan Growth

INSTITUTE OF GOVERNMENTAL STUDIES
UNIVERSITY OF CALIFORNIA, BERKELEY

Open Space for the San Francisco Bay Area:
ORGANIZING TO GUIDE METROPOLITAN GROWTH

By

T. J. KENT, Jr.
Department of City and Regional Planning
University of California, Berkeley

1970

INTERNATIONAL STANDARD BOOK NUMBER (ISBN) 0–87772–069–X
LIBRARY OF CONGRESS CATALOG CARD NUMBER 71–631477
PRINTED IN THE UNITED STATES OF AMERICA
BY THE UNIVERSITY OF CALIFORNIA PRINTING DEPARTMENT

Contents

Foreword

The San Francisco Bay Area is graced with both natural and man-made qualities that give it unusual appeal. The most prominent natural feature, of course, is the Bay itself. It is one of the world's great harbors and estuaries, with a multitude of fascinations and attractions for all who enjoy its presence. The Bay and its tidelands have helped protect the area for more than a century, influencing the directions of urban growth and preventing community builders from filling the region's center with unrelieved sprawl. The Bay also cools the land in summer, helping maintain an equable climate. Moreover, the Bay has proven to have numerous other beneficial influences on the region. The area's residents have now finally fully recognized the many essential functions performed by the broad expanse of water in their midst. Accordingly they moved to protect the Bay with strong state-enacted legislation in 1969.

Thus, with continual civic vigilance, the future of the Bay and its shoreline may be considered reasonably secure. But our principal land resources are still highly vulnerable. Level plains invite the bulldozer and the developer. Vineyards and orchards are threatened by urban growth, freeways and smog. Mountains and ridges can be quarried, excavated, and built upon. Homes have been erected on hillsides, often without regard for site safety, sometimes with tragic landslides as a result. And so it goes . . . , and goes.

The environmental features that make the Bay Area a superb place to live in are the product of geology, geography and climate. Environment exercises a profound influence, but it can also be *undermined* by people. Despite sporadic efforts, most of our surroundings are still unprotected against man's restless and often misguided energies. After the Bay, the region's terrain—its unique and fragile *open space*—is the next logical candidate for protection "by most of the people, for all of the people, against some of the people."

Open space is eminently worth conserving for its own sake, because it is a precious natural resource that people cherish. Without precautions, it can be lost forever. Furthermore, appropriate open space and land use policies can direct growth, forestalling both sprawl in the suburbs and the transformation of city centers into Gotham-like high-rise Gargantuas.

Writing clearly and persuasively in his closely reasoned Franklin K. Lane monograph, T. J. Kent has outlined the crucial roles that he sees for an open space program in the Bay Area's future. He emphasizes the

vii

need for preservation, establishes its economic feasibility, and proposes workable alternatives for getting on with the job.

The Bay Area's civic leadership appears to agree that an effective open space program is essential. Their principal differences concern ways of confirming the consensus, and of organizing to accomplish the objectives. The Kent monograph is designed to advance the discussion, helping to clarify, and hopefully to resolve, most remaining questions of policy and implementation.

Both the writer of this Foreword and the author of the monograph gratefully acknowledge the invaluable assistance given by the Institute's Editor, Harriet Nathan. We also express warm appreciation to friends and families associated with Centro Cultural Mejicano Latinoamericano de Berkeley. During a memorable Sunday picnic in Briones Park, their children, and their children's playmates, helped us prepare an excellent pictorial illustration of open space in its highest and best use (see Peter Whitney's final photograph). Gracias amigos. Hasta luego!

STANLEY SCOTT
Editor

Introduction:
Reshaping the Metropolis

Since the end of World War II, large metropolitan regions everywhere have been permitted to grow so rapidly and with such lack of effective controls that many are now dangerously disorganized. Worldwide economic competition between metropolitan regions will necessarily stimulate and compel major improvements in their organization. Locally, demands for programs to meet social and environmental needs will be even more compelling. As a consequence, most of the large metropolitan regions of the world will be physically restructured and reshaped during the next half century.

During the coming period of replanning and reorganization, two closely related regionwide physical systems will receive special attention. High-speed metropolitan public transportation services will be established and improved in the commuter-core areas of all large urban regions, in both the developed and underdeveloped nations, in the United States as well as in India and Venezuela. Metropolitan greenbelt and open space systems will also be established to serve obvious basic social needs and, in combination with rapid transit, to make the emerging metropolitan commuter-regions function effectively for economic purposes. In most areas, local governments cannot provide these two essential metropolitan physical elements; yet they are absolutely essential if today's physically disjointed urban regions are to be transformed into productive and humane metropolitan communities.

Certain extremely large metropolitan areas, such as New York and Los Angeles, are already surrounded and burdened by almost continuous suburban sprawl on a massive scale. In areas such as those, the cost of acquiring developed land for reconversion into open space will be so great that the establishment of some of the key elements of the needed open space systems will have to be delayed, perhaps for several decades.

In other as yet more fortunate metropolitan areas, such as the San Francisco Bay Area, Washington, D.C., and Seattle, with significantly smaller populations, where unusual topography and other factors have kept postwar suburban tract development within a radius that can be served by rail-transit commuter service, it is still possible to shape the central cities and their suburbs into new, larger, more unified, and more productive metropolitan communities without having to reclaim large amounts of developed land for the open space system. In these areas it

1

still is possible to "do it right the first time," in city-planning and city-building terms. Such urbanizing regions can establish large-scale open space systems to determine the shape and size of the emerging central metropolis during the next few decades, thus benefitting subsequent generations for many decades, perhaps for centuries. This will be possible, however, only if firm decisions are made and acted upon during the next few years.

Students of city planning and local government are not surprised that efforts to govern the growth of metropolitan regions in the United States are still so disorganized and ineffective. Even in Europe, where the need for controlling the growth of great cities was recognized half a century ago, it was not until after World War II that England, Holland, Denmark and Sweden finally succeeded in establishing workable city planning and urban land development systems. Now, however, the need for metropolitan greenbelt and open space programs to control and direct the growth of cities is taken for granted in all of these countries.

It will be difficult for Americans, working within the context of their three-level federal, state, and local structure—as opposed to Europe's more centralized pattern of national and local governments—to translate the lessons of European experience into terms that can be readily understood and applied throughout urban America. In the United States, once local needs have been recognized locally, they have usually been provided for sooner or later, primarily as a result of local initiative and action. State and federal actions have been important for implementation, but the crucial decisions have been made by leaders in the affected communities.

In the San Francisco Bay Area much can be gained from a regional open space system, if it can be established during the next few years. Moreover, it is now obvious to many Bay Area civic and governmental leaders that everyone will lose if the present opportunity is missed. Consequently, many individual citizens are interested in determining what will be needed to accomplish this goal. Thus we may now finally be ready to make some crucial decisions, after more than 50 years of preparatory civic and professional work. If adequate new measures are taken, they will enable us to govern and limit the growth of our unique metropolitan region in a way that may make future Bay Area generations proud of us—including our own contemporary, critical youth—not only for having done the right thing, but for having done it at the right time, before it was too late.

In recent major efforts to deal with a number of Bay Area problems, the 1963 and 1965 California Legislatures initiated several ad hoc programs, including the Bay Area Transportation Study (BATS), the Bay-Delta program, and the Bay Conservation and Development Commission (BCDC). It was hoped at the time that the programs could be coordinated as they were developed, but coordination was accomplished only to a very limited extent. In addition, many leaders anticipated that on completion of the planning phase in 1969, an integrated Bay Area regional government could be established for implementing the programs. They saw such a unified, limited-function government as a preferred alternative to further proliferation of single-purpose regional special districts. Despite much discussion, no such unified government had been established by mid-year in 1970.

Meanwhile, the reservation of metropolitan open space emerged as one of a select group of high-priority problems receiving first-round recognition from civic leaders. Their attitude gave assurance of strong support for efforts to develop an effective regional open space program.

Such a program will require an impressive combination of governmental authority and financial support. The magnitude of the effort required may be gauged in a rough way by measuring it against two other existing programs. Regional open space will require financial resources as substantial as those of the San Francisco Bay Area Rapid Transit District, and regulatory powers at least as extensive as those of the Bay Conservation and Development Commission. Consequently, proposals concerned with the regional open space needs of the Bay Area cannot avoid dealing with fundamental questions of governmental structure and authority.

This monograph has three primary objectives: First, it is intended to contribute to a broader public awareness of the great need for a regional open space program by emphasizing its economic benefits, as well as those of a more obvious social and ecological nature. The second aim is to indicate in some detail the far-reaching governmental implications of such a program, so that tough-minded realism may encourage the kind of civic and political boldness that will be essential when the time for decision arrives. Third, the first two objectives will be considered in the context of the Bay Area's evolving traditions of regional and local government home rule which, as a result of state legislative actions initiated in 1965, began their greatest time of testing in 1969.

No one can foretell whether the Bay Area is actually on the verge of an unusually creative and productive era of political action on regional issues. An impressive number of civic and political leaders in the Bay Area, however, are conscious of such a possibility. In the author's opinion the state Legislature's 1969 decision to establish the Bay Conservation and Development Commission on a permanent and strengthened basis, and to postpone action on the initial comprehensive Bay Area regional government proposals, greatly enhanced the possibilities for creating a Bay Area regional government strong enough at the outset to formulate a realistic regional open space program.

Those who believe that the future well-being of all Bay Area citizens depends on the establishment in the near future of a regional open space system, now have a new opportunity to clarify and restate their basic reasons for advocacy. They can also take advantage of the new legislative schedule to become more explicit about the governmental powers necessary to establish and develop such a system. In addition, they can consider ways in which an open space agency can be governed and fitted most constructively into the regional governmental framework that seems to be evolving in the Bay Area, slowly but surely.

Existing Bay Area Open Space:
A Gift of Geography

Individuals from every walk of life—rich and poor, longshoremen and bankers, visitors and residents—have strongly favorable impressions of San Francisco and the Bay Area. Among the great metropolitan cities of the world, the metropolis formed by the urban and suburban communities in the nine-county Bay region has a very high ranking as a place to work, to live in and to visit.

Why is this so? The social and economic forces that shaped this cosmopolitan community over the past 100 years are well documented. They are basically no different from those that have created every large metropolis since the beginning of the Industrial Revolution.

What distinguishes the San Francisco Bay Area from its metropolitan peers is the remarkable way a dramatic geographic setting has been used to accommodate the man-made system of cities. The existing open spaces in the Bay Area's metropolitan environmental structure are of critical importance: the great central open space and "blue belt" of the Bay; the headlands, cliffs, beaches and Pacific Ocean on the west; and the vast, marvelous complex of valleys, foothills, ridges, and mountains of the region's middle and outer rings, have had a decisive influence in shaping a Bay Area "way of life."

In the past, Bay Area leaders set aside tens of thousands of acres of land for watersheds on the Peninsula, in the Eastbay, and in Marin County; they succeeded in retaining, as open space, the Golden Gate headlands, Angel Island, the Eastbay regional parks, the Point Reyes peninsula and seashore, Mt. Tamalpais, and Mt. Diablo; they placed a moratorium on Bay filling, and established a permanent Bay conservation agency. If these things had not been done, we would now have a less livable, less workable, and far less distinctive metropolis.

The existing system of regional open space, however, which we tend to take for granted, also includes many privately owned areas and geographic features that have had great influence in determining the relationships between the primary and secondary cities within the region. These include San Bruno Mountain; the western slopes of Marin County; the Napa Valley vineyards; the foothills, forests, rivers, and ridges of Sonoma and Napa counties; the great broad fields of Solano County; the Livermore Valley; the slopes of Mount Hamilton; and the green foothills and mountain ranges of San Mateo, Santa Clara, and Santa Cruz counties.

5

Pressures for Urbanization

Most forecasters anticipate that the Bay Area's population will have doubled between 1960 and 1990, rising from approximately 3½ million to more than 7 million. If we do not greatly enlarge the permanent elements of our existing open space system in advance of this anticipated further urbanization, the area's distinctive individuality as a world metropolis will be lost. Moreover, our existing metropolitan physical structure will be weakened. If we fail to maintain the Bay Area's characteristic quality of concentrated, intensive development on a large framework, sprawl at the edges will cause loss of accessibility to the regional centers. Destructive development trends will emerge that are not consciously wanted by anyone, but that may prove to be irreversible if they are not stemmed during the 1970's.

Unfortunately, we already have large urbanized stretches that are indistinguishable from Los Angeles sprawl or the postwar suburban tracts on the outskirts of New York and Chicago. But the main elements of our metropolitan structure have been compactly developed along transportation routes, and are still well articulated. Thus far this has resulted primarily from the area's topography, rather than from any publicly established regional development policy. High-density San Francisco, the identifiable cities of southern Marin County, the string of well-established municipalities of the San Mateo Peninsula, and the communities in the valleys east of the Berkeley and Oakland hills delineate the pattern. Even the four-mile-wide, 40-mile-long stretch of urbanized territory from Richmond to Fremont, situated on the plain between the Bay shoreline and the Eastbay hills, has a combination of specialized industrial and commercial districts, regional shopping centers, and suburban communities that still function primarily as elements of an integrated metropolis.

The Bay Area's geographically spread out clusters of cities have functioned well because most of the urban elements are individually compact, or because they have maintained their original central districts and thus can be served, as mentioned above, by a coordinated commuter transportation system. The Bay Area's principal transit services have always been designed to strengthen the region's relatively few major employment centers, making them accessible to residents throughout the region's five county core. Consequently, Bay Area central district workers have continued to have a wider effective choice of housing than has been available in many other metropolitan communities in the United States, especially in recent years.

Shaping the Next Surge of Growth

Despite its fortunate history of city building, the Bay Area must face the possibility that acceleration of postwar sprawl during the next two decades could precipitate a major city planning disaster. The next great surge of development will in part be contained, as was most of our postwar growth, by the region's topographic barriers, but the major units of the new growth of the 1970's and 1980's should not be permitted to leapfrog and spread to more remote locations or to develop on the edge of existing communities at densities too low to enable the new areas to be integrated into the central commuter-core of the region.

To implement such metropolitan development policies, early action will have to be taken to conserve, in some fair way, major privately owned elements of the regional open space system in the outer ring. If such measures are not taken, and suburban sprawl and the automobile win the next and perhaps final round in the development battle now taking place in the outer ring of the Bay Area, these forces will weaken and then destroy the region's newly reestablished rapid transit system, cancel out the massive capital investments that have revitalized the central districts of the metropolis, and dismantle the city-system that has taken more than 100 years to build.

Ample land is available within and adjacent to existing growing communities to accommodate the estimated population growth for the next 20 years at densities lower than Berkeley's, i.e., in a compact and workable pattern, with single family dwellings available for most families. If we enlarge our permanent regional open space system, future urban growth can be shaped into such human and realistic dimensions.

The elemental importance and interrelationships of the Bay Area's open spaces, and of the region's great natural beauty, were discussed in an unusual way by the late Dr. James G. Whitney, Berkeley psychiatrist, at the Bay Area's first conference on regional open space, held in 1959. Responding to a statement that the elimination of open space would contribute to mental illness, Dr. Whitney said,

I know of no scientific proof of this proposition. Intuitively I believe it to be true, but not quite in the way it has been put. Open space is not a specific necessity for mental or any other kind of health. The failure of "the long ocean voyage" and beautifully landscaped sanitaria are demonstrations of this fact. *But a society which does not care for beauty in all its aspects and which is without a reverence for nature is spiritually undernourished. An undernourished society is weaker, sicker, and less wise. Such a society certainly will be less able to deal with all of its afflictions and challenges, one of which is mental illness.*[1] [Emphasis supplied.]

[1] Frances W. Herring ed., *Regional Parks and Open Spaces: Selected Conference Papers* (Berkeley: Bureau of Public Administration, University of California, 1961), p. 86.

Objectives of a Metropolitan Open Space System

After Congress adopted the first financial aid program for open space projects in 1961, broad support for the establishment of regional open space systems in hundreds of growing urban areas, and in every large metropolitan region, became evident throughout the country. The national goals of the program were based on pioneering work during the postwar decades by volunteer conservation groups, particularly in New York, Hawaii, Philadelphia, Washington, and the San Francisco Bay Area. These goals were restated in 1968 in the regulations of the United States Department of Housing and Urban Development. They specified that open space project applications were to be judged in terms of their potential effectiveness (1) in helping to curb urban sprawl; (2) in preventing the spread of urban blight; (3) in encouraging more economic and desirable urban development; and (4) in providing needed recreational, conservation, scenic, and historic areas.

The open space policy objectives adopted by the local governments of the Washington, D. C. metropolitan area indicate how the national goals relate to a specific region. In a 1966 report, the National Capital Regional Planning Council defined their objectives as follows:

Open space should be preserved (1) to provide ample outdoor recreation opportunities to the ever-increasing numbers of residents and visitors in the National Capital Region; (2) to conserve natural resources, scenic beauty, and rural units of economic production; and (3) to guide urban growth into efficient corridors of development and compact communities as outlined in the Year 2000 Policies Plan [for Metropolitan Development].

During the past three years, conservation leaders in several of the nation's largest metropolitan areas have begun to articulate an additional major objective for regional open space programs: the use of open space systems to slow down, and if necessary, to stop the growth of population in the larger metropolitan regions. This objective is the result of an uneasy, growing awareness of the far-reaching ecological and social damage that apparently can be caused by sustained, rapid, uncontrolled urbanization. In contemporary terms, therefore, regional open space objectives for the Bay Area should be concerned primarily with:

1. protection and enhancement of life;
2. prevention of urban sprawl; and
3. limitation of the size of the metropolis.

8

Bay Area Open Space . . . rugged,

productive,

vulnerable,

beautiful

Photographer: Peter T. Whitney

T. J. KENT, JR.

Protecting and Enhancing Life

The first objective covers a broad range of programs requiring the preservation of large open areas adjacent to or near the built-up metropolis and its outlying cities. These open areas should be safeguarded now because they will be needed in the foreseeable future for watershed protection, flood control, regional parks, wildlife protection, specialized agricultural production, fire protection, protection against earthquake and landslide hazards, and for similar basic purposes. The very large amounts of land required are indicated by the 1966 Bay Area Preliminary Regional Plan prepared by the Association of Bay Area Governments. Envisioning an estimated 1990 population of 7,200,000, the ABAG report recommended the permanent reservation of 1,209,000 acres of open space land for these purposes.

The programs outlined above are now recognized as essential to the protection of life and property in the metropolitan region, and to the future welfare of its economy. Not yet fully appreciated, however, is the *interdependence* of the system's separate elements; this becomes evident only when the system is viewed in its entirety, and in relation to basic ecological needs. Only after a regional open space plan has been outlined for a large, rapidly growing metropolitan area does it become apparent that one of the clearly articulated, conscious aims of the comprehensive program should be insurance against serious ecological disturbances. An example is the damaging effect of covering too large an area with a "suffocating" blanket of urban development. Unfortunately, until recently this aim has usually been difficult to justify until after ecological imbalance has occurred.

The potential drainage and sewage disposal problems of an interior valley, such as Nicasio Valley in Marin County, and the potential air pollution problems in such "air-pockets" as Livermore Valley in Alameda County, illustrate the need for regional ecological studies before decisions are made committing areas such as these to intensive urbanization. In such cases, ecological considerations probably would be the major factor in deciding to keep certain large areas in agricultural use, rather than permitting them to be used as sites for urban communities. In view of our uncertainty concerning ecological relationships, and the obvious examples of thoughtless—and subsequently self-damaging—urban aggression against nature that we have permitted, the objective of enhancing life in growing metropolitan areas suggests a policy of caution and conservatism in planning for urban expansion. This developmental conservatism should be evident in the large scale and the comprehensive, integrated design of our metropolitan greenbelt and open space systems.

There are, of course, other good reasons justifying permanent retention of extensive land areas in agricultural use. In metropolitan regions
such as the Bay Area many economic activities located in cities are
directly related to the nearby production and to the marketing of agricultural products. Close-in agriculture activities will be protected when
the second open space objective is achieved and the greenbelt element
of the comprehensive land development system no longer permits urban
growth by sprawl. Once urban growth is controlled, the values of existing agricultural land as real estate will be readjusted, making it normal
and economically sound for dairying, sheep and cattle raising, fruit
growing, truck farming, and other agricultural activities to be conducted in large open land areas within and adjacent to metropolitan
regions.

The objective of *enhancing* life in metropolitan areas sooner or later
will become as important as the current objective of *protecting* life in
our great cities. When this happens, we will realize that large-scale
metropolitan open space systems will once again make possible the
production of fresh vegetables, fresh fruits, fresh eggs and milk, and
other basic foods that can only be produced by the region's local resources of man and nature. Few Bay Area residents need to be reminded
of the life-enhancing difference between fresh blackberries, artichokes,
and apples, and their usual supermarket counterparts; between fresh
crab and frozen crab; between fresh and frozen salmon and sole; between fresh tomatoes and supermarket tomatoes.

Thus, a regional open space system of the scale now considered necessary, initially for other reasons, will not only insure retention of unique
and highly valued agricultural lands such as the Napa Valley vineyards.
It will also lead to an increase of our production, use, and appreciation
of local agricultural commodities, since very large areas will be available
for extensive as well as intensive agriculture. Appreciation of the cycle
and balance of nature in the region's surrounding and supporting landscape will be enhanced, as a natural consequence.

It may be a happy coincidence that a revival of our once-strong regional agricultural tradition will develop at the very time when so
many young people are actively seeking and finding ways to live and
work on the land. The too-typical reaction against this urge toward
nature—which views it as a rejection of our affluent, highly specialized
urban society—may miss the main objective and desire being expressed.
In any case, the present combination of circumstances appears most
propitious: as a consequence of the necessity to establish large scale
open space systems for a combination of other requirements, we may
be able to respond in understandable and constructive ways to the

deeply felt but subtle needs of people of all age groups and all conditions. These seem to demand a close, practical, and harmonious relationship with nature and the land—a relationship that trends of the last half century will destroy, if they are allowed to continue.

Preventing Urban Sprawl

The second primary objective of the Bay Area open space program is the prevention of urban sprawl. This has been an accepted goal of a small but steadily increasing number of city planners, political leaders, and conservation-minded civic leaders throughout the United States since the automobile facilitated the suburban tract explosion during the 1920's. Both common sense and painstakingly detailed cost-benefit studies have established the fact that disorganized, scattered, sprawling urbanization is both economically and socially a costly, wasteful way of enlarging the metropolis.

Despite the reasonableness of the objective, the United States has not thus far been able to formulate an alternative capable of achieving acceptance and of being implemented. The recent study sponsored by the Bay Area conservation group, People for Open Space, and supported by a Ford Foundation grant, is probably the first American anti-sprawl program for a major metropolitan region that has been spelled out in sufficient detail to be enacted, financed, and implemented if the civic and political leaders of the region decide to accept it. The conclusions and recommendations of the study will be considered in detail in later sections of this essay.

Two historical realities explain our failure to prevent metropolitan sprawl. The first is governmental, the second is professional, and they are closely related. When large-scale, spread-out suburban growth began in the 1920's, most of our central cities and their outlying suburban communities were organized in ways that limited their governmental jurisdictions to land that was already urbanized. Although cities that originally were geographically distinct subsequently grew together physically, they retained their separate governments. Thus there came to be many independent local governments in every large metropolitan region. No single regional government was concerned with the growth of the metropolis as a whole. Today, fifty years later, the governmental situation is basically unchanged.

Even if metropolitan regional governments had existed in the 1920's, however, the American city planning profession at that time possessed insufficient practical experience to understand the essential, economically and politically painful measures that must be taken if metropolitan sprawl is to be halted. Only in 1917 was the profession established in a formal way, as an organized group of practitioners. Since then, the only stable governmental clients in the major metropolitan regions have been individual cities and counties. During this period, city planners and their governmental superiors have made impressive improvements in the ways in which central cities have been redeveloped, and outlying individual large-tract subdivisions designed.

In the absence of a regional governmental client, however, the city planning profession has tended to think of open space measures aimed at preventing urban sprawl in terms of limited county government powers and practices. These, it will be argued, are not likely to be strong enough to prevent it on a metropolitan scale. Thus, the normal cycle of society's challenge and the profession's subsequent response now requires action by political leaders to create a regional governmental agency possessing the motivation and authority to govern metropolitan growth.

When limited regional governments have been established, the city planning profession should be able to respond with plans and programs bold enough to achieve the objective while there is still time. Efforts to establish control of metropolitan growth, and to learn how to govern it effectively in the public interest, have been late in maturing. But this has also been true of efforts dealing with health, education and human rights for the American people. Once the reasons for the delay are understood and the necessary preparations have been started, however, there still is reason to believe that a society as well intentioned as ours can succeed in doing the job.

Preventing sprawl simply means controlling the location and timing of new development in order to assure the compactness of urban patterns and the establishment of a permanent open space system. Within the context of a metropolitan region this can only be done by a metropolitan governmental agency required and empowered to govern growth in accordance with a regional development plan.

The limiting factors with which we must work in devising feasible alternatives to continued growth by sprawl include: our system of private land ownership and development; the large number of local governments which our political beliefs and traditions require; and our state and federal constitutions. Once a regional governmental agency exists, however, and once a physical development plan to govern metropolitan growth has been agreed upon, the anti-sprawl objective can be achieved as in Sweden, by public control or ownership of *all lands to be urbanized*. The other possible alternative as proposed for the Bay Area calls for public control or ownership of *all lands needed for the permanent regional open space system*. Either method can be made to work, but the latter is more suited to the traditions and conditions of the Bay Area.

Limiting the Size of the Metropolis

Once the anti-sprawl decision banning further growth by scattered tract developments has been made, some form of public debate will begin on limiting the size of the population that can reasonably be provided for in the Bay Area, so as to forestall an oppressive and unacceptable degree of overcrowding, disorganization, pollution, and congestion.

During the early 1960's such disparate commentators as the editors of *The New Yorker,* and a famous conservative, the late Lucius Beebe, both seriously questioned the continuing, ever more intensive development of New York's gigantic complex of central districts on Manhattan Island.[1] In 1968 the New York Regional Plan Association found that it had to question any population increase for the great metropolis beyond the trend estimate for the year 2000. After careful study, the National Committee on Urban Growth Policy in 1969 advocated a redirection of urban growth trends in the United States in order to facilitate the building of new large cities away from the nation's existing major metropolitan concentrations. When individuals and groups as varied as these reach such conclusions and express them publicly, it may be assumed that the time has come for a fair hearing on one of the primary objectives of a Bay Area regional open space progam: the conscious design of a system that will enable those responsible for the future of the Bay Area to regulate, and if necessary to limit, the size of the metropolis within the Bay region.

While visiting San Francisco in 1961, the British biologist Sir Julian Huxley was interviewed by a San Francisco *Chronicle* reporter. When asked about his impressions of urban growth in the Bay Area since his last visit here, in relation to worldwide urbanization trends, he responded: "We are making our cities impossible to live in because of size. A city can only become so large before it becomes an uneconomic unit. I think that New York, London, and Tokyo are already beyond that size."

The suggestion that it may prove to be in the public interest *to limit the size of the metropolitan Bay Area* will perhaps seem far-fetched to some. Others may view such a limitation as being dangerously harmful to prospects for future beneficial economic development. But it would be disingenuous not to raise the issue at this time. It is bound to come

---

[1] See Appendix I for Lucius Beebe's column "Don't Let It Happen Here," San Francisco *Chronicle,* September 19, 1965.

Metropolitan Open Space

up sooner or later, because any metropolitan open space proposal that takes into account both the requirements for ecological survival and basic metropolitan physical-structure considerations is certain to precipitate debate on this question after the proposal is adopted, if not before.

The Bay Area has already pioneered in implementing some extremely controversial regional enterprises, after several years of debate. Today the area's residents can best serve their long-term interests by facing and debating the issue of optimum metropolitan size as soon as possible. The Bay Area does not need to remain a captive of trends that have produced "overgrown" metropolises, of which New York, Los Angeles, Tokyo, and London are outstanding examples. In fact, some of these "examples" are already trying to turn back and undo what they have done.

Today more than 8 million people live within the inner boundary of the greenbelt established around London between 1938 and 1955. Beyond the metropolitan greenbelt, but still within the London region, an additional 5 million people live in growing cities and new towns that are separated by their own greenbelts.

For many years, leaders at all levels of government in the London area have agreed that the central metropolis of 8 million is too big for its own good. Since 1947, costly programs have been reducing population densities in several central London boroughs. National economic development policies have also been designed to encourage the growth of other regions in Britain. Is it wise, or is it unwise for the Bay Area, whose population increased from 1½ million to 4½ million between 1940 and 1970, to ignore this English struggle with megalopolis?

The adoption of a metropolitan open space plan and implementation program for the Bay Area would be an act of major consequence. The primary objectives of the system should, therefore, be clearly understood in advance. The program will pose formidable administrative difficulties, not the least being the need to maintain a clear distinction between two different sets of objectives. First are those of the antisprawl greenbelts, i.e., the permanent, more or less continuous, more or less circular, broad bands of open spaces around both the metropolitan commuter-core area and the outlying cities. Second are the objectives of the other regional open space programs, whose open lands will provide the main spatial resources for the entire regional city-system. Some of these lands will not necessarily be kept permanently open. They will provide the sites, for some years, for extensions of existing communities and, perhaps, for a limited number of new towns.

A full exposition and explanation of the objectives of the metropolitan greenbelt and open space system should help to encourage the boldness that will be needed if appropriate open space policies are to be adopted during the early 1970's. Public understanding of the goals will also encourage the perseverance essential for implementation of a balanced program aimed at all three primary open space objectives: protecting and enhancing life, preventing urban sprawl, and limiting the size of the metropolis.

Postwar Governmental Actions to Control Runaway Growth

During the past 25 years, civic and governmental leaders in urban regions throughout the world have recognized and responded to the need to create new regional agencies. These agencies have been necessary to control the explosive, physically disjointed manner in which existing large cities were being transformed into metropolitan communities. This period of sustained legislative activity came only after decades of indecision, when the new reality of the larger, economically unified metropolitan region was coming into being and making its existence known.

In the Bay Area, as elsewhere after World War II, the new regional agencies were established one at a time, in a piecemeal way, despite early efforts to relate them to one another. In recent years there have been new efforts to see the most important actions of the postwar period in perspective and to consider newly recognized regional needs, such as the proposed metropolitan open space program, in the context of a future regional governmental framework. This is most fortunate in terms of the open space proposal, for, as noted earlier, the anti-sprawl feature in particular will require some form of strong regional government if critically important close-in spaces are to be preserved during the early years of the program.

Postwar Regional Developments in the San Francisco Bay Area

Before considering ways to implement the regional open space proposal, it will be useful to review the most significant postwar actions taken in the Bay Area in response to problems caused by rapid, large-scale urbanization.

REGIONAL WATER QUALITY CONTROL

In 1949, the state Legislature established a statewide water pollution control agency, with regional boards appointed by the Governor and consisting initially mostly of engineers. The creation of this first regional entity for the Bay Area was significant chiefly because it was a breakthrough, leading to subsequent actions on other regional problems that could be thought of primarily as "technical" rather than political problems, such as rapid transit and air pollution.

Regional boards handle administration of the control program. In the Bay Area, the San Francisco Regional Water Quality Control Board

16

deals with a region that includes major portions of all nine Bay Area counties. The laws concerning water quality and water pollution control were revised and strengthened in the 1969 legislative session (AB 412 and AB 413), but Bay Area water pollution remains a serious problem, one that will require drastic measures for its control.

BAY-DELTA PROGRAM

The implementation of the State Water Plan, and the dumping of sewage and industrial and agricultural wastes into the Delta contributed to concern about pollution in the Bay-Delta area. In 1965, the Legislature authorized a four-year study with (1) a seven-member Board of Consultants, (2) a Technical Coordinating Committee with 25 members, and (3) a Steering Committee, to work with the State Water Quality Control Board. The project was focused primarily on the technical and engineering aspects of the problem. The study projected future pollution levels in the Bay and Delta areas, and proposed partial but extremely costly solutions through engineering means. When reported to the Legislature in 1969, the recommendations were not acted upon, but the study program was continued. Subsequently, the Board of Consultants and the two committees were superseded temporarily by an 11-member San Francisco Bay Water Quality Group.

REGIONAL RAPID TRANSIT

Shortly after World War II, pressures for improved transportation facilities caused transit studies to be made by San Francisco, Oakland, and the federal government. The San Francisco and federal studies resulted in San Francisco's first successful freeway revolt in opposition to the State Division of Highway's 1947 proposal for a second automobile bridge adjacent and parallel to the San Francisco-Oakland Bay Bridge. In 1951 the Legislature established the San Francisco Bay Area Rapid Transit Commission, which prepared the first Bay Area regional plan that was based on judgments concerning the most desirable physical structure for the future metropolis. Six years later, the commission was reconstituted as the San Francisco Bay Area Rapid Transit District (BART), and was charged with constructing and operating the regional rail rapid transit system which was, at that time, the key element in the commission's plan for the Bay Area.

Members of the BART governing board are chosen by a formula that is roughly representative of the population distribution in the district. Members are named by city selection committees in each county, by county boards of supervisors, and by the Mayor of San Francisco, but they need not be councilmen or supervisors. Most are not. In 1962, the plan and bond issue for the initial, locally financed, $800 million, 75 mile, 3 county portion of the regional system was approved by the voters. Transit service is scheduled to begin in 1972.

BART's establishment significantly influenced the ABAG decision to prepare and propose a regional open space plan in 1966, and supported individual judgments that rapid transit, compact metropolitan growth, and open space systems provided a viable alternative to a freeway-dominated pro-sprawl policy.

REGIONAL AIR POLLUTION CONTROL

The early-to-mid-1950's witnessed the relatively sudden appearance of thick, ugly, yellow smog in the Bay Area where almost everyone, almost every day, had been accustomed to enjoying dramatically beautiful, sweeping views. In response, the Legislature established the Bay Area Air Pollution Control District in 1955. The governing board's 12 members are appointed by county supervisors from among their own number and by city selection committees from among city council members, with both a councilman and a supervisor from each of six counties. (The boards of supervisors of Napa, Solano and Sonoma counties have so far failed to adopt resolutions that would make them members of the district.) The district is significant environmentally because of the intensity of air pollution problems, and politically because it was the first permanent regional district established under wholly local control.

A REGIONAL DEVELOPMENT PLAN

In 1956, after nine years of voluntary, cooperative effort, Bay Area city and county planning commissioners and professional staff members agreed on a legislative proposal defining the key elements of a regional development plan. They also stated in writing that an official nonvoluntary planning agency with specific and limited duties was needed, and urged that it be established as a new special district. The district governing board was to be appointed by city and county legislators. It was to include nonelected citizens but was to have a majority of councilmen and supervisors. The proposal thus embodied the "regional home rule" approach expressed in the legislation establishing the Bay Area Rapid Transit District and the Bay Area Air Pollution Control District. The earlier precedent of the Water Pollution Control Board was rejected; its policy-making members were appointed by the Governor.

In 1961 the city and county governments of the Bay Area formed the voluntary organization now known as the Association of Bay Area Governments (ABAG). The association was established initially to oppose the creation by the state Legislature of a regional transportation agency, the Golden Gate Authority, patterned after the New York Port

Authority. ABAG also opposed the proposed new special district for regional planning, and in 1962 assumed responsibility for a task that would inevitably prove controversial: that of planmaking for the metropolis.

In 1966 ABAG's staff completed and published a report presenting the association's recommended Preliminary Regional Plan, looking ahead to 1990. The review process started in 1966 and has continued over a period of more than three years. As a result of the review, the plan has been revised and is scheduled to be submitted to the association's General Assembly in the summer of 1970. Despite the criticisms leveled at the plan, it has unquestionably made a major contribution to the debate on the future of the Bay Area, especially because of the boldness of its regional open space proposal. The regional open space element as it stands is in direct conflict with the actual pro-sprawl development policies of the nine county governments in the Bay Area.

The association's General Assembly is organized in such a way that counties and cities vote separately. In accordance with its rules, the association can act positively only with the affirmative votes of a majority of the 84 cities *and* a majority of the counties. Thus, since Solano County is still not a member of the association, only four county votes would be needed to exercise a veto over the votes of the city members, even if the representatives of all the 84 cities were to vote unanimously in the affirmative, in support of the anti-sprawl plan.

REGIONAL TRANSPORTATION PLANNING

From 1963 when it was established by the Legislature, until its demise in 1969, the Bay Area Transportation Study Commission (BATS) spent approximately $6 million in state and federal funds compiling what was called a "comprehensive" regional transportation plan. BATS accepted a number of existing plans, including the California Highway Commission's freeway plan for the Bay Area, which was prepared in the 1950's and specifically includes several very controversial proposed freeways.

The study commission had a 41-man governing board with a heterogeneous mixture of representatives; it was not intended to be a permanent organization. The commission was required by law to include in its final report to the Legislature a recommendation for a permanent governmental agency to continue "comprehensive" regional transportation planning for the Bay Area. Under a joint agreement between ABAG and the state's Business and Transportation Agency, the BATS staff is continuing its work. The BATS 1969 plan embraces growth-by-sprawl policies that contrast sharply with ABAG's Preliminary Regional

Plan, which offers a compact, city-centered alternative. Thus the stage has now been set for what can be the long-needed, critically important, clarifying debate on the two principal metropolitan growth alternatives facing the Bay Area.

BAY CONSERVATION

As a result of an unusual combination of exceedingly competent conservation and political leaders and groups in the Bay Area, a combination sustained over a five-year period, the Legislature established the Bay Conservation and Development Commission as a permanent agency in 1969. Both ABAG and powerful private interests opposed the creation of BCDC. Its elevation to permanent status has kept open options for using it either as the framework for a limited-function regional government, or as one of the component parts of such a government.

Like the BATS board, the 27-man BCDC board was constituted on a representational formula that looked like an unworkable combination of compromises, but in fact the commission and its professional staff have performed with outstanding effectiveness.

REGIONAL HOME RULE

In 1967, and again in 1969, ABAG's General Assembly recommended to the Legislature that the association be granted the necessary authority to enable it to become a four-function regional government with a 34-man governing body. With the possible exception of the president and vice-president, members of this key governing body were to be city and county legislators selected by city selection committees and county boards of supervisors, roughly on the basis of population distribution in the nine counties.

Regional government functions were to include the preparation and maintenance of a regional plan for physical development; regional airport and regional solid waste disposal responsibilities; and the establishment and maintenance of a regional open space program, made possible by limited authority to tax and to acquire land by condemnation when necessary. Existing special districts and additional regional agencies were eventually to become departments within the regional government. As a result of ABAG's 1967 action, the crucial question was no longer whether a limited-function regional government was needed, but rather whether it should be controlled by a directly-elected council as proposed by Berkeley, San Francisco[1] and others, or by an

---

[1] See Appendix II for the complete text of San Francisco's official policy statement on home rule and metropolitan government (April 11, 1966). This statement helped to precipitate the ABAG debates, which preceded the 1967 decision to support the establishment of a unified, limited-function regional government.

indirectly-elected council, as proposed by a majority of the association's city and county members.

In 1969, ABAG reaffirmed its support of state legislation calling for a unified, limited-function regional government, and, in a major new step, approved a revenue plan that included a regional income tax.

REGIONAL GOVERNMENT STUDY

The 1950's and 1960's saw the emergence of two approaches to Bay Area regional government. A "regional home rule" approach was expressed in the method of governing and controlling the regional air pollution control agency, and, after legislative modification, the rapid transit agency. A "higher level" approach was used in creating the comprehensive regional transportation planning, Bay conservation, Bay-Delta, and Bay Area water quality control agencies. Each of those involved initiative and continuing major influence by the state government and the federal government in metropolitan Bay Area affairs.

At the end of the 1967 legislative session, a compromise produced the Joint Committee on Bay Area Regional Organization (BARO), and gave it two years to prepare a report on the need for a unified regional government in the Bay Area and the major alternatives that should be considered.

In 1969, the Legislature established the Bay Conservation and Development Commission as a permanent agency and continued, on a temporary basis, the Bay-Delta and regional transportation planning studies. As expected, the Legislature did not act on the complex regional government proposal offered by ABAG, nor on the proposal submitted by the BARO chairman, but referred them to the Assembly Local Government Committee for further study.

The proposal of both the chairman of the Joint Committee on Bay Area Regional Organization and the Association of Bay Area Governments specified that any new regional government should be given responsibility for establishing a regional open space system. Thus with the Legislature's affirmative action on the Bay conservation issue and the publication in 1969 of *The Case for Open Space* by People for Open Space (which reported the favorable results of a cost-benefit study of the regional open space element of the ABAG plan), advocates of a regional open space program for the Bay Area found themselves in a position to take the final steps that could lead to the program's creation during the early 1970's.

The Role of Non-Governmental Organizations

The preceding interpretation of post-World War II governmental actions aimed at controlling surging urban growth in the Bay Area would be incomplete and misleading if the vitally important roles played by civic, conservation, and business groups are not emphasized. The sustained interest and patient, constructive work of the 22 Bay Area local Leagues of Women Voters, and of the unified areawide group of the League, of the many conservation groups in the region, and of the areawide business community as represented by the San Francisco Bay Area Council in particular, have been and will continue to be of fundamental importance.

During the 1950's and the 1960's, the leaders of these groups, like their elected and appointed governmental counterparts at the local, state, and federal levels, have given much thought to the regional needs of the Bay Area, and to the basic principles of representative democracy that must be considered in designing a regional government capable of meeting these needs. These leaders have agreed that the open space proposal is intended to serve one of the most important of the regional needs of the Bay Area. Thus, during the 1970's we may find ourselves ready, at long last, to gain control of the Bay Area's environmental future and to put a stop to the anarchistic way in which the region's past expansion has occurred. Hopefully, we will be ready to carry out this next great metropolitan enterprise in a way that will enable us to provide for our basic metropolitan environmental needs while we make a constructive contribution to the evolution of a regional government for the Bay Area.

A Regional Open Space
System for the Bay Area:
Economics and Implementation

As we have seen, the Association of Bay Area Governments' Preliminary Regional Plan was published in 1966, and in 1967 the General Assembly acted favorably on its initial Regional Home Rule Proposal. It thus was made evident to those interested in stopping sprawl during the 1970's that the importance of creating a Bay Area regional open space system had been acknowledged by a substantial and influential body of the region's city and county legislators.

As a consequence, it might have seemed reasonable to expect that ABAG and other governmental agencies would take the next steps to assure early preparation of regional open space legislation. Early in 1968, however, it was learned that necessary next-stage professional studies on alternative methods of implementing the regional open space plan would not be undertaken before the 1969 session of the state Legislature. Since such studies normally precede decisive legislative action, it became apparent that private initiative would be needed to maintain momentum and gain added public support for an effective program.

Economic Impact of an Open Space System

The Bay Area conservation group, People for Open Space (POS), responded to the need for more research. Members of a special POS committee met with representatives of the Joint Committee on Bay Area Regional Organization and of the Association of Bay Area Governments to develop a detailed study aimed primarily at meeting the research requirements outlined by these two governmental groups.[1] The final study proposal was approved by representatives of both groups. The research was supported by a grant of $59,000 from the Ford Foun-

---

[1] Members of the POS Regional Open Space Study Committee were: Joseph Bodovitz, Leslie Carbert, Dorothy Erskine, John Hirten, T. J. Kent, Jr., (Chairman), Irwin Luckman, John Sutter, and Gary Thurlow.

People for Open Space is a voluntary informal federation of the Bay Area's most active citizen organizations interested in conservation, regional open space, and regional planning. It was formed in 1958 and has played an influential role in shaping the open space plans of the Association of Bay Area Governments and the Bay Conservation and Development Commission, in conservation-related educational activities, in the formulation of proposals for limited regional government, and in successful efforts to acquire, or maintain through governmental regulation, several major open spaces in the Bay Area. See Appendix III for a brief history of the organization.

23

dation, and was carried out by a team of consultants who were appointed by and worked closely with the Regional Open Space Study Committee of People for Open Space during 1968 and 1969.[2]

The primary objective was to clarify the probable economic impact that establishment of a large-scale, regional open space system would have on future development in the Bay Area. The quantifiable costs and benefits of such a system were carefully investigated. Thus the study estimated the costs of establishing and maintaining an open space system, and evaluated the probable effect on the sources of tax income for the different governmental jurisdictions affected. It also considered the possible effects of an open space program on the future economic development of the region and on local and regional tax levels, and analyzed the governmental organization, authority, and financing necessary to implement a regional open space plan.

THE BASIC GUIDELINE: ABAG'S PLAN

The Association of Bay Area Governments' Preliminary Regional Plan provided the basic guideline. In 1968, ABAG's plan represented the only definite regional open space proposal for the Bay Area that was also an integral element of a comprehensive metropolitan development plan. In addition, the plan included many open space proposals initially suggested by conservation groups and by the excellent open space study prepared for the state in 1965 by the consulting firm of Eckbo, Dean, Austin, and Williams. Thus the ABAG proposal was far-reaching enough to provide a good test for the kind of cost-benefit study agreed upon. It was recognized that the ABAG Plan had not been adopted, and that there were important differences between it and open space components of proposals in adopted county plans. Because it was comprehensive and far-reaching, however, the ABAG Plan supplied an extremely useful policy guide. Full use was also made of other recently completed regional studies concerned with economic development, land use and physical development trends, conservation, and governmental organization and financing.

The People for Open Space study was completed in the spring of 1969. Its findings and conclusions were presented in two reports. The first was *The Case for Open Space*, published in January, 1969, presenting a summary of the study's principal findings and conclusions. The second report, *Economic Impact of a Regional Open Space Program*,

[2] J. Richard McElyea, executive vice-president of Development Research Associates, Los Angeles, Economic Consultants, directed the study, with the assistance of John Blayney of Livingston and Blayney, City and Regional Planners, San Francisco. Legal consultation was provided by Ira Michael Heyman, Professor of Law, University of California, Berkeley.

published in April, 1969, included the consultants' background studies in detail, and presented the assumptions and methods used, together with a more complete description of the findings, conclusions and recommendations.

Early in 1969 the results of the study were presented to the members of the Joint Committee on Bay Area Regional Organization, to other members of the state Legislature, to the Governor, and to the members of the Executive Committee of the Association of Bay Area Governments. In addition, 5,000 copies of the summary report were distributed to governmental and civic leaders in the Bay Area.

Action on regional open space and related Bay Area regional government proposals was not taken in 1969 by the state Legislature, but the People for Open Space study was widely distributed and is the most recent comprehensive report on alternative methods for implementing a regional open space program. Thus it can be anticipated that the forthcoming debates preceding definitive action by the state Legislature—hopefully during the early 1970's—will be based to a considerable extent on the results of the POS study.

STUDY FINDINGS: BENEFITS EXCEED COSTS

The study's most important finding was that it was possible to develop a practical regional open space program that would have greater quantifiable *benefits* than quantifiable *costs*. As Table I indicates, developing the program by means of land acquisition plus zoning could be accomplished in two ways. The first method, Alternative A, buying land in two stages, would result in a benefit-cost ratio of .75 to 1. The "buy immediately" plan, Alternative B, would be more advantageous, giving a benefit-cost ratio of 1.1 to 1.

In addition, it was judged that *nonquantifiable* benefits and costs would shift the balance for the "Purchase-Plus-Zoning" implementation alternative even more strongly in favor of a regional open space system. (See Figure 1.) The findings make it clear that the remaining questions to receive attention will concern the way such a system can be established and maintained, rather than its economic feasibility or desirability. Those who are familiar with the histories of regional open space proposals for the major metropolitan areas of the world will recognize this as a remarkable accomplishment.

TABLE I

ACQUISITION-PLUS-ZONING ALTERNATIVES
PRESENT VALUE OF CUMULATIVE COSTS AND BENEFITS, 1970–2000
(Millions of Dollars)

	Alternative A (Buy in Two Stages)	Alternative B (Buy Immediately)
Benefits		
Lease Income (including recreational)	$ 118	$ 165
Recreational User Benefits . . .	15	15
Savings in Utilities	838	838
Savings in Governmental Services .	318	318
Total	$1,289	$1,336
Costs		
Acquisition	$1,716	$1,224
	.75:1	1.1:1
Administration and Maintenance .	4	4
Total	$1,720	$1,228

Adapted from *Economic Impact of a Regional Open Space Program for the San Francisco Bay Area*, report prepared for People for Open Space by Development Research Associates, 1969, p. 37.

The technical report's seven major findings and conclusions are presented in the following pages. They can be fully appreciated only in the context of the metropolitan physical-structure growth alternatives for 1990, which provided the basis for the study. The maps on pages 28 and 29 are based on ilustrations in the summary report, and present two contrasting alternatives for the future of the Bay Area. Figure II shows the results of growth by *sprawl*, without a regional open space system. Figure III shows growth based on a policy of *compact city-centered development*, preserving open space. The latter alternative will require establishment of a regional open space system in the early 1970's, through action by the state Legislature.

The illustrative map on page 29 also shows the physical form and magnitude of the permanent regional open space system proposed by the Association of Bay Area Governments' Preliminary Regional Plan. The following table compares ABAG's 1990 proposal with existing public open space.

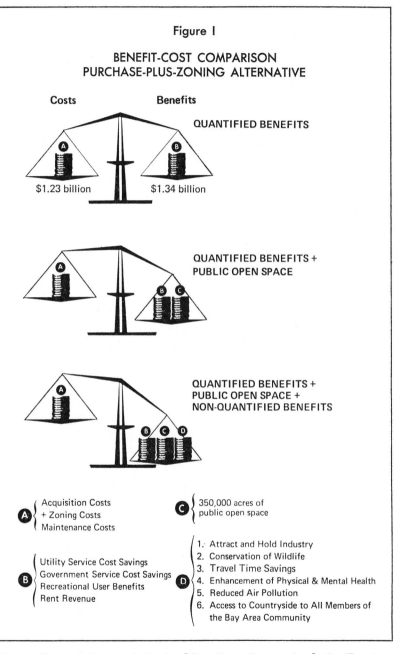

Figure I

BENEFIT-COST COMPARISON
PURCHASE-PLUS-ZONING ALTERNATIVE

Costs   **Benefits**

QUANTIFIED BENEFITS

$1.23 billion $1.34 billion

QUANTIFIED BENEFITS +
PUBLIC OPEN SPACE

QUANTIFIED BENEFITS +
PUBLIC OPEN SPACE +
NON-QUANTIFIED BENEFITS

A {
Acquisition Costs
+ Zoning Costs
Maintenance Costs

C {
350,000 acres of
public open space

B {
Utility Service Cost Savings
Government Service Cost Savings
Recreational User Benefits
Rent Revenue

D {
1. Attract and Hold Industry
2. Conservation of Wildlife
3. Travel Time Savings
4. Enhancement of Physical & Mental Health
5. Reduced Air Pollution
6. Access to Countryside to All Members of
   the Bay Area Community

Source: *Economic Impact of a Regional Open Space Program for the San Francisco Bay Area*, p. 51.

Figure II
OPEN SPACE LOST

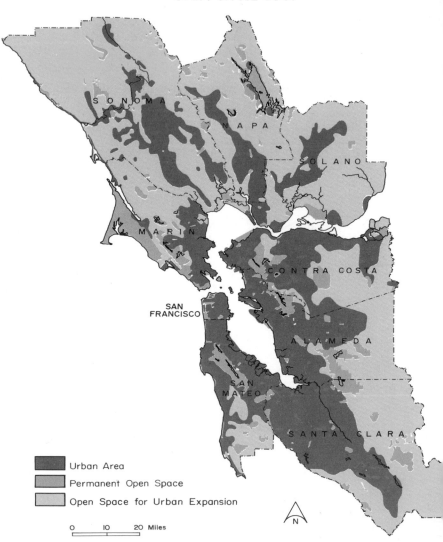

Urban Area

Permanent Open Space

Open Space for Urban Expansion

0   10   20 Miles

This map shows what the Bay Area will look like in 1990 if quick and bold action is not taken to save open space. It is assumed that a Bay agency will protect open water, and that local park agencies will buy enough land to maintain the present ratio of people to parkland. But even so, close-in open space will be nearly exhausted. For many, it will be a long, tedious drive to reach outlying regional open spaces. Much of the intervening area will be neither good city nor good countryside, but scattered subdivisions connected by ragged commercial strips. Soon urban development will fill in most of the remaining open land, smog and Bay pollution will increase, and agriculture will vanish.

Figure III
OPEN SPACE SAVED

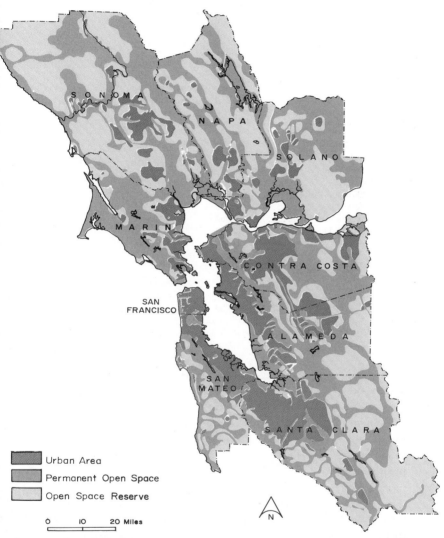

Urban Area
Permanent Open Space
Open Space Reserve

0   10   20 Miles

N

This map shows how the Bay Area's projected 1990 population of 7.3 million people can be accommodated without destroying the landscape. With prompt action, the Bay Area can retain major open spaces that will enable everyone to continue enjoying a natural environment. Sightseers, commuters, hikers, hunters, fishermen, picnickers, farmers—all have a stake in an effective open space program. The cost to the average household would be less than 10 cents a day. In fact, the dollar cost of failure to preserve open space might be much higher, if it causes the Bay Area to lose its attractiveness to new business development.

TABLE II

COMPARISON OF ABAG PROPOSAL WITH
EXISTING PUBLIC OPEN SPACE

Open Space Classification	ABAG Open Space Proposal 1990		Existing Public Open Space 1968	
	Acres Needed	Percent of Permanent Open Space Needed	Acres	Percent of 1968 total
Recreation	202,000	11	136,000	40
Agriculture	294,000	16	0	0
Wildlife Preserves: Hill Lands	197,000	11	61,000	18
Wildlife Preserves: Wet Lands	102,000	6	21,000	6
Water Resources Protection ...	312,000	17	122,000	36
Public Safety	72,000	4	0	0
Mineral Production	30,000	2	0	0
Areas to Guide Development...	592,000	33	0	0
Subtotal—Permanent Open Space	1,801,000	100	340,000	100
Open Space for Future Urban Expansion	1,633,000		0	
Total	3,434,000		340,000	

Source: *The Case for Open Space* (San Francisco: People for Open Space, January 1969), p. 7.

In considering the magnitude of the proposed permanent regional open space system—1,801,000 acres, or approximately one-third of the territory of the nine-county Bay Area—it is important to remember that the system is designed to provide for the needs of a *future* metropolitan population of 7,200,000. Even so, the proposed system is obviously large as compared with most other major metropolitan area regional plan proposals. The Bay Area's regional rapid transit system and Bay conservation plans were similarly bold in concept and generous in dimension. In view of the sizable amount of permanent open space proposed by the ABAG Plan, the favorable findings of the cost-benefit studies surprised many people, including the members of the study committee of People for Open Space and their consultants.

Tools for Implementing an Open Space Program

The People for Open Space study concluded that four strategies should be considered for preserving open space:

1. *Voluntary contracts* between owners and county governments could keep lands in agricultural use for specified periods, the properties being taxed only on their agricultural value. This is the approach of the Williamson Act.

2. *All* open space lands could be purchased by public agencies.

3. *Some* open space lands could be purchased publicly and other areas zoned to keep open space in productive use, but nevertheless insuring its preservation as open land.

4. *All* lands needed for open space use could be zoned, compensation being paid to owners whose lands lose value as a result.

Briefly, the summary report found the following advantages and disadvantages for each approach:

VOLUNTARY CONSERVATION AGREEMENTS

The California Land Conservation Act of 1965 (Williamson Act) was a creative and pioneering piece of legislation. The act was designed to preserve agricultural land by taxing *agricultural* value instead of real estate *market* value, if owners agree to keep the land in agricultural use for a specified time, usually a minimum of ten years. As county assessors increase their valuation of rural land, now typically assessed at 10 to 15 percent of market value, toward the 25 percent figure decreed by the Legislature, more and more owners of rural land are expected to sign Williamson Act agreements.

Resulting assessed value losses must be "made up for" by other taxpayers. In 1969 such losses were estimated to be about $40 million, or 0.4 percent of the Bay Area total, but ran as high as 25 percent in some school districts. A projection of recent trends indicates that the annual Bay Area loss of assessed values under Williamson Act agreements might approach $200 million. The shifted tax burden would be "spent" for open space. In return, however, the public would receive no guarantee of *permanent* preservation. Moreover, very little high quality agricultural land has been conserved by the Williamson Act even temporarily, because experience indicates that many owners place their lands under the Williamson Act only because they do not expect to develop for at least 10 years.

Nevertheless, the Williamson Act has provided a stopgap, allowing time to devise improved methods. In the absence of the Williamson Act, some valuable open space lands would already have been lost to urban development.

A Joint Legislative Committee on Open Space Lands is continuing to study various proposed modifications, in an effort to improve on the Williamson Act approach. It may prove difficult, however, to provide an incentive for landowners, without also giving a tax subsidy from which the public gains little in return.

BUYING ALL OPEN SPACE LANDS

The POS study devoted a great deal of attention to the potential costs of buying all the permanent open space proposed in the Association of Bay Area Governments' Preliminary Regional Plan. Would the costs be prohibitively high? Many people assume that the answer is "yes," and therefore dismiss open space purchase as impractical and visionary.

On the contrary, the study found that acquisition costs would be much lower than is popularly supposed—and that the corresponding future rewards would be very great. Thus, if the public were to buy all of the proposed permanent open space lands, at today's prices, the cost would be about $2 billion. In contrast, during the last 10 years alone, $1 billion has been spent in the Bay Area on right-of-way acquisition and state highway construction. The 75-mile Bay Area Rapid Transit system will have cost at least $1.2 billion by the time it is completed.

It would cost $10 annually per Bay Area resident to repay a $2 billion open space bond issue over 30 years. The real net cost would be much lower, because of important compensatory factors. Some of the open space lands could be leased to farmers for agricultural use, and the agricultural income could help finance the land purchase. Moreover, the public would save large sums on water, sewerage, and other urban services because of sprawl limitation and the compact patterns of urban development produced by the open space program. When these two additional savings are taken into account, the net annual cost for the open space purchase program may be reduced to as little as $2–$3 per person per year—or only about the cost of a good bottle of California wine and a loaf of sourdough French bread.

Looking back from the year 2000, a 1970 purchase at this price should represent a bargain comparable to the Dutch purchase of Manhattan Island for $24 in 1626. Are we as bold in our day as the early-day settlers from the Netherlands were when they bought Manhattan? No American metropolitan region has yet embarked on a full-scale open space program, but in other parts of the world excellent examples have been provided by Stockholm, London, and Ottawa.

PURCHASE-PLUS-ZONING

The study noted that zoning is frequently proposed as a way to preserve open space. But zoning presents many problems, both political and legal. On the political front, for example, evidence since 1945 has demonstrated conclusively that it is unreasonable to expect county boards of supervisors to keep close-in agricultural lands in an agricultural zone unless a majority of the owners wish their property zoned exclusively for agriculture. On the other hand, zoning on a regional basis and by a regional agency would provide better opportunities to use land in the interest of the entire area, because agency legislators elected on a one-man-one-vote basis would be responsible for and could be expected to protect the long-term interests of the metropolitan community.

Legal research for the POS study noted that the courts might find it difficult to justify a zoning policy that restricts one owner to a low return on his land, while allowing neighboring landowners to make substantial profits from urban development. In such cases the courts might well side with the injured landowners, who could argue that the zoning was intended primarily to obtain by regulation benefits that the public rightfully ought to pay for.

Purchasing some lands, and regulating the use of other lands by zoning, would reduce the initial cost of carrying out the open space plan. In the long run, however, it might result in higher costs. For example, lands held under zoning controls only temporarily might later have to be acquired at substantially increased prices. But much land could also be retained *permanently* as open space by zoning. Courts would uphold zoning for public safety, i.e., for flood plains, and might also uphold permanent, exclusive agricultural zoning for large and unique agricultural areas, such as the Napa Valley vineyards.

Purchase-plus-zoning may prove to be the most practical of the alternatives. Because of this, the study attempted to determine which lands should definitely be purchased by the public by 1990 to provide for open space and to guide urban development. Under this alternative, the costs of public purchase of 350,000 acres would be $1.25 billion, compared with $2 billion if all the lands were to be purchased. The remaining lands would be zoned as open space.

REGULATION WITH COMPENSATION

A fourth alternative, called compensable regulation, also combines purchase and zoning. This technique holds considerable promise. It has never yet been tried in the United States, although enabling legislation to permit its use has been proposed in Pennsylvania. Under compensable regulation, lands to be retained permanently as privately owned open space would be designated, mapped, and zoned for specific uses, such as intensive agriculture or dairy farming. Property owners would be guaranteed that, whenever they chose to place their land in the open market, they would receive at least the value it possessed before regulation, adjusted to changes in the value of the dollar. If the sale price were less than the guarantee, the regional agency would pay the difference. Thus, under compensable regulation the public captures future increases in land value, but guarantees to the owner any value that has accrued up to the time when regulations were imposed.

Property owners would be taxed only on the open space use of their lands. Thus owners wishing to retain their lands as open space would not be affected by the compensable regulations. This approach works no tax hardship on landowners, and leaves decisions on sales entirely up to them.

Compensable regulation poses problems because of its newness, and the consequent question of its political acceptability. It also entails appraising substantial acreages of open space, and would require a relatively complex administrative mechanism to carry out the program.

A final note on all four of the alternatives: in the long run, no single choice will prove fully satisfactory. A combination of techniques and financial sources will be needed, rather than a single alternative chosen from among the four.

Major Findings and Conclusions: Recapitulation

The seven major findings and conclusions of the study were:

1. *Open Space is Financially Practical.* A regional open space program—even a program as comprehensive as that proposed by the Association of Bay Area Governments—would not impose a major financial burden on Bay Area residents. Even the most costly technique—purchase of all proposed permanent Bay Area open space lands —would cost no more than $10 per person per year, and the net costs would approximate only $3 per person after deducting the quantifiable benefits of such a program. The total acquisition cost would be less than the combined total of BART and the Bay Area freeway system funds expended over the past ten years. The latter, of course, are depreciating assets, while the open space lands would be preserved permanently and continue to increase in value over the years.

2. *An Anti-Sprawl Policy Would Result in Dramatic Savings.* The proposed open space program would produce dramatic savings in governmental and utility costs, by shaping future urban development and limiting suburban sprawl. The projected difference between the cost of serving the growth patterns that would result *without* an open space program, and the more compact pattern *with* open space, would be approximately $300 million for municipal services, and $835 million for gas, electric, and telephone service.

3. Quantified Benefits Are Equal to Costs. The estimated quantifiable dollar benefits of an open space plan for the Bay Area are about the same as the costs required to implement such a plan. The estimated governmental and utility savings mentioned above total $1.14 billion. These quantifiable savings would make up for the dollar costs of preserving open space under the "purchase-plus-zoning" alternative.

4. The Bay Area's Environment is a Major Economic Asset. No realistic dollar value can be placed on the preservation of environmental quality in the Bay Area. The study indicated, however, that the Bay Area has attracted much of its economic activity because of its superior environment. The number of headquarters offices, industries, institutions and persons who are free to choose their environment is constantly increasing. This becomes an important factor, since in site selection decisions for many types of enterprises the Bay Area must compete with areas having lower labor, production, and distribution costs. Unquestionably, one of the Bay Area's principal economic resources today is its superior environmental quality. If the environment suffers significant degradation, the area's competitive position for encouraging desirable new development will be seriously weakened. Thus, preservation of the environment through a major open space program represents good business.

5. Assessed Values Will Be Shifted, Not Reduced. A major open space program will not cause a net loss in assessed values. Removing a large amount of land from the available regional supply will increase the value of other built-up and raw land, thus quickly restoring any temporary reductions in the tax base that may be caused by use restrictions or public acquisition. The result would be a transfer of values within the overall region. On a local basis, of course, inequities are likely to develop among small taxing jurisdictions. Methods of adjustment would have to be provided. These inequities would be less severe in many cases, however, than those created by continued use of the Williamson Act's preferential assessment provisions in their present form.

6. Increased Values Will Require New Tax Policies. As part of the regional open space program, efforts will be needed to prevent excessive increases in the market value of land available for development. On the other hand, the capture of future increases in the value of developable land offers excellent opportunities to finance the open space program. For example, capital gains taxes, real estate transfer taxes, and tax increment financing or "betterment" taxes could be used as sources of funds. Property taxes, as such, need not and should not be relied upon to provide a major source of financing.

7. *Benefits Will Be Widespread and Lasting.* With national attention increasingly focused on the crisis of the American city, is there justification for metropolitan open space? The study concluded that the answer is definitely YES. Unquestionably, public funds—and increased private investment—will be needed to attack the problems of the central city. But it must be abundantly clear that the availability of summer camps and access to beaches and countryside, are more important to the ghetto child than to the child who lives in a neighborhood having greater local amenities. Certainly, one primary goal of regional planning ought to be provision of open space—for recreation and for enjoyment—within the easy reach of the urban poor who have neither the time nor the money for long travel. In conjunction with open space, better public transportation must be provided to enable all residents to reach the open space easily and inexpensively. Finally, a balance is needed between intense attention to critical problem areas, and concern for the overall environment. If a concentrated effort to improve the quality of life in the central cities causes us to abandon concern for the *overall* quality of life in the entire Bay Region, then all of us—rich and poor, black and white, city dweller and suburbanite—will lose in the long run.

The availability of the Association of Bay Area Governments' regional open space plan, plus other recently completed regional studies, made it possible for the People for Open Space consultants to examine thoroughly the two opposite metropolitan growth alternatives: compact city-centered development with open space vs. unrelieved sprawl. The result produced some highly significant facts and figures, in addition to those included in the summary. For example, 325 square miles of land will be saved from sprawl, if adoption of the proposed regional open space system in the early 1970's shapes Bay Area growth in the 1970's and 1980's to conform with ABAG's city-centered plan. To put it another way, if present trends are permitted to continue, 325 square miles of land will be irrevocably dissipated in scattered, sprawling urban development. The fundamental inefficiency of wasting such large amounts of land—by comparison, San Francisco occupies only 43 square miles—would seem a far greater burden to society than the more than $1.1 billion in extra costs for utilities and government services that sprawl would make necessary, and which the consultants were able to quantify.

The People for Open Space summary and technical reports were prepared for concerned citizens of the Bay Area, as well as for local and state legislators and their advisers. They are being widely read. The technical report presents the detailed information needed to help individual citizens and legislators formulate their own judgments. The summary report enables one to learn quickly the principal findings and conclusions that were reached as a result of the study. The final paragraphs of the summary report below convey the sense of urgency felt by everyone who was involved in the study.

Clearly there is no single right way to create an open space system. But equally clearly, regional open space must be reserved while it is still available. If these lands are developed, there will be no second chance to keep them open.

In the Bay Area, perhaps more than anywhere else in the country, the public is increasingly demanding that a high-quality environment be maintained. The challenge is to focus our ingenuity and our energy toward creating the kind of Bay Area we want for our children and our grandchildren—and to recognize the essential importance of regional open space in this effort.

How will our generation be judged by those living in the Bay Area in 1990— will we be remembered as the generation with the vision and foresight to preserve our natural heritage, or will we be remembered as the generation whose "do nothing" attitude permitted urban sprawl to engulf the environment?[3]

---

[3] *The Case for Open Space* (San Francisco: People for Open Space, January, 1969), p. 15.

Where Do We Stand Now?

When Bay Area efforts to create a regional open space system are compared with the history of British open space and greenbelt legislation, it appears that we have reached the halfway point in what may have to be a 50-year effort. Before World War I, broad public support for policies to stop the uncontrolled, sprawling growth of London and the other large industrial cities of England and Scotland began to be evident. However, it was not until 1932—one full generation later—that the first plan for a metropolitan open space system was completed. This plan, prepared by Sir Raymond Unwin and called "London's green girdle," served for more than a decade as the basis for a voluntary action program led by the London County Council.

During the decade of the 1930's thousands of acres of open space on the outskirts of the great metropolis were purchased by local governments to provide recreation for Londoners, and to guide the growth of the metropolitan region. In 1947, Parliament enacted legislation controlling all urban growth in Britain. In 1955, the full-scale greenbelt and open space programs for London and several other British cities were permanently established, based on comprehensive city and regional development plans.[1]

The British city planning and land development system—from its inception supported and perfected by both major political parties—is acknowledged as the most advanced in the world. By comparison, our current Bay Area efforts are somewhere in the middle period of plan-making and voluntary action, which England entered in the early 1930's. If we are able to learn from the experience of others, as we are trying to, it may not be necessary to wait and watch for another 20 years, while today's more destructive forms of urban sprawl continue their unabated expansion.

It is predictable that, in one form or another, four existing Bay Area programs concerned with open space needs—those of (1) the counties, (2) the Association of Bay Area Governments, (3) the state Legislature, and (4) People for Open Space—will be continued until the main regional planning and governmental questions which are raised by the metropolitan open space issue have been dealt with satisfactorily. The extent to which these programs can be transformed into complemen-

---

[1] An excellent brief account of British experience is included in the 30-page booklet, *The Green Belts,* prepared by the Ministry of Housing and Local Government in 1962. Copies of this publication can be obtained from British Government Publications, 845 Third Ave., New York, New York 10022.

tary, mutually supportive efforts during the early 1970's will determine whether or not there is an early chance for substantial success.

If county government leaders could be persuaded to change their pro-sprawl policies prior to the creation of a regional open space agency, this would be of immense importance to the future of the Bay Area. The counties should be encouraged in every possible way to do so. If such efforts fail, however, and if we also do not establish a regional open space agency, the consequences will be drastic. For example, we will see sprawl destroy the Napa Valley, the western slopes of Marin County, and the vast open areas that still exist in Sonoma and Solano counties, as we have already witnessed, unwillingly, the destruction of the once-magnificent Santa Clara Valley.

Can the Counties Save Regional Open Space?

Knowledgeable observers are aware that county governments in the Bay region have had to devote most of their postwar efforts to the developmental problems of their growing, suburban fringe areas, rather than to the needs of the vast outlying agricultural and mountain territories, which formerly claimed their primary attention. This explains why the expansion of the Bay Area metropolis—which is taking place primarily *outside* the boundaries of the existing 91 municipal governments—is in the hands of the legislative bodies that control the region's county governments—governments created more than 100 years ago for completely different purposes.

Knowledgeable observers also know that—after urbanization takes place—residents of unincorporated suburban communities sooner or later become critical of their county's efforts to provide local services and regulations, and demand the establishment of new, locally controlled municipal governments. Since the end of World War II, thousands of acres of sprawling suburban tract developments have been encouraged by county governments. As urbanization proceeded, these areas were removed from the jurisdiction of county governments, as the number of incorporated municipalities in the Bay Area rose from 67 to 91, and as many cities pursued aggressive annexation policies.

County governments cannot effectively guide and shape metropolitan growth.[2] A two-day drive around what is now the Bay Area's middle ring of suburban tract development offers example after example of opportunities lost, of failures caused by plans based only on high hopes and expressed only as good intentions. Moreover, there is a strangely

---

[2] This blunt criticism of county governments is supported here and elsewhere by comment in the text. In addition, Appendix V presents a further critique of county government as an agency of urban land use control.

persistent unawareness of the continuing failure of county governments to implement many constructive plans.

Amid the vast amount of urban physical equipment that has been provided to accommodate the population growth during the past 25 years, the most obviously missing element is a permanent regional open space system. From the vantage point of the suburban middle ring built since 1945, one can look outward today and still see open lands. But looking outward from the inner cities, it is now apparent that a process of urban suffocation was begun about 1945. Today, few citizens wish this process to continue. Convincing arguments—based in part on past experience—suggest, however, that county governments will be unable to stop it.

Several Bay Area county governments have been recognized as leaders among the nation's urban counties. They have supported the establishment of outstanding county planning programs, and have carried out certain types of community-level and county-level general plan elements. But the earliest and strongest county planning programs have also been among the most unsuccessful in obtaining support at the crucial time for proposals designed to meet two vital postwar regional needs: effective programs for regional rapid transit and for regional open space.

Some observers expected major changes in the policies of county governments after the courts ordered county supervisorial districts reapportioned several years ago. This should have made it more difficult for agricultural interests to continue their dominant role in metropolitan Bay Area county affairs. However, not much reapportionment actually took place, despite the court decisions. Moreover, the recent record suggests that coalitions of suburban and agricultural interests have continued to win and hold control most of the time. Forces representing vested interests in the one-time profits from development of raw land also have a major influence. For metropolitan-wide social, economic, and environmental concerns, such revision of supervisorial districts as has occurred does not appear to have produced any appreciable changes for the better.

Thus, despite reapportionment and excellent work by some county planning commissions and their professional staffs, it seems unreasonable to expect county legislative bodies to define, protect and promote the long-term future interests of the metropolitan community. Regional environmental needs and the ability of county governments to meet these needs are mismatched. Unfortunately they will probably remain so.

In the past two decades Santa Clara Valley has provided a classic object lesson in growth-by-sprawl under county control. Given that experience, it would be foolish to believe that the praiseworthy action taken by the Napa County Board of Supervisors in 1968, establishing the county's specialized vineyard agricultural zone, can be sustained for the indefinite future.

If one accepts these judgments, what are the most hopeful things that can be expected while county governments still control the form and structure of metropolitan growth in the outer ring of the Bay region? First, public interest in county and regional open space proposals will continue to grow rapidly. Suburban residents will undoubtedly give encouragement and support to further development of county general plans that will become more explicit with reference to large-scale green-belt and open space proposals. The result will be a continuing increase in the number of citizens who are knowledgeable and politically astute about county and regional plans, about open space implementation methods, and about county and regional governmental powers.

Second, despite the gradual improvement of county plans for open space systems, county legislative bodies can be expected to continue to ignore, in their most important policies and actions, the pro-open space, anti-sprawl policies of their own general plans. In other words, they will continue to give lip service to admirable plans, while adopting specific zoning ordinances and capital improvement projects that promote sprawl and destroy open space. As a result of these actions—which realists must anticipate—the county electorate will be sadder but wiser. There will be a new sense of awareness of the nature of county government: a new appreciation both of what counties can do well and of what it would clearly be unreasonable to expect from county legislative bodies.

Finally, as a consequence of the hopeful experiences with the preparation of excellent county and regional open space plans, contrasted with the depressing reality of an overall record of defeat in implementing those plans at the county level, an increasing number of candidates for city and county elective offices are likely to be drawn from the growing ranks of conservationists. Thus, there will probably be a steady and significant increase in the number of elected and appointed political leaders who understand the need for a multipurpose, limited-function regional government, one that is charged specifically with conserving and enlarging the Bay Area's permanent regional open space system, and is given the power to accomplish this task.

The Bay Area's great size and unusual geography mean that each of the nine counties is a distinct subregion. The long history of county governments has produced strong county loyalties, awareness of the value of county self-government, and a spirit of county self-reliance. Thus the success of efforts to establish a Bay Area regional open space system during the early 1970's probably will depend on whether or not a significant number of county leaders are ready and willing to give outspoken public support to the creation of a regional open space agency and program—one that will be strong enough to control their own county governments in questions of metropolitan growth.

Does ABAG's Open Space Plan Have a Future?

In 1967, when the Association of Bay Area Governments made its highly significant and hopeful decision to advocate the establishment of a limited regional government, few observers realized that a second and possibly even more important decision was made at the same time. By approving the Regional Home Rule Proposal, the General Assembly also indicated its support for the reorganization of its Executive Committee in ways that would reduce the power of county delegates and increase the importance of the role assigned to the Executive Committee. Subsequently, by action of the General Assembly, the composition of the Executive Committee was modified to conform to the Regional Home Rule Proposal, and the Executive Committee's role as a legislative body was confirmed.

Thus, the relationship between ABAG's city and county delegates, who originally were on an equal footing, was modified to increase the potential influence of the municipal governments.[3] This change is of particular importance to the regional open space proposal.

As previously noted, shortly after its establishment in 1961 ABAG committed itself to the preparation of a regional development plan. With the publication of the staff's Preliminary Regional Plan in 1966, and the Executive Committee's subsequent approval of an extended review period for the plan, the association became the first advocate for a specific regional open space program in the Bay Area related to metropolitan growth requirements. Although the plan had not been acted upon by the General Assembly more than three and one-half years after its publication, and, therefore, had no official status, the staff's recommended regional open space element of the plan is now well

---

[3] These changes were the result of (1) enlarging the proportionate representation of the City of San Francisco on the Executive Committee; (2) giving the City of Oakland three Executive Committee representatives; and (3) giving the City of San Jose two representatives.

This gives city governments approximately 58 percent of the Executive Committee membership—if San Francisco is considered half city and half county. If San Francisco is considered to be a *municipal* government, the cities' share of the Executive Committee membership rises to more than 65 percent.

understood by many individuals, especially the active leaders of the Bay Area's conservation groups. Consequently the plan had developed "a life of its own."

Despite many criticisms, no one has offered an alternative to the association's regional open space proposal. Spokesmen for the Bay Area's conservation groups have urged enlargement of the areas indicated in the plan for permanent open space. They have also questioned the no-restraint policy concerning population growth between 1970 and 1990, and the completely open-ended, no-limitation policy beyond the 1990 figure of 7,200,000. Even if it is not adopted, as an unofficial policy proposal the Preliminary Regional Plan will continue to influence debates and decisions on the future of the Bay Area, and to provide the basis for arguments in support of a large-scale permanent regional open space system.

Publication of the Preliminary Regional Plan and action on the Regional Home Rule Proposal mean that ABAG has assured its continuing existence and influence in regional affairs. The association's policies and actions since 1961 help explain why the Bay Area is a national leader in the metropolitan regional conservation and open space movement. Perhaps most important of all, the existence of the ABAG plan means that the basic issue of growth-by-sprawl vs. compact, city-centered growth can no longer be ignored.

The Future of Regional Government Legislation

For the first time since the regional needs of the Bay Area began to receive serious attention more than 20 years ago, the Legislature is considering bills aimed at meeting these needs in a comprehensive way. Assembly Bill 711, introduced in 1969 by Assemblyman John Knox, Chairman of the Joint Committee on Bay Area Regional Organization, and Assembly Bill 1846, submitted by Assemblyman William T. Bagley with ABAG support, both call for a limited regional government. A number of specific responsibilities are proposed, including the preparation of a regional development plan and the establishment of a regional open space system. Although the basic approaches are different, the two bills contain more areas of agreement than of disagreement.

As a result of the Knox and Bagley proposals, continuing state legislative attention to the need for a regional open space system seems to be assured. In view of great legislative victory for Bay Area conservation forces in 1969, with the approval of the bill to establish the Bay Conservation and Development Commission on a permanent and strengthened basis, and in view of the publication of the regional open space cost-benefit study by People for Open Space in 1969, legislative leaders can be expected to prepare more realistic regional open space proposals in 1970 than would have been possible in 1969.

In long-range terms, the most significant fact concerning the relationship between the state Legislature and the Bay Area open space issue was the establishment in 1967 of the Joint Committee on Bay Area Regional Organization. Although the BARO committee may not be continued, its creation focused attention on the Bay Area's unmet regional needs in a constructive and influential way. As a result, it now seems certain that the leaders of the Legislature will give continuing attention during the 1970's to the major contemporary questions involved in the establishment of a limited regional government for the Bay Area to meet acknowledged regional needs, including the need for a regional open space system.

Will Strong Regionwide Public Support Be Forthcoming?

In our society, governmental action on major conservation issues cannot be expected to occur without a demonstration of widespread public support, usually sustained over a long period of time. The key to success in establishing a Bay Area regional open space system, therefore, is held by the leaders of the region's conservation and civic organizations.

People for Open Space is the region's one conservation organization that has focused primarily on the nine-county Bay Area. It has been in existence for more than a decade.[4] Its governing committee has, in effect, been permitted to act on behalf of many different conservation groups on matters of regional concern. At best, however, it is only a loosely knit and informal association of like-minded groups, whose leaders have learned how to work together on regional issues.

People for Open Space may or may not succeed in attracting and supporting the civic and legislative leadership that will be essential for the success of the next great Bay Area regional effort. It is certain that the organization's leadership will make the attempt. Thus, People for Open Space and cooperating Bay Area conservation and related civic groups, such as the Sierra Club and the Save the Bay Association, can be expected to maintain their active interest in the regional open space issue and to press for action during the early 1970's.

---

[4] See Appendix IV for names of the Board of Directors and Advisory Committee of People for Open Space; Appendix VI for a list of Bay Area conservation and related organizations; and Appendix VII for a letter written by Mel Lane, Chairman of the Bay Conservation and Development Commission to BCDC commissioners and proxies following the passage of BCDC legislation in 1969. Mel Lane's letter is offered as evidence that Bay Area conservation and civic groups can work effectively with interested business and government leaders.

The long postwar period of reasonably successful civic and political action on regional needs has produced a generation of leaders who are certain to be interested in preparing for the next step in shaping the future of the Bay Area. Given the availability of such experienced regional civic activists, and given the demonstrated ability of these leaders and their associates to find effective ways to marshal the strength of many different kinds of organizations, we can anticipate a strong, sustained effort to save the Bay Area's natural environment during the early 1970's.

The effort can most effectively be undertaken, however, only if there is general agreement on the major substantive provisions to be included in effective regional open space legislation. The final section of this essay will attempt to clarify the basic questions such legislation must answer.

Legislation to Stop Sprawl

Knowledge of recent open space studies and proposals, and of the historical context from which they have emerged, suggests that consideration should now be given to a two-step legislative approach. The first step calls for legislation establishing a temporary *Bay Area Regional Open Space Commission*. The second step calls for legislation that would establish, on the basis of the temporary study commission's final report, *a permanent regional open space agency* with the governmental authority and financial support required to assure the creation of a Bay Area open space system during the 1970's.

The First Step: A Two-Year Study Commission

During the 1950's and 1960's the Legislature authorized study commissions for rapid transit and for Bay conservation. The suggested temporary Bay Area Regional Open Space Commission would be based on the precedents thus established. As we know, the work of these study commissions subsequently led to the successful enactment of controversial and complex implementation legislation in 1957 and 1969.

If civic and legislative leaders who are already convinced that the Bay Area must conserve and enlarge its permanent open space system choose to follow the impressive and conservative precedents of BART and BCDC, the Bay Area may have a strong regional open space agency in the not-distant future.

It must be plainly recognized, however, that unless a way can be found to protect existing high priority open spaces during the proposed study period, the powerful forces that promote growth-by-sprawl will do great damage before they can be curbed. In response to indications that the Legislature may be preparing to change the rules that have governed urban growth in the Bay Area since the 1930's and 1940's, when county zoning and building codes were first established, pro-sprawl developments of all kinds can be expected to accelerate, in anticipation of such stringent controls.

In considering the first step for open space legislative action, therefore, it is important to be reminded of the precedents established during the BART and BCDC campaigns for what would have to be, in effect, a two-year moratorium on urban development in certain open space areas that are vital to the future regional open space system. During the 1951–57 study period that preceded establishment of BART on a permanent basis, and subsequently until 1962, when the BART bond issue was approved, no major attempts were made to revive the in-

46

herently anti-transit 1947 "parallel bridge" proposal, which would have made the financing of BART impossible.[1] Although some might not consider this to be a moratorium in the literal sense, the first successful postwar freeway revolt in the Bay Area, which stopped the parallel bridge proposal, did in fact result in a moratorium until it was determined whether the Bay Area would support BART. The BCDC precedent is more recent and more widely recognized: during the final four years of the five-year study period that preceded the permanent establishment of BCDC, control over Bay fill permits was placed by the Legislature in the hands of BCDC itself. This was done in 1965 when the authority of cities and counties in relation to such permits was temporarily withdrawn and reassigned to BCDC. The reassignment was made permanent in 1969.

Two main groups of issues must be dealt with in designing legislation to establish a temporary regional open space study commission. The first concerns the specific functions of the study commission. Second are questions of governmental organization and finance.

It is assumed that the Legislature would consider it reasonable to give the proposed temporary Bay Area Regional Open Space Commission a life-span of two years. This is shorter than the study periods preceding the permanent establishment of BART and BCDC. However, the adverse effects of urban sprawl are already well understood by many Bay Area civic leaders, and are widely observed by blue-collar and white-collar workers. Moreover, ABAG's regional open space plan has been available for study since November 1966. Perhaps most important of all, the work of the Legislature's Joint Committee on Open Space Lands, which is concerned with the entire state, has produced some excellent reports and experimental open space legislation. Thus an influential group of legislators understands the need for open space and has already had practical experience in state-level efforts to develop and test methods of open space preservation.

FUNCTIONS OF THE PROPOSED STUDY COMMISSION

Five specific assignments are proposed for the Regional Open Space Commission. In part, they reflect experience with the 1964 and 1965 legislation defining the initial duties and powers of BCDC. They are also based in part on applicable lessons learned from the experience with BART, ABAG, and BARO.

1. *The First Function of the Bay Area Regional Open Space Commis-*

---

[1] The 1947 "parallel bridge" proposal, as noted earlier, called for a second auto toll bridge parallel and adjacent to the San Francisco-Oakland Bay Bridge, which itself had been completed only eleven years earlier in 1936.

sion: to redefine and restate the public interest in the existing and po-
tential regional open space resources of the Bay Area. This would require preparation of descriptive and technical reports on the existing
and potential systems of regional open space. It would involve research
into the ecological interrelationships of the principal open space elements, and study of present and future economic, social, and environmental needs for particular types of permanent, large-scale, open space
within or adjacent to the urbanized districts of the metropolitan region.
The open spaces to be evaluated by these studies would include lands
required for regional park and recreation purposes, specialized agriculture, flood control, wildlife preservation, ecological balance, public
safety purposes, and the protection of essential natural resources. They
would also include lands needed for aesthetic and historic purposes and
for others related to the protection and enhancement of life in the Bay
Area, as determined by the commission.

2. *The Second Function of the Bay Area Regional Open Space Com-*
mission: to study the effects of further sprawl on the future of the Bay
Area. Carefully documented technical reports on the Bay Area's economy, social conditions, and physical environment would call attention
to those aspects that would be adversely affected by continued expansion
of the suburban sprawl that has characterized development in the Bay
Area's middle and outer rings since 1945. The study commission would
draw upon research by Bay Area and state governmental agencies, by
private groups, and by federal agencies. One example is the 1968 report
by the United States Advisory Commission on Intergovernmental Relations, *Urban and Rural America: Policies for Future Growth.*

This portion of the study commission's research and informational
assignment would require reiteration of many things that are already
reasonably well known. Nevertheless, the importance of this activity
cannot be overemphasized. A period of sustained public discussion,
based on the technical studies and reports envisioned, is necessary for
the development of a fully informed and concerned citizenry, as well as
a determined legislative and civic leadership. Informed and concerned
leadership will be essential if strong anti-sprawl legislation is to be
enacted at the conclusion of the study commission's work.

3. *The Third Function of the Bay Area Regional Open Space Com-*
mission: to study the implications of the policy of unlimited future
population growth for the Bay Area. Unlimited growth is the unstated
policy now being followed by all but a very few local governments, state
and federal agencies, and Bay Area public and private organizations
responsible for anticipating—sometimes more than 50 to 100 years in
advance—the region's future utility and service needs.

The development programs of the Bay Area's utility companies provide excellent examples of self-fulfilling prophecies. First, massive funds are committed to expand key elements in a utility system that will greatly increase, perhaps double, the system's capacity. Next, a steady increase in the population using the enlarged system is promoted in order to assure the success of the initial financing plan. Thus, the enlargement of the utility system creates its own need for an ever increasing population.

If the total population of the Bay Area, or the population density in central portions of the region, go beyond certain limits, it can reasonably be assured, some observers say, that the results may produce a scale and intensity of metropolitan development for which the *costs* will be demonstrably greater than the *benefits*. Large expenditures of public and private funds for utility systems—and for Bay Area freeways—have been and are scheduled to be made, based on *the opposite assumption,* i.e., on the assumption that unlimited growth will bring greater benefits than costs. It seems essential, therefore, that the policy of unlimited population growth be given a careful reexamination. The 1969 report of the National Committee on Urban Growth Policy, presented in the book entitled *The New City,* provides an excellent statement outlining the reasons for developing alternatives to the policy of unlimited growth which until recently has been the unquestioned policy of each of the nation's major metropolitan regions.[2]

4. *The Fourth Function of the Bay Area Regional Open Space Commission: to administer temporary controls over the location of urban development projects.* Controls will be needed to assure that existing priority open spaces are protected during the commission's two-year study period. The legislation will be similar in many respects to the temporary Bay fill control provisions of the Legislature's 1965 BCDC law. The availability of the Williamson Act, which (after certain conditions have been met) permits agricultural lands to be taxed at their agricultural use value, may be of particular significance in the Bay region after legislation is enacted to protect the area's priority open spaces for a temporary period. Once the Bay Area's legislative and civic leadership decides to establish a regional open space study commission, and, as a consequence, decides to protect the region's most essential and most vulnerable open spaces during the period of the study, there is no

---

[2] The committee, which was formed in 1968, is jointly sponsored by the National Association of Counties, the National League of Cities, the United States Conference of Mayors, and Urban America, Inc. Committee members represent all levels of government and both major political parties. See also *The New Towns: The Answer to Megalopolis,* F. J. Osborn and Arnold Wittick (London: Leonard Hill, 1969) (Second Edition), chapters 5, 6, and 9.

doubt that the necessary legislative provisions to accomplish this can be worked out successfully.

5. *The Fifth Function of the Bay Area Regional Open Space Commission: to prepare a comprehensive and enforceable regional open space plan for the Bay Area.* This major task will require the commission to do three things: (1) to prepare a regional open space plan; (2) to prepare an implementation program, including all measures, financial, legal, and otherwise, needed to make possible the plan's implementation; and (3) to recommend an appropriate regional governmental agency to carry out the plan.

ORGANIZATION OF THE PROPOSED STUDY COMMISSION

Given the BART and BCDC study commission experiences, it is unnecessary to reexamine questions of governmental organization and finance at any length. A determined group of civic and political leaders—adopting either of the two principal approaches used during the past 25 years—can find ways to assure establishment of a strongly motivated, representative, and able governing board for the open space study commission.

In drafting legislation for the suggested temporary study commission, it will be important to avoid unnecessary conflict with the proponents of the Association of Bay Area Governments' Regional Home Rule Proposal. ABAG's record includes constructive contributions toward developing public understanding of the need for a comprehensive regional open space system. But it also includes strong opposition to the 1965 and 1969 BCDC bills, and opposition to an earlier legislative proposal calling for a regional planning district. Thus, the association's response to the proposed regional open space study commission can be expected to be complex and, unfortunately, its net result is likely to be negative.

A regional open space program will cause major adjustments primarily only by the nine Bay Area *county* governments. A strong regional open space program should, logically, be supported by the elected leaders of all of the Bay Area's 91 city governments. As noted earlier, BCDC's work impinged not only on the nine county governments in the Bay Area: in acting on the 1965 and 1969 BCDC bills, the Legislature transferred authority for certain land use permits over Bay and Bay shoreline lands from 35 city governments having shorelines, as well. Thus, if city leadership within the association develops a clear understanding of the regional open space study commission proposal during the early stages of its consideration, ABAG opposition to the proposed open space agency should be less than it was in the case of BCDC.

It will be recalled that the chairman and other members of the Joint Committee on Bay Area Regional Organization were leaders of the 1969 BCDC legislation. These legislators have demonstrated their awareness of the need to keep moving forward in meeting regional needs while legislation for a limited regional government is being put into final form, and while attempts are made to work out the compromises that will be needed if the regional government legislation is to have a fair chance of being enacted.

The Second Step: A Permanent Regional Open Space Agency

There are many reasons for following the BART and BCDC study commission precedents in attempting to establish a strong regional open space program. However, as we have seen, the situation with respect to open space has changed substantially in recent years as a result of publication of the ABAG Preliminary Regional Plan in 1966, establishment of the Legislature's Joint Committee on Open Space Lands in 1967, and completion of the regional open space cost-benefit study by People for Open Space in 1969. Thus, open space is no longer fully comparable to the rapid transit and Bay fill situations that existed prior to 1951 and 1964, respectively, when BART and BCDC advocates were just beginning to explore and explain the need for their proposed programs. In the case of open space, substantial exploration and explanation have already been done.

The Bay Area conservation, civic, and legislative leaders who succeeded in establishing BCDC on a permanent basis in 1969 must take time for the necessary regrouping and readjustments required to shift from the subject of Bay conservation to the closely related but nevertheless quite different subject of regional open space conservation. If, after regrouping, they find they agree with the sense of urgency felt by the members of People for Open Space and others, it would, in theoretical terms, be logical to move directly, in 1971 or 1972, to obtain legislative approval for the establishment of a permanent regional open space agency. All the authority it will subsequently require could be provided in the initial legislation. Such a time schedule would be comparable to that followed by the Legislature in 1955 when it established the Bay Area Air Pollution Control District. The public health issues and sense of urgency that led to quick initial action on air pollution are also present in the urgent need to preserve regional open space and to protect the environment.

Each of the regional government proposals put forward by ABAG and BARO during the past three years has included regional open space in the group of essential new regional functions that the proposed regional government would be authorized to undertake at the outset on a permanent basis. There is also substantial agreement among many nongovernmental groups that open space preservation is a major unmet regional need. Moreover, the principal controversial implementation questions have been explored as a result of work done by the state since 1955, BCDC in 1968, and People for Open Space in 1969. Nevertheless, despite these logical justifications for avoiding the two-year delay that would be caused by following the temporary study commission precedent, this conservative course of action is the only policy that can be expected to attract the kind of large scale public support regarded as absolutely essential to the success of strong open space legislation.

Consequently, the following legislative suggestions have been developed on the assumption that a temporary study commission will be established. They are intended to highlight the principal issues that will have to be clarified when the duties and powers of the permanent agency are considered by the members of the study commission and, subsequently, by the members of the Legislature and the Governor. Hopefully, they deal with *all* of the critical questions that must be answered if the future environmental quality of the Bay Area is to be saved during the 1970's.

THE PROPOSED COMMISSION

This proposal calls for a permanent Bay Area Regional Open Space Commission to be established as the successor to the temporary study commission. The proposed agency, if created as one of the initial departments of a limited regional government, would require a combination of key elements drawn from the BARO and ABAG proposals.

As suggested by the association, the agency should have an "advocate" commission, similar to the boards and commissions of city and county governments. As suggested by both the association and the chairman of the Joint Committee on Bay Area Regional Organization, the agency should be subordinate to the legislative body of the limited regional government. And finally, as already indicated, the nature of a comprehensive regional open space program would require a governing body composed of directly elected representatives similar to that proposed by the chairman of the Joint Committee, and a strong guarantee that there will be an effective check by local governments on unwarranted expansion of the needed regional program into areas that can best be handled permanently by local governments.

Since there is no assurance of favorable action on limited regional government proposals for the Bay Area during the early 1970's, the regional open space proposal must include provisions similar to the

1969 BCDC legislation, enabling it to operate as a new and separate regional governmental agency, until a unified limited regional government is established. This means that if the sequence of legislative actions during the next few years is such that the proposed permanent regional open space commission must be established before the limited regional government, the new agency would be the first regional special district in the Bay Area to require a *directly elected* governing board. Before reviewing this controversial provision in detail, the functions and powers of the proposed permanent Regional Open Space Commission will be considered. Because the functions and powers of the agency must be so broad, and because they will require decisions of such far-reaching importance to the lives of the people of the Bay Area, they can properly be entrusted only to a directly elected governing body.

Eight Functions for the Commission

Eight functions are suggested for the Regional Open Space Commission. They are interrelated, and all are considered essential if the Bay Area's regional open space system is to be conserved, enlarged and enhanced. The functions must also be designed to insure that the people of the Bay Area are empowered to govern the future development of the metropolis in which they live. The *conservation and development* approach, which has been shown by the experience of BCDC to be both workable and acceptable, is expressed in the following proposals. As with BCDC, some observers may consider that the proposals give undue emphasis to conservation, as opposed to development. However, until it can be demonstrated that further sprawling urbanization will not irreparably damage the Bay Area, it must be anticipated that legislation to limit sprawl will be misunderstood initially as being directed against *all* new growth. This, of course, is not the case.

1. *Objectives of Regional Open Space System.* The first responsibility of the permanent open space commission would be (1) to redefine and restate the public interest in a regional open space system, (2) to study the effects of further sprawl on the future of the Bay Area, and (3) to study the implications of the present policy of unlimited population growth. On the basis of findings and conclusions made possible by these studies, the commission would state the economic, social, environmental, and ecological objectives of the regional open space system. Thus the first three functions of the proposed study commission, as already discussed, are combined into one function recommended for the proposed permanent commission.

2. *Adoption of a Regional Open Space Plan.* The commission's second responsibility would be to prepare and maintain a long-range regional

open space plan. That plan would be one element in a comprehensive Bay Area regional conservation and development plan, for which the Regional Open Space Commission would also be responsible until a limited regional government is established. A preliminary outline version of the regional plan should be completed within two years, in order to provide the basis for essential early open space action such as the regional land use ordinance described below. The legislation assigning this responsibility should require adoption of the completed regional plan (as suggested by the staff of the Joint Committee on Bay Area Regional Organization), no later than five years after the Regional Open Space Commission has been established. The legislation should also require the plan to be published in a single document that any interested citizen can obtain and understand.

The regional plan would provide a broad framework for coordinating plans for other regional elements. It would be based upon city and county plans, and would incorporate their policies and proposals to the fullest extent possible. The regional plan would also suggest how essential regionwide needs could be accommodated with a minimum readjustment of local plans. In preparing its comprehensive plan, the Regional Open Space Commission would, of course, make use of the existing plans of ABAG, BCDC, BATS, the Bay-Delta Study, the State Division of Highways, and the United States Corps of Engineers.

In addition to statements presenting the major objectives and policies of the plan and the general physical structure proposed for the future metropolis, the regional plan would elaborate on the following specifically regional issues: (1) regional centers, (2) metropolitan expansion, (3) regional open space, (4) the Bay and Bay shoreline, (5) regional transportation and transportation corridors, (6) regional utilities and public facilities, and (7) regional environmental quality and ecological issues. The relationship of the proposed regional physical development plan to regional social and economic issues would be made explicit.

The Regional Open Space Commission could be assigned the task of reviewing all regional special-element plans. But the commission should not be given authority to make final decisions in case of conflicts: this all-important responsibility must be reserved for the legislative body of the regional government. However, if the commission were to decide by a majority vote that a plan element was in serious conflict with the comprehensive regional plan, it might be reasonable to recommend that the regional special-purpose agency involved modify its plan. Such a recommendation would not be effective, however, if the board of the affected agency decided by a majority vote to proceed, despite the adverse recommendation of the Regional Open Space Commission.

3. *Adoption of a Regional Land Use Ordinance.* The commission's third function would be adoption of a regional land use ordinance to implement the regional plan. The ordinance could be patterned after Hawaii's land use law.[3] Modifications would be made, of course, to suit California's governmental structure, which is significantly different. The regional ordinance would divide the Bay Area into three land use districts: Bay, metropolitan, and regional open space districts. If the Regional Open Space Commission were part of a limited regional government, the regional legislative body would enact the necessary ordinance. Proposals to amend the boundaries of the three districts could be initiated by city or county governments, regional agencies, including the open space agency, or by the regional legislative body. The land use district boundaries would receive a comprehensive review every five years.

Except for modifications indicated by the regional plan, the *Bay land use district* would comprise the area now under the jurisdiction of BCDC. The regulations applied would be those established by the Legislature and BCDC.

The *metropolitan land use district* would include all urbanized lands in the Bay Area, plus a sufficient reserve for a 10-year expansion period. This would be the key portion of the regional land use ordinance, giving qualitative scale and definite geographic framework to both the Bay land use district and the regional open space land use district. It is needed to provide a logical and a legal basis for the boundaries and provisions of the regional land use ordinance. In certain cases, the latter would significantly alter the manner in which private property can be used, especially in the Bay and the regional open space districts. A logical regional plan, and a reasonable land use ordinance designed to implement the plan, applying to all property within the region, will be necessary under the United States Constitution and our system of land development law. As noted below, city and county zoning ordinances would govern land uses within the metropolitan land use district.

The *regional open space land use district* would include all remaining lands in the Bay Area. It would include lands designated as permanent regional open space as well as lands that might be needed for future urban development, beyond the 10-year growth period provided for by the metropolitan land use district. The Regional Open Space Commission would adopt regulations governing the uses of land within the

[3] In describing this proposal, the author has drawn on work done by Lee Beardall, graduate student at the University of California, Berkeley, in connection with the thesis he prepared for the Master of City Planning degree in 1969.

regional open space district, establishing subzones for agriculture, conservation, regional parks and recreation, and other open space uses. Within these major open space districts, counties, and where appropriate, cities, would adopt detailed land use regulations. These would take precedence over the regional land use regulations *if the local regulations were more stringent* in preserving the open character of the land. All regulations would be administered directly by city and county governments; the Regional Open Space Commission would exercise limited but controlling supervisory powers.

4. *Regional Open Space Action Program.* The commission's fourth duty would be to prepare, adopt, publish, and distribute widely an action program, including explicit short-range (one-year) and middle-range (five-to-ten-year) legislative and financing proposals. The program statement would explain how the long-range regional open space plan is currently being carried out, and how the commission proposes to carry it out during the coming decade. An annual progress report should be required.

5. *Regional "Land Bank."* The commission's fifth responsibility would be acquisition of lands needed for regional parks, subregional and local parks, and other specified open space lands needed in the future. Such lands would then be made available as required from the regional "land bank" administered by the commission. It is anticipated that an increasing number of individuals would choose to transfer their private property to the regional land bank by sale or other appropriate means, with open space conditions.

This suggestion illustrates clearly the limited role, in terms of governmental jurisdiction, proposed for the Regional Open Space Commission. The program outlined requires the continuation and strengthening of local government park departments and subregional park districts. The governmental concept is based on the assumption that in no other way can a regional park and recreation program be developed that will reflect and take full advantage of local conditions, local traditions, and local initiative. The Regional Open Space Commission would not be authorized to operate regional parks. Thus it would be required to develop a regional program by supporting existing programs, by encouraging the establishment of new city, county, and subregional park and recreation agencies, and by working cooperatively with the State Park Commission, the National Park Service, and other state and federal agencies, several of which have substantial open space lands and related programs in the Bay Area.

6. *Authority to Lease Agricultural Land.* In order to stop sprawl, it will be necessary in certain situations to purchase agricultural and

other types of open space lands, which may not be needed for regional park, conservation, public safety, or other similar purposes. The Regional Open Space Commission should have authority to retain such lands permanently, if necessary, and to lease them for agricultural or other appropriate income-producing open space uses. The commission also should be authorized to sell such lands, but only if permanent control assuring non-urban use is legally established.

7. *Compensable Regulation.* The People for Open Space report, *Economic Impact of a Regional Open Space Program,* demonstrated that a substantial amount of money—approximately $1.22 billion—would be essential for the large-scale acquisition of close-in open space lands when the new regional agency is established, *unless* the commission is given traditional land-use zoning powers with the additional power of "compensable regulation" authorized in certain defined and limited situations. Such regulatory powers would enable the commission to keep open space lands near cities and between suburban communities permanently in agricultural use. Taxation of such lands would be based on their agricultural value. Should the private owners wish to sell, they would be assured the full market value of their property, as of the date when compensable regulation ordinances and lower taxes were established.

New enabling legislation, including a financial program, would be necessary if the regional open space agency is to perform this new kind of needed land use regulatory function. Although compensable regulation offers many advantages, including the provision of strong incentives for the permanent retention of income-producing agricultural lands in private ownership, such legislation, as noted earlier, has not yet been enacted in the United States. The need for this kind of program is readily understandable in theoretical terms. But the practical arguments that will eventually lead to its implementation become evident to conservationists and legislators only when a metropolitan community finally decides to be responsible about its future and to guide metropolitan growth comprehensively, in the public interest. The Bay Area is the first large metropolitan region in the United States to have a definite anti-sprawl proposal that highlights the advantages of enlarging traditional zoning authority to permit the use of compensable regulation.

8. *Temporary Control of Development to Conserve Priority Open Spaces.* The temporary control function of the permanent Regional Open Space Commission is the same as the fourth assignment suggested for the temporary two-year study commission. Obviously, such legislation will be needed for the permanent agency only if temporary

authority to protect high priority regional open spaces was not given to the two-year study commission. The legislation will be controversial, but the BART and BCDC precedents already established and the urgent need for protecting major open spaces during the plan-making period should assure legislative support for such controls. When appropriate controls are authorized, it will be necessary to designate a reasonable time period, perhaps two years, during which the commission would be required to complete and adopt its initial Regional Land Use Ordinance. Thereafter, its authority for temporary controls would expire.

ORGANIZATION OF THE PROPOSED PERMANENT COMMISSION

Shoreline land use regulatory powers were an essential part of the 1969 BCDC legislation. These powers are normally entrusted only to general-purpose local governments having directly elected legislative bodies. Accordingly, prior to the enactment of the BCDC legislation, it was suggested several times that the proposed permanent Bay control commission ought to be composed of members directly elected, rather than appointed.[4] Likewise, because of BART's unusually large grant of taxing authority, and the powerful influence of the regional rapid transit system on the present and future social, economic, and environmental conditions of life in the Bay Area, it has been proposed several times that BART's appointed governing board should be replaced with a directly elected board.

For at least two reasons, what was proposed but not approved for BCDC and BART, seems to be essential for the Regional Open Space Commission. The first reason relates to the broad scope of the commission's work; the second to the nature of the economic and political forces at work in the Bay Area's outer ring.

Both BCDC and BART exercise powers that are altering trends and rearranging many economic and urban development forces in the central cities and in the middle ring of the metropolitan Bay Area. But neither agency has such a broad subject-matter scope that it was obvious that it should have been required to state the regionwide development assumptions upon which its special element plan was based, before proceeding with its action program.

The opposite is likely to be true for the regional open space agency. Indeed, metropolitan regional open space legislation that attempted to conceal—or failed to facilitate open acknowledgment of—the agency's underlying development assumptions would be a greater

---

[4] In March, 1970, Assemblyman John Knox introduced legislation aimed at replacing BCDC's appointed board of directors with a directly elected board.

danger for local democracy and regional home rule than could ever be justified by the *conservation* benefits it might promise. *With the regional open space issue, proponents of the special district approach will have reached the point where obviously beneficial ends can no longer be used to justify the continued use of unresponsive, autonomous and essentially anti-democratic means.*

The regional open space agency will have to be given the power to establish a regional open space zone. Under our philosophy of government and our system of law, in order to exercise that power, the commission should also be required (1) to show how the regional open space zone is logically and reasonably related to the other two regional zones needed to govern the growth of the region, and (2) to show how the comprehensive regional land use ordinance is logically and reasonably related to the agency's long-range plan for the future development of the region. An agency that is given such general and far-reaching powers—even though it is not a *multi-purpose* agency in terms of its action program—should be under the control of a directly elected governing body.

A persuasive rationale supports the recommendation for a directly elected board for the open space agency, a rationale based on our system of law as enforced and interpreted by the courts, on California's strong tradition of municipal and county home rule, and on the Bay Area's emerging tradition of regional home rule. But its logic is not self-enforcing in terms of legislative enactment. It can be ignored or disagreed with. But even if the Legislature makes an initial decision concerning the governance of the Regional Open Space Commission that does not provide for direct election, the impact of the agency's program will be so great that, sooner or later, the courts will be asked to determine the issue of regional representation.

In addition to the governmental and legal principles that recommend a directly elected board for the commission, both experienced conservationists and legislators can be expected to recognize that the commission's duties will bring it into head-on collision with the postwar pro-sprawl forces of suburban land development, including the State Division of Highways and the powerful combination of interests it seems to serve primarily. Under our existing method of expanding the metropolis, these forces are typically, and not unexpectedly, aided by county and suburban governments. (See Appendix V.)

Thus it seems unlikely that a governing arrangement for the proposed regional open space agency that gives a major role to representatives of local governments will ever be able to withstand the tremendous pressures opposing the very policies that such an agency would be intended to carry out. Despite the impressive postwar record of constructive participation by local governments and their legislators in meeting certain regional needs of the Bay Area, the scope, authority, and conflict-of-interest issues raised by the regional open space program call now for the establishment at the regional level of a system of electoral politics.

The adoption of pro-conservation or pro-sprawl policies would be determined by elections throughout the Bay Area, and by the "staying power" of the ideas and the political organizing abilities of the region's civic and conservation groups and their leaders. The time has now arrived for the Bay Area to embrace the practice of traditional, straight-forward representative democracy at the regional level. This is preferable to continuing to oppose new regional special districts in theory, and then continuing to create them in practice, one at a time. This is what we have been doing since 1949, after rationalizing the strange, temporary, and politically unhealthy compromises that have been made to insure indirect and sometimes devious control of the governing body of each agency.

CONCLUSION

There is a compelling need now to gain control of the Bay Area's sprawling growth, and to begin governing the region to protect and make secure the environmental future of the humane metropolis that man has built in the nine-county Bay Area. This need is certain to be generally acknowledged and acted upon sooner or later. Along with a number of other self-evident needs of our society, the proposed regional open space program probably has far broader and far stronger public support than either its closest friends or its strongest adversaries realize.

The city planning problem—which in this case concerns the physical structure of a great and growing metropolis—is to state as clearly as possible the policies that are needed to protect the area's still promising future. This must be done before it is too late to avoid consequences that will be economically and socially dangerous and environmentally degrading, if not ecologically disastrous.

The governmental problem—in this case primarily one of determining the relationships between an emerging limited regional government and existing local and state governments—is to find a way to create, soon enough, a strong regional agency for the necessary regional open space program, without disrupting the remarkable and still hopeful progress that has been made during the past 25 years toward the creation of a limited regional government in the Bay Area.

APPENDICES

APPENDIX I

"Don't Let It Happen Here"

BY LUCIUS BEEBE

San Francisco *Chronicle*, September 19, 1965
(Reprinted by permission of the San Francisco *Chronicle*)

The almost complete abandonment of New York City as an inhabitable place and its surrender to massive business and the towering infamies of progress are the theme of gloom and doom on the lips of every returned traveler nowadays from what, in the easily memorable past, was in everything but name the Nation's capital city and an abode of all that was enviable in the facade of living.

Even the old cliche that it was a nice place to visit has now disappeared from the national lexicon and people who have business there get in and out of town as fast as its strangled traffic and mangled agencies of transport will permit.

From being the wonderful metropolis that once, and not too long ago, offered every attraction both of the body and of the spirit Manhattan Island has become a wasteland where from the Battery to the Bronx traffic is stalled as nowhere else on earth, where the already insufficient number of luxury hotels has been further reduced to accommodate a megalopolis of offices and a population so densely concentrated that human movement and the ordinary satisfactions and convenience of urban living are all but impossible.

Hear the words of *Fortune* magazine, the Bible and acknowledged apologist for monster industry and ever bigger business:

"The truly terrible costs of New York are social and spiritual. These accrue in endless human discomfort, inconvenience, harassment, which have become part of the pervasive background, like the noise and filth, but are much deadlier. For it is people who breathe life into an environment, who create the vitality of a healthy city. If people are driven and their senses dulled, if they are alienated and dehumanized, the city is on the way to destroying itself."

The tally of New York's infamies of the current moment is far too great to bear rehearsal here, but there may be cited the barbarous destruction of the stately Pennsylvania Station to be replaced by greedy opportunists with a sports arena and the equally wanton destruction of the Savoy Plaza and Madison Hotels to be replaced by the dreary and menacing facade of General Motors. Elsewhere in the most brutally

63

congested concentration of already existing office buildings, the New York Central Railroad has raised above Grand Central Depot the world's most hideous warren of business pestilences and an additional population of 25,000 extra and unwanted people in a single city block.

The spectacle of what *Fortune* calls "a city destroying itself" is there for every other American community to witness and perhaps to ponder, but the frightening truth is that there are real estate operators every bit as avaricious, every bit as hostile to the best interests of the public, every bit as brutal in their rapacity operating in the full light of day in San Francisco as their counterparts 3,000 miles across the continent.

◇   ◇   ◇

The idea that San Francisco can be so overbuilt as to strangle on its own breath may appear fantastic, and it will be so argued by men of notable avarice and little civic responsibility. It also seemed fantastic in New York City in 1945.

The suet pudding mentality of the Governor of California admires and applauds the growth of the State's population for the same obvious reasons that all politicans with their feet in the public hogtrough admire more people: i.e., more suffrage, more ignorance and more plunder.

San Francisco still has time on its side and the example of New York if it will be warned. The equation is simple: more people, more business, more politics and more taxes equal no more San Francisco.

APPENDIX II

Policy Concerning San Francisco and the Future Governmental Needs of the San Francisco Bay Area, Establishing Guidelines and Principles to Be Observed By San Francisco's Delegates to the Association of Bay Area Governments[1]

WHEREAS, The Association of Bay Area Governments, being aware of the evolutionary developments which have taken place in the Bay Area since the end of World War II and the fact that during the past seventeen years five single-purpose area-wide governmental special districts have been created, with others in prospect, has undertaken a one-year study to reconsider its own basic policies concerning the proliferation of special districts and its own future; and

WHEREAS, The vital interests of the citizens of San Francisco and their government are directly involved in the future growth and development of the nine-county Bay Area and the solution of the increasing number of serious and complex regional problems which confront the area; and

WHEREAS, Specific additional areawide needs that illustrate the reality of the danger of proliferation of special districts, include:

(1) A proposed Bay Area greenbelt district;

(2) A proposal for areawide airport planning and financing;

(3) Suggestions concerning the need for an areawide agency to locate and operate major refuse disposal sites for the cities and counties of the Bay Area;

(4) The proposal made by Mayor John F. Shelley to ABAG in 1964 concerning the need for providing a maximum choice in housing throughout the Bay Area for families of all income levels and all ethnic groups to relieve the continuing trends that adversely affect non-white and low income citizens and the future of the central cities;

(5) Proposals for unified control of the bridges and ports of the Bay Area; and

---

[1] This resolution was submitted to the San Francisco Board of Supervisors by Mayor John F. Shelley, with a recommendation for adoption. The board unanimously approved the resolution on April 11, 1966.

WHEREAS, Developments begun during the postwar period seem to be converging, and districts which originated separately now find that the effective operation of each depends on the others, which increasing inter-dependence would indicate that the time has come to participate in the creation of a long-needed government by, of, and for the Bay Area community, which will strengthen, not disrupt or replace, the existing system of city and county government in the Bay Area, while at the same time enabling the critical needs of the metropolitan community to be provided for effectively, in a democratic way; and

WHEREAS, The City and County of San Francisco as a member of ABAG and a participant in the proposed study of the future of the Bay Area, has an obligation to provide leadership in the formation of constructive policies aimed at the solution of areawide governmental problems; now, therefore, be it

RESOLVED, That the following shall be and it is hereby established as the basic policy of the City and County of San Francisco as to the creation of means to fulfill future governmental needs of the Bay Area, and such policy shall guide the City's delegates to ABAG:

GENERAL POLICY GUIDELINES

Recognizing the danger inherent in piecemeal creation of what has been described as "a fragmented super-government for the Bay Area," San Francisco favors establishment of a unified, limited-function, metropolitan government, which is a genuinely local Bay Area Government, and not a State agency performing local governmental functions. San Francisco also favors the grouping together of all present and any essential new Bay Area functions under a single limited-function Bay Area government, with less than total consolidation of all special districts acceptable initially in order to get the framework of the new government established.

San Francisco is not committed to any detailed particular form of metropolitan limited-function government and to preclude premature dissension or disagreement concerning details, will favor discussion of metropolitan governmental needs at the level of general principles until firm agreement on this level is achieved. Normal differences regarding form may then more easily be ameliorated.

Existing areawide governmental functions which should be unified as soon as possible include: 1. Air pollution control; 2. Bay water pollution control; 3. Bay conservation and development; 4. Areawide transportation planning; 5. Comprehensive Bay Area development planning.

Eventually, the Bay Area Rapid Transit District should become an integral part of the unified Bay Area government.

BROAD PRINCIPLES

A. The Bay Area government must have an entirely local Bay Area political constituency; i.e., it must not be a State agency with some local representation on the governing board.

B. The functions of the new government must be restricted to those essential areawide functions that are not and apparently cannot be handled adequately by the city and county governments of the Bay Area.

C. The Bay Area government shall replace no local general purpose government; i.e., all existing city and county governments will continue and, in fact, will be more firmly established for the future as a result of the creation of the limited-function Bay Area government.

D. The Bay Area government's legislative body must be composed of members directly elected to it. The duties of the Bay Area legislative body will be complex and demanding; it will not be possible to continue the transition arrangements of the postwar period which placed city and county elected officials or their appointees on the governing bodies of the areawide special purpose districts.

E. Whatever method of organizing the Bay Area legislative body is decided upon, it must be in accord with the principle of equal representation. There will be issues facing the Bay Area government, such as the Bay conservation issue, that will require the urban population of the Bay Area to have a direct majority.

F. The existence of the Bay Area government should preclude the creation of any additional separately-established metropolitan special districts in the future.

G. A merger of metropolitan Bay Area functions is necessary now as an alternative to the present and future proliferation of special districts. This proliferation is not only an obstacle to an informed and interested electorate, but it diffuses our financial resources and political energies. Proliferation will make it practically impossible for the citizens of the Bay Area, as voters in a democracy, to understand and exercise effective control over the work of the increasing number of special districts. A unified, limited-function Bay Area government is needed to make democracy work at the metropolitan level and to strengthen the tradition of city and county home rule and self-government in the Bay Area.

FURTHER RESOLVED, That the City and County of San Francisco shall support the above-stated policy and principles at the meetings of the General Assembly, the Executive Committee, and, in particular, the Goals and Organization Committee of ABAG; and, be it

FURTHER RESOLVED, That the City and County of San Francisco shall support the continued existence of ABAG, whether or not the results of the study of its Goals and Organization Committee recommends the creation of a unified limited-function metropolitan government. If ABAG does support the establishment of such a government, in addition to fostering cooperative enterprises on important matters where there is general agreement, ABAG will be needed to openly and forcefully oppose the unnecessary expansion of the new government. If ABAG does not support the establishment of the new Bay Area government, the City and County of San Francisco will continue to press for further consideration of the proposal.

FURTHER RESOLVED, That the City and County of San Francisco will make special efforts to maintain liaison with the existing Bay Area Transportation Study Commission and the Bay Conservation and Development Commission as the work of the ABAG Study Committee progresses, and will encourage their concurrence in the recommendation that the creation of a unified, limited-function metropolitan government is the most effective governmental framework within which the permanent functions of their organizations could be carried out.

FURTHER RESOLVED, That copies of this resolution be forwarded to The Honorable Edmund G. Brown, Governor of California, members of the State Legislature, and officials of the Federal Government, with the request that they consider the policies and principles set forth herein to the end that all officials and agencies who will be affected by the proposed creation of a unified, limited-function metropolitan government may be apprised of the status of the ABAG study and the position of the City and County of San Francisco on the future governmental needs of the Bay Area, and with unanimity of purpose may join in a concentrated effort toward the accomplishment of the goals and principles incorporated herein.

File No. 165–66   Resolution No. 137–66

A Brief History of "People for Open Space"[1]

On June 3, 1958, the San Francisco Planning and Housing Association sponsored a conference entitled "The Peril To Our Public Lands—A Discussion of Regional Recreation." At this meeting a panel of Bay Area leaders discussed several pressing conservation issues, including the preservation of Richardson Bay and a moratorium on subdividing 6,500 acres of watershed surrounding San Pablo Reservoir. The panel stressed the need for a common policy and unity in action on a regional level to avert further desecration of the Bay Area's environment.

One of the conference speakers was Elmer Aldridge, Executive Director of the California Public Outdoor Recreation Plan Committee. The impending Outdoor Recreation Plan highlighted the lack of regional parks in California's metropolitan areas. Mr. Aldridge stressed the critical importance of such parkland and urged vigorous support for additional regional recreational areas.

Responding to these challenges, representatives from various conservation, planning and recreation groups already active in the Bay Area (e.g., Sierra Club, San Francisco Planning and Housing Association, and Marin Conservation League) met on the evening of June 17, 1958. They formed a coalition known as "Citizens For Regional Recreation and Parks." This informal federation was established as a mechanism to exchange information, develop common policy on regional conservation issues, and conduct educational programs concerning the preservation of open space.

Today this organization, now incorporated as "People For Open Space," continues these types of activities to achieve its basic, overall objective: conservation of the Bay Area's unique natural environment through the promotion of regional planning and the preservation of open space. ⋄ ⋄ ⋄

The first project undertaken by Citizens For Regional Recreation and Parks (CRRP)[2] was to compile an inventory of Bay Area land

---

[1] This report is drawn, almost entirely, from a term paper prepared by Kenneth C. Frank, graduate student at the University of California, Berkeley. The paper was developed for the course in City Planning 201, December, 1969.

[2] The name was changed to People For Open Space in 1968.

which was, at that time, publicly owned, relatively permanent, open space area. Comprised of state and local parks, water district property, military reservations, and similar lands, the inventory was distributed throughout the Bay Area. Perhaps its most influential recipient was Elmer Aldrich, who met with CRRP to discuss the inventory and its relation to the outdoor recreation plan being prepared by Mr. Aldrich's staff. Eventually, when the California Outdoor Recreation Plan proposal was released in 1960, CRRP summarized Part I of the report and distributed 300 copies to Bay Area leaders.

In order to activate citizens' organizations throughout the Bay Region, CRRP cooperated with the Extension Division of the Department of City and Regional Planning at the University of California in conducting three regional open space conferences. The initial conference entitled "Our Vanishing Open Space" was held December 11, 1959 in Richmond. This one-day affair attracted approximately 250 people, including a representative from at least one organization in each of the nine Bay Area counties. The attendees represented a broad range of interests such as conservation organizations, garden clubs and similar civic groups; city and county planners, planning commissioners and planning consultants; employees of park and recreation departments and districts; other city, county and state officials; college instructors and students; and architects and landscape architects. This conference marked the first time that Bay Area conservationists and planning experts had joined forces to consider issues of a regional nature.

A second conference was held January 27, 1961 in San Francisco. Entitled "Now or Never," this meeting focused on ways to establish a system of regional parks. Then, on January 26, 1962, CRRP, together with the University's City and Regional Planning Extension Division and the Bureau of Public Administration on the Berkeley campus, convened a third meeting. Participants discussed the topic of "San Francisco Bay—A Great Recreational Resource." Each of these three conferences served to underscore the need for prompt regionwide coordination and action to preserve the Bay Area's unique environmental setting.

Besides cosponsoring these three conferences, Citizens For Regional Recreation and Parks actively supported various specific conservation proposals. In 1960, the United States General Services Administration (GSA), which is vested with authority to dispose of surplus federal property, announced a public auction to sell 73 acres of Fort Baker. Normally, before auctioning surplus federal land to private developers, GSA provides an opportunity for local governments to purchase the acreage for half its appraised value. However, in this instance GSA cited an obscure clause allowing it to contravene that usual procedure. In addition, one week later GSA declared a similar auction for surplus property at Fort Funston, again offering land to private developers before contacting governmental agencies.

Citizens for Regional Recreation and Parks, together with other civic groups and governmental jurisdictions, brought this anomalous situation to the attention of the Congress. Besides supporting HR 12798, which directed GSA to convey the Fort Baker property to the State of California at half price, CRRP suggested that Congress amend the Administrative Services Act of 1949 to compel GSA to offer surplus property to state, county and city governments at half its appraised value before holding a public auction. Eventually, the Fort Baker auction was cancelled. Moreover, Fort Funston was offered to the City of San Francisco at half the fort's appraised value. A $1.1 million bond issue appeared on the November 1961 ballot and San Franciscans approved the purchase of Fort Funston as a recreational area.

A few months later, in June 1962, voters were confronted with a state ballot proposition to authorize $150 million for state purchase and development of recreation areas in California. Although this bond issue was announced only four weeks before the election, CRRP printed and distributed 25,000 fact sheets outlining the areas to be purchased in the Bay Region (e.g. Golden Gate Headlands, Salt Point Beach in Sonoma County, Fort Funston, etc.). Although the bond issue failed to pass because of opposition in Southern California, voters in eight of the nine Bay Area counties (Sonoma County was the exception) favored the bond issue. The dissimilarity in voting patterns can be explained in part by the active Bay Area campaigns conducted by CRRP, the Sierra Club and other local conservation groups. There were no comparable efforts in Southern California.

Recognizing the importance of establishing a continuing long range planning program for a permanent regional open space system, CRRP asked the Association of Bay Area Governments (ABAG) to develop a long range, comprehensive regional land use plan for the nine-county Bay Area. Parks and open space would be one element of that plan. With the assistance of CRRP President Mel Scott, ABAG applied for and received a federal planning grant to undertake such a study.

In order to aid ABAG in preparing the open space element of the regional plan, Citizens for Regional Recreation and Parks attempted to identify those areas with outstanding recreation and open space potential. In 1964, questionnaires were mailed to dozens of park, recreation, hunting, yachting, hiking and conservation groups and to various community leaders, asking them to indicate on maps those areas which should be reserved for recreation and preservation. The responses were processed and mapped by students in the University of California's Department of Landscape Architecture. Then a CRRP review committee, chaired by T. J. Kent, Jr., Chairman of the Department of City and Regional Planning at the University of California, Berkeley, sifted through the material and made numerous recommendations.

In his November 10, 1964 testimony before the Bay Conservation Study Commission, CRRP President John Sutter presented the shoreline sector of the survey. Later, 1,000 copies of that statement were sent to elected representatives and civic groups in the Bay Region. The complete survey, which included shoreline and inland areas, was submitted to ABAG in March 1966. ABAG's preliminary regional plan, which was published in November 1966, included most of the major CRRP recommendations. In addition to providing valuable information to ABAG and BCSC (predecessor of BCDC), the CRRP survey was important in stimulating public awareness of the plans that these agencies were formulating.

During this period, CRRP continued vigorously to present its specific views to local and national decision makers. For example, in 1965 CRRP supported State Senate Bill 309 on Bay planning; the Army Corps of Engineers were urged to withhold their permit allowing filling of the Bay near Bay Farm Island; the San Mateo County Planning Commission was requested to preclude unnecessary commercial intrusion in Coyote Point Park; and Marin County planners were urged to obtain scenic easements from the developers of the proposed Marincello Project, in order to preserve the crest of the Marin hills in their natural state.

Moreover, when the state beaches and parks bond issue was reincarnated as Proposition I on the November 1964 state ballot, CRRP publicized the measure and urged its members to mail postcards and informational leaflets to their associates. These efforts contributed to the success of Proposition I.

By 1966 the following agencies were conducting planning studies in the Bay Region: Bay Conservation and Development Commission, Bay Area Transportation Study Commission, Bay-Delta Water Quality Control Program and the Association of Bay Area Governments. Unfortunately these agencies lacked funds to make their preliminary studies widely available to the general public. Since constructive action on the final reports would eventually depend on strong public understanding and support, CRRP summarized these studies in its *Regional Exchange* publication. Almost monthly between August 1966 and November 1968, the leaflet consisted of summaries of the reports being issued by BCDC. Typical *Regional Exchange* titles are: "Tides of San Francisco Bay," "Airports on the Bay," "Marshes and Mud Flats," "Ownership of the Bay," and "ABAG's Preliminary Regional Plan."

At one time, *Regional Exchange* reached a monthly circulation of 16,000. Many civic organizations such as the Marin Conservation League, Save the Bay Association, and the Audubon Society purchased copies in bulk for distribution to their memberships. As several of these organizations incurred financial difficulty in disseminating the monthly publication, greater reliance was placed on individual subscriptions and memberships in CRRP. Schools, libraries, and elected officials were provided with complimentary copies of *Regional Exchange*. Through these channels, thousands of Bay Area residents became cognizant of BCDC, ABAG and the vital contributions these agencies could make toward preserving the region's unique environment. The overwhelming public support expressed in 1969 for establishing BCDC as a permanent agency suggests the potency of this educational endeavor.

The birth of *Regional Exchange* was not the only major CRRP activity in 1966. Local, state and congressional elections were held in that year, and in order to ascertain the candidates' positions on conservation issues, CRRP sent them questionnaires. The questionnaire responses were compiled and forwarded to newspapers, local legislative bodies and civic organizations.

Also when the Association of Bay Area Governments held hearings on its Preliminary Regional Plan during 1967–69, Citizens for Regional Recreation and Parks presented testimony favoring a strong open space element. Several changes in the Preliminary Plan were recommended. For example, in a November 1, 1967 hearing, Marcella Jacobson offered CRRP's views on ABAG's Plan as it related to San Mateo County. She suggested that any scenic parkway in San Mateo County be located outside the Crystal Springs watershed property. This is only one of several occasions in which CRRP's watershed committee has acted as a watchdog to prevent inappropriate development of scenic property owned by local utility agencies.

Nineteen sixty-eight was a significant year for CRRP. In that year the organization was active in three vital conservation issues. First, CRRP campaigned for Proposition C on the San Francisco ballot. That unsuccessful bond issue would have provided funds for the purchase of 12.5 acres around the Cliff House to prevent the construction of apartments on that picturesque site. Also, CRRP supported the Marin Conservation League in advocating that Angel Island State Park be maintained in its natural state. CRRP President John Sutter wrote to

the Chairman of the California Parks and Recreation Commission and
suggested amendments to the Preliminary Master Plan for Angel Island.
Specifically, CRRP requested a lower optimum capacity, elimination
of overnight facilities and exclusion of non-essential commercial enterprises. In a third issue, CRRP supported efforts to establish an agricultural preserve in the Napa Valley. For example, when the San Francisco newspapers were closed because of a strike, CRRP used its *Regional Exchange* to disseminate an article by Harold Gilliam entitled
"Crisis in the Napa Valley."

A second reason that 1968 was significant for CRRP was that the
organization became a nonprofit, tax-exempt corporation and changed
its name to People For Open Space. That alteration in legal status
enabled POS to obtain a $59,000 Ford Foundation grant to examine
the economic impact of preserving large amounts of open space in the
Bay Area. This study was the first of its type ever conducted in the
United States.

The overall objective was to assist the Joint Legislative Committee
on Bay Area Regional Organization and the Association of Bay Area
Governments in (a) identifying the importance of open space to the
Bay Area, (b) determining the economic feasibility of a regional open
space program and (c) recommending to the Legislature the appropriate regional governmental machinery to preserve open space.

A team of consultants was commissioned by the POS Regional Open
Space Study Committee to conduct the technical study. Using the
ABAG Preliminary Plan as the basis for their estimates, the consultants
analyzed the benefits and costs of a regional open space system in the
Bay Area. Various methods of government regulation and financing
were considered. The consultants concluded that ABAG's open space
element would be economically feasible. The main study report, *Economic Impact of a Regional Open Space Program,* and a summary
pamphlet entitled *The Case For Open Space* were issued in early 1969.
The Joint Legislative Committee on Bay Area Regional Organization,
other state legislators, the Governor, and members of ABAG's Executive Committee were presented with the results of the study. Additionally, 5,000 copies of the concise summary report were distributed to
Bay Area city and county legislators, planning and park comissioners,
conservation and other civic groups, and Bay Area leaders of business,
labor and education.

On September 27, 1969, a one day workshop was held at Stanford
University. The workshop's purpose was to equip volunteers to personally transmit the results of the open space study to public and private
bodies in the nine Bay Area counties. A coordinator was to be selected

for each county. He will be responsible for having knowledgeable speakers appear before county boards of supervisors, city councils, recreation and planning commissions, chambers of commerce, realty boards, etc. At the time this report was written, POS was vigorously using the concise summary report, *The Case For Open Space,* as a tool in striving for the preservation of specific open space land and the establishment of a viable regional open space agency in the Bay Area.

(Information on the present program of People for Open Space can be obtained from Mrs. Morse Erskine, % SPUR, 126 Post Street, San Francisco, California 94108.)

APPENDIX IV

Board of Directors and Advisory Committee
PEOPLE FOR OPEN SPACE
(formerly Citizens for Regional Recreation and Parks)

BOARD OF DIRECTORS

JOHN H. SUTTER
President
MRS. WILLIAM EASTMAN
Vice President
JOSEPH ENGBECK
Vice President
T. J. KENT, JR.
Vice President
IRWIN LUCKMAN
Vice President
MRS. DONALD McLAUGHLIN
Secretary
ROBERT LEE SIMS
Treasurer

ALAMEDA COUNTY
GARY THURLOW
WALTER TONEY
FRANK STEAD

CONTRA COSTA COUNTY
MRS. WILLIAM KRETZMER
PATRICIA WHITTLE
MRS. WARREN LARSON

MARIN COUNTY
PHILIP KEARNEY
HOWARD ALLEN
RALPH WERTHEIMER

NAPA COUNTY
HARRY TRANMER
MRS. MARSHALL EVANS
FREDERICK MONHOFF

SANTA CLARA COUNTY
LESLIE CARBERT
MRS. JANET GRAY HAYES
LAURENCE DAWSON

SAN FRANCISCO COUNTY
MRS. EDGAR WAYBURN
PUTNAM LIVERMORE
MRS. MARY HUTCHINSON

SAN MATEO COUNTY
MRS. RALPH JACOBSON
GEORG TREICHEL
MRS. RAYMOND SPANGLER

SOLANO COUNTY
DR. WILLIAM COON
PAUL BARNEY
EVERITT L. MOSSMAN

SONOMA COUNTY
DR. WILLIAM KORTUM
DR. BRADFORD LUNDBORG
WINFIELD SMITH

ADVISORY COMMITTEE

JOSEPH BODOVITZ
MRS. HOMER A. BOUSHEY
MRS. LYLE BUEHLER
BURNS CADWALADER
MRS. MORSE ERSKINE
ALFRED HELLER
LOIS CROZIER HOGLE
MRS. GREGORY JONES
MRS. MILES KRESGE
ARTHUR LAMPERT
DAN LUTEN

MRS. WILLIAM NEWMAN
THEODORE OSMUNDSON
WILLIAM PITCHER
ELIZABETH REMPEL
MEL SCOTT
LEIGH SHOEMAKER
MRS. WILLIAM SIRI
DR. LEE TITUS
JOHN TUTEUR
JACQUELINE WATKINS
LELAND WILCOX

76

APPENDIX V

A Critique of County Government as an Agency Exercising Local Land Use Controls in Urbanizing Areas

1. *Insufficient Attention to Urban Considerations.* While county boards of supervisors "represent" the entire population (or will do so when counties are equally apportioned), they do not have primary responsibility for urban matters, and especially for planning and land use control within city limits. Thus the city councilmen, who are the most experienced with problems of *built-up urban areas,* have no say over policies guiding most new urban development, which occurs in noncity areas under county planning and zoning jurisdiction.

By the same token, county supervisors are excluded from concerning themselves with most urban policy matters inside city boundaries. Thus they and their staffs are deprived of the experience, pressures and legislative support that grow out of an intimate knowledge of and need to deal with consequences of past land use policies in areas that are already built up. County supervisors are partially isolated from some of the pressures and influence that city councilmen may be subject to, including close contact—as local representatives—with some of the daily dissatisfactions resulting from inappropriate land use decisions of the past.

On the other hand, county supervisors are subjected to heavy pressures from the much narrower interests that are concerned with the one-time profit to be derived from loosely controlled building on and development of raw land in the urbanizing fringe, or even in rather remote new communities. These pressures for real estate development, in turn, have helped produce the county predisposition to "growth" and building, rather than to conservation. Finally, pressures for new development are not counterbalanced by pressures for improvement of existing development, arising from the urban populations. In most matters relating to urban policy respecting land use development, the latter are represented by their city councils.

2. *Small Boards "Representing" Large Populations.* Even if and when the supervisorial districts of all counties are reapportioned (see below), there will still be powerful reasons for questioning whether county government can provide a fully satisfactory answer to problems of urban government, and especially to problems of urban land use control. The very smallness of county boards of supervisors is one important

factor. Moreover, in a governmental entity with a small and fixed number of representatives, namely five, the "smallness factor" looms progressively larger as the county becomes more urban and more populous. Gargantuan Los Angeles County is a classic case in point. It has more than 8 million residents, yet is "governed" by a board of supervisors of only five members!

The disparity between the size of the board of supervisors and the electorate it is supposed to represent means that the counties can become very unrepresentative of their populations, especially when the latter are highly heterogeneous. Large electoral districts have a clear tendency to dilute the influences of minority voters.

3. *Supervisorial Malapportionment.* Although court decisions have held that county supervisorial districts should be equalized, many urban counties are still substantially malapportioned, thus partially disenfranchizing urban voters and reducing the influence of city dwellers over county policies on urban land use and other matters.

Conceivably, existing malapportionment may be corrected after the 1970 U. S. Census. Even so, one can expect the "tone" of county policy leadership to change somewhat more slowly, in part because legislative seniority and the system's accompanying policies and patterns of decision-making are well established, and not subject to rapid alteration.

APPENDIX VI

BAY AREA CONSERVATION AND RELATED ORGANIZATIONS

(as of March 20, 1970)
List Prepared by Ora Huth

American Association of University Women

A.A.U.W. (Martinez Branch)
Mrs. Florence Klinger, *Conservation Chairman*
072 Green Street
Martinez, California 94553

Mrs. Miriam DiPace
316 Jordan Court
Martinez, California 94553

A.A.U.W. (San Carlos Branch)
Mrs. Claude Alexander
935 Canada Road
Woodside, California 94070

A.A.U.W. (San Mateo Branch)
Mrs. Emmett Stanton
15 Plaid Place
Hillsborough, California 94010

Alameda Conservation Association
Mrs. Helen Freeman, *President*
831 Laurel Street
Alameda, California 94501

ACT (Active Conservation Tactics)
c/o Kenneth M. Sanderson
2144 Bonar Street
Berkeley, California 94703

Albany Bay Committee
Mrs. William Ganong, *President*
710 Hillside
Albany, California 94706

American Institute of Architects—
A.I.A. Northern California Chapter
Conservation Committee
John Calef, *Chairman*
254 Sutter Street
San Francisco, California 94108

A.I.A.—A.I.P.—A.S.L.A. Bay Region
Conservation Program
John Fisher-Smith, *Chairman*
Skidmore, Owings & Merrill
1 Maritime Plaza
San Francisco, California 94111

American Institute of Planners—
A.I.P Northern California Chapter
559 Pacific Avenue
San Francisco, California 94133

American Society of Landscape Architects
706 Sansome Street
San Francisco, California 94111

A.S.L.A. California Conservation Council
Hewlett Hornbeck
12 Oak Court
Orinda, California 94563

Associated Regional Citizens
Leslie Carbert, *President*
Pacific Gas & Electric Company
245 Market Street
San Francisco, California 94111

Mrs. William Eastman, *Executive Vice President*
13221 West Sunset Drive
Los Altos Hills, California 94022

Associated Sportsmen
Office: 2644 Judah Street
San Francisco, California 94122

Melvyn Fairchild, *President*
154 Cynthia Drive
Pleasant Hill, California 94523

Bay Area Council
Mortimer Fleischhacker, Jr.,
Chairman, Environment Committee
601 California Street
San Francisco, California 94108

Stanley McCaffrey, *President*
Bay Area Council
World Trade Center
Ferry Building
San Francisco, California 94111

J. E. Countryman, *Chairman*
Bay Area Council
Del Monte Corporation
215 Fremont
San Francisco, California 94105

Benicia—Save Our Shoreline
  Werner Schulz
  1035 West K Street
  Benicia, California 94706

California Garden Clubs, Inc.—Bay
Bridges District—Alameda, Contra Costa,
Martinez and San Francisco Counties
  Mrs. Leonora Strohmaier,
    Conservation Chairman
  77 Bonnie Lane
  Berkeley, California 94708

California Native Plant Society
  2490 Channing Way, Room 202
  Berkeley, California 94704

California Roadside Council
  Mrs. Helen Reynolds, *President*
  2636 Ocean Avenue
  San Francisco, California 94132

California Tomorrow
  Alfred Heller, *President;*
  Samuel E. Wood, *Consultant*
  Monadnock Building
  681 Market Street, Room 393
  San Francisco, California 94105

California Wildlife Federation
  Julius von Nostitz, *Administrative
    Secretary*
  2644 Judah Street
  San Francisco, California 94122

Californians Organized to Acquire
Access To State Tidelands
  P.O. Box 3284
  Santa Rosa, California 95402

Citizens Against Air Pollution
  101 Round Table Drive
  San Jose, California 95111

Committee for Green Foothills
  George Norton, *President*
  192 Pecora Way
  Portola Valley, California 94025

  Mrs. Pat Barentine, *Executive Director*
  40 Carmel Lane
  Redwood City, California 94062
  or P.O. Box 11511
  Palo Alto, California 94306

Conservation Associates
  Mrs. Richard Leonard
  Mills Tower
  220 Bush Street
  San Francisco, California 94104

Conservation Coordinators
  885 Oak Grove Avenue
  Menlo Park, California 94025
  or P.O. Box 548
  Menlo Park, California 94025

Conservation Law Society
  Robert Jasperson, *General Counsel*
  1500 Mills Tower
  San Francisco, California 94104

Contra Costa Park and Recreation
Council
  Alvin A. Burton, *President*
  151 Cafeto Court
  Walnut Creek, California 94598
  or P.O. Box 4322
  Walnut Creek, California 94596

Council for Governmental Responsibility
  Mrs. Ralph Jacobson, *Chairman*
  2995 Summit Drive
  Hillsborough, California 94010

Ecology Center
  2179 Allston Way
  Berkeley, California 94704

Environment Workshop
  Michael Doyle
  123 Greenwich Street
  San Francisco, California 94106

Garden Clubs of America—Zone 12
  Piedmont Garden Club
  Mrs. Gerald Brush, *President*
  68 Lincoln Avenue
  Piedmont, California 94611

  Mrs. T. Eric Reynolds,
    Conservation Chairman
  140 Estates Drive
  Piedmont, California 94611

  Hillsborough Garden Club
  Mrs. Philip M. Robertson, *President*
  2250 Redington Road
  Hillsborough, California 94010

  Woodside-Atherton Garden Club
  Mrs. Renshaw Hunter, *President*
  191 Britton Avenue
  Atherton, California 94025

  Zone 12 Conservation Committee
  Mrs. Donald Ross, *Chairman*
  335 Fletcher Drive
  Atherton, California 94025

Husicon
  Ken Thollaug, *President*
  2635 Mira Vista Drive
  El Cerrito, California 94530

Inverness Waterfront Committee
(Ad Hoc)
  T. J. Kent, Jr., *Chairman*
  84 Tamalpais Road
  Berkeley, California 94708
  Mrs. Bradley K. Holbrook, *Secretary*
  165 Vicente Road
  Berkeley, California 94705

Jenner Coastside Conservation Coalition
  P.O. Box 64
  Jenner, California 95450

Leagues of Women Voters—Bay Area
  Mrs. David Stone, *President*
  3320 Burdeck Drive
  Oakland, California 94602
  Mrs. Walther Buchen
  42 Bay View
  Belvedere, California 94920
  Mrs. Loy S. Braley
  1668 Juanita Avenue
  San Jose, California 95125
  Mrs. Carl Rosenfeld
  478 Vermont
  Berkeley, California 94707
  Mrs. Chester O'Konski
  1 Rancho Diablo Road
  Lafayette, California 94549
  Mrs. John Anderson
  280 San Benito Way
  San Francisco, California 94127

Local Initiative for the Environment
(LIFE)
  Karl G. Brosing, *Chairman*
  La Honda Road
  Woodside, California 94061

Marin Bay Watchers Committee
  Mrs. P. K. Gilman, *Chairman*
  128 Marina Vista Road
  Larkspur, California 94939

Marin Conservation League
  Harold Gregg, *President*
  Tamal Road
  Forest Knolls
  Marin County, California 94933
  Mrs. T. J. Donnelly
  125 Calumet Avenue
  San Anselmo, California 94960

Marin Council on Civic Affairs
  Mrs. Alfred S. Azevedo, *President*
  1877 Centro West
  Tiburon, California 94920

Napans Opposing Wastelands, Inc.
(NOW)
  Robert A. White, *Secretary*
  3144 Valley Green Lane
  Napa, California 94558

National Audubon Society—N.A.S.—
Bay Area Education Services Center
  Miss Mary Jefferds, *Director*
  1749A Grove Street
  Berkeley, California 94709

Bay Area Audubon Council (Chapters
and Affiliates) Golden Gate Audubon
Society
  Joshua Barkin
  P.O. Box 103
  Berkeley, California 94701
  Paul Covel, *Conservation Chairman*
  P.O. Box 103
  Berkeley, California 94701
  Sequoia Audubon Society
  Dr. Howard Gurevitz, *President*
  1505 Oak Rim Drive
  Hillsborough, California 94010
  Santa Clara Valley Audubon Society
  Dr. Joe Greenberg, *President*
  270 Kellog Avenue
  Palo Alto, California 94301
  Ohlone Audubon Society
  John Luther, *President*
  25455 Whitman Street
  Hayward, California 94541
  Marin Audubon Society
  Howard B. Allen, *President*
  P.O. Box 441
  Tiburon, California 94920
  Mt. Diablo Audubon Society
  Christian Nelson, *President*
  RFD Box 294A
  Martinez, California 94553

Northern California Committee For
Environmental Information
  Dr. Donald Dahlsten, *Chairman*
  P.O. Box 761
  Berkeley, California 94701

Pacific Inter-Club Yacht Association of
Northern California
  Richard Boswell, *Secretary*
  235 West MacArthur Blvd., Suite 600
  Oakland, California 94611

Parent-Teacher's Association—P.T.A.—
16th District
Mrs. Joseph Steed, *Recreation and
Conservation Chairman*
19030 Times Avenue
Hayward, California 94541

Peninsula Conservation Center
885 Oak Grove Avenue
Menlo Park, California 94025
or P.O. Box 548
Menlo Park, California 94025

People for Open Space (formerly Citizens
for Regional Recreation and Parks)
John Sutter, *President*
Central Building
Oakland, California 94612

Mrs. Morse Erskine
233 Chestnut Street
San Francisco, California 94133

Planning and Conservation League
Richard Wilson, *President*
909 12th Street
Sacramento, California 95814

William D. Evers, *1st Vice President*
650 California Street
San Francisco, California 94104

Redwood City Civic Association
Mrs. R. M. Barentine
40 Carmel Lane
Redwood City, California 94062
or P.O. Box 1335
Redwood City, California 94062

Regional Parks Association
Mrs. Thomas Parkinson, *President*
1001 Cragmont Avenue
Berkeley, California 94707

San Francisco Beautiful
Mrs. Hans Klussmann, *President*
260 Green Street
San Francisco, California 94133

San Francisco Nisei Fishing Club
2739 Balboa
San Francisco, California 94121

San Francisco Planning and Urban
Renewal Association
John H. Jacobs, *Executive Director*
126 Post Street
San Francisco, California 94108

Sausalito Citizens Council
Donald K. Olsen, *Acting President*
Box 276
Sausalito, California 94965

Sausalito Women's Club
c/o Mrs. Perry Brock
P.O. Box 733
Sausalito, California

Save the Scenic Coast
Mrs. Florence McKenzie
P.O. Box 363
Montara, California 94037

Save Our Bay Action Committee
Mrs. Claire Dedrick
Mrs. Janet Adams
885 Oak Grove Avenue
Menlo Park, California 94025
or P.O. Box 548
Menlo Park, California 94025

Save Our Valley Action Committee
A. W. Dunlap, *Chairman*
231 North First Street
San Jose, California 95113

Save San Francisco Bay Association
William E. Siri
P.O. Box 925
Berkeley, California 94701

Save The Redwoods League
114 Sansome Street
San Francisco, California 94104

Sierra Club
Phillip Berry, *President*
220 Bush Street
San Francisco, California 94104

Sierra Club—Action Committee
Kent Watson
3779 Harrison Street
Oakland, California 94611

Sierra Club—San Francisco Bay Chapter
Maynard Munger, *Chairman*
7 Fleetwood Court
Orinda, California 94563

Eugene Brodsky, *Conservation
Chairman*
667 47th Avenue
San Francisco, California 94121

Sierra Club—Loma Prieta Chapter
Peter Scott, *President*
1135 North Branciforte Avenue
Santa Cruz, California 95060
or P.O. Box 548
Menlo Park, California 94025

Solano County Committee For
Environmental Information
Cal Cornell
37 Court Dorado
Benicia, California 94510

South Bay National Wildlife
Refuge Committee
Art Lampert
37991 Logan Drive
Fremont, California 94536

South San Francisco Baylands Planning,
Conservation and National Wildlife
Educational Subcommittee
c/o Arthur Ogilvie
Santa Clara County Planning
Department
70 West Hedding Street
San Jose, California 95110

Southern Crossing Action Team
885 Oak Grove Avenue
Menlo Park, California 94025
or P.O. Box 548
Menlo Park, California 94025

Tamalpais Conservation Club
Laurence Stotter
2244 Vistazo East
Tiburon, California 94920

The Nature Conservancy
Huey Johnson, *Western Regional
Representative*
215 Market Street
San Francisco, California 94105

North California Chapter—NC
Dr. Howard Cogswell, *Chairman*
1548 East Avenue
Hayward, California 94541

Tuberculosis and Respiratory Disease
Association of California (TARDAC)
424 Pendleton Way
Oakland, California 94621

United New Conservationists
Eberhard H. Thiele, *Executive
Director*
487 Park Avenue
San Jose, California 95110

Urban Care
Mrs. Mary Jane Johnson
Dale Tillery, *Co-Chairmen*
office: 1749 Grove Street
Berkeley, California 94709
or P.O. Box 181
Berkeley, California 94701

APPENDIX VII

Letter from Mel Lane on the Passage of Bay Conservation and Development Commission Legislation in 1969

August 2, 1969

TO: BCDC Commissioners and Proxies

FROM: Mel Lane, Chairman, Bay Conservation and Development Commission

You no doubt were as pleased and excited as I was by the action of the Legislature on August 1st. There is good reason to believe the Governor will sign the bill.

Much of the credit for this success must go to you. I think it is safe to say that a major reason for success was that the Commission had done its homework well in preparing the Plan and that we had operated responsibly in exercising our permit granting powers.

I would like to personally thank all of you for your cooperation during the past few months. I wish I could have shared to a greater degree the problems and excitement of representing the Commission in Sacramento.

I think our policy of making every bill just like our Plan and not supporting any one bill until the major bills were merged was a sound approach. When the four authors finally agreed to get together, any one of them would have been satisfactory.

There is an army of unsung heroes in our final victory. Our staff did a fabulous job. The President pro tem of the Senate, Howard Way, was an unanticipated source of support of great importance. The Governor's increasingly strong support played a major role.

The authors of the major bills and their staffs were superb. Assemblyman Knox did an outstanding job of authoring a salable bill and guiding it through the Legislature. Senators Dolwig and Marks both sponsored excellent bills and did an outstanding job of getting the full Senate to correct the harm done to the final bill in the Senate Finance Committee and fighting off weakening amendments on the floor. Sen-

84

ator Marks gave us good liaison with the Governor and Senator Dolwig gave us some badly needed strength with the old guard of the Senate. Senator Petris did a great job—from sponsoring an excellent bill to making the final presentation of the compromise bill to the Senate.

I think it proper to particularly give credit to the Sierra Club, the Citizens Alliance (including the Save the Bay Association), the Save Our Bay Action Committee in Menlo Park, and the conservation lobbyist, John Zierold.

The real heroes of the piece are the people—through all kinds of organizations and individually, from the Bay Area as well as other parts of the State. Probably the big winner in the shortrun is Western Union. We are told that since the first of the year the Legislators and the Governor received more communications on Bay legislation than any other issue or bill.

One of the major losses in the final stages was an amendment sponsored by Westbay Associates and presented by Senator McCarthy of Marin County to eliminate proxies. We seem to be one of the few organizations where the proxy system has worked effectively, but we could not convince enough Senators of this. The same amendment also results in the unfortunate loss of our non-Supervisor Commissioners from counties.

In my opinion this amendment was ill-advised, without merit, and will be harmful to the effective functioning of the Commission. It will result in poorer attendance, with the normal disadvantages therefrom, plus placing a great hardship on all fill and shoreline development applicants who still need thirteen affirmative votes. Maybe most serious is the loss of the services of some of our most effective members.

The battle lines are already being drawn to undo next year the work of this year's Legislature. Our new legislation, A.B. 2057, calls for a lot of special planning work during the coming year. There are many projects that need to be commenced as soon as possible to make the Bay serve the citizenry better. Our work is cut out for us.

Best wishes. I wish I could be at the next meeting to share our success with you.

II

WILLIAM L. RIVERS AND DAVID M. RUBIN

A REGION'S PRESS . . .

A Region's Press:
Anatomy of Newspapers in the San Francisco Bay Area

INSTITUTE OF GOVERNMENTAL STUDIES
UNIVERSITY OF CALIFORNIA, BERKELEY

A Region's Press:
ANATOMY OF NEWSPAPERS IN THE SAN FRANCISCO BAY AREA

By

WILLIAM L. RIVERS

and

DAVID M. RUBIN

Department of Communication
Stanford University

1971

INTERNATIONAL STANDARD BOOK NUMBER (ISBN) 0-87772-072-X
LIBRARY OF CONGRESS CATALOG CARD NUMBER 71-631982
PRINTED IN THE UNITED STATES OF AMERICA
BY THE UNIVERSITY OF CALIFORNIA PRINTING DEPARTMENT

For Sarah and Tina

Foreword

More than two years ago the Institute conceived the idea of analyzing newspapers in the nine-county San Francisco Bay Area, with special reference to their treatment of public policies and community affairs. Perhaps more than in most metropolitan agglomerations, Bay Area residents have developed a substantial degree of community consciousness. Conversely, the region in which they live, with its broad Bay and numerous amenities, has acquired a high level of real and symbolic significance to its people. Treatment of the region's problems by the information media has been at least partially responsible for this image-building.

Consequently it seemed eminently desirable to examine the performance of the major medium through which public issues are discussed and opinions formulated: the region's newspapers. A research proposal was developed with the help of Harriet Nathan, and the regional newspaper study was added to the Franklin K. Lane series on Bay Area problems and issues.

William Rivers' unusual combination of training in political science and experience as a working journalist—plus his demonstrated analytic capabilities—gave him excellent credentials for his assignment. He has published numerous articles and several highly regarded books, including *The Opinionmakers* and *The Adversaries: Politics and the Press* (Beacon Press, 1965 and 1970, respectively). He is also an author, with Theodore Peterson and Jay Jensen, of *The Mass Media and Modern Society* (Holt, Rinehart & Winston, 1965); and, with Wilbur Schramm, of *Responsibility in Mass Communication* (Harper and Row, 1969).

Professor Rivers enlisted the aid of David M. Rubin, then a graduate student at Stanford University, and the work was begun. As the authors have indicated, the time periods selected for intensive reading and study of Bay Area newspapers were in late 1968 and early 1969. Like all human ventures, of course, journalism and the publishing business are subject to continual change. Much of this movement the authors have taken into account, on the basis of subsequent observation, interviews and correspondence. In any event, the "anatomy of Bay Area newspapers" prepared by Rivers and Rubin has far more than a temporary and local significance. The two authors have completed a very difficult assignment successfully and with distinction. In this they were aided by the generosity of readers, editors and working newsmen from throughout the area, who examined drafts of the manuscript carefully and made thoughtful and insightful comments on its treatment of the subject.

This remarkable response from concerned readers and newsmen who care about performance provided the authors with a wealth of information and viewpoints that were invaluable in the preparation of the book. It also indicated a deeply felt and widespread civic interest in how our newspapers do their jobs. Finally, the vigor of the response suggests that few things are closer to a region's conscience than its journalism, which thus may merit far more attention by scholars than it has yet received.

As far as we know, this is the first such study of a region's press. Perhaps it will help stimulate similar studies of other media, and of other regions.

STANLEY SCOTT
Editor

Contents

TABLES

APPENDICES

Introduction

Even in an era that is often called The Age of Television, newspapers continue to be the primary medium for transmitting substantial news and commentary on public events. We choose to analyze newspapers because it is doubtful whether anyone who cares about being informed can truly think of this as a television age. Granted that TV is the medium with the greatest impact, we are appalled by the brevity of television news reporting. How can two or three minutes of voice-over-pictures really tell us about Vietnam, or inflation, or the mayor's policies? Such reporting can, of course, give us the headline news, but not much more.

In addition, like too many of the headlines in your favorite paper, television often misleads. Indeed, we suspect that most television news—the illegitimate child of show business and journalism—not only fails to inform, but also actually distorts. No matter how dedicated to a truthful account of the day's events a television newsman may be, only through infrequent documentaries and special reports can he even try to inform us fully. He cannot transcend a news program system whose reporting is based on visual impact, a system dedicated to the proposition that a viewer's attention span is limited to one minute and 55 seconds.

The Bay Area has one program that attempts to offer more than the conventional television news fare: KQED's "Newsroom." It is valuable because it runs for an hour—a real hour, not the commercial television "hour" of only 48 minutes, with the rest of the time given over to selling soap. "Newsroom" is valuable, too, because it features reporters who know the news and can present it knowledgeably, without depending upon unseen scriptwriters. But "Newsroom" also points up some of the real limitations of television news. For example, viewers are forced to sit through all the reports that bore them, in order to see those they want to see. To a suburbanite who cares nothing about the activity in San Francisco City Hall, reports on city politics seem endless. More important, if one were to set into type all the words spoken during one whole "Newsroom" program, the resulting copy would cover less than two newspaper pages.

What the Authors Believe

So it was that we began our study of Bay Area newspapers with our primary conviction intact: *the newspaper is the basic news medium* for those who wish to be reasonably well-informed. We also undertook the study with other convictions, and with a full complement of biases.

1

Without attempting to distinguish the convictions from the biases, let us simply call them beliefs and sketch them here:

· We are political liberals. We hope that we are not doctrinaire, however, and that our opinions—on issues or newspapers—are not automatically predictable merely because we have liberal leanings.

· Whether it is called "backgrounding the news," "depth reporting," "interpretive reporting," or whatever, we consider it essential that today's newspapers go beyond the mere reporting of surface facts.

It should be said instantly that such reportage need not make a newspaper a grim instrument of determined education. We applaud the sentiments of the English publisher who said of American papers, "But they are conceived without sin, conceived without joy." We believe that a newspaper can be analytical and interpretive and still indulge itself in joy. We certainly rejoice in satire like that offered by Art Hoppe, Art Buchwald, and Russell Baker, in the humor of "Peanuts" and other comic strips, in many light stories fashioned by reporters and feature writers.

· We believe that the press must question and challenge government. As Abraham Lincoln said, "In this and like communities, public sentiment is everything." Without a challenging journalism, officials will too easily win public approval and influence sentiment. Moreover, at a time when most of the institutions of American society are involved with government, the press must question and probe into governmental relationships.

· We believe that the newspaper that attempts to report "society" news—i.e., the leisure activities of some local elite—wastes time, space and money, while injuring the community.

· Recognizing that few communities will support anything like the Los Angeles *Times,* we believe nonetheless that various kinds of newspapers must recognize their respective responsibilities to their communities. Some suggested responsibilities are outlined below.

RESPONSIBILITIES OF THE METROPOLITAN DAILY

The primary responsibility for a comprehensive report of international, national, state and major local news rests with the metropolitan daily.

The primary responsibility for interpreting (clarifying, explaining, analyzing) the news of the world, nation, state and central city must also rest with the metropolitan daily, which alone has the necessary resources.

If it carries out the above duties, the responsible paper will find it impossible to publish anything more than the most important news of the suburban cities. Moreover, the metropolitan daily that gives news space to minor meetings of clubs, civic groups, church groups and the like, however worthy the organizations or their purposes, cannot also fulfill its primary responsibilities.

RESPONSIBILITIES OF THE SUBURBAN DAILY

The suburban daily carries much the same responsibility as the metropolitan daily for providing its readers with world, national, state and city news—but its central focus and strongest emphasis should be on its locality.

RESPONSIBILITIES OF THE WEEKLY

The conventional weekly has reported the news of small towns and neighborhoods since colonial times. Such reporting is no less important today, because the metropolitan dailies and the suburban dailies, in the course of carrying out their primary responsibilities, must ignore the news of small communities and neighborhoods. The weekly remains the only medium for reporting the quality of everyday life.

The Hutchins Commission: Recommendations

Some of our own convictions grew from studying press criticisms, notably the 1947 Commission on Freedom of the Press, headed by Chancellor Robert M. Hutchins of the University of Chicago. Financed by publisher Henry R. Luce and the Encyclopaedia Britannica, the commission was composed primarily of academicians who had no journalistic experience. In its summary report, *A Free and Responsible Press,* the commission laid five demands on the press that still provide a useful starting point:

> A truthful, comprehensive, and intelligent account of the day's events in a context that gives them meaning.

> A forum for the exchange of comment and criticism.

> The projection of a representative picture of the constituent groups in the society.

> The presentation and clarification of the goals and values of the society.

> Full access to the day's intelligence.

Underlying the above demands is the assumption that an American citizen needs information—news of his local area, his state, his national government, the world—to be a responsible member of his community.

For those who have concluded their formal schooling, the newspaper (and interpersonal communication) used to be the primary sources of continuing education. Radio and television have in some ways usurped this traditional role of the press. The "Extra" is gone because speed is no longer a trait of the medium. At a minimum, radio and television are headline services and recent studies have shown that for increasing numbers of people this electronic headline service is quite enough. But most journalists, both working and teaching, agree that electronic news alone is inadequate and that the newspaper still has an important role to play.

Three Standards for Evaluating Press Quality

In translating the Hutchins principles into a workable method of press criticism, we have settled on three different standards for evaluating press quality. These are (1) objective reporting, (2) interpretive reporting; and (3) news judgment as reflected in the selection and emphasis of news stories in newspaper layout. Since we will be referring to these concepts frequently, we offer the following brief discussion of each.

Objective Reporting

Former *PM* staffer Kenneth Stewart, now Professor Emeritus at the Graduate School of Journalism, University of California, Berkeley, said of objectivity:

> If you mean by objectivity absence of convictions, willingness to let nature take its course, uncritical acceptance of things as they are (what Robert Frost calls the 'isness of is'), the hell with it. If you mean by objectivity a healthy respect for the ascertainable truth, a readiness to modify conclusions when new evidence comes in, a refusal to distort deliberately and be interpertive reporting, well and good. . . .

Philip M. Wagner, editor of the Baltimore *Sun*, contrasted objectivity with opinion, and stated that the distinction "is appealing in the abstract." He continued, "It also has certain practical virtues as a discipline to hotspur reporters, and in those cases where a publisher has the requisite qualities, it can yield brilliant results."

In brief, objectivity for reporter and copy editor is a state of mind, a point of view. It has many components: viewing a story in more than one framework, interviewing parties on all sides, considering and presenting all relevant background material, writing in an unambiguous and value-free manner, editing so as to include all important points of view and laying out the story so as not to embarrass any of the parties involved. No reporter or editor can be expected to do all this on every story, but the newsman should be aware of these strictures while reporting and editing.

We believe that a reporter's involvement in an important story does not make his writing objectively about it impossible or an unrealistic hope. Although journalism does not simply hold up a mirror to the world, the reporter can still be expected to write "impartially." As a guide, the standard of objectivity is useful. But it is not the sole determinant of newspaper quality.

INTERPRETIVE REPORTING

This is what the Hutchins report called "contextual" reporting, and it is frequently confused with opinion pieces on the news pages. Interpretive reporting—which aims to explain and clarify—is nothing more than a fact-gathering procedure intended to help the reader understand what he is reading. Former editor Carl E. Lindstrom stated:

> I do not know of an obscure or enigmatic or complicated situation in the news that cannot be explained by more facts. Facts—historical, circumstantial, geographical, statistical, reflective—can usually throw sufficient light on spontaneous news events to make them fairly intelligible. If this be interpretive reporting, well and good. . . .

Other newspapermen have stated that, considering the complexity of the world, the naked facts of a story are not sufficient to inform the reader. The facts must be buttressed with other facts from related stories: they require background. As long as the reporter's opinions are kept out of the backgrounding, the principle of interpretive reporting is acceptable to most editors.

NEWS JUDGMENT: SELECTION AND EMPHASIS

The third standard of quality lies in the choice of the news events to present from day to day, and the rather whimsical manner in which the stories are scattered about in the paper. Robert Fulford, book and art critic for the Toronto *Daily Star,* stated the problem this way: "In the papers, major stories are sometimes hinted at first, then blown up to flare headline size, then dropped to minor headline size, then eliminated entirely. The result is that readers can easily be left wondering whatever happened to the Suez Canal. . . ." Malcolm Bauer, associate editor of the Portland *Oregonian,* chastised reporters and editors for remaining "glued to the spot news break, the overnight sensation, the score of the game. They don't bother to look beyond the surface of an event—a surface that can be shown on television."

In amplifying Bauer's point, the Baltimore *Sun*'s Philip Wagner was distressed that "no real distinction is made between hard news and the elaboration of meaningless and merely distracting detail. Worse, the real story can sometimes be missed even when it is there to be told, through this absorption in sensational diversions."

This type of reportage causes the reader, according to press critic Ben Bagdikian, to question the comprehensiveness and reliability of a newspaper. The reader should be able to feel after reading his paper that at least he has seen all the news developments on the major stories that day; that they have been properly tied to background material; and that, through the paper's layout, he has a feel for what are the most important stories. Too often a daily paper offers no sense of continuity or priority in the day's events.

The Bay Area Study

In reading and evaluating Bay Area newspapers, we gathered data in three different ways. First, we read as many editions of the papers under study as possible, plus as many of the weeklies and underground papers as we could track down. Naturally, we gave major emphasis to the metropolitan papers in San Francisco, Oakland and San Jose. Second, we interviewed executives and reporters of many papers, recognizing that the choice of interviewees greatly shaped our perception of the internal workings of each paper. Third, we used some quantitative measures such as column inches and story placement to give our admittedly subjective judgments a more solid foundation. (See App. IV for summaries of topics, newspapers and dates.)

We have presented our findings in a number of ways. We have drawn "personality sketches" of the 10 papers under study; we have made a special study of the Sunday papers; we have presented case studies illustrating press coverage of stories that posed great problems for journalists—student unrest and environmental deterioration; we have taken a close look at foreign news coverage and at the weekly and underground press; and we have commented on opinion columns. Our purpose has been to describe the accomplishments and deficiencies of the Bay Area press. We have focused on news coverage because that is the most critical operation for any paper, and we can justly be criticized for having given scant attention to special interests such as sports, business and society.

In addition to political biases and a predisposition toward the conclusions of the Hutchins Commission report, we have made many judgments along the way that we can only hope will become clear in the reading. It should be stated, however, that we have the greatest admiration for the working journalists in all parts of the United States. Confronted with explosive situations, and the target of criticism by successive national administrations, they are performing more capably than ever, under increasingly difficult circumstances. Our criticism is offered in friendship.

So many Bay Area journalists, former journalists, and academicians criticized all or parts of this manuscript as it went through various drafts that it is clearly impossible to name here all those who have helped us. It is possible, however, to thank two at Stanford who were helpful at several points: Diana Winter, who typed much of the manuscript, and Charlene Brown, who was a sharply perceptive critic, as always. We are also deeply grateful to Stanley Scott and Harriet Nathan, both of the Institute of Governmental Studies at the University of California, Berkeley, who encouraged us from the beginning, then proved to be excellent critics of the various drafts.

WILLIAM L. RIVERS
DAVID M. RUBIN

The Bay Area Press: An Overview

This book must begin with a brutal truth. As long as a publisher shows decent respect for a few laws, he may do what he likes with his newspaper. If he opposes the Democratic candidate for President—and he probably does—the candidate's name can be eliminated from the paper. If he hates golf, he can instruct his sports editor to forget that the game exists. If he visualizes thousands of little circles of family readers being offended by photos revealing the sex of naked animals, he can have his art department use an airbrush appropriately. The Democrats, the golfers and the artists on his staff may rebel, readers may protest, a rival paper may thrive as a result, but the publisher's power in such cases is unmistakable.

Freedom and the Publisher's Power

His freedom springs from the libertarian philosophy on which this country was founded: that every man should speak and write his own thoughts. The clash of conflicting ideas, the founding fathers believed, would produce something called the Truth. The concept remained popular during the period when any literate man could start his own newspaper with little more than a shirt-tail full of type. The concept lost persuasiveness as conventional production processes increased in cost and newspapering became big business. (Parenthetically, in an apparent return to the earlier pattern, low-cost photo-offset techniques have recently permitted a number of community and underground presses with limited capital to function as modern-day equivalents of the frontier publishers.) But even in the early days of the republic, the quality of information and amount of Truth available may not have produced an informed electorate. As we have since learned, men have ways of holding onto their attitudes and ignoring available knowledge. Thus, despite the hopes of the libertarian philosophers, it appears that our forebears were probably stunningly uninformed.[1] And now, in this

---

[1] We speak of a free press, but whatever its Constitution states, every society restricts free expression. These are the basic controls: a law designed to protect individuals or groups against defamation, a copyright law to protect authors and publishers, a statute to preserve the community standard of decency and morality, and a statute to protect the state against treasonable and seditious utterances. Although definitions of these offenses change, the U. S. Supreme Court has consistently upheld such laws. Two justices have nevertheless offered strong opposition to them. Holding that the First Amendment means literally what it says, Justice Hugo Black argued in *Ginsburg v. United States*: "I believe the Federal Government is without power whatever under the Constitution to put any type of burden on speech and expression of ideas of any

8

era of many single-newspaper towns, even the so-called free market-place of ideas is becoming but a dim memory, if, indeed, it ever existed.

As noted, individual publishers have great freedom to publish as they like. Fortunately, they do not take full advantage of their freedom. Whether this is because they fear the financial consequences of indulging their idiosyncrasies, because they want to avoid the professional con-demnation of their peers and their employees, or because they feel a sense of social responsibility, most publishers give space to the Demo-crats and the golfers, and allow pictures of dogs and cows to run *au naturel*.

This does not mean that they are ultimately free and fair. In the beginning, publishing was controlled by the church, then by govern-ment, and now it is firmly embedded in the structure of business. Pub-lishers maintain, usually correctly, that they are controlled neither by their business friends nor by their advertisers. They do not need to be. The businessman who runs a newspaper will nearly always understand the sanctity of the business ideology. His business is different from all the others—it is the only one specifically named in the Bill of Rights, and the color of the public interest is upon it. But even though his newspaper may question the morality of individuals—sometimes those in business, more often those in government—it is not likely to question the basic structure of either the capitalist system or the governmental status quo. Only fringe papers like the San Francisco *Bay Guardian* will probe into the distribution of money and power in society.

To ask any more of the conventional, commercial newspaper may be asking too much. When one considers the wide-ranging freedom the publisher has at his disposal, and the limited amount that he uses, it becomes clear that, according to his lights, he is socially responsible.

The Bay Area's Web of Papers

In overview, the nine-county Bay Area[2] seems to be awash in news-papers. It is served by 28 dailies (10 morning, 18 evening—a total daily circulation of over 1.6 million), plus 96 weeklies and over a dozen papers that are published monthly or two or three times a week, a few of them in exotic languages: Chinese, Portuguese, Spanish and Radical.

---

kind." Justice William Douglas has stated: "The First Amendment does not say that there is freedom of expression provided the talk is not 'dangerous.' It does not say that there is freedom of expression provided the utterance has no tendency to subvert. . . . All notions of regulation or restraint by government are absent from the First Amendment. For it says in words that are unambiguous, 'Congress shall make no law . . .' " (in *The Right of the People*, New York: Doubleday & Co., 1958; p. 21.)

[2] The counties: Alameda, Contra Costa, Marin, Napa, San Francisco, San Mateo, Santa Clara, Solano and Sonoma.

Since many of these papers appear fat (and profitable), one could easily assume that the nearly 5 million Bay Area residents are being informed up to their eyeballs.

But news coverage is not neatly geographic, with each paper covering its own ground. Nearly every newspaper pushes its circulation range as far as it considers financially feasible and then attempts to cover the news in the circulation area. In many cases, the result is thin coverage nearly everywhere. Not even the home city is reported thoroughly.

Holes in the Coverage

In one Bay Area community that seemed typical, less than 50 per cent of the public meetings of governmental bodies and civic organizations were attended by a reporter from the only daily in town. Some of the others were "covered" by making phone calls to officials and officers after the meetings, or by asking someone who planned to attend to call the paper if anything newsworthy occurred. What is more, the significant actions of many such meetings have apparently been obscured by seemingly endless wrangling, and a reporter's disposition might be improved by avoiding them entirely.

But this is a sure system for ignoring the threads that tie a community together. It is even worse. An official who is truly devoted to the public interest is frustrated in his best resolves by the absence of news coverage, while an official who is furthering his own interests likes nothing better than to pick up a telephone and act as his own reporter. One need not be a cynic to suspect that the absence of coverage promotes private interests. (A newspaper cannot leave it to radio and television to report such matters, and for the simplest of reasons: they do not.) The dilemma, of course, is that there are simply too many governing bodies and organizations, too many meetings.

It is futile to ask, of course, that the newspapers cover the Bay Area neatly in order to be thorough, one covering its own area intensely, another taking up where the first leaves off, and so on. This kind of orderliness is not even desirable. Not only do regional interests cross jurisdictional lines, but such a scheme would also force a reader to subscribe to all Bay Area papers to learn the news of the region. As it is, some of the most important regional stories are available in many local papers.

Diversity of Scope and Purpose

Duplication is far from complete, however, for another facet of the local newspaper complex is diversity of scope and purpose. Only five Bay Area publications—the San Francisco *Chronicle,* the San Francisco

Examiner, the Oakland *Tribune,* the San Jose *Mercury,* and the San Jose *News*—qualify as metropolitan newspapers. They are large in number of pages and circulation, seek to serve many readers in and out of the cities where they are published, and are designed to present at some length and in some depth not only local, regional and state news, but also news of the world. There is diversity within this group, with one paper playing up stories the others minimize or ignore. We will have much to say in later chapters about the distinctive personality of each of these papers.

The other 23 Bay Area dailies are published in smaller scope. Although they carry accounts of a few of the leading national and international events and supplement these with commentaries by syndicated columnists, their thrust is local. A few, like the Berkeley *Gazette,* pursue the minutiae of city life (Boy Scout meetings, PTA socials, descriptions of the season's tallest sunflower) with the avidity of a rural weekly. Most of the other dailies tend to leave such reportage to the weeklies and concentrate on reporting pivotal local institutions: city and county government, education, courts, businesses, churches, civic organizations and the like.

The more responsible editors of the surburban dailies are nagged by the fear that their readers can learn too little of the world from their pages. Elsewhere, such dailies feel that they can depend upon the metropolitan giants to tell area residents about national and international affairs, thus permitting the smaller papers to concentrate almost exclusively on local events. But many Bay Area residents subscribe to only one paper. Suburban editors believe that even the thousands who subscribe to a metropolitan daily and a local paper may not be adequately informed because Bay Area metropolitans provide such a slender diet of world news. In recent years, one result has been an increase in the world news offerings of small dailies, in some cases because the editors know that wire-service news is less expensive than hiring reporters to cover local news.

The Suburban Daily's Dependence on Wire Copy

It is worthwhile to sketch briefly how a fairly typical Bay Area suburban daily attempts to inform its readers. Virtually all of its state, national and international news is received from an Associated Press and two United Press International wires.

It is also worthwhile to consider how AP and UPI receive their news. Some of it is gathered by hundreds of wire-service staffers scattered among news capitals around the world. But as one Bay Area reporter pointed out:

The general circulation metropolitan newspaper is the chief news-gathering source for virtually all other news agencies. When I write a story . . . a carbon copy is left on the AP spike. Another goes to UPI. At the two bureaus in the Fox Plaza, my story is perhaps given to a rewrite-man who may or may not check the facts further. The story then moves to the radio wire, the state wire, and, perhaps, the national wire.

That's how the Richmond *Independent* knows that a Richmond man has just been convicted in federal court. That's how a classical music station can report, in its five minutes of rip-and-read news every hour, that another conscientious objector has just gotten five years at Terminal Island. That's how the Berkeley *Tribe* discovers that the Establishment has struck again. That's how *Time* magazine learns that the son of a prominent New England minister has just been sentenced.

At the suburban daily, all the news is processed by a news editor and his two assistants. Besides making decisions on more than 100,000 words that come over these wires every day, these three men also edit and place all local news, which may run as high as 10,000 words a day, and select a dozen or so world news pictures from approximately 100 provided by a wirephoto machine every day. In this way, the three editors make up the general news columns.

The news editor does much of the work himself, discarding large quantities of wire copy and dividing the remaining stories among his assistants' desks and his own. Because all wire copy is received on punched tape (facilitating automated reproduction) as well as in type-script, editing consists largely of choosing between the AP and UPI versions of a story, checking for accuracy and typographical errors, and finding suitable points where stories can be cut. The punched tape can be set into type rapidly and inexpensively if few changes are made, and very rapidly and inexpensively if no changes are made. These are strong arguments against thoughtful editing.

Many a metropolitan news operation sneers at such standards. The great newspapers, and some of the merely good ones, combine the best elements of several wire service stories in preparing a single story. They set their rewritemen to work checking out wire service reports—calls to points across the U. S. and overseas are frequent, and travel by reporters to the scene of breaking news is fairly common—and in general subject the reports of wire services and special news services to scrutiny and change. Instead of the two basic wire services that are common in small daily offices, a large metropolitan paper may have 15 or 20, including special services like those provided by the New York Times and the Los Angeles Times–Washington Post combine. Many of their reports go through a checking and rewriting process; nearly all are heavily edited.

At the offices of the typical suburban daily, however, there is little re-writing, and little time for it. Thus when the suburban news editor arrived at 6 a.m. on one of the mornings when his work was being observed, he found approximately 50,000 words of wire copy. (The wire service cycle for supplying news to afternoon papers begins shortly after midnight. Thus, most news editors who start work during the dawn hours find many stories waiting for them.) He swiftly discarded all but about 8,000 words. During the next seven hours, as the wires continued to spew stories, the news editor and his assistants used more than 20,000 words of wire copy of a total of about 110,000 available. Much of it was useless because AP and UPI reported many of the same events. They edited lightly, wrote headlines, placed stories on each page, and then sent the selected stories to the composing room to be put into type.

They also edited and placed about 6,000 words of local news, and selected and placed 16 pictures. During the last hour of their working day, they prepared some material for the next day's edition—just as, yesterday, they had devoted the final hour to preparations for today's paper. During a single working day, then, they edited the rough equivalent of a small book. To emphasize the large quantity of material that must be processed quickly by daily news editors, and the short time available for their work, one can contrast newspaper and book editing. Where books are concerned, even after the author's final manuscript is in hand, a publishing house customarily devotes at least six months, and often a year or more, to editing and producing the finished work.

The Suburban Editor and His Doubts

This thumbnail description ignores some of the underlying doubts that afflict the suburban editor. He knows that many of his readers will already have read elsewhere some of the stories he plays up, and that other readers will have been satisfied with the top-of-the-news sketches of the same stories heard on their radios or seen on television. But he is concerned to provide for those readers who want more than they are able to get elsewhere.

Other questions and doubts arise. How much serious news can his readers take? How many of them will read yet another report on Vietnam, another story on the indecisive Paris peace talks, and still another report on the interminable battle between the President and Congress? On the other hand, is the editor adequately serving those who follow such matters intently—they may be few but important people—if he publishes five-inch stories rather than 20-inch stories?

Is the editor furthering the causes of rioters if he emphasizes their actions? Can a community really be informed if an editor decides to play down all news of conflict? If he answers the clamors of local critics and tries to balance stories of conflict with stories of cooperation, how many subscribers will actually read all the reports on the good works? If he boldly headlines a story of conflict, his paper will be accused of sensationalism. Reports on the New Morality—especially those using the language that is its hallmark—will offend some older readers. Failing to give adequate attention to it will persuade many younger readers that they were right all along in thinking that the Establishment press was stodgy.

Such are the demands imposed by the effort to inform and entertain a heterogeneous audience.

Thanks to court decisions made years ago, the suburban dailies now receive the same basic wire services (AP and UPI) that are available to the metropolitan papers. But they cannot obtain all the special services (such as the New York Times News Service or the Chicago Daily News Foreign Service) that most metropolitans purchase. Some of the special news services and some of the syndicates that supply news and features have contracts or "understandings," with metropolitan papers that shut out the suburban papers. The metropolitans argue that their survival depends upon their ability to provide features that are unavailable to their competitors.

This explains, for example, the dreary comic strips that appear in some Bay Area suburban papers. They are not offered because the editors believe that many of their readers will be enthralled by "Priscilla's Pop" and the like, but because the San Francisco *Chronicle* publishes "Peanuts" and "Bobby Sox" and "Dennis the Menace." The *Chronicle* will not permit its strips to appear in the suburban papers.

All metropolitan editors treasure the attractive comic strips, and some who discovered quite late which ones are attractive have used cash to wrest "Peanuts" and "Dennis the Menace" from the smaller papers, which accurately forecast the popularity of the strips when they were first offered by the syndicates. Small-town papers may be able to assert territorial rights in some cases, but their contracts with syndicates have a way of running out, whereupon syndicate salesmen draw up more profitable contracts with metropolitan dailies.

There are other hazards in the jungle of comic strip syndication. The editor who tries to jettison "Orphan Annie" because he and his staff are sickened by it soon has 40 irate readers calling him regularly at three a.m. to protest. So he drops "Buzz Sawyer" instead, only to be reminded on the first day of the strip's deletion that the publisher is a Navy veteran who dotes on Sawyer. The *Chronicle* was recently pushed by public outcry into returning the offbeat satire of the "Odd Bodkins" strip to its comic page. Later, it was dropped again.

Such are the problems of publishing suburban and small-town dailies. Like the metropolitans, these papers serve such a variety of readers— the leading banker in town and the janitor who cleans the bank, the college professor and the high school drop-out—that this variety would seem to be problem enough. But the small daily editor must cope with the appeal of the metropolitan paper that looms next door, and with the local weekly that nibbles away in his own backyard.

The Non-Dailies

In contrast, the problems of the weekly are quite different. This is also true of the semi-weekly or monthly, regardless of whether it is the conventional kind that has provided the United States with its grass-roots journalism for two centuries, or the relatively new kind that challenges aspects of the established order. These publications—"non-dailies" seems to be the only term that will encompass all of them— have one stark advantage over the dailies: a sharp focus. The focus may be geographic, expressed in reporting the doings of a small neighbor-hood or suburb or town. The focus may be ethnic or racial, concen-trating on Mexican-American or Negro life, or the Chinese community. In any case, the non-daily does not try to be all things to all men. Its scope and purpose are usually clear.

The Bay Area has numerous non-dailies of many kinds. Mort Levine publishes several of the grass-roots types in San Jose neighborhoods and in Milpitas. Others are the *Pacific Sun* of Marin County, the *Bay Guardian* of San Francisco, the *Freedom News* of Richmond. They are examples of the challenging papers that seek their readers across a wide geographic range in the Bay Area, but aim at creating a sense of com-munity among those who are irritated by the blandness of the conven-tional daily, or who suspect that the promise of American life has not been kept. Talking to those who publish such papers makes it clear that there are compensations for producing this kind of journalism.

Money is rarely the chief compensation. For every non-daily that produces a significant return, five get by only because the owner and most of his family give nearly all their waking hours to publishing. But there is a sense of dedication and accomplishment among these pub-lishers that is hard to find in the dailies.

There remains, of course, the underground newspaper, which may be best represented by the Berkeley *Barb* and *Tribe*. Such publications usually begin as challenges to the established order, with some valuable muckraking articles floating in a sea of nude pictures and four-letter words. Because few of those who work on these papers have any real interest in reporting, the muckraking becomes thin and usually comes to be based on rebellion more than on investigation. This eventually leaves little more than nudity and obscenity. There have been some startling successes in underground publishing, among them the *Barb*. The public wrangling between the staff and the owner—which resulted in the birth of the *Tribe*—during the summer of 1969 revealed just how lucrative such an operation can be. It also revealed that, like the capitalist men of the commercial press, some of those in the underground are also money-conscious.

Ray Mungo, one of the founders of the news service that provided material to underground papers for a short period (the Liberation News Service), has written of underground journalists:

> Lots of radicals will give you a very precise line about why their little newspaper or organization was formed and what needs it fulfills and most of that stuff is bullshit, you see—the point is they've got nothing to do, and the prospect of holding a straight job is so dreary that they join the "movement" and start hitting up people for money to live, on the premise that they're involved in critical social change blah blah blah. And it's really better that way, at least for some people, than finishing college and working at dumb jobs for constipated corporations; at least it's not always boring . . . that's why we decided to start a news service—not because the proliferating underground and radical college press really needed a central information-gathering agency staffed by people they could trust (that was our hype), but because we had nothing else to do. (*Famous Long Ago,* Boston: Beacon Press, 1970, p. 8)

In *The Underground Press in America* (Bloomington: Indiana University Press, 1970), Robert Glessing of Cañada College in Redwood City provided a useful definition of the underground papers: "created to reflect and shape the life style of hippies, dropouts, and all those alienated from the mainstream of American experience." (p. 3) In one sense it can be said that underground newspapers are written *by* the alienated *for* the alienated. The papers that fit under the broad canopy of Glessing's definition are wildly diverse, but he categorized them usefully under two headings that spring from their principal functions: radical political and radical cultural. The short essays Glessing received (and reprinted) after asking an editor of each kind of paper to assess the future of underground publishing, may indicate the degree of headway each category has made. Lincoln Bergman of the *Movement,* a political paper, wrote cautiously and conditionally:

> Money is needed to survive. Individuals get caught up into images of individual, not group success. The phone is tapped, agents infiltrate the group.

And so the only chance for survival is expansion. The need to speak to other people's needs. The attempt to reach and learn from the people on the bottom . . . who are the people who have the power to make the basic change. (*Underground Press*, p. 164)

Allan Katzman, editor of the radical cultural paper the *East Village Other*, is notably more confident that the underground can work basic changes:

In a very short time the underground press will erupt to the forefront of communications in this country. It will be brought there less by a radical commitment to some abstract principles than to a radical commitment to various and sundry experiences of living. It will have done the things necessary for change without, hopefully, blowing itself and others apart to do it. (*Underground Press*, p. 168)

Perhaps there are other radical political editors who are more confident of success than Bergman seems to be; and there may be radical cultural editors who are less expansive than Katzman about cultural changes that loom. It is nonetheless obvious that the undergrounders have worked more—or more obvious—changes in culture than they have in politics. Glessing is convinced that the underground is responsible for sweeping change, and he is willing to list cultural changes, such as those occurring in styles of hair, clothing, advertising, music, sex, sports and education. But observers who demand evidence that the young affect the lifestyles of others, while they are establishing their own, need do no more than ask a barber who caters to older men how his business is doing or ask a designer whether hippie styles have influenced the dress of the wealthy. Or simply look at a picture of the long locks curling over the back of the mod collar worn by former President Lyndon Johnson.

Glessing is also convinced that the underground is markedly influencing the mainstream of American journalism. He pointed to several evidences: the undergrounders cover stories that are later covered by the conventional media; many writers and editors work for underground and overground media simultaneously; and conventional media are used by the undergrounders to create and perpetuate myths.

Such influences are indisputable, but there is much more to say about the impact of the underground on the mass media. Glessing indirectly pointed up one important influence in criticizing the conventional (and devoutly conservative) Berkeley *Gazette* for shoddy reporting: "Perhaps that is why the daily *Gazette* circulation slipped from 15,502 to 14,299 from 1962 to 1968 while the underground weekly Berkeley *Barb* grew from 0 to 60,000 in the same period." (*Underground Press*, p. 145) Nothing is more impressive to the commercial press than the popularity of some underground papers. When the circulation of the Los Angeles *Free Press* approached 100,000, the editors of conventional dailies began to invite its editor, Art Kunkin, to their gatherings to explain his magic.

It is impossible to measure the extent to which daily editors have pirated or adapted the ideas and practices of the underground, but both piracy and adaptation are apparent. Some of them now print Dr. HIPpocrates, the unorthodox physician whose medical advice column started in the *Barb,* and some print the work of Nicholas von Hoffman, Washington *Post* columnist who did not get his start in the underground but whose irreverent columns would fit comfortably in the most radical sheet. The *Chronicle* prints both.

It is much too early to predict confidently that the underground press will, like the minority party, succumb because its strongest appeals are taken over and diluted to the point of mass palatability. But that may be happening. What is surely happening is that some of the strongest underground papers are achieving "conventional" success—or at least disproving the radical dictum that financial failure is the ultimate consequence of serving Truth.

Bay Area college papers may be better examples of purer, if partisan, motivation. Largely contemptuous of the values of the conventional, commercial press, and at least a bit suspicious of the values of some of the proprietors of underground papers, many college editors use their papers to promote the causes of youth. There is some excellent, dispassionate reporting in college dailies, and there are also some examples of reporting that the editors fondly suppose to be interpretive. Some Bay Area college papers deliver many of their news columns as well as their editorial columns over to frank advocacy. Reading their offerings reminded us of the era of personal journalism in the American press of 150 years ago. Ironically, this may be a wave of the future. Some of the younger journalists who work for conventional dailies applaud, because there is a growing belief that so-called "mirror to the world" journalism is dead.

The Bay Area has demonstrated that it will support most of the grass-roots weeklies and some of the papers designed for ethnic groups. Carlton Goodlett's *Sun-Reporter,* which is aimed at the Negro community, is strong locally and has developed something of a national reputation. Several Chicano papers are doing well.

The more stable of the underground newspapers make a lot of money, but it is almost as difficult to explain the precarious financial condition of the little journals of investigative reporting, challenge and protest as it is to explain why the serious approach of the old *Chronicle* and the Western Edition of the New York *Times* failed. We wonder why the San Francisco *Bay Guardian* has so much trouble reaching all the readers who would seem to welcome its excellent investigative style. Why did the *Plain Rapper,* a Resistance paper that seemed to speak directly to the concerns of the large radical community here, have to limp from one financial crisis to another? It finally died in late 1969. Why was the late *Peninsula Observer* unable to establish itself effectively with the dissident college and college-age readers who made up most of its audience?

The radical community is large enough to make such enterprises work, and if their journalistic standards are unconventional, most of their prospective readers couldn't care less. It is possible that distribution, which requires organizational ability of the sort the Establishment celebrates and practices so well, is faulty. That provides part of the answer, but not all of it. The hippie vendors who peddle the Berkeley *Barb* so successfully are evidence that the unconventional press can develop its own methods of distribution.

How Are Bay Area Papers Rated?

How do Bay Area dailies compare in American journalism? Judged in terms of prestige and prizes, not very high. When polls of editors, publishers, journalism professors and Washington correspondents are published, no Bay Area paper is ever found among the top 10. In fairness to the smaller local papers it should be noted that they have little chance of coming to the attention of many judges, and are not so much low-rated as overlooked. Small newspapers can, however, compete fairly equally with the giants for some of the Pulitzer Prizes and similar high marks of journalistic accomplishment that are geared to more inclusive nominations and wider consideration, but local papers, small and large, have had little success even in these contests. Finally, interviews with the newspapermen who have settled here indicate that they are lured more by the climate and by the Pacific than they are by the prospect of finding a great newspaper.

It was not always thus. Decades ago, San Francisco journalism was considered an important stop, or even a permanent home, for an ambitious newspaperman. The half-dozen San Francisco newspapers offered Bay Area residents across-the-board variety.

In contrast, Los Angeles was not much. Voting over 30 years ago in Leo Rosten's poll (prepared for his book *The Washington Correspondents,* New York: Harcourt Brace & Co., 1937), Washington reporters ranked the Los Angeles *Times* third among "least fair and reliable" American newspapers (just behind the Chicago *Tribune,* and two places behind all the Hearst newspapers, which together took first prize for unreliability). The *Times* was then as well known for intervening in politics as for covering it. When Rosten asked which newspapers the correspondents would most like to work for, the Los Angeles *Times* did not receive a single vote.

During this same period, Paul Smith was beginning a remarkable era in San Francisco journalism by trying to transform the *Chronicle* into a western cross between the New York *Times* and the New York *Herald-Tribune*. In one solid study, *Makers of Modern Journalism* (New York: Prentice-Hall, Inc., 1952, p. 401), Kenneth Stewart and John Tebbel called Smith's *Chronicle* "easily the worthiest major newspaper on the Pacific Coast."

By 1970, the situation had changed dramatically. A survey by *Seminar* magazine (a quarterly review for newspapermen, published by the Copley Newspapers), rated newspapers according to a scale based on positive and negative answers from 180 respondents who included members of the working press, educators, students, public relations and advertising men. The scoring system gave a plus one for each positive response and a minus one for each negative vote. Although the survey appeared to be impressionistic and made no attempt to achieve statistical significance, the results were interesting as a general indication of opinion.

The Los Angeles *Times* was rated very high, ranking fourth among all the American papers considered. It received a plus 20 rating for fairness. The *Chronicle,* on the other hand, was 21st in rank and got a minus 13 fairness rating. At the extremes, the *Christian Science Monitor* (which carried a report of the survey on page five of its August 28, 1970 issue) was top-rated with a plus 85, and the Chicago *Tribune* low-rated with a minus 52.

These bits of history point to a paradox. For today the *Times* of garish, metropolitan Los Angeles is further reputed to be the most improved newspaper in America, a worthy rival of the Washington *Post,* the *Wall Street Journal* and the St. Louis *Post-Dispatch*. It is now one of the most profitable papers in the world, publishing more news and more advertising than any other. The *Chronicle* of urbane, sophisticated San Francisco seems to be playing in a different league—one critic has suggested that it take on again the name that it had in 1865: the *Daily Dramatic Chronicle*. But in the years before its marriage of convenience with the San Francisco *Examiner,* the *Chronicle*'s circulation crept up as its quality declined.

This is all very mystifying. The Bay Area has one of the most intense concentrations of higher education facilities in the world. It is the center of a complex of industries that demand highly educated people.

San Francisco is proud of its style; some of its suburbs are no less proud of theirs. And yet the Bay Area did little to support Paul Smith's ambitious *Chronicle*. One editor who was lured here from the East years ago by Smith's promise of "a machine gun in every typewriter" now declares that Smith's vision was "all a lot of hogwash." Nor did the Bay Area wildly welcome the Western Edition of the New York *Times* when it came here nearly a decade ago. True, it was not a reasonably exact facsimile of the real New York *Times,* but support for it was even slimmer than the paper. Subscriptions were scattered, advertising was slender and the Western Edition died.

A sketchy review of the past 10 years gives us an outline of the kinds of journalism the Bay Area will support. In 1959, San Francisco was not just the home of the *Chronicle* and the *Examiner;* it boasted four major dailies, two of them circulating more than 100,000 copies each, two of them circulating more than 200,000.

Outside the City, publishing was fairly pale in 1959. Oakland was a large city, and the *Tribune* had 205,000 subscribers. But the limitations of the *Tribune*'s resources were suggested by Joseph Knowland's many titles: president, publisher, vice president, general manager and editor. The San Jose *Mercury* and the San Jose *News* were still in the hinterlands. The suburban and small-city papers were docile. The Palo Alto *Times* had a circulation of only 29,000. The San Rafael *Independent-Journal* had only 25,000 subscribers, and the Berkeley *Gazette* listed 15,025.

Now, however, of the San Francisco papers, only the *Chronicle* has a healthy circulation, 477,000. Both San Francisco papers, linked in a joint operating agreement that has them splitting profits, have a combined circulation of only 682,000. In contrast, the combined circulation of the four San Francisco papers was 724,000 ten years ago, when the Bay Area was much less heavily populated.

The circulation of the Oakland *Tribune* has risen very modestly from 205,000 to 209,000. The San Jose papers have gained readers: their combined circulation was only 116,000 in 1959; 10 years later it reached 204,000. They now rank among the top 10 newspapers in the United States in advertising linage, and the new home of the San Jose *Mercury* and *News* trumpets their wealth. Some newspapermen speak of it as "the Taj Mahal"; some of the interior appointments would do credit to a bordello.

Most of the suburban and small-city dailies are thriving. The Palo Alto *Times* and the San Rafael *Independent-Journal* will soon double their figures of 10 years ago. Nearly all of the other papers of similar size in the Bay Area have experienced increases of at least 50 percent.

Some of the success springs from stronger journalism; much of it is attributable to population growth and redistribution.

✧   ✧   ✧

We cannot provide final answers to several of the questions posed by this survey of Bay Area journalism, but the character of the Bay Area —and the kind of journalism it supports—is central to our investigation. If much of our attention is given to the established papers, and especially to the large dailies, it is because they seem to hold the key to the success of all the others. In addition, of course, they have the larger scope and the greater potential for affecting the lives of millions.

What can justifiably be asked of all these papers is that, within limits set by finances and other circumstances, they inform the community through news reports, analytical articles and opinion pieces. If they can also entertain their readers at the same time, so much the better.

Combinations and Ownership of Dailies

Appropriate fare for a weekly magazine may be positively scandalous in a weekly newspaper; and what might go unchallenged (and unnoticed) in a full-length book may cause a Senate investigation if broken in the daily newspaper. Norman Isaacs, a vice president and executive editor of the *Courier-Journal* and *Times,* monopoly newspapers in Louisville, and President of the American Society of Newspaper Editors, has put it this way: "The American citizen has different tolerances for different means of communication. He has the highest tolerance for cute books; and the next for specialized magazines. But he has the lowest tolerance of all for a paper in a monopoly situation."

If this is true, then boiling points of readers in much of the Bay Area should be as low as those of Louisville subscribers with respect to monopoly papers. The big five papers in the nine-county region have set the pattern for a combination that is proving popular for owners of newspapers at all circulation levels. The *Chronicle* and *Examiner* have carved up the San Francisco market with their joint operating agreement. It is known as the San Francisco Newspaper Printing Company, Inc., and controls, among other things, the circulation and advertising for the two papers. The San Jose *Mercury* and *News* are both owned by the Ridder family (and are therefore part of a communications empire stretching from St. Paul to Southern California). The *Tribune* is alone in Oakland and the dominant force in most of the East Bay.

In addition to these three fiefdoms, clusters of smaller papers under a single publisher can be found with ominous regularity. Peninsula Newspapers, Inc. (an employee-held operation) owns the Palo Alto *Times*, Redwood City *Tribune*, and twice-weekly Burlingame *Advance-Star*. The papers circulate in San Mateo and Santa Clara counties.

In Alameda County, Floyd L. Sparks and Abraham Kofman slug it out; Sparks runs the Hayward *Review*, Livermore *Herald and News*, and Fremont *Argus*; Kofman has the Fremont *News-Register*, San Leandro *Morning News*, and Alameda *Times-Star*. Dean S. Lesher is king in Contra Costa County with the *Times and Green Sheet* (in Walnut Creek), the Concord *Daily Transcript*, and the Antioch *Ledger*. Leo E. Owens is the owner of the Richmond *Independent* and Berkeley *Gazette*, and Warren Brown, Jr., the publisher.

This brief description of the daily power enclaves in the Bay Area is not intended as criticism per se. The authors have found both good and bad journalism in the above papers, as well as in such single properties as the San Mateo *Times* and Santa Rosa *Press-Democrat*. There is no simple rule about newspaper quality based on single versus multiple or monopoly ownership. Much of the testimony against the Newspaper Preservation Act (which has made legal a *Chronicle-Examiner* type arrangement) is equivocal on this point. It is difficult, for example, to determine the degree to which San Francisco journalism has been injured by the merger. It is much easier to document the financial consequences of such an arrangement than it is to point to a specific story and say, "This would have been covered more adequately if the city had two independent papers."

Along with monopoly and multiple ownership, however, is the offsetting fact that large numbers of daily newspapers exist in the nine-county area. The 28 separate dailies serving the Bay Area are one more than in the entire state of Kentucky; eight more than in either Oregon or Alabama; and roughly double the number in Nebraska. There are enough dailies on the Peninsula, for example, to permit a roving reader to start in San Jose and purchase a different paper every 10 miles or so. Although the papers have carved the Bay Area into spheres of influence as neatly as the world's powers have done for Europe and Asia, a determined newspaperphile can get at least three papers a day in his circulation area. (Appendix I lists the 28 dailies, their locations, circulation and chief officers.)

The American Newspaper Guild in the Bay Area

The American Newspaper Guild has a foothold in nine of the Bay Area papers, including the big five.[3] Top minimums paid to Bay Area reporters rank near the top on a national scale. Publishers have been particularly stingy, however, in offering money beyond the top minimums established by contract after five or six years of service. For this reason, while the Bay Area attracts good young talent, it is not always able to keep it. Many of the better journalists move on to higher paying jobs, leaving more youngsters with promise and those who never made it. Minimums are said to be higher for Bay Area suburban papers than for papers with similar circulations in other parts of the country, because regional collective bargaining was born in the Bay Area 20 years ago. Credit is given to strong guild leadership and philosophy for parity of pay rates in the suburbs.

With nine of the 28 papers at least partially organized, the guild in the Bay Area is well ahead of its national average. Nationally, the guild represents only about 10 percent of all U. S. dailies, including 81 of the 229 papers with circulations of 50,000 or more (including Canada). Fred D. Fletcher, Executive Secretary, San Francisco-Oakland Newspaper Guild, said that there is little progress in organizing new units locally, mainly because

> Guild organizing usually requires a combination of good in-plant leadership, good outside expertise and a need resulting from employer error or stinginess. That combination has been rare in the Bay Area largely because unorganized publishers have grown smart enough to maintain salaries and other benefits that appear, repeat appear, to match what the Guild gets in Bay Area bargaining.

Fletcher emphasized that it is usually through mistakes of the employer that the ball for organization gets rolling, and not much is rolling at present. (See Appendix II for a selected list of papers around the country, showing reporter and photographer top minimums in guild contracts as of August 1, 1970.)

What Paper Do You Read?

One of the most intriguing questions (and one most difficult to answer) about newspapers in any region is, "How much difference does

---

[3] Papers represented are the *Chronicle* and *Examiner* (editorial and white collar staffs); *Mercury* and *News* (editorial, white collar and janitorial staffs); Oakland *Tribune* (editorial staff only); Richmond *Independent* (editorial staff only); Vallejo *Times-Herald* (editorial and advertising staffs); Santa Rosa *Press-Democrat* (editorial staff only); and San Mateo *Times* (editorial not including photographers and white collar staffs).

my choice of newspaper make to my perception of the community and the world? Or, does it matter which paper I read?" Setting aside for the moment such basic information as the size of the news hole (i.e., actual inches available for news or other material after the advertising inches have been sold) and the number of subscriptions to wire services and syndicated features, two quite contradictory observations can be made of Bay Area dailies in this regard: (1) As expected, there is a definable Establishment viewpoint in all of the papers, with a relentless, numbing sameness to the tone of coverage afforded the non-Establishment, such as student demonstrators, feminists, Black militants and other stereo-typed groups. (2) Nevertheless, there are evident variations in what each of the papers feels is important both on a given day and over a period of months.

Comparisons, first of the *Chronicle* and the *Mercury,* and next of the *Tribune* and the *Examiner,* indicated the differences in news judgment among the area's top four teams of news executives. All the front-page stories, with the exception of local news items (which were different in each community), are presented below for each paper in three competing issues selected at random. Dates for the *Mercury* and *Chronicle* comparisons are January 23, 28, and 29, 1969; for the *Tribune* and *Examiner* comparisons, January 16, 17, and 30, 1969. Equivalent editions of the papers were selected wherever possible. Stories that appeared on the front pages of both papers are listed first. The page numbers in parentheses indicate where the competing paper placed a story that was not on the other's front page.

TABLE 1

NEWS JUDGMENT: FRONT-PAGE STORIES

January 23, 1969	
Mercury	*Chronicle*
Pueblo inquiry	Same
Flood tragedy—five die	Same
U. S. poor crippled by hunger	Same
Feeble support for San Jose State College teachers' strike	Same
Vote on Hickel due (6)	Fire at Wheeler Hall (not in *Mercury*)
Trustees eye talks with SFS (San Francisco State College) students (15)	Senate bill to end draft (9)
	Quiet UC strike (18)
	Appointment of Pete Wilson to state Urban Affairs Commission (2)
	Old guard purged in state Senate (2)

January 28, 1969

Mercury	*Chronicle*
Nixon's first press conference	Same
Reaction to Disney's Mineral King Project	Same
Pueblo inquiry (9)	
Southern California flooding (3)	(Remainder of front-page stories local to San Francisco)
Iraqi hangings incense Israelis (9)	
Archer wins the Crosby golf tournament (sports)	

January 29, 1969

Mercury	*Chronicle*
New Iraqi spy trial	Same
Peru seizes International Petroleum Company	Same
Nixon on crime and need for judges (13)	UC student violence (10)
Skiers snowed-in (not in *Chronicle*)	Nixon's new dog (3)
Reagan on flood aid (2)	California unions' drive to cut health costs (not in *Mercury*)
Lightning strikes United plane (not in *Chronicle*)	

January 16, 1969

Tribune	*Examiner*
Paris peace talks	Same
LBJ on wage-price spiral	Same
Two Russians in spacewalk	Same
Cabinet report warns of post-war recession (4)	
Repairs on the "Enterprise" (8)	
LBJ on breaking Paris deadlock (Not in *Examiner*)	(Remainder of front-page stories local to San Francisco)
Making an enzyme in a test tube (not in *Examiner*)	
Bomb found at SFS (not in *Examiner*)	

January 17, 1969

Tribune	*Examiner*
Soviet spacemen land safely	Same
Lack of funds haunts HHH (not in *Examiner*)	Cease-fire talks in Saigon (not in *Tribune*)

GI pullout seen by Lodge
(not in *Examiner*)

Washington courts asks
Garrison for evidence (10)

San Jose professors get letters (5)

SFS meeting (not in *Examiner*)

Regents sift independent study
plan (not in *Examiner*)

Jewish juror a problem for Sirhan
(not in *Examiner*)

LBJ says Russ plug space-gap
(not in *Tribune*)

Reagan-Hayakawa in agreement
(not in *Tribune*)

Rumor resigns in Italy
(not in *Tribune*)

Nixon statement on Vietnam
(not in *Tribune*)

January 30, 1969

Tribune	*Examiner*
Trouble at SFS	Same
Reds resist pullout and DMZ talks	Same
Allen Dulles dies	Same
Trouble at UC (4)	Jet raid charged by Iraq (5)
Pentagon to probe "Pueblo" (not in *Examiner*)	Philippine earthquake (not in *Tribune*)

The tallies from the small sample shown in Table I strongly suggest that differences in topics covered can indeed influence the reader's page one view of the world. In general, the *Chronicle* tended to give front-page space to U.C. activities, violent or otherwise. The *Mercury* put U.C. news on inside pages. The *Chronicle* emphasized San Francisco-based stories, while the *Mercury* gave more attention to non-local (i.e., non-San Jose) and non-California stories. In short, the *Chronicle's* page one leaned toward local news with a dash of student-based violence, and the *Mercury* offered its readers primarily national and international news.

The *Tribune* and *Examiner* contrast showed even less overlap in the choice of front-page stories. Like its sister the *Chronicle,* the *Examiner* presented much San Francisco-based material, while very little on the *Tribune's* page one dealt exclusively with the East Bay. The following qualitative discussions of newspaper performance explore these clues and tendencies more fully and examine the ways in which varying news judgments in Bay Area papers affect the focus and content of information presented to the reader.

Qualitative Sketches of a Ten-Paper Sample: Goals and Performance

In addition to asking whether and in what ways Bay Area residents were better informed if they read one paper as opposed to another, we also considered how well they were being served by the morning and evening papers in their areas. Over a three-month period, December 23, 1968 to March 4, 1969, we reviewed the performances of 10 dailies ranging in size from the *Chronicle* to the Berkeley *Gazette*. The sample included family papers, chain papers and papers with semi-absentee owners. The four morning papers in the study, (*Chronicle, Mercury, Gazette,* and Vallejo *Times-Herald*) represented 93 percent of the morning circulation (based on circulation figures from the *Editor and Publisher International Yearbook 1969*); the six afternoon papers (*Examiner, Tribune,* San Jose *News,* San Mateo *Times,* Palo Alto *Times,* and Santa Rosa *Press-Democrat*) accounted for 71 percent of the afternoon circulation. The 10 had the largest circulation in their respective fields.

The Metro Daily Papers

The performance of the five metro papers, i.e., the *Chronicle,* the *Examiner,* the *Tribune,* the *Mercury* and the *News,* is most important to the Bay Area community. As Joseph E. Bodovitz, Executive Director of the San Francisco Bay Conservation and Development Commission, has said, "If these five papers are not doing the job, there is nothing that can compensate for their deficiencies." The following qualitative sketches attempt to outline the philosophy of each paper, and to show how it has met its own goals and those of the community. We have tried to keep in mind the cautionary statement of one of the Bay Area's most caustic press critics, Bruce Brugmann, publisher of the monthly San Francisco *Bay Guardian:* "I put out a half-assed paper. It's the toughest thing in the world to put out a good one."

SAN FRANCISCO CHRONICLE (477,009[1])

Leaving Bardelli's restaurant one weekday afternoon, *Chronicle* executive news editor Bill German was approached by one of the paper's elderly readers, a San Francisco resident of prominent social standing. *Chronicle* film critic John Wasserman was then in the midst of a series

---

[1] Total circulation in 1969.

28

on the City's North Beach-nudie film houses, the text of which was often quite graphic.

"What is the *Chronicle* up to now?" the reader asked with a mildly reproving tone. Without waiting for German to answer, he continued, "I mean, you're a family, morning newspaper."

"If something offends you," German countered in a pleasant, off-hand manner, "you don't have to read it."

"You're all we have," the old gentleman said. "We have to read you."

Although the *Chronicle* does not straddle the Northern California market the way the colossal Los Angeles *Times* dominates the South, nevertheless it is easily the most important newspaper in the Bay Area (although not the most profitable). Its circulation is more than double that of its closest competitor, the Oakland *Tribune*. The merger with the *Examiner* left the *Chronicle* alone in the prestigious morning field, with only the South Bay's San Jose *Mercury* as competition in parts of the Peninsula. In Herb Caen, the *Chronicle* has the single most powerful columnist in the Bay Area; it has locked up most of the choice syndicated material, and it often has first pick of local writing talent.

More sassy than fat, the *Chronicle* has been lighting fires under San Francisco since the early 1950's. Publisher Charles Thieriot, editor Scott Newhall, managing editor Gordon Pates, city editor Abe Mellinkoff, and German seem to delight in making the *Chronicle* different from other metro dailies. One *Chronicle* executive has called it "the only aboveground underground paper in the United States," and he may be right. It is unlikely that there is another group of newspaper executives anywhere in the country—with the possible exception of those running the New York *Times*—that is so conscious of its audience, and of the effect of its newspaper on that audience. "Already conditioned to expect the unexpected from the *Chronicle*," German has written in a widely circulated memo, "the readers seem not even to be aware that they are being weaned into becoming readers of a more mature and responsible organ of information and opinion." Readers of the *Chronicle* do get a unique brand of journalism from a unique newspaper. Its responsibility and maturity, however, can be questioned on many counts.

The Circulation War

The *Chronicle*'s personality was formed in the great circulation battle with the morning San Francisco *Examiner*, a battle that raged from the early 1950's until the merger in 1965. Although it may come as a shock to some of the *Chronicle*'s newer readers, Scott Newhall's predecessor, Paul Smith, tried to fashion a heavy, responsible paper. How close Smith came is debatable. He had a reputation as an excellent recruiter, but no one on the staff knew what he wanted and the paper was drifting. Newhall believed the paper "gave indications of being self-consciously self-important. . . . The *Chronicle* had less coverage than it has now, and a sense of humor was somewhat lacking."

In Smith's last year (1952) the *Chronicle* was third in circulation in San Francisco with 154,608, trailing the morning *Examiner* (225,060) and the evening *Call-Bulletin* (160,271). The evening *News* was fourth at 125,625. The *Chronicle* also trailed the evening Oakland *Tribune,* which had a circulation of 191,597. That year Charles Thieriot appointed Newhall to the editor's chair; his instructions were to make the paper a commercial success. German wrote of the strategy of the circulation battle as follows:

> What strength there was in the old *Chronicle* had always been with the upper level of the population, the upper level economically and intellectually. Home-delivered circulation was proportionally high. Street sales were low. Strategy and tactics called for attracting many non-readers of our egg-headish newspaper into our tent, and, once there, keeping them from drifting out again. It was also essential that our core of serious readers not be so disaffected by the raucousness of our new spiel that they pack up and go elsewhere.

Despite the concern for serious readers, the paper plunged eagerly after circulation. The street edition received a daily banner headline, which was "no longer reserved for the most consequential news of the day." German's memo went on, "The banner, under its new concept, was to be a piece of promotional advertising for the sale of that day's edition, much in the manner of a headline on the cover of a slick magazine." Typography was also changed. Leads were set in larger type and white space around heads and pictures was increased.

Reporters were encouraged to reflect in their stories their own reactions to an event, producing something German has called the *Chronicle* "cult of personality." Newhall recognized the value of controversial and readable columnists for building circulation; thus Charles McCabe started as the "fearless spectator" dealing originally with sports, Count Marco with unorthodox women's advice, Art Hoppe with political satire, Ralph Gleason with jazz and rock, Herb Caen with his own special material, and a number of others.

The most successful circulation builders, however, were a series of wild pseudo-stories that often ran for weeks, providing the sharpest contrast to the straight journalism of other Bay Area dailies. Jonathan Root waged a campaign against poor coffee in San Francisco restaurants under such banners as "A Great City is Forced to Drink Swill." Reporter George Draper covered a campaign to clothe the naked animals of the City, which led to the founding of SINA chapters (Society for Indecency to Naked Animals). The effort received nationwide play when Draper attempted to start a chapter in the U. S. S. R.

The *Chronicle*'s attempt to out-Hearst Hearst led to one of the funniest and most celebrated incidents in San Francisco journalism—one that proved how keenly competitive newspapering can be. In 1960 the *Chronicle* sent its then outdoors editor Bud Boyd into the wilderness of the Trinity Alps as "The Last Man on Earth." Boyd, his wife and three children were to be the sole survivors of a mythical H-bomb attack, trying to test man's instincts for survival. As the *Chronicle* asked on its front page: "Could an average city dweller exist in the wilderness tomorrow with little more than his bare hands?"

Daily dispatches from Boyd appeared on the *Chronicle*'s front page, including the inevitable "night of terror" in which Boyd fought for "survival against cold and exhaustion." At the height of interest in the series, the *Examiner* sent to the mountains a reporter who learned from "unassailable sources" that the Boyds had left their camp. At the campsite the *Examiner* found (and documented with pictures) fresh eggs, empty spaghetti cans, chipped beef containers, kitchen matches, coke bottles, and enough toilet paper to start a fire.

Examiner and *Chronicle* executives waged an editorial battle over the series, with Boyd and Newhall appearing on the *Chronicle*'s television station, KRON-TV, to present a "report to the people" on the episode. A masterful, closing touch was supplied by *News-Call Bulletin* city editor Harry Press, who assigned one of his reporters to test survival in Golden Gate Park surrounded by beautiful dollies, champagne and caviar. It had the whole town laughing.

Those readers interested in serious news coverage, however, were not laughing. The "Last Man" series was receiving major headline play in the *Chronicle* at the time John F. Kennedy was battling for the Democratic presidential nomination in Los Angeles. The Kennedy story took a back seat to Boyd's escapades. Further, the Boyd series had been syndicated to many other papers around the country, and several, including the New York *Herald-Tribune* and the St. Louis *Post-Dispatch*, dropped the story midway. The *Post-Dispatch* went so far as to denounce the *Chronicle* editorially for its duplicity, a rare event in newspaper circles.

With each series the *Chronicle*'s circulation went up 15,000, and German claimed the paper held about 10,000 of these readers after a series ended. By 1958 *Chronicle* circulation had jumped to 225,409, far surpassing both the *Call-Bulletin* and the foundering *News*. The

Chronicle trailed the *Examiner* by only 32,000. During the Boyd series the *Chronicle* finally passed the *Examiner*.

In 1959 the pattern of merger began to take shape. In only six years this process was to reduce San Francisco from four independents to two. The afternoon Scripps-Howard *News* and Hearst *Call-Bulletin* combined on a 50-50 basis, Scripps-Howard maintaining editorial control and Hearst running the business, advertising, production and distribution. In 1962 Scripps-Howard pulled out of San Francisco, selling its 50 percent interest to Hearst ownership and giving San Francisco two Hearst papers.

For the next two years the Chronicle Publishing Company and Hearst media giants continued to battle for the morning field in San Francisco. In 1964 the *Chronicle* topped the *Examiner* in circulation, 351,489 to 301,356. Although the Chronicle Publishing Company was and is in excellent financial health because of profits from KRON-TV, the financial condition of the *Chronicle* has been confused by the conflicting testimony of publisher Charles Thieriot. In a July 1967 statement at the Senate Anti-Trust Subcommittee hearing on the Newspaper Preservation Act, Thieriot said that with the exception of 1956, the *Chronicle*'s losses were of "modest proportions," and that not until 1964 was the *Chronicle* "breaking even."

Thieriot claimed that monies for fighting the circulation war with the *Examiner* were coming from KRON-TV profits. In a letter to Michigan Senator Philip Hart on December 11, 1967, Thieriot reversed his position, recognizing that the use of television station profits to drive a competitive newspaper to the wall might be damaging at license renewal time (as indeed has proved to be the case). In any event, he revised his analysis of *Chronicle* profits. Wrote Thieriot,

> Before depreciation, newspaper operations showed a small and manageable loss in 1955, a profit in 1956, somewhat larger but manageable losses in 1957 and 1958 and, as indicated above, a profit for each year commencing with 1959 through September 1965, with the single exception of 1962.

Clearly Thieriot wanted to make it plausible that the Chronicle Publishing Company was able to finance the battle with the *Examiner* out of *Chronicle* newspaper profits. Since publishers have historically been unwilling to discuss finances, we can only assume from the letter to Senator Hart that the *Chronicle* was not a failing newspaper at the time of the merger.

Circulation of the *News Call-Bulletin*, however, was down to 183,176, a drain on Hearst resources. Of the three papers in San Francisco in 1964, it is safe to say only that the *News Call-Bulletin* was failing. Although the *Chronicle* had a decisive circulation lead (and since the newspaper business is one of increasing marginal return, this lead would snowball), the *Examiner* still held the lead in the profitable classified advertising department. But the Hearsts thought it more profitable in the long run to end the fight. They arranged a treaty that would kill the afternoon *News Call-Bulletin,* move the *Examiner* to the afternoon and ensure its profitability, and give the *Chronicle* undisputed control of the morning market. Since the Hearsts already owned the *Examiner* and the *News Call-Bulletin,* it is hard to understand why they did not make the move unilaterally, without involving the *Chronicle.* The only answer seems to be the profit motive, the urge to insure a guaranteed profit by uniting the City's only two remaining newspapers. The same motive held true for the *Chronicle.* As the *Guardian*'s Bruce Brugmann charged, the *Chronicle* was willing to give up its independence simply for the higher profits "promised by a joint operating agreement that would destroy the need for expensive competition."

The Merger and Its Consequences

On October 23, 1964, the two companies agreed to form the San Francisco Newspaper Printing Company, whose stock was to be owned equally by the Chronicle Publishing Company and Hearst. The new corporation would perform the mechanical, circulation, advertising, accounting, credit and collection functions for both papers. The *Examiner* was to become an afternoon paper, the *News Call-Bulletin* was killed, and the two Sunday papers were combined into the single Sunday *Examiner and Chronicle.* The agreement was submitted to the Justice Department on August 30, 1965, the attorney general replying that he did not for the present intend to institute anti-trust action. On September 1, 1965, incorporation papers were filed in Carson City, Nevada, without fanfare, and on September 12 the agreement went into effect.

The major complaint of competing publishers against such an arrangement was spelled out by J. Hart Clinton, publisher of the San Mateo *Times,* before a Senate Anti-Trust Subcommittee on July 28, 1967. The committee was considering the Failing Newspaper Act (now the Newspaper Preservation Act), intended to establish definitely the legality of such joint operating agreements between newspapers. Clinton said that after the merger in September, the basic "open" display advertising rate for space in the *Chronicle* was almost doubled, from $1.20 per line in January 1965, to $2.32 per line. The *Chronicle's* increase in circulation as a result of the merger was only 33 percent, hardly justifying such a rate increase. The *Examiner,* with lower circulation and faced with competition from other afternoon papers (although not within the City) increased its rate from $1.03 to $1.55 per line.

On the other hand, a combination rate for advertising in both papers was set at $2.58 per line, only $.26 above the rate for the *Chronicle* alone. No other afternoon paper was available at a price of $.26 per line. This naturally led businesses to advertise in both San Francisco papers, making it more difficult for other afternoon papers published in the Bay Area to compete with the *Examiner* for advertising dollars. This arrangement would also surely preclude the start of a third competitive daily newspaper in San Francisco.

Already the merger has helped kill the San Francisco *Argonaut,* a semi-weekly "shopper" with a circulation of 200,000. The *Argonaut* folded in March 1969. Its final editorial stated that "One of the main factors in the suspension was a lack of interest on the part of a substantial number of San Francisco's larger retailers in supporting a new newspaper voice." The "lack of interest" was in part attributable to the combined advertising rate. Weinstein's Department Stores, which folded in 1966, currently has a suit filed in Federal Court against the *Chronicle* and *Examiner* for triple damages, claiming that the high advertising rates of the merger forced the company out of business. The head of advertising for one large, prosperous Bay Area department store chain has said, "After the merger we no longer had any leverage. With our bargaining position removed, we no longer get the position in the paper we want. They don't care as much about us as before." Although it was difficult for large stores to pinpoint effects of the merger, this advertising director, with 15 years' experience in the Bay Area, believed that the smaller stores such as Weinstein's and Hale's (which also folded) were hurt severely:

> With even two independent papers the small stores could advertise heavily in one at half the price charged by the merged papers. Now we *have* to take space in both papers, even though there is so much circulation overlap. If we just had another daily or even two independent papers, we could concentrate on either the morning or afternoon market. With the merger, we can't.

Classified ads have brought home the effects of the merger most sharply to Bay Area residents. Although it is possible to purchase a classified ad in only the *Chronicle* or the *Examiner,* such an ad is placed at the very end of the section in a column by itself. The ad is displaced from all the usual classifications (which location is the reason most people take out a classified ad) and dumped at the back. Thus one has to advertise in both papers, when in theory an independent *Chronicle* ad might be adequate. Further, the *Chronicle-Examiner* rate of $2.19 per line is $.15 higher than that of the Los Angeles *Times,* a paper with nearly 300,000 more subscribers.

The merger has hurt news coverage, also. No longer concerned about competition, the *Chronicle* locks up its paper around five p.m., with the exception of a few later stories for which the editors were prepared. Bay Area readers receive a morning paper that is closer to an evening paper in the currency of its news. The lack of competition has also produced what one *Examiner* reporter calls "a kind of indolence in the newsroom." Many of the reporters turned to outside, freelance writing because they no longer felt a challenge in daily journalism. "On a competitive paper," an *Examiner* reporter wrote, "a reporter's lack of zeal is exposed as soon as he writes a story that suffers by comparison with the opposition. On a non-competitive paper, nobody ever knows."

It is unlikely that the merger meant much else to San Francisco readers, who seem inured to monopoly and combination, from the actions of other industries, as well as from the newspaper business.

If old claims that only one paper would have survived a prolonged circulation fight are to be believed, then San Francisco is better off with both the *Chronicle* and the *Examiner* than it would be with either alone. The authors believe that the more media outlets under separate editorial control that can exist in a city, the better. The experience of other metropolitan areas suggests, however, that San Francisco could support both a morning *Chronicle* and an afternoon *Examiner,* wholly independent of one another. The publishers prefer it the way it is now.

A New Philosophy

With the circulation battle won, and its position as the largest and most influential Bay Area daily secure, the *Chronicle* then refined and expanded its war strategy into a fullblown philosophy of newspapering. As befits this electronic age, *Chronicle* editors thought of the news product in much the same terms as they thought of television: it must both entertain and inform. "The formula at the *Chronicle* calls for a combination of fact, truth and fun," German wrote. "Each edition each day should approach the goal of informing and entertaining most of the people most of the time." Newhall likened a part of his paper to a circus barker in front of a tent, saying "Hurry, hurry, hurry, the girls are just about to take off their clothes." Once inside, readers would find a story about Vietnam, or so ran the theory.

We noted during the study period, December 23, 1968 to March 4, 1969 that the *Chronicle* was edited to be read quickly. Readers could whip through most stories in a minute or two; placing the continuation of front page stories on the back page has speeded up the process even more, and has proven to be an innovation very popular with readers. But rarely did the *Chronicle* force its readers to tax themselves. The paper's news ethic, as city editor Abe Mellinkoff saw it, was "Will someone read the story? If the story is not read, it's not news." German believed that a good test of a story's news value was the likelihood that people would talk about the subject.

> We decided not to be any more bluenosed than the society in which we lived. When a topless bathing suit was first designed and debated, we fitted out a model in the first such suit and published her picture in a prominent position in the paper. We did draw the line at any print that exposed the nipples, but that was six or seven years ago.

The emphasis on snappy, lively, readable copy with eye-grabbing pictures is antithetic to the notion of the long-running series. The *Chronicle* runs fewer series than the other four metro papers because, said Mellinkoff, "a paper should be complete in itself." One *Chronicle* reporter said that it was "unheard of" for a reporter to be relieved of his daily assignments for a long-term story. The Wasserman series on nudie movie houses, another on homosexuals, and a third on life with Jackie Kennedy Onassis did appear in the *Chronicle,* presumably because Mellinkoff thought they would be read. They probably were.

The influence of the Norman Mailer-John Hersey personal style of journalism is evident at the *Chronicle.* The rather young, liberal staff seems to be given more freedom to experiment in print, in line with Newhall's "cult of personality." The *Chronicle*'s May 1969 coverage of the People's Park trouble in Berkeley was significant for its reporter-involvement with both police and demonstrators. Some informative and readable stories resulted from the arrest and incarceration of one reporter at the Santa Rita Prison Farm, and the attendance of others at People's parties and meetings. One *Chronicle* editor felt that Mailer's approach to an event, such as the March on the Pentagon or the Democratic Convention in Chicago, resulted in more meaningful reporting than did traditional journalism. "We're feeling our way toward a new method of communication in print," he said, "without the stereotypes of what a paper is supposed to look like."

The style of city editor Mellinkoff also contributes to the freedom of *Chronicle* reporters. Unlike many city editors, including Gale Cook at the *Examiner,* Mellinkoff does not exert tight control in assigning stories to reporters. He encourages them to generate their own ideas. Editing is also very loose at the city desk. Said one young reporter, marveling, "I got some stories past the desk that I never expected would make it through."

However, in the summer of 1970, some of the younger *Chronicle* reporters complained to management that they were unhappy about the goals and purposes of the paper. Although the dissidents would disclose little about the complaints, one said that the dispute was over the desire of the younger men to "publish a real newspaper."

Despite the Republicanism of its editorial page, the *Chronicle* has been the most sympathetic among Bay papers in its handling of the contemporary cultural scene, including hippies, drugs, sexual permissiveness and student unrest. Bernard "Bud" Liebes, who has worked for both San Francisco papers said:

> The *Chronicle* appears more liberal, tolerant, and "with it" on such contemporary issues, no matter how fleeting or faddish, as pop art, op art, rock, folk music, wife swapping, and foibles of suburban America. On all these the *Examiner* has been uptight, straight.

The mood created by editor Scott Newhall makes it possible for the *Chronicle* staff to treat such subjects in a way that William Knowland's *Tribune* or Joseph Ridder's *Mercury* staffs could never attempt. In a revealing interview printed by the Berkeley *Barb* on March 7, 1969—which Newhall called an accurate statement of his position—he described the relationship of his paper to the Establishment: "We have to play it cooler than you underground papers. We have to keep the Establishment anesthetized so they don't feel the pain as we stick the needle into their archaic veins and give them a transfusion."

Some Shortcomings

The hip philosophy of the *Chronicle* is as offbeat for a serious metro as the *Chronicle*'s many sins. Despite the lengthy gestation period each night, the paper is often a horror typographically. At least one major article every morning is so garbled with slipped lines, reversals, dropped letters and the like as to be almost unreadable. The authors are still trying to decipher the words "warth to lit" from a recent issue. Usually an afternoon paper, under tighter deadlines, suffers in its makeup, but the *Examiner* is much cleaner than the *Chronicle*.

Given its list of wire services and syndicated materials, the *Chronicle* should provide excellent national and international news and opinion pieces. Newhall has contracted for the services of AP, UPI, The New York Times, The Los Angeles Times-Washington Post and others. Editors of competing Bay Area papers charged that the *Chronicle* has bought territorial rights to these services (where possible) so that other papers cannot carry them. Moreover, they contended that the *Chronicle* uses only a fraction of this material, and often not the best. Although German occasionally runs a James Reston or Tom Wicker opinion piece from the New York Times as a front-page story (a valuable and exciting idea), the bulk of the news copy comes from the AP, UPI, and Times-Post services.

The *Chronicle* puts heavy responsibility on the wire services for all non-local news; the paper has no Washington correspondent of its own, and no bureaus abroad. Considering all that is good in the *Chronicle* news philosophy, its conception of foreign coverage is hard to understand. "We have a general disinterest in detailed coverage of foreign politics and economics," an editor said. "We think our readers are more concerned with whether or not they use saran wrap in Kuala Lumpur than with New York *Times*-type foreign coverage." (See pp. 141–148 for fuller discussion of foreign news coverage.)

During the period included in this study, the *Chronicle* trailed the *Examiner, Tribune,* and *Mercury* in covering the major, continuing national and international stories. Appendix III shows the *Chronicle* in fourth position among Bay dailies on presidential news from Washington, and on Vietnam. It trailed the *Examiner* and *Tribune* on congressional news, and the *Tribune* on the Spring 1969 mid-east crisis. More important, the figures in column 3 of Appendix III show that the *Chronicle* was least likely among the metros to run such stories in the front of the newspaper. The *Chronicle* front page was heavily local and featurish. Serious legislative, non-dramatic stories (the type that make the *Tribune* "dull") were pushed to the rear. On the Presidio "mutiny" trial, however, the *Chronicle* performed best of all dailies surveyed, and was the only paper to run the story frequently on the front page. It was the *Chronicle*'s type of news.

Joseph Lyford and Spencer Klaw, of the Graduate School of Journalism, University of California at Berkeley, compared non-local news offerings in the New York *Times* and the *Chronicle* from December 12 to 19, 1968, and found some startling omissions by San Francisco's leader. On December 12 the *Chronicle* failed to carry a story from Ralph Nader about the dangers of driving a Volkswagen—there are probably as many of the German cars in the San Francisco area as anywhere else in the country—but the paper did find room for a puff story from Detroit about the Ford Maverick. The next day the *Chronicle* omitted a story on the union of Xerox and CORE to help passage of ghetto self-help bills.

On the same day, 16 publishers of newspapers with the same joint operating agreement as the *Chronicle-Examiner* asked for congressional approval of the arrangement. Lyford read about it in the Oakland *Tribune,* which has regularly outperformed the San Francisco dailies on this touchy subject. On December 19, urban expert Daniel Moynihan stated that the poverty program was a failure because it had emphasized community action over employment. Moynihan had studied the San Francisco experience, but the *Chronicle* had nothing on it. A final example (among scores of others) from December 18 typified the *Chronicle* attitude toward serious domestic and foreign news. The paper failed to mention the fact that for the first time in 40 years an opposition party had been organized in Portugal to push for election law reforms, press reforms and an end to detention laws. What the *Chronicle* did carry as foreign news was a story from Bologna that 19 men had been arrested for giving female hormones to cattle, leading the townspeople to think they would become sterile if they ate the meat.

Although the loss of the late editorial cartoonist Bob Bastian to KQED's "Newsroom" was sorely felt, according to one *Chronicle* editor, the editorial page and the stable of Newhall-nurtured columnists remains strong. The paper's talented group of reporters is led by science writer David Perlman, Keith Power, Michael Grieg, Dale Champion, Michael Harris, Carolyn Anspacher, Harold Gilliam, Scott Thurber, Bill Moore and others.

The *Chronicle's* obvious strengths make its weaknesses even harder to take. The Saturday entertainment page with the lengthy "After Nightfall" column by ad man Hal Schaefer is sheer puffery. The amount of women's page space devoted to news of the debutante-cotillion set is far larger than that given by other Bay Area papers. One city-side staffer reported that many female society writers were "frankly upset" with the tone of the society pages. They have been pushing for more articles on Black women's organizations, and on the sexual and social problems of American women. Publisher Charles Thieriot is interested in preserving the "high society" look of the pages, so they are fighting a difficult battle.

Plugs for local, cooperating businesses are also a *Chronicle* staple. A year or so ago the paper ran a contest to choose the Sultan of Yanuca, with *Chronicle* columnists as judges. Reporter George Draper sent back a series of stories about the adventures of the new sultan, each story containing a mention that Draper and the sultan flew Canadian Pacific Air. Why? Public relations officials of Canadian Pacific Air had cooked up the whole scheme and were footing air fare expenses. These indiscretions, such major problems as the absence of Washington and Saigon bureaus, and the sad state of foreign news coverage, made the *Chronicle* disappointing.

The Chronicle's *Potential*

Jerrold Werthimer, long-time journalism professor at San Francisco State College, has praised editor Newhall for providing a spot in his paper for every special public. As a monopoly paper in a sophisticated city, however, the *Chronicle* should also consider educating and elevating its readers, rather than merely catering to them. Newhall has given signs that he would like to move the *Chronicle* in this direction, if time and energy permit. "We have to educate the American people —gently, with compassion—to the fact that they are not infallible," Newhall said in a recent interview with *San Francisco Magazine*. "There's going to be a lot of trouble in this country. We are on the brink of what may be complete disaster. . . . People are trying to make sense of a senseless world. . . ."

Newhall has established the *Chronicle* as a successful barker. The people are in the tent, and they've seen the girls take off their clothes. It's time for the second act.

SAN FRANCISCO EXAMINER (204,749)

Critics of the financial arrangement that binds together the *Chronicle* and *Examiner,* and 21 other sets of papers around the country, have focused their displeasure on the combined advertising rate, the economic rewards given to a failing newspaper and the stifling of competition from other daily or weekly papers in the area. Another frequent criticism was that such an arrangement might lead to homogenization of both papers, causing them to become indistinguishable in format and viewpoint.

The Examiner's *Image*

This has not occurred in San Francisco. The character of the *Examiner,* "grey lady" of the afternoon and foil to the *Chronicle,* is evidence that some editorial separation can be maintained between merged newspapers. The *Examiner* long ago adopted a sober, conservative, often ponderous approach to newspapering. To those citizens who are confused or outraged by the *Chronicle's* antics, the *Examiner* looks more and more respectable. Purchased in 1880 by Senator George Hearst, who turned it over to son William Randolph in 1887, the *Examiner's* affiliation with the chain has only heightened its dour and prissy countenance.

Usually a paper with such matronly airs is able to view its competition from a position of strength—occasionally tolerant of the upstart's indiscretions, often grouchy and always domineering. The *Examiner,* however, is like an aged mother-in-law who has been clapped into a rest home by a son-in-law who then refuses to acknowledge her existence. The *Chronicle* calls the tune in San Francisco, and the *Examiner* may now be too old even to jump. One reason is the high average age of *Examiner* reporters (45), due to three mergers and guild seniority requirements for determining retention of staff. The mergers have also left the *Examiner* with overlapping layers of Scripps and Hearst authority, with no clear control other than at the top, where publisher Charles Gould represents the Hearst ownership. Among the committee of executives are editor Ed Dooley, executive editor Tom Eastham, associate editor Richard Pearce, managing editor Rene Casenave, associate managing editor Josh Eppinger, and assistant managing editor James McLean. All have decision-making authority.

The Shift to the Afternoon

If this imagery has been unnecessarily harsh, it is only to show that the merger placed the *Examiner* in an impossible competitive position for circulation, although its profitability was insured by the merger. Thrown kicking and screaming into the afternoon market, after generations of competition nose-to-nose with the *Chronicle,* the *Examiner* has yet to recover psychologically from the change. "The *Examiner* had a lot of esprit before the merger," said city editor Gale Cook. "It was not a happy thing. We preferred being a morning paper—it is much easier to put out."

Even a cursory study of metro papers in the United States today reveals that the morning market is the stronger, so the *Examiner's* banishment immediately put it on the defensive. The "let-them-try-to-read-it-in-another-paper" attitude has also hurt morale at both the *Examiner* and the *Chronicle,* particularly among reporters who were accustomed to working in a competitive situation. Said one *Chronicle* reporter, "The things that made for good newspapering before the merger in San Francisco are gone. The professional reporters would like to go back to the competitive situation."

The logistics of an afternoon paper give the staff less time to put it out, compel it to struggle for new leads to top the morning paper, require the sports staff to concentrate on feature writing, since game stories are all prepared by a morning staff, and force the city and news editors to be acutely aware of how far the morning paper has developed a story. If the *Chronicle's* entertainment writers did not so often decline to review operas, concerts, plays and club performances until two days afterward, the *Examiner* would be forced into second position in this respect as well. (The paper does have it a bit easier than its Eastern cousins because of the three-hour time difference, but the wire services tend to operate with only Eastern deadlines in mind, creating another problem at Western afternoon papers.) Control of the Sunday *Examiner-Chronicle* was one tidbit yielded to the Hearsts, although even here the *Chronicle* exacted its pound of flesh. The *Chronicle*'s contribution, "Sunday Punch," is entirely free of ads, while the "Datebook" and *This World* magazine have a few ads scattered about. The *Examiner*'s sections, on the other hand, are loaded with ads.

Not content with banishing its rival to afternoon "Siberia," the *Chronicle* made the move with a comparative circulation edge of better than a quarter of a million. From its final morning circulation of just over 300,000, the *Examiner* dropped to 220,000 in 1967, continuing the decline to 204,000 in 1969. The limitations of the afternoon market made it unlikely that Examiner circulation would rise above 250,000, about half the *Chronicle*'s size. This ceiling affected staff morale. Further, as indicated earlier, the *Chronicle* has contracted for the most desirable of the syndicated services. The *Examiner* was left primarily with AP, UPI, Chicago Daily News, Hearst Headline Service, and the London Daily Express, plus a few others. Editor Ed Dooley said he has all the syndicated opinion material he can use, but that he would surely like the *Chronicle*'s Times-Post service.

"We're Out to Top Them . . ."?

The merger was wholly a marriage of financial convenience. "Any time we can beat the *Chronicle* we do it with glee," Cook said.[2] "We're out to top them if we can. It's one of our few small pleasures left." There is said to be an unwritten rule that none of the *Examiner* editorial people can go over to the *Chronicle*'s editorial room. If they must get together, there is a no-man's-land in the middle. (The papers operate out of two buildings at Fifth and Mission, connected through a common print shop. The *Examiner*'s building is new. The *Chronicle* building has not been changed from the days of the *Daily Planet* in the old Superman comics.)

Although the bitterness between some *Examiner* and *Chronicle* employees is evident—Newhall seems unable to speak of the *Examiner* in a civil tone, and the worst insult city editor Mellinkoff could hurl at a reporter was to suggest that his copy read like the *Examiner*—the

---

[2] One of the ways Cook's men top the *Chronicle* is by covering the city—especially municipal politics and government—far better than the *Chronicle* has covered it in years.

authors are unimpressed with Cook's desire to scoop the *Chronicle*. In one of the juiciest incidents since the merger, the *Chronicle* was caught tailing former KRON-TV cameraman Al Kihn with private detectives in order to gather information of a compromising nature. Kihn had filed a complaint with the Federal Communications Commission detailing the manner in which the Chronicle Publishing Company, holder of the broadcast license, was said to be using the station to increase the company's profits. The *Examiner* failed to cover this incident, which Charles Thieriot later admitted did occur. The paper has also failed to cover the entire embarrassing and significant episode in which the FCC refused to renew KRON-TV's license without a public hearing. Not until the hearings began did the papers make amends. Surely if Cook were serious in his expressed desire to best the *Chronicle,* this story and others like it would have been on the front page of the *Examiner*.

In testimony before the Anti-Trust Subcommittee of the House Committee on the Judiciary, holding hearings on the Newspaper Preservation Act, Stephen R. Barnett, Acting Professor of Law at the University of California, Berkeley, indicted the *Examiner* in its handling of the *Chronicle*-KRON-TV story:

> In all the time since March (1969), when the FCC ordered the license-renewal hearing, the only story I have been able to find in the *Examiner* was the six-paragraph article . . . run on Saturday afternoon, March 22—two days late—reporting the FCC's action. The *Examiner* completely suppressed the story of the order issued by the FCC on June 5 adding to the hearing issues, at the *Chronicle*'s request, the question of the "quality" of KRON public-service programming (a question that many San Francisco citizens might want to testify about, if they were aware of the opportunity). It completely suppressed the nationally reported story of the Senate hearing on June 12, involving the private detective allegations and the alleged "blackmailing" of Mayor Alioto. And the *Examiner* has followed through by suppressing all the subsequent developments in the "private detective" story—including the *Chronicle*'s public admission that it hired the detectives, and its justification of its conduct, and including the FCC ruling adding the private-detective question to the issues to be explored at the hearing.
>
> Such is the "independent and competing" voice produced by the joint-operating agreement that this bill would foist permanently on the people of San Francisco. Such is the afternoon paper to which Thieriot referred when he told the Senate Subcommittee that "The reader has been well served under the agency arrangement in San Francisco, most particularly the afternoon reader." And such is the journalistic conduct that leads to the question: How many other stories have they suppressed that we *don't* know about?

Partially offsetting these sad findings are the *Examiner*'s opinion columns written by Dick Nolan and Guy Wright. They are valuable additions to San Francisco consciousness, far surpassing anything the *Chronicle* has to offer in the way of serious commentary on local politics. Ken Alexander is one of the better local editorial cartoonists, and the *Examiner*'s "Cartooning the Week" on Saturday's editorial page, with six of the best cartoons from both the U.S. and abroad, is an excellent idea that might be adopted by other papers searching for a weekend editorial format. Some of the foreign cartoons provided the only hints to the Bay Area of the way journalists in other countries viewed the United States. These views are often sobering. Matching the tone of the unsigned editorials, the syndicated columnists are in sum, right of center and rather ancient. Liberals include Carl Rowan and Max Lerner, while Henry J. Taylor, William F. Buckley, John Chamberlain and Bob Considine all represent the conservative view.

The paper has been much slower to react to the anti-war and related political issues of the day than has the *Chronicle*. In the two-week period studied, the *Examiner*'s coverage of the Presidio "mutiny" trial never made the first four pages (see App. III). Despite occasional good stories (see Regents' meeting at Berkeley, pp. 116–117), the *Examiner*'s coverage suffered for two reasons. First, the *Examiner* tended to emphasize strongly the numbers aspect of the demonstrations: how many days of class were missed, how many cases of arson, how many arrested. (See pp. 120–121) This was done in a regular box slugged "Campus Scoreboard," which ran in a prominent place in the paper, and the leads of the daily stories were often pegged to such statistics. We might say that the *Examiner*'s detailed attention to statistics became, after a while, like coverage of a cricket match. Second, the *Examiner* city desk was not as flexible as that of the *Chronicle* in allowing reporters to write stories out of the ordinary, to adapt to the situation.

Some Advertising Practices

Along with the *Chronicle*, the *Examiner* is guilty of running advertising puffery that passes for news. Gene DeForrest's "Around the Town" column on the Saturday entertainment page is, like Hal Schaefer's, an obvious "thank you" to regular advertisers. Editor Dooley laid responsibility for this column at the door of the San Francisco Newspaper Printing Company, agreeing that it was not "news," and he included his paper's Saturday church pages in the denunciation. The *Examiner* laid itself open for an embarrassing situation by running an ad for Brooktrails Redwood Park, a land investment company peddling recreational homesites. In the body of the ad was the picture of a Mr. Donald White, identified as a "Financial Newspaper Editor." White was at the time the *Examiner*'s financial editor, but his position with the newspaper was not mentioned in the ad, and his connection with Brooktrails (other than as an endorser) was not made clear.

Dooley confirmed a practice noted by editor Bruce Brugmann in his May 10, 1968 issue of the *Bay Guardian*. It concerned the printing of legal notices for the City of San Francisco. The city charter specified, in Section 13, that the notices be printed in a paper with a "bonafide daily circulation of at least 8,000 copies." For the past few years the *Examiner* and *Chronicle* have traded off a contract worth $135,000 a year, but the *Examiner* has had it the past couple of years.

According to the terms of the contract between the city and the newspaper, the paper of record must print the legal notices in an edition of at least 8,000 press run. Instead of running the daily column of legal notices in all editions, as most publishers appear to do, the *Examiner* only printed them in one street edition of 18,000 to 20,000 copies. Normally copies of street editions do not get into San Francisco homes unless residents purchase them from a newsstand or vendor. Thus, under this arrangement, presumably upwards of 200,000 readers of the *Examiner* never had a chance to see the legal notices.

Nothing prevents the *Examiner* from printing the notices in the home edition also, but the city does not require it. The city charter would have to be changed to require the paper of record to publish the notices in all editions, or at least in the home edition. Thus it appears that both the city charter and *Examiner* policy are responsible for this practice. Although the *Examiner* was living up to the terms of the contract, no other paper of record surveyed by the authors (including the Oakland *Tribune,* San Mateo *Times,* San Jose *Mercury* and Berkeley *Gazette*) failed to run the legal notices in all editions. Even so, the *Examiner* contended that it lost money on the city contract.

The State of the Examiner

Critical readers of the *Examiner* believe it lags behind its city in thinking; others see it as the only "responsible" voice in San Francisco. Given the current corporate arrangement, it is doubtful that the *Examiner* feels any pressure to change either its image or philosophy. This is unfortunate, because it seems to have good leadership in the news room and many excellent reporters, including Harry Johanesen (who recently won a McQuade Award of $500 for a 10-part series on the Negro in California); Jerry Belcher; Alan Cline; Gerald Adams, Mildred Hamilton, and especially political reporter Sydney Kossen. Lynn Ludlow, also an excellent reporter, supervises the best minority training program in the Bay Area. The *Examiner* has hired 16 interns for three-month periods, usually followed by a month on the reporting staff. In 1969 alumni of the program were working at the *Examiner, Chronicle, Mercury,* Sacramento *Bee,* Las Vegas *Review Journal,* Hartford *Times,* and the *Sun-Reporter.* While the Oakland *Tribune* has also made an effort to hire and train Black journalists, the *Chronicle* and *Mercury-News,* the two papers that can best afford it, have been most lax in this regard.

Forced to shift for itself, the *Examiner* would surely become a more interesting and exciting paper, and perhaps a more influential one in the process. As things stand, it appears that the *Examiner* could "scoop" the *Chronicle* every day for two weeks, and a great many San Franciscans would neither notice nor care. Certainly not the *Chron.*

OAKLAND TRIBUNE (209,120)

It may be significant that the manner of gaining entrance to the city room of the *Tribune* sets the tone for any analysis of the paper. A burly private guard mans a sign-in desk in the lobby of the building with the green-roofed towers in the center of William Knowland's Oakland. He first phones for permission and then directs the elect past a diversionary elevator to another tucked out of view. This elevator goes directly to the fourth-floor city room and executive offices. Visitors are requested to sign in and out. In its security system the *Tribune* runs a close second to the Detroit *News,* which has put iron bars over its windows. The wide-open policy at the new San Jose *Mercury* and *News* plant may as well be from another country.

Relations with the Black Community

It is not unfair to say that the *Tribune* is wary, if not downright fearful, of what its city is now and what it may become in the next few years. A number of reliable sources have speculated that Oakland may be as much as 80 percent Black within the next five to 10 years. Relations between the paper and the Black community are already strained. How the *Tribune* adapts itself to the changing urban environment in the near future makes it worth watching by the rest of the nation's metropolitan press. (The Detroit *News* has already opted to focus on the suburbs.)

A major reason for the distrust many Oakland Blacks feel for the *Tribune* was the paper's handling of a Black boycott of white merchants in the ghetto in 1968. Black citizens, disturbed at what they felt was police harassment of Black youth, complained at an open city council meeting, but did not receive what they considered a just hearing. The boycott was designed as an attempt to force the white merchants to pressure city hall over the police harassment issue. The *Tribune* responded to the boycott with a front-page editorial from the publisher, William F. Knowland, urging white Oakland residents and homeowners in surrounding areas to help break the boycott by shopping in the ghetto stores.

Although the *Tribune* had a journalistic right to take such a position, its news judgment was occasionally clouded by its editorial stance. On January 2, 1969, for example, the paper ran on its front page an AP story out of Washington, D.C. by Gaylord Shaw, headlined, "Students Get Pay as Dropouts." Shaw described deficiencies of the Neighborhood Youth Corps project in Detroit, based on data from the government's General Accounting Office. The article criticized the method of selecting trainees and implied a misuse of funds. Without making any effort to relate this story to the local Neighborhood Youth Corps project, the *Tribune* left its readers with the impression that the Detroit experience was typical. The editors ran it on page one. Among other Bay Area afternoon papers, the *Examiner,* the San Mateo *Times,* and the Santa Rosa *Press-Democrat* did not carry the story at all. The Palo Alto *Times* had a much-reduced version on page seven; and the San Jose *News* ran it on page 15.

Admitting that his paper has taken "a hard editorial position" on racial matters, city editor Roy Grimm stated,

> We try to give fair and full coverage of race problems in our community. We are criticized by some segments of the Black community as being racist, but we certainly make an effort not to be. If we ever have been racist in their eyes, it was certainly not intentional.

The conservative Republican philosophy of the Knowland family, which has run the *Tribune* since 1915, has had much to do with the paper's attitude toward Blacks. Joseph Knowland, father of the current publisher and a former congressman, purchased a one-half interest in the paper in 1915, and assumed full control in 1939 after a protracted court case. Sixty-one-year-old William Knowland, who had a lengthy career in the U. S. Senate, including service as majority leader in 1953–54 and minority leader in 1955–58, now exerts a major influence on the paper. Grimm offered this statement on the sensitive subject of writing to please a publisher:

> I like to think that we rarely knowingly slant the news. We don't have the problem of not covering a story because Mr. Knowland is against it, nor do we cover a story because he is in favor of it. But the emphasis we give a story is something else. When a piece can be handled a couple of different ways, the influence of the Publisher plays a part.

Grimm rightly claimed one of the best records of any paper in the West in the hiring of Blacks. In 1969 the *Tribune* had three Black reporters and a Black photographer, and it has given many other Black Bay Area journalists a start. Some of the *Tribune*'s Black alumni have worked for the Washington *Post*, the N.B.C. bureau in Watts, the AP Sacramento Bureau, and KQED, the educational TV station. In addition, the *Tribune* did hire reporters of Oriental descent, but apparently did not use their special talents, such as the ability of some to speak Cantonese.

The paper has not had any particular difficulties in obtaining information from the Black community, but Grimm conceded that his staff may not be getting any "real information" at all. "We can't put out a paper just for the Black population of Oakland," Grimm said. "We're selling a lot of papers in other parts of the East Bay. We've tried to cover Black issues, and we've never injected the racial question into a story. But we give no race indication unless we think it is important to the story."

Political Coverage: The Cranston-Rafferty Race

In the political area, Knowland's influence was evident in the *Tribune*'s 1968 coverage of the Cranston-Rafferty race for the U. S. Senate. The following figures (compiled by Patricia Kramer for the San Francisco *Bay Guardian*) deal with the column inches devoted to each candidate on the news pages of the *Tribune*. The figures speak for themselves:

TABLE 2

CRANSTON-RAFFERTY: COLUMN INCHES

IN THE OAKLAND TRIBUNE

October 1968

	Democratic Candidate Cranston	Republican Candidate Rafferty
October 1–4	15	54
October 6–7	0	75
October 10–16	14½	63
October 22, 24–25	22	56¼
October 28–31	17½	80½
TOTAL	69	328¾
AVERAGE PER DAY	3½	16½

The Tribune *and the Suburbs*

About three years ago the *Tribune* changed its policy of trying to "outlocal" the smaller dailies in its circulation area. Until that time there had been two separate editorial departments: a city staff and a state-suburban staff manned by bureau people. The bureau news was put on three or four pages that changed with each edition. Where a staff of 25 formerly covered the Concord, Hayward, Fremont, Martinez, Pittsburg, Richmond, Livermore, Alameda, San Leandro, El Cerrito and Walnut Creek areas, only nine now handle that job. Nevertheless, conversion to a central-city metropolitan newspaper was rejected, because 90 percent of the *Tribunes* were home delivered, many to suburban areas. The new goal was to provide the important governmental news and cover the biggest stories from the neighboring communities, and let the smaller dailies live by providing the more detailed local coverage. "We're no longer covering places like Hayward as we once did," admitted Grimm. "If I lived in Hayward, I would take both the *Tribune* and the *Review*." The paper does maintain a San Francisco bureau, not in order to sell papers in the City, but to show Oaklanders that they are not missing any San Francisco news by subscribing to the *Tribune*.

News Judgment and Page Design

Although the *Examiner* and the *Tribune* showed substantial contrast in their choice of specific front-page material, in their general news policies and treatment of certain major issues, the differences were small. During the study period of February 17 to March 4, 1969, the two papers ranked second and third behind the New York *Times* in column inches devoted to the Vietnam war, congressional news, and the President (see Appendix III); the *Tribune* did the most consistent job of the big four in its Middle East coverage. The paper performed poorly with the Presidio "mutiny" trial story, running few stories—none of them in prominent places in the paper—and prejudicing the reader against the defendants with its headlines. Headlines on *Tribune* stories concerning Vietnam and the cold war tended generally to be biased (against communists, dissenters, and the like), but on non-ideological issues the paper reacted to subjects much the same as the *Examiner* and San Jose *Mercury-News*.

The front page tended to be a bit more crowded than that of the other four major papers. The *Tribune* averaged slightly more than 11 stories per front page in the period studied, with an average story length of about 13 inches. The *Chronicle,* by comparison, averaged nine stories per front page, the *Mercury* slightly more, and the *Examiner* slightly fewer. Front page makeup was a bit on the dull side, often with a patchwork effect. *Tribune* makeup showed little imaginative use of white space or pictures, and few, if any, dramatic horizontals and diagonals (formed by headline position). Repetition of familiar layouts contributed to the unexciting appearance of the *Tribune*. The *Chronicle* and *Mercury* suffered from the same problems, and only occasionally did the *Examiner* stimulate the eye, although the latter underwent a face-lifting in the closing months of 1969.

On the editorial page, the unsigned editorials gave about equal emphasis to national and local issues; many were of the safe, "worthy of praise" variety. During the period studied, the *Tribune* congratulated S. I. Hayakawa, J. Edgar Hoover, the late State Senator George Miller Jr., David Packard and the communications industry as a whole. The opinion columns, syndicated material and feature page cried out for higher quality, more decisive writing. In a typical week's offering, syndicated columnists contributed 23 of 29 opinion pieces on national topics; five were locally written by Al Martinez on featurish subjects, and there was only one locally written item on a political topic. (Martinez has since lost his column and been put on general assignment reporting.)

The paper needs to develop its own writers who can comment intelligently on both local and national affairs, especially in view of the syndicated pundits on the "Focus" page: Hal Boyle, William S. White, Roscoe Drummond, and Dr. Max Rafferty, among others.

Finally, the editorial page devoted an average amount of space to readers' letters: 25 inches a day.

Since March 1969, the *Tribune* has converted its Saturday edition from an afternoon to a morning paper to capture more weekend advertising, the Saturday afternoon slot usually being a waste to advertisers anyway. The Saturday *Tribune* uses only UPI copy because the Associated Press would not allow the *Tribune* to use only the Saturday morning offering without paying for the rest of the week at a price that seemed prohibitive. Since the function of the Saturday morning edition is to advertise the weekend sales to shoppers, the loss of AP copy may be of minimal importance.

The *Tribune* is the only Bay Area paper to offer a weekly (Thursday) fashion section that is entirely staff written. It was begun in March 1963 by fashion editor Nora Hampton, who is presently assisted by Karen Emerson and Doris Hjorth.

The Tribune *Overall*

In sum, the *Tribune* is better than its reputation. The discussion on pages 131–132 makes it clear that the *Tribune* and reporter Fred Garretson (now spending a year at Harvard University on a Nieman Fellowship) lead the Bay Area in coverage of regional government and environmental issues. In Ed Salzman the paper is fortunate to have one of the best political reporters of the Sacramento scene. When confronted with dissident students, however, the *Tribune* bristled. Day-to-day, the paper resembles the *Examiner* in its handling of local, national and international news and its conservative approach. Considering their respective communities, the *Tribune* is certainly no further behind its readership than the *Examiner*.

The motto of the *Tribune* is "A Responsible Metropolitan News-paper." The overriding question for the paper in the next decade is: to whom must it be responsible?

SAN JOSE MERCURY (126,171) AND NEWS (77,532)

The mere mention of the *Mercury* and *News* to other Bay Area publishers is enough to set dollar signs dancing. The morning *Mercury* and afternoon *News* (plus the combined Sunday *Mercury and News*) are the most profitable papers in the Bay Area, and among the biggest moneymakers in the country. Beneficiary of this bonanza is the Ridder family, which also controls the flow of printed news in St. Paul (head-quarters for the Ridder chain), Duluth, Long Beach, Pasadena and a number of smaller cities across the nation. The *Mercury* and *News* are second in circulation to the St. Paul papers, but are the biggest moneymakers in the chain.

The *News* ranked second among all afternoon papers in the U. S. in ad linage in 1968, the *Mercury* fifth in the morning field. This was against such competition as the Los Angeles *Times,* the New York *Times,* Miami *Herald,* Chicago *Tribune* and others. The papers are fat—from 60 to 80 pages during the week and over 200 pages on Sunday.

Behind the Bonanza

There are two good reasons for the Ridders having developed a gold mine in San Jose. First, Santa Clara County and the South Bay region is the fastest-growing section of northern California. Shopping centers and tract housing are now as common as old corner drugstores. Inexplicably, the electronic media have not kept pace with the expanding market, and television has yet to make its presence felt in local advertising. The Ridder papers, which have championed the unbridled (and often unplanned) industrial expansion of San Jose, have vigorously filled the advertising gap. Thus they are, without question, the sole major advertising medium in the area.

Further, the Ridders have spared no expense in hiring topnotch advertising and promotion people to capitalize on the situation. Advertising director Louis Heindel, marketing department manager Gerold Zarwell, and public relations director Dan Stern are among the best in the business. With snappy color brochures they have demonstrated that the metropolitan San Jose market is 300,000 ahead of San Francisco County in population, $2,500 ahead in effective buying income per household, and $800 million ahead in total net effective buying income. The same comparisons have been made with Alameda County. According to Zarwell:

> There is no marketing and promotion operation in the Bay Area like the one at the *Mercury* and *News*. Only the operation at the Oakland *Tribune* comes close. The *Chronicle* has never done much along these lines, and since the demise of the Hearst ad service, the *Examiner* doesn't do much either. In the last ten years, only the Los Angeles *Times*, the Milwaukee *Journal*, and the Miami *Herald* have done the sort of thing the *Mercury* and *News* has done.

Zarwell attributed the high ad linage to the papers' concentrated coverage of the market. He said,

> We have the feeling there is no other market in the country where a paper can give such concentrated coverage of value to the retailer. We offer 80 percent coverage of the greater San Jose area, and 90 percent of our circulation is in Santa Clara County. We saturate this densely populated region, which is why we're able to draw from retailers what we draw.

He pointed to two carbon copy shopping centers, Valley Fair in San Jose and Bay Fair in the East Bay. "Valley Fair is doing very well with *Mercury* and *News* ads," Zarwell boasted, "but Bay Fair must deal with the Oakland *Tribune*, Hayward *Review*, San Leandro *Morning News*, plus direct mailing of advertising circulars to get its message across, and they are still not doing nearly as well as Valley Fair."

The new plant that opened in April 1967 symbolizes the papers' prosperity. Located on a 25-acre site near Route 101, it is the world's largest single-floor newspaper plant, and was voted one of the top 10 new industrial structures of 1968 by *Factory* magazine. Surrounded by a 136,000-gallon lagoon and hundreds of olive, sycamore and magnolia trees, the circular main entrance is unusual and inviting, the city room spacious and quiet. The facility far outclasses those of other Bay Area dailies.

The Editorial Side

There is, by the way, an editorial side to this commercial operation, and that is where the problems are found. Although there are managing editors, city editors, news editors, editorial writers and sports editors for the two papers, nearly all departments have been combined: education, society, arts, sports, travel, real estate and photo, among others. The overall operation is run by executive editor Kenneth Conn, who is responsible to publisher Joseph Ridder. Although the city desks are in a competition of sorts (Paul Conroy, managing editor of the *News,* says competition is encouraged "as long as it doesn't undermine or degrade the other paper"), such important local beats as city hall are staffed jointly by the papers. To a greater degree than in San Francisco, there is but one editorial voice in San Jose. In addition, the two have a single, forced advertising rate. It is not possible to advertise in only one of the papers.

Although the papers have been successful at knitting together a consumer market region known as San Jose, they have been much less so at creating ties with the citizenry and the community of San Jose. This is in part attributable to the papers' news philosophy. National and international news from the wires are heavily emphasized; local news, except for sports, receives short shrift.

The papers subscribe to AP, UPI, New York Times, Los Angeles Times-Washington Post, and the Copley News services. They were able to purchase the New York Times service, in competition with the *Chronicle,* only because they carried it before the abortive attempt at a West Coast edition of the *Times,* and the *Times* offered it back to them before selling it to the *Chronicle.* Because the many ads open up a large hole for news, the papers are able, both during the week and on Sunday, to run much wire material of a background and interpretive nature that never appears in the *Chronicle, Examiner* or *Tribune.* For those interested primarily in national and international news—as are many South Bay and Peninsula university people—the *Mercury* and *News* are the papers to read. (This leadership was not evident in the major, continuing stories, as the data in Appendix III make clear. Here the *Mercury* was only equal to or a bit below the other metros in total inches printed and prominence accorded in the paper. It was with stories of secondary and background importance that the San Jose papers were in front. Further, one knowledgeable observer of the San Jose scene noted that, although they were not given page one positions, *Mercury* stories on the Mexican-American community appeared frequently and were treated in depth.)

The *Mercury* publishes special sections for Monterey, Santa Cruz, and San Benito counties; southern Alameda County; the Peninsula, or "north county"; San Jose; and a street edition, which is primarily a remake of page one. Much of the coverage of outlying areas is better than local San Jose coverage. San Jose news is almost always relegated to the front page of an inside section, rarely appearing on the front page itself. In the December 23 *Mercury* the Julie Nixon–David Eisenhower wedding was front page with pictures, but no state or local item was to be found. On the 28th an Apollo shot received three stories plus pictures, but again nothing local was on the front page.

Superficial Coverage of Local Issues

When something of a local nature did appear on the front page, however, it tended to be the holdup of a grocery store or minor arson at a school. Violence at San Jose State College was also front-page material. But informative stories on industrial expansion, city government, the San Jose bus company, the waterworks, the garbage company or any other repository of local power were curiously absent. (The local television station KNTV carried more on these subjects than the *Mercury* and *News*.) There seem to be many sacred cows in San Jose, although executive editor Conn said that "there are no more policy stories [those stories specially treated or omitted through executive fiat] in our papers than in any others," a backhand admission that the papers did indeed recognize untouchables.

The refusal of the *Mercury-News* management to permit any real investigation into local business or politics is only one of the reasons for superficial local coverage. There is a standard policy among *Mercury-News* editors to trust wire service reports over the stories of staff members. One disgruntled young *Mercury* reporter stated that it was common for editors to ignore a story turned in by a staff member until it appeared on the wires. Then it was likely to be bannered.

As the largest metropolitan daily near Stanford University, the *Mercury-News* was in an excellent position to report the challenge to the university system, student unrest and related topics, the sort of thing the *Chronicle* attempted to do at San Francisco State on occasion. But the papers failed to run anything of an explanatory nature on the testimony of Stanford President Kenneth Pitzer before Senator McClellan's committee investigating student disorders: the papers carried only the bare verdict in the trial of protestors who stormed the Stanford Research Institute in May 1969, and blocked traffic on Page Mill Road; and the papers have repeatedly ignored such Black speakers in the area as Stanford Professor St. Clair Drake.

On the other hand, the editors have carried stories on the influx of radicals into businesses, on the belief of a local school official that students would turn to hard drugs if the supply of pot is cut off, and on the activities of Stanford radicals. In short, the papers have appeared to show a preference for stories depicting the less desirable aspects of young people's behavior.

Policies on the coverage of stories related to Blacks were highly conservative. One reporter stated that the office staff was aware that "it must not go too heavy on Black news at any one time." Because the *Mercury* and *News* emphasized crime stories in local news, this was the way most Blacks tended to be portrayed to the white community.

Similar policies affected the hiring of Blacks. To the surprise of many staff members, early in the summer of 1969, management rejected a proposal from the guild for the establishment of a minorities training and hiring program.

Aside from these evidences of prejudice, the more general philosophy of newspapering at the *Mercury-News* also helps explain the weak local coverage. Conn stated that three of every five readers are relative newcomers to the area, with little knowledge of or interest in local affairs. Thus it was international news and sports that held the readership together. The papers were willing to cater to these natural interests, rather than to work at creating a community spirit through increased local news coverage. Conn was aware that at some point the papers would have to tackle this task, but for now the *Mercury* and *News* are content with the second largest sports staff in the state (22 full-timers plus part-timers), which covers not only professional teams, but San Jose State, Stanford, 13 junior colleges, and over 100 high schools. (The Los Angeles *Times* boasts the largest staff—40.)

Civic Boosterism

Joseph Ridder and his papers are identified with the civic boosterism which has lured industry to the area. New businesses and job opportunities lead to more readers and advertising revenue. It is a good formula. But an electoral upset of June 1969, in which two of the three candidates backed by the Ridder papers were defeated, indicated to both Conroy and local weekly publisher Mort Levine that the homeowner was tired of continued expansion. "Citizens of San Jose are fed up with the 'growth for growth's sake' philosophy which the *Mercury* has been pushing," says Levine, publisher of the Milpitas *Post* and the San Jose *Sun* papers. "Frustrated, taxpaying homeowners are turning against the *Mercury* for its close Establishment ties." Conn agreed that the papers may be losing touch with the readers. "There is no question that we are much too close to the Establishment," he admitted. "You don't keep a man on the police beat too long because soon he will start thinking like the police." Conn added that many readers have complained that the papers did not write often enough about the planning aspects of growth.

Despite the civic boosterism, the *Mercury* does have one of the best full-time environmental writers in the state in Tom Harris. Along with the *Tribune*'s Fred Garretson, Harris has been active in forming an

Academy of California Environmental Writers. His editors give his stories more column inches and prominence than editors at either the *Chronicle* or the *Examiner* give to their environmental material. Harris has been particularly active in writing about problems of air pollution.

The local writers on the editorial and feature pages of the two papers reflect the Ridder unwillingness to confront civic problems head-on. The *Mercury*'s Leigh Weimers and Frank Freeman both write light-weight, entertaining, feature-gossip columns, as does the *News*'s Dick Barrett. Only the appearance of Harry Farrell, one of the best regional and Sacramento reporters in the state, and Lou Cannon, who wrote some good pieces on the BCDC (San Francisco Bay Conservation and Development Commission) and Leslie Salt Company, added bite to the local opinion writing.

Cannon, author of the celebrated book *Ronnie and Jesse* (N. Y.: Doubleday, 1969), is now in Washington, D.C., representing three west coast Ridder papers, including the *Mercury-News*. Incredibly, Cannon is the only local man from the Bay Area reporting from Washington. The *Chronicle* and *Tribune* rely wholly on wire services, while the *Examiner* has Hearst bureau men on call, a service better than having no one, but not to be compared with a staff employee.

The Future: A Chance for Excellence

There are predictions that San Jose may be the second largest city in the state within 10 or 15 years. With their presently secure financial base, the *Mercury* and *News* have the opportunity to become editorially excellent, as well as commercially successful. *Mercury* city editor Ben Hitt termed his paper's role in the community as "the only centralized voice in an uncentralized area." It is currently the voice for the retailers and the industrial establishment. But for the weak confederation of people, housing developments, shopping centers and highways known as greater San Jose, there is no voice now.

The Suburban Daily Papers

SAN MATEO TIMES (44,776)

Sitting in his San Francisco law office, the president, editor and publisher of the San Mateo *Times*, J. Hart Clinton, could represent the archetypical absentee owner. Each evening he receives a pouch of financial statements for the paper, including operating expenses, payroll and major purchases. He also checks over a packet of editorial material, including letters from readers, canned editorials from a special service and editorial cartoons. From this he makes up the editorial page.

Canned Editorials

Canned editorials are a bad sign—a very bad sign, indeed. The editorial and feature pages were natural places for us to begin examining the *Times,* because they demonstrated the paper's disinterest in its community. The *Times* editorial page is one of the few in the Bay Area that would be unidentifiable without its logo, or trademark. (The logotype is the newspaper's name printed from a single plate of type.) The signed and unsigned material could as easily have appeared in North Platte, Nebraska, as San Mateo, California.

Clinton apparently has not assigned very heavy editorial responsibilities to his general manager on the scene, Harold A. Schlotthauer, or to managing editor George Whitesell. Because of what Clinton called "a manpower shortage," the paper rarely editorializes on local subjects "unless they are very important." The publisher indicated that unless he wrote such pieces, they might not be properly written, and since he is an active lawyer, in addition to being a newspaper owner, he had little time to write editorials. Instead he subscribes to the Reed Editorial Service, which sends him batches of opinion pieces representing one interest group or another. The editorials from which Clinton must choose, statements that speak as the voice of the San Mateo *Times,* were ill-formed, poorly written and embarrassingly inept to anyone who is familiar with a quality editorial page. They were little better than the "odd-fact" fillers used to plug gaps on the news pages.

During the period surveyed, state and local subjects comprised just under 50 percent of the editorials in the Palo Alto *Times;* 60 percent in the Berkeley *Gazette;* 40 percent in the Vallejo morning *Times-Herald;* 50 percent in the San Jose *Mercury;* and 60 percent in the San Francisco *Chronicle.* Only 7 percent, or 1 in 15, appearing in the *Times* were on local or state subjects. What did appear? Here are two examples that lack both depth and specific relevance to the community. The first was one of two canned pieces appearing on January 2, 1969.

New National Gallery

Opening of the National Portrait Gallery in Washington came six years after approval by Congress—time enough, surely, to be sure it is a good museum, and that's what Dr. Charles Nagel, director, insists it is.

"This isn't an art museum," he says. "We are a history museum."

Right. But like other paintings portraits are of widely varying quality. As Dr. Nagel observes, "the important thing is the sitter; we want to get life portraits of each by as good an artist as we can discover."

In the "superb neo-classic" Old Patent Office Building, the collection is guaranteed worth going to see. From George Washington to John F. Kennedy, every president of the United States is represented.

Nagel likes Peter Hurd's portrait of Lyndon B. Johnson even if Mr.

Johnson called it "the ugliest thing I ever saw" and rejected it. The work is scheduled to be placed on view in the gallery after its subject is out of office.

Copying Britain's century-old tradition of the National Portrait Gallery of Art, in London, the scope of the new gallery is not limited to governmental personages.

The portraits now assembled there—most of them borrowed for the opening show—include 168 Americans "from Pocahontas and Aaron Burr to Will Rogers, Jefferson Davis and Albert Einstein."

This editorial appeared on January 18, 1969:

Money Costs More

Interest rates continue an inflationary spiral of their own, but the public doesn't seem to notice. The "prime" rate charged by most banks has changed nine times in the last two years—six times since April, 1968.

However, the problem of containing inflation remains unsolved. If the Federal Reserve banks continue to make funds available to commercial banks, although at a higher discount rate, and commercial banks continue making funds available to their customers, again at higher rates, inflation will continue to take its toll until American goods are almost completely priced out of foreign markets.

This year the U. S. trade balance could go into the red if inflation is not halted. It came perilously close last year.

It may not be popular with the outgoing administration to propose budget cuts which could ease inflationary pressures.

News Blackout on Bay Fill

Clinton's law firm represents West Bay Community Associates, a partnership comprising David Rockefeller and Associates, Lazard Frères and Company, Ideal Basic Industries (Ideal Cement) and Crocker Estate Company. They own 10,000 acres of San Francisco Bay lands between San Francisco International Airport and the Santa Clara County line, and they have designs on filling these acres for tract housing.

Many of the cities of San Mateo County are notorious for the amount of filling they have permitted in the Bay and marshlands. The question of "to fill or not to fill" is a live one in San Mateo County—or at least it could be if the newspaper were any sort of community voice. "My own convictions on Bay fill are not precisely those of my clients," Clinton said. "If I express my convictions in the paper, it might look like it was coming from my clients. So we have decided not to express any opinion on the Bay fill question on our editorial pages."

This blackout was extended to the activities of former State Senator Richard Dolwig of San Mateo. A frequent proponent of Bay fill, Dolwig was at the center of the political negotiations surrounding extension of the life of the San Francisco Bay Conservation and Development

Commission at the end of the 1969 legislative session. This action was seen by most conservationist groups as essential to the preservation of San Francisco Bay. Dolwig first introduced a bill that would have emasculated the commission; under great pressure from his constituency he then reversed his course, completely revised his bill, and made it the strongest of any considered by the Legislature. But, ironically, because of his past reputation, the conservationists distrusted it, and supported instead a somewhat weaker bill that was eventually passed. Clearly the subject of Bay fill and the activities of Senator Dolwig merited some sort of comment from the San Mateo *Times,* yet by his own admission, Clinton chose to remain silent. Why run a newspaper?

The paper has no local columnist, even of the gossip variety. "I used to have the managing editor write a local column," Clinton said, "but it turned out to be lightweight, on innocuous subjects, and it was taking up too much of his time, so I relieved him of it." Finding a replacement is not high on his list of priorities. Days go by without the appearance of any letters to the editor. In aggregate, the *Times* devoted the smallest amount of space to letters of any daily surveyed. But then the paper might not have received many letters, since it so rarely said anything controversial about San Mateo.

Syndicated columnists from Paul Harvey on the far right, to Roy Wilkins, a moderate Black, appeared frequently, along with more feature-filler material than in any other paper surveyed. The *Times* regularly carried on its editorial and feature pages Leonard Lyons, "Medical Memos" from H. S. Herschensohn, "Today's Almanac" from UPI, "Quirks in the News" also from UPI, "Junior Editors Quiz," "Sheinwold on Bridge," "Mr. Mum," "Let's Explore Your Mind," and others similarly innocuous.

The Metro Leap that Failed

Clinton has a much different goal for his paper than do the publishers of the Palo Alto *Times* or San Rafael *Independent-Journal.* When the San Francisco *News Call-Bulletin* folded, Clinton hoped to transform the San Mateo *Times* into a metropolitan paper to capture the old *Call* subscribers. He added more wire copy, and at a cost of $50,000 a year brought in the complete New York Stock Exchange closings. Thinner than the *Examiner* and generally printing only four or five pages of wire news, the *Times* was hardly in a position to compete as a metro. Yet the effort kept it from being a successful local paper. The most original idea in the *Times* (although it did not originate there), is a Peninsula news page billed as a "second front page," (not an adequate substitute for comprehensive local reporting). Said Clinton,

"We tried to persuade people that they were getting all the local news and all the wire news. Perhaps we went too far in the direction of a metro and don't emphasize local news enough."

Because of the many regional problems with which the San Mateo area is involved—including BART expansion to the airport, Bay fill, air and water pollution and highway construction—it is imperative that a strong newspaper speak for San Mateo County. (Some readers of the Redwood City *Tribune* stated that their paper does so, but that it is limited by the smallness of its circulation and newshole.)

There are so many hospitals, schools, police stations and city halls within the *Times*'s circulation orbit that its transformation into a comprehensive local paper would be a full-time job. This is perhaps the course Clinton should take. Presently the paper is floating, not really meeting the needs of any constituency.

An Uncommitted Property

An editorial change would require an investment of time and money. (Clinton does not himself own the paper, but runs the *Times* for his late wife's family who own 90 percent of the stock.) Recently funds have been spent on mechanizing the paper, to the detriment of editorial quality. The *Times* has two computers in operation, and type is set by computer-tape. "We don't want to spend our money this way," Clinton said. "We would rather put it into editorial improvement, but just to keep pace with other papers we have to spend it. Returning to the basic editorial foundation of newspapering is hard to do." Until Clinton recognizes that the *Times* is a lifeless, uncommitted property, he will never get back to the "foundations of newspapering." Meanwhile, urban and environmental problems proliferate in San Mateo County.

Berkeley Gazette (14,219)

Most of the time the *Gazette* left little doubt as to its personality—a small, local-news oriented, militantly conservative fussbudget. But then the intense, young, frequently witty editor Mike Culbert would come up with an excellent series or layout and mar the image. On three issues, however, the *Gazette* was predictable: Communists (under every bed), student demonstrators and drugs.

The *Gazette* is closely tied both structurally and financially to the neighboring Richmond *Independent,* an afternoon paper of 36,000 circulation. Warren Brown, Jr. is publisher of both papers; Leo E. Owens is owner. Neither lives in Berkeley. Nor is the *Gazette* printed in Berkeley; all the shop work is done at the *Independent.* Since it was physically impossible to print two afternoon papers in the Richmond shop, the smaller *Gazette* was forced to switch to the morning field on October 3, 1966, a day Culbert said would "live in infamy." The *Gazette* must compete in the morning with the *Chronicle,* while its real news rival is the Oakland *Tribune.*

The shift to the morning, and a subsequent loss of 2,500 readers put the *Gazette* in the red, with the *Independent* covering its losses. Only in the fall of 1968 did the *Gazette* once again show a profit, but Culbert indicated he is still working on a shoestring.

As its puny 14,000 circulation in a city of 120,000 indicates, the *Gazette* is by Culbert's own admission, seriously "out of tune with the Berkeley environment." Culbert has found five distinct communities in his circulation area, only one of which is sympathetic to the *Gazette.* Three groups—the transient University student-faculty community, the more permanent faculty and staff residents, and a large, white, liberal-left group—are either simply not interested in the *Gazette* or at odds with its editorial philosophy. The same is true for the Negro community. The conservative, 1930's-type Berkeley holdovers are the paper's sole source of strength. The *Gazette* also circulates in the Albany, Kensington and El Cerrito areas, which creates a bit of a coverage problem for Culbert, who cannot afford to publish two editions.

When Owens took over the *Gazette* in 1966 from Berkeley resident George Dunscomb, the hope was to convert the paper into a metro-like, international newspaper. "I think the idea was absurd," said Culbert. "Our entire operation is worth only a million dollars." The experiment, with heavy emphasis on wire copy, was tried for a year and a half, then abandoned. Culbert now calls the paper a "hybrid, somewhere between a local and a metro," but its heart is really the heart of a local. "The entire strength of our paper is in its local news coverage," said Culbert. "The fact that the Oakland *Tribune* does not do the job it used to do in covering Berkeley makes it possible for this paper to operate. We would go under now as a metro-wire paper; why anyone would read the *Gazette* alone for all his news, I don't know."

A Good Second Newspaper?

Unlike the San Mateo *Times,* the *Gazette* now hopes primarily to be a good second newspaper. Culbert's motto: "A local name in the paper is another paper sold." News of international importance is often underplayed in favor of local news; Culbert admitted that if he has enough good local news, "we leave out the wire stuff entirely." The paper shed one of its wire services—AP. This was not because Culbert preferred UPI, but because he felt the paper needed only one service and the AP contract ran out before that with UPI.

Given its proclivity for local news, the *Gazette*'s position at the bottom—along with the Vallejo *Times-Herald*—in coverage of six national news items was not unexpected (see App. III). But Culbert's news judgment for the frequently cluttered front page was confusing. The paper customarily ran a lengthy boxed story above the logo. There Culbert placed a story on the Knox Commission's regional government proposal (see p. 131), a better piece than a few of the larger papers carried. On January 13, 1969 he ran an excellent interview with Berkeley vice mayor Wilmont Sweeney, first Black member of the city council. The interesting and informative story was punctuated with seven candid photos of Sweeney in a masterful job of layout.

In the very same edition, however, the *Gazette* showed its concern with sensation, drugs and crime. The headline of the first lead was "Bizarre Drug 'Guinea Pig' Case Here," and the second lead had "Police Identify Man Slain in Berkeley." When in late December 1968, Red China exploded a minor nuclear device, the *Gazette* placed the story in the page one box over the logo. By way of comparison, the San Jose *News,* San Mateo *Times,* and Oakland *Tribune* placed the story on page two; the *Examiner, Chronicle,* and *Mercury* on page one below the fold; the Palo Alto *Times* and Vallejo morning *Times-Herald* did not carry it at all. On January 18 the *Gazette* gave the lead spot to a $3,500 bank robbery, rather than to the University of California Regents' meeting in Berkeley.

Although editor Culbert claimed a rapport with the Berkeley Black community, the paper supported the attempts of a parents' association to recall three members of the Berkeley Board of Education who supported integration of the public schools. Despite some recent improvement, the paper has not properly covered the Berkeley integration struggle.

Nor was it insignificant that two unsuccessful attempts have been made to challenge the *Gazette* and speak for the majority of the community. The Berkeley *Review* (which lasted about one year) and the Berkeley *Citizen* (which lasted about three) were not underground papers. The *Freedom News* is still publishing monthly in opposition to Owens' other paper, the Richmond *Independent,* which has dealt shabbily with the Richmond Black community and has done nothing about Standard Oil pollution in that city. The two Owens papers are like peas in a pod.

Editorial and Feature Pages

The *Gazette* editorial and feature pages merit mixed reviews. J. R. "Kacy" Ward's "What in the World" column is a gossipy link to the old Berkeley community to which the *Gazette* appeals. Culbert, who, for an editor, does a great deal of writing and reporting, contributes a daily column in which he regularly says more about happenings in Berkeley than writers in the *Mercury, Tribune,* or *Chronicle* say about their respective cities unexciting syndicated columnists include Holmes Alexander, Max Lerner, Bruce Biossat, Allen and Goldsmith, and Don MacLean. The *Gazette* usually ran only one unsigned editorial each day, however, and would profit from another one or two. Along with the *Chronicle* (and the Palo Alto *Times*) the paper was a Bay Area leader in space devoted to readers' letters. But too much space was given to such entertainment features as "Berry's World," handwriting expert Paul Farrar, crossword puzzles and horoscope news.

Summing Up

Clearly the *Gazette* is not a paper suited to a university community like Berkeley. About the best that can be said for it is that, unlike the San Mateo *Times,* the *Gazette* is at least willing to discuss some of the problems in the community, regardless of its own position. In the present era of indistinguishable small papers, this is no small accomplishment. But the *Gazette* is a long way from being a force in the community. At most, it is an anachronism, speaking for a Berkeley that has long since passed. It is not powerful enough to affect the flow of events in any direction.

Vallejo (Morning) Times-Herald (28,534)

Until mid-February, 1970, former State Senator Luther Gibson had one of the most tightly controlled newspaper monopolies in the Bay Area, in his ownership of the Vallejo morning *Times-Herald* and the afternoon *News-Chronicle.* Unlike the situation in San Jose, where the subscriber could take either or both of the Ridder papers, the Gibson publications were dual circulation: you could not get one without the other. This served to keep neighboring papers out of Vallejo.

On February 18, however, the afternoon paper was cut back from a daily to a weekly, appearing on Wednesday only. Oddly enough one of the big factors behind the decision was that Vallejo newsboys could not be counted on to deliver two papers. Said managing editor Wyman Riley,

> We had a monumental circulation problem. The kids just didn't seem to care. We had a turnover of a different carrier every six months; we were getting into some of the poverty kids as carriers, and often money collected was just taken home. Pretty soon our bonding company wouldn't bond the carriers anymore. We would have needed two separate circulation systems.

Costs of newsprint and labor also played a part. Although no editorial personnel were cut back, the dismissal of composing room workers led to a rocky period in February and March during which the remaining shop workers showed their displeasure by missing deadlines, losing type, misplacing page proofs and dropping lines from stories. "We had a hell of a time of it," said Riley.

Focus on Local News

While the 28- to 40-page weekly focuses exclusively on local news, or national news with a local angle, the morning *Times-Herald* tries to take up the slack. A women's section and feature page opposite the editorial page have been added from the old *News-Chronicle,* increasing the daily by four pages. Half the comics between the two papers have been dropped. "Space is a real problem now," Riley said. "We have to edit more tightly, but we still have a news hole of from 90 to 100 columns."

The papers maintain a four-man bureau in Fairfield, the county seat, and two-man bureaus in Vacaville and Napa. San Francisco and Sacramento are left to the wire services, a circumstance with which Riley is rather unhappy. In an effort to improve the paper's offerings from these areas, Riley scans the *Chronicle, Examiner, Tribune, Bee* and others for articles of regional interest. He then either deletes the bylines and runs them, or puts the information in his own daily column, which appears on the editorial page. Although the propriety of this practice is questionable, Riley is probably more aware than most other Bay Area news executives of what the competition is doing.

To Riley's credit, local news had a prominent place in the *Times-Herald.* The front page generally maintained a balance between local and national stories, and the editorial page frequently dealt with local issues. (See pp. 132–135 for the papers' campaign against regional government.) Once a week the entire editorial page was devoted to readers' letters. Although the Gibson philosophy committed the paper to a complete news package, national and international news offerings were as weak as those in the Berkeley *Gazette,* which is admittedly a local paper, and is not meant as a substitute for the *Chronicle* or *Tribune.* Appendix III shows the *Times-Herald* at the bottom, along with the *Gazette,* in its coverage of presidential stories, the cold war, the Presidio "mutiny" trial, the mid-east crisis, congressional news and Vietnam. Nor was the *Times-Herald*'s record on continuity any better than the *Gazette*'s. Stories on the above-mentioned continuing events were not run every day, nor did they generally appear in the front parts of the paper.

Mixed Views on Performance

Of all the news executives interviewed by the authors, Riley expressed the most satisfaction with the performance of his papers. He maintained that they have taken the lead in almost every worthwhile community project and that they have been a factor in the city's freedom from any major racial trouble. One former journalist, now a resident in Vallejo, did not agree. She said,

> From reading the local papers, you would never guess that Vallejo has a large and uneasy Black population, that our schools are severely racially unbalanced, that many school buildings are totally inadequate and the program is not meeting the needs of the children. I could cite other instances, but instead I'll say that generally the paper [*Times-Herald*] adopts a head-in-the-sand policy and seems to see only good in Vallejo.

With the energies of the staff no longer split between two papers, Vallejoans may soon be receiving a better morning paper. Riley is eager for editorial expansion. With the demise of the *News-Chronicle,* the afternoon San Francisco *Examiner* and the Oakland *Tribune* have an opportunity to make inroads in Vallejo, and perhaps force improvements in the *Times-Herald.*

PALO ALTO TIMES (44,684)

The reputation of the *Times* was found to be quite high among Bay Area publishers and press observers. It is viewed as one of the area's best local papers: well edited, involved and serving its community.

In bulk and appearance the *Times* was indeed impressive. It offered at least 40 to 50 pages daily, and occasionally approached 80 pages on Wednesday and Saturday. Its front page presented a good balance between local and wire stories, and the layout was often imaginative. Occasionally there was a tendency toward too much black type in the headlines, so that the eye did not know where to rest, but the news judgment was generally solid. There was an occasional wild headline, but sensationalism was kept to a minimum, except for student violence stories, particularly at Stanford.

The local papers in the Bay Area's two leading university towns, Berkeley and Palo Alto, are both politically conservative. Editor Alexander Bodi sets the tone at the *Times.* "People may not agree with me," he said, "but at least I'm honest about my feelings." Like Mike Culbert at the Berkeley *Gazette,* Bodi was most upset by student demonstrators. He was especially exercised over Students for a Democratic Society (SDS) and an ever-changing and expanding group of "subversive" activities, which Bodi has christened "communistic-fascistic." A group of

Senator Eugene McCarthy's supporters picketed the *Times* during the pre-election period in 1968 because they felt the paper was not giving fair treatment to the Senator. Bodi called the picket line a communistic-fascistic pressure device.

Although the paper dealt with troubles at San Francisco State and Berkeley with a good deal more restraint than most Bay Area papers, the advent of trouble at Stanford brought forth a different treatment. The sit-in at the Applied Electronics Lab and the April Third Movement roughly coincided with the appearance of a street sale edition of the *Times,* which carried a *Chronicle*-like banner to attract customers. Stanford radicals were frequently the subject of this banner, which emphasized their activities and statements. Nothing has so angered the student community in Palo Alto as Bodi's insistence on printing the addresses of radical groups—this during a wave of terrorist bombings engineered by rightwingers in San Mateo County. It should be noted that the *Times* was critical of the underground Los Angeles *Free Press* when the latter printed the names of narcotics agents in the state. The editor also recommended that a radical research group be hounded out of existence by city officials.

The paper has developed a relationship, although belated and tenuous, with the Black community in East Palo Alto. Bodi showed his pride in running a daily syndicated comic strip with a Black youngster as one of the main characters, and he has talked about starting an internship program for aspiring Black journalists. The paper frequently runs feature stories on Black self-help projects, and on concerned Black citizens who are working in the community. The editorial page has also shown an awareness of Black problems. Perhaps more indicative of the *Times*'s concern, however, is the fact that subscription delivery service in the ghetto was sporadic until the Black weekly *Peninsula Bulletin* was started as very weak competition. *Times* service then showed a marked improvement.

Specialty Writing and the Editorial Page

In addition to a healthy supply of wire copy—much broader national and international coverage than was offered by the neighboring San Mateo *Times*—Bodi could also be proud of his imaginative speciality writing. The "Family Leisure" section presented excellent material on food, fashions and home furnishing. Joyce Passetti and Carolyn Snyder do informative work in these areas. Dave Wik's sports pages give detailed coverage to Stanford athletics and local high school activities. In Dick O'Connor the *Times* has a perceptive sportswriter who is not afraid to print stories of team mismanagement and intrigue, as he did concerning the 1969 Oakland Athletics, Manager Hank Bauer and owner Charles Finley. One of his pieces on team dissension was pirated by the *Chronicle, Examiner* and *Tribune*. Arts editor Paul Emerson runs the best entertainment pages of any local paper in the Bay Area. Emerson hires outside talent for film, drama and music reviews; the result is a page more literate than any but those of the two San Francisco dailies.

Editor Bodi is justifiably proud of his editorial page. Most of the local editorials are written by thoughtful Ward Winslow. And the *Times* opens its columns to letter-writers on a more generous basis than any other Bay Area paper. Bodi also writes frequent columns on both local and national subjects. The editorial page of December 23, 1968, not untypical, offered a column on a state college trustee's view of Black demands; a piece by Bodi describing a speech by Saul Alinsky at the Commonwealth Club; and an unsigned editorial on the air pollution problem caused by the Kaiser-Permanente plant in Los Altos. Bodi has instituted a regular feature known as "Around the Beats" which allows staff reporters to write interpretive pieces about subjects they cover. It is undoubtedly a good outlet for the reporters' desire to analyze in print, and it gives a needed dimension to the news. Other papers could well emulate this feature. A comparison of the Palo Alto *Times*'s editorial and feature pages with those of the San Mateo *Times* makes the former's good quality even more apparent.

A Too-Small Staff

The chief problem at the *Times* seems to be that its able staff is much too small. Time after time, the Northern Santa Clara County Bureau of the San Jose *Mercury-News* covered events that were not touched by the *Times* in its home territory. And there were periods when issue after issue of the *Times* was disappointing to those who prefer depth coverage to five-inch stories. Nonetheless, the *Times* often offers something for every member of the family who is outside the activist orbit. And the local activists, especially those at Stanford, often seem to read the *Times* to get angry.

Santa Rosa Press-Democrat (47,228)
Regional Coverage

The 1970 census may show that the Santa Rosa *Press-Democrat* is one of the few newspapers in the country with greater circulation than the population of the city in which it is located. The *Press-Democrat* naturally sees itself as a regional newspaper, serving readers in Lake, Sonoma, Mendocino and Marin counties. It offers three editions: one

for northern Sonoma and Lake counties; a second for southern Sonoma
County and the Petaluma area; and a third for Santa Rosa.

To cover the territory the *Press-Democrat* has full-time bureau men
in Ukiah and Petaluma, plus part-time stringers in Fort Bragg, Willits,
Lakeport, Healdsburg, Sebastopol and other small towns.[3] Major afternoon competition comes from the San Rafael *Independent-Journal,*
which has been making inroads in southern Sonoma County circulation,
and from small dailies in Petaluma and Ukiah. Neither the San Francisco *Examiner* nor the Oakland *Tribune* represents much of a threat
to the *Press-Democrat.* The local staff has remained at 25 or so over the
past few years, with no plans in the offing to enlarge it.

The paper is owned by Mrs. E. L. Finley, widow of the publisher who
was a leading Democrat and postmaster. If the paper doesn't step on
many toes nowadays, it may be because Mrs. Finley has been friendly
with Establishment people over a number of years. A rather more
pointed complaint came from one critic who noted that the *Press-
Democrat* did not publish at all on Saturday, and that a good part of
the Monday and Tuesday papers was evidently prepared on the preceding Friday and Saturday.

Given its setting in the Redwood Empire, the paper has devoted
much attention to environmental affairs, covering coastal access problems caused by the Sea Ranch development, redwood logging and
PG & E's attempt to build an atomic power plant in the area. Managing
editor Art Volkerts described the *Press-Democrat's* editorial philosophy
on such questions as being generally "in favor of industry and users."
Although the *Press-Democrat* supported the atomic power plant, Volkerts claimed the paper's thorough coverage of the controversy played
an important part in its defeat.

A Sedate Newspaper

Also as a reflection of its idyllic setting, the *Press-Democrat* was the
least strident, emotional, or sensational paper of those surveyed. The
front page showed an equal emphasis on local-state news and national-
international, although lead stories were frequently of a local nature.
It relied wholly on UPI and Copley Press Service for non-local material,
which limited the amount of depth and background information presented.

Although approximately equal in circulation to the Palo Alto *Times,*
the *Press-Democrat* trailed in its coverage of the arts, family life and

---

[3] Stringer: one who is employed by a newspaper to report on activities in his local
area. He is retained either on a fixed monthly salary (usually no more than $100) or
is paid on a piecework basis for everything that appears in print.

fashion. The editorial page was also disappointing. It offered no local writer and confined local criticism to the one unsigned piece each day. These editorials were, however, much superior to those in the San Mateo *Times*. Jack Anderson, W. S. White, Victor Riesel and some UPI columns provided the usual opinion fare. The letters to the editor space was generous, but some of the filler—such as "Bygone Days," "Grin and Bear It," "Almanac," and the "Country Parson"—could be sacrificed to make room for some local editorial comment.

Two major problems in the next few years will be: keeping pace with the expected population growth in the northern counties, and giving the growing Mexican-American community a voice in the paper. For now, the *Press-Democrat* impresses as a responsible, sedate reflection of community sentiment, at least a part of it.

The Six Sunday Papers: Distinction or Dullness?

The circulation of Sunday papers is traditionally higher than that of dailies, indicating that many subscribers expect a little extra on Sunday—enough to allow some of them to skip the rest of the week's offerings. Many editors in the Bay Area viewed the Sunday paper as a repository for material that did not fit during the week, and as a chance to "catch up with events" and put them in perspective.

The nine-county area has six Sunday papers. In terms of circulation, one is large, two are medium-sized and three, small. The field is straddled by the Sunday *Examiner and Chronicle,* the giant hybrid resulting from the merger in 1965. The Sunday Oakland *Tribune* and the San Jose *Mercury-News* are a distant second and third, followed by the much smaller Santa Rosa *Press-Democrat,* Hayward *Review,* and Vallejo *Times-Herald.* (Although the Contra Costa *Times and Green Sheet* has a Sunday edition, it is not geared to publishing a special Sunday package. Consequently it has been excluded from this study, which covered the period between December 23, 1968 and March 4, 1969.)

Certainly the most notable characteristic of the Sundays in the study was their lack of personality or distinctive "feel." The similarities in organization, space allocation, use of local talent and special sections were obvious. Sunday magazines could be switched from paper to paper, and few readers would be aware of the substitution. The arts and entertainment in the Bay Area were, with one exception, covered with the same depth and sophistication as in Cleveland or Detroit, where offerings are perhaps one-quarter as rich. Only infrequently did a column or section shout "I am uniquely of this paper," as do the Sunday Los Angeles *Times*'s *West* magazine, the New York *Times*'s "News of the Week in Review," and the Sunday St. Louis *Post-Dispatch* editorial page.

Serving a combined readership of 1.2 million households and offering from 80 to 220 pages, the Sundays seemed to be healthy, although their uniformity and lack of distinction suggested that the readership may be held through force of habit.

The Giant Hybrid
SUNDAY SAN FRANCISCO EXAMINER AND CHRONICLE (640,004)

This Sunday combination is not a united effort of the two staffs, but rather a morning *Examiner* to which the *Chronicle* has chipped in a Sunday magazine, editorial section and comic pages. Only the cheerful face and column of William Randolph Hearst, Jr. (Editor-in-Chief of

70

the Hearst Newspapers), always appearing on page one below the fold, distinguished the Sunday *Examiner*'s news section from those of the rest of the week. Usually filling 32 pages, the front news section was a bit longer than the weekday section. A few more wire service interpretive pieces, such as one on Mayor Lindsay's problems in New York or Italian economic troubles, found their way into print. But there was nothing consistent about the Sunday news philosophy, and often during the period under study the front section was slim in news value.

The *Examiner* editorial page, with the exception of the Hearst column, was identical with weekdays: local writers Dick Nolan and Guy Wright, syndicated Sydney J. Harris and Hearst reporter Bob Considine and two or three unsigned editorials. The *Examiner*'s capable music and drama critics, Alexander Fried and Stanley Eichelbaum, were compressed into two small columns of a two-page "Lively Arts" section, a maddeningly slender Sunday obeisance to the arts. Dwight Newton on TV, Dorothy Manners with gossip, a few more pages of news, and a short section for the hobbyists customarily completed the editorial-feature section.

The Sunday Travel section, edited by Georgia Hesse, is easily the best such section in the Bay Area, with much locally written material, helpful advice on preparing for trips and excellent travel suggestions. The women's section started strong, with a profile on a female San Francisco doer, but ended in a pile of gossip columnists from Suzy Knickerbocker to Harriet van Horne. The greatest disappointment among *Examiner* contributions is the *California Living* magazine, a 40-page, full-color excuse for advertising with little redeeming social or literary value. It housed no more than three "major" articles, each including a page or two of text and accompanying pictures. Subjects were almost exclusively lightweight; political stories were avoided, and rarely was a San Francisco problem discussed, and then not in detail. *California Living*, unfortunately, is the model (and best of the lot) for all but one of the locally produced Sunday magazines. There seems to be no effort to move in the direction of *West* magazine at the Los Angeles *Times*. *West* has been focusing on articles of broader appeal, with an emphasis on travel and California politics. The quality of writing and depth of research in *West*'s articles far exceeds those in *California Living*.

The challenger to *West* is part of the *Chronicle*'s contribution to the Sunday paper: *This World* magazine. Editor Richard Demorest has chosen a news magazine format to review the week's news events. Because he does not have even one-hundredth the staff of *Time* or *Newsweek*, the review is essentially a pastiche of rewritten wire service materials assembled under standing heads. Some lengthier articles from the New York Times and Times-Post services were often placed at the rear of the magazine, but *This World*'s redeeming features comprise the most literate music and art criticism in any of the Bay Area Sundays. A typical array would include a major serious music piece by Robert Commanday; records reviews and a shorter piece by Heuwell Tircuit; Ralph Gleason on jazz; a generous book section edited by William Hogan; and Alfred Frankenstein writing on art. These would combine for an interesting and distinctive 20 pages. Harold Gilliam, one of the Bay Area's ablest conservation writers, appears every other week in *This World*.

The pink, pull-out center section of the magazine, entitled "Date Book," is another matter. Draped around movie, theater and reducing ads in 1969 were the "columns" on film and stage stars, one cut above the Earl Wilson variety, mostly wire service puffs for movies about to be released or starlets on the way up. The week's television listings were surrounded by a panoply of cheesecake photographs with sophomoric captions. Were it not for a valuable "On the Town" section listing, in tabular form, the coming events in music, art, sports, night clubs and restaurants, the pink section would be an insult to *Chronicle* readers.

"Sunday Punch," the *Chronicle* editorial and feature page edited by Carl Nolte, is among the most praiseworthy of single Sunday sections because it is distinctly the *Chronicle*'s: it has personality, it is challenging and it is fun. The handling of this section makes one wish that the Sunday *Examiner and Chronicle* were under the *Chronicle* editors' direction, just to see what they would do with it. Local columnists Herb Caen and Art Hoppe, sports editor Art Rosenbaum, traveling essayist Stanton Delaplane, Count Marco and others all contribute to "Sunday Punch." Also appearing fairly regularly in 1969 were the New York *Times*'s James Reston and Russell Baker, TRB of the *New Republic*, Stanford's Nobel prizewinner Joshua Lederberg and various other features from the *Chronicle*'s wealth of syndicated material. Add a generous helping of pictures and zany reports from Scott Newhall's far-flung foreign stringers, and you have a section of interest if not cohesiveness.

In sum, the Sunday *Examiner and Chronicle* was hardly juicy enough to curl up with for more than an hour or two. It was clear that the men behind it are aware of the type of material that succeeds in major Sunday papers (such as a weekly news review, travel, opinion, magazine-type pieces, art and theater criticism). But they have not invested enough energy in the Sunday combination to make it much more appealing than an overstuffed weekday edition. A Sunday magazine with some real punch, more analysis and feature material, and an enlarged news section are prime goals to guide needed improvement. But this may be too much to expect from a shotgun marriage.

Two Papers of Medium-Range Circulation

SUNDAY SAN JOSE MERCURY-NEWS (187,924)

The fruits of the *Mercury-News's* emphasis on ad linage and promotion were most evident in the combined Sunday creation from the two Ridder papers: a massive paper, frequently over 200 pages. In California, it is second only to the Los Angeles *Times* in bulk. The cornerstone of the paper was a substantial news offering (over 40 pages) filling the first three sections. Although the same weakness in local news reporting that afflicts the daily *Mercury* and *News* was also evident on Sundays, national and international stories were well covered by material from AP, UPI, New York Times, Times-Post and Copley news services. Many lengthy pieces that were not time bound found their way into Sunday *Mercury* and *News* columns: Duvalier and Haiti; ministates causing U.N. headaches; how model schools in Portland aid poor children; American youth revolution at the crossroads. A weekly "Sacramento Scene" column from Lou Cannon was another valuable addition to the news pages before he moved on to Washington.

The *Mercury-News* shows the greatest individuality (and potential) with "Focus," a combination news review-editorial-travel-book section. Its outstanding feature is a front page devoted to depth study of a single topic: heart transplants, man's genius for fouling his own planet, a revolution in military education and the like. Some of the material came from wire services, often supplemented with related local articles by *Mercury-News* staffers. The single-page news review seems a more sensible approach (given staff limitations) than the *Chronicle's* effort. The editorial page featured different columnists each week, including Wicker and Baker of the New York *Times,* Bill Henry and John Averill of the Los Angeles *Times,* and William Buckley and James Kilpatrick. One lively column is "The Mercury—1869" in which Daniel K. Stern of the promotion department offers excerpts from the paper 100 years ago. Careful editing of such material can produce columns that throw more light on unfolding events than do articles by many contemporary political pundits.

Travel pages at the end of "Focus" were well done, although they offered less than those in the *Examiner-Chronicle.* Real estate, which either headed its own section or formed part of another, was largely puffery received from construction and building materials firms. The

"Today's Women" section was traditional, with heavy emphasis on fashion, beauty hints and bridal announcements.

One *Mercury-News* Sunday problem is the poor quality of magazines. Two of them, *California Today* and *Entertainment Calendar*, are locally produced. *Parade* circulates nationally, but with declining popularity. Trying to please everybody, it engages no one. *California Today* is not much better, with unexciting filler on pets or decorating, and homemaker and gardening columns that seemed to avoid discussion of serious questions. *Entertainment Calendar* presented music, drama, and film criticism of a quality far below the *Examiner and Chronicle* level. Much of the 20-page section was devoted to a TV pullout, gossip columns and Hollywood notes.

The *Mercury-News* would do well to concentrate its energies on one magazine, incorporating and expanding the best of the arts criticism and gardening-homemaking articles, and adding desperately needed material on San Jose problems. Nowhere in the more than 200 pages were local concerns discussed intelligently on a regular basis during the period of our study. This kind of focus on local matters will be essential if the Sunday *Mercury-News* is to become a San Jose newspaper and develop its own personality. At present, only its bulk and the embryonic "Focus" section separate it from run-of-the-mill American Sunday papers.

SUNDAY OAKLAND TRIBUNE (237,417)

With less than half the pages of the Sunday *Mercury-News*, the *Tribune* makes up for its lack of size—and consequent dearth of national and international news—with the best local writing in the Sunday market. Stories on San Francisco Bay fill and on regional air, water and transportation problems have become Sunday fixtures at the *Tribune*. Breaking either on the front page, or on the first page of the second "Metropolitan News Section," such stories often run to 40 or 50 inches, plus pictures. For example, conservation expert Fred Garretson wrote a series entitled "Our Polluted Bay," which included articles on industry and Bay pollution, and on the San Francisco sewer plan.

The *Tribune* has also used the "Metropolitan News Section" effectively in presenting complex information on overlapping regional government jurisdictions, and in explaining what various regional commissions do. Other local stories such as the Knolls Center speech therapy program in Richmond, and little theater in the East Bay, have also been highlighted.

The total Sunday news offering was typically a rather thin 24 to 30 pages, and the editorial "News and Comment" section was the poorest of the three major Sundays. Ed Salzman provides a sharp column on Sacramento politics, but the syndicated material was less stimulating than *Chronicle* or *Mercury-News* offerings. There was no attempt at a week's news review.

In its magazine lineup the *Tribune* offers *Parade;* an unabashed home improvement tabloid entitled *California;* and *Entertainment Week.* As for entertainment, it is significant that the *Tribune* has the manpower to break away from the stereotyped movie and TV celebrity articles that dominate most such magazines (including the *Mercury-News's*), but has chosen not to do it. Music critic John Rockwell and art critic Miriam Dungan Cross were usually restricted to one page each (often less), and the book review section was a bit over a page. All were jammed unceremoniously into the rear of the magazine without being highlighted with cover displays, as is so often the case with *Chronicle* arts pieces. The *Tribune* could markedly improve its magazine by giving greater space, freedom and control to its own arts writers.

The editorial and entertainment sections of the Sunday *Tribune* could stand hearty infusions of the same imagination that goes into the "Metropolitan News Section." It is disappointing that such valuable local news coverage is offset by a pedestrian editorial and opinion section, and a dull, functional entertainment page. Even without the *Mercury-News's* bulk or the *Examiner and Chronicle's* riches of syndicated material, the *Tribune* is gamely competing in the Sunday field. But many of its best players may be on the bench.

❖   ❖   ❖

Although no one Sunday paper was clearly satisfying on all counts, an amalgam of elements of the three major Sundays analyzed above would produce an interesting newspaper. Add to the *Mercury-News's* bulk and national and international coverage the *Tribune's* local coverage, the *Examiner's* travel section, the *Chronicle's* "Sunday Punch" and emphasis on art, music, dance and drama, and some publisher would be well on his way to a superior Sunday paper. He could take his pick of available sports sections (all competent), women's pages and comics. The *Chronicle's* "Peanuts" would be essential. But for today's reader, buying all three at a newsstand cost of $1.05 (35¢ each) and wading through a combined total of 400 pages of newsprint is too high a price to pay for one decent Sunday newspaper.

Three Papers of Smaller Circulation

SUNDAY SANTA ROSA PRESS-DEMOCRAT (49,133)

The *Press-Democrat* made a few concessions to the idea of a Sunday paper, one of which showed much initiative. Each 50- to 60-page

Sunday edition included an "Empire Living" section, (with the first page devoted entirely to some subject of interest to residents of the northern counties). Staffer Bob Wells, who writes most of these lengthy features, has presented everything from shipbuilding at Mare Island and agricultural research at U. C. Davis to a driving guide through four Redwood Empire counties and a tour of the little Sonoma County town of Shellville. Wells writes clearly; the pictures were interesting and the topics never dull. The *Press-Democrat* can be proud of these Sunday pieces.

The rest of the Sunday fare, however, was mediocre. In each issue there was a single editorial page, with syndicated columns from Anderson, Buchwald, Lawrence and Hoffer. There were no major news features, background stories or news reviews. The arts were jammed together on a single page that encompassed dance, music, books and radio. The familiar Sunday magazine, *Medley,* is a bit more ambitious than its counterparts in Oakland and San Jose, although its goals are even less clearly defined. It seems to be both a news magazine and a do-it-yourself supplement, and the two approaches do not mesh well: *Medley* included fix-it columns, comics, travel notes, a feature or two from various news services, a TV pullout, fashion, decorating ideas and hobby columns. Naturally, in 16 pages (excluding the comics and TV listings), nothing was done with much depth. The nationally circulating *Family Weekly* supplements *Medley.*

Given its staff size and circulation, the *Press-Democrat* provided the minimum for a Sunday, with a bit of a bonus in Bob Wells's work. But at least the paper is more closely identified with the needs of the Redwood Empire country than is the *Mercury-News* with the needs of San Jose.

Sunday Vallejo Times-Herald (28,714)

The *Times-Herald* made the fewest gestures toward a Sunday edition of any of the Bay papers. It offered no special Sunday magazine other than the syndicated *Family Weekly,* and the single editorial-feature page was equivalent to the weekday page. Such topics as travel, the arts and entertainment, farming and ranching, which could merit an entire section, must fight for space each week.

Every Sunday the paper ran above the logo a front-page boxed story with a Vallejo angle. Some were locally written, while others came from news services. Hospital openings and other civic projects were favorite material, although such subjects as sensitivity training and pay increases for local federal workers have also been studied.

Of most interest on Sunday are three columns, two of them syndicated. Jenkin Lloyd Jones, a Tulsa newspaper editor, contributes one; Henry C. MacArthur writes another from Sacramento. Dugald Gillies, formerly an aide to publisher Luther Gibson when Gibson was in the State Senate, does a Sunday piece on Vallejo problems. Gillies, described as a "freelancer" by a *Times-Herald* staffer, is associated with the California Real Estate Association, and writes from that perspective.

The "Social Panorama" section included food and gardening news, along with the brides, and there was usually a single page for auto and travel news. Sports coverage was strong, as in all the Sunday papers under study.

Of comparable size to the Sunday *Press-Democrat*, the *Times-Herald* has nothing to match the "Empire Living" feature or even the *Medley* magazine. In contrast, a bit more effort in Santa Rosa has produced a better Sunday paper.

Sunday Hayward Review (37,977)

With 80 to 90 pages, the Sunday *Review* is the largest of this group. Some of the extra space was devoted to local news, spread throughout the news sections. The *Review* also tended to run more AP and UPI feature and background material than did the Santa Rosa or Vallejo papers; wire copy usually filled the pages at the back of the sports and women's sections.

Previewer magazine consists mainly of television listings, with a few puzzles for the kids, and a one-page "Calendar of Fine Arts" showing events in the East Bay. *Family Weekly* completes the magazine package.

The editorial and feature pages presented more syndicated columnists—including Goldwater, Hoffer, W. S. White and Childs—than the other small Sunday papers, but there was little local innovation in this part of the paper. A "Career Corner," focusing on a different career each week, was an interesting *Review* feature. A single arts page and a puff-filled real estate section were dull.

In sum, the similarities of the three small Sundays overwhelmed the relatively minor differences that enable a reader to distinguish among them.

◇　◇　◇

The importance of having good Sunday papers can be seen from the viewpoints of both the editor and reader. Many editors feel that the Sunday paper is a convenient place for much background and wrap-up reporting that is crowded out of the weekday editions. The comparatively higher Sunday circulation figures indicate that some Bay Area readers rely on the Sunday editions to perform this catch-up function. A good Sunday paper must, therefore, include a news section large enough to accommodate feature and background material, and some sort of news-in-review section. This latter might concentrate on a local news review for the previous week, since *Time* and *Newsweek* provide good national and international reviews.

One reason people spend more time with the Sunday paper than with weekday editions is the entertainment value of the Sunday offering. The comics, a magazine section, arts pages, a travel section and other specialties contribute to this entertainment package. A good Sunday paper should offer some of these entertainment and leisure specialties, concentrating on local travel and outing ideas, house and garden hints, and the local film/theater/music scene. These are some basic requirements for a Sunday paper that would be worth several hours of its readers' attention, once a week.

Papers Published Weekly, Monthly or Occasionally

In several studies of the weekly press, Professor Alex Edelstein and his associates at the University of Washington have categorized the editors of weekly newspapers in two groups, the "community-oriented" and the "journalist-oriented." If an editor is community-oriented, he will seek consensus and may gloss over even the major faults of his community to promote what he considers to be the greater good. If an editor is journalist-oriented, he will stress conflict, printing all the facts he can gather, although they may present to the community an image that many readers would prefer not to see.

This classification represents much more than an academic exercise. An editor who was told of Edelstein's conclusions said, "Sure, when the local sheriff dies, the journalist editor thinks there was foul play and tries to investigate. The community editor tries to see something positive even in this. He wants to write, 'There's a pretty new widow in town.' " Most newspapermen will agree that many of the men who run weekly newspapers tend to fall into either the community-oriented or journalist-oriented categories. They may doubt, however, that the division is quite as neat as the typology suggests.

Emphasis: Cooperation or Conflict?

Thus, it is certain the most community-oriented editor will, on occasion, print news that reveals community flaws. Conversely, the journalist-oriented editor, however dedicated he may be to disclosure, almost automatically presents many columns of news and features that promote the community's betterment and image in a way the Chamber of Commerce would approve. It may be, too, that the vast majority of weekly newspaper editors shift between community orientation and journalist orientation, depending upon the issue, the personalities involved and the circumstances. Almost any number of variables may be at work, including the editor's mood and temper on a particular day.

Neat or not, these categories are useful. For it is axiomatic that some editors stress cooperation rather than conflict, and that others stress conflict rather than cooperation. Such distinctions are useful in weighing the worth of a newspaper.

Edelstein's concepts are valuable in another way. They enable us to look at local weeklies and evaluate them against the image of an ideal: a mix of community and journalist orientations. Local progress is a satisfactory goal for any newspaper, but it is usually better served by disclosing unfortunate facts than by hiding them. On the other hand, the editor who is so sensitive to his role as an adversary that he publicly casts suspicion on nearly every action of local leaders—the crusty editor who sets himself up as the conscience of his community—may injure the community more cruelly than the editor who is in the pocket of the Chamber of Commerce. The great trick is to balance the roles by serving at once as the voice of the community's pride and the conscience of its shames and concerns. In the words of an editor of the respected Sonoma *Index-Tribune,* it is necessary to "prod and praise with equal fervor." No duty in journalism is more difficult.

As one veteran of weekly journalism pointed out,

> The problem of balancing roles is more difficult because it's hard to carry on hit-and-run journalism in a small community; you have to live with those whom you report. In a city you might expose a misfeasor and have him replaced. In a small community, he may be the best available, bad as he is. In many small towns, the citizens are happier with a mediocre physician than none at all.

The task of the small newspaper is even more difficult because of its peculiar financial problems. Many big advertisers and advertising agencies ignore weeklies. This means that the publishers of weeklies, in the words of one of them,

> must depend for 60 to 80 percent of their revenue on supermarkets. It takes 1,000 homes to support a market. The owner wants those 1,000 covered, plus another 2,000 in a concentric circle. He doesn't give a damn what else is in the paper so long as it's "safe." He just wants a copy of his ad at those homes by Wednesday afternoon. Hence the fact that virtually all successful conventional weeklies have a shopper. Papers without this kind of geographic coverage and without the market ads, have a hell of a financial problem.

Steve McNamara of the *Pacific Sun* offered a cogent explanation for the increasing number of small newspapers. He said,

> They have cropped up because there has been a need for them. *But:* it is highly important that one recognize the technological side of this. Without cold type composition and web offset printing in central plants, these papers couldn't exist. And that is a development of only the past 10 or 15 years.

Moreover, McNamara predicted,

> Smaller papers are going to be very strong in this country. It is now a nation of participants, rather than spectators. Hearst used to provide social scandals, axe murders and other vicarious thrills; TV does that now. And anyway, people are more involved in participating in their own environment. It is technically impossible for a metro to serve these small spheres of influence. The secret is finding a coherent interest group that

can provide the needed revenue either through advertising or, very occasionally, through circulation alone. Ten years from now it will all seem so simple. Right now it's rough. . . . But then if those of us who are doing it now waited for 10 years, it would all be done!

The Weeklies

The weekly press in the Bay Area presented a lively picture, with 96 newspapers in the field. They offered a significant potential for the area, and a major problem in evaluation. We tried a three-point approach in selecting and judging some of the best weekly papers. First, we began by reading a great many weeklies. Second, we asked a highly regarded editor-publisher to list those that seemed to him to be "complete" in the sense of balancing community and journalistic orientations. Finally, we wrote to the editors of every Bay Area newspaper and asked them to nominate the weekly they considered best.

Each of these methods has flaws and shortcomings. Our reading of the weekly press was not complete. We were further handicapped by lack of knowledge about the communities in which each of these papers was published. In addition, we knew that the editor-publisher's judgments might be colored by the kind of newspaper he himself produced. Finally, the editors' nominations were limited by the fact that no one could read all the papers regularly. Most of the respondents restricted their nominations to weeklies in their own counties, rather than choosing among the many published throughout the Bay Area. The ethnic papers, the religious papers, and the papers published less often than weekly thus had much less chance of being considered in such estimates than did the conventional weeklies.

Nevertheless, there was a striking similarity between the list provided by the single editor-publisher and the list based on nominations of the Bay Area editors who responded to our letters. Our own reading (primarily during December 23, 1968 and March 4, 1969) of the weeklies that were nominated, caused us to agree substantially with both lists.

NOMINATED AS "COMPLETE NEWSPAPERS" (Listed alphabetically)

The editor-publisher listed these as "complete newspapers":

Burlingame *Advance-Star* (twice a week)
Cupertino *Courier*
Livermore *Independent*
Milpitas *Post*
Novato *Advance*
Pacific Sun
San Jose *Sun*
Sonoma *Index-Tribune*

NOMINATED FOR "HIGH QUALITY"

On a second level of "high quality" newspapers, the editor-publisher listed:

Los Altos *Town Crier*
Oakland *Montclarion*
Pacifica *Tribune*
San Francisco *Progress*
Terra Linda *News*

NOMINATED AS "BEST"

Most of these selections were echoed in the editors' nominations. Those nominated as "best" by two or more editors include:

Berkeley *Post*
Burlingame *Advance-Star*
Cupertino *Courier*
Los Altos *Town Crier*
Milpitas *Post*
Novato *Advance*
Oakland *Montclarion*
Pacific Sun
Pacifica *Tribune*
San Bruno *Herald*
San Francisco *Bay Guardian*[1]
San Francisco *Monitor*[1]
Sonoma *Index-Tribune*

It is easy to understand why these papers were listed, considered "complete," or nominated as "best," especially when compared with such routine weeklies as the Menlo-Atherton *Recorder,* the Morgan Hill *Times,* and the Los Altos *News.* The routine papers sometimes seemed to avoid anything more controversial than a dogfight, and their reporting and editing were uninspired. The papers listed here, on the other hand, not only challenged local Establishments on occasion, but they also displayed a degree of specialization in reporting that enabled them to speak with authority.

When reading quality weeklies, we sometimes wondered why they are so often only way stations for reporters and editors who yearn for the world of the daily paper. The scope of the weekly is limited, and sometimes the pay of its employees is skimpy but the other compensations are great. To know a community, to be responsible for informing

---

[1] Inclusion of the *Monitor* and the *Bay Guardian* was a special tribute to those two papers, because they do not exactly fit this nomination category. The *Monitor* is a diocesan paper. The *Guardian* is a monthly.

it, to be able to alert most of the community to its own virtues and flaws —these are (or should be) excellent compensations. Certainly, some of the proprietors of the ambitious weeklies—Steve McNamara of the Pacific *Sun,* Mort Levine of the San Jose *Sun*papers and the Milpitas *Post,* and Robert Lynch of the Sonoma *Index-Tribune*—are among the many good weekly editors who seemed to be happy with their lot.

The excellence of some of the weeklies may be suggested by these items:

· The owner of the Pacifica *Tribune* once exposed shady business practices by pulling a wire loose from a television set, then sending it around to local shops for repair estimates. He did the same with a car. The stories reporting the wild estimates of the TV and car repairmen alerted his readers to a danger, and doubtless persuaded the repairmen that their estimates should have a nodding acquaintance with reality.

· In her column, "Your Dollar's Worth," in the February 12, 1969, Milpitas *Post,* Dr. Mabel Newcomer chided the San Jose *Mercury* for sloppy thinking, or worse, and warned readers:

> The answer of the "House Doctor" (whose column appears in the San Jose *Mercury*) to the woman who complained that her storm windows failed to meet the promises of the "fast-talking" salesman who had persuaded her to buy them was: "It is much better that way. Suppose salesmen told you the truth about the products or services they sell. Our economy would go into stagnation."
>
> The *Chronicle* also had published this column, omitting these introductory comments. And the business world as a whole surely would not subscribe to such a doctrine.
>
> The basic purpose of the Better Business Bureau is to protect the honest businessmen from the dishonest. But fraudulent business practices are still a common phenomenon, hard to reach in our mobile society.
>
> You are probably all familiar with the "special" offers of the sewing machine agencies that appear from time to time in this area.
>
> One of these, for Riccar machines, offers discounts on a $149 model ranging from $10 to $80, depending on the emblem noted in individual letters. The "lucky ones" get a free machine plus a four-day vacation for two in Las Vegas.
>
> There are conditions on this gift. You must call in person at the machine center (where you will probably be "switched" to a more expensive model). You must purchase a five-year prepaid Service and Instruction Policy at $12.95 a year ($64.75 total). And the "free" vacation specifies only free hotel accommodations and nightly champagne parties.
>
> I judge by the omissions that plane fare, meals, and other entertainment is at the expense of the lucky ones. An individual with firm sales resistance might save money by taking the specified model (if it ordinarily does sell for $149) and foregoing Las Vegas, but the Federal Trade Commission has cited the Riccar offer as a "bait and switch" fraud.

Dr. Newcomer went on with other matters that helped protect consumers in a forthright column of the sort that is difficult to find in the dailies.

· An editorial in the *Pacific Sun* is worth reprinting:

> Worried parents gather in Novato, demanding to know why the schools can't "do something" about the bizarre appearance and behavior of some students and teachers. In Mill Valley and Sausalito, some Tam [Tamalpais] High students get together and start their own school. They are dissatisfied with the kind of education they are getting.
>
> Behind these events lies one fact. Schools are becoming more and more like total life corporations and less like places where students go to get information with which to make their own decisions.
>
> Consider the functions which a school system performs: it runs the main in-county transportation system; it offers the principal recreation program; it has an enormous food service department, producing more meals than all the restaurants in the county combined; it runs the biggest driver-training school; it is hip-deep in the medical business, giving tests for sight, speech, hearing and psychological disorders; it is a vast "job placement" bureau; it is the main adult source of sex information; it lays down the Establishment line on drugs, and in some cases is supposed to rule on length of hair, skirts, and general physical appearance. In the time left over, it is supposed to lay on a bit of knowledge.
>
> Is it any wonder that school people become increasingly trapped in the administrative mentality? And is it any wonder that students become increasingly unhappy with the system?
>
> The blame cannot be assigned to the schools. Most school people, or at least most teachers, want mainly to teach. The blame must be assigned to the parents, who are madly loading their rightful responsibilities onto the school system.
>
> How long should your kid wear his hair? That is something for you to work out with your kid. Until you stop bringing the school system into it, your kid's chances for an education will be mediocre at best.

The foregoing discussion suggests that some significant gaps in Bay Area journalism are being filled in a few places by good weeklies. But other serious lapses require the two-fold remedy of better coverage by both dailies and weeklies throughout the area. Perhaps the weeklies' unique contribution lies in their potential—realized now and then—for providing an authentic community voice, fostering local leadership and encouraging a sense of community identity.

Published Monthly—More or Less

There is a spiritual kinship between the Bay Area weeklies—even the conventional ones—and the monthlies, because neither group is in the dominant position of the dailies. Beyond that, however, the kinship is distant. Many of the monthlies seemed to be published because their proprietors looked at the world around them, found it flawed, and decided that the flaws were caused by conspirators. There actually are a good many conspiracies, some of them criminal, others only the comfortable conspiracies that develop from easy agreements between selfish men: you help me get mine and I'll help you get yours. Consequently, there is plenty of meat for the conspiracy theorist's grinder.

Many of the theorists fail to recognize, however, that some of society's flaws are caused by accidents. Because they often do not distinguish between accidents and conspiracies, they know too many things that are not true. Yet in the end, the conspiracy theorists perform a valuable service. If the more conventional newspapers were not locked in the framework of national and local myths, not to mention their own self-interest, they would root out and publish the conspiracies. The theorists would then be left to make what they could of the accidents, and their newspapers would die swiftly. But the conventional newspapers, even the atypical *Chronicle,* ignore too many of the conspiracies and are involved in some of them. This provides both a role and a foothold for the maverick publishers.

This is far from a complete description of the reasons for the monthlies' existence, of course. Much of the fervor that goes into publishing some of the monthlies is rooted in causes that transcend particular controversies. Thus, although it is easy to imagine that there might be no *Bay Guardian* if the conventional press were more alert and devoted to the public interest, it is difficult to imagine that anything the conventional press might do would usurp the role and function of the *Freedom News* of Richmond.

It is not easy for the authors of this study to give suitable credit to unorthodox monthlies. We grew up in the tradition of so-called objective journalism as practiced by conventional newspapers. The tradition called for straightforward, dispassionate reporting, as nearly objective as fallible humans could make it. More recently, the tradition has made way for interpretive reporting: news stories that attempt to analyze, clarify, explain—but with as little of the personal opinion of the writer as can be managed. If we have sometimes wondered whether the old tradition or the relatively new one of interpretation is adequate, we have nonetheless been opposed to outright advocacy in the news columns.

The monthlies we are discussing, however, are nothing if they are not advocates. Sometimes in the news columns of the *Bay Guardian* and the *Freedom News,* the reporters were actually editorial writers. The fervor of their causes is a partial explanation. The fact that the papers are published so infrequently must provide another motive. When one has a cause, and can get at his readers only once a month, the pressure to promote a point of view must be overwhelming.

And so we were willing to consider these monthlies separately, as representative of many others that come and go in the Bay Area. We concentrated our reading during December 23, 1968–March 4, 1969, with some subsequent updating. We evaluated them in terms of what they attempted to accomplish, rather than judging them by standards that other kinds of newspapers seem to impose on all journalism. We bridled a bit at their outright advocacy; we doubted that these publications were as persuasive as they might be if they did not so often publish one point of view. At the same time, we accepted the premise that the conventional press is so overwhelming in its reach and power that extreme journalistic measures of this kind might be necessary.

BAY GUARDIAN

Bruce Brugmann's paper is so shrill, so laden with reports of alleged shady deals and under-the-table machinations, that a reader who is not a conspiracy theorist or a convinced Brugmannite tends almost automatically to reject much that his paper reports. But when one begins to look into the charges that fill the *Bay Guardian,* the reaction is quite different.

Is there really a contractual arrangement, as Brugmann reported, between the *Examiner-Chronicle* and San Francisco authorities whereby the papers can print legal notices in only a few thousand copies rather than all the copies of all editions? (This has enabled the papers to keep legal notices out of the hands of smaller publications.) Although it is consonant with city charter provisions, the arrangement appears to flout the public interest and may thwart taxpayers who want to read legal notices. The *Guardian's* account is accurate. *Examiner* executives admit it. (See fuller discussion on p. 45.)

Could it really be true that "Superchron" (Brugmann's name for the *Chronicle*-KRON-TV combination) set private investigators on the trail of Al Kihn, a former KRON cameraman? Kihn's complaints to the Federal Communications Commission about alleged shoddy KRON practices had delayed the station's license renewal, but such snooping is precisely what General Motors executives had done to Ralph Nader, the consumer affairs crusader, in 1966. Only two public apologies from James Roche, General Motors president, saved company officials from prosecution for intimidating a government witness. Surely, so soon after the General Motors fiasco, Superchron executives could not be so imprudent. But, yes, they were exactly that imprudent. They admitted it after prodding by the Federal Communications Commission.

Finally, was the overall voting record on conservation of State Senator Richard Dolwig of San Mateo County really as bad as a story in the

May 22, 1969, issue of the *Guardian* made it out to be? Could any state senator be as acquiescent to the lobbyists as the *Bay Guardian* made him seem? Dolwig's record seems to support the *Guardian*'s thesis.[1]

It was not possible to check all of Brugmann's charges thoroughly. In some cases, only the principals in the individual controversies know whether the *Bay Guardian* is reporting them accurately. Did former Mayor John Shelley get out of the last San Francisco mayoralty race because he made a deal with his probable successor, Joseph Alioto? It is certain that Shelley declined to run, and that he now holds a plush position in Sacramento, arranged by Alioto. Brugmann charged conspiracy. But only Shelley and Alioto know for sure whether the allegations are true, and they deny them.

There were many other items, including allegations against the Pacific Gas and Electric Company, the Bay Area Rapid Transit District, and the Southern Pacific Railroad. Although the responses from the officials involved were often lame and unconvincing, we cannot know the full truth about these charges—at least not yet. What we do know is that a great many of the indictments that appeared in the *Bay Guardian* were quite true. There were enough of them to lead us to believe that Bruce Brugmann's paper is one of the most valuable in the Bay Area. Perhaps if more of those who come across copies of the *Guardian* were able to check its work and weigh its value, the paper might be able to add financial success to its journalistic accomplishments.

One reporter for a Bay Area daily commented:

> My own view is that the *Guardian* has drifted further left than it ought to go for good muckraking purposes and, further, that its makeup is too reminiscent of the old *People's World* or the *National Guardian* for its own good. But it performs a vital service just by being where it is and by being willing to print the stories that come its way. Thank God it's there.

Many a local journalist is convinced that the *Guardian* provides the most penetrating reportage in the Bay Area. There is some evidence, in fact, that it has penetrated too deeply. From 1967 through 1969, Brugmann's paper won four of the nine awards open to it in the San Francisco Press Club's "Pulitzer of the West" competition. In 1970, a Press Club committee decided that the only competitive category available to the *Guardian*, that for nondailies, would be open only to weeklies, thus excluding the *Guardian*, which is published monthly or less often. Investigating the action, Brugmann reported that the committee was headed by a public relations representative of the Pacific Gas and

---

[1] As indicated on p. 59, Senator Dolwig subsequently responded to intense pressure from conservationists and, in effect, reversed his position on the Bay fill issue.

Electric Company, and was made up almost exclusively of advertising and public relations men. Nearly all of them worked for companies that had suffered from *Guardian* exposés. This shabby incident caused two respected professors to resign from the panel of Press Club judges: Kenneth Stewart, Professor of Journalism, Emeritus, at the University of California, Berkeley, and Jerrold Werthimer, Professor of Journalism at San Francisco State College.

PLAIN RAPPER[2]

The reports on student unrest that appear in hundreds of newspapers and magazines must vie for attention with reports on Congress and the President, foreign relations, tax reform and more frivolous matters. These stories of unrest may do little more than persuade readers that there are pockets of turmoil in American society. In the more active periods, when one campus is inflamed, or when several are, the reports in the conventional press may suggest more—that youth is rebelling. But when a reader turns from the generality of the American press to publications like the *Plain Rapper,* it becomes quite clear to him that a revolution, or something very much like a revolution, is underway.

No one can judge how far this revolution will go, or even how many are committed to it. Certainly, the small circulation of the *Rapper* and similar papers indicates severe limits. Perhaps an end to the war in Vietnam will mark the end of the revolution. On the other hand, the militants argue that the war exposes fundamental flaws in American society, and that thoroughgoing change is essential.

At least for the time being, however, no one who reads the *Plain Rapper* can doubt its staff's commitment to revolution, which presumably also applies to an unknown number of readers. Labelled "A National Resistance Publication," edited and printed in Palo Alto, the *Rapper* published local and national stories on draft resistance and attendant aims. Consider this statement by 15 militants in Chicago, which was published in the fifth issue:

> Today, May 25th, 1969, we enter the Chicago Southside Draft Board complex at 63rd and Western to remove and burn Selective Service records. We still have a dream of being able to communicate with this society. But we can no longer confine our peacemaking efforts to the ordinary channels of polite discourse. For we are confronting an extremely urgent situation in which the twin evils of American militarism and racism are monstrously interconnected.
> The poor people of the earth are taught to hate and kill one another in order that the powerful can enjoy the freedom to increase their fortunes through exploitative foreign investments. At the same time, the expansion

[2] Not long after this section was written, the *Plain Rapper* died.

of war-related industries diverts tax dollars away from the social programs so desperately needed here. Born and raised in poverty and oppression, young men from America's urban ghettoes are forced to burn and kill poor peasants in a land of the Third World in order to preserve a "freedom" which they themselves do not even enjoy in their own land.

It is not by accident that we perform our act of creative destruction at the draft board center which menaces the South Side of Chicago. As white Americans, we bear a special responsibility with regard to the Selective Service System and the war machine it feeds; and we can no longer allow that system to function smoothly in our name, for we cannot tolerate the atrocities it perpetrates upon our brothers in America, in Vietnam, and in other parts of the world.

Our action is negative but also creative—for there is implied in our loud "No!" a quiet but hopeful "Yes!" in our elimination of part of the death-dealing and oppressive system, the prelude to the creation of life and freedom.

Having written their manifesto, the 15 (two of them women) broke into the complex, which housed more than 30 Chicago draft boards, stuffed 50 sacks full of files of draft notices, then dragged the sacks into the alley, doused them with gasoline and set fire to them. Instead of fleeing, the militants stood around the fire singing religious songs until they were arrested.

The same issue of the *Plain Rapper* carried many other reports of similar actions, and in tones that made clear the writers' leanings. An enclosed supplement on "The Imperial University" featured several articles that linked the campus with the military-industrial complex: a sketch of the military-university research complex, a report on capitalist involvement in the Third World suggesting that universities served corporate interests, an article showing how some of Stanford's activities were tied to firms in the nearby industrial park, a report on the Spring 1969 militancy at Stanford, and an article alleging that the Urban Coalition served the ends of business at home, just as U. S. diplomacy and the U. S. military served those same ends abroad.

Much of the issue was made up of investigative reporting. Many of the conclusions, however, rested heavily upon the convictions of the authors. For example, the report on the Urban Coalition stated:

> Two factors motivated these men to discuss urban problems. One was a simple desire to cool the explosive situation in America's ghettoes. Of equal importance was the desire to tap a potentially rich socio-economic market.

The latter point might be true, but the author's statement was the only evidence offered.

The *Plain Rapper* and similar papers often relied upon their readers' faith that what was being presented was gospel. Thus, they must usually be content with "convincing" only those who are already convinced.

Perhaps they can argue that spelling out self-evident truths would be like explaining why two plus two equals four.

In any event, the reader who wishes to learn the true depths of the outrage inflaming many of the nation's youth is not likely to understand either its depths or its dimensions unless he reads a paper like this one.

FREEDOM NEWS

If the *Plain Rapper* sometimes seemed to encompass every subject even remotely connected with the Vietnam war, it was single-minded compared with the *Freedom News*. Once known as the *Peace and Freedom News*—and once strongly linked to the Peace and Freedom Party—the paper apparently tries to cover everything in Alameda and Contra Costa counties that is ignored by the conservative Richmond *Independent* and Oakland *Tribune*. That gives it a wide range.

Almost entirely the product of Elizabeth and Meyer Segal, the *Freedom News* probably feels a kinship to those who write and edit the *Bay Guardian;* but the relationship is limited to sharing a broad liberal-radical doctrine. The *Freedom News* is more wildly varied than the other papers. The issue of April 1969, for example, began with a tribute to Martin Luther King on the anniversary of his death. Then came an attack on the Nixon Administration, a report on the activities of Women Strike for Peace, and a story on the troubles of Sam Warda, a bus driver charged with removing fallout shelter signs from public buildings. This much was predictable fare.

But the next page presented two long articles on pipeline bombings in the East Bay hills. Then came "A Special Education Supplement" that was something more than the title suggested: it was interspersed with stories on the Sierra Club, on an oil workers' strike and on half a dozen other subjects that seemed to have little to do with education. This was followed by other education stories and an unclassifiable variety: a short report on a Negro youth who was to represent the East Bay in the National Speech Championships, a speculative story on the successor to the district attorney, a minor item on a retiring San Francisco police lieutenant's advice to fellow officers ("Smile"), and long reports on local censorship and local elections.

The unity of much of this melange was purely negative: *Freedom News* readers couldn't get the material anywhere else—certainly not at the length the *News* presented it.

It is especially true that readers are not likely to see as many Black faces in other newspapers as appear in almost every issue of the *Freedom News*. There are white faces as well—perhaps more white than Black—

but the *News*'s coverage is clearly the Bay Area's most thoroughly integrated.

In the end, the value of the *Freedom News* springs from its emphasis on providing what other newspapers ignore. Where else can a reader find an "Air Pollution Award of the Month" with pictures of the first-place winners—the Albany dump and the Phillips Refinery at Avon—belching smoke into the region's air?

The Opinion Columns

There was a time, not so long ago, when the opinion columns in many a newspaper were as forthright as a kick in the teeth. "The trouble with the Baptists is that they aren't held under water long enough," alleged one editorial writer. Another commented: "Tallulah Bankhead barged down the Nile as Cleopatra last night—and sank."

Those who lament the opinion columns' loss of pungency can place the blame wherever they like across a wide spectrum of causes ranging from the disappearance of the frontier spirit to the departure of incisive newspapermen into novel writing and the theater. They may even blame the dead seriousness that afflicts some of the young journalists who, having been told that newspapering is no longer a game, but has become A Responsibility, reason that writing must be grimly humorless.

But the most accurate judgment may be the simplest: when a reporter becomes a columnist or an editorial writer, he is likely to settle at his desk and forget that reporting is the basis of most effective journalism. He merely thinks, mulling a clipping that represents someone else's work, then commenting upon it. He may weave neat phrases for a time, until the arrival of a deadline invites a platitude. But he is not likely to investigate first, then think and write. This is not true of every editorial writer or columnist, of course, but it is true of far too many.

In order to place Bay Area opinion writing in context, one should first look at the current habits of most American newspapers. During recent years, many publishers and editors have become concerned, if not nervous, about the monopoly power inherent in the single-newspaper-town situation. Accordingly, even their editorial pages have become less partisan. Some of those with liberal leanings are now careful to publish at least a few syndicated columnists who lean the other way. Some with conservative leanings seek liberal columnists. This lends a semblance of balance. But many editorial pages are still frankly partisan.[1]

The Question of Availability

Does the effort to balance syndicated columnists, right and left, please readers? Not all of them. The problem begins with defining terms.

---

[1] It is true that several distinguished newspapers—and many, like the Chicago *Tribune,* which do not deserve the adjective—have distinctively unbalanced editorial pages. The Arkansas *Gazette,* which is in many respects an excellent newspaper, publishes columnists whose political tone is remarkably like that of locally written editorials, in keeping with the desire of the publisher to instruct his readers in one stentorian voice. Although some of the New York *Times* columnists quarrel with each other in print on occasion, and the editorial writers are sometimes out of step with *Times* columnists, the editorial page is hardly balanced.

92

Doctrinaire liberals—especially those on the fringe of the radical movements—doubt that there is a consistently liberal columnist outside the underground newspapers. On the other hand, the devout conservative who holds to the tenets expressed by Russell Kirk in *The Conservative Mind* would probably doubt that American syndicates have offered a consistently and devotedly conservative columnist since the late Westbrook Pegler was fired by Hearst. From such perspectives, there are no syndicated columnists who can be used to balance an editorial page because there is no one who can be placed at either end of the spectrum.

The problem of liberal-conservative balance is complicated by other factors. An editor who decides on a policy of balance may find that acceptable columnists are unavailable to him. Metropolitan papers often buy up the right to publish syndicated columnists in their areas, foreclosing publication by other metropolitan papers and smaller papers in the same territory.

Thus, an editor may decide to balance a liberal like Jack Anderson with a conservative like James Kilpatrick. He may then discover that Anderson and Kilpatrick are either unavailable or too expensive. He is able to buy and publish the column by Max Lerner, a liberal, and David Lawrence, a conservative. So instead of publishing a digger like Anderson and a cogent writer like Kilpatrick, the editor offers Lerner, who is fuzzy and pretentious, and Lawrence, who probably has not hit on a good idea for a generation.

Moreover, the editor who would like to publish James Reston's column, or Russell Baker's, finds that he must buy the entire New York Times News Service in order to get them. Any newspaper of consequence should use the Times News Service, but it is expensive, and it is often monopolized by those territorial-rights contracts so dear to metropolitan dailies.

The Voices of Dissent

Today, even an editor who avoids offering diverse opinions on the editorial page is usually careful to open his letters-to-the-editor columns to dissenting voices. If he actually provides an open forum in a substantial letters column, his own biases in editorials and column selection may not matter so much. Survey after survey has shown that letters are among the most carefully read features of any newspaper.

Does this mean that a fair-minded editor allows anyone to write at any length on any subject? No, it is obvious from many experiences that extremists, kooks and those who thirst for personal publicity flourish in such a setting—and offend other readers. The editor tries to apply a rule of reason. (Unfortunately, a fairly popular rule among some editors limits regular correspondents to one letter a month, no matter how sensibly and cogently they may write. This hardly seems reasonable when the editor propagates his own views every day.)

How does a newspaper play fair with those who oppose its policies? One distinguished editor said that he leans over backward all day long, mutters to himself that he is human and thus biased, and plays up letters from those who hold opposing views. The fair-minded editor also quells his itch to respond to the opinions of letter-writers. This does not mean that he never writes an editor's note in the letters column. Errors of fact must be corrected. If a correspondent argues that Senator Eugene McCarthy must be supported for the presidency in 1972 because McCarthy did so much to root Communists out of the State Department 20 years ago, the responsible editor must, in the public interest, note the difference between the late Senator Joseph McCarthy of Wisconsin and Senator Eugene McCarthy of Minnesota. But the editor should not respond in the letters column with a caustic note to a letter-writer who argues that Joe McCarthy purified the State Department. (Having studied McCarthyism, we doubt that the senator did much more than whip up hysteria against innocent people. But as editors considering such a letter, we would sigh and publish it.)

There is more to the philosophy of balance of opinion in many of today's newspapers, and some of it is unfortunate. Certainly, the growing reluctance on the part of editorial writers (or their superiors) to say much that is pointed makes many an editorial page increasingly useless. Some editorial writers argue, rather defensively, that they do not have all the answers, and that there is room on their pages for interpretation as well as advocacy. The point is well taken; interpretation and analysis are useful tools. Yet there is a strong suspicion that this statement is more often an excuse than an explanation. Certainly, it does not explain all the editorial salutes to Flag Day, Mother's Day and the Fourth of July. Perhaps this ought to be the rule of thumb: if an editorial writer has little or nothing to say, he should not write an editorial.

Few writers seem to be aware of the possible benefits of such a rule. In its absence one sees almost everywhere a mushy series of diffuse statements. So innocuous are most locally written editorial columns that the good ones—like those in the Washington *Post* and the St. Louis *Post-Dispatch*—are made to seem great.

With some notable and notorious exceptions, then, this is an opinion-writing era when most newspapermen believe that their freedom must be flavored with both responsibility and caution. It is not very exciting, especially if measured against an earlier era of personal journalism, when the editor and his most responsive critic might carry horsewhips. Only the underground newspapers, the new college dailies, and the radical sheets—and only a few of these—reach the level of passion and invective that characterized some of the old thunderers. We long for a more vivid note than most of the conventional newspapers strike today, although we suspect that journalism and the American people have probably gained something, even while losing color and pungency.

Where do Bay Area newspapers fit in this picture? To make a judgment, for nearly three months (roughly December 23, 1968–March 4, 1969) we read the editorial page, and the page opposite the editorial page, in each of the 10 newspapers sketched in pages 28–69: the San Francisco *Chronicle*, San Francisco *Examiner*, Oakland *Tribune*, San Jose *Mercury* and *News*, San Mateo *Times*, Berkeley *Gazette*, Vallejo *Times-Herald*, Palo Alto *Times*, and Santa Rosa *Press-Democrat*. Because some local columnists who write on general subjects are not published on either the editorial page or the op. ed. page (Herb Caen, for example) we read their columns as well. On the basis of our reading, we offer here some highly subjective judgments on letters-to-the-editor policy, columnists and editorial writers.

Letters to the Editor

We could judge certain aspects of these contributions in only a general way. Not being able to poll all those who have written letters to local newspapers, for example, we had no way of knowing how many and what kinds of letters have been rejected. We know that every Bay Area newspaper has published at least occasional letters fiercely opposed to the publisher's policy. All of the executives and journalists we interviewed maintained that they seek out opposing opinions. Undoubtedly, some letters that cut too close to the bone have been rejected. Frail humans will rationalize such actions with the easy explanation that another correspondent covered the same point, or the letter wasn't in good taste, or there was a possibility of libel—especially because at least one of these flaws is apparent in many of the letters that are received.

Some Bay Area newspapers refused to print letters supporting political candidates, on the ground that the supporters of many candidates would flood the letters column. These editors were, in effect, confessing their inability or unwillingness to select and publish the really good, the pointed and meaningful letters. In short, they were confessing their inability to edit—or their fear of the consequences of editing. Some local editors also refused to publish letters that quarreled with points of view expressed in editorials. They were thus unable to carry on a dialogue with their readers except by telephone, as they attempted to explain why certain letters cannot be published.

It seems axiomatic that such policies result in dull cut-and-dried material that is a poor excuse for a letters column. The editor who argues that opening the column to political advocacy will cause it to be inundated with letters should consider whether his paper rules out political advertising on the same ground. If it does not, he is in the peculiar position of allowing his readers a voice in local political matters only if they pay to be heard.

Some editors argued that a letters column open to correspondence supporting political candidates would enable shrewd politicians to organize letter-writing campaigns that would give them an undue advantage over their opponents. Again, however, an editor's job is to edit, and such an argument is a confession of his inability to do his job. Reflection might suggest, too, that candidates with insufficient funds for lavish billboard, television and newspaper advertising campaigns might be able to reach their constituents through the letters column, at little cost. It is doubtful that this would subvert democracy.

Nearly every Bay Area newspaper was guilty of publishing too few letters, and some papers also gave them little prominence. Our suggestion: let the editors study the readership surveys. These show that letters are far more widely and intensely read than editorials. Then let the editors attempt to justify the size of type, the headlines, the placement and the space given letters, compared with editorials. (This may be the clearest symptom of the inertia that afflicts much of journalism. Letters have always been published this way, so. . . .)

Daily Columnists

We could not assess in more than general terms the local-interest columns that could only be described as parochial pillars of tidbits. At their worst, they were riddled with the names of readers who only motored to Denver or Portland. At their best, they were made up of wry little ancedotes about local people and happenings. Because we did not live in each of the communities served by these columns, we were unable to assess their local value.

We can wonder about the style of most of them, which seems to be in Early Wisecrack. It is probably unfortunate for all the other anecdotal columnists that Herb Caen's style provided such a high standard for this kind of thing. But if none of the other columns came close to Caen's, few could be called as bad as the worst, which we judged to be Dallas Wood's "The Prowler" in the Palo Alto *Times*. It was filled with feeble anecdotage and trivia—items on a par with the fillers that tell how many ocean-going ships docked at Liverpool in 1965.

SAN FRANCISCO CHRONICLE

Assessing the *Chronicle*'s opinion offerings was a headache. The *Chronicle* presents the most provocative columnists among Bay Area dailies, including so many of them that it sometimes seems to be a "viewspaper." It is also overwhelmingly unbalanced; since the death of Lucius Beebe, who could write the most outrageously reactionary judgments in winning words, not a conservative voice is now to be heard unless one counts Joseph Alsop. Finally, the *Chronicle*'s huge package of columnists may add up to little more than a ton of feathers, a possibility of which we must take some account.

The leadership of the *Chronicle*'s columnists begins with Herb Caen and Art Hoppe. It is no more rewarding to try to define Caen's qualities than it is to try to dissect a joke, but certain values are clear. Unlike many another Bay Area columnist, Caen works. We do not know whether his work consists of sitting by the telephone and taking calls that pour in from public relations men and publicity-seekers (or having someone else take them), whether he picks up half his material from friends and makes up the other half, or whether he is the all-around-town boulevardier that his column makes him seem. The important matter is that we found his column regularly packed with pointed information and anecdotes. He sometimes filled it with one of those "essays" so dear to the columnist when he is straining for something to say that day, but ordinarily his prose poems to San Francisco came only on Sundays (he writes the Sunday column the preceding Tuesday) or when he was trying to catch his breath after a vacation.

No other Bay Area columnist is as deft as Caen. Most of his writing is lean. He has an unusually sensitive ear for the quip or the anecdote that is only marginally worth printing, and he apologizes for printing it with a deprecating phrase as effective as Johnny Carson's rueful and engaging recovery line, "That was a little bit of humor there."

Caen is much more than a gossip columnist, if only because the spread and intensity of his readership gives him unusual power. He may ride a political horse for only a sentence or two, but then another sentence appears on the same theme a few days later, and an anecdote a week later—and Herb Caen's political leanings become quite clear. They are distinctively liberal.

Beyond this, it is difficult to assess his appeal. It may be enough to say that every column, no matter how frothy the subject, suggested that an active intelligence had been at work. In the terms of what Caen produces—which is the only way to judge a journalist's work—he is an excellent writer.

Hoppe, who is less widely known than Art Buchwald and Russell Baker, may be the nation's best political satirist. Although Buchwald is better known, a genuinely funny man whose column misses as often as it hits, he seems bland compared to Hoppe. Russell Baker is probably the most gifted writer of the three, but he has trouble finding themes that will carry his wry commentary. Hoppe has more ideas, and richer ideas, than either of his rivals. It is easy to suspect, too, that Hoppe is much more the political animal than Buchwald or Baker. There is an acid quality in much of his political whimsy.

Until one tries to imitate it, Hoppe's method seems ridiculously simple. He observes the foibles of humans, especially those in government, focuses on one of their more dubious enterprises, and then imagines in print that it has been carried to its absurd conclusion. The result is political commentary of a very high order.

For all their great value, Caen and Hoppe are much more writers than reporters. Some of the specialized columnists do report and are fairly substantive. Ralph Gleason on pop culture, William Hogan on books, and Terrence O'Flaherty on television—often produce rich offerings. But Merla Zellerbach (Goerner), Stanton Delapane, Charles McCabe (an elegant stylist and a readable iconoclast), often write cleverly about very little. Count Marco writes offensively about women, and manages to offend men as well. Some issues of the *Chronicle* suggested that not a columnist left the building the day before; everything was spun off the top of somebody's head, and the reader seemed to be making his way over a mountain of whipped cream.

On Saturdays, most of the fluff writers appear to be resting. There is Lester Kinsolving, who is probably the only religion columnist a non-religionist can read both comfortably and profitably. L. M. Boyd and Milton Moskowitz pack their weekend syndicated columns with facts, a few of them valuable. Unfortunately, the Saturday *Chronicle* also carries an interminable column of puffery headed "After Nightfall." It is advertising in the guise of a column, and it is inexcusable.

The *Chronicle* reader arrives at Sunday with joy. The paper's chief contribution to the Sunday *Examiner and Chronicle* (known to some as "the Exonicle") is a section labeled "Sunday Punch." As noted earlier, it carries James Reston, Nicholas von Hoffman, "T.R.B." (a column from the *New Republic* that should lead some readers to that magazine) and others almost as good. A reader could spend as much time with the "Punch" section as with all the other Sunday sections put together.

In the absence of richer material in the locally written columns, the *Chronicle* should consider either publishing or releasing some of the syndicated columns it buys and sits on. Having contracted for the New York Times News Service, the management might consider publishing more often the perceptive work of Tom Wicker and C. L. Sulzberger. It might even consider giving full space to the columns it does publish. The list down the right side of the page opposite the editorial page— Hoppe, Jack Anderson then Abigail Van Buren—is hardly presented in complete form. Anderson's column and Abby's column usually are given much more space in other papers. If more space were needed, there is no known law requiring "Dennis the Menace" and "Bobby Sox" to appear opposite the editorial page. If a light attraction seemed essential, "Bobby Sox" might be moved, leaving "Dennis" to act as the barker who lures unsuspecting customers into the sideshow.

San Francisco Examiner

Much of the opinion writing in the *Examiner* is as old-fashioned as sarsaparilla. In one of his candid moments, the late Westbrook Pegler derided himself and all the other columnists of 30 years ago who thought they could, just offhand, deliver cosmic thoughts about absolutely anything. One usually despairs of trying to find the epitome— the example that actually stands for an entire class—but on Sunday, July 13, 1969, in his *Examiner* column, "Editor's Report," William Randolph Hearst, Jr., provided the clearest imaginable case to illustrate Pegler's point. Hearst's confession of ignorance was so striking that his exact words are worth savoring:

> Never before, to the best of my recollection, has this column been devoted to a discussion of economics and the mysterious but enormous role it plays in our national welfare.
> There are two excellent reasons for this:
> A—Economics was a subject I never studied in college.
> B—From what I have observed since then there are so many conflicting theories that only experts can pretend to understand them fully, and even then there is no general agreement, much less any semblance of unity of opinion.
> Just the same, inflation and the problem of controlling it have become so important that today I thought I'd put in my two-bits worth. And even though I am a non-expert in this non-science, most everybody else is in the same canoe.
> So here goes—a collection of thoughts, offered for what they may be worth, by one who was brought up to believe the essence of a sound fiscal policy is to be neither a borrower nor a lender.

Hearst then reported that he had become both a borrower and a lender, and continued on and on through a full double column of homilies. In essence, he was saying that he knew nothing about economics, that he was brought up to respect one kind of homely philosophy and practices another, and that, somehow, all this qualified him to instruct the 640,000 readers of the Sunday _Examiner and Chronicle._ What actually qualified him was his ownership of the _Examiner_—and that may lead some of us who are marginally intrigued by things the radicals are saying to wonder about the sanctity of property rights.

Not all of Hearst's columns were so distressing, and perhaps none of those written by the other _Examiner_ columnists were. And yet threads of this kind of thing are found throughout the paper. Bob Considine, who has a choice position in the middle of the page opposite the editorial page, has long been a prize example of the glib reporter who covers sports and war and politics and space and international affairs—just anything that interests him—as though it were really possible to do all that meaningfully. The result is dismayingly superficial.

No doubt Guy Wright and Dick Nolan, the local columnists whose work appears on the page with Considine's, have many devoted followers. They are occasionally amusing and anger easily at injustice. Sometimes, though, the page dominated by Considine, Wright and Nolan featured its best offering in a column by Sidney Harris.

To the credit of the _Examiner,_ the range of columnists on its editorial page was much greater than that in the _Chronicle_ or in most of the other Bay Area papers. Carl Rowan is perceptive, if somewhat dull. William Buckley is still interesting. Max Lerner and Henry J. Taylor represent the syndicated extremes about as well as a tired old liberal and a tired old conservative can.

Often missing from this lineup was the very element the _Examiner_ is in a good position to provide: hard-working, knowledgeable reporting about politics without regard for political ideology. This capability is represented by the team of Rowland Evans and Robert Novak, whose "Inside Report" is by far the best national political column that has surfaced in the last two decades. Evans and Novak may be wrong as often as most pundits, but they know how American government functions, especially party politics, and they work very hard.

Instead of sitting with a batch of clippings and their thoughts—a process that is indulged in by too many columnists ever since Walter Lippmann showed that a superior intelligence could make it pay—Evans and Novak make phone calls, wear out shoe leather, knock on doors, and talk to the people who are at or near the centers of power. The _Examiner_ rewards them by publishing their column occasionally.

In sum, so much of what the _Examiner_ offered was so much like what was offered years ago that it is tempting to wonder whether the paper is being edited for the emerging decade. Columnists are available who know what they are writing about, and who can write clearly and interestingly. The *Examiner* should publish more of them.

OAKLAND TRIBUNE

An almost certain sign that a newspaper avoids strong opinions—or fears offering them—is the frequent appearance of signed columns by Hal Boyle, Phil Newsom, and other wire service columnists. Boyle, an AP columnist, and Newsom, who writes for UPI, have much greater freedom than most wire service writers, and yet the wire service tradition of reporting—or, in any case, avoiding editorializing—flavors all their work. They may interpret and analyze (although Boyle seldom does), they may even venture a tentative opinion on infrequent occasion. But the thrust of strong advocacy is not in them.

There were other signs that the Oakland *Tribune* backs away from advocacy. Its local-interest columnist, Bill Fiset, is intent on amusing his readers, and does it very well. A great swatch of the page opposite the editorial page is given over to "Action Line," a service column for readers. Few of the other items that made their way to that page were any more challenging than Ann Landers, whose column is a fixture there.

Moreover, the few columns that did present a point of view were always preceded by an italicized Editor's Note: "The following views are those of the authors and are presented here to give readers a variety of viewpoints. The *Tribune's* opinions are expressed only in editorials." This is not a general note standing for all syndicated columns, but is published over every syndicate offering.

Other journalists undoubtedly understand the reason for the *Tribune's* policy, but many readers are ignorant of journalistic practice. They call to ask why the editor supports the views of Ann Landers, or President Nixon or even Al Capp. The editor explains patiently that he has done no more than print their opinions. "If you don't believe it, why print it?" comes the outraged rejoinder. There is some merit, then, in a slavish spelling out of the ground rules for publishing opinions.

But when this combines with the blandness of most of the *Tribune's* offerings—and the kind of syndicated columnists the paper publishes—it causes a degree of wonder. The editorial page includes Roscoe and Geoffrey Drummond, grappling with national politics in their low-key way, Robert S. Allen and John Goldsmith reporting from the Right, and occasional columns by Flora Lewis, Henry Hazlitt, James Kilpatrick, and a clutch of little-known writers for Long Island *Newsday* and the Washington *Star*. Except for Kilpatrick, who gouges liberals fairly effectively at times, there was little that would seem likely to heat the blood of a loyal *Tribune* reader.

It was all a bit confusing. The late Joseph Knowland was said to run the *Tribune* with one hand and Alameda County with the other. His son William Knowland, the former U. S. Senator and present publisher, is reputed to have the same power, or something close to it. One would expect such strong individuals to produce a stronger paper.

San Jose Mercury and News

The San Jose papers could be considered together, and not only because they are under a single ownership. They are alike too, in an evident regard for balance of several kinds. This is not to say that they are identical twins. The *Mercury* editorial section was much more stable and interesting than that of the *News,* although it suffered from one of the *Chronicle's* chief faults: the editors trimmed columns without regard to content. One critic pointed out:

> William Buckley, for instance, simply requires a larger compass than the *Mercury* usually allows him. He is invariably winding up to make a point when the column abruptly ends. I, for one, would prefer one full Buckley column to three half-Buckleys, largely because his style demands it.

There is political balance in the *Mercury* and *News,* with left-leaning Jack Anderson appearing in the *Mercury* (and at greater length than he is given in the *Chronicle*) not far from William Buckley's "On the Right." The *News* sometimes runs perceptive David Broder of the Washington *Post,* or a similarly liberal columnist, next to William S. White, a conservative. Art Buchwald's unclassifiable wit in the *News* is balanced by that of Russell Baker, equally unclassifiable, in the *Mercury.*

There is a kind of balance, too, in the generality of the editorial page and feature page offerings of the *Mercury* and *News*—the mix of outspoken columnists, and of those who interpret and analyze. Anderson and Buckley are examples of the first kind. Alfred Friendly of the Washington *Post* and the Roscoe and Geoffrey Drummond team stand for the interpretive variety. It was difficult to judge whether these papers carried more of one kind of columnist than of the other, especially because so few columnists appeared daily that the lineup was ever-changing. The *News's* editorial pages, in fact, seemed to be constantly in flux. Certainly, however, the weight of the editorial sections of both papers leans away from advocacy, because of the frequent appearances of light offerings like "Barb," "Potomac Fever," "Inquiring Reporter," local-interest columns, and the advice column by Ann Landers. The *News* presented more of this than the *Mercury.*

Unfortunately, another kind of balance in the *News* is represented on the one hand by the incisive intelligence of a mind like David Broder's or Joseph Kraft's, and on the other by the infinite stupidity of the column headed "Dr. Crane." We presume that benighted areas exist where "Dr. Crane" could be an ornament to editorial sections. But for a newspaper in the Bay Area to feature his inanities—and guide readers to them with a line in the front-page index—is inexcusable. In a recent defense of television, Dr. Crane wrote:

> Television also helps reduce the divorce rate, as well as drunkenness and even highway fatalities! How?
> By keeping husbands at home, in front of the TV set.
> Otherwise, they'd roam to distant taverns to spend the evenings where immoral women often try to entice them and where their excessive use of liquor makes them a terrible hazard on the automobile highways.
> Remember, over 50 percent of auto deaths involve drinking drivers!

Responding to a reader named Eva who wrote to complain that her employer was consulting a psychoanalyst and urging the same treatment on his office staff, Dr. Crane wrote a column carrying these observations:

> Eva has "horse sense" or gumption.
> The basic aim of medicine is really to free humanity from the need to consult physicians.
> So the more you can learn to handle your own problems, the more money you can retain out of your pay checks! And the lower will be taxes!
> For medicare and the current mad stampede to hospitals, is zooming our tax rates dangerously high.
> Yet many people are such "Worry Warts" about their health that they squander literally BILLIONS every year on needless drugs, vitamins and medical consultation!
> Indeed, in Hollywood, it has now become a fad to have your own personal psychiatrist!

All in all, it would seem that the *Mercury* got the choice columns and the *News* got what's left. In ordinary cases of tight finances and unavailability of some columns, that might be an adequate excuse. But both the *Mercury* and the *News* can afford a better stable of columnists. A wide variety is available because they are apparently outside the territorial-rights zone of the *Chronicle* and the *Examiner*. The San Jose papers should do better.

SOME PROBLEMS IN SELECTING COLUMNS

The five metropolitan newspapers in the Bay Area have exclusive rights to a great many of the best syndicated columnists and understandably will not share their local columnists with smaller competitors.

Consequently there is not a great deal to be said about the columns in other dailies. There offerings are limited, in part, by restrictive contracts.

Most of the editors try to balance opinion columns to some extent by posing a leftist against a rightist, thus giving their readers a wider view of the world. Many of them selected the interpretive and analytical columnists, rather than those who fall heavily to one side or the other of the political spectrum. In the end, with only a limited number of columnists to present, this might be the better course. The lack of strong advocacy in columns written by some local editors and publishers suggested, however, that they might really have chosen this course because it was safer. All in all, when one considers how column selection is closely hedged in with restrictions, it is difficult to criticize the smaller Bay Area papers for what they present or fail to present.

The only remarkable aspect of local editors' column-selecting habits was their inability to recognize a superior column when it was offered. For example, two years ago Herbert Brucker, who for 19 years was editor of the editorial page of the Hartford *Courant,* began writing a column twice a week for the Palo Alto *Times.* Brucker is 70 years old, but nevertheless is the columnist who best understands what is happening among the country's youthful rebels. In column after column he has demonstrated unusual perception, without ever condoning the violence of the militants. Nor is his scope limited to the youth rebellion. Writing only twice a week, he felt constrained to say something meaningful in each column. The result was a collection of valuable insights presented in readable prose, a record that many widely syndicated columnists cannot match. But Brucker's excellent column—which is inexpensive and readily available—was published only by the Palo Alto *Times* and the Hartford *Courant.*

The obtuseness of the editors who ignore columns such as Brucker's is not really new. For years, when they have had the opportunity to buy the "Inside Report" of Rowland Evans and Robert Novak, many editors seem to have been yawning and buying Bruce Biossat, who, in turn, caused their readers to yawn. Seeking a conservative writer, they bypassed James Kilpatrick and purchased David Lawrence, whose column would be funny if he did not believe so devoutly in what he is saying.

Such habits are deplorable, although we may be oversimplifying a bit. Thus, it is granted, somewhat grudgingly, that our views may conflict with those of editors who, in trying to get the right columnists for the right space on the right days of the week, have encountered degrees of complexity not considered here. But commentators who believe that American journalism ought to rise to its best possibilities should express their opinions. In this instance, we are convinced that editors have a responsibility to overcome, as best they can, obstacles to the presentation of quality opinion columns.

Editorial Writers

If the columnists were difficult to evaluate because of their diversity, the editorial writers were much easier to judge because of their relative uniformity. No doubt they supported some excellent causes forcefully. Perhaps many agencies of government and praiseworthy civic enterprises were grateful for local editorials, and have reason to thank those who write them. Let us grant this value and its negative corollary: that some editorials have turned up irregularities and have put a stop to some undesirable practices. But when one attempts to evaluate the work of Bay Area editorial writers against high standards, the result is disappointing.

It is not that local papers failed to write intelligent editorials, or to offer interesting little commentaries on light subjects. Indeed, some editorials presented issue analyses and judgments that have been thought through carefully and expressed vigorously. For example, a long *Examiner* editorial on "The Malice Issue in Alioto Suit" clarified many of the issues incisively:

> Citizens absorbed in the continuing drama of *Look* Magazine v. Joseph Alioto, or vice versa, must surely find themselves confused by the direction and the vehemence of some of the moves made by the principals.
>
> For example it is unusual that Mayor Alioto should direct so much of his fire at Gov. Reagan. The Mayor charges that the Governor came into possession of an advance copy of the *Look* issue alleging Alioto-Mafia ties, and disseminated that copy to the news media four days before *Look*'s distribution date.
>
> And it is extraordinary that *Look,* instead of standing quietly on its article, went before television with an elaborate rebuttal to Alioto's television reply to the article.
>
> The reason for most of these moves can be found in a 1964 landmark decision of the U. S. Supreme Court entitled Sullivan v. New York *Times.* The Court said the needs of democracy require that public officials must be subject to the broadest possible criticism. Because of this need, said the Court, a public official may not successfully sue for libel even though defamatory falsehoods are uttered against him—unless he can prove actual malice. The Court defined actual malice as the uttering of a defamatory statement knowing it to be false, or uttering it with reckless disregard for whether it is false.
>
> Mayor Alioto could prove that *Look*'s charges against him were defamatory falsehoods—and still lose in court. He has to prove that *Look* knowingly and recklessly uttered defamatory falsehoods. That is his core problem, as lawyer Alioto knows and as *Look*'s lawyers know.
>
> The Mayor might get his foot in the door on the malice if he could prove the *Look* article was transmitted deliberately for political reasons

along a certain channel: from *Look* to Reagan to the public. He is trying very vigorously to do so. *Look,* responding with equal vigor, has denied that it sent an advance copy to the Governor. Instead of a simple denial, however, *Look* made a sweeping and comprehensive denial in lawyer language.

. . . . .

The crucial malice aspect helps to explain the flurry of biting charges and prompt replies on tangential matters like racial slurs, libels on the City itself, inexperienced freelancers, etc.

More important, it goes far to explain why so much of the case is being tried before the citizenry sitting at home in front of TV. This is the court of public opinion, which to a public official is very often the highest of all courts.

Probably we are witnessing, in the *Look*-Alioto moves, the emergence of a natural pattern of conduct for cases where a public official is accused and charges libel but must prove malice. As events of recent days have shown, it is a pattern producing more of the "uninhibited, robust and wide open" give-and-take that the Supreme Court sought to encourage.

Similar valuable editorials were found in other Bay Area papers: a few in the Palo Alto *Times,* a few more in the San Rafael *Independent-Journal,* at least one in every paper. Perhaps the *Chronicle* offered more than any other local daily.

Criteria for Judging Editorials

In judging editorials, we looked for consistent value. We looked for grace of expression, clarity of writing, singularity of theme and purpose and vigor of opinion. If an editorial advocates, it should do so unmistakably. If it explains or interprets or analyzes, the writer should present more than a reporter can in the news columns. If he does not, why use editorial space that way?

Perhaps above all, we asked that editorial writers not waste their time and ours by presenting an issue in the manner of a news story, and then tacking on a short paragraph praising or vilifying the principal figure in the case. If the reader is swayed by a sentence or so of flimsy judgment, he is persuaded for a very poor reason: because an editorial writer says so. Such editorials are little better than salutes to Flag Day: they fill space. Unfortunately, Bay Area newspapers featured more of these than of the other kind, i.e. editorials presenting close argument and thoughtful opinion.

There was also a curious absence of force and passion in most editorials. We do not believe that any considerable number of editorials should be shrill, but it was possible to go for months without reading a single editorial whose tone indicated unmistakably that the writer really cared about what he was saying. Thus it was a pleasure to read

Scott Newhall's editorial reaction to a public Board of Education meeting in 1969 on the volatile issue of busing-integration. A number of citizens and a *Chronicle* photographer at the meeting were beaten by small groups of thugs opposed to the busing plan. The attackers escaped unidentified. Newhall's editorial called the men "self-appointed heirs of Hitler's brownshirts," "professional thugs" and "intellectually underprivileged . . . overnourished apes." He concluded with a challenge:

> The members of this band of social neanderthals are obviously too insecure and too frightened to come forward and identify themselves. But, if they miraculously should care to do so, they can either call GA 1-1111, extension 463, or come to this writer's office, which is Room 332 on the third floor.
>
> On the other hand, if this phantom squad of bullies cares to take umbrage at these remarks and wishes to continue its typical cowardly and disgraceful activities, it can catch the executive editor of this paper almost any week night on the darkened Fifth street sidewalk at the side entrance to the *Chronicle*. He leaves the building at approximately 8 p.m. each evening on his way home.
>
> Or, if they prefer, they can catch him quite alone in his San Francisco residence. The address is 1050 Northpoint Street. Simply ask the doorman for Apartment 708 and you will be escorted to the elevator.

We are far from suggesting that many editorials be written so pugnaciously. But it is refreshing on occasion to read an editorial that does not seem, like most of them, to have emerged from some institutional ooze.

Why Many Editorials Are Innocuous

The cause of editorial innocuousness is quite clear. An editorial writer usually finds himself in the position of the public information officer in Vietnam who is not altogether certain how far he should go in telling the truth when briefing reporters on military events. Not quite knowing how much the general would say, he plays it safe and says very little. The general might actually be more candid—although he must also play it safe and say less than his immediate superior might say, and his superior must try to guess how much the President would say in similar circumstances—but the poor staff officer cannot be certain. This is the chief reason reporters would rather talk to generals than to staff officers, and in city hall to the mayor rather than to his press secretary, or in Washington to the President rather than to the presidential press secretary.

Like the staff officer, the editorial writer may be given full instructions, usually by the editor, before he goes to work. But the editor is probably not available at the moment of composition, when the writer is putting thoughts into words. Moreover, a publisher probably looms behind the editor, and perhaps a board of directors behind the publisher. They are not always threatening figures, but they can be.

Even when the system allows an editorial writer to submit his work for clearance, removing the ultimate responsibility from him, he is not really his own man doing his own work. But this is a far better system for most writers than having to write editorials and send them directly to the composing room for printing. Such a system is almost certain to produce a number of cautious editorials; the writer tries to imagine what the objections from on high might be.

Whatever the system, if two or three figures do not loom behind the writer, the newspaper as an Institution does. Such a presence inhibits some editors-in-chief, and may even affect publishers who write their own editorials. Who can really do his best work as the voice of an Institution?

These are all stifling influences, and they make some recent changes in European journalism quite understandable. There, a good many editors—as well as sub-editors and reporters—will work for a newspaper only if the management grants them absolute freedom. In effect, they have an agreement enabling them to write as they wish, at least for the life of the contract.

The malaise of editorial pages has other causes, some just as basic. For example, institutions change more slowly than individuals. Now that we are in a period of revolution, it is not surprising that newspapers are slower to catch up than some of the reporters and the syndicated columnists.

The newspapers and their editorial columns begin with a heavy handicap. The institutions of American society are under attack, and newspapers are substantial institutions. Not only that, other institutions look to them to lead in preserving the status quo. In such circumstances, it is not surprising that even the great newspapers have only a hazy and obscured vision of the future, during this period of unprecedented institutional challenge. They are understandably slow to admit the deep fissures of hypocrisy in American culture and rhetoric, and they are quick to focus on the clearly reprehensible tactics of the militants who are trying to effect changes.

The Curious Case of Three Papers

We have noted a curious fact: the three Bay Area newspapers that are published in the home territory of the most active radicals—the San Francisco *Examiner* (San Francisco State College), the Berkeley *Gazette* (University of California), and the Palo Alto *Times* (Stanford University), often demonstrated the least editorial understanding. Perhaps this was because they have seen the militants at their most active worst. On the other hand, they also have had the best opportunity to talk to the radicals, and to try to discover what is on their minds—as well as what is in their hands. By pursuing this course, the papers might be able to write informatively about interesting facts: even though demands 1, 3, 7, 9, and 15 are either impossible of accomplishment or patently undesirable, 2, 4, 5, 6, 8, and 10 through 14 are reasonable and go to the heart of real failures of the university. Campus administrators may admit that the militants are right on these points. The editorial writers might also reflect on the fact that, whatever view one takes of militant tactics—and our view is that most of their tactics are witless and counter-productive—they often succeed. It is at least possible that the successes of the militants are decidedly temporary. It may be that the coming backlash will produce an oppressive atmosphere. But meanwhile those whose mission it is to think in print should weigh a sober question: Does anyone seriously believe that the structure of universities will be the same five years hence as it was last year?

The editorial writers might even go from there and listen to radical charges against American society. They would be likely to discover much the same thing they would have discovered about radical claims and charges against universities; some of the demands are impossible or the charges absurd, but many also point to demonstrable flaws and failures.

Finally, the writers might explore the history of revolution. With such homework, they could introduce perplexed readers to some of the thinkers who have reflected on violence, as well as to some of the behavioral scientists and philosophers who are attempting to dissect it. The next step would be to explain why so few of the "good" students are rising in protest against the interruption of their education. (To oversimplify, the explanation is that so many relatively apathetic students sympathize with the major demands—while deploring both other demands and the tactics of their fellow students—that they cannot in conscience oppose a movement promising to correct basic injustices.)

Bay Area editorial writers thus have had ample opportunity to deal more informatively with violence and protest. Perhaps they have investigated, and either have made or have failed to make the discoveries that seem to us so obvious. In any event, the results of neither judgment appeared in their work—perhaps because of the constraints mentioned earlier.

The most notable fact is that local editorial writers are not taking advantage of excellent opportunities to learn more about a great many matters beyond the youth rebellion. Three universities—Stanford,

Northwestern and Harvard—offer journalists a paid opportunity to come to campus and study anything they like for periods of up to a year. Few local editorial writers even bother to apply, presumably either because they are not interested, or because their employers will not let them go. When Stanford offered a free five-day conference on the "Second American Revolution" in June 1969, with a series of excellent lectures by authorities both in and outside academic life, Bay Area editorial writers were not among the participants. Similarly, when Stanford recently embarked on a unique and distinguished one-day-a-month seminar dealing with the problems of California's largest and least understood minority group, Mexican-Americans, representatives of the press were conspicuous by their scarcity.

This lack of evidence that editorial writers are interested in improving their product tempts us to side with the critic who held that few of them are much more than "tired reporters." In fairness, some of the obstacles we have pointed out as looming in the path of effective editorial writing may simply be too formidable. But in closing we again look at the editorials in the Washington *Post* and in the St. Louis *Post-Dispatch*—and envy their regular readers.

Case Study: Student Unrest

In assessing the performance of a number of papers in one area it was essential to find an issue common to all, thus permitting comparison. In the Bay Area this meant finding an issue with salience in such widely separated communities as San Jose and Vallejo. Student unrest was such an issue. It proved to be the most significant local story from December 1968 through April 1969, when violence exploded on campuses in many parts of the Bay Area. The situation at San Francisco State College was considered so important that papers of all sizes in all nine counties carried daily stories on activities there, and nearly the same level of coverage was given to the Berkeley Third World Liberation Front troubles.[1] Stanford University, San Jose State College, College of San Mateo, Solano College (in Vallejo), and the various locals of the American Federation of Teachers were all confronted with student unrest in the period studied.

While it was trying for police, politicans and reporters, this widespread activism was a press critic's dream. Over an 18-week period, from December 1968 through April 1969, the authors made content analyses of 10 Bay Area newspapers (see App. IV B for the choice of papers) to determine the quality of Bay Area press coverage. Extensive interviews were conducted with editors and reporters involved in the stories. The study also presented an opportunity to weigh the charges from all sides that the press was either being used by, or was catering to, students, politicans or administrators.

Although Paul Conroy, managing editor of the San Jose *News,* preferred to interpret criticisms from both sides as an indication of objective reporting, this was clearly wishful thinking. It has long been a comfortable philosophy in journalism that being hit from both sides indicates that the paper is playing it just right: straight down the middle. But it is also possible that being hit from both sides means that the reporting is so bad that everyone is outraged. The nation's press labored mightily to cover the difficult issue of unrest, and Bay Area papers have borne more than their share of such assignments. The press has heavy responsibilities, because it is often the only means of communication between dissident groups; along with television, it is the most important information source for the general public. As the nation's press corps most experienced in covering student unrest, Bay Area journalists should have some lessons to teach.

---

[1] The TWLF was the name given to a loose coalition of Blacks, Chicanos and other minority groups.

111

Dimensions of the Story

The single most important aspect of the student demonstration story was its longevity: 15 weeks of constant activity at San Francisco State; an equal period of sporadic activity at U. C. Berkeley and San Jose State; a two-week uprising at College of San Mateo. Bay Area papers plunged in and gave this story more space—much of it on the front pages—than any other issue, either local or national. *Chronicle* reporter Dale Champion has said, "Our file on San Francisco State

TABLE 3

STUDENT UNREST: COLUMN INCHES IN SIX BAY AREA DAILIES[2]

FEBRUARY 17–MARCH 4, 1969

Paper	Column Inches	
	Total	Ave. per Day
Berkeley *Gazette*	1667	119.1
San Francisco *Chronicle*	1531	109.4
Oakland *Tribune*	1419	101.4
San Francisco *Examiner*	1387	99.1
San Jose *Mercury*	871	62.2
Vallejo *Times-Herald*	683	48.0

[2] To make the content analyses more manageable in the time at our disposal, we selected from the 10 Bay Area dailies the big four (omitting the San Jose *News*), and added the Berkeley *Gazette* and the Vallejo *Times-Herald* for the sake of comparison.

looks like the file for World War II." Thus, a second aspect of the student unrest story was its sheer bulk, as measured in column inches published.

Table 3 presents the total number of inches six Bay Area dailies devoted to student stories. The period under study extended from February 17 to March 4, 1969, a time when San Francisco State, U. C. Berkeley, and San Jose State were all experiencing trouble. The totals included pictures and headlines.

Tables 4 and 5 give the column inches devoted to the Vietnam war (Saigon, Washington and Paris datelines) and the Pueblo investigation during the same time period. Figures from the New York *Times* are included for comparison.

Thus, during the period included in the sample, it was also possible to see the ratio between space devoted by the six Bay Area papers to student unrest and to the Vietnam war. The *Gazette* gave heaviest preponderance to the student story: 8.5 (student) to 1 (Vietnam). Next came the *Chronicle* with 4.5 to 1; the Vallejo *Times-Herald* with 3.9 to 1; the *Examiner* with a little over 3.1 to 1; and the Oakland *Tribune* with nearly 2.5 to 1. Last was the *Mercury* with 2.2 to 1.

The Pueblo investigation was a story of national importance carried by newspapers all across the country. This is the way the six Bay Area dailies allocated their space in comparison with the news play of the New York *Times* and with each other.

TABLE 4
VIETNAM WAR: COLUMN INCHES IN SIX BAY AREA DAILIES
AND THE NEW YORK TIMES
FEBRUARY 17–MARCH 4, 1969

Paper	Column Inches	
	Total	Ave. per Day
New York *Times*	916	65.5
Oakland *Tribune*	570	40.7
San Francisco *Examiner*	439	31.4
San Jose *Mercury*	402	28.7
San Francisco *Chronicle*	388	24.1
Berkeley *Gazette*	194	13.9
Vallejo *Times-Herald*	171	12.2

TABLE 5
PUEBLO INVESTIGATION: COLUMN INCHES IN SIX BAY AREA DAILIES
AND THE NEW YORK TIMES
FEBRUARY 17–MARCH 4, 1969

Paper	Column Inches	
	Total	Ave. per Day
New York *Times*	427	30.5
San Jose *Mercury*	285	20.3
Vallejo *Times-Herald*	277	19.8
San Francisco *Examiner*	175	12.5
Oakland *Tribune*	143	10.2
San Francisco *Chronicle*	110	7.8
Berkeley *Gazette*	68	4.8

Some of the variance in space allocation is attributable to differences between morning and afternoon papers. Also the student demonstrations were local, while the Vietnam and Pueblo stories were available by wire service only. Nevertheless, there is no question that the Bay Area papers devoted an extraordinary amount of space to the student protest story. In addition, the *Chronicle, Examiner, Tribune* and *Gazette* carried at least one front-page student story every day during the two-week period. The *Mercury* also carried a page one story every day for 10 days; and the *Times-Herald* carried stories 13 of the 14 days, 11 times on page one. Neither Vietnam nor the Pueblo investigation received such treatment. Even President Nixon's trip to Europe, which came during this period, was given less space than the student demonstrations.

Despite the massive, day-to-day coverage, the papers had a difficult time presenting the daily events in a context that made sense of the whole. This is the most difficult aspect of reporting a continuing story, whether it is a war, a strike, a trial or a demonstration. This problem was exacerbated by the large number of groups speaking to the public and contending for power, from Governor Reagan and the State College Trustees, to President Hayakawa of San Francisco State College and the many student organizations.

Issues Left Unresolved

The difficulty of providing continuity in complex and rapidly changing situations was exemplified by the fact that many issues were left unresolved in the newspaper articles from one day to the next. During the period February 3 to 7, 1969 (chosen at random) the *Chronicle* left 12 separate issues unresolved: on February 3, for example, President Hayakawa said he would reinstate striking teachers if they returned to classes on February 17, when the new semester was to begin. On February 4 the striking teachers said they would respond to Hayakawa on February 6. On February 5 the *Chronicle* reported that it was unclear whether teachers would obey a new restraining order to stop the strike, or even whether the order would be enforced. On the 7th Hayakawa informed the striking faculty who had lost their jobs that they would be rehired if they applied by February 10. Union president Gary Hawkins replied the union "probably would respond today."

And so it went with unresolved stories and events; deadlines, counter-deadlines, court dates, postponements, continuances and threatened demonstrations. The Oakland *Tribune* had eight such issues pending during the same time period for the Third World Liberation Front (TWLF) strike at Berkeley. The Berkeley *Gazette* had six. It is obvious that this caused confusion for readers, who were forced to juggle as many as a dozen events during a week or more, in order to keep things straight in only one of the strikes.

The problem was not so much that the papers did not try to fit all the pieces together—they did try—but the nature of the strike was not adaptable to the traditional demands of newspaper deadlines, pressures for new leads, and spot statements made in response to other spot statements. Most editors failed to realize that the reporting of every policy statement, demand and threat came to be counterproductive, because the reader was overwhelmed by meaningless detail. Probably not one Bay Area reader in a hundred could give even the barest outline of what happened month by month at San Francisco State. Said the *Chronicle*'s Bill German, "I'm now leaning away from reporting all the nitty-gritty specifics of all the policy statements and meetings in an SFS-type crisis. . . . I want to present the bigger picture, the larger story . . ."

The "Bridge" Story and the "No News" Story

In an effort to establish continuity, papers have developed two kinds of stories. The first is a "bridge" story, designed to keep the reader up to date. Such stories are almost always from wire services. A UPI story appeared in the San Mateo *Times* on January 2. The head was "Classes at SFS Due to Resume Monday."

> Classes are scheduled to resume Monday at San Francisco State College —and militant student groups have vowed to resume a strike which has resulted in turmoil and violence on campus since Nov. 6.
> Leaders of the Third World Liberation Front and Black Students' Union have scheduled a strike rally Sunday night at Glide Memorial Methodist Church.
> Meanwhile, mediators Ronald Haughton and Samuel Jackson planned to meet today with representatives of the college, the American Federation of Teachers and State College Trustees.
> Members of Mayor Joseph Alioto's citizens' committee, formed to find a solution to the campus problems, also planned to meet today.
> The AFT is demanding improved working conditions, a bigger voice in administrative matters and granting of 15 demands made by the TWLF and BSU.
> The teachers' union, which represents about 300 of San Francisco State's 1,100 faculty members, has threatened to strike Monday if the issues are not resolved. The AFT also has urged teachers at the 15 other state colleges to join the strike.
> Formal opposition to the threatened AFT strike has come from the 115,000 member California State Employees' Association.
> Association President Robert Carlson, who charged the AFT was capitalizing upon campus unrest to "gain by force what it failed to gain by persuasion," said members of his group would not honor AFT picket lines.

Of what use is such an article? To those who have given even minimal attention to the strike it presented no new information, no new perspective. To those not familiar with the strike, it was much too rudimentary. Indeed, as an introduction it was positively dangerous: only an anti-AFT source was quoted; student demands were only hinted at; and there was no indication of what issues Haughton and Jackson were negotiating. It was a filler article designed to keep SFS in the news; this was hardly necessary in light of the hundreds of inches devoted to the story each week.

The second type of story cloaks in a maze of unimportant information the fact that nothing happened on campus today. On December 28 the *Chronicle* ran a 30-inch piece headlined "The Crucial S. F. State Mediation Talks Begin." The key phrase came in the third paragraph: "... Ronald Haughton, the mediator ... *declined to comment* on the discussions." [emphasis supplied] That was the only real news in the piece. Seven paragraphs were devoted to who attended the meetings, plus the meetings of Mayor Alioto's citizens' committee; three paragraphs to a statement by Bishop Mark D. Hurley on what the committee hoped to do; and the remainder sketched strike background. Substantive articles on negotiations were rare. But articles about the arrangements for negotiations were many, and almost pointless.

TABLE 6

CAMPUS PROBLEMS AND THE U. C. REGENTS' MEETING:
COLUMN INCHES IN NINE BAY AREA DAILIES
January 18, 1969

Paper	Inches	Stories
San Francisco *Chronicle*	265	12
San Jose *News*	171	7
San Francisco *Examiner*	148	6
Oakland *Tribune*	124	8
Berkeley *Gazette*	123	7
Vallejo *Times-Herald*	111	8
San Jose *Mercury*	89	7
San Mateo *Times*	71	5
Palo Alto *Times*	25	3

Focus on Confrontation

Part of the blame for the inadequate strike coverage, despite the massive amount of copy, could be attributed to the news judgment of editors. All preferred to focus on confrontation rather than negotiation, and on headknocking rather than attitude changing. The greater the violence on campus—this was particularly true in San Jose and Berkeley—the more space the story was given. An excellent example of this news ethic occurred on January 17, 1969, when the U. C. Regents, including Governor Reagan, met at Berkeley to discuss University problems. Press stories noted that the Governor was jeered by students, a youngster made an obscene gesture at police, eggs were thrown at the Reagan limousine and glass was broken in University Hall. Incidentally, a number of important decisions were made at the Regents' meeting itself.

Table 6 shows that there was no lack of will or space to report the Regents' meeting at Berkeley. But what was the emphasis of this coverage?

Only the two San Francisco dailies put the disorderly incidents surrounding the meeting in the proper perspective. The *Chronicle* ran three stories: one 26-inch story on page one by Ron Moskowitz which described an important item on the agenda—the Regents' plan for overhauling the investment policies for the University's portfolio. On page eight another story of 17 inches appeared on the meeting; also on page eight Don Wegars covered the disorders in 18 inches. The *Examiner*'s education writer Lance Gilmore wrote a detailed, 63-inch, page one story on the meeting, placing particulars of the disorders in six paragraphs in the middle of the piece. Gilmore's excellent story was the best of the coverage.

The San Jose *Mercury* ran a first-page picture filling 28 column inches, showing demonstrators chasing the Reagan limousine with eggs. The story explaining the picture appeared on page 43 and was three and a quarter inches long! On results of the meeting, the *Mercury* presented 15 inches on page five from the Los Angeles Times-Washington Post News Service. The San Jose *News*, the Ridder afternoon paper having much circulation overlap with the *Mercury*, ran the same egg-throwing picture on page one with a 25-inch story combining both egg throwing and meeting results.

The Oakland *Tribune* ran a 12-inch, page one story under the head "Reagan Escapes UC Mob," accompanied by a 24-column-inch picture. The *Tribune*'s account of the meeting appeared on page three—13 inches long. Parts of the *Tribune*'s "mob" story were too dramatic to go unquoted:

> The governor, neatly attired in a black suit, hair immaculately coiffeured, emerged from University Hall relaxed and smiling to face several hundred long-haired students who had remained outside of a fenced parking lot where his Continental was parked for four hours.
> One car in the lot had already been pelted with eggs and two eggs smashed into the side of the governor's automobile as he came into view. Reagan waved cheerily as the crowd screamed obscenities and climbed inside while police pushed an opening in the throng. . . .
> Seeing the (governor's) vehicle stopped, the crowd suddenly surged into the street and went racing after it.
> The screaming mob had almost caught up when the light changed and the car moved along another block, only to get caught in some traffic.
> Sensing the possibilities, the mob poured down the middle of the street, raced through the light, which had turned red again, and were within a few feet of the car when an opening developed in the traffic and the vehicle spurted across Shattuck Avenue and out of reach. . . .

A Region's Press

An exciting and detailed play-by-play, worthy of a Mel Allen or Dizzy Dean. If the same care had been lavished on the Regents' meeting, the story might have run to a prominent 60 or 70 inches, instead of the inside 13 it received.

Among the smaller papers, the Berkeley *Gazette* bannered "Eggs Thrown at Reagan Limousine Here." But the *Gazette* also ran two front-page stories totalling 54 inches on the meeting. The Vallejo *Times-Herald* led with the violence on page one, noting in an insert that a "related story" appeared on page two. The San Mateo *Times*, in the poorest showing of all, ran two front-page pictures of activists above the fold. A 10-inch story on page two sufficed for both demonstration and meeting coverage, the violence leading the story. The five paragraphs on the Regents were so superficial as to be meaningless. On January 18 the Palo Alto *Times* ran nothing at all on either the demonstration or the meeting.

This search for confrontation was not an isolated occurrence. On January 7 both the *Chronicle* and the Berkeley *Gazette* reported the peaceful opening of the College of San Mateo by focusing on arrests, warrants issued, and police checkpoints at the school. Not until the fifth paragraph of the *Gazette*'s story was the reader told: "Meanwhile, classes resumed without incident as 8,000 students at the racially troubled junior college returned from a two-week holiday recess . . ." There was no explanation in any paper of how the peaceful CSM opening was achieved.

Explaining and Clarifying

The problem of making sense of a continuing story, and the temptation to emphasize violence, could both have been mitigated had editors done a better job with interpretive and background stories on campus troubles. During the height of the confusion the *Chronicle* ran an editorial entitled "President and Press," which stated:

> The demands of the electronic and the printed media and their pressures are different. Television and radio have supplanted the press as the instantaneous transmitters to all corners of the world of words and deeds of statesmen. It is now the newspaper's role to explain and clarify.

Without exception, newspaper editors and executives interviewed by the authors agreed that this was indeed the role of the printed media, although some expressed mock amazement that the editorial appeared in the *Chronicle*. Many agreed that this was the role wherein newspapers had been most remiss. Said one *Chronicle* news executive, "This is the area where the *Chronicle* is most vulnerable and deserves to be criticized—for its lack of interpretive and depth coverage of the San

Francisco State crisis." But he pointed out that even the New York *Times* was guilty of the charge in its first five days of reporting the Columbia University takeover. "During the first five days the *Times* was reporting discrete events, and we were aware that they were missing the larger story—what was really going on."

Editor Mike Culbert, whose Berkeley *Gazette* has been grappling unsuccessfully with student coverage since the Free Speech Movement, agreed with the *Chronicle* editorial and added,

> There is a great frustration in realizing this need for interpretive reporting and not being able to do a thing about it. We did try to run a few pieces getting at the issues of the TWLF strike (at Berkeley) but I didn't have the resources to put on it. I would like to have had many more interpretive pieces.

Manpower problems hindering such reporting were equally severe at the San Mateo *Times* and the Vallejo *Times-Herald*.

The Oakland *Tribune*'s city editor, Roy Grimm, felt that newspapers "are making some progress in the direction of interpretation, although we have not shaken off the rush to get to the next edition." Grimm discussed a backstopping method also mentioned by *Examiner* city editor Gale Cook. Said Grimm, "If I feel we didn't do an adequate job with a story the first day, we'll follow up the next day with a story or fill in on Sunday." Cook also used Sunday as the place "to catch everyone up on what happened during the week at a more leisurely pace." In this connection, the *Chronicle*'s Champion believed that, "Every week to 10 days we should have done an analytical piece on the shifting state of events, so that the readers could get a clear assessment of it."

Harvey Yorke, Director of Public Affairs at San Francisco State College, has suggested another mechanism for upgrading the level of understanding and getting administration spokesmen "out of the propaganda business." Said Yorke,

> There needs to be a time for us to talk to newsmen without talking off the record, yet not making a story of everything that is said. We have to be able to tell them what we're thinking and planning without it showing up the next day in the paper as "The college is planning to do such-and-such."

It is a sad fact that one of the more ambitious interpretations written during the period appeared in the *Chronicle* on March 3, 1969, and came from the New York Times News Service. The *Times* had investigated the loss of faculty members at Berkeley and their return to East Coast schools because of the strike. Although the accuracy of the article has been questioned, the fact that the New York *Times* had to dig this information out in the Bay Area papers' own backyard is an unfavorable commentary on the imaginativeness of assignment editors. *Chronicle* editor Scott Newhall defended his paper by saying that "it is often easier for the *Chronicle* to run a story on Columbia than on Berkeley, because we're in the middle of it here." On the other hand, one doesn't see interpretive stories about Columbia in the *Chronicle,* or in any other Bay Area paper.

Bay Area reporters have become quite skilled in writing certain types of background and interpretive stories. The interview-profile has often been done with success. Donovan Bess of the *Chronicle* presented some valuable insights into the character and motivation of President Hayakawa in a January 2 interview at his Mill Valley home. The *Examiner's* Rush Greenlee sketched Robert Hoover, center of controversy in the College of San Mateo's Readiness Program, in a December 23, 1968, story. The *Peninsula Observer,* a now-defunct weekly in Palo Alto that covered Peninsula affairs, was even more frank in its treatment of Hoover in a number of stories in December 1968, and January 1969.

Another approach was to turn news columns over to crisis participants either for short statements on a specific subject, or for a general airing of opinion. The "silent majorities" at SFS and Berkeley were not as silent as Governor Reagan and other critics of the student population would have the public believe. On December 8 the *Examiner* asked, "Why San Francisco State?" This question was presented to key actors in the crisis: State College Trustee Louis Heilbron; student body president Russell Bass; Glenn Smith, vice president of administrative and business affairs at SFS; Journalism Professor Jerrold Werthimer and others. Unfortunately, a maximum of only five or six paragraphs was allotted to any one source, making meaningful analysis impossible. Instead, each might have been given free rein, and the stories spread out into a daily series.

A third method was to turn the reporter into a selective "television camera" to describe what the campus looked like to him; how the air was charged, and what the expressions and feelings of the participants seemed to be, both on "normal" days and crisis days. Debates between two generations were popular playlets to write. Other material included banter between demonstrators and police, graffiti, crowd descriptions and accounts of innocent bystanders caught up in the action.

Although there was certainly a need for this type of reportage, it could not replace detailed probing into student demands, the history of the institution, past administration-student battles and conflicts in current negotiations. An *Examiner* article of January 7, headlined "An Almanac of Facts on SF State Crisis," was typical of the approach to these problems. Purporting, in bold type, to offer the "background" on the strike, the 29-inch piece presented the number of injuries, suspensions, arson attempts, bombings, police costs, class days lost and various monetary details. If this is background reporting, then one need only discuss the Vietnam war in terms of military hardware costs and the number killed and wounded.

Making Sense of "Demands"

Sets of demands were printed so often in Bay Area papers that the word "demand" may have become a cue for readers to flip to the comics. Yet how often were demands annotated in depth to enable the reader to make sense of them? Take, for example, the ten BSU (Black Students' Union) demands at San Francisco State, printed below:

That all Black studies courses being taught through various other departments be immediately part of the Black Studies Department and that all the instructors in this department receive full time pay.

That Dr. Nathan Hare, chairman of the Black Studies Department, receive a full professorship and a comparable salary according to his qualifications.

That there be a Department of Black Studies which will grant a bachelor's degree in Black Studies; that the Black Studies Department, chairman, faculty and staff have the sole power to hire faculty and control and determine the destiny of the department.

That all unused slots for Black students from fall, 1968 under the special admissions program be filled in spring, 1969.

That all Black students wishing to, be admitted in fall, 1969.

That 20 full time teaching positions be allocated to the Department of Black Studies.

That Dr. Helen Bedesem be replaced from the position of Financial Aid Officer and that a Black person be hired to direct it; that Third World people have the power to determine how it will be administered.

That no disciplinary action will be administered in any way to any students, workers, teachers, or administrators during and after the strike as a consequence of their participation in the strike.

That the California State College Trustees not be allowed to dissolve any Black programs on or off San Francisco State College campus.

That George Murray maintain his teaching position on campus for the 1968–69 academic year.

These demands suggested the following questions for major newspaper treatment. (1) In what ways would the Black Studies Department differ in organization from other academic departments? (2) How long have negotiations for a Black Studies Department been going on? What progress has been made? Which parties have been impeding progress, and why? (3) What would it cost to fund the Black Studies program, and where will the money come from? What was the cost of establishing other new departments at San Francisco State? How long did it take? From where did the money come? (4) What has led to the demand for replacement of Dr. Helen Bedesem as Financial Aid Officer? Answers to these questions were not available in Bay Area newspapers.

Some other matters that did not receive fully satisfactory explanations during the period under study included the order by Chancellor Glenn Dumke to suspend George Mason Murray; the role of the Coordinating Council for Higher Education; and the growth of the BSU on the campus. One was forced to the pages of *Ramparts,* the *Peninsula Observer,* and *Crisis* (a retrospective book published by SFS journalism students) for extended discussion of these issues.

Despite the massive space devoted to the strikes, Bay Area readers are probably no better prepared to understand the next student demonstration than they were the last. Too many of the stories were given over to trivial confrontations, arrests and pseudo-event rallies. Too few of them probed the "non-negotiable" positions on both sides. The Bay Area papers made laudable efforts to capture the emotion and drama of the strike—an almost impossible task. But they shirked some of the more feasible interpretive responsibilities.

Editors' Second Thoughts on Coverage

Discussions with many of the editors revealed some of the traps into which newspapers fell, and suggested means for improving coverage. The types of reporters sent to the demonstration, for example, and the order of their dispatch, had an important effect, especially on the early information gathering. Paul Conroy of the San Jose *News* said he first sent a police reporter; after the violence subsided, he assigned an education writer to determine why it happened. Roy Grimm of the Oakland *Tribune* acknowledged that "perhaps we take too much of the police beat approach to these things, and get too involved in the running battle."

A *Chronicle* editor was convinced that "the basic pattern of covering a strike at SFS is what causes trouble." He continued,

> First you react to the story with a stringer who is on the scene, on whom you have relied in the past. Then a little violence starts and you send over some reporters who are experienced at reporting headknocking. Then you start to run the handouts from the President's office. Only late in the game do you recognize what kind of story it is and begin to report it properly.

One need not minimize or condone the violence involved in campus demonstrations, to suggest that it would be better if education writers and campus specialists such as the *Examiner*'s Phil Garlington (now covering Sacramento), Lynn Ludlow, and Lance Gilmore, the *News*'s Rick Egner and the *Chronicle*'s Ron Moskowitz, be given greater responsibility. They could take some of the burden from police reporters, stringers (usually students on the paper's payroll who supply information to the staff reporter), and plants (part-timers assigned by the paper to carry out a specific job, e.g., posing as student demonstrators. This system was used by the Berkeley *Gazette*).

The five large papers and the Berkeley *Gazette* seemed to be minimally prepared in advance with either full-timers or stringers on the campuses in their area. The *Examiner*, for example, had full-time men at San Francisco State and Berkeley, a part-timer at Stanford, plus great faith in Stanford's News Bureau chief Bob Beyers (a regard shared by many other editors). The *Mercury-News* had two reporters at San Jose State, and the *Gazette* had one and a half full-time people, four stringers, and three plants at Berkeley, in what is a massive operation for a small paper. The Palo Alto *Times* had no stringer at Stanford, however, and the *Chronicle* and *Examiner* could each spare only a reporter for one day to gather background on the Stanford sit-in. Naturally, one could hope for more education news from the campuses before a confrontation starts, but such forecasting of trouble is extremely risky, readership is low and editors have difficulty finding the space.

The Press and Student Activists

Despite some advance planning, many papers were unable to establish a rapport with student militants. "Students were oriented to the TV press conference, [rather than to the newspaper interview]" said the *Examiner*'s Gale Cook. "It was hard to get a statement from them, and when you did, you still didn't know if it was representative of campus sentiment." Kenneth Conn, executive editor of the *Mercury-News*, agreed. "It was hard to talk to student dissidents. As members of the Establishment we couldn't do it. They didn't trust us." Roy Grimm speculated that his reporters were hampered by the conservative reputation of the *Tribune*'s owner, former Senator William Knowland. Such experiences suggest a marked reversal from the Berkeley FSM (Free Speech Movement) days in 1964, when, as a former University administrator reminisced, "In those days, the students were nothing if not articulate. If they won't talk to the press now, that is a distinct change."

Because of the access problem, there was a clear superiority in coverage of the participation of the American Federation of Teachers over

A Region's Press

the student participation. This was particularly true in the *Chronicle,* where one can only wish that former labor writer Dick Meister's excellent AFT coverage had been repeated for the students. Journalism professor and AFT member Jerrold Werthimer ground out AFT press releases during the strike, and had no complaints over press coverage. There was some evidence that radical communication experts among the students began to make a concerted effort at helping the press obtain strike information. This was the case at the Applied Electronics Laboratory sit-in at Stanford in April 1969. Students were assigned to shepherd reporters around the site, answer questions, suggest leads and features and do everything else a good public relations man must do. Reporters were, on the average, receptive and cooperative and strike coverage was somewhat improved.

It is imperative that relations between student activists and establishment papers be improved. The *Chronicle*'s Dale Champion pointed out chillingly that papers "have portrayed student dissidents as the enemy." He believed that many college administrators are desirous of instituting changes, but any innovations are seen as a capitulation to demonstrators, whom the public views as the enemy. This is a dangerous situation.

Because they often were unable to obtain information from militants or mediators, reporters frequently became pipelines for the establishment-administration viewpoint, which angered students. The San Jose *News*'s Dick Egner often opened the news pages of his paper to San Jose State President Robert D. Clark for comment on the AFT strike. In a 22-inch story on January 2, headlined "SJS Faculty Strike Plan 'Baseless,'" Clark not only described the demands of San Jose State's AFT chapter, but also told why each demand was spurious or indicated how it was already being remedied. Not one AFT spokesman was quoted. The Vallejo *Times-Herald* failed to pursue any of the leads provided by Solano College President N. Dallas Evans in municipal court testimony about a sit-in disturbance at the college. Defense counsel for the 19 Negro student defendants, Robert K. Winters, allegedly caught Evans in distortions and mis-statements of fact, yet the paper failed to investigate the sit-in, beyond using the official channels.

Wire Services and TV

Among Bay Area editors and executives there was unanimous agreement on the extremely poor quality of wire service coverage of local disorders. This was particularly evident in AP and UPI stories on student demonstrations. Repeatedly wire stories overplayed the head-knocking, the sensational and the bizarre. They did not provide the types of background-interpretive pieces that staffs of the larger papers turned out. The *News*'s Paul Conroy—along with Vallejo publisher Luther Gibson, has complained for 20 years about the deteriorating quality of San Francisco wire coverage. The wire services' treatment of the demonstrations was unimaginative and superficial. The Berkeley *Gazette*'s Mike Culbert was most vocal in his criticism. "AP and UPI could not even be relied on to report the headknocking correctly," said Culbert. "The wire services didn't know what was going on in the first stages of the TWLF [Third World Liberation Front] strike [at Berkeley]. The early leads in the first days of the strike were atrocious. At one point AP was taking down my *speculation* on what was happening and moving it as the early lead." It should be remembered that a wire service staff is about one-tenth the size of the *Examiner* or *Chronicle* news staff.

Poor wire coverage hurt such papers as the Santa Rosa *Press-Democrat,* San Mateo *Times,* Vallejo *Times-Herald,* Palo Alto *Times* and Berkeley *Gazette* much more than it did the big five dailies. The latter were at least able to cover major demonstrations on a regular basis. When a smaller paper could free one of its own men for duty, such as for the opening of SFS after the Christmas cooling off period, the results were not happy. Said San Mateo *Times* publisher J. Hart Clinton, "We sent a reporter and a photographer to SFS but they might as well have stayed at home. Covering SFS and similar disturbances requires more sophisticated people than we have working in the news room." Stories turned in on the January 7 reopening of SFS by the *Press-Democrat*'s Peter Golis and the Palo Alto *Times*'s Ron Goben and Ken Rowe contained much of the same material moved by the wire services that day. Golis described in rather pedestrian terms the "scene" at Nineteenth and Holloway (SFS), and threw in some press conference quotes from SFS President Hayakawa and AFT President Gary Hawkins for good measure. Goben and Rowe did virtually the same thing. The *Times*'s story ran 18 inches, the *Press-Democrat*'s only 16. Clearly both the papers and the readers were shortchanged.

Pressure on Editors

In the future, manpower allocation by both large and small dailies will represent important policy decisions. The two San Francisco papers frequently had up to 10 men assigned to the student story. "It was a real drain on our resources," said the *Examiner*'s Gale Cook. Roy Grimm of the *Tribune* called it "damn expensive coverage"; and the *Mercury*'s Kenneth Conn said such coverage "pulled other reporters off their beats, burned up many columns of our news hole, and lost

us a lot of time just keeping people on alert." Part of this may be due
to what Cook called "the escalation effect." He said, "We all got caught
up in one of those things where it's a question of who is going to be
the first one to let go of the story. But each paper was afraid of getting
beaten if they did let go. This had an escalation effect on the coverage."
Despite this, two editors—German and Culbert—plan to send in more
manpower earlier for the next demonstration.

Another, more visible, pressure on editors came from television.
Grimm, Cook, and Vallejo managing editor Wyman Riley knew that
the local television stations would feature the headknocking on their
evening news reports. They felt impelled to follow television's lead
in their own news presentations. "If you know what TV is going to
show that evening," said Grimm, "you feel you have to show it too."

The great difficulty in portraying campus events accurately and
fairly has been pointed out by two members of the Berkeley faculty—
Joseph Lyford and Spencer Klaw. Klaw, a former associate editor of
Fortune magazine, believed it would have taken "instant historical interpretation to put all the events in place, which is too much to ask
of the medium." Lyford and Klaw invited 60 of their students to submit papers on what the TWLF strike at Berkeley meant to them, and
Lyford found some interesting opinions that defended the press. "Many
student papers criticized the media for reporting so much violence at
the expense of other kinds of coverage," Lyford said. "But we noted
that about 90 percent of the comments made by students in their
papers were concerned with violence and the reaction to it, so perhaps
the violence was more important than some people think."

Another student pointed out that the *Daily Californian*—which was
in sympathy with the strike, like most student newspapers—was just
as guilty as its bigger cousins in failing to report the background issues.
In the months before the actual strike began, the University administration and various minority organizations were negotiating at length on
setting up a Black studies program in a Third World College. The
Daily Californian reported none of this, concentrating instead on the
issue of credit for Eldridge Cleaver's proposed course 139X. The *Daily
Californian*, like the rest of the media, paid sole attention to what was
happening at the moment. Because of the silence concerning TWLF-
Administration negotiations, when the strike started many U.C. students were uninformed as to why there was a strike, on what issues the
students and the administration differed, and on what had already
occurred. If Berkeley students were confused, is it any wonder that Bay
Area newspaper readers were confused?

It is encouraging that most editors admit their failings in presenting interpretive pieces, overplaying the violence, and identifying too closely with the Establishment. Most are also aware that the age difference between editors and demonstrators makes it difficult, as Scott Newhall says, "for editors to know what in hell the kids are thinking." Another *Chronicle* editor described "a very live argument currently raging at the *Chronicle*" over the best way to cover demonstrations: is it to be the interpretive, lengthy, more personal article in the Norman Mailer-John Hersey-Truman Capote style of reporting; or is it to be the more old-fashioned, straight news reporting, with the elusive standard of objectivity? The *Chronicle* leans to the former. The other papers do not seem to have reached this stage yet. But the problems created in covering student demonstrations have begun to obscure the distinction between "article" and "news story." The *Chronicle*'s German has expressed willingness to break the stereotypes of traditional news coverage. Moreover, pouring the 1968–1969 student revolt into the old news molds may have irreparably cracked the molds. The new methods that editors and reporters adopt will affect media coverage of all events.

Case Study: Regional Organization and the Environmental Crisis

In the past few years, the proliferation of Bay Area citizens' groups that fight the redwood loggers, Bay fillers, air polluters, and even the Army Corps of Engineers, has testified to the environmental awareness of Californians. Elected officials in the nine-county Bay Area have demonstrated a willingness—unmatched in many other urban areas—to examine regional problems of transportation, open space, air quality, water pollution, sewage and related ecological matters. Witness the many "alphabet" commissions in the Bay Area, including: The San Francisco Bay Conservation and Development Commission (BCDC), the Bay Area Air Pollution Control District (BAAPCD), San Francisco Bay-Delta Water Quality Control Study (Bay-Delta), The Bay Area Transportation Study Committee (BATS), the Association of Bay Area Governments (ABAG) and others.

The Story of the '70's

A gathering of journalists in late June, 1969, arranged by Stanford's Professional Journalism Fellows program, heard former ABC commentator and chief correspondent of the Public Broadcast Laboratory Edward P. Morgan offer this perspective on inadequate environmental coverage by the daily press. "In the 1950's," he said, "the big story was reporting the cold war. Reporters completely missed the major stories of the 1960's: the Negro revolution and campus unrest. I wonder what the major story of the 1970's will be that the press has failed to report?" Morgan answered his own question—he believed it would be environmental deterioration.

Among the many academicians who agree with Morgan is Joseph Lyford, Professor of Journalism at Berkeley. Lyford believes that the reporting of "environmental aggression" stories is the chief current duty of a newspaper. "If such stories are not covered because they are invisible, or because there is no news peg, then we may face irreversible ecological erosion in the years ahead."

The genuine conservationist spirit in the Bay Area, manifested in a prevailing sense of urgency about ecological matters that is in the vanguard of American sentiment, encourages the expectation that Bay Area newspapers would be enterprising in their environmental coverage. Although the overall picture has yet to be determined, there are many definitely bright spots. The Oakland *Tribune*'s Fred Garretson

128

and the San Jose *Mercury*'s Tom Harris (now writing in place of Bailey and Cannon) have earned recognized and respected by-lines in environmental reporting.[1] Among the better environmental writers is Harold Gilliam, who writes twice each month for the *Chronicle*'s Sunday magazine; Paul Peterzell of the San Rafael *Independent-Journal;* Scott Thurber of the *Chronicle;* and Al Cline of the *Examiner,* all of whom do what they can in a limited amount of time.

But most papers and almost all broadcast stations do not have the manpower or the will to staff regularly the many meetings of regulatory agencies that bear responsibility for quality of the environment. Many such meetings are covered by only one or two papers, if at all. The wire services contribute little.

Bay Area Regional Organization

Many ecological problems tend to be peculiar to one area, making it difficult to deliver an overall evaluation of environmental coverage in Bay Area newspapers. Instead, we have chosen coverage of a regional issue of uniform importance to all nine counties: the report of the Joint Committee on Bay Area Regional Organization (popularly known as BARO), chaired by Assemblyman John T. Knox. The committee was charged by the California State Legislature with "studying the possibilities of establishing a regional organization in the San Francisco Bay Area to insure the region's effective and orderly planning, growth, and development in conjunction with the conservation of its physical and environmental resources." The joint committee went out of existence at the end of the 1970 session of the California Legislature, but Bay Area regional organization is still a lively issue.[2]

In a massive investigation, the joint committee considered the following multi-county, multi-jurisdictional concerns to evaluate the desirability and feasibility of incorporating them into some form of regional governmental organization:

Regional planning;
Air and water pollution;
Solid waste disposal;
Regional parks and open space;
Transportation, including airports, bridges, rapid transit and ports;
The socio-economic impact and desirability of regional government;
The necessary powers required for a regional government to function effectively;

---

[1] Gilbert Bailey, who did a good job on the environmental beat for the *Mercury,* now works for the Long Beach *Independent Press-Telegram.*

[2] We monitored the newspapers for the BARO story for the period from December 23, 1968 to March 4, 1969. Basic data are drawn primarily from this period.

Membership composition and selective methods for said regional government;

Methods for including existing regional and sub-regional multi-county districts and agencies, where appropriate, into said new regional government;

The determination of an appropriate definition for "the San Francisco Bay Area" with respect to regional organization; and

All other functional matters relevant to regional organization.

Clearly the legislative recommendations resulting from this study should have held a high interest for all papers in the Bay Area. At a December 17, 1968 press conference, Assemblyman Knox first unveiled his plan for a Bay Area regional government (also rather ambiguously referred to by the same acronym as the Joint Committee, BARO). The Joint Committee report was complex and required thoughtful interpretation and careful explanation. In response, all of the 10 papers on which our study focused carried prominent, and frequently lengthy, articles on the proposal.

How effective was the newspapers' treatment of the story? In part this is an unfair question, because the first agent controlling the flow of information was the committee's public information officer, C. Dennis Orphan, a former newsman in Baltimore and Chicago. Orphan wrestled with the problem of presenting the committee findings to the press so that the information would be intelligible to reporters, and subsequently to the readers. "Most papers do not have the staff to interpret a 150-page report and present it to the public," said Orphan. "If I do a digest of the report, I'll be guilty of imposing my judgment of what is important on the papers." Orphan tentatively thought of preparing a different digest for each of the nine counties, emphasizing points of local interest, but in the end, under deadline pressure, he issued a single 15-page report.

Orphan first outlined the four general functions of the proposed regional government: (1) taking over the functions of BCDC; (2) beginning work on a billion-dollar regional sewage facility; (3) designating major transportation corridors for the region; and (4) acquiring and operating regional parks and open space. Next he presented a section on organizational detail, including officers, salaries and standing committees.

He then listed the powers and duties of the proposed regional government, beginning with a description of the general regional plan to be prepared. The nucleus of the plan would consist of five mandatory elements—relating to transportation, environmental quality, regional parks and open space, San Francisco Bay and public service facilities. Eight additional factors of less importance which the plan should contain were also outlined. Next came specific land use powers with respect to the Bay, and a statement concerning control over policy and management of other existing agencies to be exercised by the regional government. The report closed with a brief statement of possible revenue sources to finance the regional government, including an income surtax, sales and use taxes, environmental quality fees, and general obligation and revenue bonds. Although this outline is sketchy, it gives some idea of the scope and emphasis of Orphan's report, which none of the papers printed in full.

Newspaper Attitudes and the Gatekeeper's Role

Despite the fact that reporters were virtually handed the basis for their stories in Orphan's short report, each paper's policy on the regional government question, and on environmental problems in general, played an important gatekeeper role.[3] Stories on December 17 and 18, 1968 appeared as banner leads, above the paper's name in the Berkeley *Gazette,* with red headlines in the Oakland *Tribune,* as a page one second lead in the San Jose *Mercury,* on page 14 in the San Francisco *Examiner,* and as far back as page 36 in the San Jose *News.*

The *Mercury's* Gil Bailey called the regional organization a "controversial" proposal with "broad power over local governments." The San Francisco *Chronicle's* Mike Harris saw it as "a series of gentle steps . . . toward the formation of limited regional government. . . ." Fred Wyatt of the Berkeley *Gazette* called it "a sweeping proposal." The Oakland *Tribune* devoted 86 inches to the proposal in two days; the Vallejo *Times-Herald* 51 inches on December 18; the *Chronicle* 33 inches; the *Examiner* 30; the San Mateo *Times* 18 inches; and the Santa Rosa *Press-Democrat* a paltry 11 inches. Clearly it made a great difference which reporter in which paper one read, when seeking information even of the relatively simplified press-conference variety. It also indicated that Orphan was probably correct in his judgment that at least the suburban papers could not adequately deal with a 150-page report.

The Oakland *Tribune* and Fred Garretson presented by far the most complete and accurate stories. The *Tribune* was the best Bay Area paper for environmental coverage, largely because of Garretson's work. The day of the conference, the *Tribune* ran a 34-inch story on page one outlining the Knox recommendations in rather value-free terms. Garretson acted essentially as a conduit: he included verbatim the five mandatory elements of the report; the general functions; and

---

[3] With respect to newspapers, the gatekeeper is one who decides which items shall be admitted to a place in the columns, and which items shall be excluded.

some of the material on powers and responsibility, financing, and organization. The next day—and this was the crucial element—Garretson brought his own special expertise to bear in an analytical piece of 52 inches. With intelligence and perception he discussed the need for a regional framework; he outlined the agencies that most likely would be subsumed under BARO; and he posed the question of power levels in Washington, Sacramento, the regional level and the local level. No other paper matched this one-two punch of careful reporting and close analysis.

In its own disturbing way the *Mercury-News* came the closest to the *Tribune*. On December 17 Gil Bailey wrote for the *News* a 22-inch factual report of the BARO proposal, containing most of the essential information. In the *Mercury* the next morning Bailey wrote an analytical piece slightly hostile to BARO, but full of his knowledgeable observations. He discussed potential points of controversy raised by the proposal and questioned the costs involved. It was the necessary companion piece to the *News* article. Unfortunately, they appeared in two different newspapers that do not have full circulation overlap. What the 50,000 or so *Mercury* readers who did not subscribe to the *News* made of Bailey's analytical piece (and therefore of the BARO proposal) is hard to say. Readers taking only one or the other of the two papers were shortchanged. This happens often with the *Mercury-News* combination.

With one exception, the other Bay Area papers either presented the story without analytical comment, or mixed the two in one piece. Both approaches were inferior to that taken by the *Tribune*. The services of an expert in this area are essential if a paper hopes to comment intelligently about future BAROs. Former *Gazette* reporter Fred Wyatt and the Palo Alto *Times*'s Jay Thorwaldson were clearly in too deep in an admittedly complex subject. The *Chronicle*'s Michael Harris presented more of his own views on regional government than those of Assemblyman Knox. The *Examiner*'s H. W. Kusserow, wrote a good, factual piece on December 17, but there was no follow-up story.

At least, however, the above-mentioned papers recognized the importance of the story, and had representatives at the press conference. In contrast, the San Mateo *Times*, Santa Rosa *Press-Democrat*, and Vallejo *Times-Herald* used wire stories that were dull and perfunctory. For the *Times*, in an area already bursting with fill projects and related controversy, this was inexcusable. The *Times-Herald*'s use of AP was disturbing for a different reason. Publisher Luther Gibson attacked the BARO proposal with a vengeance. Most other Bay Area papers ran one or two editorials on the subject from December 1968 to March 1969 (with the exception of the San Mateo *Times,* which ran none). But the Gibson papers carried lengthy denunciations of BARO on December 21, December 27, December 31, January 27, February 20, March 4 and March 18. As expected, Gibson opposed the concept because of his stated fear that less populous areas, such as Sonoma, Solano and Napa counties, would be dominated by the larger urban areas and would be dragged into problems of neither their concern nor making. The editorials argued this position, and challenged the one man-one vote, majority rule approach taken by Knox. Gibson also asked for local option on joining the regional government. Journalistically this was a perfectly reasonable position, and because managing editor Wyman Riley admitted that reader interest in the issue (judging by letters to the editor) was very low, the Gibson papers were probably smart to crusade in order to build interest in the subject. But Riley knew what to expect from the Knox committee, and he owed Vallejo readers more than a 15-inch AP story, countered by 36 inches from local Assemblyman John F. Dunlap, a member of the Knox committee, who registered his criticisms (juxtaposed with the AP article). The arguments presented by Dunlap and the newspaper editorials were indistinguishable.

Presentation of the Amended BARO Proposal

In Sacramento on March 3, Assemblyman Knox formally presented newsmen an amended legislative proposal for regional government. Only the articles by the *Tribune*'s Ed Salzman and the *Chronicle*'s Sacramento bureau made the connection between the December proposal and the March revision. The rest of the papers (with the exception of the Vallejo *Times-Herald*) either used wire service copy or wire copy disguised as Sacramento bureau stories. The regional government story was sufficiently complicated without newspapers adding to the confusion by presenting the March proposal as something discrete from the December proposal. Only the *Tribune* and *Chronicle* handled the story properly: they described the revisions; summarized the basic provisions and assessed the political chances of the bill. Wire stories concentrated on organization of the government—all old material— and presented the five mandatory elements of the regional plan as if they were new.

The Vallejo *Times-Herald* used the occasion as a news peg on which to present more of Assemblyman Dunlap's negative views. Following is the *Times-Herald*'s coverage of the Knox press conference—the page two story ran four-and-a-half inches:

A Region's Press

Dunlap Opposes Knox Proposal

Assemblyman John Dunlap, D-Napa, yesterday told his opposition to a bill by Assemblyman John Knox, D-Richmond, calling for formation of a limited super-government in the Bay Area, Dunlap said:

"Despite the fact that this bill changes the so-called staff report recommendation so that the area of the proposed regional agency would exclude Dixon, Rio Vista and Vacaville, I still am opposed to it.

"Its provisions for a referendum are based on a regional referendum rather than one which will allow local communities, including counties or cities, to decide individually for themselves whether they want in or out.

"Although I have always recognized that we have regional problems, I don't think we can solve them by a mandatory regional government. I think the people have to want something before it's going to work."

It would be virtually impossible for a reader to piece together the facts of Knox's March proposal from such an article as this.

Beyond the December and March press conferences, coverage of regional government followed the same patterns already established. At the top, the Oakland *Tribune* ran an excellent piece in its Sunday, December 3, 1968, "Metropolitan News Section" describing all the existing agencies with overlapping regional authority. The article was accompanied by a diagram of regional authority over Oakland which made the picture quite comprehensible. On December 25 Garretson presented a report by Stanley Scott and John Bollens, published by the University of California's Institute of Governmental Studies at Berkeley. The report tended to support main elements of the Knox proposal. Garretson followed this on December 29 with a discussion of regional government in the Minneapolis-St. Paul area, and showed how the Twin Cities' experience might be applicable to Bay Area problems. The *Tribune* periodically reviewed the status of the Knox proposal, covered debates on regional government throughout the Bay Area, and reported the changes in the Knox proposal a week before the second press conference.

The *Mercury-News*'s Gil Bailey also discussed the Twin Cities Metropolitan Council in a January 7 piece. A lengthy article on December 22, headed "Just What Is Regional Government?" provided a valuable analysis of overlapping regional authorities, much like Fred Garretson's. Urban affairs writer Jack Fraser (who also has since left San Jose) contributed a couple of sharp political analyses of the Knox proposal, plus information on the philosophy of the Bay Area Council's Citizens for Active Discussion of Regional Organization (CADRO). The subsequent departure of Bailey and Fraser is reflected in the poor March coverage offered by the *Mercury-News*. Executive editor Kenneth Conn was hard pressed to replace these two until he hired Tom Harris.

From December through March neither the *Examiner* nor the *Chronicle* provided anything comparable to the work of Garretson and Bailey. The *Examiner* even used AP for its March 3 story on Knox. Of the smaller papers only the *Times-Herald,* which was printing every anti-Knox comment it could find, gave any attention to the matter. On December 19, Don Engdahl of the Santa Rosa *Press-Democrat* wrote an excellent 40-inch piece analyzing the Knox proposal from the perspective of the northern counties, but the *Press-Democrat*'s article of March 3 may as well have been written the previous December. Coverage in the San Mateo *Times,* Palto Alto *Times* and Berkeley *Gazette* was also weak.

In dealing with the issue of regional government, the newspapers treated the matter in a mixed and uneven way, a circumstance not entirely of their own creation. Some of the problems surrounding the BARO report are suggested by this statement made by a knowledgeable reporter who attempted to cover the BARO story:

> The BARO report, commissioned when the 1969 legislative fight appeared likely to concern regional government rather than the future of the Bay Conservation and Development Commission (BCDC), was badly goofed up and seriously delayed, although many of the fine young men and women who were dragooned to work on sections of it probably didn't know this. The report was actually supposed to have been prepared months before, and was to have been much more of a blueprint for action than it actually turned out.

By March 3, when an amended proposal was issued, many viewed it as being largely window dressing and were convinced that the battle had shifted to saving BCDC.

> Knox was the commander in the latter fight and deserves the credit he got for "saving the Bay." But what should have been reported on BARO . . . was that the deadline for the report had not been met, that the nature of the report (some of it still in "notes") was far different from what had been promised, that the committee work was in a mess, and that the Legislature had given up on the proposal for the time being, both because of the lobbyist counter-attack on BCDC and their dissatisfaction with the progress of BARO. Knox, who was just beginning to take the steps in behalf of BCDC that ultimately proved so decisive, received a lot of favorable free publicity for BARO . . . and then put the report on ice, where it was destined to go anyway.

The Chronicle, the Tribune and the Environmental Beat

While, in retrospect, the entire BARO idea gave way to the fight to save the Bay Conservation and Development Commission, the type of treatment it received is important if one is to understand the generally uneven coverage given environmental matters by the Bay Area press.

Are all alphabet reports from government and university commissions handled in such a fashion? Will only a crisis such as the Santa Barbara oil slick prompt detailed coverage? Can the press be expected to provide some sort of early warning system on environmental matters? These are just some of the questions that could be answered by detailed study of media performance in reporting air and water pollution, overpopulation, urban crowding, mass transit and solid waste disposal. A small step in this direction has been provided by Penny Hermes, a Berkeley graduate student with a background in biology and journalism. From December 1968, through March 1969, Miss Hermes compared the coverage of air and water pollution stories in the *Chronicle* and *Tribune*. Her conclusions tended to support those presented above.

"During this period," she said, "the *Tribune* ran three times as many stories as the *Chronicle* on those subjects, with 920 more column inches. The *Tribune* has three writers (including Garretson) on the environmental beat, while the *Chronicle* has only Scott Thurber." Miss Hermes believes that the *Tribune* considered such stories to be of high priority, while the *Chronicle* played them down because they were not "sexy" or interesting enough. *Tribune* city editor Roy Grimm is convinced that one of the reasons his paper is considered dull or drab by some critics is its emphasis on complex environmental stories. "The problem with material like that is making it readable," said Grimm. But the *Tribune* has been willing to pay the price, whereas the *Chronicle* has not.

When the *Chronicle* did take notice of such questions, its coverage was discontinuous, and lacked both backgrounding and follow-up. The *Chronicle* was especially negligent in its coverage of Bay pollution by San Francisco's sewage system. The *Tribune* began covering this story in December; the *Chronicle* did not pick it up until March 12.

Miss Hermes also contended that the *Chronicle* has avoided some controversial issues that would have required stepping on the toes of influential persons. She said that the paper has steadily failed to report the maneuverings of West Bay Community Associates, the group that is hoping to fill part of San Mateo County's shoreline for tract housing. Garretson, in contrast, has consistently named names in his stories. He told Miss Hermes that during one of his series, publisher William Knowland told him to be even more specific and to name even more names. The fact that the late Joseph R. Knowland, Sr., and his wife were among the founders of the Save the Bay Association and were active on the Save the Redwoods campaign and the California State Park Commission has influenced the *Tribune*'s coverage.

Echoing many editors, Miss Hermes criticized AP and UPI for unexciting coverage of environmental issues. "They do no digging on their own," she said. "They read the *Chronicle* in the morning and pick up what they have. Very little of what the *Tribune* does gets on to the wire, so almost nothing of interest gets outside the Bay Area."

One man can have much influence on the quality of wire coverage of the environment in the Bay Area. The *Tribune's* Fred Garretson reported that while Doug Willis of AP was assigned to the local environmental beat in mid-1969, he did an excellent job. When Willis was transferred to Sacramento, however, coverage returned to its usual level.

Regional environmental stories are impossible for the wires to cover using present methods, anyway. Since so much wire coverage of all types of stories is a rewrite of the metro papers, a rewrite of a story of regional importance would require the wire man to gather local reports from papers all around the Bay in order to put the story in a perspective of regional interest. If this were done (which it is not) the story would be one or two days old—too old for other papers in the state or the West to carry.

Miss Hermes also criticized all Bay Area papers for not regularly covering the air and water pollution control agency meetings. "The *Chronicle* won't travel to Oakland for meetings, and the *Tribune* won't go into San Francisco."

The Santa Barbara Oil Leak Story

The oil well leak in the Santa Barbara Channel was surely one of the most significant environmental pollution stories of the decade, particularly for California. Nevertheless, none of the Bay Area papers covered the story with their own reporters, although all ran varying amounts of wire copy. The authors examined this coverage in six of the Bay papers, and the New York *Times,* for the two-week period February 17 to March 4, 1969. Tables 7 and 8 present (1) the total number of column inches each paper ran on the Santa Barbara oil slick story and, for comparison, on the Sirhan trial, which was another California-based event that received only wire coverage in Bay Area papers; (2) the number of days (out of a total of 14) a story appeared; and (3) the number of times a story appeared in the first four pages of the paper.

The two tables showed that, judging by the attention it received, the oil slick story ranked just behind the Sirhan trial in perceived news value. It was most significant that the continuity of coverage of the oil slick story was comparable to that of the Sirhan trial. Editors recognized the importance of the story, gave it space almost every day for

TABLE 7

Oil Leak: Summary of Treatment in Six Bay Area Dailies and
the New York Times, February 17–March 4, 1969

Paper	Total column inches	No. of days in paper	No. of days on first four pages
San Francisco *Chronicle*	265	13	10
San Jose *Mercury*	222	12	5
New York *Times*	191	7	5
Vallejo *Times-Herald*	147	12	4
Oakland *Tribune*	131	11	2
San Francisco *Examiner*	130	10	4
Berkeley *Gazette*	25	4	2

TABLE 8

Sirhan Trial: Summary of Treatment in Six Bay Area Dailies and
the New York Times, February 17–March 4, 1969

Paper	Total column inches	No. of days in paper	No. of days on first four pages
New York *Times*	435	11	3
San Jose *Mercury*	381	11	8
San Francisco *Chronicle*	272	12	2
Vallejo *Times-Herald*	241	12	11
Oakland *Tribune*	209	13	9
San Francisco *Examiner*	148	10	3
Berkeley *Gazette*	128	10	4

two weeks, and frequently featured it in the first four pages. During this period the Pueblo investigation, the Presidio "mutiny" trial, and the Mid-east crisis all received daily coverage of lesser magnitude than the Santa Barbara oil slick.

With the exception of the Berkeley *Gazette*, which virtually ignored the oil slick, Bay Area papers seemed receptive to covering stories of an ecological nature. The current problem is that editors are not taking the initiative in seeking out and exposing instances of what Joseph Lyford called "environmental aggression." When a federal task force indicated it would help California groups in preventing tampering with San Francisco Bay, the papers reacted with varying coverage. When a group of experts issued a report citing the dangers of continued Bay pollution, papers gave the story prominent space for a day and then moved on. This is normal, long-standing newspaper practice.

Covering the ecological and environmental story, however, demands a more dynamic newspaper ethic. The urgency of the environmental issue, and the danger of waiting for news pegs on which to hang environmental stories at a time when the problems are festering all around must lead to new approaches.

The AP's Bill Stall, inspired by William Bronson's book *How to Kill a Golden State* (Garden City, N.Y.: Doubleday, 1968), wrote a three-part series that ran in the San Jose *News* and Palo Alto *Times* on January 13, 14 and 15, 1969. An editor's note to the first piece explained Stall's purpose: "For nearly 200 years, man has exploited California's natural resources in an effort to build and live 'the good life.' Here is the first of three articles on how Californians now are trying to repair the scars of that exploitation." Stall briefly touched on the philosophical differences between Dr. Edgar Wayburn of the Sierra Club and Larry Kiml, natural resources director for the State Chamber of Commerce; zoning along Interstate 5; slum conditions and pollution at Lake Tahoe; comprehensive city planning by the Irvine Company in Southern California; and smog and motor vehicle pollution. This kind of series, but done in much greater depth, would help focus attention on local environmental and ecological problems. Stall had no news peg and no specific axe to grind, yet the series presented a readable and valuable overview of California's problems.

Priority Concerns of Weekly and Monthly Papers

Many of the area's weekly and monthly newspapers have made environmental problems one of their top priority concerns—and consequently are far outstripping the daily newspapers. The *Freedom News*, Richmond's monthly alternative to the daily *Independent*, has done much that is worth imitating. Contributor Clifford C. Humphrey writes regularly on the "Politics of Ecology," and in the April 1969 issue he covered the Sierra Club Wilderness Conference in detail. The May 1969 issue had a special supplement titled "Diagnosis of San Francisco Bay," which offered a detailed map showing Bay fill plans; a discussion of such Bay Area concerns as earthquakes, refuse, open space and the Bay-Delta Plan; and the names and addresses of all Bay Area groups concerned with environmental problems.

Freedom News editor Betty Segal has also challenged Standard Oil for its "wreaking" of Richmond (February 1969) and criticized a redevelopment project for downtown Richmond (October 1968). The paper is militantly protective of the East Bay environment, and it is performing a service for its community that the *Chronicle, Examiner, Mercury* and *News* are shirking in their respective cities.

Mrs. Segal admitted that the *Freedom News* borrowed many of its ideas for environmental coverage from the defunct *Peninsula Observer*, a Palo Alto weekly edited by David Ransom. Although the strict revolutionary left "line" of the *Observer* prejudiced much of its political coverage and affected the overall credibility of the newspaper, its air pollution coverage by Ned Groth was first rate. In a series of articles beginning on November 18, 1968, Groth took a hard look at the Bay Area Air Pollution Control District and what it was not doing. In the November 18 cover story, entitled "Breathing More Now and Enjoying It Less?" Groth assessed the regulatory spirit of the commission and its close links to the industries it was created to regulate. He also published a list of leading smog makers in the Bay Area.

On January 6, Groth turned to Los Altos Hills' pollution problem caused by the Kaiser-Permanente Cement Company, a subject also tackled by the Los Altos *Town Crier*. Uncontrolled emissions from Kaiser's clinker-coolers were settling as a fine powder all over the south Peninsula. Groth moved on to the Monterey area in the January 20 issue to examine pollution from the PG&E steam-generator electric power plant at Moss Landing. The dangers of fluoride pollution from industrial smoke stacks received his fire on January 27. Next to the "coming revolution," the *Observer* made control of environmental pollution its top priority concern, and Bay Area dailies (especially on the Peninsula) could have learned much from it.

The Burlingame *Advance-Star,* the twice-a-week sister paper of the daily Palo Alto *Times* and Redwood City *Tribune,* provided further evidence that the nondailies can do an excellent job in this area. The Sunday, March 2, 1969 issue provided a better advance story on the Knox proposal in Sacramento than most papers ran *following* the news conference. A banner story on February 9 explained the controversy between the Bay Conservation and Development Commission and San Mateo Senator Richard J. Dolwig. The bylined story by George Newman also provided a map of the Bay (reprinted from *California Tomorrow*) depicting lands already diked or filled and potentially fillable Bay lands. The following week the *Advance-Star* ran the official Bay Plan map submitted to the state legislature by the BCDC, picturing waterfront land uses that would be allowed under the plan.

If Bay Area dailies had the enthusiasm and sense of urgency pervading these weeklies and monthlies, environmental coverage would improve dramatically. In addition, the larger dailies should take their cue from the Oakland *Tribune* and the San Jose *Mercury* by cultivating writers like Fred Garretson and Tom Harris. Otherwise, the Bay Area may be overwhelmed by industrial and governmental inertia.

Case Study: Foreign News
(If Anyone Cares)

Now that the world has become a global village—and the moon's surface seems hardly more exotic than a piece of the Mojave desert—it should not be surprising that the American press would devote more space to foreign news. Some students from abroad—who are enrolled in colleges and universities in the United States—still subscribe to their homeland newspapers on the theory that our domestic press has always been too insular to care about the rest of the world. Of course, reading one's homeland newspapers is sensible strategy, whether American newspapers are insular or not. No amount of international news coverage can take the place of a free press and its ability to report and comment on the domestic affairs of its own country. Although foreign students visiting the United States would probably be agreeably surprised by the way the American press now treats foreign news, typical American newspaper coverage is still far from adequate.

Even the most enthusiastic assessment, therefore, does not suggest that foreign news dominates the pages of American newspapers, or even that our press is as internationally minded as those abroad. In one comparison of English and American newspapers (*Journalism Quarterly*, Autumn 1966), Professor Jim Hart of Southern Illinois University found that the slender English papers were more attentive to the world than even the best of the bulky American papers. But the margin was not great.

The proportion of space devoted to foreign news in the American press is no longer scandalously meager. Moreover, leaders like the Los Angeles *Times* and the Washington *Post* are not alone in flavoring their offerings with more foreign news. Professor Hart's study showed that a newspaper on the second level, the Minneapolis *Tribune*, and some that are at least a cut below the *Tribune*, such as the Philadelphia *Inquirer*, gave almost as much of their news space to international affairs as did the *Post*. Thus, it is not uncommon for an average metropolitan daily to carry 300 column inches of foreign news every day.

Bay Area Papers Compared with Others

In proud San Francisco, where cosmopolitanism is supposed to be a way of life and the foreign born are everywhere, one would assume that the major newspapers would devote substantial proportions of

141

DISTRIBUTION OF NEWS, FEATURES AND O[

Newspapers	Local, County, State Politics and Gov't		National Politics and Gov't		International Affairs		Crime, Accidents, Disasters	
	Col. In.	%	Col. In.	%	Col. In.	%	Col. In.	%
Bay Area Papers:								
Oakland *Tribune*	127.5	2.4	115.5	2.1	129.5	2.4	201.0	3.7
San Francisco *Chronicle*	123.5	3.1	57.5	1.4	126.5	3.2	335.5	8.4
San Francisco *Examiner*	72.5	1.8	151.0	3.7	111.0	2.7	202.0	4.9
San Jose *Mercury*	422.0	8.7	147.5	3.0	87.5	1.8	287.0	5.9
San Jose *News*	136.5	3.4	160.5	4.0	153.5	3.8	148.0	3.7
Comparison Papers:								
Atlanta *Constitution*	252.0	7.9	116.5	3.7	163.5	5.1	72.5	2.3
Buffalo *News*	178.5	5.0	182.5	5.1	229.5	6.5	222.5	6.3
Los Angeles *Times*	256.5	5.3	230.5	4.7	259.0	5.3	181.0	3.7
New York *Times*	474.5	8.1	229.0	3.9	430.5	7.5	102.0	1.7
Toronto *Globe & Mail*	98.5	2.6	158.0	4.1	251.0	6.5	199.5	5.2

ᵃ Percentage totals rounded.

their news space to international affairs.[1] But the assumption is not supported by the facts. In preparing the information summarized in Table 9, we first analyzed the contents of single issues of the San Francisco *Chronicle* and *Examiner,* and found surprisingly small percentages of total news space devoted to foreign news. We then examined two other issues of these papers, with similar results.

Next we analyzed the contents of the other three metropolitan dailies published in the Bay Area, first a single issue, then two other issues.[2] The Oakland *Tribune* and the San Jose *Mercury* and *News* were no more sensitive to the need for foreign news than the two San Francisco dailies. We then compared the Bay Area's major dailies with four other dailies published in other parts of the country, and one in Canada. Two of these papers were the New York *Times* and the Los Angeles *Times*. Because it may not seem fair to compare the Bay Area's local papers only with such giants, the other three chosen were less prestigious—less likely to consider themselves newspapers of record—the Atlanta *Constitution,* the Buffalo *News* and the Toronto *Globe and Mail.*

One of our analytical methods gave an advantage to the Bay Area

[1] San Francisco ranks third among major U. S. cities in its percentage of foreign born residents.
[2] All tallies in Table 9 are based on January 9, 1969 editions.

s, BY MAJOR SUBJECT AREAS, JANUARY 9, 1969

	Sports		Amusements		Opinion		Economics, Business, Labor		Miscellaneous		Total Col. Inches	Total %ᵃ
	Col. In.	%	Col. In.	%	Col. In.	%	Col. In.	%	Col. In.	%		
	1113.0	20.7	474.0	8.8	342.0	6.4	915.0	17.0	79.5	1.5	5382.0	100
	638.0	16.1	500.5	12.6	413.0	10.4	506.5	12.7	80.5	2.0	3975.0	100
	781.0	19.1	701.0	17.1	318.0	7.8	625.5	15.3	76.0	1.9	4094.0	100
	588.0	12.1	547.5	11.3	166.0	3.4	633.0	13.1	127.5	2.6	4840.0	100
	562.0	13.9	526.0	13.0	326.0	8.1	598.5	14.8	96.0	2.4	4033.0	100
	465.0	14.6	282.5	8.9	291.5	9.1	417.0	13.1	25.0	.08	3180.5	100
	369.0	10.4	387.5	10.9	190.5	5.4	517.5	14.6	48.0	1.4	3552.0	100
	485.0	9.9	714.5	14.6	343.5	7.0	906.5	18.6	82.0	1.7	4878.0	100
	366.0	6.3	162.0	2.8	244.5	4.2	791.0	13.5	87.0	1.5	5855.5	100
	556.0	14.5	185.0	4.8	380.5	9.9	1214.0	31.6	34.0	.09	3844.0	100

dailies, and reduced the foreign news percentages of the New York *Times* and the Los Angeles *Times* considerably (to seven percent and five percent respectively).[3] But the two still remained well above the low levels of the Bay Area papers. No method of juggling and figuring could alter the fact that, either in terms of a percentage of total news space or total column inches, each of the five major Bay Area dailies carried less foreign news than any of the five other papers chosen for comparison. It is not surprising that Bay Area papers carry less foreign news (see International Affairs, Table 9) than the New York *Times* and the Los Angeles *Times*. But less than the Toronto *Globe & Mail*? Less than the Atlanta *Constitution*? Less than the Buffalo *News*?

---

[3] Instead of placing in the "International Affairs" category the opinion columns that dealt with foreign news and letters-to-the-editor that commented on foreign affairs—the usual practice in such studies—we assigned all opinion columns and letters to the "Opinion" category. This worked to the advantage of the Bay Area's papers, because few of their opinion columns and letters commented on international affairs. Thus exclusion of opinion columns and letters from the "International Affairs" percentages gave the Bay Area papers a better chance of comparing favorably with the New York *Times* and the Los Angeles *Times*, both of which carried many opinion columns and letters on international affairs.

The New York *Times*'s and the Los Angeles *Times*'s percentages in the "National Politics and Government" category were also reduced more than those for the other papers. Both carried many opinion columns and letters on national affairs—considerably more than most other American papers.

What Does the Chronicle Print?

The kind and character of reports that newspapers offer are more important than either the percentages or the column inches devoted to foreign news. With nearly 500,000 subscribers, the *Chronicle* has more than double the circulation of any other Bay Area newspaper. Thus it was appropriate to focus on the quality of foreign coverage provided by the *Chronicle*. We chose the final home edition of January 9, 1969, for the evaluation.[4]

The front page carried stories of a police-student clash at San Francisco State College, a raid on a hippie mansion, and several other eye-catchers. Nearly every story the *Chronicle* featured on page one originated in San Francisco. The exceptions were: one story from Los Angeles, one from Sacramento and a third from Monterey. The front page had no stories that originated outside of California. (One observer pointed out that the *Chronicle*'s policy on departmentalization assigned local news to the early pages and foreign news to later pages.)

Page two, in turn, was almost as parochial as page one. Only a short report, "Winds Kill 2 in Colorado," suggested to readers that there were other climes, other people. Foreign news first appeared on page three—a five-inch report on "Raging Fires in Australia." Another foreign news item turned up on page four, a one-inch story that can be reprinted here in its entirety: "Canadian Prime Minister Pierre Elliot Trudeau missed a session of the Commonwealth Prime Ministers Conference yesterday after coming down with a cold."

Under ordinary circumstances, the record thus far might suggest to anyone who cared about "the world somewhere out there," that he should jettison the *Chronicle* and have a more serious paper delivered—if necessary, flown in daily from the outside. But let us ignore those first four pages, and grant a major premise of *Chronicle* philosophy, i.e., the reader must be given a certain amount of pap so that he will be lured inside to more substantial fare.

There was no foreign news on page five, but on page six the *Chronicle* included a 23-inch story headlined "Witches and Things," about modern witchcraft in Portugal. Above the main head ran a smaller headline: "Lisbon is Talking About."

Such stories represent one of the *Chronicle*'s chief innovations in American journalism. Instead of printing the kind and variety of foreign news that commonly appears in serious newspapers, the editors have instructed their foreign operatives—nearly all of them part-time employees, or "stringers"—to try to determine what people are talking

---

[4] The record would look somewhat better on a Sunday, when *This World* uses foreign news from some of the wire services.

about over lunch in cities around the world.[5] Judging by the results, these are peculiar lunchtime conversations. For example, the reporters appeared to find that the French never talked about Pompidou, De Gaulle, the Common Market, French glory, or French philosophy; the English never talked about the government's austerity program, the rise of the red-brick universities, taxes or the problem of the pound. In fact, lunchtime conversations over the world seemed startlingly alike. Everyone everywhere was apparently talking only about sex, voodoo, witchcraft, drinking (in India, the City of Trivandrum is talking about "Toddy Tapping"), or some form of eccentric behavior.

Page eight featured another variety of the *Chronicle's* favorite foreign news story, "Trial of Six Opens in Swiss 'Devil Girl' Slaying." It was exactly as long, nine inches, as that day's first conventional foreign item, a page seven story that reported on the plans of Ambassador W. Averell Harriman to leave Paris after months of conducting peace talks.

Other items of foreign news appeared in the January 9 issue, of course, and a few were serious reports. But it is significant that the three longest stories—the only ones running more than 20 inches—reported on witchcraft in Portugal, the fact that 1969 was a lucky year in Japan because it was the "Year of the Cock," and "Bloody Flight from Cuba," a story on the escape from Cuba of 80 rebels, which appeared on page 15. In short, the major foreign news emphasis in the *Chronicle* issue of January 9 was assigned to two items of superstition and one of bloodshed. This was par for a very peculiar course.

The reader should note further the alternative treatments of the Cuba escape story as discussed in the following section of this study. Significantly, the good foreign news story gives a framework for understanding. The mediocre story does not.

The Chronicle and the New York Times News Service

It is not ordinarily considered fair to compare other newspapers with the New York *Times*. The latter does its utmost to provide posterity, as well as current readers, with a full record of each day's events. But there is one justification in comparing the *Chronicle* with the *Times:* the *Chronicle* buys the New York Times News Service, thereby preventing it from being used by any other Bay Area newspaper, except the San Jose *Mercury* and *News*. This means that every day the *Chronicle* receives nearly 30,000 words of the best news, features and opinion

---

[5] Although nearly all of the "Talking About" series are written by *Chronicle* stringers, some are winnowed from news service reports. The item on witchcraft in Portugal was provided by, of all unlikely services, the New York Times News Service. The *Times* did not see fit to publish the story in its own columns.

offerings the *Times* has, most of which the *Times* will publish. The amount of this *Times* material the *Chronicle* uses is determined by the *Chronicle*'s editors.

On January 9, there was some duplication—of a sort—in *Chronicle* and *Times* offerings. For example, the *Chronicle* had the one-paragraph item already mentioned on the Commonwealth Prime Ministers Conference—the one that featured Canadian Prime Minister Trudeau's head cold. The *Times* story on the conference was not about Trudeau's head cold but about one of the most sensitive issues facing the Commonwealth: race relations.

There was not much difference in the length of the *Chronicle* and *Times* stories on the escape from Cuba, but what a difference in substance! Like the *Chronicle* (which used the Los Angeles Times-Washington Post report) the *Times* reported fully on action, shooting and bloodshed. But the last half of the *Times* story placed the bloody event in context. The *Times* reporter offered full details on an airlift that brought Cuban refugees to the United States five times a week as a result of an agreement between the U. S. and Cuba. In operation more than three years, the airlift had already brought in more than 130,000 Cubans. But males between 15 and 26 years, and some technicians and specialists who are older, were not allowed to leave, the *Times* reported. Those who successfully applied for the airlift faced a waiting period of about two years, and could take only a few possessions with them. It was to avoid such restrictions that the fleeing Cubans fought their way to the United States base at Guantanamo. The *Times* story ended with four paragraphs explaining that the U. S. maintains the 45-square-mile base to serve the fleet, and that Castro had spent millions to build a fortified no-man's land on a wide strip of terrain adjoining the base.

The *Chronicle* report was all derring-do. The *Times* story put derring-do in a framework of understanding. The difference called to mind a *Times* editor's explanation of his paper's attitude toward reports of violence: "When other papers cover a murder, it's sensationalism. When we cover a murder, it's sociology." The editor spoke half arrogantly, half in jest, but his statement sketched the *Times*'s policy regarding most news items, and it emphasized a distinct difference between the philosophy of the *Chronicle* and the philosophy of the *Times*.

The dividing line between the *Times*'s coverage of the world and that of all the other Bay Area papers—except the *Chronicle*—is less clear, partly because the other local papers have not adopted the *Chronicle*'s philosophy of titillation as an absolute good. As the table above shows, however, the rest of the Bay Area metropolitan dailies have not extended themselves to expand their readers' knowledge of world events.

Moreover, although they pay lip-service to the ideal of providing background information—i.e., the *Times* story of the fleeing Cubans—as well as action, the background is sparse or nonexistent.

Going through the local papers and matching their foreign news coverage with that of papers which energetically seek to inform their readers about world events is a tedious and depressing exercise. One who undertakes it sees clearly the inadequacy in the performance of most Bay Area newspapers. There must be an explanation that goes beyond merely suggesting that the local editors are either parochial or don't give a damn.

Who Cares to Read Foreign News?

How many readers really care whether newspapers offer a nourishing menu of foreign news? No doubt there are professors of international relations in Bay Area universities who care deeply. It is not much of a leap of the imagination to include other professors and their students, and businessmen and professional men whose work has an international flavor. Add a smattering of Northern Californians who care because of a wide variety of reasons, including some readers who have no more incentive than a laudable curiosity to know how the world is going.

If reader interest is to be a crucial factor, it seems that there are not enough of these persons interested in foreign news to make a decisive difference. We have alluded to the period when the *Chronicle* was trying to become the New York *Times* or *Herald Tribune* of the west. We have mentioned elsewhere the abortive Western Edition of the New York *Times* itself. Both were failures. They failed in part because an insufficient number of readers seemed to care for them.

It is dangerous to attribute these failures solely to their heavy share of foreign news. It is like trying to assign the reason for a failing political campaign—or a successful one—to a single cause. Did Pat Brown fail to be re-elected to the governorship of California because the voters were tired of him? Because he was tired? Did the voters elect Ronald Reagan because he is handsome? Because he has mastered television? Because he is conservative? Because his program appeals to many Californians? Brown was defeated and Reagan was elected, perhaps, for all these reasons—and others.

By the same token, the old, serious *Chronicle* may have failed because it gave so much space to all that dreary foreign news. Today's *Chronicle* may have reached its present level of success because its foreign news is titillating rather than useful. And because its columnists are provocative. And because it is generally entertaining. And . . . on and on.

The fact remains that few Northern Californians seem to clamor for a serious newspaper. This led us to jettison the first title for this chapter: "The Lack of Foreign News in Bay Area Papers, Or Why Northern Californians Don't Know Any Better." A more accurate title might be "The Lack of Foreign News in Bay Area Papers: Who Cares?"

Bruce Brugmann has argued that Bay Area residents have never really had a chance to show whether they would support a quality daily. Neither the old *Chronicle* of the Paul Smith era nor the Western Edition of the New York *Times* was given sufficient resources to succeed, he maintains. His position is debatable, at least, but we do not propose to contest it further here. Let Brugmann's argument comfort those San Franciscans who are too proud of their city ever to believe that it refuses to embrace quality.

Conclusion

The great question that remains is why the many capable journalists we have cannot lift Bay Area journalism above mediocrity. If we ever had doubts that local journalism *is* mediocre, they were dispelled during our interviews with reporters and editors. One was quite proud of his paper, a few were complacent, but the great majority were dissatisfied with—and often even contemptuous of—significant aspects of their own papers. As for the many readers with whom we discussed local journalism, nearly all were overwhelmingly negative about the papers they read. When one of the authors began to mention to a World Affairs Council audience that a critique of the Bay Area press would soon be published, he was interrupted by a burst of applause that was surprising in its intensity.

The answer to the question of why the Bay Area does not have a great daily newspaper, or even one of undisputed high quality, begins quite simply but becomes exceedingly complicated. The first necessity is an owner who is determined to produce a great paper and knows how to go about it. This is the most important factor, but there are others. The market for the paper must be large enough to provide revenues enabling the owner to pay for a quality product. The community served by the paper must be large. The intellectual level must be such that the readers will feel rewarded by an informative paper, rather than repelled by it. The effort to set the paper on the path toward greatness must be properly timed. For example, the current period of recession or near-recession coupled with inflation (1969–1970) might be a ruinous time to attempt to convert a mediocre paper into a great one.

All these factors are so difficult to mesh in one locale at one time that the creation of a great newspaper might be deemed an accident rather than a considered policy. And, indeed, considering how few of the 1,764 daily newspapers in the United States are of high quality, that may be a reasonable conclusion. Nevertheless, publication in New York, Washington or Chicago is not a prerequisite for obtaining the income necessary to accomplish the task. In the 10 years that he has been publisher of the Los Angeles *Times*, Otis Chandler has transformed it from a family trumpet to one of the four or five best newspapers in the United States. In relatively small St. Petersburg, Florida, Nelson Poynter has been so serious and intelligent about informing his audience that his St. Petersburg *Times* must be ranked with fine newspapers published in much larger cities. The Louisville *Courier-Journal*, which is also published in a relatively small city and in a poor state, is deservedly ranked on nearly every list of great newspapers.

149

We cannot know whether all the factors listed above will ever be combined so that the Bay Area can produce a great paper. Certainly, we must await the coming of a publisher whose first purpose is quality, whose vision is sharp enough to recognize it, and who works for high profits only because they enable him to provide a more significant public service. (The hard-headed publishers who treat newspapers like any other business have a right to snort derisively at such a prescription. They also have the unquestioned right to milk their newspaper businesses of profits, leaving nothing to improve the product. They are wrong only because they seem to think we should respect them for such performances.)

Even in the absence of an ideal publisher, Bay Area newspapers can be improved markedly. Let us suggest two steps.

First, pay scales for reporters and editors should be raised dramatically to attract and retain first-rate talent. The experience of the Los Angeles *Times,* which lured fine journalists from high-paying magazines by paying them better, suggests what a strong salary scale can accomplish. The list in Appendix II of guild scale minimums (and we are aware that some journalists are paid above minimum scale) indicates that reporters on Bay Area metropolitan papers are being paid comfortably but not professionally. This is a period when top reporters on great papers may earn $25,000 to $35,000, with bureau chiefs earning more. Too many Bay Area editors do not recruit actively. They sit back and riffle through a stack of letters from people who want to come to California, selecting one who looks promising—and who doesn't expect much money.

A former editor said that he was

> constantly flooded with job applications from those who want to come to California at almost any pay scale. This helps to keep pay scales down, despite the upward influence of the guild on all Bay Area newspaper salaries. But you would still find, I would guess, that some of the non-guild papers still pay atrociously, a condition that has always influenced the quality of newspapering in the Bay Area.

Most Bay Area newspapers must take the second step of disentangling themselves from local Establishments. One knowledgeable local critic chided us for worrying unduly about the penchant of publishers for making money, and asserted that we should pay attention to the "publishers' real concerns—running their communities."

That brings us to an important consideration: the stance of Bay Area newspapers. The press is the only business institution specifically mentioned in the Bill of Rights, and thereby given a degree of protection from government regulation. This means, of course, that the founding fathers envisioned the press as a check upon government. For this function to be performed effectively, the modern political reporter must do much more than question officials in an abrasive manner, or rub two politicians together to produce newsworthy sparks. The reporter must recognize that we live in the age, not of just a military-industrial complex, but of a government-industrial-labor-education complex. He must be alert to the powerful inducements often employed to lure the communications industries into equal and tranquil partnership with the complexes.

The Skeptical Adversary

Because government seldom constructs its own offices, builds roads, develops parks, writes textbooks, or directly carries on the myriad other activities of modern governance, government has a multitude of inextricable links to business and to all the other pivotal institutions of society that do perform these tasks for government. Professional journalists must serve as adversaries to this system—not belligerently, but questioningly and skeptically.

How well does Bay Area journalism perform this task? To answer the question, one need only look at the destruction of the local environment, the pollution of everything from air to human relationships and at the timidity of the press in failing to expose the contaminators.

At the risk of oversimplification, this comment by Arnold Elkind, chairman of the National Commission on Product Safety, can stand for a whole catalogue of inadequate reporting:

The news media to whom our records and hearings are available have generally not availed themselves of the opportunity to alert the public to product hazards. With few exceptions, they have deleted brand names and identifying information from reports about product hazards.

This reportorial failure is of crucial importance. Not only is the press the sole knowledgeable adversary to government, but also it is the primary source of the contemporary information with which we organize our lives. We can know very little: there is not much that the citizen can be sure of through direct experience and observation. The world is too big and complex, and our daily paths in it are too narrow and limited—from home to office or classroom, to a store, to club or restaurant or theater, then back home again—for us ever to see and experience more than a tiny sample of the world. We depend upon the press—and radio and television, of course—to provide us with the vast majority of what we understand about contemporary affairs. The information they give us is synthetic—we do not know it at first-hand—but we depend upon it. We have no other choice.

Another problem is the fragmenting of traditional newspaper reporting, which, as one reader said,

> contributes directly and continuously to the inability of newspapers to confront the problems of our times and communities until they are so clear that University students force us to confront them.

In a country like the United States it is especially necessary for the press to recognize its own importance. As James Madison said,

> Knowledge will forever govern ignorance, and a people who mean to be their own governors must arm themselves with the power knowledge gives. Popular government without popular information or the means of acquiring it is but a prologue to a farce, or a tragedy, or perhaps both.

It is especially important that the Bay Area press recognize its responsibility. It is essential that Bay Area editors and publishers commit themselves, not only to slashing at those few politicians who arouse their anger, but also to a role of *speaking truth to power*. If significant power resides in the Pacific Gas and Electric Co., or Pacific Telephone and Telegraph, or Stanford University, or the University of California —and surely it does—the only honest and valuable journalism must confront these power centers with the same stance that is struck before political and governmental power.

Further, in addition to practicing confrontation, the papers need to develop depth and breadth of view both in judgment and in performance.

Shortcomings and Future Directions

In this book we have attempted to point out some of the strengths and shortcomings of Bay Area newspapers. Publishers in the nine-county area have to grapple with every important print media problem and development in the country today. The directions taken by Bay Area newspapers in the next few years should be accurate indicators of what we can expect from newspapers throughout the United States.

Suburban papers will decide whether it is more profitable to concentrate on local news—as is the case in Berkeley and some of the smaller communities in Contra Costa County—or to provide a complete news package, in competition with the metropolitan dailies—as is now the case in San Mateo, Richmond and Vallejo. What will be the role of the underground press, of the semiunderground weeklies and monthlies such as *Freedom News* and the *Bay Guardian?* Answers to these questions will also probably emerge in the next few years.

We have tried to show both the good and bad aspects of joint operating agreements; the successes and failures of the suburban dailies; the solid contributions and questionable extremism of the weeklies and undergrounds. We have commended some papers and criticized others. Our overriding impression of the whole of the Bay Area press can be expressed simply:

We are in a period of revolution. If most of the journalists in the Bay Area, and especially the proprietors of Bay Area papers, think that their present performance is sufficient unto the needs of the hour, then they do not know what time it is.

APPENDICES

APPENDIX I

Bay Area Newspapers:
A. Dailies

(in decreasing order of circulation)

Source: *Editor and Publisher International Yearbook 1969*

Legend: m = morning
      e = evening
      S = Sunday

Name of Newspaper	County of Publication	Circulation	Publisher
San Francisco *Chronicle* (mS)	San Francisco	480,233	Charles de Young Thieriot
Oakland *Tribune* (eS)	Alameda	225,038	William F. Knowland
San Francisco *Examiner* (eS)	San Francisco	208,023	Charles L. Gould
San Jose *Mercury* (mS)	Santa Clara	126,382	B. H. Ridder
San Jose *News* (eS)	Santa Clara	75,531	B. H. Ridder
Santa Rosa *Press-Democrat* (eS)	Sonoma	45,504	Mrs. E. L. Finley
San Mateo *Times* (e)	San Mateo	45,394	J. Hart Clinton
Palo Alto *Times* (e)	Santa Clara	44,520	Charles T. Tyler
San Rafael *Independent-Journal* (e)	Marin	43,649	Wishard A. Brown
Richmond *Independent* (e)	Contra Costa	36,170	Warren Brown, Jr.
Hayward *Review* (eS)	Alameda	35,510	Floyd L. Sparks
Vallejo (morning) *Times-Herald* (mS)	Solano	29,219	Luther E. Gibson
Contra Costa *Times and Green Sheet* (eS)	Contra Costa	23,001	Dean S. Lesher
Redwood City *Tribune* (e)	San Mateo	21,923	Frank J. O'Neill
Napa *Register* (e)	Napa	16,992	J. V. Brenner
Berkeley *Gazette* (m)	Alameda	14,448	Warren Brown, Jr.
Fremont *News-Register* (m)	Alameda	9,618	Abraham Kofman
Concord *Daily Transcript* (e)	Contra Costa	9,355	Dean S. Lesher
Fairfield-Suisun *Daily Republic* (eS)	Solano	9,282	Don R. Hancock
San Leandro *Morning News* (m)	Alameda	9,205	Abraham Kofman
Alameda *Times-Star* (m)	Alameda	8,897	Abraham Kofman
Antioch *Ledger* (e)	Contra Costa	8,737	Dean S. Lesher
Livermore *Herald and News* (m)	Alameda	7,896	Floyd L. Sparks
Fremont *Argus* (m)	Alameda	7,262	Floyd L. Sparks
Petaluma *Argus-Courier* (e)	Sonoma	6,942	Phil Swift
Pittsburg *Post-Dispatch* (e)	Contra Costa	6,705	Mrs. T. R. Bishop
Martinez *Morning News-Gazette* (m)	Contra Costa	3,200	Luther E. Gibson
Gilroy *Evening Dispatch* (e)	Santa Clara	3,166	George R. Kane

Bay Area Newspapers:
B. Weeklies, Bi-Weeklies, Monthlies
(alphabetically by counties)

Source: *Editor and Publisher International Yearbook 1969* and local inquiries. To obtain circulation figures on all weeklies, bi-weeklies and monthlies would have been beyond the scope of this project, and was not attempted. The *Yearbook* noted above is a useful source of information for those newspapers included in its listings.

Name of Newspaper	County of Publication	Day of Issue	Publisher
Albany *Times*	Alameda	Wed.	Ila Mae Wilson
Berkeley *Barb*	Alameda	Thurs.	Max Scheer
Berkeley *Tribe*	Alameda	Thurs.	Red Mountain Tribe, Inc.
Black Panther	Alameda	Sat.	Black Panthers
California Voice (Oakland)	Alameda	Fri.	E. A. Daly
Castro Valley *Reporter*	Alameda	Thurs.	Floyd L. Sparks
Freedom News	Alameda	monthly	Elizabeth Segal
Jornal Portugues	Alameda	Thurs.	Alberto S. Lemos
Montclarion	Alameda	Wed.	Fredric Graeser
Neighborhood Journal	Alameda	Wed.	Peter Victor
Oakland *Observer*	Alameda	Sat.	Marion G. Tibbits
Piedmonter	Alameda	Wed.	E. Clayton Snyder
Pleasanton *Times*	Alameda	Wed.	John B. Edwards
The Post (Berkeley)	Alameda	Thurs.	Thomas L. Berkley
San Lorenzo *Sun-Journal*	Alameda	Thurs.	Floyd L. Sparks
Union City *Leader*	Alameda	Thurs.	Richard L. Folger
Voz de Portugal (Hayward)	Alameda	1st, 14th, 21st of the month	Gilberto L. Aguiar
Brentwood *News*	Contra Costa	Thurs.	William H. Brewer
Concord *Journal*	Contra Costa	Thurs.	L. E. Stoddard
Contra Costa *News Register* (Walnut Creek)	Contra Costa	Tues. & Fri.	Ruth E. Davidson
Crockett *American*	Contra Costa	Thurs.	E. C. & R. V. Frates, Dr. C. J. Smith
Diablo Valley *News*	Contra Costa	Thurs.	
El Cerrito *Journal*	Contra Costa	Wed.	Frank J. Maloney
El Sobrante *Herald Bee Press*	Contra Costa	Thurs.	I. Eddie Galli
Lafayette *Sun*	Contra Costa	Fri.	Dean S. Lesher
Orinda *Sun*	Contra Costa	Fri.	Dean S. Lesher
Pinole-Hercules *News*	Contra Costa	Thurs.	Andrew M. Peters
Pleasant Hill *Post*	Contra Costa	Thurs.	L. E. Stoddard
Pleasant Hill *Sun*	Contra Costa	Fri.	Dean S. Lesher

Name of Newspaper	County of Publication	Day of Issue	Publisher
San Pablo *News*	Contra Costa	Wed.	Frank J. Maloney
Tri-City News (Rodeo)	Contra Costa	Fri.	Andrew M. Peters
Valley Pioneer (Danville)	Contra Costa	Wed.	R. Semmes Gordon
Walnut Creek *Sun*	Contra Costa	Fri.	Dean S. Lesher
Walnut Kernal	Contra Costa	Thurs.	L. E. Stoddard
Corte Madera-Larkspur *Courier*	Marin	Wed.	John Luc
Corte Madera *Times-Herald Tribune*	Marin	Wed.	Frank Marchi
Ebb Tide (Tiburon)	Marin	Wed.	John Luc
Fairfax-San Anselmo *Reporter-Sun*	Marin	Wed.	Peter Edwards
Larkspur-Corte Madera *Times-Herald-Tribune*	Marin	Wed.	Frank Marchi
Mill Valley *News-Herald-Tribune*	Marin	Wed.	Frank Marchi
Mill Valley *Record*	Marin	Wed.	Edward M. Mills & Katharine S. Mills
Novato *Advance*	Marin	Wed.	George A. Barnwell
Pacific Sun (San Rafael)	Marin	Thurs.	Stephen McNamara
Point Reyes *Light*	Marin	Thurs.	Don De Wolf
Ross Valley *Times-Herald-Tribune*	Marin	Wed.	Frank Marchi
San Rafael *Herald-Tribune*	Marin	Wed.	Wayne Swift
Sausalito *News-Herald-Tribune*	Marin	Wed.	Harry Johnson
Terra Linda *News*	Marin	Wed.	Eric C. Colby
Tiburon *Pelican-Herald-Tribune*	Marin	Wed	Frank Marchi
St. Helena *Star*	Napa	Thurs.	Starr Baldwin
The Weekly Calistogan	Napa	Thurs.	Ted J. Libby
Yountville *Weekly News*	Napa	Thurs.	John A. Nemes
Bien	San Francisco	Thurs.	Barbara R. Stribolt
Chinese Pacific Weekly	San Francisco	Thurs.	Gilbert Woo
Dock of the Bay (incorporated the *Peninsula Observer*)	San Francisco	Sat.	Bay Area Media Network
Good Times	San Francisco	Wed.	Waller Press
Jewish Community Bulletin	San Francisco	Fri.	Eugene J. Block
Monitor	San Francisco	Thurs.	Roman Catholic Archbishop of S.F.
The Movement	San Francisco	monthly	The Movement
Northern California Industrial and Business News	San Francisco	alternate Mon.	
Richmond *Banner*	San Francisco	Fri.	Frances C. Trimble
Rolling Stone	San Francisco	bi-weekly	Straight Arrow Pub.
San Francisco *Bay Guardian*	San Francisco	monthly	Bruce Brugmann

Name of Newspaper	County of Publication	Day of Issue	Publisher
San Francisco *Progress*	San Francisco	Wed. & Sat.	Henry J. Budde
Sun Reporter	San Francisco	Thurs.	Carlton B. Goodlett, M
Swiss Journal	San Francisco	Wed.	Mario Muschi
Vestkusten	San Francisco	Thurs.	Karin W. Person
Belmont *Courier-Bulletin*	San Mateo	Wed.	L. K. Rhodes
Brisbane *Bee-Democrat*	San Mateo	Thurs.	Logan Franklin
Burlingame *Advance-Star*	San Mateo	Wed. & Sat.	Edwin W. Rice
Coastside Chronicle (Pacifica)	San Mateo	Wed.	Alton I. Cloud
Foster City *Progress*	San Mateo	Wed.	R. M. Buren
Half Moon Bay *Review*	San Mateo	Thurs.	Edward M. Bauer, Jr.
Menlo-Atherton *Recorder*	San Mateo	Wed.	Richard Nowels
Millbrae *Sun and Leader*	San Mateo	Wed.	Anne Loftus
North County Post	San Mateo	Wed.	J. Hart Clinton
Pacifica *Tribune*	San Mateo	Wed.	William A. Drake & Margaret B. Drake
The Record and Westlake Times (Daly City)	San Mateo	Wed. & Fri.	Logan Franklin
San Bruno *Herald and Recorder-Progress*	San Mateo	Wed. & Thurs.	Alton I. Cloud
San Carlos *Enquirer*	San Mateo	Wed.	A. H. Dorinson
San Mateo County *Union Gazette*	San Mateo	Mon.	A. J. Remmenga, Gen.
San Mateo *Post*	San Mateo	Wed.	J. Hart Clinton
South San Francisco *Enterprise-Journal*	San Mateo	Wed. & Fri.	Logan Franklin
Almaden-Cambrian *Sun Guide*	Santa Clara	Wed.	Morton I. Levine
Cambrian Weekly News (San Jose)	Santa Clara	Wed.	Wilton von Gease
Campbell *Press*	Santa Clara	Wed.	George Vierhus
Cupertino *Courier*	Santa Clara	Wed.	David MacKenzie & William J. Norton
East San Jose *Sun*	Santa Clara	Wed.	Morton I. Levine
Los Gatos *Times-Observer*	Santa Clara	Tues., Thurs.	George R. Kane
Milpitas *Post*	Santa Clara	Wed.	Morton I. Levine
Morgan Hill *Times* and San Martin *News*	Santa Clara	Thurs.	Ralph W. Slauter
North San Jose *Sun*	Santa Clara	Wed.	Morton I. Levine
San Jose *Sun*	Santa Clara	Wed.	Morton I. Levine
South San Jose *Sun-Graphic*	Santa Clara	Wed.	Morton I. Levine
Sunnyvale *Scribe*	Santa Clara	Thurs.	David MacKenzie & William J. Norton
Town Crier (Los Altos)	Santa Clara	Wed.	David MacKenzie & William J. Norton

e of spaper	County of Publication	Day of Issue	Publisher
ow Glen Sun-Times an Jose)	Santa Clara	Wed.	Morton I. Levine
icia Herald	Solano	Thurs.	Thomas M. Banks
Benician	Solano	Thurs.	H. D. Frane
n Tribune	Solano	Thurs.	Frederic N. Dunnicliff
r News-Herald & leton Journal	Solano	Wed.	Esther T. Pierce
ville Reporter	Solano	Mon. & Thurs.	John Rico
erdale Reveille	Sonoma	Thurs.	Jerome J. Tupy & Terrance L. Thompson
serville Press	Sonoma	Thurs.	Jerome J. Tupy & Terrance L. Thompson
dsburg Tribune, nterprise & Scimitar	Sonoma	Thurs.	Dean Dunnicliff
s-Herald (Santa Rosa)	Sonoma	Wed.	George R. Chase
ma County Herald-ecorder	Sonoma	Mon., Wed., Fri.	Dale Sipe
ma Index-Tribune	Sonoma	Thurs.	Robert M. Lynch
es (Sebastopol)	Sonoma	Thurs.	Ernest V. Joiner
World (Cotati)	Sonoma	Wed.	Kvan, Inc.
World (Rohnert Park)	Sonoma	Wed.	Kvan, Inc.

APPENDIX II

Top Minimum Weekly Salaries for Reporters and Photographers in Selected Newspapers:

American Newspaper Guild Contracts as of August 1, 1970
(Figures supplied by the American Newspaper Guild)

Name of Newspaper	Minimum	After
Washington *Post*	$263.25	5 yrs
Washington *News*	260.00	5 yrs
NY *Times*	ª255.25	2 yrs
Washington *Star*	249.50	4 yrs
Chicago *Sun-Times & News* (2)	246.92	5 yrs
NY *News*	ᵇ242.30	6 yrs
ᵈOakland *Tribune*	240.75	6 yrs
Sacramento *Bee*	240.75	6 yrs
ᵈSan Francisco *Chronicle & Examiner* (2)	240.75	6 yrs
St. Louis *Post-Dispatch*	240.00	5 yrs
NY *Post*	ᶜ239.20	4 yrs
ᵈSan Jose *Mercury & News* (2)	233.59	6 yrs
Stockton *Record*	233.00	6 yrs
Sacramento *Union*	230.83	6 yrs
ᵈRichmond (Cal.) *Independent*	230.00	6 yrs
ᵈSanta Rosa *Press-Democrat*	230.00	6 yrs
ᵈVallejo *Times-Herald*	230.00	6 yrs
St. Louis *Globe-Democrat*	229.00	5 yrs
ᵈSan Mateo *Times*	226.16	6 yrs
Cleveland *Plain Dealer*	225.00	4 yrs
Detroit *Free Press*	222.35	4 yrs
Pittsburgh *Post-Gazette*	220.00	4 yrs
Baltimore *Sun & Evening Sun* (2)	220.00	5 yrs
Toledo *Blade & Times* (2)	219.50	4 yrs
East St. Louis: *Metro E. Journal*	217.60	5 yrs
Seattle *Post-Intelligencer*	215.00	5 yrs
Seattle *Times*	215.00	5 yrs
Gary *Post-Tribune*	213.35	5 yrs
Long Beach *Independent & Press-Telegram* (2)	208.80	5 yrs
San Diego *Union & Tribune* (3)	205.75	6 yrs
NY: Long Island *Press*	200.00	3 yrs
Vancouver *Sun & Province* (2)	193.63	5 yrs
Bakersfield *Californian*	192.50	5 yrs
Toronto *Globe & Mail*	192.00	5 yrs
Chattanooga *Times*	186.00	5 yrs
Fall River *Herald-News*	180.00	4 yrs
San Pedro *News-Pilot*	176.80	5 yrs
Los Angeles *Herald-Examiner*	174.80	5 yrs

162

Name of Newspaper	Minimum	After
San Antonio *Light*	170.01	5 yrs
Sioux City *Journal*	162.75	4 yrs
Terre Haute *Tribune & Star* (2)	156.50	5 yrs
Alexandria *Gazette*	135.00	6 yrs
Lowell *Sun*	134.00	5 yrs

a Includes $5.25 cost-of-living increase.
b Includes $5.00 cost-of-living increase.
c Includes $4.90 cost-of-living increase.
d Bay Area newspapers.

Note: A contract signed in San Francisco in November 1970, like a number of others signed recently, requires that after five or six years of experience, reporters and photographers will be paid more than $300 a week, or about $16,000 a year. In the near future, additional new contracts will increase the minimums paid by other publishers in large metropolitan areas. It is assumed, however, that the long-term salary relationships shown above will not be changed appreciably.

APPENDIX III

Comparative Treatment of Six National News Items
February 17–March 4, 1969

Newspaper and story	Total column inches	No. of days on first four pages	No. of days out of 14 story run	% of headlines "biased"[a]
VIETNAM				
New York *Times*	916	9	14	.10
Oakland *Tribune* . . .	570	14	14	.45
San Francisco *Examiner* .	439	11	14	.39
San Jose *Mercury*	402	11	14	.41
San Francisco *Chronicle* .	388	5	14	.36
Berkeley *Gazette*	194	10	12	.47
Vallejo *Times-Herald* . .	171	7	10	.33
MID-EAST CRISIS				
New York *Times*	815	13	14	.09
Oakland *Tribune*	337	9	14	.11
San Francisco *Chronicle* .	322	6	13	.20
San Francisco *Examiner* .	296	7	14	.30
San Jose *Mercury*	296	4	13	.25
Berkeley *Gazette*	145	9	11	.30
Vallego *Times-Herald* . .	73	5	6	.00
CONGRESS				
New York *Times*	775	10	14	.04
San Francisco *Examiner* .	338	9	11	.36
Oakland *Tribune*	246	9	12	.30
San Francisco *Chronicle* .	222	5	14	.27
Berkeley *Gazette*	177	6	7	.17
San Jose *Mercury*	139	2	12	.38
Vallejo *Times-Herald* . .	103	1	9	.27
THE PRESIDENT				
New York *Times*	1600	11	14	.04
San Francisco *Examiner* .	776	13	14	.35
Oakland *Tribune* . . .	671	13	14	.29
San Jose *Mercury*	589	7	14	.17
San Francisco *Chronicle* .	538	8	14	.36
Vallejo *Times-Herald* . .	255	7	10	.00
Berkeley *Gazette*	159	5	8	.40

Newspaper and story	Total column inches	No. of days on first four pages	No. of days out of 14 story run	% of headlines "biased"[a]
COLD WAR				
New York *Times*	832	12	14	.08
San Francisco *Chronicle* . .	332	6	13	.35
San Jose *Mercury*	291	8	14	.42
Oakland *Tribune*	273	11	13	.40
San Francisco *Examiner* .	216	10	13	.20
Berkeley *Gazette*	147	7	11	.25
Vallejo *Times-Herald* . .	99	2	6	.28
PRESIDIO MUTINY[b]				
San Francisco *Chronicle* .	246	4	10	.15
San Francisco *Examiner* .	229	0	10	.36
San Jose *Mercury* . . .	80	1	7	.14
Oakland *Tribune*	68	0	6	.28
Vallejo *Times-Herald* . .	57	0	6	.00
Berkeley *Gazette*	28	1	3	.00

[a] In our working definition, a biased headline is one that contains a value-laden word for which an equivalent and less value-laden word could have been substituted. For example in headlining a murder story, "slaughter" is more value-laden than "kill."

[b] Data for the New York *Times* are not included, because the *Times* ran nothing on the mutiny during the 14-day period of analysis.

APPENDIX IV

Newspaper Source Materials Used in the Study

A. MAJOR TOPICS EXAMINED AND WHY THEY WERE CHOSEN FOR QUALITATIVE ANALYSIS

Topic or Category	Notes on Bases for Selection
Goals and Performance	These qualitative topics revealed basic information concerning every paper under study, and helped us formulate an overview of each one. Time periods covered were related to the development of major stories.
Sunday Papers	The personality of a Sunday paper may be quite different from that of the daily. Further, Sunday reading offers the rare opportunity for some busy people to follow news developments and to reflect on what they read.
Weeklies	Because every sizeable community has one, the weekly has an important role to play in community awareness and local politics. Some of the best journalism in the Bay Area is found in weeklies.
Monthlies	The world of underground journalism is largely that of monthlies. Since the Bay Area is in the forefront of the underground movement, we thought it appropriate to take at least a brief look at selected monthlies.
Opinion Columns	An editor's choice of syndicated material provides a useful clue in evaluating the quality of the editorial page. The nature of the home-grown columns can also indicate a newspaper's involvement with the community and the editor's own philosophy of newspapering.
Student Unrest	This was chosen for study because it comprises one of the most important local stories that all of the papers in the sample could be expected to cover on their own, apart from the wire services.
Regional Organization and the Environmental Crisis	This topic was particularly appropriate for a regionwide study of newspaper performance. In addition, the environmental story was unusually significant because the Bay conservation commission was strengthened and made permanent in 1969. Local newspapers could be expected to have their own staff members covering the story.

166

Topic or Category	Notes on Bases for Selection
Foreign News	This material is usually the most neglected part of a newspaper's coverage. Moreover, the topic permits comparisons with newspapers outside the Bay Area, an examination that cannot be performed with local news. Finally, it seemed likely that important differences on this score might be found among the five major Bay Area papers.

For the group of comparison papers, the New York *Times* and the Los Angeles *Times* were chosen as embodying accepted standards of quality; the other three were selected because they serve central cities that are roughly the same size as the larger Bay Area cities, because they are usually *not* listed among the "great" papers in the United States (as the New York *Times* and the Los Angeles *Times* usually are), and because they are based in metropolitan areas.

No particular significance is attached to the date of January 9, 1969. Comparable editions of all papers under scrutiny were available for that date.

B. SUMMARY OF TOPICS, NEWSPAPERS AND DATES
IN THE QUALITATIVE DISCUSSION

Topic	Newspaper	Dates
Goals and Performance	Sample includes: San Francisco *Chronicle* San Francisco *Examiner* Oakland *Tribune* San Jose *Mercury* and *News* San Mateo *Times* Berkeley *Gazette* Vallejo *Times-Herald* Palo Alto *Times* Santa Rosa *Press-Democrat*	Period between December 23, 1968 and March 4, 1969
Sunday Papers	All those in the 9-county area: Sunday San Francisco *Examiner and Chronicle* Sunday San Jose *Mercury-News* Sunday Oakland *Tribune* Sunday Santa Rosa *Press-Democrat* Sunday Vallejo *Times-Herald* Sunday Hayward *Review*	Period between December 23, 1968 and March 4, 1969
Weeklies	Nominated from among 96 weeklies in the Bay Area	Period between December 23, 1968 and March 4, 1969
Monthlies	Nominated as among the best: *Bay Guardian* *Plain Rapper* *Freedom News*	Period between December 23, 1968 and March 4, 1969
Opinion Columns (editorial page and the page opposite)	Same sample as for "Goals and Performance" study: San Francisco *Chronicle* San Francisco *Examiner* Oakland *Tribune* San Jose *Mercury* and *News* San Mateo *Times* Berkeley *Gazette* Vallejo *Times-Herald* Palo Alto *Times* Santa Rosa *Press-Democrat*	Period between December 23, 1968 and March 4, 1969

Topic	Newspaper	Dates
Student Unrest	Same sample as for "Goals and Performance" study, used for nonquantitative analysis	Eighteen weeks in period during December 1968 through April 1969
Regional Organization and the Environmental Crisis	Same sample as for "Goals and Performance" study, used for nonquantitative analysis	Period between December 23, 1968 and March 4, 1969
Foreign News	San Francisco *Chronicle* San Francisco *Examiner* Oakland *Tribune* San Jose *Mercury* and *News* New York *Times* Los Angeles *Times* Atlanta *Constitution* Buffalo *News* Toronto *Globe & Mail*	January 9, 1969

C. SOME QUANTITATIVE ANALYSES

Topics for Tables	*Notes on Bases for Selection*
News Judgment, Front-Page Stories: Table 1	Variations in the news judgment of editors, as seen in the contents of their papers' front pages, demonstrate how the reader's perception of the world can be affected. We paired two sets of newspapers (the *Mercury* and the *Chronicle*; the *Tribune* and the *Examiner*), for three dates chosen at random, to see whether distinctive differences in content would show up. They did.
Cranston-Rafferty Race: Table 2	The *Tribune*'s treatment of this story was used to illustrate the way political philosophy can affect coverage in terms of column inches.
Student Unrest, the Vietnam War and the Pueblo Investigation: Tables 3, 4 and 5	These three topics were all issues of major importance during the observation period of February 17 through March 4, 1969. The treatment of a local, a national and an international issue during this period thus made meaningful column inch comparisons possible. To simplify quantitative comparisons during the two-week sample period, six Bay Area papers (instead of the 10 used in the Major Topics examination in section A) were followed for the local student unrest story. To these six, the New York *Times* was added for comparison in the Pueblo and Vietnam stories.
Campus Problems and the U. C. Regents' Meeting: Table 6	January 18, 1969, the day after the Regents' meeting, presented an opportunity for observing the way in which Bay Area papers covered a substantive event closely related to the student unrest story. It was also a Saturday, when the Santa Rosa *Press-Democrat* does not publish an edition. Thus, the overall comparisons include nine instead of 10 Bay Area papers.
Treatment of Santa Barbara Oil Leak and Sirhan Trial: Tables 7 and 8	The same six local papers and the New York *Times* were compared during the two-week period for quantitative treatment to discern news judgments concerning a story of statewide ecological importance and one of national political importance.

Topics for Tables	Notes on Bases for Selection
Distribution of News, Features and Opinion: Table 9	This tally was, of course, closely linked with the examination of foreign news described in section A. The 10 additional categories shown in Table 9 permitted substantial comparisons between the performance of the five major Bay Area papers and the five out-of-state papers.
Treatment of Six National News Items: Appendix III	The tally expanded on the Vietnam war treatment noted above. The same newspapers were examined on the same dates, with the addition of two topics of international importance: the Mid-East crisis and the cold war, and three of national importance: the President, the Congress and the Presidio mutiny story.

D. SUMMARY OF TOPICS, NEWSPAPERS AND DATES IN THE QUANTITATIVE STUDY

Topic	Newspaper	Dates
Column Inches on Cranston-Rafferty Race	Oakland *Tribune*	October 1968
Column Inches on Student Unrest	Berkeley *Gazette* San Francisco *Chronicle* Oakland *Tribune* San Francisco *Examiner* San Jose *Mercury* Vallejo *Times-Herald*	February 17– March 4, 1969
Column Inches on Vietnam War	New York *Times* Oakland *Tribune* San Francisco *Examiner* San Jose *Mercury* San Francisco *Chronicle* Berkeley *Gazette* Vallejo *Times-Herald*	February 17– March 4, 1969
Column Inches on Pueblo Investigation	New York *Times* San Jose *Mercury* Vallejo *Times-Herald* San Francisco *Examiner* Oakland *Tribune* San Francisco *Chronicle* Berkeley *Gazette*	February 17– March 4, 1969

Topic	*Newspaper*	*Dates*
Column Inches on Campus Problems and the U. C. Regents' Meeting	San Francisco *Chronicle* San Jose *News* San Francisco *Examiner* Oakland *Tribune* Berkeley *Gazette* Vallejo *Times-Herald* San Jose *Mercury* San Mateo *Times* Palo Alto *Times*	January 18, 1969
Treatment of Oil Leak	San Francisco *Chronicle* San Jose *Mercury* New York *Times* Vallejo *Times-Herald* Oakland *Tribune* San Francisco *Examiner* Berkeley *Gazette*	February 17– March 4, 1969
Treatment of Sirhan Trial	New York *Times* San Jose *Mercury* San Francisco *Chronicle* Vallejo *Times-Herald* Oakland *Tribune* San Francisco *Examiner* Berkeley *Gazette*	March 4, 1969 February 17–
Distribution of News, Features and Opinion	Atlanta *Constitution* Buffalo *News* Los Angeles *Times* New York *Times* Oakland *Tribune* San Francisco *Chronicle* San Francisco *Examiner* San Jose *Mercury* San Jose *News* Toronto *Globe & Mail*	January 9, 1969
Treatment of Six National News Items	New York *Times*[a] Oakland *Tribune* San Francisco *Examiner* San Jose *Mercury* San Francisco *Chronicle* Berkeley *Gazette* Vallejo *Times-Herald*	February 17– March 4, 1969

[a] Included in all tallies except that for the Presidio mutiny, because the *Times* did not use that story during the period studied.

3m-2,'71 (P1022)   141

III

STANLEY SCOTT AND JOHN C. BOLLENS

GOVERNING A
METROPOLITAN REGION . . .

Governing a Metropolitan Region:
The San Francisco Bay Area

INSTITUTE OF GOVERNMENTAL STUDIES

UNIVERSITY OF CALIFORNIA · BERKELEY

Governing a Metropolitan Region:

THE SAN FRANCISCO BAY AREA

By

STANLEY SCOTT
Institute of Governmental Studies
University of California, Berkeley

JOHN C. BOLLENS
Department of Political Science
University of California, Los Angeles

1968

LIBRARY OF CONGRESS CATALOG CARD NUMBER 68-65254
PRINTED IN THE UNITED STATES OF AMERICA
BY THE UNIVERSITY OF CALIFORNIA PRINTING DEPARTMENT

Preface

Most of the material on which this volume is based was originally prepared as part of a research effort for the San Francisco Bay Conservation and Development Commission.* When created in 1965, the commission was given a legislative charge with wide-ranging implications reaching far beyond the Bay itself, requiring the commission to formulate some basic recommendations for the future government of the nine-county metropolitan region. In doing this the commission needed to take into account other concurrent investigations of the region's problems and system of governance. Furthermore, it was essential that the commission review and rethink some of the fundamental issues raised by alternative proposals for regional government.

Although many of the concrete illustrations presented here relate to the San Francisco Bay Area and the concerns of the Bay commission, much of the discussion is also applicable to almost any regional governmental problem, in almost any major metropolitan area. Perhaps the San Francisco region is unique, or nearly so, in that the chances of establishing a regional government—or at least of achieving a substantial rationalization of the existing governmental system—appear to be better here than in most large metropolitan areas in the United States.

But in some form or other the issues confronting the Bay Area—organization, representation, finance, the extent of governmental powers—urgently demand the attention of all metropolitan areas. For example, with the build-up of pressures for metropolitan decision-making—signaled by requirements for metropolitan areawide review of requests for federal grants—the importance and design of the decision-making machinery is increasingly highlighted. Furthermore, there are potentially conflicting thrusts of influence from the governmental branches. For example, the federal administration is actively encouraging the formation of voluntary regional councils of government and their employment in major regional decisions. Second, the courts are pursuing the one-man, one-vote principle, to which few of the regional councils conform. The resulting tension will probably emphasize even more the significance of regional governmental organization and representation—the issues which this volume addresses.

S.S. and J.C.B.

---

* Stanley Scott and John C. Bollens, *Government: Regional Organization for Bay Conservation and Development* (San Francisco: San Francisco Bay Conservation and Development Commission, October 1967).

Contents

PART THREE: Summary and Conclusions

TABLES

MAPS

PART ONE

Problems of Governmental Organization

Introduction

In 1961–65, the uncontrolled filling of San Francisco Bay began to arouse intense public interest. The use of tidelands and shallow portions of the Bay to create new "made" land for residential and industrial sites was increasing, and threatened to accelerate sharply. A combination of growing citizen concern, most prominently represented by the Save San Francisco Bay Association, and University research efforts, primarily the work of Mel Scott,[1] resulted in the creation of a special study commission to make a preliminary investigation. Early in 1965, the study commission reported to the Legislature that a serious problem did indeed exist, and recommended a new temporary agency to deal with it.[2] The Legislature and the Governor responded by establishing the San Francisco Bay Conservation and Development Commission. The commission was authorized to regulate Bay filling during the 1965–69 interim, and was directed to prepare a comprehensive and enforceable plan for the Bay and its shoreline. In addition, the commission was asked to recommend "the appropriate agency" to maintain and carry out the comprehensive plan.[3]

Study of Comprehensive Regional Governmental Reorganization

The commission's legislative charge emphasized the multifunctional nature of the problems confronted, as well as their regional character. It recognized not only that all parts of the Bay are interrelated, but also that what happens in the surrounding region affects the Bay and shoreline, and vice versa. Thus the commission soon realized that restriction of its initial investigation to organizational alternatives capable of dealing only with the Bay and shoreline would be completely inadequate, in view of the breadth and scope of the Legislature's intent. Accordingly, the commission was obliged to look beyond limited organizational means for regulating Bay fill and shoreline development, and to contemplate the inclusion of those functions with other regional functions and programs. This led to a thorough study of the problems and available alternatives for comprehensive regional governmental reorganization.

---

[1] Mel Scott, *The Future of San Francisco Bay* (Berkeley: Institute of Governmental Studies, University of California, September 1963).

[2] California. San Francisco Bay Conservation Study Commission, *A Report to the California Legislature* (Sacramento: January 7, 1965).

[3] *Cal. Stats.,* 1965, ch. 1162 (*Government Code,* sec. 66651).

Current Interest in the Bay Area

Other concurrent activities in the Bay Area also argued for an exploration of comprehensive approaches. In 1966–67 the Association of Bay Area Governments (ABAG) sponsored a proposal for a four-purpose agency, to be created through a modification of the association's own structure. Currently, the Bay Area Transportation Study Commission (BATS) and the Bay-Delta Water Quality Control Study are considering organizational means of implementing their plans. Most important of all, the possible establishment of a multipurpose government in the Bay Area is under examination by the Joint Committee on Bay Area Regional Organization (BARO), aided by an advisory committee (Senate Concurrent Resolution No. 41, 1967 General Session). In addition, other nongovernmental organizations and agencies, such as the Bay Area Council, Associated Regional Citizens (ARC), San Francisco Planning and Urban Renewal Association (SPUR), The Leagues of Women Voters of the Bay Area, and People for Open Space, to name a few, are actively engaging themselves in discussions of regional problems and the possible need for a regional government.

Furthermore, the hearings by BARO, as well as preliminary reports of a leadership opinion survey conducted by the Institute of Governmental Studies, point to a strong consensus on the need for a limited-function regional government in the Bay Area.[4] In its study of governmental alternatives, BCDC has taken advantage of this widespread interest in and acceptance of comprehensive approaches. Thus the commission has furthered its own aims, and has also given a significant impetus to the other regional study efforts, by its investigation of organizational alternatives and their implications.

Importance of the BCDC Recommendations

Whatever institutional recommendations are made by BCDC will, if adopted, have major long-term impact on the future of the region and its governmental structure. Once created, new institutions tend to be perpetuated, particularly if they serve a useful purpose. The nature of the institutional arrangement finally devised to deal with the Bay and shoreline (and possibly other problems) is not a minor or incidental matter. On the contrary, the new arrangement will, as a result of the way its governing body is constituted, plus the scope of the powers as-

[4] Stanley Scott and Willis D. Hawley, "Leadership Views of the Bay Area and its Regional Problems: A Preliminary Report"; and "Organizing to Solve Regional Problems in the San Francisco Bay Area," *Public Affairs Report* (Berkeley: Institute of Governmental Studies, University of California) 9 (1, 2), February and April 1968.

signed, means of financing, and other features, largely determine the nature of public policies to be developed in updating the plan, modifying its conditions, and exercising powers of implementation.

Implications for the Future

The institutional recommendations should be carefully drafted, with a long time span and long-term goals in view. Population growth, technological change, and environmental modification have already put tremendous pressures on natural resources in urban areas. These pressures will increase in the future. Only institutions that are inherently strong, and deliberately structured for adaptability to unforeseen change, will be able to meet the long-term challenges of the future. This argues for *comprehensive* solutions rather than the adoption of provisional makeshifts.

Although planning for the long-term future presents an almost insuperable task, two devices can help scale the job down to a reasonable size. First, the recommendations can be based on the best estimate of future regional problems and programs of the next five to fifteen years. Second, the institutions established can be designed to insure their later reexamination and possible modification if and when changed circumstances so require.

Already, therefore, a number of criteria are beginning to emerge. First, the institutional recommendations must be based on consideration of *all* the regional programs in existence or which are likely to be undertaken within five to fifteen years. Second, the arrangements must take into account the interrelations among all regional activities and the complex ways in which different regional programs affect each other. Third, the *minimum* goal should be the best feasible coordination of regional efforts, and the *maximum* goal establishment of a comprehensive agency comprising them all. Fourth, a periodic objective review should be "built into" the system, to facilitate future modification, as needed. This would provide insurance against organizational obsolescence and institutional resistance to change.

A Central Task—Analyzing Areas of Conflict

Among other things, this study poses some of the critical issues confronting BCDC—the tough problems of organization, administration, and finance that must be resolved in the course of the commission's work. As noted above, these issues include the interrelationships between existing and future agencies with major impact on current or probable future regional problems and programs. All these interrelationships involve actual or potential competition in future development and resource allocation. Hence they are surrounded by conflicts between interested parties, and many are highly controversial.

These conflicts and controversies, as well as the impact of different kinds of development, must be studied and analyzed. The review process must explore the policy implications of the different viewpoints and interests. This evaluation will shed additional light on the feasibility and probable results of various organizational and financial arrangements. Too often in the past, public discussions and negotiations have not illuminated the real issues clearly, and the actual reasons for many decisions, or "non-decisions," have remained obscure, hidden beneath the cliches and "conventional wisdom" in which much public discussion of controversial matters is often clothed.

Organization of the Study

Following this introduction, the study presents an overview of the Bay Area's regionalism, which was established very early in California's history. Experimentation with various governmental arrangements is discussed briefly, bringing the review of Bay Area developments up-to-date. This should provide necessary perspective to facilitate evaluation of a variety of organizational approaches presented later. The third chapter sketches general guidelines for further study and policy determination, including elements in the decision process, criteria and methods for establishing a regional policy-making body, leadership, functions and powers, financing, and relationships with other agencies. The subsequent three chapters review experience with and ideas about alternative approaches to metropolitan governmental organization in other regions and in the Bay Area itself. The seventh chapter contains a detailed examination of the recent Association of Bay Area Governments proposal. The eighth chapter presents two other concrete suggestions for ways of choosing a Bay Area regional government. The ninth and final chapter summarizes the findings and recommendations of the study.

As used in this report, "The Bay Area" means the nine counties bordering on San Francisco Bay.[5] The authors believe that either a single- or a multipurpose regional agency formed to carry out plans for the Bay must include these nine counties, We note, however, the suggestions made by others that the geographic area included be either smaller or larger than the nine counties.

---

[5] The nine counties are: Alameda, Contra Costa, Marin, Napa, San Francisco, San Mateo, Santa Clara, Solano, and Sonoma.

The Nine Counties' Regionalism: An Historical Overview

An overview of the San Francisco Bay Area's development as a region, including a look at its history of experimentation with solutions to regional and subregional problems, is essential background for an understanding of the current situation and the continuing pressures for organizational change. The Bay Area covers some 7,000 square miles of land area, and contains approximately 4.5 million people. The region is thus nearly as large as either Massachusetts or New Jersey. Most of the population, however, is clustered near the Bay shoreline on relatively narrow plains ringed by hills: some 1,300 square miles comprise the "urban segment."

The Bay and the Region

The Bay itself has had a crucial role in directing urban growth. From the early days of American domination, beginning with the Gold Rush of 1849, the use of shallow-draught steam-powered boats knit together the various settlements around the Bay. The protected waters not only offered safe harbor for ocean-going vessels, but also served as an incomparable early-day means of local and regional transport. Thus, while the Bay separated the region's communities spatially, its strong sinews of waterborne communication and commerce gave the area a very real sense of economic interdependence.

As geographer James Vance puts it:

The San Francisco Bay Area was, from the beginning, characterized by *an open extensive settlement pattern* with a few major nuclei ... and with large areas of intervening space. Spreading the population "thin" and carrying them about on water, the Bay Area metropolis was able to stake out the limits of its ultimate site, even by the mid-point of the nineteenth century. Subsequent events have merely filled in this initial frame.[1]

Thus, the Bay Area's "regionalism" was established very early, although most matters of commerce and government—i.e., government below the state level—were much too localized for treatment by a governmental entity as large as the Bay Area. The region was soon divided into nine counties for purposes of many local governmental functions, and individual cities were created to serve the dispersed but growing urban settlements.

---

[1] James E. Vance, Jr., *Geography and Urban Evolution in the San Francisco Bay Area* (Berkeley: Institute of Governmental Studies, University of California, 1964), p. 35.

7

Thus geography and historic circumstance, plus more than a century of growth, have made the San Francisco Bay Area one of the most complex metropolitan communities in the United States—at least in terms of governmental organization. For comparison: Los Angeles County encompasses a population of 7 million persons in a single county, and has capitalized on that fact by transforming the county into an agency of regional and subregional government that, at least until recently, has been unique in the United States. The existence of the dominant City of Los Angeles, with its approximately 460 square-mile area and nearly 3 million population, also provides a central governmental framework which has no counterpart in the Bay Area. The San Francisco Bay Area's 4.5 million people are distributed among nine counties—thus precluding use of a county as a regional governing mechanism; and San Francisco, the largest city (a consolidated city-county), contains only 42 square miles of land area and 740,000 people.

Similar comparisons may be made with many other major metropolitan areas which have dominant central cities, or only one or two county governments, or both, thus giving these regions relatively well-defined centers of political power, as compared with the Bay Area. For example, the New York region of 13 million population has at its core the great central city (in effect, a consolidated city-county) of 8 million; the Chicago area has a dominant central city, and much of its metropolitan population is contained in Cook County; the same may be said of Pittsburgh and Allegheny County, Cleveland and Cuyahoga County, Miami and Dade County, and of many other urban centers.

This is not to deny the fact that almost all major metropolitan areas in the United States suffer from severe governmental fragmentation. But San Francisco suffers more than most. Paradoxically, however, the weakness has also been a source of strength: it has encouraged experimentation.

Experimentation: A Product of Diversity

The complexity of the Bay Area's governmental structure—especially the absence of a single dominant county—has made peculiarly difficult the handling of regional problems, the conduct of regional planning, or the construction of needed regional facilities. Several attempts to achieve comprehensive governmental reorganization by creating some kind of general purpose (or multipurpose) government in the region have met with failure.[2] The existing local governments have viewed such proposals as a threat to their autonomy, if not to their existence. This

---

[2] The efforts before 1948 are analyzed in John C. Bollens, *The Problem of Government in the San Francisco Bay Region* (Berkeley: Bureau of Public Administration, University of California, 1948).

attitude, bolstered by the persistent Jeffersonian-Jacksonian tradition of the political primacy of *local* government has defeated all efforts at comprehensive reorganization.

Strong resistance has also come from various portions of the private sector. Many business firms, labor unions, and other groups with workable arrangements protecting their interests have preferred a less-than-satisfactory status quo to the uncertainties of comprehensive change. The existing "system" represents a complicated balance of power whose deliberate modification, except at a slow pace, many of the participants have viewed with concern. Nevertheless, almost all recognize that the problems of urban growth make *some* change essential.

Until quite recently, moreover, regional problems have tended to reach the critical stage one at a time. The pressures to obtain new domestic water supplies for the Bay Area preceded by some years the demand to build the major bridges crossing the Bay. Similarly, awareness of the regional water pollution problem came several years before acceptance of the need for regional air pollution control. And the state was well along with the planning and construction of an urban freeway system for the Bay Area before community leaders decided to build a 75-mile rail rapid transit system.

Thus, regional problems have been confronted singly and solved individually through a variety of mechanisms. Further, the personnel of civic and governmental leadership which developed solutions differed markedly from problem to problem, making for further diversity. Whatever may be said of such a piecemeal policy of ad hoc solutions versus a comprehensive solution, the recent history of the Bay Area represents a great deal of governmental experimentation.

Without attempting a full enumeration of the regional and subregional institutions created, the most important ones are listed here in the chronological order of their dates of establishment: East Bay Municipal Utility District (1923), Golden Gate Bridge and Highway District (1928), East Bay Regional Park District (1934), San Francisco Bay Regional Water Pollution Control Board (1949),[3] Bay Area Air Pollution Control District (1955), Alameda-Contra Costa Transit District (1956), San Francisco Bay Area Rapid Transit District (1957), West Bay Rapid Transit Authority (1964), and Marin County Transit District (1964).

The Governor's Commission: 1959–1961

After 1957 there was a temporary halt in the establishment of permanent new regional entities, and an effort was made to reevaluate the

---

[3] Now renamed Water *Quality* Control Board.

situation.⁴ A Governor's Commission on Metropolitan Area Problems
was appointed in 1959. Its report to the Governor and Legislature in
1960–61 urged the creation of one multipurpose regional district in
each of the state's metropolitan areas, to be responsible for *regional
planning*⁵ and at least *one* additional function taken from the following
list: (1) air pollution control, (2) metropolitan water supply, (3) metropolitan sewage disposal and drainage, (4) metropolitan transportation,
terminals and related facilities, (5) metropolitan parks and parkways,
(6) metropolitan law enforcement functions, (7) metropolitan aspects
of fire protection, (8) metropolitan phases of urban renewal, (9) civil
defense, and (10) any other areawide function requested by the residents and leadership of the individual metropolitan region concerned.

In order to implement this proposal, the commission recommended
that the state Legislature authorize establishment of a multipurpose
district by majority vote within each of the state's metropolian areas.
Such a district would have been governed by a council selected by, and
from the membership of, the governing bodies of the cities and counties
within the district. This recommended pattern of *constituent-unit*
representation was derived largely from experience in the Bay Area
(see below, pages 24 and 25, for a discussion of this experience).

The proposal, although imaginative and potentially of great significance, proved unacceptable. It met first with relative indifference
and later with a wave of hostility. The officials of many small and
medium-sized cities, in particular, opposed the creation of something
they referred to as "metropolitan supergovernment." This emotive term
evidently suggested to many that one *single* government would be
established in a metropolitan area, replacing and absorbing all existing
local governments.

Obviously the Governor's Commission was proposing something
quite different. No responsible leader has ever seriously suggested a
change as drastic as the creation of a single unitary government for a
region as large and diverse as the Bay Area. But the "supergovernment"
label helped crystallize concern that the multipurpose district might
alter some of the existing power relationships—as it almost certainly
would have done. In any event, pressure from the two associations representing California's city and county governments effectively shelved the

---

⁴ There was, however, no lull in activity. In addition to the efforts of the Governor's
Commission, several groups were pressing for various kinds of action, as will be noted
below.

⁵ The commission was recommending *advisory* regional planning only. In California, the "police" power of zoning and land use control traditionally rests with the
municipalities for areas within city limits and with the counties for areas outside
the cities.

proposal. But the commission's deliberations did help focus attention on the Bay Area's experimentation with regional machinery of government through 1960, and afforded an opportunity to assess the consequences.

Developments: 1960–1966

Despite the post-1957 lull in forming new regional districts and the state's failure to enact the metropolitan multipurpose district proposal, some extremely significant new developments in the Bay Area have occurred since 1960.

The Association of Bay Area Governments

First among these developments was the creation of the Association of Bay Area Governments (ABAG) in 1961. This move was stimulated by a growing awareness of the need for a regional forum of local officials, and was probably hastened by powerful efforts in 1959 and 1961 to establish still another permanent special district in the Bay Area: a "Golden Gate Authority." This proposed agency, later called "Golden Gate Transportation Commission," would have had jurisdiction over the toll bridges, and authority to acquire or build seaports and airports. Although the 1961 proposal contained many good features and received strong support from parts of the business community, its dependence on revenue bond financing was questioned by many observers. In addition, some officials opposed it as constituting a threat to their locally-owned seaports and airports. Others fought the move because they considered its proposed use of the region's bridge tolls to support airport and seaport development illogical and unwise. This financial arrangement would have established a close linkage between rather unrelated forms of transportation, while leaving out transportation modes (i.e., various forms of transit) more directly related to the money-making bridges.

The 1959 proposal resulted in a study commission and a report to the Legislature urging creation of the "Golden Gate Transportation Commission."[6] The 1961 bill was narrowly defeated, primarily through the efforts of the chairman of the Senate Transportation Committee. But the proposal's real or implied threat to local governments in the Bay Area, and its demonstration that they were poorly organized to influence proposals affecting the Bay region, hastened the creation of the Association of Bay Area Governments.

---

[6] California. Golden Gate Authority Commission, *Final Report on the Feasibility of a Regional Agency to Coordinate Transportation Facilities ... with Recommendations for a Golden Gate Transportation Commission for the San Francisco Bay Area* (February 1, 1961).

The association began essentially as an agency for research, study, and discussion of mutual problems. A voluntary organization, but with legal status, it was formed by intergovernmental contracts under California's "Joint Exercise of Powers Act."[7] All cities and counties in the Bay Area are eligible to join, and eight of the nine counties and 80 of the 91 cities are now members. The association is governed by a General Assembly consisting of one representative chosen by and from the governing body of each member city and county (the constituent-unit principle). City and county representatives vote separately, however, and a majority of a quorum of each is required for action. Thus, the General Assembly is essentially a "bicameral legislature meeting in a single room." From 1961 to 1967, a smaller Executive Committee of 19 members provided continuity and conducted the organization's affairs under policies established by the General Assembly.[8] The association is financed by annual assessments levied against all member governments on a population basis.

Shortly after ABAG was established, the Berkeley city representative requested that the organization support proposed legislation creating a San Francisco Bay Area Regional Planning District. This proposal was considered by the association, but was rejected in favor of an ABAG-sponsored attempt to accomplish regional planning by coordinating the planning activities of the area's individual cities and counties. With tremendous effort, city and county planning staffs contributed their time to ABAG in an attempt to inventory existing plans and prepare a single nine-county base map.

Difficulties encountered in this first step toward "regional planning" convinced most local officials that effective planning would require a staff employed by ABAG. In 1962 ABAG endorsed the proposal that the association itself become the area's advisory regional planning agency. At the same time an application was made to the U.S. Housing and Home Finance Agency (now absorbed by the Department of Housing and Urban Development), for urban planning assistance funds, to be supplemented by local contributions in money or staff time. An initial federal grant of $170,000 was announced in February, 1964. Subsequent federal, state and local support enabled ABAG to employ a full- or part-time staff of 13 persons, and to produce a preliminary regional plan in November, 1966.[9]

[7] *California Government Code*, secs. 6500–6578.

[8] The Executive Committee was enlarged to 20 members in 1967, and reorganized as of January 1, 1968 to provide for a 34-member body.

[9] Association of Bay Area Governments, *Preliminary Regional Plan for the San Francisco Bay Region* (Berkeley: November 1966).

THE TRANSPORTATION STUDY COMMISSION

Meanwhile a large committee comprising business, government, and civic leaders had been working to promote a comprehensive program of transportation planning for the Bay Area, also to be financed primarily by federal funds. A proposal approved by the state Legislature and Governor in a 1963 act created the Bay Area Transportation Study Commission (BATS). This commission has 41 members, 19 of whom are representatives of the cities and counties and of ABAG. In effect, the ABAG Executive Committee sits on the commission, affording a basis for close liaison between the two planning efforts.

Funds from the U.S. Bureau of Public Roads, Department of Housing and Urban Development, State Department of Public Works, and ABAG are being contributed to the joint BATS-ABAG planning endeavor. Because BATS is a temporary agency established only for the initial crash program of transportation planning, the BATS legislation provides that the study commission "shall take steps to provide for an orderly transition of its responsibilities to appropriate permanent agencies. . . ." To this end, BATS is directed to give first consideration to existing agencies, but "if the study commission finds that the purpose and intent of this section may be advanced thereby, it may make studies and develop recommendations for a possible reorganization or realignment of responsibilities of public agencies dealing with transportation problems in the Bay Area."[10]

THE COMMISSION ON BAY FILLING

While plans for the joint BATS-ABAG program were being laid, another regional problem of major proportions was beginning to arouse intense public interest. The filling of shallow portions of the Bay to create new land for residential and industrial sites had been increasing and threatened to accelerate sharply. Vocal citizen concern resulted in the creation of a special study commission to make a preliminary investigation. Early in 1965, the study commission reported to the Legislature that a serious problem did indeed exist and recommended a new temporary agency to deal with it.[11] The Legislature and the Governor responded by establishing the San Francisco Bay Conservation and Development Commission, which was instructed to prepare a comprehensive and enforceable plan for the Bay and its shoreline.

---

[10] *Cal Stats.*, 1963, ch. 911 (*Government Code*, secs. 66500–66515).

[11] California. San Francisco Bay Conservation Study Commission, *A Report To the California Legislature* (January 7, 1965).

The prestige of ABAG has suffered somewhat from these events. When the issue of Bay filling first arose, ABAG had difficulty arriving at a consensus on policy. Member cities and counties with extensive fillable shallow Bay lands were reluctant to forfeit opportunities for what they believed to be potential additions to their economies. As the controversy grew heated, however, some local governments realized that all would lose if unrestricted filling were continued indefinitely and at an accelerated pace. ABAG finally supported the idea of a state-imposed system of regulation, but urged that it be administered by the association. This suggestion was not accepted, because several interested parties, including the state (which owns half the Bay), believed the proposal would result in weak enforcement.

Instead, the San Francisco Bay Conservation and Development Commission was established. Nevertheless, local governments and ABAG presumably have a measure of influence on BCDC. Three members of the 27-man commission are appointed by ABAG to represent the cities of the Bay Area. Nine more are appointed by each of the county boards of supervisors—one to a county. BATS, which is closely tied to ABAG and local government, appoints one representative. The remainder of the commission consists of two representatives of the federal government, four of state governmental agencies, one from the Regional Water Quality Control Board, and seven "representatives of the public," five of whom are appointed by the Governor and one each by the Senate Rules Committee and the Speaker of the Assembly. These complicated and seemingly unwieldy arrangements were necessary to accommodate the unusually wide range of groups and agencies that are concerned with the Bay and its future.

A Plan To Avert Large-Scale Water Pollution

Waste waters from reclamation and drainage projects in California's Central Valley, and the fertilizers and pesticides they carry, have a potential for serious pollution of the Bay waters. This threat resulted in another ambitious program, which was launched by 1965 legislation designed to avoid large-scale pollution of the Bay waters and those of the Sacramento and San Joaquin River Deltas that feed into the Bay.[12] To guide the San Francisco Bay-Delta Water Quality Control Program, a steering committee was created representing BCDC, ABAG, four regional water quality control boards, nine interested state agencies, and the two houses of the Legislature. In addition, a technical com-

_____
[12] *Cal. Stats.*, 1965, ch. 1351.

mittee has been created representing the above agencies, the University of California, several agencies of federal government, local governments, and private industry.

As was suggested before, the Bay Area may be engaged in the process of converting an inherited governmental weakness into a policy-making strength. The weakness: governmental complexity and the absence of any dominant institutional framework to take the lead in solving regional problems. The strength: experimentation with regional solutions is made both easier and more necessary because there is no dominant center and the region's governmental structure has not "frozen" into the relative immobility characteristic of many areas.

Geography, climate, history and assorted good fortune have made the Bay Area one of the choice places for human habitation on this planet—or so most residents fondly believe. And believing this, they are convinced they have a great deal to lose from uncontrolled growth. The public is finally beginning to realize that our ever-more-powerful technology and economy have unleashed formidable and increasing forces tending to modify the environment. Many Bay Area leaders now see that much of the region's excellence will be destroyed unless strong public and private countermeasures are taken.

This is what the current flurry of activity is all about, with the varied array of commissions and committees, and large cast of characters. A great deal is at stake, but with statesmanship and luck, California and the Bay region may be able to initiate the necessary processes of comprehensive planning and control. In this effort, not only should the Bay Area's own experimentation be drawn upon, but also thought should be given to the experience of other areas with different approaches to governmental reorganization. Valuable positive and negative guidance —i.e., suggestions as to what might be attempted as well as hazards to be avoided—may be obtained from others' accomplishments and failures. This material is summarized in Part Two. Before reviewing experiences elsewhere, however, we present the following discussion of guidelines for analyzing the governmental issues in the Bay Area—or indeed in any metropolitan region.

Some Guidelines for Further Study and Decision

This chapter opens with a discussion of criteria that should be relevant to *any* governmental agency proposed, whatever its functions and powers may be. These guidelines, which are stated in general terms, will be useful in evaluating organizational proposals intended to deal with a single governmental function, as well as more broadly based, multipurpose regional governmental concepts. Potential major policy determinants are then reviewed, the implications of representational systems analyzed, and some concrete possibilities sketched. Next, the dimensions and demands of the regional legislative responsibility are outlined, and the critical problem of leadership examined. The chapter closes with a review of the range of functions that might be assigned, the scope of organizational and financial choices available, and possible relations with other governments.

Criteria for a Regional Government

An effective regional governmental agency must be able to search out needs in its area of concern, formulate proposed programs, and insure full consideration and public disclosure of all the implications of the proposals. Then, after due discussion, the agency must be able to reach decisions on highly controversial issues. It must also have the authority and financial resources to implement those decisions.

Full Analysis and Disclosure

All aspects of proposed programs and their probable implications should be examined carefully before final decisions are made. It may be as important to analyze and disclose the implications of a *negative* decision as of a positive one. In other words, the decision process should be designed to consider the effect on the region of both *action* and *inaction*. Also, the arrangements for thorough study should be explicitly for that purpose. The study machinery should not be converted into a mechanism for unnecessary delay or the exercise of vetoes.

Thus searching study and analysis are essential to the decision process. Many examples could be given of incomplete analysis of the implications of proposed new programs, as well as incomplete disclosure of all relevant information. In fact, deliberate failure to publicize may be practiced as a means of getting an action either accomplished or blocked. But the implications of *public* sector actions should always be analyzed and publicly reported prior to final decision. This does not, of course, mean day-to-day reporting of all plans and negotiations; it does mean disclosure before a public action has become an accomplished fact.

16

Without this, public decision-making may become "one-upmanship," the outcome depending on which group manages to obtain an advantage over another by guile, stealth, intrigue, or simply by outwitting the "other side." In the private sector nondisclosure is part of the game, and is even protected by law, e.g., census and income tax nondisclosure protection. In the public sector such nondisclosure is normally contrary to the public interest. Any new governmental system to deal with regional problems should be carefully designed to minimize if not eradicate the practice of achieving "public" policy decisions by inadequate analysis or nondisclosure of their consequences.

REPRESENTATION OF "INTERESTS"

The policy body itself should not deliberately contain representatives of special interests. Representation of interested parties, as such, can be best accomplished through the hearing process, through advisory councils, or perhaps through ad hoc committees established to consider specific questions. Interested representatives could be placed directly on the advisory councils or committees. This has both advantages and disadvantages. It would insure the representation of specified interests, but the advisory council might become largely a sounding board for the expression of interest viewpoints, rather than the watchful guardian of the penetrating and wide-ranging review function envisioned above. Probably the better way to handle the problem would be full and fair public hearings during which interest representatives appear before the policy body, or before an advisory council, or special ad hoc committees.

CAREFUL STUDY—BUT LEADING TO A FINAL DECISION

Ample study and consideration of all interests and alternatives should not be permitted to postpone final decisions indefinitely. The major aim is to develop a feasible and workable process for coming to grips with issues, developing solutions, and implementing decisions. Among other things, this suggests minimizing the number of persons or groups holding the power of veto, if the new decision process is to result in action.

RELATING THE PROCESS TO THE NEED

The findings and accomplishments of science and technology make it clear that the many *systems* operating in the region—physical, social, economic, ecological—are deeply and increasingly interrelated. Almost anything done in one field in any part of a metropolitan area has an influence in other fields and throughout the area. Good policy decisions must be based on the fullest possible understanding of their ramifications.

The finest and most up-to-date tools of data processing, model build-ing and systems analysis should be available to the agency or agencies charged with the overview function on major regional questions. Proper use of such resources as part of an appropriately designed political de-cision process, could go far toward eliminating unforeseen or undis-closed adverse impacts of new policies.[1]

Goals: The End Product

But the technology of systems analysis alone will not provide adequate solutions to the policy and planning problems to be faced by the region. Painful, difficult, and hard-headed work must go into the quest for regional goals if the agency or agencies in charge are to do more than preside over partially coordinated processes of strangulation and envi-ronmental degradation. The following are needed if planning is to be effective: goals[2]; powers of land use control; financial authority; such additional police powers as may be necessary to handle regional, inter-acting systems; and governmental mechanism(s) for making decisions and carrying them out.

Implementation: Many Levels

Perhaps the same mechanism(s) that sets the goals can carry them out. On the other hand, there are many "levels" of goals, ranging from decisions on major, long-term regional policies to matters primarily of local concern. Thus more than one level of goal-setting mechanism would appear both inevitable and desirable.

Some basic large-scale goals can be adopted as *fundamental regional guidelines*. The more detailed goal decisions at the local level must be accommodated within these guidelines, through (1) persuasion, (2) exercise of the police power at the regional or state level, (3) regional or state-level fiscal transfer payments, or (4) combinations of the first three.

ACCOUNTABILITY

A legislative policy-making body should be both accountable and responsive, while retaining sufficient independence and authority to confer effective decision capability. "Accountability," as the term is employed here, means a generalized ultimate responsibility to the public served. Its converse would be a long-term or permanent insulation from the influences of public opinion.

[1] Melvin M. Webber, "The Roles of Intelligence Systems in Urban-Systems Plan-ning," *Journal of the American Institute of Planners* 31: 289–296, November 1965.
[2] See for example: John W. Dyckman, "Social Planning, Social Planners and Planned Societies," *Journal of the American Institute of Planners* 32:66–76, March 1966; also the article in the same issue by Robert C. Young, "Goals and Goal-Setting," 76–85.

RESPONSIVENESS

"Responsiveness" must be differentiated from accountability. Responsiveness suggests a willingness to consider the views and desires of various affected interests and groups *during* the process of policy development. Thus responsiveness designates the degree to which the legislative body responds to pressures from interested parties.

DECISION CAPABILITY

The final term, "decision capability," refers to the capacity of the legislative body to make and implement a firm and final decision on a public policy matter, once the evidence is heard and adequate public discussion has taken place. Responsiveness and decision capability may be viewed as partially countervailing tendencies. That is, a legislative body relatively insulated from pressures and possessing adequate authority is likely to manifest a high level of decision capability—of freedom to "get on with the job" regardless of stiff opposition. This can be good and constructive, yet if carried too far, may result in arbitrariness or failure to consider the impact of the agency's decisions on other agencies and interests in the region.

But a legislative body that is overly sensitive and responsive to current pressures from interested groups may be unable to make the hard positive decisions necessary to develop and implement new public policies. Additional problems are created if the body is responsive to pressures of certain groups but not others. When this occurs, and adequate disclosure does not redress the balance, the public interest may not be well served.

Thus the need for decision capability partially conflicts with the need for a degree of responsiveness. The aim should be *accommodation* of both requirements through an appropriate balance. The region needs a policy-making body with the ability to decide difficult and controversial issues, but it also must be protected against the risk of creating an excessively independent, unresponsive, and potentially irresponsible agency.

Determinants of Policy

The policies of an organization are determined by a multitude of influences, including the scope of questions and controversies confronted, the system of representation employed, the terms on which financial resources are made available, and the functional responsibilities assigned.

These points are illustrated in the following discussion drawn from the Scott-Bollens BCDC report. Special attention is given those factors that should be weighed in designing a governmental mechanism to further the planning, conservation, and development of San Francisco Bay and its shoreline.

QUESTIONS AND CONTROVERSIES: THE BAY ALONE

Why is "the controversial Bay"—and the question of filling Bay tidelands—an object of such intense conflict? In a sentence, it is because there are so many diverse interests concerned with Bay filling, on one hand, and with Bay and shoreline conservation, on the other. One of the great pressures for Bay filling is the potential high value of close-in "made" land. Long-term owners of submerged lands—with clear or clouded titles—as well as recent speculative investors, stand to gain from the large appreciation in value that occurs when filling and development are permitted. Prospective developers also have an interest, because made land gives them a place to locate new housing or industrial parks.

Local governments may consider filling a means to make room for future growth and thus to enhance their tax bases. Bay fill can provide a relatively cheap location for new freeways because it avoids the need to acquire right-of-way in built-up areas. Also, Bay frontage has been widely used for garbage and refuse disposal. Tideland filling has provided for expansion of airports and seaport facilities. Furthermore, filling has been employed to dispose of spoils from dredging operations.

Powerful pressures are also working against further Bay filling, except on a small-scale and highly selective basis. One of the most important sources of counter-pressure is grounded in a combination of esthetic-psychological-economic factors. The Bay is perhaps *the* most important and unique open space feature of the region, which gives it form and character. The physical beauty of the area is primarily dependent on its topography, i.e., the hills, the flatlands and the Bay itself. Psychological awareness of the Bay—whether directly through observation from vantage points, or implicitly in the knowledge that "it is there" to be viewed and enjoyed at leisure—is one of the reasons why so many residents consider the Bay Area one of the finest places to live in the United States. And these very real but imponderable factors translate into economic values, i.e., the ability of the area to compete effectively in national specialty labor markets, the value of view lots, and so forth.

The Bay is one of the crucial reasons why the urbanized community of the nine counties has grown up in a relatively dispersed pattern, with "elbow room" and a sense of spaciousness. The Bay has shaped the "Area." And the Bay as permanent open space can help to limit the future congestion which a filled-in Bay would permit.

Conservationists view the Bay as a major natural phenomenon eminently worthy of being preserved, not unlike Yosemite, Lake Tahoe, or the Redwood stands. It is an important wildlife preserve and a crucial link in the Pacific Flyway for migratory birds. Directly or indirectly the Bay supports a recreational and commercial fishery of major magnitude. The mudflats are an important source of nutrients for aquatic life, and the salt water-fresh water gradations in the Bay's estuaries are essential to the life cycle of anadromous fish, which must migrate from the sea to fresh water at spawning time. The Bay and its shoreline also possess actual or potential recreational uses of very great value: for sailing and boating, for beaches, waterfront parks, marinas, and similar facilities.

Proximity of the active Hayward and San Andreas earthquake faults have raised serious questions regarding the wisdom of filling and building on tidelands. Under certain conditions, structures on such land are prone to earthquake-caused damage.[3] Finally, further extensive filling of the Bay's shallow areas would adversely affect the region's climate, temperature variations, and air pollution.

This brief discussion only outlines some of the major interests in the Bay and tidelands. It does, however, indicate the range of concerns which make "the controversial Bay" one of the most fascinating, frustrating, and significant land-use policy issues now confronting the region.

QUESTIONS AND CONTROVERSIES: THE BAY PLUS OTHER REGIONAL ISSUES

Considerations affecting the Bay obviously do not terminate at the shoreline. They include the whole continuum of problems and issues confronting the region. The question of Bay fill affects the location and enlargement of port and airport facilities, as well as of freeways. It has a direct impact on the future of solid waste disposal in the region. The Bay is a variety of open space, different in character but related to the other kind of open space—the hills and mountains. Together these open spaces have a major role in determining the form and quality of life in this urban region. These are only a few examples of the multitude of interrelationships between the Bay and the region.

Furthermore, complex interrelationships increase when a multifunctional agency is considered to control Bay fill and to accomplish other regional purposes. In addition to Bay conservation and development, functions most frequently discussed in the Bay Area for possible treatment by a multipurpose agency include regional planning, solid waste disposal, open space and parks, air and water pollution control, and

---

[3] California. San Francisco Bay Conservation and Development Commission, *Fill: Three Reports on Aspects of Fill in San Francisco Bay* (San Francisco: May 1967).

transportation. Beyond these, it is conceivable that "wholesale" *aspects* of many other public functions could be handled on a regional basis, including but not limited to water supply, education, housing and renewal, police, fire protection, finance of major capital facilities, and so forth. The realm of functions regionalized will delineate the scope of new questions and issues presented. These will, in turn, both influence and be resolved by the public policy determinations finally made.

REPRESENTATION AS A POLICY DETERMINANT

Additional considerations beyond the generalized criteria discussed previously enter into the representation equation and will act as powerful policy determinants. Especially important is the expression of regional vs. local viewpoints. Some people tend to take a regional view of things; others tend to give priority to matters of immediate concern to themselves and their local communities.

What factors are involved in a person's outlook, especially as it might be reflected in the policies of a regional legislative body of which he is a member? The internal value system of the individual is important, of course. This is the cumulative result of all his past experience. The external influences brought to bear upon him by friends and business or professional associates, as well as his means of earning a livelihood, will also help determine his policy positions. The method of selecting a local or regional representative and the nature of the constituency to which he is responsible will be influential. Long-term tenure may give a representative sufficient security and confidence to express a regional view, and, when occasion demands, to rise above local interests bringing pressure on him.

For a variety of reasons one individual may consider himself primarily a resident of a region, while another may concentrate on localized social or business interests that determine his outlook. Businesses whose markets are regional in scope may impart to their staff a regional outlook in public matters. Thus the young, upward-mobile business executive may be a good candidate for a post requiring a regional outlook. On the other hand, he may be too single-mindedly concerned with personal advancement to take controversial stands on public issues. Or he may fear that time devoted to public service will jeopardize his future in private enterprise.

Both local and regional interests embody values deserving consideration and reasonable representation. How should they be weighed and balanced? Direct involvement of locally oriented individuals is one means of protecting local interests. But this may impede regional programs if the "locals" are strictly negative. On the other hand, their involvement may be useful (1) as a means of expressing legitimate views, (2) as a method of educating them to the reality of regional needs, and (3) as a means of communicating regional feedback to their fellow "locals".[4] If the "locals" dominate, however—or even exercise a minority veto power—regional programs probably will not be implemented. This must be kept in mind when evaluating concrete proposals for establishing systems of representation.

Different systems of representation will thus bring forth different mixes of viewpoints and result in the adoption of different policies. In other words, *representation* is a critical matter.

OTHER POLICY DETERMINANTS

In addition to representational systems, there are still other policy determinants. Methods of finance and the scope of functional responsibilities are significant factors. For example, if an agency is given no taxing power or other independent revenue sources, but is required to finance its activities on a commercial basis, this will go far toward determining what projects it will or will not undertake. An agency limited to revenue bond financing cannot be expected to undertake costly capital outlays unless there is clear evidence of the installation not only being self-supporting, but also producing sufficient surplus to pay off the bonds. Similarly, an agency given responsibility for a single function—or a limited geographic area—will behave differently from one charged with several functions—or a large geographic area. In part, this is a matter of institutional jurisdiction, and in part of financial arrangements and constraints. In part, also, this relates to the influence of agency staff members, who have an interest in the organization's continued existence (and their jobs), its growth, and *appearance* of success. The essential point is that *finance* and *responsibilities* are important determinants—along with systems of representation—of the policies an agency will enunciate, as well as what it will actually do or fail to do.

Representation: Constituting the Policy-Making Body

An imaginative governmental draftsman with a penchant for speculation could devise dozens of organizational arrangements for choosing a regional policy-making body. Nevertheless, most of these are variations on a few familiar organizational themes that will be explored in Part Two of this report. Some of the alternatives and their probable consequences—as they relate to the San Francisco Bay Area—are now outlined briefly.

---

[4] The acceptance by ABAG members of the need for regional planning in the Bay Area is, in part, a result of the direct involvement of local councilmen and supervisors in the association's planning effort.

CONSTITUENT-UNIT REPRESENTATION

The Bay Area's own experience provides an instructive commentary on the possible uses of the constituent-unit principle of representation. After many experiments with various forms of regional and subregional organization, by 1960 a school of thought had grown up in the San Francisco Bay Area about the desirability of various kinds of areawide governmental organizations.[5] It may be summarized as follows:

> The continued creation of separate and independent regional or metropolitan special districts will make it increasingly difficult to deal with *interacting* or regional public problems, services, and facilities. Hence, according to this view, some attempt should be made to design a single multipurpose agency, to which any new regional functions could be assigned. This would consolidate the various regional activities, and make certain that fiscal and other requirements of *each* function would be considered in the context of all the remaining needs of the area—and by an agency capable of taking or initiating action.

> All major regional public functions affect and interrelate with the local activities and interests of the *basic units of government* in the metropolitan area—the cities and counties. For this reason, close coordination between the cities and counties, on the one hand, and any regional agencies, on the other, is essential to effective operation. One way, although not the only way, of facilitating coordination between the regional agencies and the cities and counties is through the selection of governing bodies by means of "constituent-unit representation." This arrangement can take many forms as long as it provides for a federated structure in which the basic units of local government (cities and counties) are represented on the governing board of the regional district. Constituent-unit representation has the advantage of building into the regional district's structure a mechanism likely to insure its close coordination with the local governments.

In the Bay Area, the constituent-unit principle was first embodied in the air pollution control district, established in 1955. Another version was incorporated in the rapid transit district, established in 1957. The principle also underlay the unsuccessful multipurpose metropolitan district recommendation of the Governor's Commission on Metropoli-

---

[5] For a discussion of Bay Area experience to 1960, see: Stanley Scott ed., *Metropolitan Area Problems* (Berkeley: Bureau of Public Administration and University Extension, 1960), pp. 20–25.

tan Area Problems.[6] It has since been employed as a basis for the Association of Bay Area Governments, the local agency formation commissions, the West Bay Rapid Transit Authority, and the Marin County Transit District. Elements of constituent-unit representation are also found in the ad hoc Bay Area Transportation Study Commission and San Francisco Bay Conservation and Development Commission.

The Bay Area's constituent-unit approach was based on the assumption that the governments thus formed would be *single-purpose* in scope. Late in 1966, however, the Association of Bay Area Governments approved a statement by its Goals and Organization Committee urging extension of the principle—as embodied in a modified ABAG—to three new governmental functions, in addition to the regional planning effort now in progress. At the same time, ABAG approved a statement that a suggestion for absorption of BCDC and other regional bodies by the reorganized ABAG "should be given high priority for study, discussion and decision. . . ."

Some implications of this proposed extension of the constituent-unit principle to a multipurpose Bay Area government are examined below at pages 32–34 and 75–76, as well as in the fourth chapter of Part Two.

APPOINTMENT BY THE GOVERNOR

Appointment of the entire membership of metropolitan or regional governing bodies may be appropriate in certain situations, but none of these situations is currently present in the Bay Area; therefore, gubernatorial appointment of the entire membership has been and is now rejected as a concept.

The circumstances which could make gubernatorial appointment appropriate for some or all members of such a body include:

(1) When the metropolitan area reaches into two or more states (example: the New York Metropolitan Area, which includes parts of New Jersey and Connecticut).

(2) When one major metropolitan area in a small state contains a large portion of the state's population (Boston and Massachusetts).

(3) When there are "up-state vs. down-state" political splits, the metropolitan area often being dominated by one political party and the state government by another (Chicago and Illinois).

---

[6] The Governor's Commission appears to have considered the constituent-unit principle to be transitional, and commented as follows in the report of December 1960: "The Commission recognizes that as a metropolitan area *multipurpose* district is given an increasing number of functions it may be desirable to have some or all of the members of the metropolitan council chosen directly by the electorate in order to broaden representation by a cross section of groups in the metropolitan area. . . ." [Emphasis supplied]

(4) When special or unique situations exist, or existed in the past. (For example, the Port of San Francisco was taken out of the hands of the municipal government approximately 100 years ago, partly because the local officials of that time were not considered trustworthy. It was not returned to local control until 1968.)

DIRECT ELECTION

Direct election is the prevailing method of selecting what we hope are accountable, responsive and vigorous legislative bodies to govern general-purpose public agencies—the city councils, county boards of supervisors, state legislatures, and the U. S. Congress. Clearly direct election would be the preferred method for selecting accountable, responsive and vigorous *multipurpose* regional governments.

But as noted below, the success of the electoral process depends upon the importance and "visibility" of the agency whose members are elected, on the methods of filling vacancies, on the size of the electoral district, the closeness of contest, and upon partisanship or lack of it. Generally, direct elections of members of single-purpose district boards have rarely involved real contests or summoned the sustained popular attention necessary if direct election is to be effective. While directly elected single-purpose regional policy-making bodies have proven in many instances to be very high in decision capability, they are often low in responsiveness to outside pressures (at least to those publicly expressed), and because the elections are not contested, practically speaking the members are not accountable to the public.

Possibly a single-purpose agency with important responsibilities and extensive regulatory authority—such as control of Bay conservation and development—could call forth enough attention and involve such a multiplicity of interests that direct election of its members would work. But we have no experience in the United States with single-purpose districts possessing such extensive regulatory power. So, although we insist that multipurpose districts or governments must have a substantial proportion, at least, of directly elected members, we believe that the governing body of a *single-purpose* regional agency probably should not be directly elected. Any future move to create a single-purpose district governed by directly elected officials should be approached cautiously, and should be employed only as a last resort, subject to carefully designed safeguards.

Whether a decision is made in 1969 or at some later time, the problem of designing a regional agency that will be accountable, while maintaining an appropriate balance between responsiveness and decision capability, will have to be considered in depth. The matter is much more complicated than simply choosing among the three methods of selecting board members (1) by direct election, or (2) by appointment by the Governor, or (3) by indirect election (the constituent-unit method).

We shall return (on page 31) to the possibility of combining, in the regional legislative body of a multipurpose agency, members selected by two or more different methods. At this point, however, let us examine in detail the factors influencing the effectiveness of direct election.

Political Visibility

An agency whose political "visibility" is low cannot be expected to generate much interest or awareness on the part of voters. Visibility may be influenced by many factors, but one of the most potent relates to the number and importance of the functions with which the agency is entrusted. And importance means more than the *real* significance of the agency's decisions to the community. That is, the agency must not only *be* important, it must *be seen to be important* to the voter. The voter's image of an agency may not coincide with the actual significance of its decisions on the future of the region. Image, for example, is influenced by such matters as the treatment of an agency's affairs by mass media. If the media tend to ignore the agency, voters do not know about its activities, and voter interest in elections will be low.

Choosing Replacements

Under some arrangements, midterm vacancies are filled temporarily by appointees selected by the remaining members of the governing body. If the person selected runs for the office at a subsequent election, he is listed as an incumbent. Incumbents are seldom defeated in elections involving low political visibility. Consequently the practice encourages autonomy and self-perpetuation. The appropriate antidote is a requirement of midterm elections to fill vacancies, or a provision for interim appointment by an independent outside official or agency.

Size of Electoral Districts

Influence of the size—in area or population—of the electoral districts is a complex matter depending on many circumstances. A few of the more important will be reviewed here. First, the larger the district, the lower will be political visibility, unless the post is viewed as very important and the election contests are traditionally hard fought.

Second, the larger the district, the greater will be the influence of the major mass media—and of persons or groups with the ability (including sources of finance) to make effective appeals to the voters through the mass media.

Third, the larger the electoral district, the greater will be the effort and expense of conducting an effective campaign. Unless campaigns are supported from public sources, the need for assistance can increase a candidate's vulnerability to influence by those (1) who have the necessary funds and (2) who have a financial interest in the outcome of the agency's policy decisions.

Fourth, the smaller the district, the greater will be the influence of localized forces within the district, i.e., community newspapers, formal or informal community power structures, and concentrations of racial and ethnic minorities, or other geographic concentrations of persons having like interests and socioeconomic characteristics.

Fifth, small districts may consequently make for parochialism, while large districts may encourage candidates to give greater attention to regional matters .

Sixth, large electoral districts may tend to dilute the influence of concentrations of minority voters. The difference between the number of non-Caucasians in the Bay Area's nine-member Senate delegation (none) and that of the eighteen-member Assembly delegation (three) is a concrete example of this effect.

Seventh, on the other hand, if a large-district election is closely contested, cohesive minorities may constitute extremely influential "swing vote" factors that can determine the outcome of the election. If the "swing vote" phenomenon is to be effective, however, the elections must be contested and the races close. Low political visibility, nonpartisanship, the advantage of incumbency, and gerrymandering to produce "safe" seats can all operate to reduce the effect of the swing vote.

The significance of size is also related to the demographic composition and residential patterns of the area. For example, a large district in portions of San Mateo or Marin counties might be comparatively homogeneous. On the other hand, a district cut from a few city blocks in Oakland, San Francisco or Berkeley could be designed to approximate a cross section of the population. Lines in the core areas, however, could also be so drawn as to group Negroes in one district, upper-middle-class whites in another, lower-class whites in a third, and so on.

One desirable aim is to achieve a reasonable cross section of the population in as many districts as possible. Another goal is to avoid diluting and perhaps nullifying the influence of racial, ethnic, or other minorities. Obviously these two ends may conflict. How can an appropriate balance be achieved? Clearly, decisions on electoral districts must consider more than just the "one man, one vote" principle, which, laudable as it is, can mask other inequities that may be equally disenfranchising.

Consequently, electoral districting should give consideration to the distribution of the population and its racial, ethnic, and socioeconomic makeup. That is, the influence of the size and shape of districts, and their geographic location, require superimposition—actually or figuratively—of any proposed system of electoral districts on a map showing the region's demographic patterns, if all the representational implications are to be brought out. To our knowledge no metropolitan representational system has openly and explicitly taken into account the complex effects of population composition and distribution. Because this is such a difficult and controversial task, it may be preferable to use districts already established for some other electoral purpose, if they meet the representational needs of an elected Bay Area regional government.

Closeness of Contest

As suggested above, several factors can influence the closeness of electoral contests. The importance of the post sought is a major determinant of the vigor with which seats are contested. So will be the "political visibility" of the agency concerned. Gerrymandering of districts to produce safe seats obviously minimizes contests. Plurality elections—which allow many candidates to try for one seat, the person receiving the most votes winning without a runoff—almost certainly reduce the effectiveness of contests by scattering the voters' attention and permitting candidates to win with less than a majority.

Close contests and well-fought campaigns can be encouraged by several devices. For example, the post can be made significant by elevating the agency and its functions in the eyes of the voters. Electoral districts can be devised that will create a minimum of "safe" seats and thus encourage competition.

Partisanship

The delicate issue of political partisanship in local or regional elections must be raised. "Conventional wisdom," as well as what appears to be a majority view of California's leaders—both nonpartisan and partisan—holds that partisan elections at the local and regional levels are undesirable. The rationale for this position is based in part on the scandals afflicting machine-ridden local and state partisan politics in the late 19th and early 20th centuries. In part, it is grounded in such reasoning as "there is no Republican or Democratic way to pave a street or clean a sewer." In part, it rests on a conviction that local nonpartisanship is so universally accepted in California as to be beyond change.

There is growing evidence, however, of attempts to rethink the fundamental assumptions of nonpartisanship, in California and elsewhere. Local and regional governments are concerned with a great deal more than routine matters like street maintenance. They are becoming deeply involved with some of the most fundamental issues confronting society. The new and expanded federal programs will increase this involvement.

Thus, the activities of all governmental levels—federal, state, and local—are converging, as they intensify their efforts to solve the physical, social, and economic problems of the metropolis. An emerging governmental region, such as the Bay Area, represents a new level. Should its system of governance continue to be developed according to the fifty-year-old nonpartisan formula? Or is it time to rethink the philosophy of nonpartisanship as it applies to metropolitan regions?

Furthermore, both political parties are recognizing that urban-metropolitan problems are matters of central concern, and important sectors of both parties define urban problems as being among the critical issues of American partisan politics. Also, partisanship appears to be entering many of California's local elections more and more openly. The time may come when the best interests of all concerned will be forthright recognition of the trend by making the elections legally partisan.

Partisan elections tend to stimulate voter interest and awareness, increase the turn-out at the polls, and provide the citizens with basic reference points which help to identify major policy differences between candidates. The parties and partisan elections can also serve as recruiting mechanisms in bringing forth candidates representing a wide range of interests. Finally, the parties provide an organizational base for a continuing "opposition," facilitating the development and presentation of alternative policies to those followed by the groups currently in power. This function of constructive opposition is, of course, an important element in a healthy democratic process.

For the record, the authors express two opinions on partisanship at the regional level, when direct elections are employed to choose part or all of a regional legislative body. First, we believe a good case can be made—theoretically at least—for the formal introduction of partisanship. In a state like California, which is practically devoid of political "machines"—in the turn-of-the-century sense—at either the state or local levels, partisan elections could be an effective means of selecting a regional legislative body and holding it accountable to the electorate. Second, we are convinced that the need to create regional problem-solving machinery in the near future is urgent, and that the chances of doing so within the next several years should not be jeopardized by attempting to introduce too many new ideas, such as partisan elections, all at once.[7]

---

[7] Some aspects of the partisanship vs. nonpartisanship issue, as it relates to the regional governmental proposal of the Association of Bay Area Governments, are discussed below, pp. 114–120.

SOME CONCRETE POSSIBILITIES FOR REPRESENTATION ON A
REGIONAL POLICY-MAKING BODY

A few of the more likely possibilities for organizing a regional policy-making body—either single-purpose for the Bay alone or multipurpose—are outlined here.

An Elected Governing Body

The entire policy body could be directly elected, from districts, on a nonpartisan or partisan ballot. The electoral areas might be the existing 18 Assembly districts, or nine Senate districts, or a combination of both. The last chapter in Part Two discusses the slight modification necessary to make these districts adequate for election of Bay Area regional legislators. Districts could also be especially drawn for the regional agency,[8] or each county could be assigned a quota of representatives, based on its population, and the board of supervisors asked to apportion the quota among electoral districts within the county.

The ABAG Proposal and Variations

The ABAG proposal for a regional government is discussed in some detail later in this study. The reader is referred to the appropriate chapter, pp. 92–121.

A Continuation of BCDC

BCDC can be considered among the logical contenders to succeed itself, perhaps on a permanent basis, especially if it is decided that the successor should be concerned only with those matters now assigned the commission, i.e., Bay and shoreline planning and policing. Or a temporary extension of BCDC might appear desirable if it proves impossible to create a more broadly based regional government in 1969.

Other Kinds of "Mixed" Bodies

There are, of course, many other possible mixtures in addition to that represented by BCDC. Three illustrative alternatives are presented here.

1. The legislature could be composed in equal parts of (1) members directly elected from districts, (2) members appointed by the Governor with legislative consent, and (3) members selected by counties and cities and/or by ABAG.

2. The legislature could comprise 18 members elected from the Assembly districts, plus nine chosen by ABAG.

3. A two-house legislature might be created. The lower house—whatever its size—could be directly elected. The ABAG Executive Commit-

---

[8] If districts drawn especially for a regional government are a real possibility, a study of the use of computer models in designing electoral districts could be commissioned.

tee—as modified under the ABAG proposal—could then be designated as the upper house. It could be a "House of Lords" of sorts, possessing the power to review and delay legislation, but subject to an override by the elected lower house.

The Regional Legislative Responsibility: Time, Effort, Tenure, Compensation, Size of Body

The demands of time and effort placed upon the regional legislators will depend on many factors. The number of functions assumed will be important, as will the size and effectiveness of the legislature's organization. The availability of high quality and dependable staff support will be important.[9] Another factor will be the legislators' other public responsibilities: if the constituent-unit principle is used, some individuals will be members of two, three, or even more public bodies, and the consequent time demands could make it difficult to participate effectively in all.

Tenure relates to term of office, in the case of elected officials, and to either term or susceptibility of removal by the appointing agency, in the case of appointive or constituent-unit selections. The prevailing term of office for elected officials of most local governments in California is four years. There is no obvious reason to depart from four-year tenure in the case of an elected regional legislature.

In the case of appointive or constituent-unit representation, tenure would depend on the extent to which it was considered desirable to make the legislator immediately and directly responsive to influence by the appointing agency. Appointment and removal "at the pleasure" of the appointing agency would maximize dependence on the latter. Selection for a specified term with removal only "for cause" would maximize the legislator's independence, as would longer terms of office.

Directly elected legislators responsible for a multipurpose regional district should receive adequate salaries. Officeholding should not be "priced out of the market" for all but the affluent, or those who may be obligated to special interests. However it is possible that the payment of salaries to some members of a mixed legislative body could create problems. For example, if both local representatives and directly elected legislators were included, would it be reasonable and fair to pay one but not the other? Probably not. Are there persuasive reasons for differential

---

[9] The possible influence of staff can hardly be overemphasized. Good staff support is extremely important, in order that an adequate and accurate flow of information and suggestions can be maintained to the legislative body and policy leadership. Also, it is essential that the legislators be able to devote sufficient time and effort to insure that staff do not "take over" key policy decisions. That is, the staff contribution should be influential and of high quality, but not dominant.

treatment? We doubt it. If the salaries are substantial, but not munificent, and if the responsibilities and demands on time are also substantial, it is unlikely (1) that people would seek the posts solely for money, or (2) that the indirectly elected positions would be given as sinecures to "deserving" persons in financial need, but with relatively few other qualifications.

In 1966 a constitutional amendment and legislation raised state legislator's salaries from $6,000 to $16,000. The latter figure would not appear excessive for members of a multipurpose regional legislative body with major powers. Of course, substantial salaries should be accompanied by parallel conditions such as the strong "conflict of interest" provisions embodied in the state legislative pay raise "package."[10] Similarly, it might be appropriate to consider making salary payments dependent on the recipient's maintaining a good attendance record at meetings of the regional body and of its committees.

The size of the body will depend on many factors. The number of interests that have to be accommodated in achieving political acceptability is one consideration. But there is no "magic" formula for determining how large a legislature should be—one of almost any size can be *made* to function. The U. S. House of Representatives, for example, has 435 members, yet it works, however creakily on occasion, through an elaborate committee system. California's lower house has 80 members and its upper house 40. California counties other than San Francisco are served by five-member boards of supervisors, regardless of county size. Los Angeles County, for example, with 7 million people, is governed by a five-member legislative body.

Thus there is no theoretical standard as to size, and there is a tremendous range in actual practice. Local experience in the Bay Area, however, may suggest some useful guidelines. The six-county Bay Area Air Pollution Control District would be governed by an 18-member board if the district were expanded to nine-county scope, as envisioned in the law creating it. The three-county San Francisco Bay Area Rapid Transit District is governed by an 11-member board. The nine-county Bay Area Transportation Study Commission consists of 41 members. The nine-county San Francisco Bay Conservation and Development Commission consists of 27 voting members. Most of the policy work of the nine-county Association of Bay Area Governments has taken place in the 20-member Executive Committee—now enlarged to a maximum of 34—and is subsequently ratified or rejected by the 88-member Gen-

---

[10] A conflict of interest prohibition is the other half of the compensation-regulation equation embodied in the recently enacted Proposition 1A and collateral legislation: (*Cal. Const.,* Art. IV. secs. 4–5; *Cal. Stats.,* First Ex. Sess., 1966, ch. 163).

eral Assembly, which normally meets only twice a year. This suggests that a legislative body of between 20 and 40 members should be both workable and sufficiently large to represent a wide spectrum of regional interests in the nine-county area.

Leadership: Selecting a Chief Executive

A crucial feature of an effective government is leadership—the ability of individuals or groups within the agency to recognize present and foresee future needs, and to formulate the policies required to meet them. One means of developing leadership is direct and at-large election of the chief executive—equivalent to the governor at the state level or the mayor at the city level.[11] Candidates contending for the top office could go to the electorate with alternative programs. The campaigns could serve some of the purposes of the political parties at the state and national levels in offering voters reasonably clear policy choices. The victorious executive would have a popular mandate to work for adoption of his programs and to devise new policies as needs arise.

On the other hand, some observers question the wisdom of forcing candidates to conduct at-large campaigns throughout the Bay Area. In large part, this is due to concern over the high cost of such campaigns.[12] An alternative method—selection of the chief executive by the regional legislature, from its own membership or outside—would avoid these high costs. Under this method the executive would need to be appointed for a specified term and not be subject to replacement at the pleasure of the legislature, in order to give him sufficient tenure and independence to exercise effective leadership. This system has worked well in Toronto.

But the "musical chairs" method of choosing the presiding officer—as practiced by the Bay Area Air Pollution Control District and the Association of Bay Area Governments—should be avoided. Such a system, with its traditions of only one-year tenure and alternation between city and county members,[13] encourages discontinuity and restricts the choice of successors. Such a plan also makes it almost inevitable that

---

[11] Dade County (Miami) and Davidson County (Nashville) both employ this method of selecting the metropolitan mayor. The Dade County experience also suggests the importance of elected policy leadership to protect the appointed top administrative staff. Absence of such leadership in the early years of the reorganized Dade County government placed an intolerable burden on the county manager.

[12] In the City and County of San Francisco alone, for example, the two principal contenders in the mayoralty election of November, 1967, spent a combined total of nearly $700,000. It would obviously be extremely expensive to finance areawide campaigns of equivalent intensity throughout the nine counties.

[13] Possibly the leadership problem in a constituent-unit system could be solved by a slight departure from current practice. ABAG has proposed election of the President and Vice President by secret ballot of all councilmen and supervisors of the area.

members with limited leadership ability will eventually act as presiding officers, if they only retain their seats long enough. Finally, not only is tenure short, but also the formal powers of the presiding officer are few. Primarily they comprise his presumed greater knowledge and involvement in agency activities during his year in office, the parliamentary powers of chairman, appointment of committees, and the opportunity to take the initiative in encouraging or discouraging the presentation of new programs.

Agency Functions and Powers: A Minimum

A minimum allocation of power would be continuation of the existing functions of BCDC, enabling it or the successor agency to maintain a permanent planning process, thus keeping the Bay and shoreline plan up-to-date. It would also include the power to grant or withhold permits for Bay fill. This assumes, of course, that there will be no recommendation for a return to the preexisting situation, i.e., every local government for itself, which seems a most unlikely prospect at this writing.

But a long-term continuance of these minimum powers will result in strong pressures for adverse development which BCDC or its successor may be hard put to withstand. Thus a strong grant of power to control land use along the shoreline will be an essential tool in the program to implement a plan for the Bay and shoreline. This authority will also need to be accompanied by ample financial resources and the power of eminent domain. A combination of land use control, condemnation, and purchase will be necessary to guide development—where control is sufficient—and to acquire and develop portions of the Bay and shoreline, or lease or resell them, under conditions, where those are appropriate means of plan implementation.

Finally, if it is decided that Bay and shoreline control should be combined with—or closely related to—other regional functions, now or later, the powers necessary to sustain a *multipurpose* regional government would be required.

Agency Functions and Powers: A Multipurpose Body?

The possibility of establishing a multipurpose agency introduces a number of new considerations. These include the rationale for a multipurpose body, the major choices available and the allocation of functions among levels of government.

THE RATIONALE

One of the crucial reasons for urging a multipurpose agency is to insure recognition—by the system of governmental decision-making—of the *interdependence* of the physical, economic and social systems within a region. A multipurpose agency can bring the interdependent systems under one policy-making roof and help achieve compatibility between the scope of policy decision-making and the regional needs these policies attempt to meet.

In addition, a multipurpose agency should possess enhanced political visibility, thus helping insure accountability as well as public awareness of regional problems and needs. Grouping regional functions requiring public support is probably the best way to encourage reasonably rational allocation of scarce resources in a democratic system.

The federal government is increasingly recognizing the interdependence of all its programs at the regional level, and is requiring a multifunctional review by a single regional agency of a wide range of projects receiving federal aid. This review process will increasingly be of enormous importance in determining the way in which the region lives and grows.[14] It would benefit the Bay Area to take steps insuring that, ultimately, the agency conducting the review meets the criteria outlined above for the decision process and for a regional policy-making body. A well-designed multipurpose regional government would do this; anything less would not.

THE CHOICES

If the arguments for a multifunctional structure are found persuasive, several possible choices are available. These choices involve (1) the degree of integration sought for the several functions, and (2) the number of functions to be included.

An Operating Agency: Consolidation

Full-scale integration or *consolidation* would combine several regional functions, setting them up as subsidiaries or departments within the regional government. If the new government absorbed existing regional agencies, such an effort would probably need to be phased over a transitional period, perhaps of several years, in order to insure an orderly transfer.

A Coordinating (or "Umbrella") Agency:
Integration Without Consolidation

On the other hand, it may be possible to achieve a good deal of integration short of actual consolidation, particularly when existing regional agencies are concerned, and institutional resistance to dissolution is high. The concept of an "umbrella" agency with a general overview

[14] Charles M. Haar, "Budgeting for Metropolitan Development: A Step Toward Creative Federalism," *Journal of the American Institute of Planners* 34:102–104, March 1968.

function holds sufficient appeal to warrant further exploration. The umbrella agency could be designed to keep a watchful eye on selected major regional programs, and especially on their mutual interrelationships. Employment of an umbrella government could prove to be the only practical means of accomplishing regional objectives without major surgery on existing agencies—either regional or local.

But to be effective the umbrella government would need significant powers. It could, for example, be authorized to appoint part or all of the boards of directors of the other agencies. Another important sanction would be the power to review and say "yes" or "no" to proposals of whatever scale embodying potential conflicts with stated regional goals. The umbrella government could also be given major financial resources. Perhaps it could serve as the distributor for state and federal money paid into the region, in addition to dispensing funds from independent revenue sources of its own. Through the distribution and redistribution of resources, the umbrella government could encourage interagency coordination and facilitate the difficult decisions that *should* be made when, in the best interest of the region, one agency ought to defer to another.

Interagency transfer payments could help ease the difficulties caused by continuation of agencies which are limited either functionally or geographically. For example, an agency capable of making transfer payments could assist the Alameda-Contra Costa Transit District by absorbing the losses the latter may sustain if it adjusts its bus routes, rates, and schedules to maximize the effectiveness of the rail service provided by its "competitor," the San Francisco Bay Area Rapid Transit District. Without a higher-level government able to cushion and absorb such adverse effects, intraregional competition of many other kinds, analogous to the potential conflict between A/C Transit and BARTD, could harm the region's overriding public interest.

Finally, if all else failed, and deleterious conflicts or inabilities to act appeared likely to jeopardize the well-being of the region, still stronger powers to order necessary consolidation or other governmental reorganization could be held in reserve. These powers could be placed directly in the hands of the umbrella government, or could be exercised by the state Legislature, acting on recommendations by the former.

Which Regional Functions?

As noted above, the functions most frequently mentioned in the Bay Area for possible assumption by a regional government include one or more of the following: regional planning, regional refuse collection and disposal, regional parks and recreation, open space programs, air pollu-

Governing a Metropolitan Region

tion control, water pollution control, and transportation.[15] In addition to these, the Governor's Commission on Metropolitan Area Problems mentioned water supply, regional sewage disposal and drainage, regional aspects of law enforcement and fire protection, regional aspects of urban renewal, civil defense, and any other areawide function which might be requested by the residents and leadership of the individual metropolitan area concerned.

Many considerations must enter into the selection of regional functions to be brought under either a consolidated or umbrella agency. First, is the function being dealt with at all on a regional basis under existing arrangements? (If not, it may be a prime candidate for a regional agency's list of functions.) Second, how adequate is the treatment of each function now receiving regional attention? (This inevitably leads to the next question.) Third, how closely interrelated is the function with other functions being considered for linking? Fourth, how entrenched and politically powerful are the existing agencies possessing a vested interest in the present arrangement?

The emphasis on *regional functions* may suggest an oversimplification that should be clarified. Actually, few public functions are *exclusively* regional or *exclusively* local. Most can be separated into local and regional *components*. This leads to another important set of choices determining which *components* of certain functions must be treated regionally for effective action, and which *components* can appropriately be left in the hands of local government without endangering regional interests.

There are several reasons to regionalize only those functional components that cannot otherwise be dealt with satisfactorily. First, retention of significant local powers will help strengthen local government. Second, removal from local units of responsibility for components of functions with which they cannot cope effectively will also strengthen local government, as well as further regional programs. Third, sorting functions into their regional and local components should help minimize the reluctance of local governments and other interests to accept essential changes.

Financing Regional Programs

The agency's need for fiscal powers would obviously depend on the substantive responsibilities assigned to it. If it is only to conduct con-

---

[15] The study of Bay Area regional organization under Senate Concurrent Resolution No. 41, adopted in 1967, is specifically asked to determine which of the following functions, among others, should be handled wholly or partially on a regional basis: (1) regional planning, (2) air and water pollution, (3) solid waste disposal, (4) regional parks and open space, and (5) transportation (including rapid transit, ports, airports, and bridges).

tinuing studies and keep the Bay plan up-to-date, an annual budget of a few hundred thousand dollars would probably suffice. If implementation is to be solely through the police power, fiscal requirements would remain limited. But if implementation is to be effected in whole or in part by negotiated purchase or condemnation of properties, or through physical development of the shoreline by the agency—and this will almost certainly be required for an effective program—then financial resources of major magnitude will be essential.

Property tax inadequacies, both real and alleged, do not make this long-established source of public revenues a likely candidate for raising large sums of money, over and above the heavy support it already provides for school districts (the major user), counties, cities, and other special districts. In most California urban areas the property tax rate runs to $10 per $100 of assessed valuation or even higher. Further, the property tax is difficult to administer, is often erratic as well as regressive in its incidence, and is subject to abuses, some of which were highlighted by California's recent county assessor scandals. The main virtue of the property tax is its apparent ease of employment. A new district or agency can readily be authorized to add a few more cents per $100 assessed valuation. But if large monetary outlays are anticipated, other sources should be utilized.

There are many possibilities:

1. A regional addition to the income tax, perhaps computed as a flat percentage of the state or federal income tax to simplify paperwork.

2. Taxes or charges levied specifically upon benefits derived from the Bay.

3. A long-term commitment of a portion of tolls from bridges across the Bay.

4. A "property appreciation" tax (similar to the new British "betterment" charge by which a property owner pays a percentage—in the British case, nearly 50 percent—of the increase in the value of his property that has resulted over a period of time from public improvements or planning decisions, as opposed to increased value resulting only from the owner's own efforts).

5. A property transfer tax (levied on property when it changes hands, the amount of the tax being based on the sale price).

6. A regional addition to one or more state taxes, such as the gasoline tax, cigarette tax, alcoholic beverage tax, general sales tax or other state levies.

A regional addition to the income tax appears to be one of the most equitable and attractive possibilities. If a multipurpose agency is to be established, however, a whole "family" of taxes should be considered, perhaps with the income tax as the most important single source.

Taxes related to property value appreciation should not be viewed *only* as likely sources of revenue. They can also have a very significant impact on the land market, and on the rate and location of value appreciation. If properly utilized, tax policies can curb land speculation and land-value inflation. These taxes are two-edged swords. They provide public funds with which to acquire land. And they can reduce materially the costs of land acquisition. Further, they can help influence the course of future urban development, short of actual public acquisition of property. Thus land value taxes are *both* a source of funds *and* a means to the implementation of regional plans. The impact of property tax policies on urban land is indicated by the following comment:

[The planners] . . . should know that the assessor is *de facto* using and misusing the property taxation tool and that this is part of the reason why the other planning tools are not working as well as they should. They should make the practice of using property taxation for land-use planning purposes a tool of their own. In this respect, the Hawaii experiment [with a combination of zoning and graded taxation] is well worth noting and following.[16]

The implications for the Bay Area of these intricate but very real and potentially powerful interrelationships between taxation and land use deserve careful exploration by any group concerned with the future directions of the region's growth.

If BCDC or its successor is to undertake long-term plans requiring major capital outlays, two other matters should be considered. First, the agency will need to break loose from the annual budgetary cycle. A five- to ten-year plan, or an even longer-term plan for capital finance, will be required for an effective property acquisition program. Second, a means of capital finance through a simple majority referendum, as is the case with state bond issues, must be found to replace the archaic 90-year old constitutional two-thirds vote requirement now handicapping California's cities, counties and school districts.[17]

It should be pointed out that an agency empowered to acquire land for preservation, development, leasing, or resale could become at least

---

[16] Donald G. Hagman, "The Single Tax and Land-Use Planning: Henry George Updated," *UCLA Law Review*, 12: 762–788, March 1965.

[17] The federal interstate highway program, California's own state freeway program, and the Feather River Project provide illustrative cases in point. The three represent some of the most massive public works programs undertaken in the history of mankind. All involve major capital outlays, and are financed on a long-term basis. In each case, once the initial decision was made, there were no further budgetary reviews, thus permitting long-term planning of the programs. Did any of them have to pass a two-thirds referendum requirement? No. The federal and state highway programs were undertaken with no referendum vote at all—federal and state legislation, respectively, authorized the two long-range programs. The Feather River Project had only to get a simple statewide majority vote, as state general obligation bonds

partially self-supporting, once it has become operative. Nevertheless, the agency should not be made heavily dependent on dealings in land for its financial resources. Otherwise there would be the risk of encouraging it to adopt policies tending to fill its coffers, rather than policies adjudged best for the region.

Finally, federal and state financing should not be overlooked. The state might see fit to establish a special program for the Bay Area, provided some counterbalancing benefits were conferred on other California regions. And a channelling of some of the federal and state funds available for land acquisition, renewal, and urban improvement to or through the agency could provide it with a good deal of leverage. All the state and federal funds now spent in the Bay Area that have a regional impact could be required to be expended in accordance with the regional plan. This policy alone would represent a significant step toward effective plan implementation, even without additional appropriations or other powers.

Relations With Other Governments

The importance of functional and governmental interrelationships has been a recurring theme in this chapter. It appeared in the discussion of the decision process. Also, the need for effective interrelationships is one of the stated rationales behind the constituent-unit principle of representation. The umbrella agency concept, and the division of functions into local and regional components, are both predicated on the primary importance of intergovernmental relationships.

Many agencies are involved in policies and programs that affect the Bay and shoreline, either directly or indirectly. The State Division of Highways builds freeways along the shoreline; the Division of Bay Toll Crossings constructs bridges across the Bay; BARTD is building a tube under it. The air pollution control district regulates the quality of air over the Bay; the regional water quality control board determines the purity of water in it. The federal government owns a small portion of the Bay, as well as some critical shoreline areas. Also the federal government has an ultimate regulatory authority over navigable waters, such as the Bay and its tributaries. The state government is a major owner. BARTD and its three-county transit system, BATS and its nine-county transportation plan, and individual cities' and counties' zoning and developmental planning all involve significant impacts on future uses of the Bay and shoreline.

---

require only a simple majority. New forms of financing bearing some of the characteristics of these highly effective programs will need to be devised if the Bay Area is to accomplish the massive land acquisitions that may be required under the BCDC plan, and that are proposed by ABAG's preliminary regional plan.

The successor agency recommended by BCDC should be designed to take these many impacts and interrelationships into account. If a regional government is created, it would be designed specifically to undertake the task. If a more limited agency must be established, however, the need to consider relationships with other governments would be all the more critical.

Several kinds of federal and state interests must be considered, regardless of whether one is discussing (1) only the implementation of a plan for the Bay and shoreline, or (2) a broad-gauge multipurpose regional government for the Bay Area. As noted, the federal and state governments own portions of the Bay and shoreline, and have important police and regulatory responsibilities over it. Furthermore, what happens in an area as large and richly endowed as this region carries both state and national import. Degradation of the Bay, or of the Bay Area, would represent a major loss to both the state and nation. Furthermore, the federal and state governments invest large sums of money in the Bay Area every year. They have a legitimate interest in seeing the money well spent, and in guarding against locally or regionally initiated programs conflicting with those intended to be furthered by the federal and state investment.

Any regional agency capable of implementing a plan for the Bay and shoreline, or of handling a number of other regional problems, will need major financial resources in addition to the state and federal moneys mentioned above. This will require state legislative authorization for regional taxes, and perhaps additional state and federal subsidies. The state will need to retain general legislative jurisdiction over any agency that may be created, in order to facilitate modification later if experience or changed circumstances so require.

Finally, and above all, there must be a mutual exchange of information and ideas, and cooperation in programs, between state and federal agencies and the regional agency.

How can the variety of state and federal interests in the Bay region be accommodated and protected? In part, certain existing regulatory functions, if continued, would help do this. Also, strings attached to state and federal moneys going into the region can accomplish the same end. To the extent that federally owned lands or federally controlled waterways are involved, obviously the national government would have an ultimate and overriding authority. But arrangements should also be made to insure maximum federal consideration of local and regional interests.

Should state and federal representatives sit on the regional policy body? We think not. There is something a bit awkward or anomalous about state or federal civil servants sitting on a regional legislature. And it would be completely infeasible to have top-level political appointees such as the State Director of Finance or the Secretary of the Interior designated as members.

The state's interest is perhaps best protected by its ultimate retention of full legislative authority to restructure the regional agency, should that prove desirable. Similarly, the federal interest may best be protected not only by its utlimate authority over the areas under federal jurisdiction, but also by national encouragement of the development of strong regional planning processes. And the vital processes of liaison and cooperative program development can be encouraged without representation of the state or federal govenments on the regional policy-making body.

It is now appropriate to examine other thought and experience on the North American continent directed toward devising governmental solutions for regional problems. Although the variations in detail can be almost endless, only a few basic responses to regional problems have been tried or suggested in the Anglo-American world. For discussion, most of these are grouped as one- and two-tier approaches. The term "one-tier approach" designates organizational arrangements involving only one level of general-purpose local government. The two-tier approaches employ an upper-level government, which is assigned certain functions, usually regional in nature, as well as lower-tier governmental units, which are responsible for designated local functions.

Among the one-tier approaches are city-county consolidation (discussed in the first chapter of Part Two) and municipal annexation. This is followed by a review of two-tier approaches, including federation, the comprehensive urban county, and metropolitan-scale special districts. The voluntary regional councils of governments are treated next. A separate chapter considers in some detail the governmental proposals for the San Francisco Bay region emanating from the Association of Bay Area Governments. Finally, two possibilities for direct election, using slightly modified Assembly and Senate districts, are examined in the last chapter of Part Two.

A Survey of Alternatives

A One-Tier Approach:
City-County Consolidation

While city-county consolidation *as such* does not offer a solution to regional problems of many areas, the experience with consolidations and consolidation attempts can provide valuable procedural and substantive guidance for almost any region. Properly adapted to a region's governmental situation, these clues can be most instructive in suggesting both ways of proceeding and things to be avoided in the search for better methods of handling regional problems.

Typically, city-county consolidation proposals would merge the major city—or all cities in a metropolis—with the county government.[1] Less often, consolidation proposals also provide for the absorption of additional local governments, including school districts and other special districts.

The idea of consolidation has considerable appeal. A single government, it is reasoned, possesses both the authority and territorial size necessary to deal with areawide problems in a unified fashion. It is also contended that a consolidated government, endowed with both metropolitan and local functions, can achieve economies of scale, making possible lower unit costs. Efficiency would be improved because the single government would eliminate duplication of services or poor coordination—conditions often prevailing when many local governments are involved. Proponents of consolidation further point to the ability of a consolidated government to allocate financial resources on the basis of need, thereby eliminating the discrepancies between resources and requirements that characterize many fragmented governmental systems.

Despite considerable advocacy and attention, city-county consolidation has only rarely been employed. In fact, only seven metropolitan areas have chosen this route to governmental reform.[2] Four of the con-

---

[1] City-county *separation*, such as that which created the City and County of San Francisco in 1856, should not be confused with city-county *consolidation*. As employed here and in the other cited examples, however, separation is a separatist or non-regional measure, opposite in intent to the regional devices we are examining. Thus separation involves the detachment of a city, sometimes after enlargement of its area, from the remainder of a county. The separated city government subsequently carries out both municipal and county functions and is often legally regarded as a city-county. Except in Virginia, where separation takes place automatically in every city when it reaches a population of 5,000, all U. S. city-county separations occurred many years ago. In addition to San Francisco, they include Baltimore (1851), St. Louis (1876), and Denver (1902).

[2] We exclude a few city-county consolidations in Virginia, which were resorted to as a defensive measure against that state's unique practice of removing from county jurisdiction all land annexed by a city.

47

solidations were accomplished in the 19th century—New Orleans (1813), Boston (1821), Philadelphia (1854), and New York (1898)—and a fifth, Honolulu (1907), resulted from action of the territorial legislature and was retained when Hawaii became a state. Until 1967, only two such consolidations had taken place in any state during this century—Baton Rouge (1947) and Nashville (1962).[3]

The Early Consolidations

The five city-county consolidations that became operative between 1813 and 1907 were all accomplished by state legislative action[4] and did not require local voter approval.[5] The number of existing local governments involved in these consolidations varied. In Honolulu, the territorial legislature created a local unit to perform both city and county functions where there had been neither a city nor a county before. The Boston and New Orleans consolidations each involved only one county (termed *parish* in Louisiana) and one city.

The New York and Philadelphia consolidations were quite different, bringing many local governments together, and including public education in the system. Moreover, the New York consolidation encompassed four preexisting counties. Another unique feature of the New York consolidation was the establishment of local entities, called boroughs. The boroughs were made territorially coterminous with county boundaries and given limited administrative functions, but no legislative powers.[6] All these consolidated governments still exist. The original boundaries have been changed little, if at all, and in most instances they now include only a small portion of the territory of the metropolitan area in which each is situated.

Opposition and Defeats

As metropolitan areas and their governments grew during the early decades of the present century, the continued high interest in city-county

---

[3] On August 8, 1967, the electorate of Jacksonville and Duval County, Florida, voted almost two-to-one for a charter consolidating the two governments. After a transitional period, the charter became fully effective October 1, 1968. The new government has a population of about 500,000 and an 800-square mile area. The charter provides for a full-time elected chief executive with strong-mayor powers, and for a 19-member council, five of whom are elected at large, and the others from districts of equal population. The charter also provides for general and urban service districts, making it possible to levy higher taxes in areas receiving urban services than in those which do not.

[4] It was an act of the territorial legislature in the case of Honolulu.

[5] A comprehensive historical treatment of consolidation is found in John A. Rush, *The City-County Consolidated* (Los Angeles: privately printed, 1941).

[6] The most up-to-date analysis of the New York City government is Wallace S. Sayre and Herbert Kaufman, *Governing New York City: Politics in the Metropolis* (New York: W. W. Norton, 1960).

consolidation failed to pay off anywhere. Many new suburban communities sprang up, forming powerful blocs of opposition to consolidation because of their desire to control local finances and land development, and because of real or fancied fears of the unresponsiveness of a single big government for the metropolis. Stiff legal obstacles to city-county consolidation were enacted. Subsequently the advocates of this approach have confronted two kinds of hurdles. First, they have had to obtain passage of a constitutional amendment or a state enabling law permitting metropolitan areas to adopt city-county consolidation. Second, it has been necessary to obtain approval of the consolidation plan by the local voters, usually involving at least two separate mapority votes—in the central city and in the remainder of the area—and sometimes more than two. From 1900 to 1945, most consolidation attempts failed even to clear the first hurdle, and only three proposals got to the voters. All were defeated.

Adoption in Baton Rouge

The Baton Rouge-East Baton Rouge Parish consolidation, approved by a slim areawide majority in 1947, is actually only a partial merger. The legal existence of the two governments was continued, but they were interlocked. The seven city councilmen of Baton Rouge, plus the parish mayor-president, govern the city area. These eight, sitting with two other members elected from the rural section of the parish, make up the consolidated city-parish governing body.

The mayor-president, elected on a parishwide basis, is the chief administrator of both governments and presides over both councils. He appoints the public works director, personnel administrator, finance director, and purchasing agent, who serve both the city and parish. He also appoints the police and fire chiefs, who operate only in the city. Thus, the two governments are interlocked in important ways, although they still have separate governing boards, separate budgets, and separate accounting for city and parish funds.

DIFFERENTIAL ZONES

The Baton Rouge consolidation was innovative in another respect, one subsequently copied in many other such proposals, including the one adopted in Nashville more than a decade later. This is the provision for differential taxing and service zones throughout the consolidated area on the basis of differing needs and land use. The City of Baton Rouge was extended to the limits of major urban development and designated as the urban zone. A rural zone and two industrial zones were also established.

The city government furnishes fire and police protection, traffic regulation, street lighting, sewerage, garbage and refuse disposal, and inspectional services in the urban zone, which is subject to both city and parish taxes. Parish taxes are also levied in the rural zone and the two industrial zones. Bridges, highways, streets, and airports are provided throughout the parish by the consolidated public works department and financed by parish taxes.

In the industrial zones the industries supply the needed city-type services at their own expense. No municipal-type services, except those from the sheriff, are available in the rural zone unless the parish council sets up special taxing districts in areas desiring added services, which are thus locally financed. Portions of the rural zone adjacent to the city may be annexed into the urban zone, as they become urbanized, by majority consent of the owners of property in the affected area, and after approval of the city council. No further incorporations are permitted. (Two small preexisting municipalities were not made part of the consolidation, but they are prohibited from enlarging their areas.)

PERIODIC REVIEW

The Baton Rouge-East Baton Rouge Parish consolidation has been reviewed periodically by official study committees. In each instance changes, mostly minor, have been suggested and usually implemented by voter approval of charter amendments, or through council or administrative action. The first study group helped substantially to increase public confidence in the new governmental system. It was a prestigious body and permitted all parties to air their views at open hearings. The extensiveness of its discussions produced greater citizen understanding of the rather complex reform that had been instituted.[7]

The second review committee, which reported in 1956, and the third, active mainly in 1959–60, expressed the increasing general confidence in the consolidation growing out of its successful experience. The third group gave this well-tempered evaluation:

. . . this plan appears to be eminently well suited to the efficient and responsible conduct of local government in the area. The Committee is well aware that the future growth and development of this Parish will necessitate adjustments and we believe that the Charter provides an excellent framework within which this development can take place.[8]

---

[7] William C. Havard, Jr. and Floyd L. Corty, *Rural-Urban Consolidation: The Merger of Governments in the Baton Rouge Area* (Baton Rouge: Louisiana State University Press, 1964), p. 42.

[8] Plan of Government Study Committee, *Report of the Plan of Government Study Committee to the City-Parish Councils* (Baton Rouge: June 1960), p. 10.

Revived Interest

Activity in support of city-county consolidation picked up again in the 1950's and early 1960's, but no further adoption was accomplished until 1962. During that period, proposals were turned down by the voters of many metropolitan complexes, generally in medium- and small-sized metropolises and chiefly in the South. Almost without exception, the proposals were required to obtain separate voter majorities in both the central city and the remainder of the county. In most instances the central city voters approved, but the other majority was not forthcoming. In several instances neither majority was obtained.

The Nashville Consolidation

The fifteen-year interlude in adoptions ended in 1962 when the voters of Nashville and the remainder of Davidson County, Tennessee, approved a city-county consolidation. The two required approvals were given by almost identical voter majorities—approximately 57 percent in each case. Four years previously, the electorate outside Nashville had rejected a comparable proposal, only 42 percent casting affirmative ballots. In the interim between the two elections, however, the City of Nashville had annexed about 50 square miles of county territory. This large-scale annexation activity, accomplished by unilateral action on the part of Nashville, converted many anticonsolidationists of the first election into proconsolidationists in the second contest. Some changed because they felt they would have better representation in a consolidated government than in the Nashville city government, which might subsequently annex them. Others, who lived in the new sections of Nashville that had been annexed involuntarily, chose consolidation as a revenge against Nashville's incumbent mayor, who led the city annexation movement and by 1962 was the major opponent of countywide consolidation.

GENERAL AND URBAN SERVICE AREAS

A major feature of Nashville's consolidation is the creation of two districts or zones. One is the *urban services district,* composed at the outset only of the former City of Nashville—about 75 square miles. The other zone, a *general services district,* consists of the entire county, including Nashville, with an area of 533 square miles and a population of about 415,000. Six small suburban municipalities were initially left outside the urban services district, which may be enlarged by the metropolitan government whenever new areas require urban services. These municipalities, however, are in the general services district and therefore subject to the metropolitan government's jurisdiction for areawide services and control.

Functions performed by the metropolitan government and financed on an areawide basis—that is, through the general services district—include schools, police, courts, public welfare, streets and roads, traffic, transit, library, public housing, urban renewal, public health, refuse disposal, and the enforcement of building, electrical, housing and plumbing codes. Functions performed only in the urban services district, and financed by it, include water supply, sewage disposal, fire protection, intensified police protection, and street lighting and street cleaning. The metropolitan government possesses both city and county taxing powers.

MAYOR, COUNCIL, AND REDISTRICTING

A metropolitan county mayor is elected at large for a four-year term, and may not serve more than three consecutive terms. He is the chief administrative officer and also has a veto power over legislative actions. The metropolitan council—the legislative body—is made up of 40 members, who are also elected for four years, five at large and 35 from single-member districts. Redistricting of the council must take place every 10 years, beginning with the 1970 decennial census.

A FAVORABLE EVALUATION

Daniel R. Grant, a veteran analyst of Nashville metropolitan developments and a professor of political science at Vanderbilt University, has made a highly favorable appraisal of the early years of the consolidated governmental operations.[9] The community decision-making process has been considerably simplified, and it is now easier to focus public attention on officials and their decisions. Many duplications have been eliminated and some economies have been achieved—although the consolidation has stimulated rising public expectations and will thus probably bring future increases in expenditures and taxes. Specialization and professionalization of public personnel, and equalization of certain services on a countywide basis (most notably schools and parks) have been accomplished. A number of city-county financial inequities have been eliminated by shifting various services formerly financed solely or largely by city taxpayers to a countywide tax base. In all these instances, the predictions of consolidation proponents have come true. On the other hand, only one major substantive claim of the opponents has been borne out: rural residents have had to pay higher taxes without gaining major benefits.

[9] Daniel R. Grant, "A Comparison of Predictions and Experience With Nashville 'Metro'," *Urban Affairs Quarterly*, 1:34–54, September 1965.

Lessons From Experience With City-County Consolidation

1. In most large metropolitan areas city-county consolidation is of limited value. In the San Francisco Bay Area, for example, the complete consolidation of all 91 city and nine county governments into a single entity is exceedingly unlikely. Such an approach is completely impractical politically. Even if it could be accomplished, it would probably be highly inadvisable. A single government encompassing 7,000 square miles and a current population of 4.5 million would actually *be* the "supergovernment" that is raised as a specter in some sectors of the area as a means of preventing more realistic and workable governmental reorganization plans from being implemented.

2. City-county consolidation within various *individual* counties of multicounty metropolitan areas, however, conceivably could produce a stronger *local* level of government.

3. The concept of tax and service zones employed in the Baton Rouge, Nashville and Jacksonville consolidations may be of value whenever the area of need within a region varies among services.

4. Periodic review of the results of metropolitan reorganization, as practiced in Baton Rouge, is a logical procedure that could well be emulated elsewhere.

5. Baton Rouge, Nashville, and Jacksonville, the three city-county consolidations effected in the present century by voter approval, all have directly elected chief executives. These offices were created expressly to provide leadership.

6. Mandatory redistricting of metropolitan legislative seats may be necessary to avoid the development of inequitable representation as the population distribution changes.

Two-Tier Approaches

Introduction

In multi-county situations, such as the San Francisco Bay Area's, two-tier approaches are clearly more acceptable and have more to offer than one-tier arrangements. Complete consolidation of local governments in multi-county regions is usually not only politically infeasible, but in most cases would also be highly questionable on practical grounds. Two-tier approaches make it possible to build upon or to leave relatively undisturbed the existing structure of local government. Thus, experience with the two-tier variants—federation, the urban county, and regional districts—whose basic similarities are far more important than their differences in form, should prove most instructive.

What can we expect to learn from the discussion of two-tier approaches? First, the division of functions and powers between the two levels will indicate which activities have been treated elsewhere as "regional" and which as "local." Second, the process by which two-tier government was established will be of great interest. Third, the actual workings of two-tier governments, including their successes and difficulties, as evaluated by informed observers, will give essential guidance on goals to be sought and pitfalls to be avoided.

Federation

Governmental federation differs significantly from city-county consolidation. As we have seen, the latter produces a *one-level* system wherein a *single* areawide government carries out both metropolitan and local public operations. Federation, in contrast, is a *two-level* approach, the first of three to be discussed in successive sections of this chapter. A federation establishes a new general or multiple-purpose metropolitan government to handle areawide functions, while local units continue to perform local activities. The two levels are federated or interlocked in two respects, as in our national federal system. First, powers are allocated between the metropolitan and local governments. Second, local areas—but not necessarily local *governments*—are used as the representational base for choosing members of the metropolitan legislature.

The Movement

The idea of metropolitan federation received its greatest attention in the United States in the closing years of the nineteenth century and the first three decades of the present century. Thus, although the initial

54

efforts on behalf of city-county consolidation preceded those for federation, strong interest in both was evident during the latter part of the period.

Most proponents of federation considered this approach to be intrinsically superior to consolidation and not a stepping stone to it. They judged the complete merger of a number of governments to be unnecessary and inappropriate. Not all needs in a metropolis, they reasoned, were areawide in scope, and consequently the assignment of both metropolitan and local functions to a single areawide government was irrational. In their view, the logical arrangement would allocate metropolitan responsibilities to a new general metropolitan government, and continue the local governments for local purposes.

Although much discussed, the idea of federation was seldom shaped into a concrete proposal and even less often voted upon. It first received serious attention in 1896, when a three-member commission appointed by the Governor of Massachusetts to analyze types of metropolitan organization recommended the passage of a legislative bill calling for a referendum on the question of federation in the Boston area. The bill failed to pass, and federation received almost no consideration anywhere in the nation for the next two decades. In 1916 a significant effort began in Alameda County, California (Oakland-Berkeley), which produced the first federation charter ever presented to the voters anywhere in the nation. The electorate rejected the proposal.

The second and final federation plan to be submitted for popular approval by a metropolis was defeated by Allegheny County (Pittsburgh) voters in 1929. The following year Missouri voters killed a proposed constitutional amendment that would have authorized St. Louis and St. Louis County to draft a federation charter for presentation to the electorate. In the late 1920's, a private organization prepared a detailed federation plan to link San Francisco and San Mateo County; the plan was partially incorporated in the new San Francisco charter of 1931, but the movement to get the federation proposal implemented by voter approval sputtered and died the following year.[1] Attempts to revive the idea in San Francisco-San Mateo counties, Alameda County, and Allegheny County later in the 1930's and to install the approach in Dade County (Miami) in the 1950's proved shortlived.

A concrete plan of federation has not subsequently been formulated in any metropolitan area in the United States. The inability to get fed-

---

[1] The federation efforts in Alameda County and San Francisco–San Mateo counties are considered in detail in John C. Bollens, *The Problem of Government in the San Francisco Bay Region* (Berkeley: Bureau of Public Administration, University of California, 1948), pp. 65–94.

eration adopted anywhere in our nation and the transfer of such effort to other forms of the two-level approach punctured the federation movement. Interestingly enough, the decline of federation in this country coincided with its rise in Canada. Metropolitan federation went into operation in the Toronto area in 1953 and has been in effect there ever since.[2]

THE OBSTACLES TO ADOPTION

Legal Impediments

Federation attempts in the United States have generally been hampered by two legal obstacles. First, because formal means of activating such plans did not exist, the proponents had to seek authorization through constitutional amendment or state statute. Second, the legal authorizations obtained usually embodied difficult hurdles in their requirements for local adoption. A number of them required approval by referendum and stipulated multiple majorities, sometimes a majority in each city (in some instances coupled with countywide majorities); or an extraordinary majority in more than half of the municipalities plus a countywide majority. In contrast, it should be noted, many metropolitan special districts, which are examples of another form of the two-level approach, needed only a single areawide popular majority. Moreover, some metropolitan districts have been established directly by action of the state legislature, without referendum, the procedure which was also followed in creating Toronto's federation.[3]

Internal Problems

Federation efforts also have been impeded by other obstacles. One difficulty—an appropriate and acceptable distribution of powers between the metropolitan and local units—is inherent in all multipurpose two-level systems. Determining which level should have what responsibilities is often a troublesome and perplexing issue—a dilemma not posed by city-county consolidation. Should the powers of both governmental levels be specified or should the functions of *only one or the other* be enumerated explicitly? (Actually, all three possibilities have been incorporated in different federation plans.) Also, should all aspects of a function be assigned to one level, or is it more logical in certain functional fields to allot some components to one level and the remain-

---

[2] The Quebec and Manitoba provincial Legislatures passed federation acts pertaining to the Montreal and Winnipeg areas in 1959 and 1960, respectively. The metropolitan governments established by these laws, however, have far fewer powers than their Toronto counterpart.

[3] Most regional and subregional districts established in the Bay Area during the post-World War II years were created by legislative acts without referenda.

der to the other? For example, refuse *collection* might continue to be handled by the local governments, while regional refuse *disposal* might be made the responsibility of the metropolitan government. Again, the allocation of entire functions to one level, and the division of other functions between the two, have been laid out in various federation plans. Obviously, a great many combinations are possible.

The other difficulty has related to the composition of the governing body of the upper level. All federation proposals, except some prepared for the Boston area, provided for direct election of all governing board members, and for either the nomination or election (and in some instances both) of some or all members from sub-districts within the metropolitan boundaries. Constructing the metropolitan governing body has therefore involved decisions about whether representation should be based solely on population, or whether other factors, such as existing local units, should be considered. It has similarly involved judgments on ways to insure adequate representation without swelling the metropolitan board to an unwieldly size. These have frequently proved to be very delicate questions.

AREA AND THE BOROUGH CONCEPT

Some proposed federations have concerned only a single county. This was true of the proposals for Alameda, Allegheny, and Dade counties, where a new metropolitan government would have replaced the existing county. Other proposals have encompassed more than one county. The Boston area proposals pertained to a whole county and portions of three others. The San Francisco and St. Louis arrangements related, in effect, to a consolidated city-county on the one hand and a county government on the other.

A number of the federation plans would have renamed the local governments "boroughs," frequently after territorially enlarging them so that, altogether, they would encompass all the land within the boundaries of the metropolitan government. Thus, in the case of the Alameda County plan of 1916, all the ten existing cities would have been called boroughs. Four of them would have been substantially increased in size and two augmented slightly, by the addition of unincorporated area. The eleventh borough would have been created *de novo* from unincorporated land in Washington township.

Thus, boroughs may constitute the lower-tier governments in a federation. (But they are not necessarily employed as the local areas from which members of the metropolitan legislature are chosen; sometimes larger election districts have been proposed for this purpose.) As a result of this new nomenclature for the local governmental level, federation is sometimes called the *borough plan*.[4]

THE TORONTO AREA FEDERATION: HOW IT CAME TO BE

Despite Toronto's many differences from our governmental tradition and geographic circumstance, its experience is clearly the most instructive evidence available that a metropolitan federation can be installed and that it will work. As noted earlier, the Toronto area's leap into federation in 1953 was the first successful attempt on the North American continent. Like its counterparts in the United States, the Toronto metropolitan area had serious problems of areawide impact. The needs of some local communities, especially in education, were far outdistancing their financial resources, sometimes to a point of near bankruptcy. Growing deficiencies in water supply and sewage disposal were afflicting many suburban localities. Other unmet needs—in highways, mass transit, housing, and land use control, for example—were also reaching a state of considerable aggravation.

But there were—and are—similar needs in many areas of the United States. Federation became a reality in the Toronto area chiefly due to a combination of two factors, both of which have been absent in all the many metropolises in the United States where this approach has been discussed or proposed. First, an impartial official board was available with power to propose a plan of governmental reorganization. Second, action of the provincial (state) Legislature was sufficient to accomplish reform.

The Ontario Municipal Board is a quasi-judicial, administrative agency—appointed by the provincial government of Ontario—which is generally without equal in the American states. (Probably its closest kin in the United States is the Alaska Local Boundary Commission.) Besides exercising control over local public finance, the Ontario board may order, without a local vote, various types of boundary adjustments, including the consolidation of localities, or the establishment of certain new governmental units.

---

[4] The term "borough" is at times employed in ways unrelated to federation, however. For example, in New York City it identifies administrative entities, which have no legislative powers, and consequently are not governments. The term is also used to identify various types of local governments in certain states, Alaska, New Jersey and Pennsylvania, for example. But none of these represents the use of the term *borough* as employed in a federation, i.e., to designate the local unit of government in a metropolitan-local system. A historical discussion of the term is contained in Orval Etter, *The Metropolitan Borough: What Is It?* (Portland, Oregon: Portland Metropolitan Study Commission, January 1966).

Amid a setting of growing problems, separate applications were made by three municipalities—Toronto, Long Branch, and Mimico—asking the Ontario Municipal Board for various changes in the governmental structure of the Toronto area. The board held hearings of many months duration in 1950 and 1951. There was strong participation by local governmental officials and private individuals, who presented several million words of testimony and submitted some 300 items of evidence. The board took the matter under advisement in mid-1951, but did not publicly announce its decisions and recommendations until early 1953.

The board denied the applications before it, but concluded that the applicants had effectively demonstrated a pressing need for major reform of the existing governmental system. The board offered its own proposals for a suitable form of metropolitan government in the Toronto area.[5] The provincial Premier was sympathetic and had a bill introduced which largely complied with the recommendations of the Ontario Municipal Board, and it was promptly passed by the Legislature in April, 1953. The metropolitan council was organized in the same month, and the legislation went into full effect on January 1, 1954. Thus was a federation of 13 municipalities installed in an area of 240 square miles containing about 1,200,000 people.

The Toronto Area Federation: The First Thirteen Years

The original Toronto plan of metropolitan federation had several prominent characteristics. One was the creation of an areawide government to carry out functions judged essential to the entire area. This government, called the Municipality of Metropolitan Toronto, embraced the territory of all 13 contiguous municipalities. A second characteristic was the retention of the central City of Toronto and the 12 suburban municipalities to handle functions not allotted to the metropolitan unit. A third feature granted each municipality constituent-unit representation in the metropolitan legislature.

Metropolitan Powers and Shared Functions

The new metropolitan government was initially given specified powers in many functional fields—water supply, sewage disposal, arterial roads, transit, property assessment, health and welfare services, metropolitan parks, public housing and redevelopment, and planning. Its powers were enlarged by provincial legislation in 1957 to include law enforcement, air pollution control, civil defense, and most phases of licensing.

---

[5] Ontario Municipal Board, *Decisions and Recommendations of the Board* (Toronto: January 20, 1953), p. 42 ff. This publication is also known as the Cumming Report, named for the board's chairman, Lorne Cumming.

From the beginning, some functions were given exclusively to the metropolitan government (property assessment, for example) while some functions (libraries) remained entirely with the municipal governments. In other matters, the principle of shared functions was utilized in various ways. For instance, in certain shared activities the metropolitan government took on the role of wholesaler. This was true of water supply: the metropolitan government was obligated to construct and maintain pumping stations, treatment plants, trunk mains, and reservoirs. Water was then sold wholesale to the municipalities, which in turn retailed it to consumers. This was also true of sewage disposal: the metropolitan government was assigned the building and maintenance of trunk sewer mains and treatment plants, whereas the municipalities administered the local sewage collection systems.

The principle of shared functions was also employed to make the metropolitan government a financial overseer. Thus, the metropolitan government reviewed the bond proposals of municipalities, and issued bonds in its own name for those proposals receiving its sanction. Also, the metropolitan unit, on advice of an independent metropolitan school board, determined the amounts of the funds to be approved for school site purchase and building construction, and issued bonds for such purposes against its own credit. Eleven locally-elected school boards, however, were responsible for public elementary and secondary education in the municipalities.

A further application of the shared-function principle gave the metropolitan government authority over aspects of other services for which an areawide need had been conclusively demonstrated. Accordingly, the responsibility for constructing and maintaining an arterial highway system was given to the metropolitan unit, while local streets remained in the hands of the municipal governments. Similarly, the development and operation of large metropolitan parks went to the new government, and responsibility for local parks stayed with the municipal governments.

Two other powers of the metropolitan government should be mentioned. It selects the members of the Toronto Transit Commission, which was made the sole supplier of public transportation in the area. The metropolitan government was also authorized to adopt a general areawide plan, which would be controlling in the municipalities, after being approved by the appropriate provincial minister (formerly the Minister of Planning and Development, now the Minister of Municipal Affairs).

Balanced and Ex-Officio Representation

Another prominent characteristic of the original Toronto governmental plan related to the balance of representation on the metropolitan council. First, an equal number of members came from the central city and the suburbs, both being granted 12 representatives, although at the time the City of Toronto had 60 percent of the area's population. Second, each of the 12 suburbs was allocated a single member, regardless of size. Accordingly, the metropolitan council was composed of 24 members if it selected its chairman, the chief executive officer, from its own membership, or 25 members if it chose an outside person. (To date the council has always chosen its chairman from outside.)

The federation act also provided for officials of the constituent municipalities to serve as the members of the metropolitan council. Consequently, Toronto's representatives were the mayor, the two controllers[a] receiving the largest number of votes in the last citywide election, and the nine aldermen (councilmen) receiving the largest number of votes in the last municipal election. In turn, the heads (mayors and reeves) of the other municipalities represented the suburbs. The terms of office of metropolitan council members and the chairman were initially set at one year.

Accomplishments and Criticism

The metropolitan government registered important accomplishments during the 13-year period before basic changes went into effect on January 1, 1967. The greatest progress was made with needs considered critical in pre-federation days—water supply, sewage disposal, and education. Water supply and sewage disposal capacities were greatly increased and many new school structures and additions were built. Significant advances were also made in mass transit, expressway construction, air pollution control, and law enforcement. Another major accomplishment was the establishment of an excellent metropolitan credit rating, facilitating the financing of capital improvements and saving millions of dollars in interest charges. By the end of the 13-year period, none of the 13 member muncipalities wished to return to the pre-federation arrangement.

Despite these accomplishments, the federation was criticized during

---

[a] Four elected Toronto controllers, along with the mayor, constitute a board of control possessing important financial and personnel authority in the Toronto city government.

this period.[7] Some of the critical comment centered on the lack of assertiveness in public housing and areawide planning. Other complaints pointed to the priority given public works programs—where concrete results could be quickly demonstrated to the public—to the virtual exclusion of the more controversial, socially-oriented problems in such a field as welfare. (But it should be pointed out that metropolitan officials deliberately chose to concentrate first on high priority physical and service problems which could readily be alleviated, as a means of showing the value of the new metropolitan-local system.)

The most frequent point of criticism involved the formula of representation in the metropolitan governing body. From the outset, there was strong opposition to the allocation of one seat to each suburban municipality, irrespective of population. In the beginning, each of the three smallest municipalities had only about 8,000 or 9,000 people, while the three most populous suburbs had populations of approximately 110,000, 79,000, and 70,000. Thus, the largest outlying municipality had more than 13 times as many inhabitants as the smallest. These suburban population discrepancies, great as they were at the outset, increased during the subsequent 13 years.

Opposition to the equal division of seats between the central city and suburbs did not develop at the inception of federation, although Toronto then had almost three-fifths of the total population. Toronto was deliberately underrepresented to avoid control of the metropolitan government by the central city. Opposition to this aspect of the representation formula crystallized, however, as the years passed and the suburbs outgrew Toronto, which now has only about 40 percent of the area's population.

THE TORONTO AREA FEDERATION: THE REORGANIZATION OF 1966

In 1966, new provincial legislation made significant changes in the federation, while reaffirming support for the two-level approach.[8]

---

[7] For criticism and discussion of accomplishments, see Albert Rose, "The Case Against Total Amalgamation in Metropolitan Toronto," *Public Affairs Report* (Berkeley: Institute of Governmental Studies, University of California) 4:1–5, April 1963; Municipality of Metropolitan Toronto, *Metropolitan Toronto, 1953–1963: A Decade of Progress* (1963), and comparable later reports; Frank Smallwood, *Metro Toronto: A Decade Later* (Toronto: Bureau of Municipal Research, 1963); and Harold Kaplan, *Urban Political Systems—A Functional Analysis of Metro Toronto* (New York: Columbia University Press, 1967).

[8] Preceding the legislation, a royal commission, consisting of a single commissioner, H. Carl Goldenberg of Montreal, undertook a two-year study of the existing federation. The findings and recommendations, which were partly followed by the provincial Legislature, appeared as *Report of the Royal Commission on Metropolitan Toronto* (June 1965).

Municipal Consolidation

The most important alterations were consolidation of the 13 municipalities into six, increase in the size of the metropolitan council, and reapportionment of the membership. The six new municipal governments consist of the City of Toronto and five boroughs. The limits of the central city and three boroughs were enlarged through mergers of two, three, or four units. The boundaries of the two remaining boroughs were unchanged; these two had been the most heavily populated suburban governments under the original federation. (Also, the 11 local school boards were consolidated into six and their territorial jurisdictions made coterminous with those of the six municipalities.)

Redistribution of Representation

The metropolitan council was expanded to 32 members (or 33 in the event its chairman should be selected from outside the body). The enlarged City of Toronto was allotted 12 members and each suburban borough was granted between two and six members. The crucial point, however, was that representation of the boroughs was based upon the 1964 population of the City of Toronto, as enlarged, divided by 12. Consequently, at the outset each member of the metropolitan council represented about 55,000 to 60,000 residents. The new representation formula was made subject to periodic review by the provincial government, the first review being scheduled to take place between seven and nine years after the reorganization of 1966.

The new formula drastically changed the previous arrangement. Furthermore, it closely approximates equality of representation for all voters, a criterion which has been employed in the court-enforced reapportionment of most state legislatures in the United States—as well as even more recently in reconstituting various county boards of supervisors, city councils, and school boards.[9]

[9] The strikingly close relationship between the allocation of the 32 seats to the member municipalities and their proportion of the total population is shown below:

Municipality	Population	Allocation of Metro Council seats	Allocation based on population (rounded)
Toronto	695,000	12	11.9
North York	396,000	6	6.8
Scarborough	277,000	5	4.7
Etobicoke	263,000	4	4.5
York	144,000	3	2.5
East York	95,000	2	1.6
	1,870,000	32	32.0

Other Alterations

Some other changes resulted from the 1966 provincial legislation. The terms of office of the chairman and other members of the metropolitan council were increased from two to three years; the terms had been one year from 1953 to 1956. The council's executive committee was enlarged to 11 members, including the chairman, four Toronto council members and the mayor, and the five mayors of the suburban municipalities. (Previously, the executive committee first had five members and later was enlarged to seven.) It is a powerful committee, responsible for preparing the annual budget, awarding all contracts, nominating all heads and deputy heads of departments, and initiating policy proposals. As before, it takes a two-thirds vote of the council to overrule the executive committee on the award of contracts and nomination of officials.

The powers of the metropolitan government were increased in such fields as welfare and waste disposal. In addition, the metropolitan government was empowered to provide greater equalization of school finances. It was also authorized to provide local school boards sufficient funds to furnish adequate educational services, on the basis of estimates submitted by an independently selected metropolitan school board.

Major Unchanged Features

Some fundamental aspects of the metropolitan federation were not changed. No powers possessed by the metropolitan government were given to the municipalities. Elected officials of the municipalities still constitute the entire membership of the metropolitan council (unless the chairman should be selected from outside). The overall territorial boundaries of the Metropolitan Toronto federation remain the same.

LESSONS FROM EXPERIENCE WITH FEDERATION

1. Action by the provincial (state) legislature, based upon recommendations by an independent investigating body, is an effective way to accomplish metropolitan reform. Moreover, the adoption of metropolitan reform by legislative act alone, instead of with popular referendum, retains for the legislature the authority to effect further reorganization later if it should prove necessary.

2. The areawide and local levels of government may logically share some functions, the former handling regional aspects and the latter taking care of others.

3. The metropolitan government may appropriately serve as an "umbrella" agency for specific purposes: approval of local bond pro-

posals, equalization of financial resources, and appointment of other governing boards responsible for particular activities—transit in the case of Toronto. Thus an upper-level government can influence local and regional policies, insuring consideration of the regional welfare, without engaging in direct *management* of all regional and local functions.

4. Regional planning is an important power of the upper-tier government in a federal system. In Toronto, for example, the metropolitan government can draft general regional plans which, after provincial approval, are binding on the local governments. The latter are responsible for local planning and zoning.

5. A powerful executive committee is essential when the governing body of the federation is large. Toronto's experience suggests that a 25-member body requires a smaller executive committee if it is to function effectively.

6. Periodic review by an independent agency—possibly a committee of the legislature—plus freedom to reorganize in the light of experience and changed circumstances, are crucial if the regional government is to be kept up-to-date.

The Comprehensive Urban County

The comprehensive urban county, a second kind of two-level system, features a general metropolitan government in addition to local units, thus resembling federation. The major difference is that under the urban county plan, an existing county government is converted into a general-purpose metropolitan agency by the simultaneous transfer of a number of functions from other local governments. Accordingly, the urban county—rather than a metropolitan-level government created by federation—handles activities of an areawide nature, while municipalities and other local entities continue to provide local services. Because of this, and the fact that Dade County encompasses an entire metropolitan area, the Miami experiment, although based on a single preexisting county, is fully as relevant to the study of functional reallocation at the metropolitan level as the experience of a true federation like Toronto's.

Dade County (Miami): The Plan in Action

The first comprehensive urban county system to become operative in the United States went into effect in Dade County (Miami), Florida, in July 1957, and has been functioning there ever since.[10] Dade County comprises a large population and area: more than a million people and 2,054 square miles, a portion of which, however, is uninhabitable swampland. It also is one of the nation's fastest growing metropolitan areas, having tripled its population in 20 years.

Background and Adoption

There had been some functional consolidation in Dade County during the 1940's. A countywide health department was established, the county acquired the area's principal hospital, and a county port authority was created. But reorganization received its real impetus when voters in the City of Miami only narrowly defeated a citywide referendum to abolish the municipality and transfer its responsibilities to the county government. This prompted the steps leading to installation of the comprehensive urban county system. A professional survey of the need for governmental reorganization was financed in 1954, and a proposed constitutional home rule amendment for Dade County was approved by the state electorate two years later.[11] In May, 1957, the county voters approved, by a slim majority, the comprehensive urban county charter prepared by a gubernatorially-appointed board. The charter was required to obtain only a single countywide majority, which it did by a margin of less than 2,000 votes. A heavy affirmative electoral response in the City of Miami tipped the scales in favor of the charter.

The Structural Renovation

The charter provided for a county government strengthened both structurally and functionally, and for the retention of all existing municipalities, then numbering 26 (in 1961 the number increased to 27). Most of the cities had fewer than 10,000 population. In contrast to the municipalities in the Toronto federation, which are contiguous and encompass all the population, the municipalities in Dade County include

---

[10] Support for the comprehensive urban county plan has been growing in the last 20 years. This is particularly true of metropolitan areas situated within the limits of a single county, as well as others which are intercounty, but have most of their population in one central county. (Most metropolitan areas are still of one-county size.) The greatest attraction of the plan is its ability to employ an existing unit for metropolitan purposes instead of establishing a new government. Recent efforts in support of the comprehensive urban county approach have been made in five metropolitan areas—Cleveland, Dayton, Pittsburgh, Houston, and Miami. The attempts failed in the first four areas during the 1950's and early 1960's, but succeeded in Miami (Dade County).

[11] Public Administration Service, *The Government of Metropolitan Miami* (Chicago: 1954).

only about three-fifths of the total population. In other words, almost two-fifths of the county's inhabitants reside in unincorporated territory that is often urban in nature.

Charter adoption accomplished substantial internal reorganization. It converted the assessor, tax collector, surveyor, supervisor of voter registration, and purchasing agent from elected officials to appointees of the county manager. The manager, who was given responsibility for the county's administrative operations, was made appointive and removable by the board of county commissioners, the legislative body of the metropolitan county. The charter also authorized the county board to convert the sheriff and constables from elective to appointive status, which they did.

Under charter provisions that went into effect in 1958, the entire county was divided into five districts for purposes of representation. Voters in each district elected one commissioner to the county board. In addition, another commissioner from each of the districts was elected by a countywide vote. (This represented a compromise between the proponents of a ward or district system and those who preferred countywide elections.) Finally, a commissioner was elected from each city with an official population of not less than 60,000. All were chosen for four-year terms. Accordingly, the first application of these charter sections produced a governing body of 11 commissioners, Miami being the only city of over 60,000. Hialeah and Miami Beach both qualified for additional representation after the federal census of 1960, whereupon the number of commissioners increased to 13.

Enlarged Powers

The county government also was granted considerable new authority under the charter. It may build arterial roads, own and operate transit systems and transportation terminals, and regulate traffic. It may provide for hospitals, health and welfare programs, park and recreational sites, public housing, urban renewal, air pollution control, flood and beach erosion control, and drainage. It may regulate or own a broad range of public utilities and promote the area's economy. It may provide central records, training, and communications for fire and police protection. In addition, the county government was given the authority both to prepare and enforce comprehensive plans for the county's development, and to adopt and implement zoning regulations, as well as uniform building and related technical codes throughout the county.

The county government was also given authority to set reasonable minimum standards for all governmental units in the county for the performance of any function, and to assume responsibility for any local service failing to meet the standards. Approval of the county governing body is required—as well as consent of the local voters under most circumstances—for any proposal to form a new municipality or to annex territory to an existing city. On the other hand, no municipality in existence when the charter was adopted may be abolished without the sanction of a majority of its electors voting in a special election called for that purpose.

Challenge and Support: Attempts to Alter the Plan

The reorganized Dade County has been subjected to repeated attempts to secure basic changes, most of them designed to weaken the reform arrangements. However, the efforts at change have subsided in the last few years, in part because some of their goals were realized, and, in part, because the system now seems to have attained a degree of stability.

One line of attack tried unsuccessfully both in 1957 and 1961, was to reinstate almost without exception the distribution of functions in existence before the charter's adoption. A second line of attack attempted to reinstate some or much of the precharter organization of the county government.[12]

Another set of efforts was aimed at strengthening the metropolitan level of government. One move called for a basic alteration in the procedure for choosing the county governing body. It provided for reduction of the county commission from 13 to nine members. Eight commissioners were each required to be residents of eight newly formed districts, but the ninth member, the chairman-mayor, could live anywhere in the county; all nine were to be elected from the county at large. This proposed amendment was approved by the electorate in 1963.

The other suggested change would have supplanted the council-manager form of county government with the strong-mayor form. It was, in part, an outgrowth of repeated criticism of the county's political leadership, which was generally termed inadequate under the reformed system—as it also had been under the preexisting form of government. A serious effort was made on behalf of this proposal in 1964, but it failed to get enough signatures to qualify for the ballot.

---

[12] A substantial part of this effort was directed at returning the offices of sheriff and assessor to elective status. After three such attempts in four years, the sheriff's position was again made elective by a close vote in 1963. Another part of this second line of attack was designed to replace the council-manager form with the previously existing commission form; this proposal, included within a sweeping amendment, met defeat in 1961.

Problems of Leadership and Finance

Leadership and finance are two major problems confronting the metropolitan governmental system in Dade County. No form of governmental organization is able to *guarantee* top quality leadership, but it is evident that neither of the first two county managers, both of whom were dismissed by decisive votes of the county commission, could find the right combination of techniques under the prevailing conditions. The rapid turnover of managers—two removed in the first seven years—also contributed to the early vicissitudes of the reform.

Some observers hold hope for strengthened leadership from the recently established office of mayor, the holder of which is elected on a countywide basis. But countywide election may not be enough; a definite assignment of policy-making responsibilities to the mayor may be needed to generate the necessary leadership capabilities. In any event, the charter's original council-manager arrangement, with no elected executive, has given way to one containing such an executive. It remains to be seen whether the small-commission-mayor-manager "mix" will provide the requisite elements for effective leadership.

Financial problems are severe. The county has been forced to continue with the old, highly restricted tax structure of pre-reform years, despite a great increase in responsibilities. These include furnishing more areawide services, in addition to providing municipal services for the large and continually growing population of the unincorporated areas. Due in part to legal difficulties and uncertainties, the county has been unable to install an equitable means of financing municipal services in the unincorporated sections. Furthermore, the state has not yet taken on additional obligations in certain important fields, such as welfare and health, nor has it authorized a broader financial base for Dade and other heavily populated counties.[13]

The Problem of Divisiveness

The most fundamental problem of Dade's comprehensive urban county system has been the continuing conflict between the "consolidationists," who wish to abolish the cities, and the "localists," who wish to eradicate the metropolitan powers of the county government. A strong effort to make the system work is needed, instead of repeated divisive attempts to implement such contradictory aims. Furthermore, although the municipalities are formal partners in the two-level system, many of their officials have been obstructionists, opposing almost every effort to institute areawide services and facilities. Their tactics proved

[13] Edward Sofen, *The Miami Metropolitan Experiment*, 2nd ed. (Garden City, N.Y.: Doubleday Anchor, 1966), pp. 209, 232.

so harassing that in 1962 the county manager recommended consolidation of the 27 municipalities and the county into a single unit. If the two-level system is to emerge as an effective and long-range answer for Metropolitan Miami, a better spirit of cooperation must somehow be developed between the two interlocked elements, the county and the municipalities.

LESSONS FROM EXPERIENCE WITH THE COMPREHENSIVE URBAN COUNTY

1. In most multi-county metropolitan areas the comprehensive urban county approach probably would be useful chiefly to improve the existing county governments' ability to deal with those problems that can be solved by single-county action.

2. The areawide powers granted to the metropolitan government in Dade County to adopt and enforce comprehensive plans, zoning regulations, and uniform building and related technical codes, constituted a major breakthrough at the metropolitan level in the United States. These powers are widely recognized as crucial instruments for the intelligent direction of urban growth, but they are also some of the most jealously guarded prerogatives of local governments in virtually all metropolitan areas.

3. Endowing a county or areawide government with authority to determine and enforce reasonable minimum standards of service for cities and non-school local special districts could be a method for strengthening the local government level.

4. An independently elected chief executive may be useful in helping develop effective public leadership in an areawide government.

5. Extremist positions for and against metropolitan reform may have a seriously debilitating effect on any newly formed regional government, before it has had an opportunity to be tested fairly. Referenda and threats of referenda have been employed as a major weapon in the continuing campaign of harassment of Dade County. Contrast this with the Toronto experience, where reform enacted by legislation without referendum protected the new government and gave it a chance for a fair trial.

Regional and Subregional Multi-County Districts and Agencies

Regional and subregional multi-county districts provide one of the most promising approaches to metropolitan problems. They lend maximum flexibility, and can be installed with a minimum of disturbance to existing units, if that is desired. They may be assigned as few or as many functions as circumstances require. Normally they are given only a small number of functions. In this, they differ somewhat from the other two-level approaches, federation and the comprehensive urban county, which usually have multiple purposes and thus are considered to be *general-purpose* governments. Theoretically, of course, a district could be assigned as many powers as a full-fledged federation. In practice, however, they have not been: most provide only a single service.

This section will concentrate on regional and subregional multi-county districts—hereinafter usually referred to as metropolitan districts—that are independent governmental units. They meet the same test as do cities, counties, and other governments, i.e., they are organized entities of a public character. For instance, their officials are elected by the voters, or appointed by elected officials, and the districts possess considerable fiscal and administrative independence.[14]

MANY FUNCTIONS, MANY DISTRICTS

Metropolitan districts across the nation undertake a wide variety of activities.[15] Most common are the provision of port facilities, sewage disposal, airports, mass transit, regional parks, public housing, and water supply. In recent years there has been a noticeable increase in mass transit districts. Other activities less commonly carried out by metropolitan districts include air and water pollution control, bridge construction and maintenance, electricity supply, flood control, hospital facilities and care, and libraries. Still others include insect pest control, public health services, transport terminal facilities, and tunnel construction and maintenance. In aggregate, then, these districts have attacked some of the most serious areawide physical problems confronting metropolitan regions.

The growth of metropolitan districts, especially in the past 20 years, is one of the most pronounced trends of governmental change in the United States. They are now functioning in a large number of metropolitan areas, primarily in the heavily populated centers. In many areas they are the only form of metropolitan government in existence.

---

[14] The districts (sometimes called authorities) thus are separate governments. They should not be confused with the dependent districts that are subordinate agencies of state and local governments and have no effective autonomy.

[15] Three general studies of metropolitan districts have been made: John C. Bollens, *Special District Governments in the United States* (Berkeley: University of California Press, 1957); Max A. Pock, *Independent Special Districts: A Solution to the Metropolitan Area Problems* (Ann Arbor: Legislative Research Center, University of Michigan Law School, 1962); and Advisory Commission on Intergovernmental Relations, *The Problem of Special Districts in American Government* (Washington: 1964).

REASONS FOR GROWTH OF METROPOLITAN DISTRICTS

A Last Resort

One reason for the expanding number of metropolitan districts is the frequent view of them as a device of last resort, installed only after more thoroughgoing changes have been rejected. In the St. Louis region, for instance, areawide difficulties continued to mount after the defeats of city-county consolidation in 1926 and of federation four years later.[16] Subsequently St. Louis has used the district mechanism twice, first in 1949 with the formation of the Bi-State Development Agency through an interstate compact, and again in 1954 when the Metropolitan St. Louis Sewer District was formed through dual voter consent in St. Louis and St. Louis County. An epidemic of encephalitis, attributed by some people to the serious sewage problem in the suburbs, helped substantially to elicit popular support for the sewer district proposal. In 1963, the Bi-State Development Agency, which initially restricted itself to providing limited dock facilities, completed the purchase of all privately-owned mass transit companies in the area. Two years later it began operating an airport.

A Mild Method

The previously mentioned mildness of the metropolitan district method has been another contributor to its growing use. It causes a minimum of disturbance among units of the existing governmental system. Consequently it has considerable appeal to many local public officials and employees who believe major reorganization would affect them detrimentally—through loss of position, power, or job seniority. A metropolitan district furnishes a means of dealing with a specific problem, often on an isolated basis without regard for related metropolitan matters. This avoids the politically painful task of formulating a rational general plan of governmental organization. A district can thus be an "easy" resort as well as a last resort.

Limited Finances

The narrow financial base of many metropolitan districts has also proved attractive in some quarters and has fostered the trend. Many of these units must depend completely or chiefly on non-tax sources—service charges, tolls, and rents—and on revenue bonds whose principal

[16] For a recounting of the various reorganization efforts in Metropolitan St. Louis, see John C. Bollens, ed., *Exploring the Metropolitan Community* (Berkeley: University of California Press, 1961), pp. 61–69, 97–178; Henry J. Schmandt, Paul G. Steinbicker, and George D. Wendel, *Metropolitan Reform in St. Louis* (New York: Holt, Reinhart and Winston, 1961).

and interest must be paid from operating funds. Withholding the power to levy taxes and to incur general obligation indebtedness may appeal to those who would minimize expenditures, but it also limits the activities in which districts may participate.

Certain areawide functions simply cannot be performed on a profit-making or self-sustaining basis, and districts not endowed with broad financial authority are unable to deal with some of the most important problems of the metropolis. For example, when the Massachusetts Bay Transportation Authority was formed in 1964 to provide mass transit in the Boston area, the state Legislature realized that fare receipts would be insufficient. Accordingly it earmarked the returns from an increase in the state cigarette tax to provide additional money for the transit system.

Ease of Formation

The ease with which metropolitan districts may be formed has also sped their numerical growth. Seldom has a state constitutional amendment been required to authorize activation of a district. This contrasts markedly with the legal obstacles to the federation and comprehensive urban county approaches. State enabling legislation is the usual means of establishing metropolitan districts. Frequently metropolitan districts are established without any local referendum. Often when a popular referendum is required for formation, only a single areawide majority is specified.

Three methods of district activation without referendum have been utilized. Some districts, including the air pollution control and rapid transit districts in the San Francisco Bay Area, and the rapid transit district in the Los Angeles area, were created by special state legislative acts. Others, including the Cleveland Metropolitan Park District, were created under state legislation requiring action by local public officials.[17]

Indirect Methods of Selection

In many instances the members of the district governing board are selected by appointment and not through direct election by the voters.[18] Furthermore, the method of indirect selection may be so devised as to

---

[17] Still others, including the Port of New York Authority and the Bi-State Development Agency of the St. Louis area, are based on interstate compacts passed by the respective state legislatures.

[18] As was noted earlier, pp. 26–30, direct election of single-purpose regional or sub-regional districts is probably inadvisable. Certainly experience in the San Francisco Bay Area, with the East Bay Municipal Utility District, the East Bay Regional Park District, and the Alameda-Contra Costa Transit District, substantiates this conclusion. Their record is one of low political visibility, ineffectual contests against incumbents, and nearly meaningless elections.

render public accountability of the governing body membership virtually impossible. The members of the Cleveland Metropolitan Park District, for example, are appointed by judges of the common pleas court. Sometimes the appointing authority is distributed among several different agents, and a consenting requirement added, producing a complex scheme. In the St. Louis area, for instance, three members of the Metropolitan St. Louis Sewer District are chosen by the mayor of St. Louis with the approval of the judges of the circuit court in the city. The other three members are appointed by the elected county chief executive of St. Louis County with the consent of the local district judges. Even more complex and bewildering is the method of selecting the governing body of the Chicago Transit Authority. The mayor of Chicago selects four members with the consent of the Governor and the city council. The Governor chooses the other three members, one of whom must live outside Chicago. The Governor's appointees must be approved by both the state Senate and the mayor of Chicago!

Constituent-Unit Concept

In some district legislation, mostly of recent origin, representation is based on the constituent-unit principle. This means that members of the governing body are appointed by the governing boards of the general governmental units situated within the district. Sometimes but not always, the governing boards must choose the representatives from among their own members. Such a procedure is said to promote greater intergovernmental cooperation and coordinated planning. It also assures that control of the metropolitan district will rest with officials of the general local units. Consequently local officials often take the lead in advocating the constituent-unit concept.

In the Municipality of Metropolitan Seattle—which is actually a metropolitan district—the governing body consists of the mayor and seven councilmen of the central city, the three members of the county board of commissioners, mayors or councilmen from the area's three largest municipalities other than Seattle, a mayor or councilman from one of the remaining eight municipalities, chosen by vote of their mayors, and a chairman, who must be a private citizen, selected by the fifteen.

The Bay Area Air Pollution Control District and the San Francisco Bay Area Rapid Transit District, also employ the constituent-unit principle. A portion of the membership is selected by county supervisors, and the other portion by city selection committees, i.e., by countywide conferences of mayors. All air pollution control district directors must be mayors, councilmen, and supervisors, equally divided between city and county officials. By contrast, laymen may be and have been appointed to the rapid transit district board.

The recently established Southern California Rapid Transit District employs still another variation of the constituent-unit principle. Five members are appointed by the county board of supervisors, two by the mayor of Los Angeles with the council's confirmation, and four by a suburban city selection committee. The selection committee is made up of one council member from each city within the district, other than Los Angeles. In choosing the four non-Los Angeles city representatives, each member of the selection committee is entitled to cast one vote for each $10 million, or major fraction thereof, of assessed property value for district purposes in his city. However, each committee member is entitled to at least one vote, and no member may have more votes than those of all the other cities combined.

For the purpose of determining representation, a novel procedure was written into the law. The city selection committee may group or combine the areas of the cities within the district, except Los Angeles, into corridors based on existing or proposed transit lines or in any other manner, irrespective of contiguity.[19] The cities have been placed in four groupings to provide a representative from each of the four major proposed travel corridors as outlined by the district engineers. The directors of the Southern California Rapid Transit District may be, but are not required to be, members of the governing bodies of the cities and the county within its boundaries; a number of directors are private citizens.

Criticisms of Appointment Method

The appointment method of selecting metropolitan district governing board members—including the constituent-unit principle—has been criticized on the ground that such districts are insufficiently accountable to the public. Certainly when local public officials serve as the metropolitan district board members, the process of public control becomes indirect and rather ineffective. The *local* public, for example, may remove a public official from the metropolitan board by defeating him for re-election to the local post (or in some states, including California, by recalling him from his local office). But the "regional public" has no way of registering its dissatisfaction with such a representative at the polls. Even the local public may not do so if it is satisfied with the representative's performance in his city or county post, and judges his *local* record to be more important than his performance in the metro-

---

[19] *Cal. Stats.*, 1964 Extra. Session, ch. 62 (*Public Utilities* Code secs., 30000–31520).

politan unit. In practice, therefore, a *metropolitan* district board made up of local officials is not directly accountable to the voters or the "public."

Utilization of the district mechanism for a series of single or very limited purposes has produced a formidable problem of representation and democratic control. Appointment fails to provide adequate accountability to the public. Election of a district governing body provides a semblance of direct accountability and control, but is often a fiction because there is little competition for the offices and little voter attention to the elections, due in part to the narrow functional base of operation. Moreover, as these districts of limited scope grow in number, popular control becomes attenuated to the point of nonexistence because the voters simply cannot follow the activities of multiple districts.[20]

THE MULTIPURPOSE DISTRICT IDEA

Experience with the problems of *single-function* metropolitan districts—which include lack of coordination in dealing with areawide problems, the irrational allocation of financial resources, increased governmental complexity, and the dilemma of representation—has stimulated interest in *multipurpose* districts. Such units could be created in several ways: granting existing districts more functions, consolidating those already in operation, or establishing new districts empowered to provide a broad range of areawide functions. Thus far, little has been accomplished along any of these three lines. Single-purpose districts continue to operate under their narrow power grants. No important consolidations have taken place. The few broad authorizations have not been employed to full advantage but instead have been utilized in a very restricted manner. For example, multipurpose district legislation was enacted in the State of Washington in 1957, but the district formed under the law in the Seattle area, called the Municipality of Metropolitan Seattle, performs only sewage disposal. Twice it has unsuccessfully sought to undertake additional functions.[21]

AN "UMBRELLA" DISTRICT: THE TWIN CITIES METROPOLITAN COUNCIL

In one of the most significant recent metropolitan reorganizations, the Minnesota state Legislature established a Metropolitan Council for the seven-county region encompassing the twin cities of Minneapolis and Saint Paul (approximate population: 1.8 million; area: 2,800 square

---

[20] Bollens, *Special District Governments in the United States*, pp. 252–254.

[21] League of Women Voters of King County, *The Municipality of Metropolitan Seattle,* 3rd ed. (Seattle: 1965), pp. 4, 9.

miles).[22] The primary motivation of the region's leadership was to retain general policy control over areawide functions as they develop, to coordinate existing and future local and regional programs, and to create a representative body for the planning review functions required by recent federal legislation.

The new legislation was based, in part, on an extensive program of research and consensus building that culminated in a report by the Citizens League.[23] The original legislative proposal called for a *directly elected* council that would have taken *operating responsibility* for major regional functions. The proposal received bipartisan support, and, partly because it was limited to areawide programs, got strong backing from municipal officials in both the suburbs and central cities. A counterproposal for an *appointed* council and an agency with *coordinating* responsibilities resulted in a closely fought contest between the two concepts. The appointed-coordinating concept won by a very narrow margin. There is evidence of strong continuing support for direct election, however, and the representational arrangement may be changed in the future.

As established, the council has a 15-member governing body. Fourteen members are appointed by the Governor, one being selected from each of fourteen 100,000-population appointive areas formed by grouping (approximately) two state Senate districts. The Governor makes his appointments in consultation with the two state Senators and four state Representatives from each appointive area. The fifteenth member is the chairman and principal executive officer, who is appointed by the Governor, at large. Council appointments are made for staggered six-year terms, and the chairman serves at the Governor's pleasure.

The council is intended to be nonpartisan, and, in fact, no clear partisan political alignments have appeared in its deliberations. "Politics" is realistically recognized, however, because the member representing each appointive area is normally of the same party as the majority of the elected state legislative delegation from that area.

Among the council's major responsibilities are regional planning, a function taken over from the preexisting Metropolitan Planning Commission, which was abolished and whose staff and facilities were absorbed by the new council. The council was given a number of potentially very influential powers to encourage implementation of its plans and to prevent their being contravened by other regional or local

[22] *Minna. Session Laws* 1967, ch. 896.
[23] Citizens League, *Citizens League Report. A Metropolitan Council for the Twin Cities Area* (Minneapolis: February 9, 1967).

programs. First, the council has authority to review the proposals and projects of independent commissions, boards, or agencies whose plans have a multicommunity effect and (except for sewage treatment plant construction) may suspend any proposal found inconsistent with the council's plan. Such vetoes may be appealed to the state Legislature. The scope of this power is indicated by the following list of agencies whose plans the council may suspend: (1) the Minneapolis-Saint Paul Sanitary District, (2) the Minneapolis-Saint Paul Metropolitan Airports Commission, (3) the Metropolitan Mosquito Control District, (4) the Metropolitan Transit Commission, (5) the Hennepin County Park Reserve District, (6) the North Suburban Sanitary Sewer District, (7) two hospital districts, (8) the Dakota-Scott Library District, (9) the Lake Minnetonka Conservation District, (10) six soil conservation districts, and (11) four watershed districts.

In addition, the council is directed to appoint from its membership a nonvoting member of the airports commission, the mosquito control commission, and the Minneapolis-Saint Paul Sanitary District. It also may appoint a nonvoting member of any other metropolitan area commission or board authorized by law.

Second, the council reviews all comprehensive municipal plans in the Twin Cities area. It may hold hearings, and comment on and criticize such plans, but is not directly empowered to veto them. The council's influence over municipal plans, however, is greatly strengthened by its third power, the review function provided for under "section 204" and other federal requirements for areawide review of grant applications. This power is reinforced by *state* legislation also specifically requiring such a review. The review requirement includes a veto power in the case of open space land acquisition proposals.

A fourth council function is preparation for the state Legislature of a statement of consensus within the metropolitan area on what should be done. In effect the Legislature has said to the council: "If you agree among yourselves that you want something done, and if it doesn't conflict with general state policy, we'll give you the authority to do it."[24] In preparing the groundwork for the consensus, the council is directed to engage in a continuous program of research and study in the following subject areas: air pollution control, acquisition and financing of major parks and open spaces in and adjacent to the metropolitan area, water pollution control, long-range planning, solid waste disposal, tax structure and equalization of tax resources, assessment practices, the

<hr>

[24] "Local Officials and Metropolitan Reorganization," (remarks by Ted Kolderie, Executive Director, Citizens League, delivered to officials of the Ohio-Kentucky-Indiana Regional Planning Council, March 2, 1968), p. 7.

consolidation of common services of local governments, and advance land acquisition for development purposes. Each study is to include recommendations as to the governmental organization or agency best suited to discharge the functions recommended.

Other council responsibilities include operating a data center, handling urban research and demonstration projects, coordinating civil defense planning, and intervening on behalf of the metropolitan region in annexation and incorporation proceedings before the Minnesota Municipal Commission.

In addition to its eligibility to accept gifts and grants from the federal and state governments and other sources, the council may levy a property tax of not more than 0.5 mill per $1.00 of assessed valuation. For its first full year of effort, the council adopted a work program requiring an expenditure of approximately $1,200,000.

The council's crucial work of regional planning and plan implementation took a step forward with the publication in June 1968 of the Joint Program Metropolitan Development Guide. This culminated six years of study and planning that had been initiated by the Metropolitan Planning Commission, the Minnesota Highway Department, and local planning and engineering departments within the metropolitan region. The guide is now being reviewed by the Metropolitan Council as it prepares its own edition. A recent issue of the council's *Newsletter* (June 1968) describes the way the council will use the guide to coordinate and direct growth, and provides a useful summation for this brief discussion of the Twin Cities experiment:

The Metropolitan Development Guide being published for the Joint Program describes the basic technique for coordinating metropolitan development. That is, to influence the development of certain metropolitan "shapers" that will, in turn, influence and coordinate other development.

The so-called shapers are major shopping and office centers, transportation facilities, utilities, and open spaces. By their location, by their size, and by the timing of their development, those four kinds of development effectively determine the overall pattern of growth within which other kinds of development fall more or less naturally into place.

The tool for coordinating the four shapers is the Development Guide itself. Its policy recommendations prescribe how development should take place and be coordinated if a desirable metropolitan environment is to be maintained.

STATE AND INTERSTATE AGENCIES

Metropolitan District Commission

At times a state agency, instead of a locally-controlled metropolitan district, is formed to handle certain areawide functions. A prominent example is the Metropolitan District Commission, which has been operating in the Boston area since 1919, when it was created to take over the responsibilities of two other state agencies, a metropolitan park commission and a metropolitan water and sewerage board. Accordingly, the commission provides regional park facilities, supplies water, and disposes of sewage. It serves a total of 49 cities and towns, which embrace about 2.5 million people and 544 square miles. In effect, there are separate service and financing areas for each of the three functions, and differing numbers of cities and towns are included in each area—30 for water, 37 for parks, and 40 for sewerage. All three include Boston.

The commission consists of a commissioner, who is the chief executive, and four associate commissioners, all appointed by the Governor for staggered five-year terms and all residents of the district (one of whom must live in Boston). The commission is a state agency, although its activities are carried out for the metropolitan cities and towns and not for the whole state. All its property is held in the name of the Commonwealth of Massachusetts, and its budget is subject to state legislative appropriations. All expenses incurred in the construction, operation, and maintenance of its services and facilities are first paid by the state and then assessed back to the municipalities within the particular service area (district).[25]

Delaware River Basin Commission

A recent notable illustration of the use of the compact device is the Delaware River Basin Commission, organized in 1961 for the four-state area centering on Philadelphia. The commission is unusual in several important respects. First, it is based on an interstate-federal compact, the national government for the first time becoming a partner with the states—New York, Pennsylvania, New Jersey, and Delaware—in such an agreement. Second, the national government chooses one of the five members of the governing body; the President of the United States makes this appointment. (The other four appointees are selected by the four governors.) Third, the commission has broad powers. It is authorized to undertake river basin planning and water resource project development and operation. Moreover, the commission is empowered to review, and thereafter disapprove or require modification of, proposals by other agencies that substantially affect the region's water resources—proposals relating, for instance, to flood protection, hydroelectric power, recreation, and water withdrawals or diversions. The commission has no taxing power, but it may issue revenue bonds when it has capital improvements capable of supporting them. During its

[25] *Origin, Development and Activities of the Metropolitan District Commission* (Boston: The District, 1964), pp. 6, 9.

early years, the agency has been largely financed by appropriations from the participating states and the national government.[26]

The Tahoe Regional Planning Agencies

Legislative acts in 1967 and 1968 created the California Tahoe Regional Planning Agency (for the California portion of the Lake Tahoe basin) and the Tahoe Regional Planning Agency (for both the California and Nevada portions of the basin).[27] The overlapping two-agency structure makes it possible to employ the California body on a standby basis, with the same membership as that representing California on the bistate agency. The purpose of this was to permit adoption and enforcement of higher planning and development standards on the California side whenever the California membership concludes that bistate agency requirements are insufficient.

Both agencies' duties and powers are extraordinary. They include preparation, adoption, review and maintenance of a comprehensive long-term general plan for the development of the Tahoe region, including land uses, transportation, conservation, recreation, and public services and facilities. The agencies shall adopt all necessary ordinances, regulations, and policies to effectuate the adopted regional plan. They shall, for example, lay down general regional standards for (among other things) zoning, solid waste disposal, sewage disposal, shoreline development and flood plain protection. And the agencies have power to insure compliance with the regional plan and with all related ordinances, regulations and policies by legal action, on finding that they are not being enforced by a local jurisdiction. Significantly, the California agency has the power to veto any public works project of which it does not approve.

Financing for the agencies, to the extent that they are not financed by fees, subventions, and state and federal grants, will be obtained by annually allocating among the member counties the amount necessary to support the agency, in proportion to the assessed valuations of property located within the region. In California, each county will place a levy on taxable property within its boundaries sufficient to pay the amount allocated to it.

---

[26] For a case study of the steps leading to the formation of the commission, see Roscoe C. Martin, *Metropolis in Transition: Local Government Adaptation to Changing Urban Needs* (Washington: Housing and Home Finance Agency, 1963), Chapter X.

[27] The California legislation consists of two acts—*Cal. Stats.*, 1967, ch. 1589, and *Cal. Stats.*, 1968, ch. 988—including a proposed interstate compact, which must be ratified by Congress. The Nevada Legislature also enacted similar legislation in 1968. The legislation was based on the *Report* [dated February 15, 1967] *of the Lake Tahoe Joint Study Committee.*

The California agency's five-member governing body consists of a county supervisor from each of the two California counties in the region, appointed by the respective boards; one councilman of the City of South Lake Tahoe appointed by the council; one member appointed by the Governor of California, subject to Senate confirmation, who shall not be a resident of the region and shall represent the public at large; and the Administrator of the California Resources Agency or his designee.

The Nevada membership of the bistate agency will include one member of the board of commissioners of each of the three affected counties, one member appointed by the Governor of Nevada, and the Director of the Nevada Department of Conservation and Natural Resources.

New York Experience and the Case Against Authorities

When service or regulatory problems straddle state lines, interstate agencies—some of which are independent district governments—are increasingly being established to deal with them. Best known of such agencies is the Port of New York Authority, created in 1921 by an interstate compact entered into by the legislatures of New York and New Jersey and approved by congressional resolution. According to the compact, improved coordination of the terminal, transportation, and other facilities of commerce serving the Port of New York would result in great economies, benefiting the nation in general and both states specifically. The authority's governing body consists of 12 commissioners, six resident voters of New York and six of New Jersey, appointed by the governors of the respective states with the consent of their senates. The authority has no taxing power, but it may make charges and incur indebtedness. Its current debt is approximately $850 million. The initial mission of the authority was to develop and implement a comprehensive plan that would have given every railroad serving the port access to all parts of the port. This was not achieved, however, and the authority has registered its principal accomplishments in other aspects of transportation, most notably airports, bridges, and tunnels.[28]

The Port of New York Authority has acquired or built and now operates four airports, two heliports, six interstate bridges and tunnels, six marine terminal areas, two union truck terminals, a truck terminal for rail freight, and a union bus terminal. Since 1962 the authority has also operated the Hudson and Manhattan Railroad, a commuter line, now renamed the Port Authority Trans-Hudson System (PATH). Although

---

[28] Robert G. Dixon, Jr., "Constitutional Bases for Regionalism: Centralization; Interstate Compacts; Federal Regional Taxation," *George Washington Law Review*, 33: 59, October 1964.

the authority has increased the variety of its activities over the years—usually through additional authorizations by the state legislatures—it is still limited to elements of a single major function: transportation.

The Port of New York Authority failed to achieve its original purposes, in part because it had no independent resources to finance the necessary improvements. Instead, it moved in other directions by acquiring, constructing, and operating remunerative facilities. In doing this, it exhibited the usual subservience of such authorities to the forces of the money market.

Professors Wallace S. Sayre, Columbia University, and Herbert Kaufman, Yale University, authors of a definitive work on the government of New York City, have commented at length on the area's experience with the port authority and similar agencies. Such authorities, they report, must interest investors if they are to obtain financing. Investors, in turn, naturally demand security for their investments. They favor money-making facilities and user charges that insure a steady income. They are not interested in new capital investments that may not begin paying high returns quickly. Furthermore, investors oppose construction of other facilities that may compete with existing authority projects. Often prohibitions against such competition are written into the bond covenants.

The authorities tend to operate more like private businesses than like public governments. They are not subject to public budget hearings as are general-purpose governments. They do not have to justify their spending before the fact. Like private corporations, they have only to explain afterward what they have done, but normally do not have to defend their projects beforehand, or to modify their policies after review by superior agencies.

The following statements about "one-sided" agencies such as the Port of New York Authority deserve consideration:

In sum, their operating policy decisions, as these are reflected in their budgets, are made internally rather than in dealings with outside agencies and officials, in private rather than in public, and the authorities are the undisputed masters of their own operating resources.[29]

The authorities are relatively well shielded against outside influences by their security of tenure, their fiscal independence, and their administrative freedom.[30]

The authority chiefs . . . are distinguished by their singular success in effectuating policies and programs they prefer personally. Their insulation has stood

[29] Wallace S. Sayre and Herbert Kaufman, Governing New York City: Politics in the Metropolis (New York: W. W. Norton, 1965), p. 331.
[30] Ibid., p. 337.

them in good stead, and their strategies have made the most of the advantages insulation affords them.[31]

The very triumphs of the authorities have given rise to searching, increasingly skeptical second-looks at this administrative device. It has been questioned on the grounds that public functions should not be several steps removed from constant control by the elected executives of the city, and that decision about the quality, quantity, and kinds of public service, and the charges for it, should not be shielded from public pressures any more than decisions about taxation are. . . .

The skewing of governmental resources, particularly public investment, away from service functions that do not pay their way and toward enterprises that make money has also engendered anxiety. And the more rapidly the authorities grow, and the more self-directing they appear, the more profound are the uncertainties and anxieties about their position.[32]

Lessons From Experience With Metropolitan Districts

1. Much recent and current discussion of approaches to regional problems, in the Bay Area and elsewhere, has centered on metropolitan districts, in one form or another.

2. The formation of metropolitan districts by state legislative action without referendum has ample precedent.

3. Most special districts are subject to severe financial limitations. For example, some are forced to depend heavily on the property tax, while others may be restricted to user charges and revenue bond financing. Such limitations should be minimized if a new district is to be created or an old one reorganized.

4. The disposition to establish governing bodies that prove insufficiently accountable to the people is a basic and unresolved issue in the use of the district approach.

5. Regional problems are interrelated. The continued formation of single-purpose metropolitan districts further proliferates governments and disperses public authority. Such districts cannot effectively solve a range of regional problems, and the public has great difficulty in keeping them accountable.

6. If established, a multipurpose metropolitan district should be assigned signficant responsibilties and powers, both to enhance its problem-solving capability and to increase its political visibility. Further, in order to reduce fragmentation and increase accountability, possibly some of the functions now allocated to single-purpose districts should sooner or later be assigned to the multipurpose district.

---

[31] Ibid., p. 342.
[32] Ibid., p. 343.

7. Requiring *local* plans to adhere to a regional general plan should be an important method of fostering better planning in the development of an area, while retaining a degree of flexibility and control at the local level.

8. A metropolitan district can embody the "umbrella" agency concept, as does the Metropolitan Council in the Twin Cities area. The newly created council was given extensive powers to engage in regional planning, to conduct research on a wide range of problems affecting the area, and to veto proposals found in conflict with its regional guidelines. The council was not, however, given any *operating* responsibilities, and thus did not displace existing local or regional agencies.

Councils of Governments

Metropolitan or regional councils of governments (COG's) represent a method of dealing with areawide problems that is strikingly different from the other methods analyzed in the preceding chapters. Whereas all the methods discussed previously involved the reorganization of established governments or the creation of new units, the COG idea rests on *voluntary cooperation* of existing governments. Consequently, it is the mildest of all approaches, building on the status quo without disturbing its formal organization. Moreover, unlike the other methods, each of which produces a metropolitan *government,* the COG approach does not create an areawide government, but instead simply provides a voluntary mechanism for the local units to consider metropolitan or regional needs.

What is currently being proposed by ABAG should not be confused with the *voluntary* council of government concept. The ABAG proposal would build on the existing voluntary COG framework in the Bay Area, modify it somewhat, and convert it into a general-purpose, limited function regional government: see the next chapter, pp. 92–121.

Major Characteristics

A FORUM, NOT A GOVERNMENT

A council of governments is a voluntary association of governments formed to provide an areawide mechanism for local officials to study, discuss, and determine solutions to metropolitan or regional problems. It is a continuing forum in which governmental representatives are convened for deliberations and the making of recommendations. Since a council of governments is not a government, however, it has no authority to enforce decisions. Instead, its decisions are merely suggestions, whose implementation depends on the concurrence of the various governments that have joined the association.

VOLUNTARY NATURE

Membership in a COG is a voluntary act taken at the discretion of the individual local governments in a metropolitan area. Any member may withdraw at any time.[1] Local financing is obtained from contributions

---

[1] Recent legislation requiring regional review of local applications for federal grants supporting a wide variety of projects will entail some qualification of the word "voluntary" as applied to those regional councils of governments that are certified by federal authorities to conduct the necessary review.

86

by the member governments, the specific shares usually based on a population formula. Professional staffs, often very small, are a common feature.

MEMBER GOVERNMENTS

The members of COG's are solely or principally local governments, predominantly cities and counties. However, there is considerable variation as to whether or not other governments—both local and non-local—are eligible for membership. In some cases, all local governments, including school districts and other special districts, may join.[2] In others, state governments are participants; in the Washington, D.C., organization, two states, the national government, and the government of the District of Columbia are members.

Most representatives in councils of governments are elected officials, rather than appointed employees of member jurisdictions or private citizens. When many governments belong and the councils are large, much of the work is often handled by an executive committee. The full membership assumes the role of a ratifying body, and meets only occasionally, thus affording it only a perfunctory role as a "regional legislature."

A Recent Movement

The council of governments approach is of recent origin: the first COG, unique in that its membership was restricted to counties, was the Supervisors Inter-County Committee, organized in 1954 in the Southeastern Michigan region (Detroit). Next came the Metropolitan Regional Council in the New York region in 1956, followed by the Metropolitan Washington Council of Governments (Washington, D.C.) and the Puget Sound Regional Governmental Conference (Seattle-Tacoma) in 1957.

To this early group of COG's was added the Mid-Willamette Valley Council of Governments (Salem, Oregon) in 1959, the Association of Bay Area Governments (the nine-county San Francisco Bay Area) and the Regional Conference of Elected Officials (Philadelphia) in 1961, and the Southern California Association of Governments and the Metropolitan Atlanta Council of Local Governments in 1964. These COG's were formed for either or both of two reasons: (1) a conviction that intelligent decision-making about areawide problems must be based

[2] In recent discussions of a restructured council in the Detroit area, the school superintendent of the central city has urged the inclusion of school districts. For an extended treatment of the reorganized Detroit area council, see Metropolitan Fund, Inc., *Governmental Organization in Metropolitan Southeast Michigan*, Parts One and Two (Detroit: 1965).

on collaborative judgments by the governments in the area and (2) a fear that local governments were otherwise likely to lose important powers to proposed metropolitan governments.

INITIAL SLOW GROWTH

Notwithstanding its simplicity and mildness, the COG idea was slow to catch hold. By 1964 only nine metropolitan areas had COG's, more than a decade after the movement was begun. This was true despite the wide praise and support given to the idea, particularly by national organizations made up partly or completely of local officials. For instance, in 1962, the national Advisory Commission on Intergovernmental Relations acclaimed the COG idea to be "one of the more significant recent developments in local government in metropolitan areas" and later prepared model state legislation authorizing such organizations.[3] In similar supportive action, the American Municipal Association (now the National League of Cities) and the National Association of County Officials (now the National Association of Counties) inaugurated a joint service to their memberships "to encourage the formation of and to strengthen the operation of voluntary governmental regional councils."[4]

VARIED DIFFICULTIES

The COG idea not only was slow to grow but also encountered numerous difficulties in its early years. Professor Royce Hanson of American University, who made the first general study of the original nine COG's, concluded that "all of them suffered from uncertainties, inexperience in metropolitan cooperation, and lack of adequate financial resources."[5] Also, some councils did not have very active programs.

[3] Advisory Commission on Intergovernmental Relations, *Alternative Approaches to Governmental Reorganization in Metropolitan Areas* (Washington: 1962), p. 85. A recent commentary and draft law on councils of government are to be found in: Advisory Commission on Intergovernmental Relations, *1968 State Legislative Program of the Advisory Commission on Intergovernmental Relations* (Washington: 1967), pp. 388–391.

[4] Joint letter from American Municipal Association and National Association of County Officials, Washington, May 25, 1962. In the following year the two groups jointly issued a collection of exhibits about COG's.

[5] Royce Hanson, *Metropolitan Councils of Governments* (Washington: Advisory Commission on Intergovernmental Relations, 1966), iv. Separate studies have also been made of three of these councils. They are: Royce Hanson, *The Politics of Metropolitan Cooperation: Metropolitan Washington Council of Governments* (Washington: Washington Center for Metropolitan Studies, 1964); Randy H. Hamilton, *ABAG Appraised: A Quinquennial Review of Voluntary Regional Co-operative Action Through the Association of Bay Area Governments* (Berkeley: Institute for Local Self Government, 1965); and David G. Mars, *The Formation of SCAG [Southern California Association of Governments]: A Case Study* (Los Angeles: Center for

The New York COG, for example, led a precarious existence and at one time was practically defunct. A number of councils, including those in the Bay Area and the Southern California region, had difficulty persuading the largest cities to join.

COG Activities

INTERGOVERNMENTAL COMMUNICATIONS

In the judgment of Professor Hanson, intergovernmental communication is the most significant activity of these nine councils of governments.[6] In serving as metropolitan communication systems, these COG's, with the exception of the one in the New York region, have reduced inter-local suspicions and hostilities, thus providing a basis for further cooperation. However, these COG's have had two major difficulties in their metropolitan communications role. First, only the members of executive committees meet frequently, thereby limiting the number of local officials engaged in meaningful discussion of regional issues. Second, since the councils of governments are known only to civic leaders and media representatives—the public being almost totally unaware of them—they are not very useful in *general* political education.

PLANNING, LEGISLATION, COOPERATION

The COG's have given planning and development issues considerable attention. Some COG's, including the Association of Bay Area Governments and the Puget Sound Governmental Conference, have become official advisory regional planning agencies. A number also have been engaged in legislative activity, such as recommending to member governments adoption of uniform ordinances concerning gun sales, air and water pollution, and teen-age drinking. In general, COG's have been less active and less successful in the state legislative field. Further, the associations have provided cooperative services to their members, including studies of mutual problems, and sometimes joint action programs. A prominent example of the latter was the establishment by the Metropolitan Atlanta Council of Local Governments of an areawide fugitive squad through the cooperation of local police departments.

Training and Career Development, School of Public Administration, University of Southern California, 1966). For a short case study of the Mid-Willamette Valley Council of Governments, see Roscoe C. Martin, *Metropolis in Transition: Local Government Adaptation to Changing Urban Needs* (Washington: Housing and Home Finance Agency, 1963), Chap. III.

[6] Hanson, *Metropolitan Councils of Governments*, pp. 6–8.

Expansion of the Movement

In contrast to its sporadic acceptance in earlier years, the COG idea is now being extensively adopted. Nearly every standard metropolitan statistical area now has some form of intergovernmental council or regional planning agency in existence or in the process of formation.[7]

FEDERAL STIMULATION

Amendments in 1965 to the Federal Housing Act of 1954 have served as the major stimulant to the spread of councils of governments. Under Section 701 (g), COG's became eligible to receive grants from the Department of Housing and Urban Development for a wide variety of activities. Included are financial underwriting for studies, data collection, regional plans and programs, and other types of efforts designed to solve metropolitan or regional problems. Also included are expenses for general administration and professional, technical, and clerical staffing. Federal grants may be used to pay as much as two-thirds of the cost of the work for which they are allocated.[8]

Because of this legislation, a number of COG's will have, among other responsibilities, the functions of an advisory regional or metropolitan planning agency. In areas having both a council of governments and a separate metropolitan or regional planning agency, both are eligible for metropolitan planning grants under Section 701, although normally such grants are made to only one applicant in any area.[9] When dual grants are authorized, the two applicants must develop a fully unified program of metropolitan planning.[10]

---

[7] Interview with Victor Jones, Professor of Political Science, University of California, Berkeley, and Senior Research Fellow (1967), Washington Center for Metropolitan Studies, who is currently examining the organizational response of local governments to the new federal aid review requirements.

[8] Housing Act of 1954, Section 701 (g).

[9] Housing and Home Finance Agency, *Planning Agency Letter No. 50,* August 16, 1965. The Association of Bay Area Governments was recognized as the official regional planning agency before the enactment of the 1965 amendments.

[10] Many areas have had metropolitan or regional planning agencies for some time. As in the case of councils of governments, they are almost always advisory and "free floating," possessing no metropolitan governmental base. Due in large part to these characteristics, the "technical accomplishments [of metropolitan planning] have far exceeded its influence on government decisions." U. S. House of Representatives. Committee on Government Operations. Intergovernmental Relations Subcommittee, *Metropolitan America: Challenge to Federalism* (1966), p. 112. For additional details on planning organizations, see two reports of the U. S. Senate Committee on Government Operations. Subcommittee on Intergovernmental Relations: *National Survey of Metropolitan Planning* (1963) and *The Effectiveness of Metropolitan Planning* (1964).

COORDINATING THE REVIEW FUNCTION

Councils of governments—or other appropriate areawide governments or agencies—authorized to undertake regional or metropolitan planning, are given the significant additional responsibility of coordinating various federal grant applications under the Demonstration Cities and Metropolitan Development Act of 1966. The law states:

All applications made after June 30, 1967, for Federal loans or grants to assist in carrying out open-space land projects or for the planning or construction of hospitals, airports, libraries, water supply and distribution facilities, sewage facilities and waste treatment works, highways, transportation facilities, and water development and land conservation projects within any metropolitan area shall be submitted for review . . .

. . . to any areawide agency which is designated to perform metropolitan or regional planning for the area within which the assistance is to be used, and which is, to the greatest practicable extent, composed of or responsible to the elected officials of a unit of areawide government or of the units of general local government within whose jurisdiction such agency is authorized to engage in such planning. . . . (sec. 204)

Lessons From Experience With Councils of Governments

1. No council of governments has been transformed from a voluntary association into a metropolitan government, although the Association of Bay Area Governments has initiated an effort to effect such a change.

2. The plan of representation employed by a council of governments may be inadequate as the basis for a regional legislature with significant powers.

3. Councils of governments so far have not generally registered many major concrete accomplishments in solving regional problems, although some important research and planning efforts have been undertaken.

4. Recent federal grant and review legislation has virtually assured a growing importance for the councils in areas that do not have alternative regional governmental agencies.

5. It remains to be seen whether councils of governments generally will become significant and long-term instrumentalities for metropolitan or regional problem-solving.

6. If the councils should assume major responsibilities for regional decision-making, the possible impact on them of the Supreme Court's "one-man, one-vote" rulings will need to be given careful consideration.

The ABAG Proposal for Regional Government

The Association of Bay Area Governments has urged that ABAG, now a voluntary council, be reconstituted by the Legislature as a formal regional government with limited functions, but with the intent of eventually assuming responsibility for Bay conservation and development, as well as other regional programs. Thus it is essential to examine the ABAG proposal carefully. Furthermore, ABAG's organizational recommendation represents a proposal-in-being, designed specifically for the Bay Area, to which can be applied many of the criteria and lessons learned from the preceding discussion.

A skeleton bill based on the ABAG proposal was presented to the Legislature in 1967, but was neither perfected nor enacted. Instead, as was noted earlier, a compromise arrangement created a Joint Committee on Bay Area Regional Organization. The committee will report to the Legislature in 1969 on the need for some form of regional government in the area. Meanwhile, the ABAG General Assembly voted to enlarge the Executive Committee to a potential maximum of 34 members, along the lines of the reorganization envisioned in the regional governmental proposal. This change was implemented January 1, 1968. Consequently much of the following analysis dealing with the representational aspects of ABAG's *governmental* proposal applies with equal force to the association's voluntarily reorganized Executive Committee.

ABAG and the Origin of its Proposal

A notable accomplishment of the association has been its demonstration to leading city and county officials—through study and mutual discussion—that the nine-county Bay Area constitutes a single region and is the primary focus of a number of unsolved problems shared by its constituent communities. Furthermore, ABAG's efforts have convinced local officials that effectively staffed regional planning is essential, and that new organizational and financial arrangements will be required to deal with unmet problems. A primary question remaining is: what kind of regional mechanism or mechanisms should be established?

For more than a year, the association's Goals and Organization Committee addressed all these matters, and, during the latter period of its assignment, concentrated primarily on the question of governmental organization in the Bay Area. At the end of September, 1966, the committee submitted a plan for "regional home rule" and government of the Bay Area.[1] The plan was reviewed by the Executive Committee and has been debated, modified and approved in principle during subsequent meetings of the General Assembly. At these meetings a number of amendments and other proposals were made, explicitly raising many questions relating to the basic ABAG proposal which are still to be resolved, in addition to further questions which lie beneath the surface and require careful study. The latter part of this chapter will explain the proposal and variants on it, and make a start on the necessary analysis.

Important Contributions of the Proposal

Despite shortcomings to be discussed later, concepts underlying the ABAG proposal represent significant contributions to thinking about Bay Area problems. One of the most constructive elements in the proposal is the clear recognition that a limited-function, multiple-purpose regional government is necessary in the nine-county Bay Area. Although only three functions are outlined to start with—in addition to advisory regional planning—the subsequent assumption of other regional functions is envisioned. Purely local functions would remain with the cities and counties.

Another meritorious feature is the proposed method of establishment by direct legislative action. This recognizes the inability of a voluntary agency to perform the difficult acts of government, acknowledges the need to avoid referenda on organizational issues of such great complexity, and retains for the state Legislature jurisdiction to reorganize the regional agency later in the light of experience.

The proposal selects three functions that are now or soon will become critical—functions that are not being well cared for—and that consequently entail a minimum challenge to existing agencies. The proposal also recognizes that important powers will be essential, including long-term capital financing for property acquisition, and the power of eminent domain.

Furthermore, the proposal embodies an effort to adjust voting power in the ABAG councils to reflect in rough fashion the comparative populations of the constituent units. Also the ABAG action has helped raise public awareness of the issues of regional government to a higher level than ever before. Finally, both the basic proposal and the suggestions put forth for discussion by individual ABAG members, have highlighted some of the critical questions of organization, representation, powers

---

[1] Association of Bay Area Governments, *Regional Home Rule and Government of the Bay Area: Report of the Goals and Organization Committee to the General Assembly* (Berkeley: September 29, 1966).

and financing that must be resolved if a satisfactory regional governmental solution is to be achieved. In doing this, ABAG has performed a signal service for the Bay Area, in the tradition of its function as a public forum.

Functions and Powers

FUNCTIONS

The ABAG proposal would, by legislative act, reconstitute the voluntary Association of Bay Area Governments as a limited-function regional government encompassing the nine counties. The proposal would continue ABAG's advisory regional planning function, and, in addition, give it responsibility for regional refuse disposal needs, regional open space and park needs, and regional airport needs. Furthermore, the General Assembly meeting of December 16, 1966, approved a Goals and Organization Committee statement of further objectives clearly indicating the intention to go beyond the three enumerated functions:

The Regional Home Rule proposal is directed at creation of a limited-function, general-purpose regional agency to accomplish three primary objectives:

1. Deal immediately with existing priority problems which are not being attacked by existing regional agencies.
2. Prevent the creating of additional fragmentation at the regional level in the future by anticipating problems.
3. Absorb, as appropriate over time, existing regional special purpose agencies and programs.[2]

A multi-functional approach such as this appears to have much to recommend it. But the three initial functions chosen for ABAG are limited in scope, and in effect ABAG is open to the criticism that it would begin as a limited-purpose special district of the kind the Goals and Organization Committee finds undesirable in principle.

The criticism would be rendered moot if, in the future, the association absorbed all other regional functions. But this would be a "backdoor" approach to multipurpose regional government. That is, an organization would be created first, then gradually regional functions would be attached to it. Perhaps a better approach would be *to look at regional problems first,* including but not limited to solid waste disposal, airports and open space, and *then design an organization*—or organizations, if several groupings of functions appeared to make sense —whose powers, finance and governmental structure would be tailor-

[2] *Report to General Assembly, From Goals and Organization Committee* (Berkeley: November 30, 1966), p. 4.

made to solve the problems confronted. This is the approach now being attempted by BCDC and BATS, i.e., first, look at the problems assigned; second, propose plans and solutions; and third, think about organizational and financial arrangements to accomplish the ends set forth. It is also the approach being employed by the Joint Committee on Bay Area Regional Organization.

Adoption of the ABAG proposal for the three functions (plus regional planning) and use of other independent organizational means to accomplish the aims of BCDC and BATS, would obviously be contributing to the continued proliferation of regional agencies. Furthermore, having solid waste disposal, airports and the terra firma variety of open space under one jurisdiction, the Bay and shoreline under another, and transportation under a variety of others, would create a situation containing substantial possibilities for conflict, impasse, poor planning and duplication of effort.

The Bay Area has had many object lessons in the failure of one agency to consider the impact of its decisions on others, and vice versa. The termination of open dump refuse burning is an excellent example. This was ordered many years ago by the Bay Area Pollution Control District as a first step in its program to clean up the basin's airshed. Open dump burning had been a primary method for disposing of the region's solid wastes. With some notable exceptions, however, the agencies responsible for solid waste disposal—primarily the cities—failed to prepare themselves for the long-term impact of the open burning ban.

This occurred despite the constituent-unit representation principle on which the air pollution control district was based, partly for the purpose of establishing lines of communication with the cities and counties. These communication lines failed to provide the foresight necessary to avoid the now-imminent solid waste disposal crisis. Had air pollution control and solid waste disposal been the responsibility of a single agency, that agency's governing body might have listened to its staff's warnings about the future impact of the burning ban. Presumably they would have proceeded quickly to develop new means of disposal, and perhaps have phased the cessation of burning to coincide with the availability of alternate methods.

The unresolved dispute between the East Bay Regional Park District and the East Bay Municipal Utility District over who should be responsible for all regional recreational facilities in the area both serve, supplies another example of conflict and duplication of effort. And the potential for destructive competition between the Alameda-Contra Costa Transit District's bus operation and BARTD's rail rapid transit system provides still another object lesson in the kind of damaging interagency conflict caused when too many governments begin getting in each other's way.

The ABAG proposal, partial as it is, would not improve the situation very much, initially. Real improvement would require creation of a regional agency with significant power to effect coordination, or consolidation, if necessary.

POWERS

ABAG's powers under its governmental proposal would include (1) a continuation of advisory regional planning, (2) levying an assessment prorated among the nine counties on the basis of both population and assessed valuation—the maximum sum that may be raised could not exceed the equivalent of $0.01 per $100.00 of the region's assessed valuation; (3) issuance of general obligation bonds and taxation to finance their repayment; and (4) adoption of one or more of three specified regional plan elements for an airport system, parks and open space, and refuse disposal, and (5) eminent domain.

Plan implementation would call for separate General Assembly votes (with both city and county majorities) on the general regional plan, each special plan element, and on the proposal for implementation. This would have to include a finding that the "problem is regional and that it cannot be solved by existing city and county governments."

Furthermore, a city or county having ownership or jurisdiction or both over property proposed to be taken could "veto" the action. In this event, an affirmative General Assembly vote of either (1) two-thirds of those present and voting, or (2) one more than 50 percent of the membership, whichever is larger, would be required in order to overrule the local veto.

The aims outlined in the ABAG preliminary regional plan would necessitate massive public acquisition of open space. Total open space requirements by 1990 are estimated at 864,000 acres. The preliminary plan recommends a public open space acquisition program to provide for resource protection and preservation, open space for health, welfare and well-being, public safety (flood plains, unstable soil areas, etc.), public service corridors, and finally, open space for urban expansion. The plan emphasizes the importance of the last-mentioned space need:

The largest open space category—for urban expansion—is generally designated in areas having lesser resource value as open space, and which can be held as a reservoir for future development. Ideally, the release of these lands for development would be based upon demonstrated need within a regional context.[3]

Land acquisition on the scale and for the purposes envisioned would require (1) strong exercise of the police power in the form of land use controls to preserve open space that is to be held open for a long period or in perpetuity, (2) the power of eminent domain, and (3) excellent financial resources to support the "land bank" function in reserving open space for future urban expansion.

The ABAG proposal omits the police power altogether. It includes eminent domain, but with such a strong minority veto provision as to render the authorization virtually useless for large-scale projects.[4] General obligation bond financing, requiring a two-thirds majority vote, would represent a further imposition on the already overburdened property tax, and probably militate against authorization of the necessary funding.

New revenue sources will be essential if a regional plan as bold as that suggested by ABAG is to be implemented. Income and sales taxes are likely possibilities:

States should encourage local governments to supplement property tax revenues with other revenue sources. In the case of some large municipalities and in some metropolitan areas, sales and income taxes hold most promise, particularly where they can be piggy-backed on State-imposed taxes with attendant economies of collection.[5]

Representation

One of the critical issues confronted in devising a new regional government is the representation formula to be followed. As the chapter on "guidelines" demonstrated, many considerations enter into the choice, and the final decisions will do much to determine the future policies of the new agency. Furthermore, court decisions on the "one man, one vote" principle may force proponents of any new government to consider carefully the concept of equal representation when working out their formula.

---

[3] Association of Bay Area Governments, *Preliminary Regional Plan for the San Francisco Bay Region* (Berkeley: November 1966), p. 40.

[4] If all General Assembly members were in attendance, negative votes by either four county members *or* 31 city members would block an attempt to override a local veto of property acquisition. Given a more typical attendance, for example, seven county and 70 city members, either three negative county votes or 24 negative city votes would block an override. In the latter instance, either the three smallest counties, containing 6.9 percent of the region's population, or the 24 smallest cities, with a mere 1.8 percent of total population, could sustain a local veto.

[5] Municipal Finance Officers Association, *Report of the National Conference on Local Government Fiscal Policy* (Chicago: November 1966), p. 4.

THE MAJORITY PROPOSAL AND OTHERS

The Majority Proposal

As noted above, ABAG attempted an adjustment of its formula to achieve a rough approach to equal representation. This was done in several ways. First, the Executive Committee would be increased to 34 and the membership distributed to give the larger cities and counties more votes (see Table 1). Second, the reorganized Executive Committee would become the association's *legislative body*, although its actions in planning, financing, and the acquisition of property would be subject to the required General Assembly approval.[6] Third, the President and Vice President would be selected for two-year terms by secret ballot of all city councilmen and county supervisors in the region, voting as one body.[7]

The other members of the Executive Committee would be chosen by and from the mayors, councilmen and supervisors as follows:

San Francisco:

Two by the board of supervisors; two by the mayor; fifth member to be selected alternately by the board and the mayor.

San Mateo and Contra Costa (each):

One by the board of supervisors; one by the conference of mayors; third member to be selected alternatively by the board and the conference of mayors.

Santa Clara:

Two by the board of supervisors; two by the conference of mayors; two by the San Jose city council.

Alameda:

Two by the board of supervisors; two by the conference of mayors; three by the Oakland city council.

Marin, Sonoma, Solano, and Napa (each):

One by the board of supervisors; one by the conference of mayors.

ABAG Members' Minority Proposals

A number of other methods of representation were suggested by association members but were not accepted. Several are outlined below for illustrative purposes:

---

[6] The General Assembly would remain as now constituted: "a bicameral body meeting in a single room," with all cities having equal votes on the municipal side and all counties having equal votes on the county side.

[7] The President and Vice President would not have to be councilmen or supervisors, and would be ex officio voting members of the Executive Committee.

1. Choose city members of the governing body (the Executive Committee) on the basis of (1) nomination by petition of at least 15 percent of the mayors and councilmen within each county, and (2) election by secret ballot of all mayors and councilmen in the county.

TABLE 1

VOTE DISTRIBUTION: 34-MEMBER EXECUTIVE COMMITTEE

(ABAG Proposal)

The first three columns of Table 1 were taken from ABAG Goals and Organization Committee Report to the General Assembly, February 7, 1967.

County area	Percent of Bay Area population[a]	Vote distribution[b]		Vote distribution[c]	
		Votes	% of total	Votes	% of total
San Francisco	17.5	5	14.7	5	15.6
San Mateo	12.3	3	8.8	3	9.4
Santa Clara	20.6	6	17.6	6	18.8
Alameda	23.9	7	20.6	7	21.9
Contra Costa	11.8	3	8.8	3	9.4
Marin	4.4	2	5.9	2	6.2
Sonoma	4.1	2	5.9	2	6.2
Solano	3.7	2	5.9	2	6.2
Napa	1.7	2	5.9	2	6.2
President and Vice President	....	2	5.9	..	....
	100.0	34	100.0	32	99.9

[a] Based upon published figures as used by the state for subvention purposes as of January 1966.
[b] This vote distribution includes the President and Vice President, but leaves their percentage unallocated because of uncertainty as to which counties they will come from.
[c] This distribution excludes the President and Vice President.

2. Create a governing body composed solely of city councilmen and county supervisors, the number of representatives for each area being assigned on the basis of population.

3. Create a governing body composed solely of directly elected representatives, the districts to be drawn on the basis of population.

4. Create a governing body consisting partly of directly elected representatives and partly of city councilmen and county supervisors.

5. Modify the majority proposal in two ways: (1) Increase the Executive Committee to 39 members by adding one representative each from the counties of San Francisco, San Mateo, Santa Clara, Alameda and Contra Costa. (2) After two years, require one-half of the Executive Committee members to be directly elected by the voters.

"One Man, One Vote": The Principle of Equal Representation

"One man, one vote" is a term currently applied to the philosophy underlying recent decisions holding that courts can and will apply the equal-protection clause of the 14th Amendment in determining the constitutionality of state and local legislative apportionments. As court interpretations currently stand, the "one man, one vote" rule means that when state or local legislators are elected by and from single-member districts, the districts must be substantially equal in population.

Application at the state level—A series of U. S. Supreme Court decisions, most important of which were *Baker v. Carr,* 369 U. S. 186 (1962) and *Reynolds v. Sims,* 377 U. S. 533 (1964), declared jurisdiction over what had formerly been considered a "political question"·beyond adjudication, and held malapportionment in either house of a bicameral state legislature to be unconstitutional under the equal-protection clause. The court began outlining standards and mandating reapportionment schemes. In *Silver v. Jordan,* 241 F. Supp. 576 (1964) a federal district court applied this new interpretation in California, holding the state Senate apportionment unconstitutional, and giving the Legislature until July 1, 1965 to reapportion. The decision was affirmed by the U.S. Supreme Court in *Jordan v. Silver,* 381 U.S. 415 (1965). Acting under this mandate, the Legislature redrafted Senate district lines in time for the November, 1966 election.

Application to local government—Until recently, federal and state court decisions appeared to be moving toward a nearly universal application of the "one man, one vote" requirement to general-purpose local governments. California State Supreme Court decisions, among them *Griffin v. Board of Supervisors of Monterey County,* 33 Cal. Rep. 101 (1963), and *Miller v. Board of Supervisors of Santa Clara County,* 63 Cal. 2d 343 (1965), have been applying the rule to county supervisoral districts. And the recent U. S. Supreme Court decision in *Avery v. Midland County,* 36 *United States Law Week* 4257 (April 2, 1968) held that:

the Constitution permits no substantial variation from population in drawing districts for units of local government *having general governmental powers* over the entire geographic area served by the body. [Emphasis supplied]

But several of the recent decisions have also made exceptions and raised new questions. The court seems to be saying that answers to two questions are important in assessing the constitutionality of a system for choosing local officials: (1) Is the officials' function legislative? If not, the constitution requires no particular scheme of selection. (2) Are the officials elected by as well as from districts? If not, the rule requiring districts of equal population would not apply except in special cases.

Defendants in the *Avery* case, for example, attempted to elicit a "no" answer to the first question by maintaining that Midland County did not have a legislative function. The Supreme Court held otherwise, however, resting its reasoning on the existence of a general responsibility and power for local affairs:

... virtually every American lives within what he and his neighbors regard as a unit of local government with general responsibility and power for local affairs. . . . The Midland County Commissioners Court is such a unit.

The court itemized the following as evidence of such responsibility:

It sets a tax rate, equalizes assessments, and issues bonds. It then prepares a budget for allocating the county's fund, and is given by statute a wide range of discretion in choosing the subjects on which to spend. In adopting the budget the court makes both long-term judgments about the way Midland County should develop . . . and immediate choices among competing needs.

In commenting on the second question, the court also explicitly limited the impact of its *Avery* ruling as follows:

Our decision today is only that the Constitution imposes *one ground rule* for the development of arrangements of local government: a requirement that units with *general governmental powers* over an entire geographic area not be apportioned among *single-member* districts of substantially *unequal population*. [Emphasis supplied]

The *Avery* case commented further on certain situations wherein the court has drawn back from full application of the equal-representation principle to local entities. In *Sailors v. Board of Education,* for example, the court did not apply the requirement to a school board, both because of the essentially *administrative* (rather than legislative) nature of the board's function, and because of the *appointive* method whereby members were selected. In *Dusch v. Davis,* relating to the City of Virginia Beach, the court countenanced city council districts with unequal populations, in part because *voting* on the candidates was *at large*. But the court also took note of the fact that the *newly consolidated* city was *heterogeneous,* and that, at least *transitionally,* there was need for knowledge of rural affairs on the city council. Furthermore, the court commented on the possibility that the plan represented an *accommodation* between urban and rural communities that may be important in solving metropolitan problems. Clearly the court viewed the Virginia Beach arrangement as an experiment, hopefully a constructive one, but one that also should be watched to see how it works out. The court referred to the possibility that the plan might operate to reduce the voting strength of racial or political groups, and indicated that such a development would be cause for *reconsidering* the system's constitutionality.

Possible application of the principle to metropolitan organizations— Although metropolitan organizational structures with a legislative function—such as the ABAG proposal[8]—will have to bear scrutiny in the light of the equal representation requirement, it is obviously not clear at this time precisely how the requirement will be interpreted, in the metropolitan context. The court's reasoning as outlined above, plus the following comment from the *Avery* case, would allow some leeway for experimentation in dealing with problems of governmental organization and representation in metropolitan areas:

> The *Sailors* and *Dusch* cases demonstrate that the Constitution and this Court are not roadblocks in the path of innovation, experiment and development among units of local government. We will not bar what Professor [Robert C.] Wood has called "the emergence of a new ideology and structure of public bodies, equipped with new capacities and motivations. . . ."

How much and what kinds of representational experimentation the court will permit remains to be seen. Certain clues emerge from the above discussion, but they remain only clues. For example, entities whose representational arrangements do not conform to the principle of equal representation may be accepted, if a part or all of the membership is appointive; or if their responsibilities are so narrowly defined in the underlying statute or charter as to render them "administrative" rather than "legislative"; or if the system appears to be a constructive, fair-minded experiment, whose formula represents a workable compromise among opposing groups, and is necessary to solve important metropolitan problems. Even when one or more of these conditions is present, however, the court also dropped a hint suggesting that designers of any new metropolitan machinery should be extremely cautious about obviously disenfranchising elements of the population. When approving

---

[8] The regional government proposed by ABAG would be responsible for regional planning, and the implementation of three special plan elements: regional refuse disposal facilities, regional parks and open space, and a regional airport system. In implementing the three plan elements the regional government could acquire land and other facilities, over the objections of local governments, by an extraordinary vote in the General Assembly. The agency would also be empowered to levy taxes and issue general obligation bonds, revenue bonds, special assessment bonds and tax anticipation notes in the same manner as city and county governments. Further consideration would be given to the assumption of a wide range of additional regional activities. In short, the ABAG proposal would create a multipurpose agency with a legislative function.

the Virginia Beach plan in *Dusch v. Davis,* the court commented:

As the plan becomes effective, *if it then operates to minimize or cancel out the voting strength of racial or political elements of the voting population,* it will be time enough to consider whether the system still passes constitutional muster. [Emphasis supplied]

Regardless of the effect of future court decisions, however, the principle of equal representation is important in its own right, and deserves consideration *on its merits* when regional governmental proposals are being analyzed.

The Majority Proposal—Departures from the Principle

The *Avery* case, the most recent U.S. Supreme Court decision applying the principle of equal representation to local government, does not directly concern organizations such as that proposed by ABAG, because the latter would not have elected representatives standing from single-member districts. Consequently, the question of whether and when the principle may be applied to an ABAG-like organization remains to be answered by future court decisions. Nevertheless, it is useful to study the representational structure embodied in the ABAG proposal to determine how it departs from the philosophic if not the legal concept of "one man, one vote."

On examination, the proposal is seen to depart in a number of ways. Certain departures involve relative voting strength on the Executive Committee and General Assembly, respectively. Others relate to the appointing authorities, i.e., the counties and malapportioned supervisorial districts, on one hand, and the possibilities for minority control of the mayors' conferences, on the other.

Departures involving the Executive Committee—The proposed formula for allocating Executive Committee seats among the county *governments* substantially over-represents the small counties. The end result is shown in Table 2, which compares the proposed voting strength of county governments, as such. The four smallest counties would be over-represented, Alameda and Santa Clara counties would be under-represented, and a close approximation to population would be achieved in the case of Contra Costa, San Francisco and San Mateo counties. A single vote would give Napa County 435 percent and Solano 200 percent of their proportionate shares. The Alameda and Santa Clara County governments, on the other hand, would receive only 62 and 72 percent, respectively, of their proportionate shares of votes.

Compare the extreme cases presented by the governments of Alameda and Napa counties. The former would be given two votes and the

Governing a Metropolitan Region

latter one vote, although Napa contains less than one-fourteenth the population of Alameda County. Thus a Napa County voter, as represented on the Executive Committee through his county government, would in effect have seven times the voting strength of an Alameda County voter, as similarly represented. Analogous but smaller disparities occur in the cases of other counties.

TABLE 2

County Governments' Voting Strength Compared with Population

This table compares the Executive Committee voting strength of county *governments*, as such. Thus it excludes the city seats allocated municipal governments in each county area.

County	Percentage of Bay Area population	Executive Committee vote allocation	Percentage allocation of Executive Committee vote— ABAG proposal	Vote allocation as percentage of population distribution
Alameda......	23.9	2	14.8	62
Contra Costa .	11.8	1.5[a]	11.1	94
Marin.........	4.4	1	7.4	168
Napa.........	1.7	1	7.4	435
San Francisco.	17.5	2.5[a]	18.5	106
San Mateo....	12.3	1.5[a]	11.1	90
Santa Clara...	20.6	2	14.8	72
Solano........	3.7	1	7.4	200
Sonoma.......	4.1	1	7.4	180
	100.0	13.5	99.9	

[a] Contra Costa, San Francisco and San Mateo counties would alternate one delegate between the city and the county governments. These delegates are shown as 0.5 vote. Also, the President and Vice President are excluded from this table because there is no way of knowing from which counties either would come.

Because the Alameda and Santa Clara County *governments* would be underrepresented on the Executive Committee, residents of their unincorporated areas would be partially disenfranchised. This results from the move to give the cities of Oakland and San Jose additional members, to approximate the population distribution between those two central cities and the other municipalities in their respective counties.[9]

The small cities would have a disproportionate influence in the

---

[9] In Alameda County, 13.7 percent of the registered voters live in non-city areas, and would thus be represented on the Executive Committee by two county supervisors, whom they would have to "share" with the city residents. The latter, however, would also be represented by the five members of the Executive Committee from the cities in Alameda County. In mathematical terms, the 61,000 non-city voters could be said to have 0.274 of a vote in the Executive Committee (13.7 percent of 2). The 444,000 city voters would have 6.726 votes, or 3.4 times their proportionate share.

Looking at it another way, the Alameda County government would be granted two selection of Executive Committee members. In every county except San Francisco, the conference of mayors would choose city representatives. Further, the conferences of San Mateo and Contra Costa counties would alternate with their respective boards of supervisors in selecting an additional Executive Committee member. Thus the mayors' conferences of the eight counties would choose between 10 and 12 of the 34-member Executive Committee.[10]

Each mayor has one vote in the mayors' conference. Thus the mayor of Richmond, representing Contra Costa County's largest city with 82,000 population, would have no more voice than the mayor of Hercules, representing a city of only 310 people. Or the mayor of Berkeley, representing the second largest city in Alameda County[11] with 120,000 population, would have no more voice than the mayor of Emeryville, representing a city of 2,700 population. Or Sunnyvale, the second largest city in Santa Clara County[12] with 75,000 population, would be equated with Monte Sereno, whose population is 1,300. These three examples of disparities between the mayors' votes and the cities' comparative populations can be repeated in all the other counties except San Francisco, where there is no problem because there is only one mayor.

Another way of viewing the possibilities for inordinate small-city influence involves the "minimum controlling population" of cities represented in the mayors' conferences. This measure is based on the aggregate populations of the smallest cities in each county which constitute a potential voting majority. The possibilities for minority control are obvious (see Table 3). In no county does the minimum controlling percentage approach 50 percent, one of the accepted measures of "equal" representation. For the most part, minorities of from one-tenth to one-quarter of total municipal population could control the conferences and determine their selections for Executive Committee seats.

Departures involving the General Assembly—All cities have equal

---

votes on the Executive Committee. Because of the special provision giving Oakland three votes, the city governments within Alameda County would have a total of five votes. Similarly, Santa Clara County would have two votes, whereas its cities would have four.

[10] The report does not say so explicitly, but it is presumed that the two additional members, President and Vice President, would be elected by secret ballot of all supervisors, mayors and city councilmen within the region, as outlined in Exhibit C of *Regional Home Rule and Government of the Bay Area,* the report of the Goals and Organization Committee submitted September 29, 1966.

[11] Alameda County's largest city, Oakland (386,000 population) would be given three representatives on the Executive Committee, to be selected by the city council. Oakland would also participate in mayors' conference selections.

[12] Santa Clara County's largest city, San Jose (360,000 population) would be given two representatives on the Executive Committee, to be selected by the city council. Like Oakland, San Jose would also participate in mayors' conference selections.

voices in General Assembly voting, irrespective of their populations.
The City of Oakland, for example, with 380,000 population, is equated
with the City of Hercules, with 310 people. Also on the city side, San
Francisco, with 740,000 population has no more voice than Colma, with
its 500 residents. Similarly, all counties have an equal voice in the
General Assembly's dual roll call voting. Alameda County, with more
than 1,000,000 residents is equated with Napa County, which has a
population of 76,000.

TABLE 3

MAYORS' CONFERENCES: POSSIBILITIES FOR MINORITY CONTROL

City and county population estimates employed throughout this report are based
on information from the Financial and Population Research Section,
California State Department of Finance.

County	Total city population	"Minimum controlling population"[a]	"Minimum controlling population" as percent of total population of cities in county
Alameda...............	942,000	101,000	10.7
Contra Costa...........	330,000	72,000	21.8
Marin.................	128,000	34,000	26.6
Napa..................	40,000	11,000	27.5
San Francisco..........	--------- Not relevant ---------		
San Mateo.............	466,000	102,000	21.9
Santa Clara............	772,000	85,000	11.0
Solano................	142,000	17,000	12.0
Sonoma...............	81,000	16,000	19.8

[a] Smallest aggregate population of cities having a potential voting majority in the mayors' conference.

Unincorporated area residents are partially disenfranchised in the
General Assembly. This is because city residents are, in effect, represented twice in General Assembly voting. That is, they are "represented"
by the city members when the city roll is called, as well as by the county
members when the county roll is called. In contrast, residents of unincorporated communities have no representation on the city "side" of
ABAG's two-house General Assembly.[13]

[13] The percentage of non-city voters ranges from 11.4 in Solano County to 51.7
in Sonoma County (see Table 4). Thus 51.7 percent of Sonoma County's voters would
be represented in the General Assembly by a single county member and would have
no voice on the city side. But the remaining 48.3 percent of the county's voters would
be represented *both* on the county side by the single county member *and* on the
city side by the eight city delegates. Thus a majority of the county's voters would be
completely disenfranchised on the city side due to the "accident" of their location
outside municipal boundaries. Analogous but smaller discrepancies and inequities
can be found in all counties except San Francisco, which has no unincorporated
territory.

A recent Michigan Supreme Court county apportionment case could, is applied in California, have great significance with respect to the under-representation of non-city voters in both the General Assembly and the Executive Committee.

... we may take the law to be that the Equality clause of the Fourteenth Amendment requires the States to render substantial equality between citizens except where there exist differences justifying the classification of citizens, in which event there must be equality within the classes, and that the differences which may justify classification must be such as bear reasonable relation to permissible State objectives sought to be achieved by classification and not such as are merely arbitrary and capricious. *Brouwer v. Bronkema,* 141 N.W. 2d 98 (1966).

TABLE 4

VOTERS IN CITIES AND UNINCORPORATED AREAS

NOVEMBER, 1966

| County | Registered voters in thousands | | Total | Registered voters in unincorporated areas |
	In cities	In unincorporated areas		
Alameda	444	61	505	13.7%
Contra Costa	147	93	240	38.7
Marin	60	29	89	32.5
Napa	20	16	36	44.4
San Francisco	372	0	372	0.0
San Mateo	221	32	253	12.6
Santa Clara	326	60	386	15.5
Solano	54	7	61	11.4
Sonoma	42	45	87	51.7
Nine-county total	1,686	343	2,029	16.9

Obviously the "discrimination" against residents of unincorporated areas would be an unintentional side effect of the basic voting system proposed, plus the "accident" of residential location. But this emphasizes the difficulty of justifying the proposed "classification." Residents of unincorporated territory almost certainly have as much at stake in the region's problems and their solution as do city dwellers. And area-wide taxes levied equally on property in unincorporated areas and in cities would, by definition, place the same burden on all. Thus the basis for a classification justifying differential treatment of city and non-city residents is not apparent.

Malapportionment of supervisorial districts—County governments are one of the two basic building blocks in ABAG's constituent-unit system of representation. Thus any departures from the principle of equal representation in electing county governments would affect the regional government as proposed by the association. Consequently it is essential to examine the basis on which supervisorial districts are allocated in all the counties except San Francisco, which elects its supervisors at large.[14] The measure of malapportionment employed is the percentage points by which the number of registered voters in the smallest and largest districts in each county depart from the countywide average (see Table 5).

Only Alameda County appears to be well-apportioned, with deviations from the average of –6 percent and +6 percent, respectively. All the other seven counties showed marked departures from the average, the greatest being –67 percent in the case of Solano County's smallest district and +64 percent in Sonoma County's largest district. Such discrepancies, until removed, suggest caution in employing the county as a basic unit on which to erect a Bay Area regional government.

Could ABAG Comply With the Principle?

It obviously would be no simple task to bring ABAG into compliance with the principle of equal representation, should that prove necessary. Probably the easiest obstacle to surmount is the malapportionment of county supervisorial districts. In fact, it appears almost certain that either the courts or the state Legislature will require equitable districting of all counties in the near future.

Inequalities among the counties would not be so easily dealt with, because the redrafting of county boundaries is unlikely. Perhaps some of the smaller counties could be grouped together. The following four-way combination was suggested to a BATS study group for discussion purposes: (1) San Francisco and San Mateo, 1.3 million; (2) Contra Costa, Marin, Napa, Solano and Sonoma, 1.2 million; (3) Alameda, 1.1 million; and (4) Santa Clara, 1.0 million.[15] Similar groupings of cities could be devised, analogous to the "corridor" categories and weighted voting employed in choosing city representatives on the Southern California Rapid Transit District Board (see p. 75). Grouping cities not only would help minimize noncompliance with equal representation, but also would reduce the size of the General Assembly.[16]

---

[14] San Mateo County nominates its supervisors from districts, but they must be elected at large. Thus it can be argued that unequally apportioned districts in San Mateo County do not violate the equal-population principle, because of the at-large general election. As noted above, a recent U. S. Supreme Court ruling held constitutional an analogous plan under which a district or borough residency requirement was applied to seven members of an eleven-member council, all of whom are elected at-large. *Dusch v. Davis*, 35 *United States Law Week* 4461 (1967). This decision, however, seems to have been based upon certain factual considerations not present in San Mateo County.

[15] Suggested by John C. Beckett, study group chairman, in letter of April 4, 1967, directed to Richard M. Zettel, Bay Area Transportation Study Director.

[16] Weighted voting should be a last resort, however, and any such system should

TABLE 5

COUNTY SUPERVISORIAL DISTRICTS: DEVIATION IN APPORTIONMENT[a]

County and district number	Percentage deviation from countywide average
Alameda	
1st (smallest)	−6
4th (largest)	+6
Contra Costa	
5th (smallest)	−31
4th (largest)	+51
Marin	
5th (smallest)	−34
3rd (largest)	+30
Napa	
4th (smallest)	−38
5th (largest)	+21
San Mateo	
1st (smallest)	−28
4th (largest)	+26
Santa Clara	
3rd (smallest)	−15
4th (largest)	+30
Solano	
5th (smallest)	−67
1st (largest)	+43
Sonoma	
4th (smallest)	−47
3rd (largest)	+64

[a] The countywide average equals the total number of registered voters divided by the number of supervisorial districts. The percentage deviation from the average is a measure of the departure from "perfect apportionment." These figures are based on 1966 voter registration rather than population. Population would have been preferable, but reliable estimates are unavailable, whereas the Secretary of State has published firm figures on the voter registrations of all supervisorial districts at the time of the November, 1966, general election.

be designed with extreme caution. Careful study of apparently equitable systems shows that they may over-represent or disenfranchise, often quite drastically and in unexpected ways which superficial examination does not disclose: "... weighted voting does not allocate voting power among legislators in proportion to the population each represents because *voting power is not proportional to the number of votes a legislator may cast.*" [Emphasis in original] Also: "The mathematical accuracy which proponents of weighted voting have claimed ... is illusory." See John F. Banzhaf III, "Weighted Voting Doesn't Work: A Mathematical Analysis," *Rutgers Law Review* 19:317–345, 1965. The intricacies of weighted voting are further examined in R. Roland Pennock and John W. Chapman, eds., *Nomos X—Representation* (New York: Atherton Press, 1968), see articles by William H. Riker and Lloyd S. Shapley, "Weighted Voting: A Mathematical Analysis for Instrumental Judgments," pp. 199–216; and Robert Nozick, "Weighted Voting and 'One-Man, One-Vote'," pp. 217–225.

Although complicated formulas would be required to bring ABAG into conformity with the "one man, one vote" principle, no doubt they could be devised, if needed. On the other hand, the courts have tended to take a rather simplistic view in applying the equal representation principle. Thus they may look with disfavor on agencies established under complicated formulas of indirect representation. At the very least, the Michigan case suggests the exercise of great care in setting up a "mixed" legislative body containing both directly and indirectly elected members. Still, if the state Legislature should establish a mixed regional legislature, stating clearly that it is intended to be a provisional and experimental attempt to deal with unique metropolitan organizational problems, the courts might well leave the agency undisturbed, at least for a trial or transitional period.

Method of Selection: Further Comments

The indirect method of choosing the governing body under the ABAG proposal merits further comment on its necessity and advisability, its possible future legal status, the role and performance of the mayor's conferences in the selections, and the partisan effects of a representational system based on "nonpartisan" local governments.

Should Multipurpose Legislative Bodies be Directly Elected?

Appointment and other methods of indirect election are widely employed to choose the members of special-purpose agencies and authorities. Such a system of "representation" is tailored to the specific circumstances confronted, as well as to the limited purposes and projects to be accomplished. Furthermore, indirect election has been justified (1) as a means of avoiding the known drawbacks of directly electing special district boards, (2) as a method of encouraging close cooperation between the special district and local governments in the area, (3) as a device for winning local acceptance of regional programs that might otherwise be opposed, and (4) as a transitional stage in the development of a more nearly representative regional government.

On the other hand, direct election is the accepted method of choosing the legislative bodies of general-purpose governments—local, state, and national. Can the principle of indirect election safely be applied in proposals such as ABAG's, that might soon either become general-purpose governments, or at least be assigned many important functions and decisions crucial to the region's future? This question can be argued in terms of good public policy, as well as more narrowly on the basis of future tests of constitutionality. The Michigan case raised the latter issue by implication, when it suggested that indirect election was not "equal" to direct election. The issue obviously cannot be settled here. But there may be grounds for litigation testing the constitutionality of representational systems choosing multipurpose or general-purpose regional legislatures by indirect election.

THE ROLE OF THE MAYORS' CONFERENCE

The mayors' conferences (city selection committees) deserve careful attention because of the appointive role they would play under the ABAG governmental proposal in selecting a majority of the city representatives on the Executive Committee.

Reasons for Creation

The city selection committees were first legally established in 1955 under the Bay Area Air Pollution Control District Act. They were created for three basic reasons: First, it was recognized that the air pollution problem required creation of a new regional agency, and that the political realities of the time meant that it would have to be another single-purpose special district. Second, the region's leaders were reluctant to establish a district with a directly elected governing board, because of their belief that the low political visibility of single-purpose districts, plus voter unawareness, make direct election a highly questionable means of holding such regional agencies accountable. Third, the cities of the region preferred to have a voice on the district board, rather than follow the arrangement in the Los Angeles area, where air pollution control was a function of county government alone.

The "Bay Area Pattern"

The "Bay Area pattern" of constituent-unit representation was devised to meet the needs and conditions outlined above. The method of selection on the county side was a foregone conclusion from the start: Each county board of supervisors would select one of its own members. It was agreed that city governments should receive representation equal to that of the county governments, but the municipalities far outnumbered the counties, thus obviously necessitating some kind of adjustment. After deliberation, it was decided that one city representative per county should be chosen by the county's conferences of mayors, building on the informal discussion groups that had been organized in Alameda and Contra Costa counties a few years earlier.

Thus the "Bay Area pattern" was formed. It was employed subsequently in connection with the San Francisco Bay Area Rapid Transit District, the Executive Committee of the Association of Bay Area Governments, the local agency formation commissions, the West Bay

Rapid Transit Authority (San Mateo County), and the Marin County Transit District. It is employed to select part of the membership of the Bay Area Transportation Study Commission, and the San Francisco Bay Conservation and Development Commission.

Advantages

Experience with the "Bay Area pattern" suggests that it has proven a useful and constructive political invention, at least on an interim basis. It appears to have had modest success in improving relationships among the districts. It has established lines of communication—although sometimes tenuous—between several regional single-purpose districts and local government. It has given a common or parallel structure to the new regional districts, and has made it possible to avoid creating additional directly elected single-purpose district boards.

Drawbacks: Mayor's Conference Weaknesses

On the other hand, an examiantion of the mayors' conferences suggests that they may leave something to be desired as the possible appointing authority of a significant number of the regional legislators who may eventually *run a multipurpose regional government.*

Perhaps the primary problem is the lack of cohesion of the mayors' conferences. Unlike the county boards of supervisors—their counterpart appointive authority on the county side—the mayors' conferences are not legislative bodies in their own right. They are informal social-discussion groups normally meeting no more than once a month to review mutual city problems within the county. Their "life histories" show that they may become quite active for a time, when the cities are significantly concerned about special problems, these often being their relationship with the county government in such matters as the sales tax distribution or the division of county highway funds. But at other times the conferences may be hard put to find something to do.[17]

A related problem, and perhaps the chief cause of the lack of cohesion or sense of purpose, is the frequent change in membership. Many cities whose mayors are chosen by the council rotate the post every year, and much of a mayors' conference membership changes annually. Unquestionably this feature has made it difficult to develop continuity and

---

[17] The following comments from field notes taken during interviews with mayors and city managers may be helpful. One respondent commented that, while the conference "promoted inter-city communication and relations ... it does have a problem in justifying its existence." Or: "It permits an exchange of ideas ... [but] there's a lot of criticism of the conference. Sometimes it does go for months dead on its ... [feet]."

leadership.[18] In practice, it has forced the conferences to rely heavily on the leadership of those few mayors who are directly elected to their posts, or who by custom are retained by their councils for a number of years.

A more subjective matter—one which obviously could be debated—relates to the attitudes of some of the mayors as they affect the tone of the conferences. Comments from field interviews: "Cities are 'too provincial—each city is concerned too much with its own utility, not with urban government generally'." Or: "The [. . .] County Conference of Mayors is very, very weak. It is primarily social, with no formality of organization." Again: "What is wrong is that it is treated as a social affair." ". . . there is a valid point of criticism in asserting that the conferences over-emphasize the social aspects."

Turning specifically to criticisms relating to the conferences' appointive function in choosing regional representatives, one finds such comments as: "Elections . . . are usually routine." The evidence suggests that, at least until recently, appointments have been made rather casually, and on the basis of limited consideration of the candidates and their abilities.[19]

Possible Changes

This rather negative view of the city selection committees should be qualified a bit. First, if the appointive role of the mayors' conferences takes on added significance, as it surely would if the ABAG governmental proposal were enacted, the appointments would undoubtedly be given a great deal more careful thought than in the past. Second, a change in some cities' practice of rotating mayors frequently would almost certainly give the conferences much greater stability and continuity of leadership. Third, the same result could be achieved by changing the composition of the city selection committee and providing for a long-term appointment by each council to that body. Fourth, modification of the ABAG proposal to provide for weighted voting, or for

---

[18] These comments are illustrative of the problem: "The trouble is that when you switch mayors annually, it takes five or six meetings to find out what is going on." "The mayor has just developed a good rapport when it is time for him to be turned out."

[19] These comments are relevant: "[. . .] was selected because he expressed an interest and asked for the nomination." Or: "He had the time and they had known him in the conference." Or: "One of the real weaknesses is that a candidate is nominated and elected the same evening . . . unless you're contacted by letter or phone you don't know how you're voting. Too often, nominations are opened, the names presented, and a move made the nominations be closed. There is no time to consider the concrete qualifications of the names." Or: "One election took only three minutes."

groupings of smaller cities for voting purposes, would help reduce the disproportionate voting strength of the small cities.[20, 21] These changes would alleviate—but not eliminate—some of the drawbacks outlined above. Until these or other changes are made, however, the ABAG proposal will rest on rather weak organizational underpinnings in the form of the mayors' conferences.

THE PARTISAN EFFECTS OF SELECTION BY "NONPARTISAN" LOCAL GOVERNMENT

All proposals to create a regional government would establish a new entity "halfway" between traditional local governments and the state government. California state government is deliberately and distinctly partisan. California local government is legally nonpartisan. In which tradition should a new regional government fall? What is the impact of legal nonpartisanship on the city and county governments that would be constituent units of the proposed regional government? On ABAG? These questions merit discussion in this analysis of the ABAG regional government proposal.

More than 50 years ago, city, county, and school district elections were made legally nonpartisan,[22] following the leads of several other states, in the Progressive effort of Hiram Johnson to end domination of the party machinery by the Southern Pacific Railroad. The reform was also related to revelations of the connection between city party machines and the state's political structure brought out by San Francisco Boss Abe Ruef's maneuvering at the Republican State Convention of 1906. The bad reputation of local party activity and machine control of city halls, plus proven corruption, strengthened the hand of the Pro-

---

[20] The Southern California Rapid Transit District Act of 1964 attempted to meet the third and fourth objections. The law makes long-term appointments possible in the case of a special city selection committee which chooses several members of the district governing board. Also, each selection committee member's vote is weighed according to the assessed valuation of the city he represents. See p. 75.

[21] The disproportionate role of the smaller cities provides a minor irony. Voting in the mayors' conferences and the ABAG General Assembly favors those areas and communities that have fractionated their governments into little municipalities, some of which may be inadequate, and many of which have created unnecessary competition for tax base. Thus a prize—additional votes in the mayors' conference and the General Assembly—is given to those whom some might call shortsighted. On the other hand, communities with more foresight or better luck, which organized themselves in a superior fashion, i.e., into larger cities possessing greater competence to deal with local problems, are penalized in the councils of the mayors' conferences and the General Assembly. The unintended but real result is to give premiums for parochialism and demerits for the exercise of good judgment.

[22] _Calif. Elections Code,_ sec. 41.

gressives in their efforts to clean up. Introduction of nonpartisanship at the local level was a part of the campaign.[23]

As noted earlier in the third chapter, however, local nonpartisanship in California has been debated on several grounds. First, considering the radical improvement in the character and quality of California's local government, does nonpartisanship still serve a useful purpose? Second, given the increasing involvement of local government in some of the most fundamental issues of our society, would the legal introduction of partisanship at the local level be a constructive act, thus recognizing the fact that local governments are no longer—if indeed they ever were—limited to such reputedly nonpartisan matters as paving sidewalks and pruning street trees? Third, there is increasing evidence of covert and sometimes overt activity in local elections by politically oriented groups, including party organizations. Fourth, many observers believe that nonpartisan local government is neither nonpartisan nor politically neutral, but that more often than not the system operates to the substantial advantage of candidates who are Republican by party registration. No effort will be made here to resolve all these issues. Some are matters of opinion and value judgment, and perhaps cannot be decided on strictly objective grounds.[24]

Two things will be attempted here. First, attention will be called to a remarkable, imaginative and relevant document produced by the Republican Policy Committee of the United States Senate. Second, because the data are readily available, an effort will be made to determine whether or not there is anything in the allegation that nonpartisanship at the local level favors candidates of Republican party registration.

A Case for Partisan Involvement in Urban Problems

A striking and persuasive set of arguments for partisan involvement in the problems besetting local government and the metropolitan regions recently emanated from Republican sources. This policy is being urged as part of an effort to take advantage of "the decade ahead [which] offers Republicans their first opportunity in nearly forty years to establish themselves once again as the majority party in the United States."[25]

---

[23] In 1915 the Legislature attempted to extend the principle to *all* state offices, but this effort suffered a resounding defeat of 58 percent to 42 percent at a 1916 referendum.

[24] The history and debate over nonpartisanship are thoroughly covered in Eugene C. Lee, *The Politics of Nonpartisanship: A Study of California City Elections* (Berkeley: University of California Press, 1960).

[25] U. S. Senate. Republican Policy Committee, *Where the Votes Are: A Profile of America in the Mid-1960's* ... (89th Congress, 2d Session, Document No. 106, 1966), p. 1.

The report continues :

... these problems—education, environmental health, transportation—will bear in upon us with increasing weight over the next decade. Whichever party offers the most rational solution may well win the respect and long-term allegiance of this new electorate. [The new electorate referred to comprises a power group described by Peter Drucker as "... a professional, technical, and managerial middle class—very young, affluent, used to great job security and highly educated."][26]

Later the report refers even more explicitly to both the urgency and the political relevance of the kinds of problems with which local government in the Bay Area, the Association of Bay Area Governments, the San Francisco Bay Conservation and Development Commission, the Bay Area Transportation Study Commission and other groups are trying to deal:

Planning, zoning, urban renewal, and large-scale expressway construction have become important forces in America in only the last 10 years or so. The metropolitan issues will not disappear, they will only intensify. If they look impossibly complicated today, and we fail to do something about them, they will look far worse next year ...

If a political party wishes to stay in the game of politics, it must tackle the public problems affecting the most persons, and those problems ... are centered in the American metropolis.[27]

If this is all true, it suggests that the time may be near for rethinking the roles of partisan politics at both local and regional levels.

Is Local Government Politically Neutral?

For discussion, assume that the legal nonpartisan status of city and county government also means that the processes whereby local elected officials are recruited and selected are completely neutralized and sealed off from partisan political influences. Or to put it another way, assume that partisanship and factors associated with the individual's partisan registration are statistically neutral and have no influence on or correlation with the outcome of local elections. What would be the result if these assumptions were well founded? The partisan composition of elected councils and boards of supervisors would approximate that of the city or county from which they were chosen. Thus the hypothesis can be tested by comparing the partisan registrations of county supervisors and city councilmen with those of the populations they serve.[28]

---

[26] Ibid., p. 3.
[27] Ibid., p. 13.
[28] The analysis on which this discussion is based appears in full in the Appendix. In the interest of brevity, some of the detail is omitted from this textual discussion. Information on the partisan registration of voters was taken from: California. Secre-

County boards and partisan registration—In eight of the nine Bay Area counties the partisan registration of the supervisors was significantly different from that of their electorates in 1966–67 (see Table 11[29]). In six counties the differences favored the Republicans by 5 to 50 percentage points. In one striking case the reverse was true: A combination of at-large elections in a county that is 66 percent Democratic, active participation in elections by politically oriented groups, and the filling of vacancies by mayor's appointments, accounted for San Francisco's county supervisors being 100 percent Democratic. The registration of supervisors in Contra Costa and Marin counties also favored the Democrats, but a good deal more modestly.

To describe the phenomenon somewhat differently, Solano County, which showed the greatest divergence, had the highest Democratic registration of the nine counties, 70 percent. But the Solano board was made up of four Republicans and one Democrat, and thus was only 20 percent Democratic. Other counties whose divergence strongly favored the Republicans included Napa (–39 percent), Santa Clara (–36 percent), and Sonoma (–36 percent).[30]

In another approach to the problem, the supervisorial districts of eight counties were arrayed from lowest to highest in terms of Democratic registration (see Table 12). Republicans had a distinct advantage in the first three quartiles: these districts elected supervisors who were 70 percent Republican. Only in the fourth quartile, including districts above 65 percent Democratic, did Democratic supervisors predominate (70 percent).

These facts tell us a number of things. First, there is a relationship between the partisan affiliation of voters and of the supervisors they elect. Second, "nonpartisan" county government is not politically neutral. The Republicans have a pronounced advantage which is not overcome until Democratic registrations of approximately 65 percent and above are reached.

This Democratic "handicap" is translated into an even larger Republican advantage in the partisan composition of the area's supervisors. Although their combined electorate was 60 percent Democratic, the eight counties were governed by 40 supervisors who were 40 percent Democratic in registration.

Cities and partisan registration—Measures such as those applied to

---

tary of State, *Report of Registration for Nov. 8, 1966, Gen. Election* (1966). Information on the registration of supervisors and councilmen holding office in 1966–67 was obtained from the respective county clerks.

[29] Tables 11 through 16 have been placed in the Appendix.

[30] Here and elsewhere minus signs (–) designate deviations which favor Republicans and plus signs (+) designate deviations which favor Democrats.

county government were also used to test the political neutrality of city government. For example, an analogous array of cities was prepared, ranging from Hillsborough, the city with the lowest Democratic registration (21 percent) to Pittsburg, which has the highest (84 percent).

The results are strikingly similar to those obtained from the array of supervisorial districts (see Table 13). Republican councilmen predominate in the first three quartiles. And to an even greater extent cities controlled by councils whose members are Republican by registration dominate the first three quartiles. Only in the fourth quartile— composed of cities with Democratic voter registrations ranging from 67 to 84 and averaging 73 percent—does one find a majority of Democratic controlled councils. While there is no definite "breaking point," councils with a majority of Democrats predominate when the Democratic voter registration of the city exceeds 69 percent. Below that level one finds a preponderance of councils with Republican majorities.

In still other ways the cities reveal differences between the partisan flavor of councils and electorate, analogous to those shown above for counties (see Table 14). In seven of the eight counties the city councilmen were less Democratic than the registered voters within incorporated areas, the differences ranging from six to 21 percentage points. In Solano County, for example, where 71 percent of the cities' voters were registered Democrats, only 50 percent of the city councilmen were so registered.

The end result: a municipal electorate that is 60 percent Democratic selects a "delegation" of city councilmen who are 45 percent Democratic. Further, because the small cities tend to be Republican, 60 percent of the city councils in the region are controlled by Republican majorities. Whatever the value of these attempts to quantify the differentials, one clear fact emerges: City election procedures favor Republicans more than Democrats in the selection of councilmen.

Local Government Is Not Politically Neutral

If influences related to partisanship were neutral in a statistical sense, city councilmen and county supervisors would approximate their jurisdiction's voters in partisan registration. A normal distribution— assuming complete neutrality of the partisan registration factor—would see approximately as many local councils and boards exceeding their electorates in Democratic registration as falling below.

But the evidence shows that local government as a representational mechanism is not politically neutral. It confers a distinct—although not universal—advantage on persons of Republican registration.[31] The implications of this fact should be given consideration in reviewing various methods of choosing policy makers to govern a new regional agency.

Partisanship and ABAG

The "Republican advantage" in local legislative bodies also influences the composition of the Association of Bay Area Governments (see Tables 15 and 16). In 1968 for example, the official representatives of county governments on the ABAG Executive Committee consisted of seven Republicans and six Democrats, i.e., 46 percent Democratic.[32] The city representatives included 12 Republicans and six Democrats, i.e., 33 percent Democratic.

Because the Executive Committee votes as a single body, and not by the General Assembly's dual roll call, the overall percentages are more meaningful than the separate city and county figures. In 1968, 31 Executive Committee members were made up of 19 Republicans and 12 Democrats, i.e., 39 percent Democratic. That was the de facto partisan composition of the important steering group developing policies for a regional population that was approximately 60 percent Democratic in composition.

The General Assembly's official county representatives were 63 percent Republican and 37 percent Democratic. On the city side, the figures were 57 percent Republican and 43 percent Democratic.[33] But, because of the "two-house" voting requirements in the General Assembly, an effective veto in the General Assembly could be wielded by a county

---

[31] Although there has been some change over the years, this phenomenon appears to have been a long-term characteristic of local government in the Bay Area, and presumably throughout California. Information on Bay Area cities for 1955 shows that their councils tended to have a lower percentage of Democratic composition than their electorates. The amount of the (negative) deviation in 1955 for all cities approximated 18 percentage points, as compared with the 1966 (negative) deviation of 15 percent. Thus the overall discrepancy in partisan composition between councils and electorates was reduced slightly during the 11-year period, but still remains substantial.

[32] These figures are based on the association membership list as it stood in the summer of 1968.

[33] The following is worth noting here. A combination of equal voting in the General Assembly by all cities, regardless of size, and a tendency toward Republican control of the councils of many small cities, could combine to produce a peculiar potential for minority control of the assembly. The 46 smallest cities in the Bay Area—which contained only about 7.5 percent of the total city population (San Francisco included as a city)—would have theoretical voting control over the General Assembly. The councils of nearly two-thirds of these 46 cities contained Republican majorities.

representation that was only 37 percent Democratic, in a region whose electorate was 60 percent Democratic.

Independence of View and Voting by Regional Legislators

Is Independence Desirable?

Complete independence is neither possible nor desirable, otherwise the representative represents only *himself*. On the other hand, some independence is important if the legislator is to weigh conflicting interests fairly and reach an informed judgment on the best policy for the community.

Furthermore, a degree of independence is essential to the legislative process, which requires the exchange of ideas and accommodation of conflicting aims. The frequent practice of "instructed voting" on the part of ABAG delegates provides a case in point. When delegates come to the meetings with explicit voting instructions from their appointing authorities, they are precluded from participating in a true legislative process.

A directly elected legislature is composed of members who have been chosen to represent a constituency and to vote according to their own judgment on issues brought before the legislature. They are not "instructed" by the electorate how to vote on specific issues, and, in fact, cannot be. They may use such means as they choose to evaluate the state of opinion among their constituents, but they remain free to deliberate, negotiate with fellow legislators, vote on amendments and modified versions of proposals, and so forth, without having to report back to a parent body for new instructions. There may be an appropriate role for instructed voting, but it is not in a true legislature. The inflexibility and lack of "give-and-take" introduced by instructed voting would impair the legislative process as we know it.

Would Independence be Possible Under the ABAG Proposal?

Members of the General Assembly and Executive Committee of the Association of Bay Area Governments are vulnerable to (1) local community pressures, and (2) replacement by their boards of supervisors or mayors' conferences at any time. For example, a councilman might incur the displeasure of the voters in his city, in which case he would be subject to immediate recall, or to defeat at the next regularly scheduled municipal election. Loss of a representative's seat in his city council or county board of supervisors would also remove him from ABAG automatically. Or a position taken by a city representative sitting on the Executive Committee, for example, could offend his mayors' conference, which could then replace him forthwith. These vulnerabilities to immediate local pressures could make it risky for an ABAG representative to vote his convictions on the proper balance between regional and local concerns when the most difficult issues are under consideration.

Conclusions

The ABAG governmental proposal—and the subsequent voluntary reorganization of the Executive Committee—is the outcome of a remarkable opinion shift and process of self-education conducted by city and county officials during the preceding six years or more. The governmental proposal and ABAG's preliminary regional plan, taken together, represent a significant expression of local awareness of the area's basic regionalism, and of the need to attack a number of large-scale problems on a unified, nine-county basis.

On the other hand, the ABAG governmental proposal clearly bears the imprint of its source: the city and county governments of the Bay Area. This is as it should be. Local government is one of a series of mechanisms through which opinion is expressed, leadership developed, and policies formulated. In their work on the ABAG proposal, local governments in the Bay Area are playing their roles in such policy development.

But there are other actors in the regional drama, each of whom can be expected to play still other roles and espouse other views. These include, but are not limited to the San Francisco Bay Conservation and Development Commission, the Bay Area Transportation Study Commission, the area's Senate and Assembly delegations to Sacramento, and organized groups such as labor, industry, conservationists, the Bay Area Council, the League of Women Voters, Associated Regional Citizens, and so forth. For that matter, the individual local governments can be expected to express different and often conflicting opinions on the future of the Bay Area, and have done so in recent ABAG debates.

Obviously, there are many ways—and combinations of ways—to "represent" the Bay Area public and to develop leadership for and from it. Each will have its own advantages and drawbacks. This chapter has attempted a critical analysis of aspects of the current ABAG governmental proposal, viewed in this light. For added perspective, therefore, it is now appropriate to present a brief review of another method of representation and leadership development: direct election.

Direct Election:
Two Possibilities

In addition to the constituent-unit principle of representation embodied in the ABAG proposal, several other methods of choosing some or all of the members of a regional legislative body have been discussed in the Bay Area.

One suggestion is that the state Senators and Assemblymen elected from the Bay Area could also serve as the regional legislature. It seems obvious, however, that the pressure of state legislative business, especially with the new annual general sessions, would render any such arrangement totally out of the question. Furthermore, the state's voters and taxpayers can justifiably expect the legislators to concentrate on state matters, and not let themselves be diverted by direct and permanent involvement in a regional legislative situation.

Accordingly, we must examine other methods of constituting a regional elected legislature. Many varieties and combinations of methods are conceivable, of course, but this chapter is limited to two possible sets of districts for direct election of Bay Area regional legislators, i.e., the districts already employed for electing Assemblymen and state Senators.

Election From Assembly Districts

The area covered by 18 of the state's Assembly districts coincides almost, but not quite, with the area of the nine counties (see Map 1). With a minor shift, therefore, the entire nine-county Bay Area would be coterminous with the area covered by 18 Assembly districts.

The minor "problem area" is the northern portion of Sonoma County, containing 51,342 of the county's 87,023 registered voters, which is included in the 2nd Assembly District, along with Mendocino County and part of Humboldt County. For purposes of Bay Area electoral requirements, this discrepancy could be corrected by either of two adjustments (see Table 6). The northern portion of Sonoma County could be attached either (1) to the area comprising the 7th District (containing the remainder of Sonoma and all of Marin County) or (2) to the area of the 5th Assembly District (Napa and Solano counties).

The first alternative has the advantage of keeping Sonoma County intact as an electoral district, but would create a very large voting jurisdiction, containing 176,000 registered voters, as compared with 139,000 in the Bay Area's largest Assembly district, the 22nd (see Table 7). The

122

MAP I.

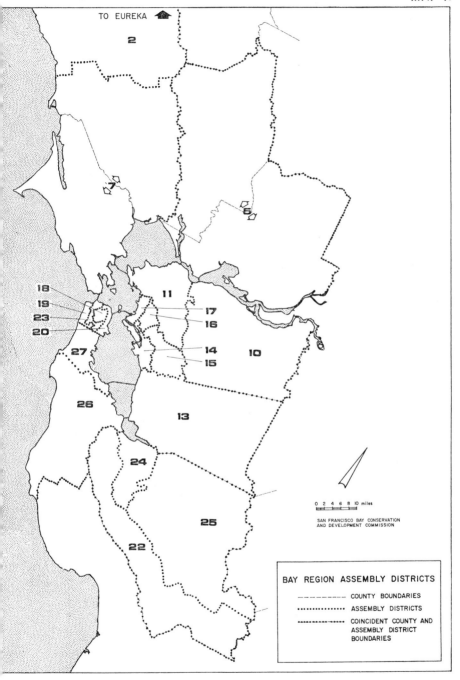

TO EUREKA

2

7

6

18
19
23
20

11

17
16

27

14
15

10

26

13

24

25

22

0 2 4 6 8 10 miles

SAN FRANCISCO BAY CONSERVATION
AND DEVELOPMENT COMMISSION

BAY REGION ASSEMBLY DISTRICTS

--------- COUNTY BOUNDARIES
················· ASSEMBLY DISTRICTS
·····•► COINCIDENT COUNTY AND
ASSEMBLY DISTRICT
BOUNDARIES

second alternative would create an electoral district with 147,000 registered voters, admittedly large, but not a great deal larger than the 22nd District. The percentage deviation from the Bay Area average for Assembly districts is shown in Table 6 and Table 7.

TABLE 6

POSSIBLE ASSEMBLY DISTRICT MODIFICATION
FOR BAY AREA ELECTORAL PURPOSES

	Number of registered voters	Percent deviation from average of Bay Area districts[a]
1. First Alternative		
Detach Sonoma portion of 2nd District.....	51,000	
Attach to 7th District		
7th District............................	+125,000	
Augmented 7th District.................	176,000	+60
2. Second Alternative		
Detach Sonoma portion of 2nd District.....	51,000	
Attach to 5th District		
5th District............................	+ 96,000	
Augmented 5th District.................	147,000	+34

ᵃ See Table 7 below.

EIGHTEEN ELECTORAL DISTRICTS AND "AUTOMATIC" REAPPORTIONMENT

Either of these changes would give the region 18 electoral districts, with numbers of registered voters ranging from 76,000 to either 147,000 or 176,000.[1] There would obviously be some question as to whether such an array would meet the equal-population requirement. Presumably, however, if the Assembly districts as now apportioned do meet it, regional electoral districts based on them would also be considered in compliance.

Such an arrangement would have both advantages and hazards with respect to future redrawing of Assembly district boundaries. The advantage is that no special arrangement would need to be made for reapportionment; electoral districts based on Assembly districts would be periodically reapporitioned "automatically," whenever Assembly district boundaries were re-drawn. On the other hand, however, the areas covered by future Assembly districts might require greater adjust-

[1] The 18 could, of course, be grouped in pairs to form nine electoral districts, or split to form 36.

ments than that involving northern Sonoma County in order to make the electoral districts coincide with the nine-county area.

In any event, assuming that an 18-member body is approximately the right size, there are advantages to using existing electoral districts because "they are there." Later, after the regional body is operative, the map could be re-drawn by an appropriate agency on the basis of experience and of the area's representation needs.

TABLE 7

BAY AREA ASSEMBLY DISTRICTS, 1966 VOTER REGISTRATION
(Rounded)
The average number of registered voters in the 18 Bay Area districts, unmodified,
is 110,000.

Assembly district	Number of registered voters	% deviation from average of Bay Area districts	Assembly district	Number of registered voters	% deviation from average of Bay Area districts
5th.......	97,000	−12	18th......	89,000	−19
7th.......	125,000	+14	19th......	103,000	− 6
10th.......	127,000	+15	20th......	76,000	−31
11th.......	113,000	+ 3	22nd......	139,000	+26
13th.......	124,000	+13	23rd......	104,000	− 5
14th.......	85,000	−23	24th......	124,000	+13
15th.......	105,000	− 5	25th......	123,000	+12
16th.......	103,000	− 6	26th......	133,000	+21
17th.......	88,000	−20	27th......	120,000	+ 9

THE IMPLICATIONS OF USING ASSEMBLY DISTRICTS

If Assembly districts were employed for the election of regional legislators, the resulting electoral process would resemble Assembly elections. The resemblance would be striking if political partisanship were introduced into the campaigns on either a formal or informal basis. At this writing, the formal introduction of partisanship appears unlikely in view of the prevailing nonpartisan ideology at the local level. Recent developments in a number of Bay Area local governments suggest, however, that partisan influences can be expected to affect many of the regional elections, even if they remain legally nonpartisan.

In any event, the results of the 1966 Assembly election were analyzed to determine some possible implications of using Assembly districts (see Table 8). Twelve of the 18 Assemblymen elected were Democrats and six were Republicans. Thus the Bay Area, with a 61 percent Democratic registration, managed to choose an Assembly delegation that was 67 percent Democratic despite (1) the statewide Republican trend of 1966,

TABLE 8

1966 California Assembly Election Results: San Francisco Bay Area

District number	Regis. % Democratic	Republicans Name	Residence	District number	Regis. % Democratic	Democrats Name	Residence
7	50.5	Bagley	San Rafael	5	65.7	Dunlap	North Napa
10	58.0	Dent	Concord	11	61.2	Knox	Richmond
16	51.2	Mulford	Piedmont	13	65.0	Bee	Hayward
22	44.4	Milias	Gilroy	14	65.7	Crown	Alameda
25	63.3	Crandall	San Jose	15	65.1	Fong	Oakland
26	48.7	Britschgi	Redwood City	17	68.4	Miller	Berkeley
				18	76.9	Brown	San Francisco
				19	64.6	Meyers	San Francisco
				20	68.5	Burton	San Francisco
				23	64.8	Foran	San Francisco
				24	60.4	Vasconcellos	San Jose
				27	65.2	Ryan	Burlingame
		6 Republicans				12 Democrats	

and (2) the well-known difficulty Democrats have in translating voter *registration* majorities into equivalent *electoral* majorities at the polls.

How can this result be explained? No doubt many factors were at work, but some of the most likely possibilities are presented here. First, of course, the "incumbency factor" helped. The Bay Area's 1964–66 Assembly delegation was made up of 13 Democrats and five Republicans. Eight of the Democrats and five of the Republicans elected in November, 1966, were incumbent Assemblymen.

Second, Assembly districting, accomplished in 1965 under a Democratically controlled Legislature, shows a definite tendency to group the more strongly Republican areas into larger districts. Thus, other things being equal, Republicans can be expected to elect fewer Assemblymen than they would if the districts were all the same size. The converse holds true for some of the more strongly Democratic areas.[2]

Finally, the district lines create a large number of "safe" seats. A Democratic incumbent in a heavily Democratic district is very difficult to oust, as is a Republican incumbent in a district that is either predominantly Republican or that has only a narrow Democratic margin. But in the Bay Area, safe Democratic districts far outnumber safe Republican districts; one count places the current proportion at 11 to four.

What are the implications of these findings for a Bay Area regional government? They suggest that use of existing Assembly districts as the voting areas for electing a regional legislative body might tend to favor Democrats more than districts otherwise drawn. The situation would change, no doubt, if the Republican party were to regain control of one or both houses of the California Legislature and then reapportion, or if Congress or the courts place restrictions on "safe-district" gerrymandering.[3]

[2] This phenomenon can be highlighted by looking at the largest and smallest Bay Area districts. The 20th district, which is the smallest, has 76,000 registered voters, is 68.5 percent Democratic and elected a Democrat. On the other hand, the 22nd district, which is the largest, has 139,000 registered voters, is 44.4 percent Democratic and elected a Republican. The same trend appears when the smallest one-third of the districts is compared with the largest one-third. The six smallest Assembly districts are more Democratic in registration (65.7 percent) than the Bay Area average (60.6 percent), and send an even more strongly Democratic delegation to Sacramento (83.3 percent). On the other hand, the Democratic registration in the six largest districts is six percentage points below the areawide average—54.3 percent compared to 60.6 percent—and they send a predominantly Republican delegation to Sacramento (66.6 percent Republican).

[3] "As legislative districts become more equally populated within a state through legislative and judicial action, attention will likely turn to combatting the gerrymander." Joseph E. Schwartzberg, "Reapportionment, Gerrymanders, and the Notion of 'Compactness'," *Minnesota Law Review* 50:443–452, January 1966.

Election From State Senate Districts

State Senate district boundaries would need two adjustments to make them fit the nine-county area (see Map 2 and Table 9). First, for Bay Area electoral purposes, Sonoma County would have to be detached from the 1st District, which extends to the Oregon border, and attached to another Bay Area Senate district, presumably the 4th, which includes Marin and Napa counties, as well as almost all of Solano.

Second, a small corner of Solano County containing 2,706 registered voters, now included in the 2nd Senate District along with eight other Northern California counties, would also presumably be attached to the 4th Senate District.

The augmented 4th District would be just short of eight percent larger than the next largest Bay Area Senate district, and should qualify under the principle of equal-population. It would be slightly smaller than the state's largest, the 35th Senate District in Los Angeles and Orange counties, with 281,000 registered voters. Its percent deviation from the Bay Area average is not much greater than those of San Francisco's two at-large districts (see Table 9).

Use of Senate districts would provide nine electoral areas averaging twice the size of Assembly districts. Furthermore, four of the districts—the 9th and 10th, and the 8th and 11th—are in effect multimembered, each coterminous pair electing two Senators-at-large. If these areas were used, candidates for four of the nine Bay Area regional legislative posts would have to mount campaigns capable of reaching *four times* the average population of Assembly districts.

The 1966 elections resulted in a Bay Area Senate delegation more evenly divided in terms of party than the Assembly delegation (see Table 10). Despite this near-equality in party affiliation, further analysis reveals that the Senate district lines drafted in 1965 favor Democrats, just as do the Assembly district boundaries. The three smallest Senate districts, for example, are predominantly Democratic in registration (63.3 percent) and send a predominantly Democratic delegation to Sacramento (66.6 percent). The Democratic registration in the three largest districts is significantly below the Bay Area average (55.5 percent compared to 60.6 percent). They elected a predominantly Republican delegation (66.6 percent).

Further Comments and Conclusions

With minor adjustments, the areas of either Assembly or Senate districts could be employed for direct election of all or part of a Bay Area regional legislative body. Democrats would probably be favored some-

MAP 2.

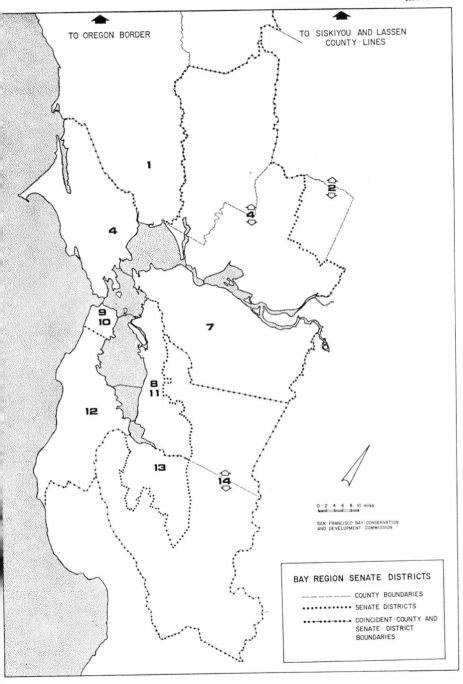

TO OREGON BORDER

TO SISKIYOU AND LASSEN
COUNTY LINES

1

4

2

4

9
10

7

8
11

12

13

14

0 2 4 6 8 10 miles

SAN FRANCISCO BAY CONSERVATION
AND DEVELOPMENT COMMISSION

BAY REGION SENATE DISTRICTS

————— COUNTY BOUNDARIES
•••••••••••• SENATE DISTRICTS
•••••••••• COINCIDENT COUNTY AND
SENATE DISTRICT
BOUNDARIES

TABLE 9

POSSIBLE SENATE DISTRICT MODIFICATION FOR BAY AREA ELECTORAL PURPOSES
The average number of registered voters in the nine districts, including voters
added from the 1st and 2nd districts, is 225,000. The countywide 8th and 11th districts in San Francisco, and the 9th and 10th districts in Alameda County, were
treated as if they were each single member districts containing half the county's
registered voters.

Senate districts	Number of registered voters per Senator, 1966 (rounded)		Percent deviation from average of nine Senate districts
4th			
Marin, Napa and part of Solano.........	183,000		
Add Sonoma County (detached from 1st District).......................	87,000		
Add portion of Solano County (detached from 2nd District)....................	3,000	= 273,000	+21
7th			
Contra Costa County..................		= 240,000	+ 7
8th and 11th			
Alameda County (two Senators elected at large)...........................	448,751 (÷ by 2)	= 224,000	negligible
9th and 10th			
San Francisco (two Senators elected at large)...............................	372,000 (÷ by 2)	= 186,000	−17
12th			
San Mateo County....................		= 253,000	+12
13th			
Part of Santa Clara County............		= 205,000	− 9
14th			
Part of Alameda and Santa Clara Counties...........................		= 238,000	+ 6

what, because of the ways in which the boundaries are drawn. However,
if nonpartisanship, as such, favors Republicans, nonpartisan elections
based on Senate or Assembly districts might cancel out this influence.
On the other hand, if the regional legislative posts assume considerable
significance in the area, it is probable that the political parties will attempt to exert an informal influence in the "nonpartisan" campaigns
and elections.

The major difference between the Senate and Assembly districts lies in their size, the 18 Assembly districts averaging half the registered voters contained in the Senate districts. Campaigns based on Assembly district areas would thus be less expensive and require less effort. Also, there is less likelihood that minorities of various kinds would be diluted or "washed out" in the smaller districts. The Bay Area's 18-member Assembly delegation, for example, contains three non-Caucasians. The Bay Area's nine Senators, on the other hand, are all Caucasians. This suggests that ethnic or other minority populations, especially those that may be comparatively concentrated in their distribution, are less likely to be overlooked if smaller electoral districts are employed.

One of the advantages of using either Senate or Assembly districts is that they are ready-made and will be redistricted periodically, thus obviating the need to design election areas especially for a Bay Area regional government. Of course, there are other important counter-balancing considerations which may justify the employment of other criteria for designing alternative election districts. For example, specially drawn areas may be preferable in order (1) to avoid the partisan gerrymandering which often accompanies the mapping of state legislative districts; or (2) to avoid changes in the total number of districts, which may occur every ten years in state legislative districting; or (3) to increase the likelihood of equitable minority group representation by making the areas smaller and more numerous; or (4) for any of several other considerations, some of which have been discussed on pages 26–32.

Would incumbent Senators or Assemblymen be concerned at the prospect of other persons being elected from districts *identical* to their own? If the regional legislative posts become important, and if young, politically upward-mobile individuals are elected, some will eventually become rivals of incumbent, or successors of retiring, Senators and Assemblymen. This would probably happen regardless of the geographic areas covered by the election districts, but it might be accentuated by the creation of identical districts.

In any event, establishment of a body of directly elected regional legislators should promote the public interest by improving the area's leadership capabilities. The recruitment channels for elected public office are rather limited, and relatively few county supervisors and city councilmen move on to higher elected positions. Thus, if also justified on other grounds, the establishment of 9, 18, 36, 40 or more new directly elected legislative posts in the Bay Area should be a welcome enlargement of the existing machinery for leadership development.

TABLE 10
1966 California Senate Election Results: San Francisco Bay Area

District number	Regis. % Democratic	Republicans		District number	Regis. % Democratic	Democrats	
		Name	Residence			Name	Residence
4.........	57.3	McCarthy	San Rafael	7	59.5	Miller	Martinez
8 [a].........	65.3	Sherman	Berkeley	9 [b]	66.3	[McAteer] [c]	San Francisco
12.........	56.5	Dolwig	Atherton	10 [b]	66.3	Moscone	San Francisco
14.........	50.2	Bradley	San Jose	11 [a]	65.3	Petris	Oakland
				13	62.5	Alquist	San Jose
		4 Republicans				5 Democrats	

[a, b] Districts 8 and 11, and 9 and 10 are paired.
[c] At a special election in 1967, San Francisco voters chose Judge Milton Marks, a Republican, to fill the vacancy caused by Senator McAteer's death.

PART THREE
Summary and Conclusions

Summary and Conclusions

Introduction

1. Under its broad legislative charge, the San Francisco Bay Conservation and Development Commission is considering comprehensive functional objectives, and not limiting its studies solely to the Bay and shoreline. Similarly, it is investigating comprehensive organizational arrangements, and not limiting itself to a single-purpose Bay conservation agency. Highly restricted studies and evaluations would ignore many crucial interrelationships between the Bay and the region, and fail to take advantage of the current interest in exploring comprehensive governmental approaches to regional problems.

2. Consequently, the range of functions is broad enough to include mutual implications—political, administrative, economic, esthetic—of Bay and shoreline planning and the *many other* regional activities and needs in the area. In doing this, the commission is examining policy implications of many regional programs, both those now institutionalized and those likely to be developed in the foreseeable future.

3. Because planning for the long-term future is hazardous, it is preferable to recommend institutional arrangements based on the best estimates of likely needs in the next five to 15 years. Further, any recommended organizational structure should be so designed as to require later reexamination, and possible modification when circumstances change, as they are sure to do.

4. The Bay Area's own experience is rich and instructive. Its existence as a *region* was established early. From the beginning the Bay, both as a transportation artery and as "open space," played a crucial role in shaping the area's development. A much greater than average governmental decentralization has encouraged organizational experimentation. Dissatisfied with directly elected single-purpose districts, the area's leaders invented the "Bay Area pattern" of constituent-unit representation in 1955, and years later, organized the Association of Bay Area Governments. But pressing problems are now forcing the region's leaders to think about further experimentation. This is going on through the work of the Association of Bay Area Governments, the San Francisco Bay Conservation and Development Commission, the Bay Area Transportation Study Commission, the Bay-Delta Study, the Joint Committee on Bay Area Regional Organization and many civic groups.

5. An almost unparalleled public concern with solving urgent problems sparked by an acute awareness of the need, and supported by a conviction that the Bay Area possesses a unique excellence which could

Governing a Metropolitan Region

be lost through inaction, have combined to bring effective regional reorganization nearer to realization than ever before.

6. This combination of factors affords the Bay Area a virtually unprecedented opportunity to improve on what it has already learned—and to draw upon relevant experience elsewhere—in designing a regional decision-making process fitted to the realities and needs of the 20th century's closing decades.

Guidelines for Further Study

CRITERIA FOR A REGIONAL GOVERNMENT

1. Any regional decision-making system should provide for full analysis and disclosure of the implications of proposed new programs. The implications of *failure to act* should be studied at least as carefully as proposed action, perhaps more carefully. The best techniques of systems analysis should be available to give members and staff of the regional agency up-to-date information on the consequences of proposed action—or inaction.

2. Special-interest representation should be accommodated through the public hearing process, rather than by giving interest groups representation on the governing body.

3. The decision process should lead to *decisions,* and not to indefinite procrastination and postponement. This suggests minimizing veto provisions.

4. The geographic *area* and the *functions* of the regional agency should be as broad as the regional needs that are to be met.

5. Regional goals must be developed and the authority to implement them made available.

6. The implementation of agreed-upon regional goals may take place on many levels. But the regional agency must have the means to insure that local or "fine-grained" decisions do not contravene the regional interest.

7. A legislative body should be both accountable and responsive, while retaining decision capability. "Accountability" is an ultimate and periodic responsibility to the public served. "Responsiveness" means a readiness to consider fairly the concerns of all interested parties who may be affected by a proposed decision. It suggests also an absence of rigidity and a willingness to modify proposed plans when such change seems appropriate and in the public interest. "Decision capability" refers to the capacity of a legislative body to make a *decision* and move ahead, once the evidence has been collected and analyzed. These three

terms designate overlapping and partially countervailing criteria. The ultimate aim should be to achieve an appropriate and necessarily delicate balance among them.

SOME DETERMINANTS OF POLICY

Many factors help influence the outcome of policy decisions. These include the nature of the controversies and conflicting interests involved, the system of representation, financial resources, and the functional responsibilities of those charged with making decisions.

1. The Bay is an extremely important and controversial feature of the region. Pressures for filling come from those who would take advantage of the high potential value of tidelands as close-in "made" land: owners or speculative investors, developers, and local governments wishing to increase their tax base. The Bay may also be used as a location for freeways, garbage dumps, and airport and seaport expansion, among other purposes.

2. Pressures against filling also come from a variety of sources. The esthetic and psychological value of the Bay, its contribution to the beauty and openness of the region, and the residents' sense of identification with the Bay are all important. The beauty, ethos and mystique of the "Bay Region" translates into many forms of economic value, such as premiums on view lots and the area's strong competitive position in the national specialty labor markets.

To many conservationists the Bay is worth preserving as a natural phenomenon, like Lake Tahoe or the Redwood stands. It is part of the "Pacific Flyway" for migratory birds. The Bay supports a major recreational and commercial fishery. It also has other great recreational potentials, for sailing and boating, for beaches, marinas, and similar facilities.

The earthquake hazard and known instabilities of deep mud raise serious questions about building on filled land. Finally, extensive filling could make the area's climate less equable and increase air pollution. The interplay of these conflicts, and the accommodations reached in resolving them, will determine future policy governing "the controversial Bay."

3. If a multipurpose agency is established for Bay conservation and development, the assignment to it of other regional functions and controversial issues will expand the range of interests to be considered. This will influence the public policy determinations finally made.

4. The way the representation system works will be a major policy influence because it will determine the kinds of individuals who are recruited as community leaders and decision makers. Especially im-

portant will be the relative influence of persons having a local orientation as compared with those tending to take regional and long-term views of controversial matters.

5. Other policy determinants include the kinds of financial resources available to a regional agency, and the limitations on their use.

REPRESENTATION ON THE POLICY-MAKING BODY

A regional legislative body could be constituted in any of many ways, most of which are variations on a few well-known organizational themes.

1. The region's own experience has resulted in development of a "Bay Area pattern" of *constituent-unit representation,* now embodied in a number of regional and sub-regional institutions in this area. The pattern is in part an outgrowth of dissatisfaction with directly elected special district boards. It also represents an effort to devise forms tied to existing cities and counties more closely than either directly elected or gubernatorially appointed boards would be.

The constituent-unit philosophy was originally based on the assumption that the units so formed would be single-purpose in scope. Now, however, the Association of Bay Area Governments is proposing that the principle be extended—through ABAG—to four functions immediately, and eventually to a wide range of regional activities to be undertaken by ABAG. This puts the principle in a new context and necessitates a rethinking of its possible application to a multipurpose regional government.

2. Appointment of the entire membership of metropolitan or regional governing bodies may be appropriate in certain situations, but none of these situations is currently present in the Bay Area. Therefore, appointment of the entire membership by the Governor and/or the state Legislature has been and is now rejected as a concept.

3. Direct election is the prevailing method of selecting what we hope are responsible, responsive, and accountable legislative bodies to govern general-purpose public agencies such as cities and counties. Clearly direct election would be the preferred method for selecting accountable, responsive and vigorous multipurpose regional governments. As the Bay Area experience has shown, however, direct election is not the only answer, and almost certainly not the best answer when single-purpose agencies are concerned. So, although we insist that multipurpose districts or governments must have a substantial proportion, at least, of directly elected members, we believe that the governing body of a *single-purpose* regional agency should not be directly elected.

4. Many different factors and variables affect the nature and character of direct election. These include:

Political visibility. An agency with low political visibility cannot be expected to generate much interest or awareness on the part of the voters, and direct elections under such circumstances will not be effective.

Filling of vacancies. Under some arrangements, interim vacancies on directly elected boards are filled by appointment by the remaining members of the board. The new member subsequently runs as an *incumbent* at the next election. Because incumbents are seldom defeated, this leads to excessive autonomy and a "closed club" setting.

Size of electoral district. The size of the electoral district—in either area or population—exerts significant, complex and sometimes conflicting influences on elections.

For example, large districts may: reduce political visibility, increase the influence of television and the metropolitan press, increase the effort and expense essential for effective campaigns—and thus also increase vulnerability to influence by well-financed interests—dilute the influence of concentrations of minority voters, and encourage candidates to give greater attention to regional matters.

Conversely, small districts may: increase political visibility, increase the influence of community newspapers and the formal or informal community power structure, reduce the effort and expense of the campaigns, and increase the likelihood that concentrations of minority voters will get some voice. But small districts will also make for parochialism.

Degree of contest for election. Close contests are encouraged by making the posts important, increasing their political visibility, avoiding "plurality" elections, and designing electoral districts that create a minimum of "safe" seats.

Partisan v. nonpartisan elections. "Conventional wisdom," and, apparently, the view of a majority of California's leaders, holds partisan elections at the local and regional levels to be undesirable. On the other hand, there is growing evidence of efforts to rethink this position in California and elsewhere. Local governments are increasingly concerned with basic issues of our society. Also, partisan influences are entering a number of local election contests in California. Partisan elections tend to identify major policy differences between candidates, stimulate voter interest and awareness, and increase voter turnout. Partisan elections could be an effective means of selecting a regional legislative body and holding it accountable to the electorate.

5. The design of a regional legislative body should seek to assure that it will be accountable, but will also maintain an appropriate balance between responsiveness and decision capability. This is a complicated matter.

Some obvious possibilities for organizing a regional policy body include: (a) electing the entire body from districts, on a partisan or nonpartisan basis; (b) employing the ABAG proposal or modification of it; (c) continuing BCDC, either as it is now constituted or with modifications, or (d) having members of the body appointed by the Governor and/or the state Legislature. Other possibilities to be considered include various kinds of "mixed" legislative bodies, including directly elected members, representatives selected by cities and counties and/or by ABAG, and appointees by the Governor and/or the state Legislature. A directly elected legislature could be designated as the lower house in a bicameral system; the ABAG Executive Committee could constitute the upper house, with a suspensory veto that could subsequently be overridden by a special vote of the lower house.

THE REGIONAL LEGISLATURE: TIME AND EFFORT, TENURE, SIZE, COMPENSATION

Innumerable factors affect the degree of burden imposed by membership in a legislative body, the members' willingness and ability to assume the burden, and their freedom to discharge the responsibilities of office. This, of course, is true of members of the legislative body of any existing or prospective regional agency.

1. The number of functions assigned to the agency will affect time demands on its members, as will the legislature's size, and the efficiency of its organization. The availability of top-quality staff will be important. The individual legislator's other responsibilities also enter the equation, especially if the constituent-unit principle is employed and a regional legislator is also a member of a city or county governing board, with its own time demands.

2. Elected officials of most local governments in California serve four-year terms. There is no obvious reason to depart from this practice in the case of a directly elected regional legislative body. Length of term of indirectly elected legislators is important, however, because it helps determine their degree of independence .

3. Regional legislators of a multipurpose agency with significant responsibilities should receive adequate salaries. The salaries currently paid members of the state Legislature—$16,000 per year—would appear to be the appropriate order of magnitude, because office-holding should not be limited to those with independent means. Adequate salaries should be accompanied by a strong guarantee against conflicts of interest.

4. A legislative body of almost any size can be *made* to function. Recent Bay Area experience suggests that a legislative body of between

20 and 40 members would be both workable and sufficiently large to represent a wide spectrum of regional interests, but the optimum size can best be determined when the organizational design of an agency is actually being drafted.

LEADERSHIP: SELECTING A CHIEF EXECUTIVE

A crucial feature of an effective government is leadership—the ability of individuals or groups within an agency to recognize existing problems, anticipate future needs, and formulate policies and programs to meet them.

1. The "musical chairs" method of choosing the presiding officers of the Bay Area Air Pollution Control District and ABAG, with one-year tenure and alternation between city and county representatives, does not make for strong and continuing executive leadership.

2. Acceptable means of developing leadership would be (a) direct, regionwide election of the chief executive—equivalent to the Governor at the state level or the mayor at the city level, or (b) selection of the chief executive by the legislative body for a specified term of office.

3. The executive's formal powers are also important in establishing him in a leadership position. Absence of an executive with a leadership role may place too great a burden on the top-level appointed staff.

AGENCY FUNCTIONS AND POWERS: A MINIMUM

A continuation of the existing functions of BCDC on a permanent basis would represent the minimum allocation of power necessary for Bay conservation and development. But this would not be enough. A combination of land use regulation, purchase and condemnation will be necessary to limit and control Bay filling—where control is sufficient —and to acquire and develop lands, or lease or resell them subject to conditions, where these are appropriate means of Bay conservation and development.

AGENCY FUNCTIONS AND POWERS: A MULTIPURPOSE BODY

1. A crucial function of a multipurpose agency can be to insure *recognition* of the essential interdependence of the large-scale decisions made in a region. A multipurpose agency can bring under one policy-making roof the decisions now made by independent bodies—or not made at all—which affect the physical, social, economic and environmental situation throughout the Bay Area.

2. Several alternatives are possible in moving to create a multipurpose agency. These relate to the degree of integration sought and the number of functions included. Full-scale integration or *consolidation* of

functions is one possibility. On the other hand, it may be possible to achieve a good deal of integration short of actual consolidation. One promising alternative is an "umbrella" agency with powers to encourage interagency cooperation, and, as a last resort, to enforce coordination or even require consolidation. The umbrella government concept may represent the only feasible method of accomplishing regional objectives without major surgery on existing agencies—either regional or local.

3. Which functions should be administered regionally? Senate Concurrent Resolution No. 41 (1967) specifically mentions the following functions for regional study: regional planning, air and water pollution, solid waste disposal, regional parks and open space, and transportation (including rapid transit, ports, airports, and bridges). In addition to these functions, the Governor's Commission on Metropolitan Area Problems (1960) mentioned others for possible administration by a regional agency, including water supply, regional sewage disposal and drainage, regional aspects of law enforcement and fire protection, regional aspects of urban renewal, and civil defense. This listing emphasizes the fact that few public functions are exclusively regional or local. Most can be separated into local and regional components.

As a general rule, there is no point in regionalizing those things that can be handled adequately locally. Basic criteria for the decision are the quality of existing provisions for the function in question, the closeness of the relationships between functions proposed to be linked, the degree of entrenchment of existing agencies with a vested interest in the present arrangement, and the possible existence of important decision areas that are being left unattended.

FINANCING REGIONAL PROGRAMS

The agency's need for fiscal powers would obviously depend on the responsibilities assigned to it. Financial resources of major magnitude will be essential, if implementation of the plan is to be in whole or in part by negotiated purchase or condemnation of lands in the Bay.

1. The overworked property tax is not a likely source for major new funds.

2. Other possibilities include: (a) a regional addition to the income tax, (b) taxes or charges specifically upon benefits derived from the Bay, (c) a long-term commitment of a portion of tolls from bridges across the Bay, (d) a "property appreciation" tax, (e) a property transfer tax, (f) a regional addition to one or more state taxes, such as the gasoline tax, cigarette tax, alcoholic beverage tax, general sales tax or other state levys.

3. A regional addition to the income tax is probably the most equitable, attractive and productive possibility, especially if it could be established on a withholding basis, like the federal income tax.

4. If a multipurpose agency is established, a whole "family" of taxes should be considered, perhaps with the income tax as the most important single source.

5. Taxes related to property value appreciation are both possible sources of revenue and tools for implementing plans. Thus they can be employed to influence the course of future urban development and help to achieve regional goals.

6. The new agency will need to be freed from the one-year budget cycle if it is to plan and implement on a long-term basis, and given access to capital financing arrangements that bypass California's archaic requirement for a two-thirds favorable referendum on general obligation bonds.

7. If the agency develops a land bank function—buying, selling, and leasing land to help carry out its plan—this activity could become partially self-supporting.

8. If some of the federal and state funds made available in the Bay Area were channelled through the new agency, this could provide it with both revenues and leverage for plan implementation.

RELATIONS WITH OTHER GOVERNMENTS

1. Many federal, state and local agencies are involved in policies and programs that affect the Bay and shoreline, either directly or indirectly. The successor agency recommended by BCDC should be designed to take these many interrelationships into account.

2. Several kinds of state and federal interests must be considered. A prime fact, however, is that further degradation of the Bay, or of the Bay Area, would represent a major loss to the state and nation. In addition, both the federal and state governments invest large sums of money in the Bay Area every year. Consequently, they have a legitimate interest in seeing the money well spent.

3. The state's interest is perhaps best protected by its ability to encourage rational planning and by retention of ultimate authority to restructure the new regional agency, if that should prove desirable later on. Similarly, the federal interest may best be protected not only by its ultimate authority over areas under federal jurisdiction, but also by national encouragement of the development of strong and effective regional planning processes.

Alternative Approaches to Metropolitan Governmental Organization

This section summarizes the survey of alternative approaches, and attempts to indicate the lessons that may be learned from these experiences.

THE ONE-TIER APPROACH: CITY-COUNTY CONSOLIDATION

Typically, city-county consolidation proposals feature the merger of the major city—or of all cities in a metropolis—with the county government.

1. The complete consolidation of all local governments in most large metropolitan areas is not only exceedingly unlikely, but also probably highly inadvisable. (With its 7,000 square miles of area and 4.5 million people, for example, the Bay Area is much too large and has too many diverse interests for any such massive consolidation.)

2. City-county consolidation within individual counties could conceivably produce a stronger local level of government. It is debatable, however, how feasible or helpful such consolidation would be, and whether it would further the solution of *regional* problems such as Bay conservation and development.

3. Concepts employed in the consolidations in the Baton Rouge and Nashville areas may be helpful here: that is, having separate service areas for urban and non-urban sections, with different tax levels reflecting different levels of service.

4. Periodic review of the results of a metropolitan reorganization, as practiced in the Baton Rouge area, should be emulated elsewhere.

5. Both the Baton Rouge and Nashville areas have directly elected chief executives (metropolitan mayors). These offices were created expressly to provide areawide policy leadership.

6. Mandatory redistricting of metropolitan legislative seats can prevent the growth of representational inequities when population shifts. The Nashville-Davidson County charter, for example, requires electoral district revision every 10 years.

TWO-TIER APPROACHES: INTRODUCTION

Two-tier approaches clearly are more acceptable than any one-tier arrangement, and have more to offer in complex, multicounty metropolitan regions. These approaches include Toronto's federation and Miami's comprehensive urban county (Dade County), and in addition, other less comprehensive examples, including multicounty special districts and authorities, and councils of governments.

TWO-TIER APPROACHES: FEDERATION

A federation establishes a new general or multiple-purpose metropolitan government to handle areawide functions, but retains local governments to perform activities designated as local. The best known and most successful example of federation on the North American continent is the Municipality of Metropolitan Toronto, created in 1953. The following generalizations are based primarily on the Toronto experience.

1. Action by the provincial (state) Legislature is an effective way of accomplishing metropolitan reform. Moreover, adoption by legislative act, instead of popular referendum, preserves the Legislature's authority to effect further reorganizations when changed circumstances so require.

2. The areawide and local levels of government may logically share functions, the former handling regional components and the latter taking care of local components. Furthermore, the allocation of functions, or components of functions, between levels of government, can be "tailored" to fit the institutional situation in the area where federation is being installed.

3. The metropolitan government may appropriately serve as an "umbrella" agency for specified purposes. In Toronto these include approval of local bond proposals, equalization of financial resources, and appointment of the governing board of the regional transportation agency. Thus an upper-level government can influence or determine local and regional policies without engaging in direct *management* of the specified functions.

4. Regional planning is an important power of the upper-tier government in a federal system. In Toronto, for example, the metropolitan government can draft general regional plans which, after provincial approval, are binding on the local governments. The latter are responsible for local planning and zoning.

5. A powerful executive committee is essential when the governing body of the federation is so constituted as to be unwieldy. Toronto's experience suggests that a legislature of 25 or more members needs a smaller executive committee with considerable authority.

6. Periodic review by an independent agency, plus legislative freedom to effect reorganization in the light of experience and changed circumstances, are essential if the regional government is to be kept up-to-date.

TWO-TIER APPROACHES: THE COMPREHENSIVE URBAN COUNTY

Under the comprehensive urban county approach, an existing county government is converted into a metropolitan agency, which handles regional functions. Municipalities or other local entities continue to provide local services. The following generalizations are based on the experience of Dade County (Miami). Because Dade County encompasses an entire metropolitan region, the single-county Miami experiment is fully as relevant to the possible allocation of functions at the regional level as is the experience of a true federation like Toronto's.

1. In multi-county areas, the comprehensive urban county approach probably would be useful chiefly to improve the existing county governments' ability to deal with those problems that can be solved by single-county action.

2. The areawide powers granted to the metropolitan government in Dade County to adopt and enforce comprehensive plans, land use regulations, and uniform building and related technical codes, constituted a major break-through at the metropolitan level in the United States. These powers are widely recognized as crucial instruments for the intelligent direction of urban growth, but they are also some of the most jealously guarded prerogatives of local governments in virtually all metropolitan areas.

3. Endowing a county or areawide government with authority to determine and enforce reasonable minimum standards of service for cities and non-school local special districts could be a method for strengthening the local government level.

4. An independently elected chief executive may be necessary for effective public leadership in an areawide government.

5. Extremist positions for and against metropolitan reform may have a seriously debilitating effect on any newly formed metropolitan government, before it has had an opportunity to be tested fairly. Referenda and threats of referenda have been employed for many years as a major weapon in the continuing campaign of harassment of Dade County—in contrast with the Toronto experience, where reform enacted by legislation, without referendum, protected the new government and gave it a chance for a fair trial.

Two-Tier Approaches: Regional Districts and Agencies

Use of regional and multicounty districts and agencies is one of the most promising approaches to metropolitan problems. They afford maximum flexibility, and can be installed with a minimum of disturbance to existing units, if that is desired. They can be assigned as few or as many functions as circumstances require, and their service areas can readily be designed to fit the area of need.

1. Much recent and current discussion of approaches to regional problems has centered on metropolitan districts, in one form or another.

2. The formation of metropolitan districts by state legislative action without referendum has ample precedent.

3. Most special districts are subject to severe financial limitations. For example, some are forced to depend heavily on the property tax, while others may be restricted to user charges and revenue bond financing. Such limitations should be minimized when a new district is created or an old one reorganized.

4. The disposition to establish governing bodies that prove insufficiently accountable to the people is a basic and unresolved issue in the use of the district approach.

5. Regional problems are interrelated. The continued formation of single-purpose metropolitan districts further proliferates governments and disperses public authority. Such districts cannot effectively solve a range of regional problems, and the public has great difficulty in keeping them accountable.

6. Requiring *local* plans to adhere to a regional general plan could be an important method of fostering better planning in the development of an area, while retaining a degree of flexibility and control at the local level.

7. A multipurpose metropolitan district should be assigned significant responsibilities and powers, both to enhance its problem-solving capability and to increase its political visibility. Further, in order to reduce fragmentation, and increase accountability, possibly some of the functions now allocated to single-purpose districts should sooner or later be assigned to the multipurpose district.

8. A metropolitan district can embody the "umbrella" agency concept, as does the Metropolitan Council in the Twin Cities area. The newly created council was given extensive powers to engage in regional planning, to conduct research on a wide range of problems affecting the area, and to veto proposals found in conflict with its regional guidelines. The council was not, however, given any *operating* responsibilities, and thus did not displace existing local or regional agencies.

COUNCILS OF GOVERNMENTS

The experience with voluntary councils of governments, as such, has little to offer the Bay Area that is not already well known here. This is true because the region's local leaders, working through a council of governments, have agreed (although not unanimously) that voluntary cooperation is not sufficient to solve regional problems. The Association of Bay Area Governments and its recent governmental proposals demonstrate this. Thus what is being proposed by ABAG should not be confused with a voluntary council of governments. The ABAG proposal would *build onto* an existing voluntary council framework, modify it somewhat, and convert it into a limited-purpose regional government.

The ABAG Proposal for a Regional Government

In 1966–67 the Association of Bay Area Governments urged that it be reconstituted by the Legislature as a formal regional government with limited functions, but with the intention of eventually taking over Bay conservation and development, as well as other regional programs.

IMPORTANT CONTRIBUTIONS OF THE PROPOSAL

1. The proposal recognizes the necessity for a limited-function, multiple-purpose regional government in the nine-county Bay Area.

2. The proposed regional government would be given its powers by direct legislative act. This recognizes the inability of a voluntary agency to perform the difficult acts of government, admits the need to avoid referenda, and thus retains in the state Legislature the power to reorganize the agency later in the light of experience.

3. The proposal selects three functions that are critical regional needs, or soon will be so, and that involve a minimum challenge to existing agencies.

4. The ABAG recommendation recognizes that important powers will be essential to the proposed open space acquisition program, including long-term capital financing and eminent domain.

5. The proposal attempts an adjustment of voting power to reflect in rough fashion the comparative populations of the constituent units, the cities and counties. (Although the ABAG governmental plan was not implemented by legislative action, the association has since voluntarily reorganized its Executive Committee along the lines of the proposal.)

FUNCTIONS AND POWERS

1. The proposal would continue ABAG's advisory regional planning functions, and, in addition, give the new government responsibility for satisfying regional refuse disposal needs, regional open space and park needs, and regional airport needs. Furthermore, the proposal envisions expansion of the functions to include other regional problems as they develop, as well as absorption of existing special-purpose agencies over time.

2. Despite a number of constructive features, this must be considered a "back-door" approach to regional government, attaching functions

gradually to a preexisting "forum-type" agency. A more direct and logical way would be to look *first* at *problems,* and *then* devise organizational *solutions.*

3. If the ABAG proposal should be adopted, but the later expansion of its functions not take place, ABAG would have contributed to the proliferation of limited-function agencies in the region. This is true because some kind of agency or agencies will have to take over the BCDC and BATS functions, as well as other emerging regional needs.

4. Achievement of the goals outlined by ABAG's preliminary regional plan would require strong exercise of the police power (which is left out of ABAG's proposal altogether). It would need the power of eminent domain (which would be granted under ABAG's proposal, but subject to such stringent veto requirements as to render the authorization virtually useless for major projects). Excellent financial resources would be essential. (Under its regional governmental proposal, ABAG would have to depend primarily on a $0.01 per $100 property tax, plus general obligation bond financing.)

REPRESENTATION

There appears to be substantial agreement on the need to form a limited-function regional government in the San Francisco Bay Area. One of the critical undecided issues, however, is that of representation: how the regional legislative body should be constituted. The ABAG proposal presents a concrete recommendation which needs analysis and to which the criteria outlined in the third chapter can be applied.

1. The proposal endorsed by a majority of the ABAG General Assembly attempts to establish a rough proportion between representation and population. It would increase the Executive Committee membership to 34, and give the larger cities and counties additional votes. The reorganized Executive Committee would become the association's *legislative body,* although its actions in planning, financing, and acquiring property would be subject to approval by the General Assembly, in which each city and county would continue to have an equal vote. The President and Vice President would be elected for two-year terms by secret ballot of all city councilmen and supervisors voting as a body. The President and Vice President would not have to be councilmen or supervisors.

2. During the ABAG discussions, a number of "minority" proposals were put forth. Most of these urged that representation be more closely proportional to population, or that all or part of the legislative body be directly elected, or both.

3. The "one man, one vote" issue must be considered in two ways.

First, will principles underlying the series of U. S. Supreme Court decisions requiring reapportionment of state legislatures also be applied to the legislative bodies of local and regional governments? At present this matter is very complicated and the answer unclear. New and seemingly conflicting cases are being decided all the time. Second, regardless of current or possible future requirements imposed by court rulings, the principle of equal representation is so important that it must be considered *on its own merits* when regional governmental proposals are being contemplated.

4. In many ways, the ABAG proposal for regional government departs from the principle of representation in proportion to population. Several departures involve voting strength on the Executive Committee and choice of its members. Others involve General Assembly member selection and relative voting strength. Still others relate to the malapportionment of county supervisorial districts.

Departures involving the Executive Committee:

(a) The four smallest counties would be over-represented, Alameda and Santa Clara counties would be under-represented, and a close approximation of population would be achieved only in the cases of Contra Costa, San Francisco, and San Mateo counties.

(b) The Alameda and Santa Clara County governments would be under-represented, as compared with their cities, thus partially disenfranchising unincorporated area residents in those two counties.

(c) The small cities would have a disproportionate influence in the selection of Executive Committee members. Each mayor has one vote in his mayors' conference. Thus the mayor of Richmond, representing a city of 82,000, would have no more voice than the mayor of Hercules, representing 310 people.

Departures involving the General Assembly:

(a) All cities have equal voices in General Assembly voting on the municipal side, irrespective of their size.

(b) Similarly, all counties have an equal voice in General Assembly voting on the county side. Alameda County, with more than one million residents, is treated equally with Napa County, which has 76,000 people.

(c) Unincorporated area residents are partially disenfranchised in the General Assembly, being represented only on the county side of the bicameral body.

5. Malapportionment of county supervisorial districts is surprisingly widespread. Only the supervisorial districts in Alameda County appear to be well-apportioned. Seven counties showed marked variations in the size of supervisorial districts.

6. The ABAG proposal's noncompliance with equal representation

could be reduced in several ways. (a) County supervisorial districts could be reapportioned. (b) Smaller counties and smaller cities could be grouped for the purpose of selecting representatives. (c) A "mixed" legislature could be created, some members being chosen under the constituent-unit principle and others by direct election from acceptably apportioned districts.

7. The mayors' conference has several limitations as a means of selecting representatives. Weaknesses of the mayors' conferences:

(a) Unlike county boards of supervisors, the mayors' conferences are not legislative bodies. They are monthly social-discussion groups, lacking cohesion and continuing responsibilities.

(b) Many cities rotate their mayors frequently, causing rapid turnover in mayors' conference membership. This intensifies the problem of developing leadership, cohesion, and a sense of continuing purpose.

(c) The conferences often tend to be provincial, each city being concerned primarily with its own immediate problems.

(d) Appointments to regional agencies, including ABAG, appear to be made rather casually, on the basis of limited consideration of the candidates and their abilities.

Possible changes in the mayors' conferences:

(a) If the appointive role takes on greater significance, the selections would probably be considered more carefully.

(b) Longer tenure for mayors would reduce conference membership turnover.

(c) Alternatively, each city could appoint a long-term representative, not necessarily the mayor.

(d) A plan for weighted voting or grouping of cities, if carefully designed, would reduce the disproportionate voting strength of the small municipalities.

THE PARTISAN EFFECTS OF SELECTION BY NONPARTISAN LOCAL GOVERNMENT

1. Should a new regional legislature be partisan or nonpartisan? The preponderance of California opinion still appears to favor nonpartisanship, in local and probably regional elections, although there are a number of reasons for reconsidering this position: (a) Party machines of the corrupt turn-of-the-century variety no longer exist. (b) Local government is increasingly involved with basic social issues, the same issues with which the parties concern themselves on the state and national levels. (c) Conversely, political parties are involving themselves—directly or indirectly—in many local elections in California.

2. Local government is not politically neutral. By and large, it gives a distinct and material advantage to Republicans. This is true of both city and county government.

3. The partisan deviation of local government is also transmitted to the ABAG councils. Thus the "Republican advantage" manifested by local government is reflected—and sometimes magnified—in the ABAG Executive Committee and General Assembly.

INDEPENDENCE OF VIEW AND VOTING BY REGIONAL LEGISLATORS

1. Some degree of independence is desirable if a regional legislator is to weigh policy conflicts fairly and reach informed judgments that are in the best interest of the entire area. Furthermore, the legislative process requires a flexibility and freedom to negotiate, which is denied by the local practice of sending "instructed" delegates to the ABAG sessions.

2. ABAG delegates are vulnerable to local community pressures, and to replacement by their boards of supervisors or mayors' conferences at any time. These vulnerabilities to immediate local pressures can make it hazardous for an ABAG member to vote his convictions on the proper balance between regional and local concerns, especially *when the most important and difficult issues are under consideration.*

CONCLUSIONS

1. The ABAG proposal is the outcome of a remarkable opinion shift toward acceptance of the need for a regional *governmental* approach to a number of areawide problems.

2. The proposal quite properly bears the imprint of its source, the city and county governments of the Bay Area.

3. But there are other actors in the regional drama as well as other and perhaps better ways of representing local and regional interests. These also need to be considered.

Direct Election: Two Possibilities

In addition to the constituent-unit principle of representation embodied in the ABAG proposal, several other methods of choosing some or all of the members of a regional legislative body have been discussed in the Bay Area. One suggestion is that the state Senators and Assemblymen elected from the Bay Area could also serve as the regional legislature. Although the pressures of state legislative business render this suggestion infeasible, election of regional legislators on the basis of either Assembly or Senate districts is a definite possibility.

ELECTION FROM ASSEMBLY DISTRICTS

1. Given either of two minor adjustments, 18 electoral areas based on Assembly districts could be created—see Map 1, page 123.

2. If Assembly districts were used, the resulting electoral process would resemble Assembly elections in some respects.

3. The present Assembly districts tend to favor Democrats. Assembly districting, accomplished in 1965 under a Democratically controlled Legislature, tends to group the more strongly Republican areas into larger districts and the more strongly Democratic areas into smaller districts. Thus, other things being equal, Republicans could be expected to elect fewer Assemblymen than if all districts were of equal size.

4. The district lines create a large number of "safe" seats. Safe seats are those whose voter registrations are such that an incumbent of the appropriate political party will, under normal circumstances, be very difficult to oust. In the Bay Area, safe Democratic districts far outnumber safe Republican districts: one count places the current proportion at 11 to four (representing a total of 15 safe seats out of the 18 in the Bay Area).

ELECTION FROM STATE SENATE DISTRICTS

1. Two adjustments would modify state Senate districts sufficiently to create nine electoral districts coterminous with the Bay Area—see Map 2, page 129. This would provide nine electoral areas averaging twice the size of Assembly-based districts. Alameda and San Francisco counties each have two coterminous and countywide senatorial districts. These four districts are thus approximately *four* times the size of the average Assembly district.

2. The Senate district lines generally favor Democrats, just as do the Assembly district boundaries.

3. Again, the district boundaries create a large number of safe seats, and again, the Democrats are favored. One current estimate is that either five or six seats may be considered safely Democratic under normal circumstances, and two or three seats safely Republican.

CONCLUSIONS

1. With minor adjustments, either Assembly or Senate districts could form the basis for electing a regional legislature.

2. Democrats would be favored somewhat, because of the way district boundaries are presently drawn.

3. Size is the major difference between the two sets of districts. On the

average, Assembly districts have half the number of registered voters of Senate districts. However, two pairs of the Senate districts are coterminous and countywide, and are thus twice as large as they otherwise would be.

4. Size of district is significant: (a) Campaigns based on present Assembly district areas would require approximately half the expense and effort of those based on present Senate districts (one-fourth as compared with the Alameda and San Francisco Senate districts). (b) The smaller districts would make it less likely that minority populations would go unrepresented. The Bay Area's nine Senators, for example, are all Caucasians, while the 18-member Assembly delegation contains three non-Caucasians. Thus electoral areas even smaller than Assembly districts may be desirable to maximize minority representation and for other reasons.

5. Districts based on either Assembly or Senate districts would be redistricted automatically from time to time.

6. Because the recruitment ladder into elected public office is limited, the addition of 9, 18, 36, 40 or more new elected posts in the Bay Area should be welcome.

Local Government and Political Partisanship: A Preliminary Analysis

Counties and Partisan Registration

In eight of the nine Bay Area counties the party registrations of the county supervisors were significantly different from those of the electorate in 1966–67 (see Table 11): In six counties the differences—which range from five to 50 percentage points—favored the Republicans. The reverse was true in one striking case: because of a combination of (1) at-large elections in a county that is 66 percent Democratic, (2) active participation in elections by politically-oriented groups, and (3) the filling of vacancies by mayor's appointments, San Francisco had a board that was 100 percent Democratic in registration. The registration of supervisors in Contra Costa and Marin counties also favored the Democrats, but somewhat more modestly.

To describe the phenomenon another way, Solano County, which showed the greatest divergence, had the highest Democratic registration of the nine counties, 70 percent. But the Solano board was made up of four Republicans and one Democrat, i.e., it was 20 percent Democratic. Other counties whose divergence between registration and electorate strongly favored the Republicans were Napa (–39%), Santa Clara (–36%) and Sonoma (–36%).

An array was made of the supervisorial districts of eight counties, in another approach to the problem of verifying and measuring the fact that present procedures for selecting local governing boards tends, with some exceptions, to favor the election of Republicans.[1] Districts were grouped in quartiles, from the lowest to highest in Democratic registration. The results are summarized in Table 12.

Republicans had a distinct advantage in the first three quartiles, electing supervisors who ranged from 60 to 80 percent Republican. The voters in each of the three quartiles were 47, 56, and 63 percent Democratic, respectively. Thus, the percentage point deviation favoring Republicans was –27, –16 and –33, respectively.

Only in the *fourth* quartile did the situation change. Supervisorial

---

[1] The consolidated city-county of San Francisco with its at-large elections was excluded.

districts in the fourth quartile, which ranged from 65 percent to 77 percent in Democratic registration, elected seven Democrats to three Republicans. Thus in the fourth quartile, the average partisan compositions of the supervisors and the electorates were quite similar, 70 percent and 71 percent, respectively.

The transition from a distinct Republican advantage to an approximation of Democratic "equality" appears to take place in the vicinity of a 65 percent Democratic voter registration. At about the 65+ percentage level of Democratic voter registration, Republicans ceased to be favored; consequently, the fourth quartile supervisors and electorate were very similar in partisan composition.

These facts tell us a number of things. First, there is a relationship between the partisan affiliation of voters and of the supervisors they elect. Second, if partisan affiliation or other factors related to partisan affiliation were statistically neutral—i.e., had no discernable effect on the outcome of local elections—the supervisors would approximate the partisan registrations of the populace from which they are chosen. This is not the case. Third, the Republicans have a pronounced advantage, which is not overcome until county Democratic registrations of approximately 65 percent and above are reached.

This indicates the existence of a Republican advantage of roughly 15 percentage points. The percentage-point advantage is translated into an even larger advantage in the proportion of Republican-registered supervisors elected. With an electorate that is 60 percent Democratic, the eight counties are governed by 40 supervisors who are 40 percent Democratic in registration—representing a differential of 20 percentage points.

Cities and Partisan Registration

Measures such as those applied to county government were also used to test the political neutrality of city government. For example, an analogous array of cities was prepared, ranging from Hillsborough, the city with the lowest Democratic registration (21 percent) to Pittsburg, which has the highest (84 percent)—see Table 13.

The results were strikingly similar to those obtained from the array of supervisorial districts. Republican councilmen predominated in the first three quartiles, and to an even greater extent so did cities controlled by councils with a majority of Republican members. Only in the fourth quartile—composed of cities with Democratic voter registrations ranging from 67 to 84 percent—did Democratically-controlled councils prevail. While there is no definite "breaking point," councils with a majority of Democrats predominate when the Democratic voter registration of the city exceeds 69 percent. Below that level one finds a preponderance of councils with Republican majorities.

In still other ways the cities reveal differences between the partisan flavor of councils and electorate, analogous to those shown above by counties. Table 14 was obtained by grouping the cities within each county. In seven of the eight counties the city councilmen were less Democratic than the registered voters within incorporated areas, the differences ranging from six to 21 percentage points. In Solano County, for example, where 71 percent of the city voters were registered Democrats, only 50 percent of the city councilmen were so registered. Or, to look at the matter another way: Bay Area city residents in the eight counties were approximately 60 percent Democratic and 40 percent Republican. Their elected city councilmen, on the other hand, were 45 percent Democratic as compared with 55 percent Republican.

The end result: A municipal electorate that is more than 60 percent Democratic selects a "delegation" of city councilmen who are 45 percent Democratic. Further, because the small cities tend to be Republican, 60 percent of the region's cities are controlled by Republican majorities. A comparison of councilmen with electorate suggests a Republican advantage of approximately 15 percentage points. And the city "breaking point" of 69 percent mentioned above suggests that the advantage may run even higher. Whatever the value of these attempts to quantify the differentials, one clear fact emerges: present methods of electing city councilmen tend to favor Republicans over Democrats.

Local Government Is Not Politically Neutral

If influences on the outcome of local elections which are related to partisanship were neutral in a statistical sense, city councilmen and county supervisors would approximate their judisdictions' voters in partisan registration. There would be variations, of course, but a normal distribution—assuming complete neutrality of the partisan registration factor—would see approximately as many local councils and boards exceeding their electorates in Democratic registration as falling below.

On the contrary, however, the evidence shows that local government as a representational mechanism is not "politically neutral." It confers a distinct—although not universal—advantage to persons of Republican registration. The implications of this fact should be given consideration in reviewing various methods of choosing policy makers to govern a new regional agency.

Partisan Registrations of ABAG Officers

The "Republican advantage" in local legislative bodies influences the composition of the Association of Bay Area Governments (see Tables 15 and 16). For example, the 13 official representatives of county governments currently members of the ABAG Executive Committee consist of seven Republicans and six Democrats, i.e., 46 percent Democratic. The city representatives include 12 Republicans and six Democrats, i.e., 33 percent Democratic.

Because the Executive Committee votes as a single body, and not by the General Assembly's dual roll call, the overall percentages are more meaningful than the separate city and county figures. The 31 Executive Committee members are made up of 19 Republicans and 12 Democrats, i.e., 39 percent Democratic. That is the de facto partisan composition of the steering committee of the voluntary "legislature" for a regional population that is more than 60 percent Democratic in composition.

The General Assembly's official county representatives are 63 percent Republican and 37 percent Democratic. On the city side, the figures were 57 percent Republican and 43 percent Democratic[2] but, because of the "two-house" voting requirements in the General Assembly, an effective veto power in the General Assembly was wielded by a county representation that was only 37 percent Democratic, representing a population that is over 60 percent Democratic.

---

[2] The following is worth noting here. A combination of equal voting in the General Assembly by all cities, regardless of size, and a tendency toward Republican control of the councils of many small cities, could combine to produce a peculiar potential for minority control of the Assembly. The 46 smallest cities in the Bay Area—which contain only about 7.5 percent of the total city population (San Francisco included as a city)—would have theoretical voting control over the General Assembly. The councils of nearly two-thirds of these 46 cities contain Republican majorities.

TABLE 11

VOTERS AND COUNTY SUPERVISORS:
DIFFERENCES IN PARTY REGISTRATION, 1966–67

County	Registration percent Democratic	Board of Supervisors percent Democratic	Percent deviation[a]
Alameda	65	60	− 5
Contra Costa	60	80	+20
Marin	48	60	+12
Napa	59	20	−39
San Francisco	66	100	+34
San Mateo	57	40	−17
Santa Clara	56	20	−36
Solano	70	20	−50
Sonoma	56	20	−36
Total	60		

a Difference between the registration of the electorate and the supervisors is expressed in percentage points. A minus (−) sign means that the percent Democratic registration of the supervisors is lower than that of the electorate; a plus (+) means that it is higher.

TABLE 12

VOTERS AND COUNTY SUPERVISORS:
QUARTILE GROUPINGS OF SUPERVISORIAL DISTRICTS, 1966–67
(San Francisco Excluded)

Supervisorial districts	Voter registration % Democratic	Supervisors % Democratic	Percent Deviation[a]
1st Quartile (lowest Democratic registrations)	47	20	−27
2nd Quartile	56	40	−16
3rd Quartile	63	30	−33
4th Quartile (highest Democratic registrations)	71	70	− 1
Total	60	40	−20

a Difference between the registration of electorate and supervisors expressed in percentage points. A minus sign (−) means that the percent Democratic registration of supervisors in the specified quartile is lower than that of the voters; a plus (+) means that it is higher.

TABLE 13

VOTERS AND CITY COUNCILMEN: CITIES GROUPED BY QUARTILE, 1966–67

(San Francisco Included)

	Voter registration % Democratic	Councilmen % Democratic	Percentage point deviation[a] (councilmen compared with electorate)	% of city councils with majority of Democrats	Percentage point deviation (Democratic-controlled councils compared with electorate)	Total voter registration (rounded)
1st Quartile (lowest Democratic registrations)	38	22	−16	18	−20	160,000
2nd Quartile	53	41	−12	35	−18	260,000
3rd Quartile	64	47	−17	35	−29	667,000
4th Quartile (highest Democratic registrations)	73	68	−5	73	0	227,000
Total	61	45	−16	40	−21	1,314,000

[a] A minus sign (−) indicates that the total of councilmen or councils in the quartile were less Democratic in party registration than the electorate, a plus (+) indicates that they were more Democratic.

TABLE 14

VOTERS AND CITY COUNCILMEN:
CITIES GROUPED BY COUNTIES, 1966–67

County	Electorate % Democratic	Councilmen % Democratic	Percent Deviation[a]
Alameda	65	53	−12
Contra Costa	65	59	− 6
Marin	48	29	−19
Napa	61	65	+ 4
San Mateo	56	39	−17
Santa Clara	55	37	−18
Solano	71	50	−21
Sonoma	54	40	−14
Total	60	45	−15

[a] A minus sign (−) means that the percent Democratic registration of councilmen is lower than that of the voters; a plus (+) means that it is higher.

TABLE 15

PARTISAN COMPOSITION OF GENERAL ASSEMBLY:
ASSOCIATION OF BAY AREA GOVERNMENTS, 1968

County	County side				City side			
	Democratic #	%	Republican #	%	Democratic #	%	Republican #	%
Alameda	0	0	1	100	8	62	5	38
Contra Costa	1	100	0	0	7	54	6	46
Marin	0	0	1	100	5	45	6	55
Napa	0	0	1	100	1	25	3	75
San Francisco	1	100	0	0	1	100	0	0
San Mateo	1	0	0	100	6	37	10	63
Santa Clara	0	0	1	100	5	33	10	67
Solano	..	..	..	..	1	20	4	80
Sonoma	0	0	1	100	3	37	5	63
Total	3	37%	5	63%	37	43%	49	57%

TABLE 16

PARTISAN COMPOSITION OF EXECUTIVE COMMITTEE: ASSOCIATION OF BAY AREA GOVERNMENTS, 1968

County	County delegation				City delegation				Total			
	Democratic #	%	Republican #	%	Democratic #	%	Republican #	%	Democratic #	%	Republican #	%
Alameda	0	0	2	100	3	60	2	40	3	43	4	57
Contra Costa	2	100	0	0	0	0	1	100	2	67	1	33
Marin	0	0	1	100	0	0	1	100	0	0	2	100
Napa	0	0	1	100	0	0	1	100	0	0	2	100
San Francisco	3	100	0	0	1	50	1	50	4	80	1	20
San Mateo	1	100	0	0	1	50	1	50	2	67	1	33
Santa Clara	0	0	2	100	1	25	3	75	1	17	5	83
Solano	:	0	:	:	0	0	1	100	0	0	1	100
Sonoma	0	0	1	100	0	0	1	100	0	0	2	100
Total	6	46%	7	54%	6	33%	12	67%	12	39%	19	61%

IV

KARL V. STEINBRUGGE

EARTHQUAKE HAZARD . . .

Earthquake Hazard in the San Francisco Bay Area:
A Continuing Problem in Public Policy

INSTITUTE OF GOVERNMENTAL STUDIES

UNIVERSITY OF CALIFORNIA · BERKELEY

Earthquake Hazard in the San Francisco Bay Area:
A CONTINUING PROBLEM IN PUBLIC POLICY

By

KARL V. STEINBRUGGE

Department of Architecture

1968

LIBRARY OF CONGRESS CATALOG CARD NUMBER 68–65260
PRINTED IN THE UNITED STATES OF AMERICA
BY THE UNIVERSITY OF CALIFORNIA PRINTING DEPARTMENT

Foreword

With this monograph the Institute of Governmental Studies is pleased
to resume its series of Franklin K. Lane reports on public policy problems and issues confronting the San Francisco Bay Area. In the work
presented here, Karl V. Steinbrugge attempts to advance a crucial educational process. The people of the Bay Area, including a great many
state and local officials, have only begun to think about the governmental implications and public policy needs posed by the region's
serious and omnipresent—but silent and unseen—earthquake hazard.

Two major earthquake faults run through—or very near—much of
the Bay Area's urbanized territory. All portions of the nine counties can
anticipate severe or violent shaking in future great earthquakes, which
the experts tell us are inevitable. The Farallon Islands, 30 miles west of
San Francisco, are moving in a northwesterly direction with respect to
Mount Diablo, 30 miles east of the City. Year by year, stresses continue
to build up in the intervening geological formations. Sooner or later
something will give, producing a major earthquake. Although its date
and epicenter cannot now be predicted, the authorities emphasize that
the Bay Area's next big jolt could occur any day. And that great earthquake will, in turn, be followed by others, each in its own time.

Fortunately, we are not doomed simply to sit and wait. A great deal
can be done. So far, however, actual accomplishment is lagging badly.
More effort should be devoted to *pre-earthquake* programs of *disaster
prevention,* as well as to plans for *post-earthquake rescue, assistance,
rehabilitation and reconstruction.* Effective policies must be based on
greatly improved public understanding of the hazard, and of the many
kinds of preventive measures that are essential to minimize losses of
life and property, and to facilitate post-earthquake recovery. Karl V.
Steinbrugge is to be complimented for this pioneering effort in translating scientific and engineering knowledge about earthquakes and
their consequences into the realm of public policy, and for outlining
some of the governmental programs that urgently need undertaking.

STANLEY SCOTT
Editor

Acknowledgments

A study such as this, which crosses over many disciplines, cannot be the sole work of one man. Whatever measure of success this study might have, more than a normal amount of credit will be due to Lloyd S. Cluff, who guided the author through many problems involving geologic hazards. Additionally, George O. Gates, Robert E. Wallace, and Dorothy Radbruch of the U. S. Geological Survey provided many valuable suggestions, as did Gordon B. Oakeshott and Harold B. Goldman of the California Division of Mines and Geology. S. T. Algermissen of the U. S. Coast and Geodetic Survey clarified some seismologically oriented problems.

Frank E. McClure and Henry J. Degenkolb, both of whom are consulting structural engineers with very substantial earthquake engineering experience, gave the author many insights into the current problems involved in evaluating seismic risk to buildings. William W. Moore of Dames and Moore, provided helpful criticism on soils engineering problems as they relate to the practical world of Bay Area growth. Architects George P. Simonds and Gerald McCue contributed interesting thoughts on planning problems.

Lastly, and certainly not least, were the thought provoking comments of Professor Perry Byerly, who has greatly influenced the thinking of the Bay Area engineering professions for many years in seismologically oriented matters.

The responsibility for the thoughts and conclusions belongs solely with the author, and it would be unfair to imply that all who assisted would agree with the author's findings. On the other hand, their thoughts and criticisms have been invaluable.

KARL V. STEINBRUGGE

Contents

ix

Introduction

Public concern with earthquakes and their effects has risen sharply in the past decade. This increasing interest has been reflected in local governmental circles, as well as at the state and national levels. Currently, large expenditures on earthquake research are being proposed by the scientific and engineering communities in the hope of predicting: (1) the occurrence of earthquakes, (2) the dynamic behavior of different kinds of ground, and (3) the dynamic behavior of various structures in relation to different kinds of ground. Despite this interest, there are substantial public policy voids in the San Francisco Bay Area with respect to earthquake-resistive construction and its relationships to earthquake geologic hazards such as faults, ground with poor bearing capacity, and potential landslide areas.[1]

The 1964 Alaskan earthquake emphasized the fact that extensive damage can occur even in sparsely populated areas. It also showed that modern cities can be vulnerable. A number of local and federal government agencies took a major role in the redevelopment and rehabilitation of the 1964 Alaskan earthquake disaster areas. Many of these local and federal agencies were involved in this type of activity for the first time. Others have expanded their participation. Private organizations with diverse backgrounds, such as the Red Cross and the insurance industry, were also involved in the aftermath of the 1964 Alaskan earthquake. Federal government policies formed after the Alaskan disaster have set trends that, in one form or another, will affect many levels of governmental operation, and will influence the roles of private organizations in seismic disasters within the Bay Area, as well as the United States as a whole. Present Bay Area policies must be reviewed, revised, and extended where necessary. As a first step, it is important to understand and to evaluate the earthquake hazard in the San Francisco Bay Area so that public policy can be better formulated to respond to this danger. Consequently, a substantial portion of this monograph is directed towards an understanding of the local earthquake hazard.

The extent of the *post-disaster* assistance, and the involvement of federal, state and local governments will, of course, largely depend on the public's reactions to the loss of life and to the amount of property damage. The effectiveness of the governmental response, however, may be greatly improved by *pre-disaster* planning. Such planning of public

---

[1] For the purposes of this study, the San Francisco Bay Area is defined as those counties having shorelines on the Bay: Alameda, Contra Costa, Marin, Napa, San Francisco, San Mateo, Santa Clara, Solano, and Sonoma counties.

1

policy has two distinct components, which can be studied separately:

1. Policy with respect to the planning and development of earthquake protection for a community or metropolitan area, prior to an earthquake disaster.

2. Policy with respect to the emergency operations during and immediately after a disaster, and subsequent post-earthquake planning and reconstruction.

Both of the foregoing components have received increased attention in recent years. For example, in May of 1966 a national symposium on emergency operations was held in Santa Monica, California. It provided a multidisciplinary forum for the discussion of all types of post-disaster emergency operations conducted by federal, state and local governments, as well as by other organizations.

A second important example was the earthquake seminar held in San Francisco on June 13-14, 1967, sponsored by the U. S. Office of Emergency Planning. This seminar was intended "to stimulate thinking about the problems that might face organizations having disaster responsibilities should a major earthquake occur" in the Bay Area. The resulting *Report of the Earthquake Seminar* was published by the U. S. Office of Emergency Planning (September 1967) and is worth careful attention.

This Lane monograph, however, directs attention towards the public policy aspects of *pre*-earthquake planning, which can minimize the effects of a disaster. In other words, this is to be a discussion of the steps that should be taken to assure maximum feasible protection against life hazard, and reduction of potential property damage to optimum levels. Public policy towards pre-disaster planning can and should differ greatly from region to region, in order to reflect the varying probabilities of a disastrous earthquake occurring. It should also reflect the extent and quality of the earthquake resistance in existing structures in a region, as well as the special geological hazards, such as faults, unconsolidated materials (such as Bay mud), and earthquake-induced landslide potential.

Present earthquake engineering techniques, when conservatively and intelligently applied, can make new construction adequately safe. In most cases they can substantially reduce property damage. In the near future it may be possible to develop techniques which reduce the earthquake damage potential, for all classes of new construction, sufficiently so that a large earthquake will be an expensive nuisance but not a financial disaster. Unfortunately, it probably will not be economically feasible to apply these new techniques to the collapse-hazard types of construction built years ago.

Other problems relate to the permissible degree of experimentation: (1) with the use of new structural materials for low as well as high-rise buildings, (2) with the development of fills over poor ground conditions, such as Bay muds, for building construction, and (3) with reductions in the safety factor due to a presumably better understanding and control of building materials. There can be no progress without experimentation or venture. But experiments and new ventures are not necessarily safe. Buildings that embodied some of the most modern design and construction techniques suffered collapse or serious damage during the 1964 Alaskan shock.

The following three sections of this monograph will examine pre-earthquake disaster planning. In each instance, emphasis will be placed on hazard-planning needs, and the discussion will be organized as follows:

Frequency of damaging Bay Area earthquakes.

Geologic hazards such as active faults, structurally poor ground, and earthquake-induced landslides.

Expected earthquake performance of existing and new buildings and other structures.

Definitions and Discussion of Terms

Any evaluation of the earthquake hazard must be based on an understanding of fundamentals of the subject. In this case, the subject matter is rather technical and involves several disciplines. Consequently, for the nontechnical reader's convenience, the following seismological and geological terms are defined and discussed in Appendix A. The terms are listed here in the order of their appearance in Appendix A, pp. 65–72.

Fault	Field epicenter
Fault zone	Fault dip
Fault trace	Epicentral distance
Active fault	Intensity
Dead (inactive) fault	Isoseismal line
Focus	Isoseismal map
Epicenter	Magnitude
Instrumental epicenter	Tsunami (seismic sea wave)

Frequency of Damaging Bay Area Earthquakes

As a first step towards formulating public policy, it is necessary to evaluate the potential frequency of damaging earthquakes in the San Francisco Bay Area. Strictly speaking, it is not now possible to predict earthquakes accurately as to time, place and severity. Prediction is, however, a distinct future possibility. The federal government is both proposing and receiving elaborate plans that may someday produce a well-founded method for earthquake prediction.

The best practical approach to earthquake prediction to date is to study the historic seismic activity in a region, to temper this information with geologic knowledge and geodetic survey data, and then to judge the future earthquake potential, using all of these data. In the Bay Area the founding of the first mission in 1776 limits the continuous historic record to under 200 years. Quite possibly the earthquakes in October 1800, which caused cracks in the ground near the Pajaro River, were also felt in the San Francisco Bay Area. But the known non-instrumental historic record for the San Francisco Bay Area begins on June 21, 1808 with the statement, "There were twenty-one shocks at the Presidio of San Francisco" from June 21 to July 17 of that year.[2]

One study of the seismic history of Alameda, Contra Costa, Marin, San Francisco, San Mateo and Santa Clara counties made for the author showed that about 12 damaging earthquakes have occurred per century during the brief historical record. The term "damaging earthquake" means that damage occurred in at least one location; by no means does it imply that the shock was necessarily felt through the entire San Francisco Bay Area. The 12 earthquakes per century were not evenly spaced in time, strength, or geography. Nor is it easy to determine a reasonable periodicity from a review of all recent damaging earthquakes centered in the Bay Area and adjoining counties (see Table 1).

Figure 1 shows the time distribution of damaging earthquakes in the San Francisco Bay Area, plus those in adjacent counties.[3] The fact that the literate population in the San Francisco Bay Area and adjoining counties was sparse prior to 1849 could have left several strong earthquakes unrecorded in outlying regions. The information presented in

---

[2] S. D. Townley and M. W. Allen, "Descriptive Catalog of Earthquakes of the Pacific Coast of the United States 1769 to 1928," *Bulletin of the Seismological Society of America* 29:22, 1939.

[3] Appendix B presents a brief earthquake history of the San Francisco Bay and Monterey Bay regions.

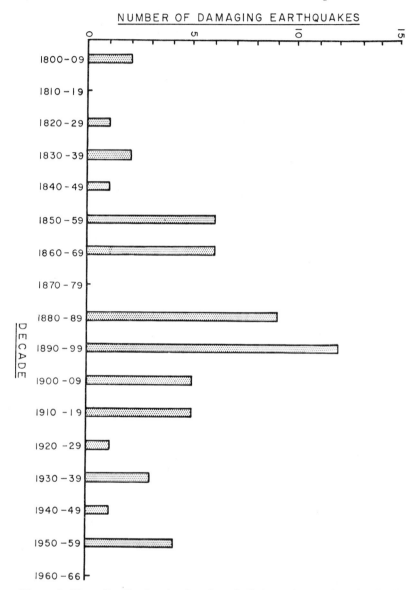

Figure 1. Time distribution, by decades, of all damaging earthquakes in the Bay Area and adjoining counties. Based on Don Tocher's "Seismic History of San Francisco Region," in *San Francisco Earthquakes of March 1957*, Gordon B. Oakeshott ed., California Div. of Mines Special Report 57 (1959), 39–48.

TABLE 1
RECENT BAY AREA EARTHQUAKES

Date	Location	Richter Magnitude
April 25, 1954	Watsonville	5.3
September 4, 1955	San Jose	5.8
October 23, 1955	Walnut Creek	5.4
March 22, 1957	San Francisco (Daly City)	5.3
September 14, 1963	Chittenden	5.4

Figure 1 indicates an increasing seismicity prior to the San Francisco 1906 shock. There is no similar evidence of increasing seismicity today. At present, data from compilations such as that shown in Figure 1 can only indicate that the region is earthquake active.

It is more pertinent to study the occurrence of *great* earthquakes than of the more frequent moderate shocks, because the great earthquake defines the full scope of seismic risk. The historical record has five entries generally accepted to be the largest known shocks in the Bay Area. These are as follows:

1. June 10, 1836, on the Hayward fault. At 7:30 A.M., cracks and fissures opened up along this fault from San Pablo to Mission San Jose.

2. June, 1838, probably on the San Andreas fault. A fissure was described as extending from near San Francisco to near Santa Clara.

3. October 8, 1865, probably on the San Andreas fault. Considerable damage occurred in San Francisco. The earthquake presumably had its epicenter on the San Andreas fault in the Santa Cruz Mountains.

4. October 21, 1868, on the Hayward fault. At 7:53 A.M. cracks and fissures from this earthquake formed from about San Leandro to about Warm Springs. Very heavy damage occurred in the town of Hayward, and there was also extensive damage in sections of San Francisco.

5. April 18, 1906, on the San Andreas fault. At 5:13 A.M., the well-known San Francisco shock occurred. Faulting extended from southern Humboldt County to near San Juan Bautista in San Benito County.

Although all of these earthquakes were undoubtedly of different Richter magnitudes, they all appear to have been of sufficient size to approach or equal the maximum probable future earthquake intensities to be expected in at least major sections of the San Francisco Bay Area. Instrumental data do not exist for the pre-1906 shocks, and even the historical data are meager for the 1836 and 1838 shocks.

Obviously the time distribution of these major earthquakes is not at all uniform. This phenomenon has also been noted elsewhere in the world on a larger time scale. For example, the time distribution of Japanese earthquakes since 684 A.D. shows three periods of great seismic activity, with periods of lesser activity between. This uneven time distribution poses an additional unknown in the attempts to estimate earthquake frequency based on the historical record.

The foregoing tabulation of largest Bay Area earthquakes shows that these earthquakes are related to known major geologically active faults. In general, in the western United States, large earthquakes with large surface ruptures can be related to clearly defined geologic faults. Geologists cannot guarantee that there are no major active faults under the Bay, except possibly for the northerly extensions of the Hayward and Calaveras faults. In addition, gravity studies indicate two northerly trending faults in the southern part of the Bay, but there appear to have been no damaging historic earthquakes related to them. Further, data from seismic instruments show that many small earthquakes in the Bay Area do not necessarily occur on known faults (Figure 2.)

The most geologically recent movements on the principal active faults in the Bay Area have been of the strike-slip type—i.e., the ground surface on one side moves horizontally with respect to the other—with only small vertical components. Similar ground movements can be expected in the future. Based on this reasoning, some geologists believe that the ratio of vertical to horizontal fault displacements on the San Andreas fault system may be in the order of 1:10 or 1:20, making a 1 foot to 2 foot downdrop or uplift a reasonable maximum for a great earthquake. Thus it is not likely that an otherwise stable shoreline will disappear beneath the Bay due to the drop or rise of bedrock over thousands of square miles, such as occurred in Chile in 1960 and in Alaska in 1964.

Returning to the problem of earthquake frequency, since accurate surveys were first conducted in 1868, precise triangulation by the U.S. Coast and Geodetic Survey has shown repeatedly that the earth's surface in the San Francisco Bay Area is being measurably strained. For example, the Farallon Islands west of the Golden Gate are moving northwesterly with respect to Mt. Diablo in Contra Costa County. The situation is similar wherever points on opposite sides of the San Andreas fault are measured, namely, locations on the west side are moving northerly with respect to those on the east side of this fault.

It is a commonly held theory that, when the strains within the earth's crust become too great, a rupture will take place. A sudden rupture (faulting) generates the seismic waves that define an earthquake. These measured accumulating strains in the earth's crust in the San Francisco Bay Area have allowed earthquake prediction calculations to be made.

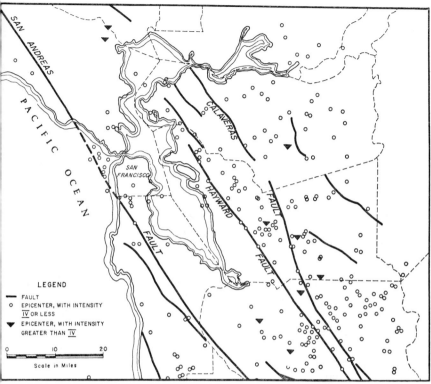

Figure 2. Map of San Francisco Bay Area showing principal active faults (heavy black lines) and the instrumental epicenters of earthquakes that occurred during the periods of 1930–41 and 1941–48. From Perry Byerly's "History of Earthquakes in the San Francisco Bay Area," in *Geologic Guidebook of the San Francisco Bay Counties*, California Div. of Mines Bulletin 154 (1951).

These calculations are based on the average of the largest fault displacements in the 1906 earthquake divided by the average rate of measured accumulating strain. This number comes to a reasonable figure of 60 to 75 or more years between major or great earthquakes, depending upon the interpretation given to the data.

With the very recent discovery of fault creep from San Pablo to Fremont on the Hayward fault, however, these earthquake prediction calculations are now even more open to question. It is now known that the Hayward fault slipped, or faulted, for about half a foot in the area of the City of Fremont, sometime between 1949 and 1957, without a recorded earthquake. No movement is now being observed. Other sections of the Hayward fault are performing differently. For example, movements are currently damaging the University of California stadium in Berkeley.[4] We can conclude that the strains in the Bay Area are continuing to accumulate, although part of them are probably being released by fault slippage. It is reasonable to assume that both the large historic earthquakes and the recent fault slippage represent typical characteristics of the Hayward fault, and that future strong earthquakes are therefore to be expected on this fault.

The foregoing discussion is a brief overview of the problems of predicting earthquakes in the San Francisco Bay Area. On the basis of the historical record, and in view of the accumulating strains, *for planning purposes* it is reasonable to anticipate a major or great earthquake in the San Francisco Bay Area once every 60 to 100 years.

The San Francisco 1906 shock is the largest Bay Area earthquake for which detailed information is available. It is fair to ask whether this is the largest credible earthquake to be expected in the future. The question has been answered reasonably well by seismologists on the basis of seismographic records from which earthquake magnitudes have been determined.[5] The largest earthquakes in the world, recorded by seismographs for over half a century, have not been much greater in magnitude than the 1906 San Francisco shock. Therefore the forces generated by the 1906 San Francisco earthquake appear to be a reasonable upper limit. The *duration* of the damaging intensities, however, may be substantially longer than that experienced in 1906, which is estimated to have been from 40 to possibly 60 seconds. Experience from the 1964 Alaskan earthquake showed that the duration of damaging intensities in Anchorage was probably three times as long as that in San Francisco's 1906 earthquake.

In recapitulation, the frequency of major or great earthquakes strongly affecting at least large sections of the San Francisco Bay Area, may reasonably be assumed to be from 60 to 100 years, for *planning* purposes. (These figures should *not* be used for prediction purposes.) Further, the forces released by the 1906 San Francisco shock appear to be a reasonable maximum for future great shocks, but the duration could be substantially longer than that of 1906. Finally, all sections of the Bay Area can have earthquakes, but the largest ones will probably be associated with the well-known active faults.

---

[4] Further information may be obtained from the several papers on the subject in the *Bulletin of the Seismological Society of America* 56:257–323, 1966.

[5] The magnitude of an earthquake is a measure of the earthquake's size; the numerical value of the magnitude is related to the earthquake's energy.

Geologic Hazards

The discussion of geologic hazards is directed towards the application of certain excellent geologic studies related to earthquakes in the Bay Area, which have become available in recent years. Bay Area geology, per se, is not within the scope of this discussion.[6] The broad application of the results of geologic mapping and other geologic research to planning in the Bay Area requires an interdisciplinary approach involving civil engineering and geology. Unfortunately, such studies are rare, and this monograph will only scratch the surface.

In the discussion that follows, each earthquake-related geologic hazard will be examined from a civil engineering viewpoint, and the conclusions will be given from an engineering planning standpoint.

Geologic Faults

Earthquake-active geologic faults in the Bay Area have been mapped in considerable detail by the U. S. Geological Survey, and at scales suitable for general planning studies. The *Miscellaneous Geological Investigations Map I-522,* "Approximate location of fault traces and historic surface ruptures within the Hayward fault zone between San Pablo and Warm Springs, California" by Dorothy H. Radbruch (1967) is one such example. A map of a portion of the San Andreas fault, where it crosses the heavily populated sections of the San Francisco Bay Area, was compiled by J. Schlocker, E. H. Pampeyan, and M. G. Bonilla (1965) and is also available in the USGS open file report "Approximate trace of the main surface rupture in the San Andreas fault zone between Pacifica and the vicinity of Saratoga, California, formed during the earthquake of April 18, 1906." Finally, reference can also be made to "Most conspicuous strands of the San Andreas and related faults, Southwestern Marin County" by Robert D. Brown, Jr. (1967). This is also a USGS open file report. In summary, basic mapping data are now available for city planning in Bay Area fault zones.

The Engineering Significance of Faults

Before considering the planning of urban development in and around active earthquake faults, however, it is important to understand their civil and structural engineering significance. It is generally held that

---

[6] Persons wishing to study geologic literature of the Bay Area should investigate the resources of the California Division of Mines and Geology, Ferry Bldg., San Francisco. The U.S. Geological Survey's Public Inquiries Office in San Francisco is also an important source of information.

sudden fault movement is the cause of earthquakes. The accumulated strains in the earth, when suddenly released along a fault, are the sources of seismic energy. The energy from the released strains travels through the earth in the form of seismic waves; it is this energy that causes the vibrational damage to buildings. Interestingly, some competent scientific opinion in countries such as Japan and New Zealand holds that faulting is a product of and not the primary cause of earthquakes. In any event, the surface ruptures along a fault can be disastrous to water lines, dams, and other man-made structures astride the fault rupture. In California, surface faulting often accompanies moderate as well as large earthquakes. As much as six inches of surface faulting has been measured in several small earthquakes.

The actual fault break in an earthquake may be confined to a very narrow width. The 1906 San Francisco faulting had the appearance of a furrow turned by a plow, although the horizontal fault displacement reached as much as 21 feet. On the other hand, the width of the disturbed *zone* may vary considerably, and can amount to hundreds of feet for certain types of faulting. Width depends on four variables: (1) attitude of the angle of the fault plane with respect to the ground surface, (2) the amount of displacement, (3) the direction of movement, and (4) the near-surface geologic conditions. An excellent compilation of these variables, based on earthquake experience, may be found in "Historic surface faulting in continental United States and adjacent parts of Mexico," M. G. Bonilla, USGS open file report, 1967.

Obviously, the services of competent and experienced geologists are mandatory for estimating the probable width of the disturbed zone in which future movements on any particular fault may occur. The fault zone of a major fault may be, and usually is, much wider than the actual breakage in a single earthquake. Such a zone often consists of a series of approximately parallel bands containing shattered and broken rock and gouge material (clay-like powdered rock). Both the San Andreas and the Hayward faults have fault zones one-half to one mile wide along certain portions of their length.

Since the ground ruptures—individual breaks caused by single earthquakes—on the San Andreas and Hayward faults probably have occupied a width of usually not more than a few feet, it is reasonable to infer that the half-mile wide fault zones were formed by numerous instances of earthquake faulting occurring over a long period of geologic time. The planes, or very narrow bands of slippage represent the weakest sections of the fault zone. It follows, then, that these slippage planes or bands are the most likely places for future earthquake faulting, considering the lifetime of a man-made structure. Over millions of years, however, numerous exceptions must have occurred to have created the wide fault zone.

GRADES OF RISK

Based on the foregoing reasoning, it is possible to suggest three grades of risk—ranked from lowest to highest—with respect to surface faulting:

Grade 1: Outside of the fault zone.

Grade 2: Within the broad fault zone, other than on the traces of faulting listed for Grade 3.

Grade 3: On the trace of the faulting which occurred in the last earthquake, and on the trace of fault creep. Also on the trace of other ruptures not significantly modified by erosion.

Figure 2 is a generalized map of the San Francisco Bay Area showing the principal geologic faults from a seismic hazard standpoint. As has been mentioned, the San Andreas fault has been associated with three major earthquakes: 1838, 1865, and 1906. The Hayward fault has been associated with two major earthquakes: 1836 and 1868. Both faults are in heavily populated areas. Any planning to reduce risks should certainly give these two faults the highest priority, and attention probably should also be given to the Calaveras fault.

Present city planning provisions and building ordinances in and adjacent to the Hayward and San Andreas fault zones usually ignore the possibility of surface faulting. In recent years individual architects and engineers have sometimes been able to persuade owners to build elsewhere—only to have the fault site built upon by others who may be unaware of the hazard. At present there are no soundly established criteria to guide local building departments and planning agencies in these matters. Apparently the first city to recognize the hazard and attempt to do something about it was Fremont, where the building department, since its inception in 1957, has been requiring a fault-location study before issuing a building permit. Despite the lack of precise fault-zone land-use designation and building code criteria, developers have been encouraged not to locate buildings and structures of significance on known or suspected fault traces. Rather, they have been encouraged to utilize those areas for accessory landscaping and recreational features, vehicle parking and similar low-value and low-density uses.

A second example of public awareness of the need for planning in and near fault zones may be seen in the work being conducted by the Geologic Hazards Committee, appointed by the adjoining towns of Woodside and Portola Valley. The San Andreas fault lies within the city limits of both of these San Francisco Peninsula communities, and the location of the trace of the 1906 faulting has been well identified. At the time the first draft of this was written (December, 1967), the Geologic Hazards Committee had recommended that:

1. Both cities retain an engineering geologist on a continuing basis to advise on matters relating to geologic hazards, including relevance to city ordinances.

2. All local ordinances and regulations bearing on geologic hazards be revised where necessary so as to minimize potential losses from these hazards.

3. A geologic hazards map of the towns be compiled as a continuing guide to planning and development.

In other cities, major structures have been built recently in the Hayward and San Andreas fault zones. For example, a telephone building, having underground trunk lines, has been built in the Hayward fault zone. At this writing the San Francisco Bay Area Rapid Transit District is constructing a tunnel through the Hayward fault zone, although it is now well known that the Hayward fault has slipped (fault creep) in recent years. It is reasonable to expect a major earthquake, with substantial fault displacement, through the BART tunnel within its lifetime.

Freeways run along portions of the San Andreas and Hayward faults. A major fault displacement along a freeway probably would cause overpasses to collapse, thereby causing more serious interference with emergency vehicular movements than would be true of city streets without overpasses. Housing projects have covered large sections of the fault zones in recent years, and the construction has proceeded virtually without considering the possible effects of fault displacements.

FAULT-ZONE PLANNING

The present situation has undoubtedly resulted in part from the lack of adequate fault-zone planning and construction criteria. Legal uncertainties have also contributed. Thus, in years gone by, the possible threat of legal action by property owners has reportedly kept some geologists who were familiar with the location of the Hayward fault from publishing their knowledge in detail. But blame lies with no one group.

The U. S. Geological Survey's recent fault maps show these previously unpublished data, as well as the results of other recent USGS field work. With this information now in the public domain, it is appropriate to consider the design criteria for planning efforts in and near fault zones. This planning effort should have a two-fold approach: (1) it should guide *future* construction in and across fault zones, and (2) it should also include policies with respect to *existing* construction in and across fault zones. To implement these two approaches, the USGS fault maps should be converted into planning maps which show the location and width of the broad fault zone, as well as recent rupture traces.

It will not be easy to establish this planning map and related design criteria. It may not even be possible, given the present state of the art. But the *attempt* should be made, requiring group action by government geologists, along with those in private practice. The consultant group must also include civil and structural engineers, soils engineers, seismologists, and city planners, in order to give a suitable balance to the results. The planning map will have to be a living document, as new geologic information will constantly change the zone boundaries. In order to keep the map and other design criteria current, the consultants must be a continuing body working within a duly constituted governmental agency.

The planning map would not, however, be a *hazard* map, because only a detailed site investigation can finally determine the actual degree of hazard. But the planning map would constantly be revised to reflect the results of detailed site investigations made in conjunction with planned construction.

The term "fault" tends to create an exaggerated fear in the public's mind. There is, of course, ample reason to believe that—*provided all other factors are equal*—the greater the distance separating a given structure from an active fault, the less the damage that is to be expected when a major earthquake occurs on the fault. But "all other factors" are rarely equal. Consider the cases shown in Figure 3, which is based on the simplified assumption that an earthquake's energy can be represented as being concentrated in a relatively small volume. Structure "B" in Figure 3 (top) is only slightly farther from the energy source than is structure "A." On this simplified basis the intensity at "B" should be only little less than at "A," based on the respective distances from the energy source. And in Figure 3 (bottom), the structure at "C" could receive about the same amount of seismic energy as the structure at "A," under the given idealized conditions, although "C" is much farther from the trace of the fault.

RISK-GRADE ZONES AND DESIGN CRITERIA

Detailed criteria regarding construction should be developed after the establishment of risk zones in and around a fault. As a starting point for discussion, the following are suggested as reasonable guidelines for new construction, unless special safety features described elsewhere in this study are embodied in the planning, design, and construction. Grades are numbered 3, 2, and 1, with the highest number denoting areas of greatest hazard.[7]

Grade 3: On the trace of the last known faulting, or the trace of other ruptures not significantly modified by erosion. Across the trace of fault creep.

No new structure should be built across the trace of the last known rupture, if it has not been specifically designed to accommodate the maximum probable displacement to be expected in the maximum probable earthquake. Normally, buildings could not be constructed economically under these circumstances. Pipelines and roadways, however, could be constructed economically, since they can be designed to accommodate large lateral offsets without significant loss of function.

Obviously, it will be impossible to locate accurately the trace of the most recent ruptures on extensive sections of the faults. Thus it will be necessary to establish criteria stating the minimum distance from the *probable* fault trace that a structure can be built. This distance probably will vary, depending upon local conditions.

Piping and other underground facilities for vital functions must be valved adequately or otherwise designed for rapid shutoff, and must be accessible for emergency repairs. As an alternative, it is reasonable to expect that facilities for gas lines, water lines, and telephone cables can be designed to accommodate substantial fault displacements. Such construction can easily be done for facilities above grade level, but may entail substantial costs for facilities below grade level.

Freeway grade separation structures must be designed to accommodate anticipated displacements. Possibly structures of this type should be eliminated from Grade 3 areas altogether.

Long-range planning should zone Grade 3 areas for parks, golf courses, roadways and similar usages wherever reasonable. All construction should be minimized in this risk zone.

Grade 2: In the fault zone, but not across the traces of the last known rupture, or other ruptures not significantly modified by erosion.[8]

It seems reasonable that new building construction might be limited to one- and possibly two-story wood frame dwellings, and to one-story wood frame mercantile and office buildings not exceeding 7,500 square feet in area, unless special design features are provided. Zoning re-

---

[7] These risk grades are the same as those outlined above, p. 13.

[8] The criteria for Grade 2 zoning will be difficult to apply, and may not be appropriate, in areas covered by deep alluvial soils.

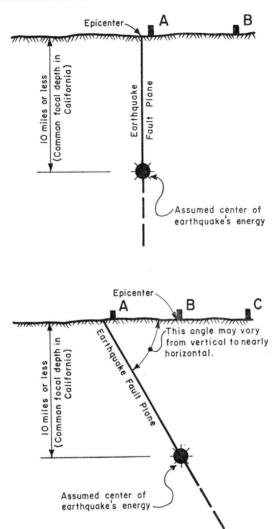

Figure 3. Two idealized earthquake faults. See text for discussion of relationships between surface intensity and trace of the fault.

quirements specifying large lot sizes would be desirable, in order to reduce the population density. In the unlikely event that the next fault breakage does not follow the last rupture, the above mentioned wood frame construction could be torn asunder. Even so, the hazard to life would be limited; life safety is quite a different thing from property

damage in wood frame dwelling construction. Experience has demonstrated that wood frame dwelling construction, with its many partitions,
will hang together even when severely damaged. Occupants probably
will survive even when the wood frame dwelling is a total loss, having
been torn apart by faulting. This might not be equally true for wood
frame mercantile structures, which normally have few partitions.

Warehouses, storage areas, and similar minimum population density
occupancies might be allowed, but their offices should be no larger than
that necessary to accommodate these occupancies. Appropriate special
design features should be required.

Grade 1: Not in the fault zone.

No restrictions. (Grade 1 risk areas, even when very close to the fault
breakage, probably represent no major increase in risk, despite their
proximity. Damage as a result of ground *vibration,* however, is quite
different from damage as a result of fault displacement.)

Intensities in large earthquakes, as typified by damage to man-made
structures, may be an approximately constant factor for at least a mile
or two from the surface expression of the fault, provided all other
factors are equal. (This is not to say that the ground *motions* are the
same at the fault as those a mile or two from the fault.) Experience has
also shown that buildings near the fault breakage will not necessarily
be destroyed. Figure 4 is a classic photograph of a house adjacent to the
San Andreas fault. The 1906 faulting moved the house, as well as all
of the land, 15 feet 9 inches to the right, from the photographer's viewpoint, yet the house remained standing. Figure 5 illustrates an even
more extreme case: a small wood frame structure is shown on the Dixie
Valley (Nevada) fault, after the earthquake of December 21, 1954. This
well-built frame structure survived without structural damage. Indeed,
a cup sitting on a shelf remained on the shelf. And the 1959 Hebgen
Lake shock in Montana clearly showed that the earthquake intensity,
as observed in building damage adjacent to the fault, was not noticeably different from that found in similar buildings several miles from
the fault. Again, this is not to say that the ground motions were the
same at each location, but that the *effects* of the motions were not sufficiently different to be discernible in building damage.

Existing construction in fault zones presents a very different problem
from that of new construction. It is obviously not feasible to tear out
the old construction and rebuild to meet improved standards each time
an additional safety improvement is developed. On the other hand, a
permissive attitude does not reduce the hazard. Judgment governing
the disposition of old construction has generally been very lenient in

Figure 4. House adjacent to San Andreas fault. The center lines of the path and the house steps (see the two arrows) were coincident before the 1906 San Francisco earthquake. Afterwards the offset was 15 feet and 9 inches, as shown in this photo. The fault trace is identified by the heavy broken line. Location is Skinner's ranch in Marin County. Plate 38B, *The California Earthquake of April 18, 1906,* Report of the [Calif.] State Earthquake Investigation Commission (Washington, D.C.: Carnegie Institution of Washington, 1908–10).

Figure 5. Undamaged wood frame structure in rupture zone of the 1954 Dixie Valley (Nevada) earthquake.—*Karl V. Steinbrugge photo.*

the United States. Therefore, in the light of today's attitudes towards retroactive building construction laws, one politically reasonable compromise policy might be to allow present construction to remain, *except for high-population-density structures and vital public structures.* Grades 2 and 3 earthquake fault risk areas containing high population density structures—such as apartment houses and other structures with occupant loads of possibly 50 or more, theaters and other places of public assembly—as well as public structures, such as city halls, fire stations and schools, should be redeveloped into usages compatible with the hazard. Obviously, careful planning is required because this will be costly to the city and disruptive to the community. (This also strongly emphasizes the need for intelligent planning *in areas that are not now heavily populated,* such as the San Andreas fault zone of western Marin County.)

The foregoing recommendations, especially those for new construction in presently undeveloped areas, can be implemented feasibly from an economic standpoint. One outstanding example is provided by a large planned community in Santa Clara County south of San Jose, containing a section of the Hayward-Calaveras fault zone, which anticipates a population of 100,000 within 20 years. The designers of the development have considered this fault problem in detail. Their consultants, Woodward-Clyde-Sherard and Associates, recommended that the active fault zones be utilized for parks, roadways, general open spaces and other similar usages. Fewer land use restrictions would be imposed on less hazardous areas. This is the first example of large-scale planning of its type known to the author. It represents a commendable effort in promoting the public welfare and safety.

Structurally Poor Ground

Structurally poor ground (such as San Francisco Bay muds and the deep alluvial soils near San Jose and in Santa Rosa) has been associated with intensified earthquake damage. Significant portions of San Francisco Bay have been filled, and additional large fills have been proposed. At this writing, the State of California's San Francisco Bay Conservation and Development Commission (BCDC) is preparing a plan for the conservation of San Francisco Bay and the development of its shoreline. This plan is to be submitted to the Governor and the Legislature in 1969. While the plan is being prepared, BCDC controls all filling and dredging in the Bay through a permit procedure. It is apparent that any long-range plan for the development of the Bay's shoreline must consider the seismic risk to life and property on the proposed fills. Accordingly, earthquake hazard is one of the criteria on which BCDC is basing its planning recommendations.[9]

EARTHQUAKE EFFECTS ON BUILDINGS ON BAY FILLS

Much of the criticism directed against the development of and construction on San Francisco Bay fills is based on their past performance in large earthquakes. Furthermore, some fills have performed poorly during earthquakes elsewhere throughout the world. Thus it is of value to review critically and in detail the historical record for the Bay Area.

There are insufficient data on the 1836 and 1838 earthquakes to establish firm conclusions, but the 1865, 1868, and 1906 shocks have been described in varying but adequate detail. San Francisco, being the only city having significant portions of its land area on man-made fills at the time of these earthquakes, was the location of most of the property damage related to such fills. It is appropriate to point out that in Santa Rosa there was also intensified 1906 earthquake damage to buildings located on the deep naturally deposited alluvial soils. Thus, naturally deposited soils can be as hazardous as the poorest man-made fill. The available data have been well summarized in Andrew C. Lawson's report of the (California) State Earthquake Investigation Commission, *The California Earthquake of April 18, 1906* (Washington, D.C.: Carnegie Institution of Washington, 1908–10, 2 volumes and atlas), henceforth referred to as *Commission Report*.

The earthquake of October 8, 1865. The earthquake of October 8, 1865 apparently was centered in the Santa Cruz Mountains. The *Commission Report* states on page 449 of vol. 1:

On the marshy lands in the vicinity of Howard and Seventh Streets the ground was heaved in some places and sank in others. Lamp-posts were thrown out of perpendicular, gaspipes were broken, etc.

The earthquare of October 21, 1868. This earthquake on the Hayward fault also caused damage in San Francisco. The *Commission Report* states on pages 436–37 of vol. 1:

The portion of the city which suffered most was that part of the business district, embracing about 200 acres, built on 'made ground'; that is, the ground made by filling in the cove of Yerba Buena. The bottom of this cove was a

---

[9] BCDC has released three closely related reports dealing with structurally poor ground in the San Francisco Bay Area. They are as follows: "Seismic Risk to Buildings and Structures on Filled Lands in San Francisco Bay," by Karl V. Steinbrugge; "Seismic Problems in the Use of Fills in San Francisco Bay," by H. Bolton Seed; and "Bay Mud Developments and Related Structural Foundations," by Charles H. Lee and Michael Praszker. These three reports, in expanded form, are also to be published by the California Division of Mines and Geology. They are currently in press.

soft mud varying from 10 to 80 feet in depth, and the material used to fill it was largely 'dump' refuse, much of which is organic and hence perishable. Many of the buildings of that period were built flat on this filled mud, without piling, and before the land had had time to become firm . . . .

At the corner of First and Market Streets, the ground opened in a fissure several inches wide. At other places the ground opened and water was forced above the surface. At Fremont and Mission Streets the ground opened in many places. The general course of damage in the city was along the irregular line of 'made land,' or low alluvial soil, where it met the hard or rocky base beneath it . . . .

The earthquake of April 18, 1906. The 1906 earthquake on the San Andreas fault has been studied in great detail by many authorities. Probably the most thorough and generally accepted study of the intensity and the relationship of damage to ground conditions in San Francisco was made by H. O. Wood. The article was entitled "Isoseismals: Distribution of Apparent Intensity in San Francisco," and was published in the *Commission Report,* vol. 1, pp. 220–241. It is useful to quote some of the major points made in this study:

About the Ferry Building, at the foot of Market Street, is a district of 'made' land shown on map [See Figure 6 of this monograph] in which high intensity was manifested. Here buildings of all sorts were crowded close together. Wooden buildings, 1 story to 3 stories high, with brick or stonework fronts, were interspersed among ordinary brick buildings from 2 to 6 or 8 stories in height. Mingled with these was a considerable number of modern, class A, office buildings. . . . After the fire had past, standing walls revealed ugly, sinuous cracks, in rudely parallel systems, which were not due to fire nor to dynamite. Masonry blocks in the walls of excellent modern buildings were broken as by a blow. Rivets were sheared off in parts of the framework of steel structures, and tension rods in such frames were badly stretched. . . . In spots the streets sank bodily, certainly as much as 2 feet, probably more. Accompanying this depression, concrete basement floors were broken and arched, as if to compensate for it. The surface of the ground was deformed into waves and small open fissures were formed especially close to the wharves. Buildings on the water side, along East Street, generally slumped seaward, in some cases as much as 2 feet. The damage was greatest close to the water's edge, growing less as the solid land was approached, gradually at first, then more rapidly. (p. 233)

It is important to recognize that, despite the great intensity manifested near the water-front, first-class modern buildings, such as the Ferry Building, built on deep piling or grillage foundations, were not imperiled by injuries to their walls or framework. Some rivets were sheared off; some tension rods were stretched; an occasional girder was dislodged, and cracks were formed here and there in the brick and stone walls. Large financial loss was unquestionably occasioned, but buildings of this type were not in serious danger of collapse nor of being toppled over, either during or after the shock. (p. 235)

Wood concluded:

This investigation has clearly demonstrated that the amount of damage produced by the earthquake of April 18 in different parts of the city and county of San Francisco depended chiefly upon the geological character of the ground. Where the surface was of solid rock, the shock produced little damage; whereas upon made land great violence was manifested. (p. 241)

Figure 6 shows, in modified form, the earthquake intensities of the 1906 shock, as determined by H. O. Wood for a portion of San Francisco. Intensity obviously varied greatly within short distances, and the differences correlate with geological variations.

A critical reading of the reports of the 1906 earthquake also reveals statements such as these:

Buildings erected upon good foundations withstood the ordeal well, even when the streets around them were depressed and fissured. (*Commission Report*, p. 236)

Foundations did not suffer at all, no instances of damage having come to hand. ("The Effects of the San Francisco Earthquake of April 18, 1906 on Engineering Constructions," in *Trans. Am. Soc. Civil Engineers* 59:235, 1907)

The context in which the foregoing statements appear suggests that the writers may have had in mind the taller fire-resistive buildings, although no specific qualifying statements were made.

The description of material, and of the natural marsh areas, leaves a strong impression that the "made ground" was of poor structural quality. For example, a most vivid description of poor ground in San Francisco was given by Hittell:

The peat in the marshes that had their heads near the site of the new city hall was strong enough to sustain a small house or a loaded wagon, though a man, by swinging himself from side to side, or by jumping upon it, could give it a perceptible shiver. There were weak places in it, however, and a cow which in searching for sweet pasture undertook to jump from one hard spot to what appeared to be another, made a mistake, for it gave way under her and a gentleman hunting nearby was surprised to see her go down, and still more to observe that she did not come up again.... Many ludicrous scenes occurred in filling up the swamps. When streets were first made the weight of sand pressed the peat down, so that the water stood where the surface was dry before. Sometimes the sand broke through, carrying down the peat under it, leaving nothing but water or thin mud near the surface. More than once a contractor had put on enough sand to raise the street to the official grade, and gave notice to the city engineer to inspect the work, but in the lapse of a day between the notice and inspection, the sand had sunk down six or eight feet; and when at last a permanent bottom had been reached, the heavy sand had crowded under the light peat at the sides of the street and lifted it up eight or ten feet above its original level ... so that houses ... were carried away from their original position and tilted....[10]

[10] John S. Hittell, *A History of the City of San Francisco* (San Francisco: A. L. Bancroft, 1878), pp. 433–434.

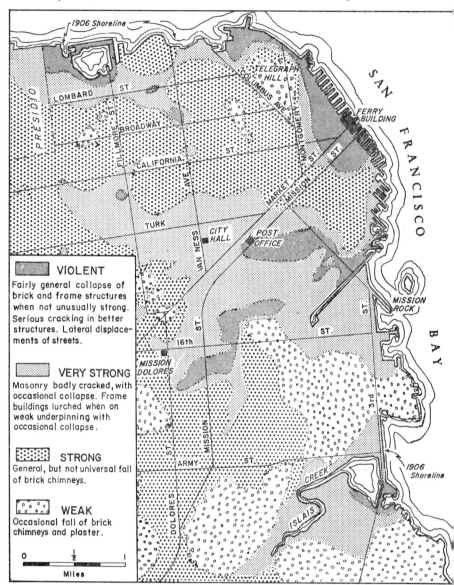

Figure 6. Map of a portion of San Francisco, showing apparent 1906 earthquake intensities. The San Andreas fault is located about 10 miles west of the Ferry Building. Note large variations in intensity for areas approximately the same distance from the fault. "Violent" intensities are associated with poorest ground areas. (This figure is simplified from Map 19 of the atlas to the *Commission Report*.)

Even if the foregoing description was considerably exaggerated, the collapse of buildings on such soils during an earthquake would not be unexpected. The historic record certainly shows that the seismic risk to buildings and other man-made structures is much greater on weak alluvium than on firmer ground. Studies of great earthquakes elsewhere throughout the world have usually, but not universally, given similar results. But Bay Area experience also shows that buildings on piling performed better as a class than did those on footings resting directly on the soil.

Recent advances. In recent years, and especially since World War II, the science and profession of soils engineering has greatly expanded its knowledge. This knowledge is being almost universally applied in the design of major structures in the Bay Area. Thus developers of housing tracts generally make extensive use of soils engineering data. Soils engineers are now able to give the architect and structural engineer vastly better information on the structural characteristics of soils, and their probable earthquake performance, than was available at the time of the large Bay Area earthquakes.

Because of the recency of these developments, however, there has been very little seismic experience with buildings on modern engineered fills. Only the moderate shock of March 22, 1957, can be cited. This earthquake, centered in Daly City, south of San Francisco, was investigated by the author and others in a study of "Damage to Buildings and Other Structures During the San Francisco Earthquake of March 22, 1957."[11] The following quotation summarizes their findings:

Cuts and fills exist throughout the Westlake Palisades tract, and some of the fills exceed 35 feet. All grading work was under the supervision of a qualified soils engineering firm. . . . Further, considerably greater cuts and fills of similar soils exist to the east of Skyline Boulevard and such occasional damage as was found was not related to the soils. We may conclude that the recompacted soil was not a significant factor in the damage. . . . (p. 81)

Although these fills were not placed over Bay mud or other compressible Bay soils, their performance certainly demonstrates that man-made fills, per se, can give quite satisfactory performance *in moderate* earthquakes. In contrast, slight damage at the San Francisco International Airport, about 10 miles southeast of the epicenter, was attributed to both differential settlements and horizontal vibratory forces. Almost all of these airport structures were built on piling.

[11] Karl V. Steinbrugge, Vincent R. Bush, and Edwin G. Zacher, in Gordon B. Oakeshott, ed., *San Francisco Earthquakes of March 1957,* California Div. of Mines, Special Report 57 (1959), pp. 73–106.

The Anchorage experience during the 1964 Alaskan earthquake is instructive. It appears that liquefaction of certain types of soils, under vibratory forces of long duration, caused the spectacular land movements involving many city blocks. While soil liquefaction was observed and described after the 1960 Chilean shock and other earthquakes, apparently it was not adequately studied until the 1964 Alaskan earthquake. This brings up the troublesome question of the seismic risk entailed by Bay fills that have been placed in recent years without benefit of this newer knowledge of the soil liquefaction problem. Restudy of these pre-1964 fills may disclose unsuspected hazards, but any resulting remedial action would involve the philosophically and politically troublesome question of retroactive building code provisions.

Soils engineering has developed quite rapidly in recent years, including the very recent accumulation of substantive knowledge on the potentially major hazard of soil liquefaction. However, there is still much to be learned from further study and research concerning the seismic risk on Bay fills, marsh lands, and other poorly consolidated materials. Thus, in view of the meager experience with modern Bay fills, laboratory and theoretical approaches must be fully utilized. These approaches are often employed with only the judgment of the practitioner extrapolating the results to reality.

It is general practice for soils engineers to give ground settlement figures (or differential settlement figures), often as a function of time, for structural engineers to use in the design of buildings to be located on poor ground. At this point economics must be weighed against seismic risk, as well as other factors. The present state of the art does not allow the formulation of a numerical equation relating economic factors to seismic risk without very substantial judgmental determinations. Consider two extreme and quite impractical cases:

1. Remove the compressible Bay soils and replace them with firm materials (to extend this to absurdity: replace all soils from bedrock to the ground surface with concrete).

2. Place a structure not having special footing design directly on poor soils, such as those described by Hittell and referred to earlier in this monograph.

The first solution is impractical because of cost, while the second is impractical because of safety hazard.

EFFECT OF DIFFERENTIAL SETTLEMENT ON SEISMIC RISK

Building settlements that occur prior to an earthquake, particularly those involving one portion of a building settling more than another portion (i.e., differential settlements), can produce measurable strains

Figure 7. Differential settlements have caused the center of this building to "hump." Note curve formed by the sidewalk and by the window sills. The building has many cracks in its brick walls due to differential settlements.

in a building. These strains may result in stresses that substantially weaken a structure. Figure 7 illustrates an extreme case of differential settlements in a building constructed many years ago, prior to the development of present-day soils engineering techniques. These differential settlements have cracked the walls badly and otherwise weakened the building. Nearby buildings have settled differentially to such an extent that doors had to be rehung. It becomes obvious that differential settlements can (and normally do) weaken a building and cause it to perform poorly in an earthquake.

In the author's opinion, differential settlements prior to and during an earthquake are a major reason for greater observed earthquake damage on made land. The author has had considerable personal experience to substantiate this observation. For example, in the case of the 1954 earthquake in Eureka, California, previous differential settlements caused damage in the brick wall of a major structure: moss was growing in the crack. The crack moved slightly ("worked") during the earthquake, and paint and plaster bridging portions of the crack fell to the floor. It was impossible to convince persons unfamiliar with earthquake engineering that the crack had existed prior to the shock, and that the flaked paint on the floor was merely the result of the failure of a subsequent coat of paint bridging the crack. The point of this paragraph is not to discount the heavier damage that has been found in these structurally poor ground areas, but to provide a partial explanation of its occurrence. Reasons for the comparative lack of damage to pile-supported structures (which are less prone to differential settlements) become clearer.

Even in modern structures, stresses are almost always increased when the theoretically predicted differential settlements actually occur as predicted. These stresses can be kept within tolerable limits by careful and sophisticated structural design. But serious stresses may result if actual differential settlements should prove to be greater than anticipated. Experienced and competent judgment is essential in evaluating anticipated differential settlements, but this need is not necessarily satisfied by a man who becomes a licensed civil engineer and opens a consulting office.

The margin of judgment error can be and has been considerable in some cases. Also, the structural engineer is under economic pressures to increase the amount of "acceptable" differential settlements in his design. There is, therefore, a greater likelihood for the average modern building on Bay fills to be subject to greater pre-earthquake stresses within it than is the case of a similar building on structurally firm soil or on rock. This possible danger can, however, be substantially eliminated by appropriate design and construction of special foundation and structural systems.

Methods for minimizing differential settlements in buildings on Bay fills vary with the kind of building and the type of foundation. Economics has a major role in determining the latter. Piling has had overall excellent earthquake experience throughout the world. Large monolithic mat footings beneath a structure have also performed well— differential settlements for this foundation type could cause a building to "tilt," affecting the operation of elevators and other functional aspects, but not necessarily causing serious strains. Indeed, major buildings in a recent Japanese earthquake tilted so far as to rest almost on their sides, and yet remained structurally intact. These are, of course, extreme examples of buildings remaining intact after foundation failure. Individual footings that are not interconnected are the least expensive, but also are the least satisfactory.

The foregoing dealt with footing types, rather than with soils beneath the footings. Today's general practice in the case of one- and two-story

TABLE 2

TOTAL OBSERVED SETTLEMENT OF SELECTED MULTISTORY BUILDINGS
IN FINANCIAL AREA OF SAN FRANCISCO

Height of Building	Period	Total Settlement (at various columns) Maximum Minimum (to nearest inch)	
17 stories	1925–47	3″	0″
29 stories	1922–50	7″	5″
22 stories	1922–50	10″	6″

Source: Data based, in part, on Charles H. Lee, "Building Foundations in San Francisco" (*Proc. Am. Soc. C. E.*, Vol. 79, Separate No. 325, 1953).

buildings is to place a blanket of carefully selected and compacted soil several feet thick over the compressible Bay soils. This blanket will act as a mat, and light structures with conventional footings resting on the mat should not settle differentially.

It is usually the province of the structural engineer, architect, and/or developer to weigh the soils engineer's recommendations against the estimated costs of reducing differential settlements to some tolerable limit. This tolerable limit is a matter of judgment; there is no commonly accepted standard. Probably there have been too many instances where cost unduly influenced judgment, and this may explain some of the observed differential settlements in relatively recent fills.

The historical record of Bay Area earthquakes demonstrates that tall buildings in poor ground areas have performed well, but this information must be used with care. Table 2 shows differential settlements observed in buildings on poor ground in downtown San Francisco. This suggests that significant stresses may have developed in these tall buildings since construction. Presumably, more modern buildings will have experienced smaller differential settlements.

GROUND MOTIONS ON BAY FILLS

Research, particularly in Japan, is showing that the ground motions in structurally poor soils are different from those in rock. Actual soils beneath a particular building are usually very complex, with varying soil strata having different dynamic characteristics. Consequently, the practical case of Bay fills is very complicated. In general, ground oscillations become slower as seismic waves progress from bedrock through less competent materials to the building foundation. Evidence from small earthquakes also indicates that the amplitude of the ground motions becomes substantially greater in structurally poor grounds, as compared to rock. In other words, ground motions are amplified as they pass through less competent materials. This amplification has often been demonstrated in a crude fashion by vibrating a bowl of jellylike material.

The foregoing factors have not yet been incorporated into American building codes, partly because the information on them is too new and too incomplete. But these phenomena theoretically can become troublesome to long-period structures. (In lay terms, long-period structures are most commonly the high-rise buildings.) A classic example of selective damage to tall buildings (i.e., long-period structures) compared to rigid one- and two-story buildings occurred in the Mexican earthquake of July 28, 1957. The earthquake was distant, its epicenter being reported as from 170 to 220 miles from Mexico City. There was pronounced damage to many of the tall reinforced concrete and steel frame buildings in downtown Mexico City. Several of them collapsed. In contrast, small one- and two-story "collapse hazard" buildings performed well.

Soils in downtown Mexico City consist of unconsolidated lake bed and other materials, and they are of exceptionally poor structural quality. Ground motions from this distant earthquake selectively damaged the long-period (multistory) buildings. But multistory building damage was far more pronounced in the poor ground areas than in the nearby firmer ground areas. (Differential settlements obviously played a role in some of the damage, but the author's observations indicate that it was minor in most cases.)

POLICING

The number of local soils engineering firms has increased substantially in recent years, and the number is still rising. Thus it is conceivable that a land developer can "shop" for experts, thereby finding one who will approve or recommend procedures involving judgment-evaluated risk which the large majority of other practitioners would question. Admittedly, of course, all professions require a substantial amount of judgment, and differences of opinion are to be expected among competent professionals.

Life safety in buildings is subject to a set of checks and balances in the form of minimum standards found in building codes, and enforced by local building officials. These checks and balances are effective to a degree, and relate to everything from concrete foundations to roofs. However, most building departments are not staffed to review the reports of *soils* engineers. Further, the state of the art of estimating soil response to seismic forces appears to be sufficiently limited that no generally accepted set of minimum standards has been developed.

It seems, therefore, that the higher *risk* to buildings on Bay fills receives less "check and balance" attention than do the superstructures (buildings), themselves. Thus it is fair to ask whether these risks do not justify greater supervision from the building departments.

RECOMMENDED PUBLIC POLICY: RISK ZONING FOR BAY FILLS

A conservative engineering design approach is appropriate in order to compensate for a different seismic risk on Bay fills. Land use for fills over the deeper compressible soils should be so restricted as to minimize population density unless special precautions are taken. Such precautions may involve substantial costs where multistory buildings with large life occupancies are permitted. Experienced, licensed structural engineers must give special attention to the foundations as well as to the superstructures. Water and gas systems should be specially valved in Bay fill areas to minimize the effects of possible pipe breakage. Provision of an independent water-supply system for fire protection, using Bay water, is desirable for particularly hazardous occupancies and locations.

In view of the earthquake hazard, the use of engineered fills over compressible deep Bay soils for building foundations must be considered in some degree experimental. Many answers regarding the degree and type of increased seismic risk—and methods to reduce it—can be derived from seismic records, even after only moderate shocks. In the interests of long-range land-use planning, strong-motion seismic equipment should be installed and housed on each major Bay fill development, as well as on other kinds of natural and artificial ground. For best results, each installation should be coordinated with and become a part of the U. S. Coast and Geodetic Survey network. One solution would have the installation and housing of these instruments done at the expense of the developer, and with the condition that the records therefrom be in the public domain. Somewhat similar programs are already in existence in southern California for high-rise buildings.

In developing a constructive and useful program to control earthquake risk, it is important to recognize that urban facilities are normally constructed at locations which meet the economic and functional needs of people, rather than those that fit natural geologic features. In any overall land-use planning program, it would obviously be quite imprudent to ignore all unfavorable geologic features. On the other hand, avoiding all unfavorable geologic features is equally unrealistic.

Therefore, the emphasis of zoning and control measures should be directed towards establishing special requirements for design and construction, which provide appropriate protection for public safety, rather than attempting to establish completely arbitrary land-use requirements.

Man-made facilities have a margin of safety in order to allow for adverse combinations of human limitations (such as errors in design and construction), material limitations (such as normal quality variations), and forces of nature (such as earthquake, wind, and flood), exceeding those anticipated from normal past experience. Such safety factors are based on judgments, and they represent a necessarily arbitrary, but realistic estimate of economics vs. life safety, and economics vs. property damage. In a similar vein, any land-use planning for geologic hazards will require a value judgment of the increased risk, against which will be balanced a value judgment of the steps to be taken in reducing this risk to tolerable levels. It is important that land-use planning be based on more than economic considerations alone. On the other hand, the people of the Bay Area will not be well served if land-use conditions are created which *unnecessarily* discourage development in the Bay Area.

Implementation of the foregoing recommendations requires a number of value judgments on matters for which there are few precedents. As a starting point, it seems reasonable to divide all potential developable San Francisco Bay fill areas into zones, based on the degree of increased risk caused by building on fill, and to have a map prepared showing these zones. The zones should provide for decreases in population density with increases in seismic risk. A broad outline of some possible alternative requirements for a four-zone system follows:

Zone 1: Zone of minimum increased risk
  I. All structures three or more stories in height shall have a structural engineer of record who, upon completion of the construction and before occupancy, must file a statement with the local building department that he or a specified structural engineer on his staff, has knowledge that the structural engineering aspects of the plans and specifications have been complied with during construction. (There is precedent for this in regulations governing California public school construction. Undivided responsibility for a building's structural integrity will lead to better construction.)

Zone 2: Zone of moderate increased risk
  I. All requirements of Zone 1, plus the following: Single-family and

multiple-family occupancies shall be limited to two-story wood frame construction. Other occupancies shall be no higher than one story plus mezzanine.

A structural engineer of record shall be required for all buildings having concrete, brick, and/or hollow concrete block walls, in which these walls constitute more than 25 percent of the total exterior wall area.

No city halls, hospitals, or places of detention shall be permitted in Zone 2. *or*

II. Moderate degree of special design and construction requirements.

Zone 3: Zone of substantially increased risk

I. All requirements of Zone 2, plus the following:

Occupancies shall be limited to warehouses, storage areas, and similar minimum population density occupancies. Offices shall be only those necessary to accommodate these occupancies. Dwellings shall not be permitted. Structures shall be one story in height.

Only public buildings which are necessary to service the area shall be permitted. Fire stations may be placed in this zone if such location is mandatory because of other considerations. *or*

II. Substantial degree of special design and construction requirements.

Zone 4: Zone of maximum increased risk

I. Parks, golf courses, and similar land uses may be permitted. Appurtenant structures (such as storage sheds) may be permitted if of one-story wood frame construction, or of equivalent light mass and inherent strength. This zone could include former refuse dump areas. *or*

II. Maximum degree of special design and construction requirements.

It is important to note that the zoning recommended above is to be based on *minimal engineering requirements*. There is no reason why, possibly at extra expense, superior engineering criteria could not be established adequate to overcome even the worst site deficiencies.

Zone 1 may constitute most of the developable land. Special provisions for waivers must, however, be incorporated into any rules. Obviously, even in Zone 4, it would be possible—although not necessarily economical—to put in special foundations and structural systems capable of overcoming site deficiencies for major buildings or other large structures.

Technical and detailed specifications involving several disciplines will have to be established in order to zone the Bay Area equitably, and to further implement the foregoing. Guidelines for differential settlements may be established if feasible. Existing soils data will have to be evaluated for each zone. Criteria for the locations of seismic instruments are needed. Minimum standards for soil reports and engineering geology reports, and the policing of engineered fills, will have to be considered. Detailed standards will have to be developed for special risks, such as oil storage tanks, airports, docks, etc.

The development and implementation of the foregoing program must be the function of a continuing body of technically qualified personnel, if the risk zoning and its technical regulations are to keep up with the rapidly changing state of the art. The qualified personnel should probably be a group of consultants, and must include soils engineers, structural engineers, geologists, and city planners, in order to give suitable balance. In order to keep the zoning map and other design criteria current, this group must be a continuing body working within a duly constituted governmental agency.

Earthquake-Induced Landslides

Landslides are common in the hillside sections of the Bay Area, especially during a very wet winter. In addition, landsliding is also an *earthquake* geologic hazard, since the landslides could become catastrophic in the event of a major earthquake during or immediately following an extended period of heavy rainfall.

Public policy with respect to landslides has been given considerable study in the Los Angeles area since the heavy rains of January 1952, which resulted in approximately $7,500,000 damage to public and private property in the City of Los Angeles. The heavy rains of 1955 caused further landsliding: this was followed by the Portuguese Bend landslide which started in August 1956 and which destroyed or severely damaged 150 homes.

Because of this experience, the City of Los Angeles has pioneered in several aspects of land-use control in potential landslide areas. The city passed a grading ordinance in 1952, and later established a Geologic Hazards Committee, and an Engineering Geologist Qualification Board, to evaluate the qualifications of geologists submitting reports to the city. Since then, other jurisdictions, principally in southern California, have adopted similar ordinances. The *Uniform Building Code,* which is the generally accepted document for building departments in California, now contains excavation and grading rules giving local building departments a minimum amount of control over the landslide hazard.[12] The landslide problem in the Bay Area is somewhat different from that of land-use planning in fault zones. Each landslide is normally independent of other landslides in time and location, whereas fault movement represents a common problem simultaneously to many Bay Area cities. Therefore, any plans to cope with earthquake-induced landslides should, in a large part, be considered along with the almost annual landslide problem.

The problem of enforcing grading ordinances in southern California has been well stated by Scullin:

. . . the Building Officials generally are not staffed with the desired professionals necessary for coordinating and inspecting extensive grading operations. As more of the earthwork failures go to the courts, the more the legal counsels advise us of the necessity of employing such personnel with the appropriate backgrounds and experience for controlling and regulating the hillside urban development codes. The governmental agencies approve the plans, issue the permits, and approve the construction. . . . If the agencies do not know what is necessary for competent professional work they certainly don't know whether the professionals are doing the work necessary for insuring the public safety and welfare. Over 50 percent of our work is involved with making sure the professionals have been retained by the developers to do the work and they are on the job during the job. (pp. 233–234)

With respect to the Bay Area, the February 1967 newsletter of the San Francisco Section of the Association of Engineering Geologists contained the following information, given to them by their Building Codes Committee:

A discouraging report from this Committee is that the use of engineering geology reports as required by several Bay Area grading ordinances is not being enforced. A quick survey of the various cities and counties shows the major reasons are either ignorance of what constitutes an engineering geology report or ignorance of geologic hazards within the area. . . .

It should be pointed out that a report made by an engineering geologist may have a different viewpoint from one prepared by a soils engineer. For example, the engineering geologist would note and map such things as bedrock differences and their behavior, and faults and their characteristics. The soils engineer might test the surficial and near-surface materials with regard to their competency as a building foundation. Often, both kinds of reports are necessary.

---

[12] International Conference of Building Officials, *Uniform Building Code* (1967 ed., Vol. I.) For a much fuller treatment of the landslide problem in the metropolitan Los Angeles area, and its development into code restrictions, see C. Michael Scullin, "History, Development, and Administration of Excavation and Grading Codes," in *Engineering Geology in Southern California* (Ass'n Engr. Geolog., 1966).

The minimum standards recently established in the *Uniform Building Code* probably should be given an adequate trial by local building officials in the Bay Area before any different major procedural methods are considered. It remains to be seen, however, whether the grading ordinances can be administered effectively in small Bay Area cities having minimum staffs of building officials.

Buildings and Structures

Up to this point, discussion has been limited to the performance of the foundation materials supporting buildings and structures. Should these materials fail because of faulting, soils sinking or lurching, or landslide, then the structure may be subjected to excessive forces, and serious damage can result. Foundation failure is quite different from *vibration damage* to buildings and structures. In the latter case, the foundation materials beneath the structure may remain intact, while the structure itself is destroyed by ground vibration. The vast majority of buildings have to contend only with vibrational forces, and damage from earthquake-induced geologic hazards may be comparatively rare in many earthquakes.

Seismic Risk from Vibrational Forces

Architects and structural engineers have given more attention to the effects of vibrational forces in buildings than they have to the geologically oriented problems. Extensive engineering research, particularly in the last 10 to 20 years, has developed the basic theory for the understanding of earthquake forces on buildings, the response of the buildings to these forces, and design methods to reduce life hazard in these structures. All of these problems have by no means been fully solved, but expanding research is underway on remaining problems.

The fact that all problems have not been solved is clearly evident from the extensive damage to many buildings in Anchorage during the 1964 Alaskan earthquake. Most of the damaged buildings were designed to be earthquake resistive in some degree, most buildings were designed by recognized professional engineers, and most damaged buildings were built under construction standards common to many parts of the United States. Unfortunately, similar circumstances are found in other cities where a large earthquake can cause similar damage. In the next great earthquake, some Bay Area cities quite possibly will also witness the collapse of modern buildings, which probably had their counterparts in Anchorage in 1964.

Seismic risk can be viewed from different standpoints, with quite different results. For example, severe earthquake *damage* does not necessarily imply an equivalent *hazard* to human life. An earthquake may crack a building so extensively that repairs are uneconomical. Despite such damage, however, collapse—and consequent injury or death of occupants—may not be a serious threat. During the 1964 Alaskan earthquake, major multistory buildings up to 14 stories suffered damage ranging up to 40 percent of a building's replacement value, without

37

accompanying life loss. Conversely, the failure of light fixtures and shelving, or lighting loss in an auditorium, resulting in panic, are examples of life hazards in structures that sustain only minimum damage. The collapse of nonstructural hollow concrete-block partitions around stairs has also caused injury and death.

A commonly accepted viewpoint on seismic risk is to take such engineering design steps as may be necessary to minimize life hazard, and to restrict property damage to reasonable limits in the event of a great earthquake. There is, however, no consensus on what constitutes a "reasonable limit" to earthquake-caused property damage. Some engineers take an extreme viewpoint, being willing to allow total loss to their client's property, provided that life safety is assured. This viewpoint is also sometimes held by speculative developers who, through sale of the developed property, transfer the hazard to the unsuspecting buyer.

The basic philosophy behind the seismic provisions of most American building codes appears in the *Recommended Lateral Force Requirements and Commentary* by the Seismology Committee of the Structural Engineers Association of California (1967). This publication states that the code intends buildings to "Resist major earthquakes of the intensity or severity of the strongest experienced in California, without collapse, but with some structural as well as nonstructural damage." It goes on to state, "In most structures it is expected that structural damage, even in a major earthquake, could be limited to repairable damage." By using certain types of flexible, but "safe" framing systems in certain occupancies, such as hotels and hospitals, it is quite possible to suffer a 50 percent property loss without serious structural damage. (Design for damage control usually includes life safety, but design for life safety —i.e., minimum code standards—does not necessarily include damage control.)

In most cases the earthquake provisions of a building code, plus the design engineer's judgment, normally determine the seismic risk as it affects the design of any particular building or structure. Expert advice may have been obtained from engineering geologists, seismologists, soils engineers, and others, but the design engineer must evaluate all reports and synthesize them into a judgment decision, sometimes influenced by the minimum standards of the building code. Unfortunately, in some cases all efforts are directed towards barely meeting the minimum earthquake standards of a building code. In fact, such minimal compliance places a building on the verge of being legally unsafe.

The foregoing is a brief statement of the nature of seismic risk for new construction. In summary, earthquake-*resistive* construction, which protects life, is realistically feasible, although earthquake-*proof* construction is not guaranteed in new buildings. Older existing structures are quite a different matter, on the other hand, and will be discussed in detail in the following paragraphs.

Non-Earthquake-Resistive Construction

A significant portion of the buildings in the Bay Area are not earthquake resistive. Despite the historical record of previous destructive shocks in most of the major Bay Area cities, ordinances placing strong earthquake-bracing provisions in building codes were not passed until around 1950. Some of the reasons for this laxity are rather interesting.

After the 1906 San Francisco earthquake, it soon became clear that persons controlling the eastern financial resources needed to rebuild the Bay Area, and San Francisco in particular, were more afraid of earthquakes than of fires. The Baltimore and Chicago fires were catastrophes which they understood, as they could understand the fire following the 1906 shock. Thus, in the years after the 1906 earthquake and fire, it became fashionable locally to refer to the disaster as "the fire"— the word "earthquake" was mentioned seldom or not at all. In the March 1911 issue of the *Bulletin of the Seismological Society of America,* Professor Andrew Lawson stated that a discussion of earthquakes was as welcome in San Francisco as a discussion of the plague; consequently, funds for earthquake research could not be obtained. Published reports tended to reduce the estimated percentage of earthquake damage as compared to fire damage. The press mentioned the word "earthquake" as little as possible. Ray Spangler commented on this in the May 26, 1955 issue of the *Redwood City Tribune:*

... there has been a great change of attitude in the past 25 years. I remember that as a student correspondent for a San Francisco newspaper I once questioned the geology department at Stanford about a minor 'quake. The professor gave me the information but told me my newspaper wouldn't print it. He was right.

It wasn't until 1947 that the City of San Francisco adopted its own strong earthquake-bracing laws. As noted, most other Bay Area cities adopted strong earthquake-bracing provisions around 1950. Berkeley and Palo Alto, however, passed adequate laws somewhat earlier.

Hazard Abatement: Some Limitations

Many of the existing non-earthquake-resistive buildings present serious hazards. Financially and technically it would be difficult to strengthen most of these older buildings to meet today's earthquake-bracing requirements. Certainly the thousands of buildings with bearing

TABLE 3

HAZARD COMPARISON OF NON-EARTHQUAKE-RESISTIVE BUILDINGS

Note: This table is intended for buildings not containing earthquake bracing, and in general, is applicable to most older construction. Unfavorable foundation conditions and/or dangerous roof tanks can increase the earthquake hazard greatly.

Simplified Description of Structural Type	Relative Damageability (in order of increasing susceptibility to damage)
Small wood-frame structures, i.e., dwellings not over 3,000 sq. ft., and not over 3 stories..................	1
Single or multistory steel-frame buildings with concrete exterior walls, concrete floors, and concrete roof. Moderate wall openings................................	1.5
Single or multistory reinforced-concrete buildings with concrete exterior walls, concrete floors, and concrete roof. Moderate wall openings......................	2
Large area wood-frame buildings and other wood-frame buildings.	3 to 4
Single or multistory steel-frame buildings with unreinforced masonry exterior wall panels; concrete floors and concrete roof.	4
Single or multistory reinforced-concrete frame buildings with unreinforced masonry exterior wall panels, concrete floors and concrete roof.	5
Reinforced concrete bearing walls with supported floors and roof of any materials (usually wood).	5
Buildings with unreinforced brick masonry having sand-lime mortar; and with supported floors and roof of any materials (usually wood).	7 up
Bearing walls of unreinforced adobe, unreinforced hollow concrete block, or unreinforced hollow clay tile.	Collapse hazards in moderate shocks

Source: Abridged from Pacific Fire Rating Bureau Tariff Rules.

walls of non-reinforced brick, held together by sand-lime mortar, are extremely vulnerable to earthquake damage. Many of these will suffer partial or total collapse in a great earthquake. Also open to question are many of the multistory buildings speculatively constructed during the boom years of the 1920's.

When Bay Area communities added earthquake-bracing provisions to their building codes, the requirements were not intended to be retroactive. This followed general custom throughout the United States. Building ordinances are not retroactive except in most serious cases, and then with qualifications. Any other course for Bay Area cities would have required the virtual destruction and rebuilding of most major structures. This would, of course, have been economically infeasible. As a result, retroactive building laws are rather lenient in their application, despite the following clause that is usually found:

All buildings or structures which are structurally unsafe . . . or otherwise dangerous to human life . . . by reason of obsolescence . . . as specified in this Code or any other effective ordinance, are, for purposes of the Section, unsafe buildings. All such unsafe buildings are hereby declared to be public nuisances and shall be abated by repair, rehabilitation, demolition, or removal. . . .[13]

From experience it appears that the foregoing clause is rarely used. A more politically acceptable and more common method for upgrading the safety of buildings is to require improvements *when building permits are issued for additions or repairs*. The *Uniform Building Code* then calls for: (1) full compliance of old and new construction with all current code requirements if the work being done exceeds 50 percent of the value of the existing structure; and (2) full compliance of only the *new* construction with all current code requirements if the work being done exceeds 25 percent but not 50 percent of the value of the existing structure.[14]

The recently issued pamphlet entitled *Dangerous Buildings* (Vol. IV of the *Uniform Building Code*, 1967 ed.), was intended to offer building departments reasonable procedures for the classification and abatement of dangerous buildings. The code contains the following language in sec. 302, item 13, defining a dangerous building as:

any building . . . [that] has in any . . . supporting part, member, or portion less than 66% of the strength . . . required by law in the case of newly constructed buildings . . .

It is apparent from the foregoing discussion that *legal tools* are available to deal with buildings presenting an earthquake collapse hazard. The *economic* consequences of a literal enforcement could, of course, cause political repercussions. As a result, retroactive ordinances, such as those discussed above, are usually applied leniently. A good illustration is provided by the actions of a group of engineers, who were recently in an authoritative position to make earthquake safety recommendations for existing major buildings in part of a Bay Area city proposed for redevelopment. In the opinion of some engineers, this presented a good opportunity to bring these substandard buildings up to

[13] *Uniform Building Code* (1967 ed.), sec. 203a.
[14] Sec. 104 of the *Uniform Building Code* should be consulted for complete details.

current safety standards. But the group's final recommendation was to allow certain structures to remain in the redevelopment area if they met only about 50 percent of the present code's earthquake standards.

PARAPETS: A SPECIAL PROBLEM

It is reasonable to proceed with the abatement of all types of hazards to human life on a relative safety basis, tempered by economic considerations. Earthquake-caused damage or collapse is only one of many hazards to buildings. Probably the *greatest* life hazard from earthquakes will result from the failure of unreinforced unit masonry, particularly unreinforced brick parapets on buildings.[15] Earthquake-induced failure of dams also could be a great life hazard in the Bay Area, but dams have their special problems (to be discussed in the following section).

Unreinforced brick parapets of older non-earthquake-resistive buildings can fall onto sidewalks; examples of the potential life hazard may be seen in Figures 8 and 9. Persons in the streets, as well as inside buildings, can be killed or injured by the fall of this obsolete type of brickwork. The hazard also extends to unanchored ornamentation, such as veneers, which can be as lethal as parapets. Fortunately, parapet corrective work is relatively inexpensive in most cases.

Although Bay Area cities have not yet responded realistically to this significant hazard, the Structural Engineers Association of Northern California is endeavoring currently to interest San Francisco authorities, as well as other civic bodies, in taking the necessary corrective steps. The San Francisco Chamber of Commerce is supporting the engineers. In 1968 the Chamber issued the following policy statement "The building codes of the City and County of San Francisco should, to the fullest extent economically possible, require construction standards designed to minimize dangers from structural failure due to earthquake forces."

Unlike Bay Area cities, Los Angeles has approached the parapet problem in a realistic and orderly fashion, providing a most instructive example. In brief, Los Angeles passed a retroactive building ordinance requiring the elimination or strengthening of hazardous parapets and appendages. Next, carefully selected city personnel inspected parapets, determined the extent of the hazard, and approved realistic solutions proposed by the individual owners and their engineers. Instead of a crash program, this was a long-range plan, taking years to accomplish. It allowed the owners time to finance the reconstruction, and to meet the often peculiar engineering problems involved. The abatement program

---

[15] Brick parapets are those portions of walls which extend above the roof level. In addition to their aesthetic value, these walls may also prevent fire from spreading from the roof of one building to another.

Figure 8. Typical life hazard due to failure of unanchored brick parapet, and portion of wall below parapet.

Figure 9. Life was lost in this building because of the collapse of a parapet and brick wall of adjoining building.

was thought out carefully, and it has proven to be both economically and politically feasible. In view of this experience, failure of Bay Area cities to proceed in a similar direction seems to represent an unreasonable risk.

Los Angeles' clear demonstration of what can be done will place a heavy burden of explanation on Bay Area governments and building officials, if a great earthquake knocks down unanchored parapets, causing hundreds or thousands of casualties. The responsible authorities will be in an unenviable position if, after such an event, they have to admit that they had taken no preventive measures.

There is no simple, realistic or economic way of eliminating hazardous non-earthquake-resistive buildings quickly, and no specific program is proposed here. But cities should *begin planning* for ways and means to develop programs. A hazardous-parapet abatement program should certainly be started immediately in the major cities.

A Major Hazard: Fire Following Earthquake

The great fires that followed San Francisco's 1906 earthquake and Tokyo's 1923 earthquake are still vividly remembered. Today, however, the conflagration hazard is far smaller than it was in 1906, because there is a better supply of water, better fire-fighting equipment, and less vulnerable construction. San Francisco is also now equipped to use water from the Bay as a second source of fire-fighting supply.

IN SAN FRANCISCO

This section will be limited to summary comments on the performance of the San Francisco water system in the 1906 shock, and to a review of the relationships of today's water systems to active faults. Detailed studies of fire protection systems, and the conflagration potential of specific cities, have been made by the American Insurance Association (formerly the National Board of Fire Underwriters) and the Pacific Fire Rating Bureau. Their reports should be studied for detailed recommendations.

It will be useful to review some of the facts regarding the 1906 fire. The National Board of Fire Underwriters published a report *before* the earthquake (in 1905), summarizing their findings as follows:

In view of the exceptionally large areas, great heights, numerous unprotected openings, general absence of fire-breaks or stops, highly combustible nature of the buildings, many of which have sheathed walls and ceilings, frequency of light wells and the presence of interspersed frame buildings, the potential hazard is very severe.

The above features combined with the almost total lack of sprinklers and absence of modern protective devices generally, numerous and mutually aggravating conflagration breeders, high winds, and comparatively narrow streets, make the probability feature alarmingly severe.

In fact, San Francisco has violated all underwriting traditions and precedent by not burning up. That it has not done so is largely due to the vigilance of the fire department, which cannot be relied upon indefinitely to stave off the inevitable.

Reality proved worse than the prediction, because portions of the water system were severely damaged by the earthquake. Two of the three main storage reservoirs serving San Francisco were located on the San Andreas fault in the Peninsula south of the city. The third reservoir was near the fault but not on it. The reservoirs, the earth-fill dams, and one concrete dam survived excellently. However, all of the three conduits from the main storage reservoirs to San Francisco were damaged or destroyed where they crossed the fault, or where they crossed marshy areas. Of the three distributing reservoirs only the Lake Honda Reservoir was injured by the earthquake. However, when the fire in San Francisco was under control, this reservoir still contained over one-sixth of its capacity. One supply conduit from the main storage reservoirs was repaired in three days. At no time during the conflagration were all of the distribution reservoirs empty. Thus the belief that there was no water available in San Francisco after the earthquake is in error. Instead, the fire-fighting problem was one of *distribution,* and not of dam and reservoir failure.

Hundreds of pipe breaks occurred in the city distribution system, principally where the lines crossed filled ground and former swamps. Equally serious was the fact that thousands of service pipes were probably broken by earthquake motion and by the collapse of burning buildings. In vital portions of the distribution system, water was therefore not available to fight the fire, although it was available in the Western Addition residential section during the entire conflagration.

The burned district in San Francisco covered 4.7 square miles, comprising 521 blocks, of which only 13 were saved and 508 burned. As a result, the three-day conflagration following the earthquake caused substantially more damage than the earthquake. Furthermore, as noted earlier, in the years that followed it became "proper" to call the event the 1906 *fire,* and to omit any reference to the earthquake. Consequently, estimates of the ratio of direct earthquake damage to fire damage decreased with the passage of time. But a recent restudy of all available records indicated that earthquake losses amounted to perhaps as much as 20 percent of the combined earthquake and fire loss in San Francisco, based on today's insurance methods of estimating losses.

Future earthquake damage patterns for the water system in San Francisco can be expected to follow those of the past, but on a substantially diminished scale because of continuing improvements. However, potential damage patterns for East Bay cities and Peninsula cities on the Hayward or San Andreas faults do not appear to be nearly as clear. For example, the Hayward fault passes through most of the East Bay cities, including the heart of Hayward and Fremont. This gives rise to several problems of design and operation of water systems, and of public policies related thereto.

IN THE EAST BAY

The situation of the East Bay Municipal Utility District (EBMUD), which supplies water for most East Bay cities, is a case in point. The district's principal storage reservoirs are on the east side of the Hayward fault, which thus separates them from the majority of the consumers, located west of the fault. Water is delivered to the East Bay cities by two underground supply tunnels that are intersected by the Hayward fault, a third tunnel feeds two supply conduits that cross a branch of the Hayward fault, and one grade-level conduit crosses a line thought to be a northerly extension of the Hayward fault.

In 1964, during the course of a routine inspection of the 9-foot horseshoe reinforced-concrete Claremont water tunnel, EBMUD discovered that a six-and-one-half-inch fault offset had occurred near the tunnel's western extremity. This was evidently the result of recent slippage (creep) on the Hayward fault, and gives a clear indication that the fault is active. The offset apparently caused three circumferential cracks, with a transverse displacement of about an inch, at a point approximately 1000 feet from the tunnel's western portal. The district has awarded a contract to effect major improvements in this tunnel, specifically including additional strengthening of the section affected by the fault, in order to minimize damage by additional movement or by a major earthquake.

In reducing its dependence on long supply lines that may be ruptured in an earthquake, the EBMUD has pursued a policy of constructing large numbers of distribution system reservoirs in its 280 square mile service area, located as near as possible to the users. The district's system now has a total of 141 distribution reservoirs, with an aggregate capacity of 738 million gallons, or nearly four times the average consumed in one day. This local storage complements the storage capacity behind the major dams, which contain another 90-day supply, as a minimum. All the major dams, however, are located east of the Hayward fault.

Nevertheless, it is recognized that seismic hazards can only be reduced, not eliminated. The detailed water distribution map of Oakland, for example, shows numerous examples of large and small conduits crossing and recrossing the Hayward fault zone. In view of this and other hazards, on July 20, 1967, EBMUD initiated a reconnaissance seismicity survey with the objectives of determining (1) how the system is likely to be damaged by seismic disturbances, (2) how well it would function to extinguish the fires that frequently break out after an earthquake, and (3) what further measures, if any, are necessary and justifiable to make the system more secure against seismic forces.

It would be quite proper for all water utility districts and companies serving areas in the Hayward and San Andreas fault zones to reassess the water distribution problems posed by future fault movement, if they have not done so already. Their efforts should include basic detailed geologic studies intended to give a better understanding of the nature and possible extent of future fault displacements, to determine the boundaries of the fault zone, and to guide development of a distribution system planned to minimize the effects of earthquake faulting.

Governmental Agencies

Many local, state, and federal agencies are directly or indirectly involved in programs intended to mitigate future earthquake disasters. The following discussion is limited to the existing and planned programs of the principal agencies that, to the author's knowledge, are primarily involved in planning hazard-reducing measures to be taken *before* a disaster—in contrast to measures intended to minimize the effects *after* its occurrence.

The State of California and its Programs

SAN FRANCISCO BAY CONSERVATION AND DEVELOPMENT COMMISSION

The role of the San Francisco Bay Conservation and Development Commission (BCDC) has already been discussed briefly. There appears to be no specific directive in the enabling act for BCDC that requires the commission to consider the seismic risk to developments on Bay filled lands.[16] However, it is reasonable to assume that such considerations are envisaged under sec. 66651 (b), which requires a final BCDC report containing, in part, a ". . . comprehensive plan . . . for . . . the development of its shoreline. . . ."

In the Spring of 1967, seismic risk problems were presented to BCDC in reports mentioned previously.[17] On June 1, 1967 BCDC adopted the following nine statements as possible Bay planning conclusions:

1. To reduce risk to life and damage to property, special consideration must be given to construction on poor soils throughout the Bay Area, including soft natural soils, steep slopes, earthquake fault zones, extensively graded areas, and filled lands in San Francisco Bay. The BCDC is concerned about the safety of construction that might be permitted in its plan for the Bay.

2. The safety of construction on fills depends upon (a) *the stability of the ground or Bay bottom* on which a fill is placed (i.e., the original mud, sand, rock, etc.), and (b) *the manner in which and the material of which the fill* is built.

3. In regard to the *stability of the ground or Bay bottom,* specific analysis must be made in each case by competent specialists, but approximate indications are: (a) building foundations on *bedrock* are generally the safest; (b) the *older Bay mud,* which includes firm sediments, generally provides good foundation support for piles and other foundations; and (c) the *younger Bay mud,* is the weakest soil and generally requires special engineering to overcome its deficiencies.

---

[16] *Cal. Stats.,* 1965, ch. 1162.
[17] See note 9, above.

48

4. In regard to the *manner in which a fill is built,* construction of a fill or building that will be stable enough for the intended use requires (a) recognition and investigation of all potential *hazards,* and (b) construction of the fill or buildings in a manner specifically designed to minimize these hazards. *Hazards* include (a) settling of a fill or a building over a long period of time, and (b) ground failure caused by the manner of constructing the fill or by shaking in the event of a major earthquake. If these hazards cannot be overcome adequately for the intended use, the fill or building should not be constructed.

5. There are no minimum construction codes regulating construction of fills on Bay mud because of the absence of sufficient data upon which to base such a code. Recognition and investigation of all potential hazards of constructing a fill and the design of the fill and any construction thereon to minimize these hazards therefore requires the highest order of skilled judgment, utilizing the available knowledge of all affected disciplines, in the absence of adequate data or of any minimum codes.

6. *In preparing its final plan* for the Bay, the Commission shall appoint a Board of Consultants consisting of geologists, civil engineers specializing in soils engineering, structural engineers, and other specialists to review, on the basis of available knowledge, all new fills that might be permitted in its plan so that no fills would be included upon which construction might be unsafe.

7. In the absence of adequate codes or data, public safety in regard to construction of Bay fills requires an instrument such as an adequately-empowered Board of Review competent to (1) set and then constantly adjust standards as rapidly as new information becomes available, (2) review all fill proposals on the basis of available knowledge, and (3) prescribe an inspection system to assure placement of the fill according to the approved design. As one of its recommendations for *carrying out the plan* for the Bay, the Commission should propose methods of providing such review and inspection, such as by boards, including all affected disciplines. The Board of Consultants referred to in Conclusion No. 6 will be requested to recommend to the Commission such methods as it deems advisable.

8. The BCDC recommends that cities, counties, and the Association of Bay Area Governments give similar consideration of or to life and property hazard in other parts of the Bay Area where fault zones, hillsides, excessive grading and general soil conditions may pose special construction problems.

9. To provide vitally needed information on the effects of earthquake on all kinds of soils, the BCDC recommends that installation of strong-motion seismographs be required on all future major land fills, in other developments on problem soils, and in other areas recommended by the U. S. Coast and Geodetic Survey for purposes of data comparison and evaluation.

It is of vital concern to the Bay Area that BCDC finally recommend a reasonable plan that is scientifically sound as well as politically and economically feasible. This may not be easy to accomplish, because opposing economic pressures are to be expected. They must be weighed against the need for appropriate seismic safety control measures.

An excellent start towards implementing the foregoing was BCDC's appointment on February 16, 1968 of a Board of Consultants to Review Safety of Proposed Fills. As a first step, this board began the study of the criteria which would be necessary to establish a satisfactory level of safety in a field where no generally accepted technical standards currently exist. At this writing, August 1968, the board has almost completed its work of preparing a technical report, which will be a substantial beginning towards fulfilling the author's "Recommended Public Policy: Risk Zonings for Bay Fills" (pps. 31–34 of the monograph). It is expected that the report to BCDC will be submitted to the California Legislature in January, 1969, as a part of the BCDC "San Francisco Bay Plan."

RESOURCES AGENCY: GEOLOGIC HAZARDS ADVISORY COMMITTEES

A thoughtful study of California's earthquake hazards has been made through the Resources Agency of the State of California. This study was the outgrowth of two state conferences organized by the agency's administrator. The first was an Earthquake and Geologic Hazards Conference held in San Francisco on December 7–8, 1964. It was followed by a second conference on landslides and subsidence.

Two geologic hazards advisory committees were appointed immediately after the first conference: one on program, and one on organization. The two committees were instructed to advise the Resources Agency on the kinds of programs the agency should institute, and on the way these programs should be organized. The two committees took a broad view of the problems, yet remained realistic. The product of the program committee provided a well-thought-out balance among pure research, applied research, and the implementation of this research for the State of California, as well as state cooperation with other governmental and private organizations. The organization committee completed its work in 1967. Because of its relevance and importance, sections of its final report have been included here:

. . . we recommend that the State make optimum use of the potential represented among the universities, both public and private, State and local government agencies, Federal agencies such as the Geological Survey, the Environmental Science Services Administration and the Corps of Engineers, and various private organizations whose expertise and capabilities are especially pertinent. To do this will require additional budgetary and supervisory support, some directed toward the State's own operations and some toward those of other organizations. We do not recommend the formation of a single agency to undertake all of the work pertinent to earthquake and geological hazards. . . .

The planning, organizing and implementing of the programs recommended . . . will be a major long-term effort requiring knowledgeable and perceptive guidance on a continuing basis. It is apparent that all of these cannot, and probably should not, be undertaken immediately. . . .

To provide the required guidance and judgment, we therefore recommend the establishment of a Board of reputable and knowledgeable persons, not employees of State agencies, who would be consulted on all State earthquake and geological hazards programs. . . . We recommend that this State Earthquake and Geological Hazards Board be composed of twelve to fifteen individuals of recognized competence and reputation in civil engineering, geology, seismology and other pertinent technical and scientific fields, and that they be appointed by the Governor and serve without remuneration. The Board should have the services of a full-time paid Executive Secretary and office staff employed and discharged at the discretion of the Board. It would be the function of the Board to keep itself informed concerning earthquake and geological hazards and what the State is doing about them, to advise, approve, and coordinate research programs for State agencies, to recommend programs to the legislature for implementation and financing, to assist in obtaining funds for research on geological hazards, and to make contracts for research with State agencies, universities and private organizations. . . .

1. *Prepare for Future Earthquakes*—As a first step we strongly recommend that State agencies draw up plans and prepare for appropriate action in regard to facilities and construction under their jurisdiction upon the occurrence of a destructive earthquake. It should be tacitly assumed that such an earthquake will occur somewhere in California in the near future. . . .

2. *Study Earthquake Safety of Dams*—The great potential destruction attending the failure of a dam that retains a large body of water is an especially important problem in California where many dams are in locations liable to severe earthquake damage.[18] The present imperfect state of knowledge of the earthquake resistance of dams makes this a problem of high priority. Research should be done on the dynamic behavior of dams during earthquakes, and on methods of achieving a safe and economical design for new dams. As part of this research, strong-motion seismographs and related instruments should be installed on selected dams throughout the State; it should be made obligatory that all future major dams constructed in the State should be instrumented to record the dynamic behavior during earthquakes. . . .

A matter of particular concern is the problem of evaluating the safety of existing dams that do not meet present-day standards for earthquake design. We recommend that the Division of Safety of Dams of the Department of Water Resources give this problem the most careful scrutiny. . . .

3. *Strengthen the Urban Mapping Program*—We recommend that the Division of Mines and Geology expand and accelerate its program of urban geologic mapping. The resulting maps should embody data needed for the recognition and appraisal of geological or geology-related hazards, so that the public will be alerted to the need for seeking expert advice in the development of such land.

---

[18] Author's note: There are a number of dams in the Bay Area whose failure would cause large losses of life and property. See discussion below entitled "Resources Agency: Division of Safety of Dams," p. 53ff.

4. *Develop Central Clearinghouse for Information Pertinent to Geological Hazards*—We recommend that the Division of Mines and Geology be given the responsibility for gathering, storing, and releasing geophysical information bearing on California earthquake and other geological hazards. This information should be organized and maintained on modern principles of information retrieval so that it will be readily available in useful form to interested State agencies and to the public. Information should be collected on such diverse topics as sedimentary basins, active faults, geological maps, earthquake statistics, landslides, soil investigations, logs of borings, theses, and reports.

5. *Study the Physical Behavior of Potentially Hazardous Soils*—A recurrent geological hazard that is of great practical importance to the public is the adverse behavior of natural materials as expressed by landsliding, creeping, subsidence, and liquefaction. Such unstable behavior can result in partial or total loss of superincumbent structures and also can affect relatively large areas, particularly when initiated by an earthquake. Present knowledge of properties and behavior of soils and rocks, and their response to earthquake shaking is not adequate to solve the problems already known to exist. . . . We believe this research would best be done at universities and by private professional organizations with adequate research capabilities.

As part of this program, strong-motion seismographs and related instruments should be installed at selected locations on different kinds of foundation material to record their behavior during earthquakes.

6. *Strengthen and Support Seismographic Networks in California*—Basic information on California earthquakes is now collected by networks of seismographs installed and operated by the University of California in the northern part of the State, and by the California Institute of Technology in the southern part. These organizations provide data on such important features as the magnitudes of shocks occurring in California, the locations of epicenters, the depths of foci, and the general seismicity of the State. The data collected by the networks, and the consequent analyses are basic to coping with the problems of earthquakes. These networks require a modest expansion to provide a more complete and well-balanced coverage. . . . We recommend that the State provide funds to accomplish this and to assist in meeting the operating expenses.

7. *Record Destructive Ground and Building Motions*—There is a special engineering need for measurements of the strong ground shaking of destructive earthquakes, and the consequent oscillations of buildings. Such recordings are fundamental for earthquake engineering research aimed at developing safe and economical earthquake-resistant buildings, and the State has a responsibility to provide such recordings. In particular, it is recommended that all future major State-owned structures be equipped with strong-motion recording instruments, as is now required of important buildings by the Los Angeles Department of Building and Safety. Selected existing State-owned structures should also be instrumented so as to form a network that gives adequate statewide coverage.

8. *Promote Earthquake Education*—To be useful, information on geological hazards and how to cope with them must reach not only practicing geologists, design engineers, architects, building officials, and contractors, but the informed

public as well. The University of California Extension System is well suited for conveying existing information to the people who will make use of it and who will be affected by it. We recommend that the University Extension System expand its program in this direction. The Division of Mines and Geology also should be a prime source of scientific information on earthquake and geological hazards. . . .

The report of the program committee goes on to state:

As plans for the above described activities are developed by the appropriate agencies and institutions, it is recommended that the State Earthquake and Geological Hazards Board be charged with analyzing the proposed programs with respect to technological feasibility, economic practicality, and organization and responsibility for the projects. It is further recommended that this Board establish project priorities based on relative potential for most rapidly and practically reducing the undesirable effects of geological hazards.[19]

The author participated in the Earthquake and Geologic Hazards Conference, and was a member of both the program and organization committees. Without qualification, he believes that the organization committee report, partially quoted above, must be implemented. As of November, 1967, the Administrator of the Resources Agency had accepted the recommendations of the geologic hazards advisory committees, and asked its Department of Conservation, through the Division of Mines and Geology, to implement these recommendations, within current limits of funds and personnel. Departmental legislation was enacted at the 1968 legislative session to increase the five-man State Mining and Geology Board to seven members, rather than set up a new State Earthquake and Geologic Hazards Board.

RESOURCES AGENCY: DIVISION OF SAFETY OF DAMS[20]

Possible hazards from the failure of dams in the Bay Area were brought to public attention by the failure of the Baldwin Hills Dam in Los Angeles on December 14, 1963. This disaster caused the loss of five lives and approximately $15 million in property damage. The cause of the failure—currently in litigation—was stated this way: "Earth movement occurred at the reservoir on December 14, 1963, following an apparent long-term development of stress and displacement in the foundation. The movement was apparently not seismic but took place at faults which were planes of foundation weakness." (See California.

---

[19] *Earthquake and Geologic Hazards in California.* A report to the Resources Agency by the Geologic Hazards Advisory Committees for Program and Organization, April 26, 1967.

[20] The author is grateful to F. W. Blanchard, East Bay Municipal Utility District, and to Robert B. Jansen, California Division of Safety of Dams, for the factual information in this section.

Dept. of Water Resources, *Investigation of Failure, Baldwin Hills Reservoir,* April 1964, p. 3.) The dam was located within the earthquake-active Inglewood fault zone.

Under the State of California's *Water Code,* all dams and reservoirs in California, except those under minimum legal size and those owned by the federal government, are under the jurisdiction of the State of California for safety of design, construction, operation, and behavioral surveillance. This program, in continuous operation since 1929, is administered by the Department of Water Resources, Division of Safety of Dams. As of July, 1967, Bay Area counties contained 203 completed dams that were large enough to be under the jurisdiction of the State of California.

Because the consequences of a storage-dam failure are often much greater than those caused by collapse of even a large building, safety factors for dams must be more conservative than those for buildings. Since 1964, the state's program has included reevaluation of older dams for the adequacy of spillway capacities, safe structural and stability factors, and possible materials and foundation deterioration related to safety. Assembly Bill 1051, 1965, extended jurisdiction to offstream dams and reservoirs, and generally strengthened California's dam safety program in recognition of the increasing hazards presented by the state's population growth, and the construction of new storage facilities. The reevaluation of dams which have been under state jurisdiction for many years is now, for the first time, being applied to these existing offstream dams.

One segment of this reevaluation effort has emphasized the probable seismic stability of dams during tectonic disturbances, such as faulting. Embankment dams and multiple-arch dams are receiving particular attention.

Selected dams in the Bay Area are being reevaluated. First attention is being given older dams, and those that are potentially more hazardous. In some cases, dam owners have been asked to have their structures evaluated by qualified engineers of their own selection, whose findings are then reviewed by the state. Cooperation from the owners has been good. Several multidam owners have been exceptionally amenable to the state's requests. Several dams have already been strengthened where it was found desirable to do so. Where necessary, such investigations and improvement requirements apply retroactively to structures under state jurisdiction since the original law was enacted in 1929; they also apply to existing offchannel dams that were first brought within the state's jurisdiction in 1965.

Administrative measures are available to remedy situations considered hazardous, if the owner should be uncooperative. The authorized use of all dams is controlled by conditional and revocable certificates (sections 6355, 6357–6357.4, 6363, 6461, Division 3, *Water Code*). Although revocation has not yet been found necessary, use restrictions have been imposed in several instances. These will continue until improvements allow full or conditional use.

An example of attention recently given to dams includes the survey conducted by the East Bay Municipal Utility District of their facilities in 1964. One result of this survey was the expenditure of more than $350,000 to increase the seismic resistance of 47-year-old San Pablo Dam.

OFFICE OF ARCHITECTURE AND CONSTRUCTION: REGULATION OF
PUBLIC SCHOOLS

California's Field Act, controlling public schools construction—principally new schools—has set the highest current standards for earthquake safety of any law-enforcing agency. The act was passed after the disastrous 1933 Long Beach earthquake, and is administered by the state's Office of Architecture and Construction.

The Field Act does *not* apply to places of general public assembly (such as privately owned theaters and auditoriums) or to vital public service buildings (such as city halls, fire stations, etc.). Thus, some publicly owned buildings that should be either strengthened or demolished are still in use. The responsible political jurisdictions are remiss in not making hazard studies of these facilities, and developing remedial programs where necessary.

The Field Act does not control the site selection of public schools. Until 1967, a school district could purchase a site having a geologic hazard such as an earthquake fault, and build on the fault. In 1967, however, the Legislature added the following language to the *Education Code*:

The governing board of a school district, prior to acquiring any site on which it proposes to construct any school building . . . shall have the site . . . investigated by competent personnel. . . . The investigation shall include such geological and engineering studies as will preclude siting of a school over or within a fault, on or below a slide area, or in any other location where the geological characteristics are such that the construction effort required to make the site safe for occupancy is economically unfeasible. . . . (sec. 15002.1)

No provisions were enacted for enforcing the foregoing section of the *Education Code*.

One instance of school site planning is the Contra Costa College campus in San Pablo, lying astride the Hayward fault. Shortly after the college district acquired the site, the possibility was raised that it was crossed by the then largely unknown and unmapped northerly extension of the Hayward fault. The location of the Hayward fault was determined as accurately as possible by detailed geologic studies, which followed immediately. A "greenbelt" was laid out around the fault trace, and buildings were planned for locations some distance away from the fault. This pioneering planning concept of 1954 is still being used by the college when locating new buildings on their campus.

In 1967, the Bureau of School Planning of the California State Department of Education made a statewide survey of the number of non-Field Act schools remaining in California. Their questionnaires drew about an 80 percent statewide response. School board response from the nine Bay Area counties, correct to March 1, 1968, was made available to the author and may be partially summarized as follows:

Number of Bay Area school districts responding:...................... 102
Number of Bay Area school districts having non-Field Act schools:...... 65
Number of non-Field Act schools in the Bay Area:..................... 295
Number of Bay Area school districts having _no_ correction plan:......... 16

Despite the elapse of 35 years since the Field Act was passed by the Legislature, about two-thirds of the Bay Area school districts still have one or more buildings which are legally unsafe. It seems clear that the local leadership has been insufficient in many cases.

In 1967, the Legislature also added sections to the _Education Code_ which may speed the replacement of older schools that do not conform to the Field Act. (It should be pointed out that the Field Act was not retroactive with respect to existing construction.) Governing boards are now required to have all non-Field Act schools examined and reported on by January 1, 1970. If the buildings are found to be unsafe, the board must make repairs (or replace the buildings) from their funds. If available funds are insufficient to repair or replace the structure(s), the board must call an election authorizing bonds, or an increase of the maximum tax rate. Should the voters reject these means of obtaining funds, the proposals must be resubmitted to the electorate within five years.

To make the 1967 legislation more effective, the 1968 Legislature enacted a law stating that no known earthquake-unsafe public school building could be used as a public school building after June 30, 1975.[21]

OTHER STATE AGENCIES IN RELATED ACTIVITIES

Most of the other agencies are principally concerned with building

---

[21] _Cal. Stats.,_ 1968, ch. 692.

construction. In the Bay Area, the roles of these state agencies are relatively minor, compared with those already discussed. Accordingly, they receive no further treatment here.

Federal Agencies and Programs

The principal federal agencies that play a direct and substantial part in dealing with the earthquake problems discussed here are the U. S. Coast and Geodetic Survey of the Environmental Sciences Services Administration (ESSA) and the U. S. Geological Survey. Others, such as the Corps of Engineers, which handles considerable construction work in rivers, harbors, and dams, have very important functions not as directly related as those of the first two agencies. Most of the federal agencies are considerably more research-oriented than the local agencies that must deal with the ordinary day-to-day problems.

U. S. COAST AND GEODETIC SURVEY

The U. S. Coast and Geodetic Survey has been active in several scientific fields in the Bay Area. Their operation and maintenance of the strong-motion seismographic network is of major importance. These instruments, usually located in large buildings, are quite different from those customarily in continuous operation at university seismographic stations. The latter instruments are designed for extreme sensitivity in order to record distant earthquakes. They go "off scale" during even a moderate local earthquake. On the other hand, the strong-motion seismograph does not operate until triggered by a strong earthquake. When thus activated, the strong-motion instrument will record for a given period of time before automatically shutting off.

The largest American earthquake for which strong-motion seismograph records are available is the 1940 El Centro, California, earthquake. Strong-motion instruments located in San Francisco buildings have been there for decades, but only the moderate earthquake of 1957 was strong enough to trigger them.

The records of the strong-motion seismographs are vital to basic earthquake engineering research because they describe the actual motions that occur when earthquake forces become destructive. These instruments should be located in many different building types and on varying geologic environments, since ground motions and buildings' responses to these motions have many variables. The present network in the Bay Area is too "thin," and more instruments are needed for adequate coverage.

The Coast and Geodetic Survey field-investigates felt earthquakes and prepares reports on them. Isoseismal maps are prepared for stronger earthquakes. The survey also studies the vibration characteristics of structures.

All of the foregoing are vital activities directed towards better design of safer structures. They need to be intensified.

U. S. GEOLOGICAL SURVEY

The Geological Survey's principal concern with the subjects discussed in this monograph, as the agency's title suggests, relates to the foundation materials beneath man-made structures, or other geologic conditions that constitute hazards to life and property. Broadly speaking, this agency's interest stops where the U. S. Coast and Geodetic Survey begins its studies. Much of the Geological Survey's work in the Bay Area is in the same general direction as that of the State of California's Division of Mines and Geology.

The vital work of the Geological Survey in connection with the San Andreas and Hayward faults has already been described. The survey has stated its additional role in the Bay Area as follows:

The objectives of the program are to provide large-scale, detailed geologic maps and reports on the bedrock and surficial rocks, and to provide basic information on foundation conditions and construction materials and their relations with geologic processes, in one of the most rapidly expanding urban areas of the nation. Geologic data, obtained by systematic mapping, helps minimize or avoid planning and engineering problems by permitting the engineer to design his structure to better fit into the limitations imposed by the natural conditions.

The maps and reports in no way pretend to supplant detailed site studies. . . . The reports and maps supply background and regional information that can be used to plan a meaningful site investigation program, both in the field and in the laboratory, that is required in the design of specific engineering projects.

The geology of San Francisco Bay itself is presently being studied by the Geological Survey. The study area includes all of San Francisco Bay including San Pablo and Suisun Bays and bordering areas underlain by bay deposits. The objectives of the study are:

1. To establish the geometry and physical and chemical characteristics of the sediments of San Francisco Bay and bordering marshlands.

2. To elucidate the geologic history of the bay and the estuarine processes pertinent to sedimentation and to planning, constructing, and maintaining engineering structures.

3. To evaluate the relations between geology of the bay and engineering behavior of bay sediments, including seismic response and the potential for landsliding and subsidence.

The foregoing program is important and must be continued.

EARTHQUAKE PREDICTION

After the 1964 Alaskan earthquake, the Director of the President's Office of Science and Technology convened a panel of experts to examine the possibilities of earthquake prediction. The panel recommended a program costing an estimated $137 million over a period of 10 years. Since then, the proposed program has been under study by a federal interagency group. This group has broadened the program's emphasis on the applied aspects, namely life safety and control of property damage. Although the program has not been funded by Congress, scientific interest remains high. There is no assurance that the proposed program will result in a usable earthquake prediction system, but the additions to geophysical knowledge will undoubtedly be of very substantial value. Furthermore, the resulting progress in earthquake engineering will certainly reduce the seismic hazard to life and property.

The ability to predict earthquakes—partially or precisely—will pose problems. Suppose, for example, that the public were told that there was a 50–50 chance of a destructive earthquake occurring within three years of the announcement. What might be the response? In many cases, major industrial and commercial construction would probably be postponed until after the anticipated event, or relocated elsewhere, thus resulting in a major dislocation for large segments of the local economy. Painting and other maintenance work on dwellings, as well as other buildings, would probably be postponed until after the predicted earthquake, if possible. In many instances, inventories subject to damage would be reduced or relocated elsewhere, in anticipation of the earthquake.

Suppose, in addition, that the earthquake did not occur on schedule, but that it actually took place two years later than expected, i.e., five years after the first announcement. During the two-year period after the predicted event failed to happen, many who had postponed construction or maintenance might well have gone ahead with their delayed plans. Thus they would suffer both the inconvenience of delay, and the earthquake damage they had hoped to avoid. Such an experience would obviously have political and economic consequences. Other problems can be cited. For example, should people be allowed to remain in non-earthquake-resistive buildings if there were a 50–50 chance of a destructive earthquake occurring in the next three years? If persons were required to vacate these hazardous buildings for three years, and if no serious earthquake then occurred, it would be reasonable to expect political consequences. Similar problems can be posed for other prediction possibilities.

The foregoing are not suggested as reasons to oppose a program of earthquake prediction. Instead they are urged as reasons to learn more about how society will respond to such predictions. Seismologists will surely learn enough about the interior of the earth to predict earthquakes successfully. Consequently, it is essential that we *immediately* begin research on the social and economic consequences of earthquake prediction, and on how to cope with them.

For its own part, a major Bay Area contribution would be to develop and implement a program leading to the abatement of the building-collapse hazard, effective planning in fault zones, and the like. Hopefully all construction will eventually be highly earthquake-resistive. Then an earthquake could be an exciting experience, unsettling, perhaps, but not necessarily hazardous. In any event, the social and economic consequences of a successful—or partially successful—earthquake prediction program are more far-reaching than most persons realize.

Local Agencies and Programs

BUILDING DEPARTMENTS

The building departments of cities and counties are the principal effective policing agents for all construction that is not government owned. Certain specialized structures, such as privately owned dams, fall under the purview of agencies other than cities and counties. For all practical purposes, however, most building construction is policed by local building departments.

The *Uniform Building Code,* or adaptations thereof, is the basic document for the building departments in most Bay Area cities. The code is constantly being updated, and a new edition is released every three years. It is a quite satisfactory code and has served well.

The Structural Engineers Association of California has synthesized the basic research findings of universities, government agencies, and structural engineers into functional earthquake code provisions. These recommended code provisions have been adopted by the International Conference of Building Officials in the *Uniform Building Code.* This has been a laborious process, but it has provided a reasonable set of checks and balances. The final earthquake code provisions are invariably a compromise involving economics, safety, and practical design methods, but the provisions are usable and generally satisfactory.

The responsible local body, i.e., a city council or county board of supervisors, may adopt the *Uniform Building Code* as the law applicable to its jurisdictional area. These political subdivisions may also add amendments to the plumbing, electrical, and other sections of the code, including revisions to the earthquake-bracing provisions. While minor variations exist, the earthquake-bracing provisions adopted by the various political subdivisions usually conform exactly to the *Uniform Building Code.*

Each city and county normally has its own building department. Very large local governments, such as the City of Los Angeles, can and do have a variety of technical specialists capable of handling the most complex design and construction problems. The cities of San Francisco and Oakland, being considerably smaller than Los Angeles, find it more difficult to be comparably staffed. The very small cities—which are often growing rapidly and in which much new construction takes place—may not even have a technically qualified engineer at the head of the department, because of salary limitations. Often the supporting staff is not technically competent to handle complex engineering problems.

Effective code enforcement must see to it that the construction drawings approved by the building department are faithfully followed during construction. This is usually done, but not always. For example, the author has a number of photographs of hollow concrete block walls which, when cut open, revealed reinforcing steel, but had no concrete (grout) around the steel. Such faulty construction negates the earthquake effectiveness of the steel reinforcement. Other examples with other materials can also be cited.

Construction in landslide areas, in fault zones, and on poor soils also requires much more attention by building departments. But, as noted, local building departments are generally not staffed with soils engineers and engineering geologists, whose knowledge is essential for adequate control in these matters.

PLANNING COMMISSIONS

Building departments—through the earthquake, plumbing, electrical, and other provisions of their building codes—protect the public safety and health in man-made construction. Planning commissions, on the other hand, consider land use from aesthetic and other general public welfare standpoints. These are quite different from the safety concerns emphasized by building departments.

Thus the planning commission may assume that life-safety matters are the principal concern of the building department. Consequently, a planning commission may inadvertently zone an area containing a major landslide, earthquake fault, or unstable Bay fill on a basis entirely unrelated to the hazards present.

Given a sufficient amount of money, proper engineering can eliminate hazards from any site, or at least minimize them. For example, an engineer could design a structure able to withstand a 20-foot fault displacement, or he could level a whole hillside in order to eliminate a landslide potential. But appropriate solutions may often impose economic limitations that either postpone or possibly even prevent certain types of developments. As a practical matter, an owner who has purchased property containing an earthquake geologic hazard often is unaware of the hazard until he plans to develop the site, whereupon his consultants inform him of the situation. Because of the investment already made, the owner is at least partially committed to go ahead and build on the difficult site, if at all possible. Appropriate zoning based in part on geologic hazards could help owners avoid such unforeseen problems.

Although several attempts have been made to control land usage in order to minimize earthquake geologic hazards, not all have been successful. In 1966–67, the Marin County Planning Commission considered a proposal to study earthquake hazard and related land-use problems in the San Andreas fault zone in western Marin County, but at this writing no studies had been authorized. Beginning in 1967, the State Division of Mines and Geology was expending one-half man-year, per year, on Marin County geologic mapping.

In 1965, Redwood City made a detailed engineering study for the development of portions of its shoreline areas. The final report made use of the best available scientific and engineering information. It included a discussion of the seismic design considerations required for the development of the shoreline area. Other examples of land-use planning could be cited, but to the author's knowledge no comprehensive policy regarding all earthquake geologic hazards has been established by any Bay Area planning commission.

Summary and Recommendations

In the Bay Area, earthquakes are sufficiently frequent and severe to justify requiring that all building construction be earthquake resistive. This principle is recognized and enforced by the various local building ordinances. The ordinances apply to new construction, but are essentially inapplicable to construction built prior to the enactment of earthquake provisions. The standards for earthquake-resistive design for the Bay Area are among the highest in the world. But this does not mean that all of the earthquake problems have been solved, particularly in the area of geologic hazards, where there is little or no control.

Two principal problem areas require public policy attention:

A. Planning for best land use where earthquake geologic hazard may exist:

1. *In and across active fault zones:* This is a problem primarily with the active San Andreas and Hayward faults. It is recommended that studies be directed towards the development of planning maps and other criteria to delineate the risk with respect to fault location. One such approach, using three grades of risk for fault zones, appears on page 13 and following.

2. *Bay fill lands:* It is recommended that studies be directed toward the development of planning maps and other suitable criteria to control the possibilities of increased seismic risk in these areas of San Francisco Bay. Approaches to this problem are given on page 31 and following.

3. *Potential landslide areas:* The landslide problem would be serious if a major earthquake were to occur after a long wet season. While further study is recommended, however, changes from present public policy do not seem warranted at this time.

B. Reducing the life hazard of older non-earthquake-resistive, collapse-hazard structures:

Solutions to this problem involve political and economic issues, as well as engineering considerations. It is realistic, however, for the cities to begin planning ways and means of developing programs to minimize the hazards of older buildings.

Comprehensive land-use planning for earthquake geologic hazard areas has not been systematically and rationally attempted anywhere in the United States. If steps are taken in the Bay Area to develop such a comprehensive plan, it must be a pioneering effort, involving economics, geology and engineering.

63

One organizational approach to regional land-use problems would assign them to some type of regional government. To be effective, such a regional government would have to be adequately staffed and funded, and given sufficient authority to act in cases where earthquake geologic hazards exist. A regional governmental organization would probably be better able to resist political pressures that might otherwise influence the leaders of a small community, especially one encompassing large undeveloped land areas in earthquake geologic hazard zones.

A regional government would also have enough earthquake geologic hazards work to justify an adequate staff. Technical standards involving several professional and scientific disciplines would have to be established. These standards must be the work of a professional and scientific group, and not that of an individual, since broadly based and sound judgment is very important. The professional and scientific group should serve as consultants, or as an advisory board. The group should include geologists, soils engineers, city planners, structural engineers, business economists, and others. Their jurisdiction should include publicly owned utilities, as well as private property.

In conclusion, the principal earthquake *geologic* hazards in the Bay Area are significant regional land-use problems best solved by some type of regional government. This government must have adequate funds and authority to plan, and to implement its plans, using a competent professional interdisciplinary approach. The *nongeologic* earthquake hazards, principally older non-earthquake-resistive buildings have been and probably should continue to be the responsibilities of the cities and counties.

APPENDIX A

Some Seismological and Geological Terms

Fault

A geologic *fault* may be defined as a fracture or fracture zone, along which there has been movement of the two sides relative to one another. Scarps (cliffs) will form on the earth's surface if the relative movement along the fault is vertical; fences and roads will be horizontally offset if the relative movement is horizontal. Surface effects are, of course, in part dependent upon the topography. A purely horizontal displacement of several feet, for example, might bring together a small hill and a depression creating an apparent vertical scarp several feet high. All sorts of combinations of vertical and horizontal movements can also take place. The total relative movement, or displacement, over millions of years may be only a few inches, or it may amount to many miles. The fault movement occurring at any one time generally lies within a preexisting *fault zone*.[1] In the case of major faults, the fault zone may be more than a mile wide in some places.

A *fault trace* is a line on the surface of the earth formed by the intersection of the fault with the earth's surface.

An *active fault* is one that has experienced displacements of sufficient geologic recency to suggest that future displacements are to be expected. A fault may be active, despite the fact that it may not have moved in historic times.

A fault is presumed to be a *dead fault* (inactive) if it shows no evidence of movement in recent geological time. There can, of course, be borderline cases. For example, the "dead" White Wolf fault in Kern County, California, came back to life in 1952, and the resulting earthquake caused damage in Tehachapi, Bakersfield, Los Angeles, and elsewhere.

The foregoing definitions lack a key figure, namely, how many years a fault must be inactive before it is considered dead. Some competent geologic opinion holds that a fault should be considered active if it has displaced Recent alluvium. One New Zealand viewpoint, which is reflected in their city planning in seismic areas, considers a fault active

---

[1] The term *fault zone* is described more fully in the context of the Hayward and San Andreas faults, which are discussed elsewhere in this monograph.

65

if movement along it has occurred at least once in the last 1000 years.[2] Another viewpoint tentatively held by some in the United States would consider a fault to be active if it had experienced surface movements in the last 10,000 years. Obviously the foregoing figures must be used with caution.

Recent (1966) experience in California suggests that small amounts of surface faulting occur in relatively frequent small-magnitude shocks, and that surface faulting may take place more often than previously suspected. It is hoped that tighter definitions for active and dead faults will be established before long. (The discussion of active vs. dead faults applies primarily to some western states; in other areas it is difficult to correlate earthquake activity with known faults.)

Focus

The *focus* of an earthquake is usually an instrumentally located point below the earth's surface where the faulting first occurs, presumably on a fault. *Focal depth* refers to the depth of the focus below the earth's surface. In California, the usual focal depth of most earthquakes has been estimated to be about 10 miles, although there is evidence that the March 1957 San Francisco shock may have had a focal depth of as little as six miles. Studies of smaller shocks in California also show focal depths substantially less than six miles. However, in some parts of the world, focal depths may reach hundreds of miles.

A shallow focal depth implies that the earthquake's energy is released close to the earth's surface. Damage from such a shallow shock is or can be more concentrated and intense than in the case of a deep-focus earthquake releasing an equal amount of energy.

Epicenter

The term *epicenter,* which is commonly mentioned in today's newspapers in connection with earthquakes, should more properly be called *instrumental epicenter,* but custom has dropped the first word. The instrumental epicenter is the point on the earth's surface directly above the focus, and must be located by instrumental means. It is commonly theorized that the beginning of the fault rupture causing an earthquake is at the focus, which in turn is directly below the instrumental epicenter.

The *field epicenter* defines the location of the greatest or most pronounced earthquake effects—it may not coincide with the instrumental

[2] New Zealand, Ministry of Works, Town and Country Planning Branch, "Town Planning and Earthquake Faults," *Town and Country Planning Bulletin* (No. 7, May 1965).

epicenter. For example, the field epicenter of the September 4, 1955 San Jose earthquake was located eight miles west of the instrumental epicenter; the field epicenter in this instance was based on the observed maximum building damage. When major surface faulting occurs, however, the field epicenter may sometimes be defined as the location of the maximum observed fault displacement. In the 1906 San Francisco shock, the San Andreas fault had its maximum displacement of 21 feet in Marin County. On the basis of this displacement some authorities have placed the field epicenter there.

The instrumental epicenter need not fall on the surface rupture of the faulting, and indeed it often does not. Instrumental inaccuracies, the angle that the fault makes with the vertical *(fault dip)*, as well as other factors can explain the apparent variances.

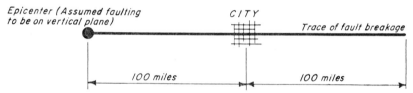

Figure 10. Illustration of the concept of epicentral distance, which may not always be meaningful. In the case shown, with the epicenter at one end of a fault rupture, maximum damage from vibration and fault rupture may be in the city rather than at the epicenter. See text for fuller explanation.

It would, indeed, be convenient if the instrumental epicenter, the field epicenter determined from building damage, and the field epicenter determined from maximum fault displacement would coincide.

The distance between any location on the earth's surface and the instrumental epicenter, or the *epicentral distance,* is a convenient figure to state in earthquake reports. In many cases this distance may be related to the severity of damage. However, the instrumental epicenter may not be located above the center of the energy release occurring during fault movement. For example, the epicenter may be at one end of a rupture that extends for many miles, whereas the center of the energy release may be at or near the midpoint of the fault rupture. It is the released energy, reduced by damping and dissipation as it travels by wave motion from its source, that causes vibrational damage to a building. Suppose that an earthquake has an epicenter 100 miles from a city and that the fault rupture extends from the epicenter to, through, and beyond the city for another 100 miles (Figure 10). The city's epicentral distance of 100 miles would certainly not be a measure of the damage in the city, which might be located directly above the center of the energy release.

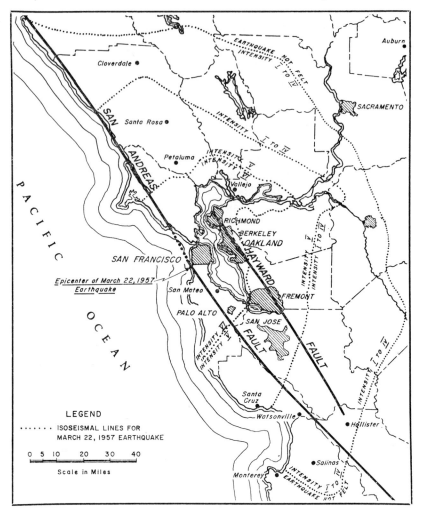

Figure 11. Isoseismal map of the March 22, 1957 San Francisco (Daly City) earthquake. From California Department of Natural Resources. Div. of Mines, *San Francisco Earthquakes of March 1957* (Special Report 57, 1959).

Intensity

The *intensity* of an earthquake is a measure of earthquake effects of all types. Lowest earthquake intensities are based principally on human reactions, such as "felt indoors by few," since other effects, such as damage, are usually not present. The highest intensities are largely measured by geologic effects, such as broad fissures in wet ground, numerous and extensive landslides, and major surface faulting. The middle intensity range is based largely on the degree of damage to buildings and other man-made structures. Thus it should be clearly understood that intensity ratings are non-instrumental, and rely on human observations and interpretation. The reader should also be warned that human reactions, building damage, and geologic effects are not fully compatible in any single intensity scale.

During an earthquake each location experiences an intensity measured by the earthquake effects noted at that location. A person gathering reports on a widely felt earthquake can find literally thousands of intensity locations. Intensities at the various locations may be plotted on a map. A line, called an *isoseismal line,* can be drawn so as to separate areas experiencing different intensities. Figure 11 is an *isoseismal map* of the Bay Area showing intensities experienced during the earthquake of March 22, 1957.

Isoseismal maps are useful since they describe, in summary form, the geographic patterns of damage. They can also relate damage to soils and geology. Intensity studies suffer from necessarily subjective interpretations of the data, but they still have not been superseded by a more useful method for summarizing damage.

The maximum intensity on the Modified Mercalli scale is XII—by definition, damage is total at that intensity, objects are thrown upward in the air, and similar maximum effects are observed.[3] However, there have been no cases of total destruction of well-constructed earthquake-resistive buildings subjected only to ground vibration. Total damage *may* occur as a result of an earthquake-induced landslide, faulting through the site, or other geologic event. But there is ample reason to believe that—when adequate measures are taken to overcome or avoid geologic hazards—the maximum intensities to man-made construction can be limited to VIII for most modern earthquake-resistive structures.

Magnitude

The approximate *magnitude* of an earthquake can be quickly obtained from seismic records—and this is the number commonly published by the daily press in connection with earthquakes. In contrast, maximum *intensity* determinations may take many days, because field work is involved. The magnitude scale has been defined as follows by Professor Charles Richter, its inventor and original developer:

Magnitude is intended to be a rating of a given earthquake independent of the place of observation. Since it is calculated from measurements on seismo-

[3] The Modified Mercalli Scale has been used in the United States since 1931. See Table 4 for a summary description.

grams, it is properly expressed in ordinary numbers and decimals. Magnitude was originally defined as the logarithm of the maximum amplitude on a seismogram written by an instrument of specified standard type at a distance of 100 kilometers (62 miles) from the epicenter. . . . Because the scale is logarithmic, every upward step of one magnitude unit means multiplying the recorded amplitude by 10. . . . The largest known earthquake magnitudes are near 8¾; this is a result of observation, not an arbitrary 'ceiling' like that of the intensity scales. (*Elementary Seismology*, W. H. Freeman & Co., 1958, p. 17)

TABLE 4

MODIFIED MERCALLI INTENSITY SCALE OF 1931 (ABRIDGED)

Note: The parenthetical R. F. listings below indicate equivalent intensities on the Rossi-Forel Scale.

I. Not felt except by a very few under especially favorable circumstances. (R. F. I)

II. Felt only by a few persons at rest, especially on upper floors of building Delicately suspended objects may swing. (R. F. I to II)

III. Felt noticeably indoors, especially on upper floors of buildings, but many people do not recognize it as an earthquake. Standing motor cars may rock slightly. Vibration like passing of truck. Duration estimated. (R. F. III)

IV. During the day felt indoors by many, outdoors by few. At night some awakened. Dishes, windows, doors disturbed; walls make creaking sound. Sensation like heavy truck striking building. Standing motor cars rocked noticeably. (R. F. IV to V)

V. Felt by nearly everyone; many awakened. Some dishes, windows, etc., broken; a few instances of cracked plaster; unstable objects overturned. Disturbance of trees, poles, and other tall objects sometimes noticed. Pendulum clocks may stop. (R. F. V to VI)

VI. Felt by all; many frightened and run outdoors. Some heavy furniture moved; a few instances of fallen plaster or damaged chimneys. Damage slight. (R. F. VI to VII)

VII. Everybody runs outdoors. Damage negligible in buildings of good design and construction; slight to moderate in well-built ordinary structures; considerable in poorly built or badly designed structures; some chimneys broken. Noticed by persons driving motor cars. (R. F. VIII minus)

VIII. Damage slight in specially designed structures; considerable in ordinary substantial buildings with partial collapse; great in poorly built structures. Panel walls thrown out of frame structures. Fall of chimney, factory stacks, columns, monuments, walls. Heavy furniture overturned. Sand and mud ejected in small amounts. Changes in well water. Disturbs persons driving motor cars. (R. F. VIII plus to IX minus)

IX. Damage considerable in specially designed structures; well-designed frame structures thrown out of plumb; damage great in substantial buildings, with partial collapse. Buildings shifted off foundations. Ground cracked conspicuously. Underground pipes broken. (R. F. IX plus)

X. Some well-built wooden structures destroyed; most masonry and frame structures destroyed with foundations; ground badly cracked. Rails bent. Landslides considerable from river banks and steep slopes. Shifted sand and mud. Water splashed (slopped) over banks. (R. F. X)

XI. Few, if any, (masonry) structures remain standing. Bridges destroyed. Broad fissures in ground. Underground pipe lines completely out of service. Earth slumps and land slips in soft ground. Rails bent greatly. (No R. F.)

XII. Damage total. Waves seen on ground surfaces. Lines of sight and level distorted. Objects thrown upward into the air. (No R. F.)

Crude correlations have been developed for the relationship of an earthquake's magnitude with its maximum intensity. These correlations are often based on "ordinary ground conditions in California." When the ground conditions vary, as they usually do, the error introduced in using these correlations becomes exceedingly gross (see Figure 6). In other regions, where focal depths may be greater, the correlations become even poorer.

The magnitude can also be related to the earthquake's energy. A one-unit increase in magnitude corresponds roughly to a 30-fold increase in energy. A two-unit increase in magnitude, such as from 5 to 7, leads to a 30 times 30 (or 900) increase in energy, and so forth.

Tsunami (or Seismic Sea Wave)

Tsunami is the Japanese word for an ocean wave—sometimes called tidal wave[4]—that may be of great height when it approaches shorelines. It usually is accepted that most tsunamis are generated by sudden changes in the elevation of the sea bottom occurring during earthquakes. Submarine landslides may also be the cause of some tsunamis. The downdrops or uplifts of the ocean floor cause water to move to or from the area, generating waves which can have velocities of 500 to 600 miles per hour in the deep ocean.

Tsunamis have not been a significant hazard to the San Francisco Bay Area in historic times. In the rare event of a major tsunami striking the Golden Gate, extensive damage within the Bay would be unlikely. The narrow mouth of the Bay restricts the quantity of water that can flow through it in a short period of time, and also minimizes ocean waves that pass through it. Changes in water level between the ocean

---

[4] The term "tidal wave," is usually and erroneously applied to tsunamis, or seismic sea waves. Tidal waves are actually waves related to tidal forces. Nevertheless, common usage apparently has made the term "tidal wave" an acceptable part of the popular vocabulary for seismic sea wave.

and the Bay result in swift currents within the Bay, however, and this may damage moored boats and shoreline developments with submarginal freeboard. The 1964 Alaskan tsunami, for example, caused a five-foot drop in the water level at the Alameda Naval Air Station for a short period of time, as well as swift currents in the Bay. Tsunami damage could be extensive to low lying coastal regions of Bay Area counties fronting on the Pacific Ocean, although there is no local history of such a disaster.

Major Earthquakes in The Bay Area

The historic Bay Area earthquakes which have had an observed intensity of VII or greater are listed below. Through 1930, intensities are given on the Rossi-Forel scale; for 1931 and later, intensities are given on the Modified Mercalli scale. Appreciable damage begins to occur at intensity VII on both of these scales.

The following catalog of earthquakes was originally compiled by Don Tocher for his article "Seismic History of the San Francisco Region," and was published by the California Division of Mines in *San Francisco Earthquakes of March 1957,* Special Report 57 (1959). This catalog has been updated to include the more recent earthquakes.

1800 October 11. Strong shocks at San Juan Bautista, continuing at least through October 31. Every building damaged; cracks appeared in the ground of the rancheria, and a deep fissure near the Pajaro River.

1808 June 21. Eighteen shocks [some say twenty-one] at the Presidio of San Francisco up to July 17. Adobe walls were seriously damaged (VIII). Date of main shock not known.

1822. The church at the Santa Clara Mission was badly injured. The Mission San Jose may also have been damaged by this shock.

1836 June 10, 7:30 a.m. One of the five largest earthquakes centered in the San Francisco Bay region in historic times. Ground breakage along the line of the Hayward fault at the base of the hills east of the bay, extending from Mission San Jose to San Pablo. As strong or stronger than the shock of October 21, 1868, which had its center along the same fault. At least one foreshock; numerous aftershocks for at least a month.

1838 June. Just after noon. Another of the five largest shocks in the area. Surface breakage along the San Andreas fault zone, probably extending at least from San Francisco to a point near Santa Clara. Serious damage to walls at the Presidio of San Francisco and at the Missions San Jose, Santa Clara, and San Francisco. Comparable with the earthquake of April 18, 1906.

1841 July 3, 2:07 p.m. Intensity VII at Monterey. Also felt at sea.

1851 May 15, 8:10 a.m. Severe shocks (VII) at San Francisco. Also felt on ships in the harbor.

1851 November 26. Eleven shocks felt along the coast from Santa Cruz to Mendocino. This may be an incorrect reference to strong shocks in southern California on October 26, 1852, or November 27, 1852. None of the 11 are known to have been destructive.

73

1852 November 22, 11 p.m. Intensity VIII on the San Francisco peninsula. Severe 8 miles to southwest of San Francisco, where considerable fissuring of the ground allowed the waters of Lake Merced to drain into the ocean.

1856 February 15, 5:25 a.m. Intensity VIII at San Francisco, where there was considerable building damage. Felt from Santa Rosa south to Monterey, and as far east as Stockton. Water in San Francisco Bay disturbed.

1858 November 26, 12:35 a.m. At San Jose (VIII) nearly every brick, adobe, or masonry building was cracked or injured in some way. There was some damage to buildings in San Francisco (VII), especially on made land.

1859 October 5. Intensity in San Francisco has been estimated as VII, although details are lacking.

1861 July 3, 4:11 p.m. Intensity IX (?) near the present site of Livermore. Adobe houses damaged, men in the fields thrown down.

1864 March 5, 8:49 a.m. Widely felt, but apparently strongest at San Francisco (VII+). Intensity VII at San Jose and Santa Clara, VI at Stockton. At San Francisco, plate glass windows were shattered and plaster cracked.

1865 March 8, 6 p.m. Intensity VIII in east-central Sonoma County. Severe in Santa Rosa and upper Bennett Valley, a few miles from Santa Rosa. Plaster cracked, clocks stopped, and chimneys thrown down.

1865 October 8, 12:44 p.m. One of the five largest earthquakes in the region in historic times, and first of the two large shocks of the 1860s. Apparently centered on the San Andreas fault in the Santa Cruz Mountains, where cracks in the ground, landslides, and dust clouds were observed. Intensity at least IX. In San Francisco, damage was most severe on made ground; the Old Merchants' Exchange Building at Battery and Washington Streets was ruined, and a fissure appeared in the ground on Howard Street from Seventh to Ninth.

1866 March 26, 12:30 p.m. Felt in San Francisco, Stockton, Monterey, Sacramento, and San Jose. Minor damage may have occurred in San Francisco, although existing reports do not agree sufficiently well to estimate the maximum intensity.

1868 October 21, 7:53 a.m. One of California's great shocks, and second of the two large Bay Area shocks of the 1860s. Surface breakage was observed on the Hayward fault from Warm Springs to San Leandro, a distance of about 20 miles. The maximum horizontal offset was about 3 feet. Intensity X at Hayward, where every building was damaged, and many demolished. Intensity IX at San Francisco, where, as in earlier large shocks, damage was chiefly confined to buildings on filled ground along the bayshore. About 30 persons lost their lives in this shock. This earthquake was felt at places 175 miles from the source.

1882 March 6, 2 p.m. Newspaper reports suggest an epicenter near Hollister, with an intensity there of VII. Felt to the southeast at least as far as San Luis Obispo and Visalia.

1883 March 30, 7:45 a.m. Intensity VII at Hollister. Plaster knocked loose and windows broken. Also strong at Watsonville and Santa Cruz. Felt from Martinez to San Luis Obispo.

1884 March 25, 4:40 p.m. Severe, possibly VII, at San Francisco. Felt from Santa Cruz to Petaluma, and at Grass Valley.

1885 March 30, 11:56 p.m. Intensity VIII at Mulberry, on the San Andreas fault southeast of Hollister, where chimneys were thrown down. Plaster fell at Hollister (VII), and the soft river banks were fissured extensively at the junction of the Pajaro and San Benito Rivers.

1885 July 31, 4:10 p.m. Intensity VII at Cloverdale, Sonoma County. Details lacking.

1888 February 29, 2:50 p.m. Intensity VII or perhaps VIII at Petaluma, where walls were cracked. Strong at a number of points north and west of the bay.

1888 November 18, 2:28 p.m. Five chimneys knocked down along 23d Avenue in Oakland. This shock was not felt over a very wide area.

1889 May 19, 3:10 a.m. Strongest at Antioch and Collinsville (VIII), where chimneys were damaged, plaster cracked, and crockery and glassware broken. Slight damage at Lodi, Napa, Rio Vista, and San Francisco. Felt over a wide area in central California.

1889 July 31, 4:47 a.m. Intensity VII in the San Francisco Bay region. One chimney fell in San Leandro; the brick pier of the 8-inch telescope at Chabot Observatory in Oakland was cracked. Felt from Gilroy to Santa Rosa.

1890 April 24, 3:36 a.m. Intensity VIII to IX in the Monterey Bay region. Many chimneys down at Watsonville, with somewhat less damage at Gilroy and Hollister. Ground fissures in the San Andreas fault zone near Chittenden. The railroad bridge over the Pajaro River was displaced, and nearby track moved. Felt from Salinas to Santa Rosa.

1891 January 2, 12:00 m. Ceilings cracked and plaster down at Mount Hamilton (VII). Strong, but no significant damage at San Jose, Gilroy, and Lathrop (San Joaquin County).

1891 October 11, 10:28 p.m. Intensity VIII to IX at Sonoma and Napa. More or less damage to every house in the Sonoma Valley, where chimneys fell and people were thrown from their beds.

1892 April 19, 2:50 a.m. Intensity IX to X in Solano and Yolo Counties. In Vacaville, nearly every brick building was wrecked, and many frame buildings damaged. The shock was nearly as severe at Dixon and Winters. This was probably the largest shock in the San Francisco Bay region between 1868 and 1906. Felt from Fresno to Healdsburg, and east to western Nevada.

1892 April 21, 9:43 a.m. A very strong aftershock of the preceding earthquake. Intensity was fully IX at Winters, where many buildings which withstood the earthquake of April 19 were totally wrecked. At Vacaville, 12 miles south of Winters, damage was considerably less than on April 19. Felt from Fresno to Red Bluff, and east to Reno.

1892 November 13, 4:45 a.m. Intensity VII+ at Monterey, where chimneys were cracked. Minor damage at Salinas and Hollister. Felt as far north as Petaluma.

1893 August 9, 1:15 a.m. Intensity VII to VIII at Santa Rosa, where chimneys fell, windows were broken, and plaster was damaged.

1897 June 20, 12:14 p.m. Felt from Napa and Sacramento south to Templeton, and east to Modesto, Merced, Fresno, and Visalia. Source probably on the

San Andreas fault in San Benito County. Intensity VIII to IX at Hollister, where nearly every brick building was damaged, and at Salinas, where walls and chimneys were thrown down.

1898 March 30, 11:43 p.m. Considerable damage at Mare Island Navy Yard (VIII), where only the late hour of occurrence averted many fatalities. Chimneys twisted and considerable minor damage in San Francisco (VII). Felt over much of central California, and at Carson City, Nevada.

1899 April 30, 2:41 p.m. Epicenter probably on the San Andreas fault northeast of Watsonville. Intensity VII to VIII at Watsonville and toward Corralitos; chimneys and cemetery monuments damaged in Green Valley.

1899 July 6, 12:10 p.m. Two separate shocks within one minute of each other. One, apparently centered a few miles south of the earthquake of April 30, 1899, knocked down chimneys in Watsonville and broke lamps and windows at Salinas. The other was a very local shock, but did more or less damage to nearly every brick building in Pleasanton, 50 miles north of Watsonville.

1899 October 12, 9 p.m. Plaster knocked from walls and some chimneys down at Santa Rosa (VII to VIII). Some damage in Petaluma.

1902 May 19, 10:31 a.m. Intensity VIII at Elmira, Solano County, where nearly all chimneys were thrown down; VII to VIII at Vacaville, VII at Fairfield and Suisun.

1903 June 11, 5:12 a.m. Epicenter probably on the Hayward or Sunol (Calaveras) faults north of San Jose. Intensity VIII. Chimneys down in San Jose, Hayward, Livermore, and near Niles.

1903 July 24, 12:26 p.m. Several brick walls were cracked and much plaster fell at Willows (VII).

1903 August 2, 10:49 p.m. Intensity VIII at San Jose and Mount Hamilton. In San Jose, there was much damage to brick and stone buildings and to chimneys. Chimneys fell and plaster was cracked at Mount Hamilton. Felt over an area of about 50,000 square miles.

1906 April 18, 5:12 a.m. One of the greatest shocks in California, caused by movement on the San Andreas fault between San Juan Bautista and southern Humboldt County. Maximum horizontal ground offset at the fault was 21 feet, near the head of Tomales Bay. The ground southwest of the fault moved toward the northwest relative to the northeast side. Vertical movement was small (not more than 3 feet), and was generally confined to the region northwest of the Golden Gate.*

1910 March 10, 10:52 p.m. Intensity VII in the Monterey Bay region, strongest at Aptos and Watsonville, but nearly as strong in much of the Pajaro Valley. Nearly everywhere in the epicentral region the motion was a slow rocking of alarming energy. Although the intensity nowhere exceeded VII, the shock was perceptible over an area of more than 60,000 square miles, sug-

---

* The 1906 earthquake is discussed in considerable detail elsewhere in this study, and therefore most of the catalog material has been deleted. Not mentioned elsewhere, however, is the estimate that total life loss was probably 700 to 800. Direct property loss due to earthquake and fire within the city of San Francisco probably amounted to $400 million (1906 values), with earthquake losses accounting for about 20 percent of the dollar figure.

gesting either that the focus was rather deeper than usual for a California earthquake, or that the focus was well offshore in Monterey Bay.

1911 March 11, 1:30 p.m. Plaster cracked, some damage to chimneys, and things knocked from walls at Hollister (VII).

1911 July 1, 2:00 p.m. Intensity VIII to IX at Coyote in the Santa Clara Valley. In the region around San Jose, Gilroy, and Morgan Hill, the intensity was VII to VIII; many chimneys were destroyed and some brick walls cracked. The 36-inch refracting telescope at Mount Hamilton shifted three-quarters of an inch on its base, and a three-story brick dormitory building was damaged so badly that it had to be condemned. According to Gutenberg and Richter (1954), the instrumental magnitude of this shock (6.6) was higher than any in central California since 1906. The epicenter was most likely on the Hayward fault in the rugged hills east of Coyote. The shock was felt over 60,000 square miles.

1914 November 8, 6:31 p.m. Intensity VIII at Laurel in the Santa Cruz Mountains. Felt from St. Helena south to Soledad. Epicenter probably on the San Andreas fault near Laurel.

1916 August 6, 11:38 a.m. Intensity VIII at Paicines, VII at Hollister. Region of perceptibility about 30,000 square miles.

1926 October 22, 4:35 a.m. Center on the continental shelf off Monterey Bay. Intensity VIII at Santa Cruz, where many chimneys were thrown down; VII at Capitola, Monterey, Salinas and Soquel. Felt from Healdsburg to Lompoc, and east to the Sierra, an area of nearly 100,000 square miles. Another shock one hour later was similar to the first in almost every respect.

1933 May 16, 3:47 a.m.* Intensity VIII near Overacker Station, between Niles and Irvington, where all chimneys were down and other damage was done to buildings, and in Niles Canyon, where rockfalls blocked the road. Intensity VI to VII at Hayward, Martinez, Mission San Jose, and Walnut Creek.

1937 March 8, 2:31 a.m. Damage to chimneys, plaster, retaining walls, and sewers in north Berkeley, Albany, and El Cerrito (VII). Felt over an area of 5,000 square miles.

1939 June 24, 5:02 a.m. Epicenter on the San Andreas fault 7 miles south of Hollister. Damage to chimneys of farmhouses and to the walls of a winery building in a small area south of Hollister (VII). Some cracks in the ground.

1949 March 9, 4:28 a.m. Felt over an area of 20,000 square miles from Santa Rosa south to Santa Margarita. At Hollister (VII) damage consisted of fallen chimneys, cracked walls, sprung elevator shafts and door frames, and broken windows. Intensity was VI over a rather wide area from Pinole to Soledad.

1954 April 25, 12:33 p.m. Intensity VIII in a small region along the Chittenden Road on the south bank of the Pajaro River. Several houses severely damaged, ground cracked, and loose earth slid onto the road. Epicenter doubtless on the San Andreas fault, which crosses the Pajaro River at this point. Felt over 12,000 square miles from Santa Rosa to San Ardo, and east to Fresno.

*Commencing with this shock, intensities listed are based on the Modified Mercalli scale.

1955 September 4, 6:01 p.m. Damage at San Jose (VII) consisted mainly of damaged chimneys (75 in the Willow Glen district, east of San Jose) and cracked walls. Some underground pipe damage. Felt from Santa Rosa to San Ardo and east to Madera.

1955 October 23, 8:10 p.m. Epicenter between Walnut Creek and Concord. Maximum intensity VII; moderate property damage (estimated at $1,000,000) over a considerable area. Damage was mostly confined to broken windows, cracked walls and plaster, and loss from broken merchandise. A few chimneys were knocked down, including two in Berkeley. Felt from the Carmel Valley to Zamora, and east to Copperopolis.

1957 March 22, 11:44 a.m. Epicenter on the San Andreas fault near Mussel Rock. Principal building damage was to frame houses in the Westlake Palisades tract west of Daly City. Damage was principally exterior plaster cracks, but several dwellings sustained more serious structural damage, and a number of chimneys were cracked. Maximum intensity VII.

1963 September 14, 11:46 a.m. Felt over an area of about 5,000 square miles. Maximum intensity was VII in a small area along the San Andreas fault about 7½ miles east of Watsonville in the vicinity of Chittenden.

Selected Background Reading

The publications listed below are intended as guides for informed laymen. A substantial number of important scientific publications have not been listed because their use requires a technical background on the part of the reader. Some of the listed publications are out of print, but probably all are available at university libraries as well as at the California Division of Mines and Geology library, Ferry Building, San Francisco.

Association of Engineering Geologists. *Geology and Urban Development*. Glendale, Calif.: 1965.

California. Department of Natural Resources. Div. of Mines. *San Francisco Earthquakes of March 1957*. (Special Report 57) ed. Gordon B. Oakeshott. Ferry Building, San Francisco: 1959.

———. The Resources Agency. [Dept. of Conservation. Div. of Mines and Geology]. *Earthquake and Geologic Hazards Conference [Proceedings]*. San Francisco, December 7 and 8, 1964.

———. ———. *Landslides and Subsidence: Geologic Hazards Conference [Proceedings]*. Los Angeles, May 26 and 27, 1965.

———. San Francisco Bay Conservation and Development Commission. "Bay Mud Developments and Related Structural Foundations," by Charles H. Lee and Michael Praszker; "Seismic Problems in the Use of Fills in San Francisco Bay," by H. Bolton Seed; and "Seismic Risk to Buildings and Structures on Filled Lands in San Francisco Bay," by Karl V. Steinbrugge; in *Fill, Three Reports on Aspects of Fill in San Francisco Bay*. 1967.

———. ———. *Geology of San Francisco Bay*, by Harold B. Goldman. February 1967.

———. State Earthquake Investigation Commission. *The California Earthquake of April 18, 1906*. (Report of the State Earthquake Investigation Commission . . .) 2 vols., atlas. Washington, D.C.: Carnegie Institution of Washington, 1908–10. Andrew C. Lawson, Chairman of the Commission.

Geologic Hazards Advisory Committees for Program and Organization. *Earthquake and Geologic Hazards in California*. (A Report to the Resources Agency). Privately printed. April 26, 1967.

Iacopi, Robert. *Earthquake Country*. A Sunset book. Menlo Park, Calif.: Lane Book Co., 1964.

New Zealand. Ministry of Works. Town and Country Planning Branch. "Town Planning and Earthquake Faults," *Town and Country Planning Bulletin No. 7*. May 1965. pp. 1–6.

79

Redwood City Seismic Advisory Board. "Report of Seismic Investigation for Redwood City General Improvement District." September
1965. [Not generally circulated]

U. S. Geological Survey. "Approximate Location of Fault Traces and
Historic Surface Ruptures Within the Hayward Fault Zone Between
San Pablo and Warm Springs, California," by Dorothy H. Radbruch.
Miscellaneous Geologic Investigations, Map no. 1–522. 1967.

————. ————. "Approximate Trace of the Main Surface Rupture in
the San Andreas Fault Zone Between Pacifica and the Vicinity of
Saratoga, California, Formed During the Earthquake of April 18,
1906," by J. Schlocker, E. H. Pampeyan, and M. G. Bonilla. Open
File Report. [unpublished map available for public inspection] 1965.

————. ————. "Historic Surface Faulting in Continental United
States and Adjacent Parts of Mexico," by M. G. Bonilla. Open File
Report. 1967.

————. ————. "Most Conspicuous Strands of the San Andreas and
Related Faults, Southwestern Marin County," by Robert D. Brown,
Jr. Open File Report. 1967.